OXFORD STUDIES IN DEMOCRATIZATION

Series Editor: Laurence Whitehead

·····································

DEMOCRATIC CONSOLIDATION
IN EASTERN EUROPE
Volume 2

OXFORD STUDIES IN DEMOCRATIZATION

Series Editor: Laurence Whitehead

....

Oxford Studies in Democratization is a series for scholars
and students of comparative politics and related disciplines.
Volumes will concentrate on the comparative study of the
democratization processes that accompanied the decline and
termination of the cold war. The geographical focus of the
series will primarily be Latin America, the Caribbean,
Southern and Eastern Europe, and relevant
experiences in Africa and Asia.

OTHER BOOKS IN THE SERIES

The New Politics of Inequality in Latin America:
Rethinking Participation and Representation
*Douglas A. Chalmers, Carlos M. Vilas, Katherine Roberts Hite,
Scott B. Martin, Kerianne Piester, and Monique Segarra*

Human Rights and Democratization in Latin America: Uruguay and Chile
Alexandra Barahona de Brito

Regimes, Politics, and Markets: Democratization and Economic Change in
Southern and Eastern Europe
Jose Maria Maravall

Democracy between Consolidation and Crisis in Southern Europe
Leonardo Morlino

The Bases of Party Competition in Eastern Europe:
Social and Ideological Cleavages in Post-Communist States
Geoffrey Evans and Stephen Whitefield

The International Dimensions of Democratization: Europe and the Americas
Laurence Whitehead

Citizenship Rights and Social Movements:
A Comparative and Statistical Analysis
Joe Foweraker and Todd Landman

The Legacy of Human Rights Violations in the Southern Cone:
Argentina, Chile, and Uruguay
Luis Roniger and Mario Sznajder

Democratic Consolidation in Eastern Europe Volume 1
Jan Zielonka

The Politics of Memory: Transitional Justice in Democratizing Societies
Alexandra Barahona de Brito, Carmen González-Enriquez, and Paloma Aguilar

Democratic Consolidation in Eastern Europe

Volume 2
International and Transnational Factors

....

EDITED BY

JAN ZIELONKA
and
ALEX PRAVDA

OXFORD
UNIVERSITY PRESS

OXFORD

UNIVERSITY PRESS

Great Clarendon Street, Oxford OX2 6DP

Oxford University Press is a department of the University of Oxford.
It furthers the University's objective of excellence in research, scholarship,
and education by publishing worldwide in

Oxford New York

Athens Auckland Bangkok Bogotá Buenos Aires
Cape Town Chennai Dar es Salaam Delhi Florence Hong Kong Istanbul
Karachi Kolkata Kuala Lumpur Madrid Melbourne Mexico City Mumbai
Nairobi Paris São Paulo Shanghai Singapore Taipei Tokyo Toronto Warsaw

and associated companies in Berlin Ibadan

Oxford is a registered trade mark of Oxford University Press
in the UK and certain other countries

Published in the United States
by Oxford University Press Inc., New York

British Library Cataloguing in Publication Data

Data available

Library of Congress Cataloging in Publication Data

Democratic consolidation in Eastern Europe / Jan Zielonka, and Alex Pravda, editors.
p. cm. (Oxford studies in democratization)
Includes bibliographical references and index.
Contents: v. 1. Institutional engineering
1. Democratization—Europe, Eastern. 2. Democratization—Former Soviet republics.
3. Europe, Eastern—Politics and government—1989- 4. Former Soviet republics—Politics
and government. 5. Constitutional history—Europe, Eastern. 6. Constitutional
history—Former Soviet republics. I. Zielonka, Jan, 1955- II. Series.
JN96.A58 D43 2001 320.94′091717—dc21 00–046509
ISBN 0–19–924168–6
ISBN 0–19–924409–X (pbk)

1 3 5 7 9 10 8 6 4 2

Typeset by Graphicraft Limited, Hong Kong
Printed in Great Britain by
TJ International Ltd., Padstow, Cornwall

Preface

This study of international and transnational pressures on post-communist countries is one of three books prepared within the Project on Democratic Consolidation in Eastern Europe. The European University Institute in Florence and its Research Council sponsored the project. The two other volumes in the series deal with (a) institutional engineering and (b) civil society and democratic orientations within Eastern Europe. The aim of the project is to contrast a set of democracy theories with empirical evidence accumulated in Eastern Europe over the last ten years. We try to avoid complex debates about definitions, methods, and the uses and misuses of comparative research. Instead we try to establish what has really happened in the region, and which of the existing theories have proved helpful in explaining these developments. This volume, like the others, starts with a presentation of conceptual and comparative frameworks, followed by detailed analyses of the countries undergoing democratization and democratic consolidation.

We are especially grateful to the European University Institute and its Research Council for their generous financial support and intellectual leadership. Individual members of the Research Council such as Roeland In't Veld, Pierre Hassner, Johan Olsen, Vincent Wright, and Fritz Scharpf gave us the initial encouragement to undertake this ambitious project and guided us through its successive stages.

We particularly thank Dov Lynch for his excellent editorial work on the volume, and Alexandra George who undertook the final polishing and prepared the book for publication. Remy Salters helped us to keep some chapters up to date as the speed of change in some Eastern European countries threatened to overtake the rate with which the manuscript could be prepared for publication, and Liz Webb provided valuable secretarial assistance. And, most of all we are indebted to the authors of the individual chapters, without whose knowledge and insight, effort and patience, this volume and project could not have come to fruition.

Finally, we would like to thank Dominic Byatt of Oxford University Press for his willingness to take on this large publishing project and for ensuring its smooth completion.

J. Z.
A. P.

Contents

List of Figures

List of Tables

List of Contributors

KYRIL DREZOV is Lecturer in Politics at the University of Keele.

TOM GALLAGHER is Professor of European Peace Studies at Bradford University.

LESLIE HOLMES is Professor of Political Science at the University of Melbourne.

GEOFFREY EVANS is a Fellow of Nuffield College at the University of Oxford.

ANTONI Z. KAMIŃSKI is Professor and Chair of International Security and Strategic Studies at the Institute of Political Studies, Polish Academy of Sciences in Warsaw.

S. NEIL MACFARLANE is Lester B. Pearson Professor of International Relations and Director of the Centre for International Studies at the University of Oxford.

TARAS KUZIO is Senior Research Fellow at the Centre for International and Security Studies at York University, Toronto

MARIE MENDRAS is Professor at Sciences-Po and researcher with the CNRS and the Centre d'Études et de Recherches Internationales in Paris.

EWA MORAWSKA is Professor of Sociology and History at the University of Pennsylvania in Philadelphia.

IVER B. NEUMANN is Head of the Centre for Russia at the Norwegian Institute of International Affairs in Oslo.

VELLO PETTAI is Lecturer in Political Science at the University of Tartu.

ALEX PRAVDA is a Fellow of St Antony's College at the University of Oxford.

Ivo Samson is Executive Director of the Slovak Foreign Policy Association in Bratislava.

Reimund Seidelmann is Professor of International Relations at the University of Giessen and Professor for Political Science at the Institute for European Studies, Free University Brussels.

Karen E. Smith is Lecturer in International Relations at the London School of Economics and Political Science.

Susan Senior Nello is Research Fellow in the 'Richard Goodwin' Faculty of Economics at the University of Siena.

Milada Anna Vachudová is Postdoctoral Fellow of the Center for European Studies at Harvard University and of the European Union Center of New York City at Columbia University.

László Valki is Professor of International Law at Eötrös University, Budapest.

Radovan Vukadinovic is Professor of International Relations at the University of Zagreb.

Stephen Whitefield is a Fellow of Pembroke College at the University of Oxford.

Jan Zielonka is Professor of Political Science at the European University Institute in Florence.

Introduction

Alex Pravda

All students of democratization now agree that international factors matter. This recent consensus is the result of a long academic journey, starting with the study of Latin American transitions from authoritarian rule, passing through regime change in southern Europe, and climaxing in the attempt to make sense of the cascade of events in the East following the collapse of communism. This journey is a story of analytical adjustment to those enemies of Grand Theory, events. As democratization has travelled east, so it seems to have become more obviously entangled with international factors. Analyses of transition from authoritarianism in Latin America initially relegated the international dimension to a marginal role, one which deserved no more than passing reference.[1] Perhaps because their *dependencia* school predecessors had made sweeping generalizations about the centrality of the international, later students of transitions reacted by focusing overmuch on the domestic. Their myopia became increasingly visible when analysts reflected on Latin American transition from the perspective of regime change in Spain and Portugal. There the international context was too obvious and important to minimize. Subsequent work on Latin American transition, notably that of Laurence Whitehead, has produced a more rounded analysis which gives due weight to the international dimension. Similarly, one stage on, appreciation of the role international factors have played in southern European transitions has benefited from analysis of their more recent role in Eastern Europe. The way in which analysis of developments in different regions at different times has improved understanding across both dimensions is a good example of the value of comparative political studies, an instance of positive transregional influence in the academic sphere.

[1] Philippe Schmitter, 'Transitions from Authoritarian Rule: Prospects for Democracy', in Guillermo O'Donnell and Philippe C. Schmitter, *Transitions from Authoritarian Rule: Tentative Conclusions about Uncertain Democracies* (Baltimore: Johns Hopkins University Press, 1986), 5.

Distinctiveness and Distinctions

The East European wave of democratization stands out from others in three respects: the salience of the international environment; the outward orientation of elites and peoples; and the simultaneity of democratization and marketization. Few would dispute that the international environment, notably the collapse of the Soviet inner and outer empires, played a more central role in initiating transition from totalitarian and authoritarian rule in this wave than in previous ones. We have to go back to the years immediately following the Second World War to find anything of similar intensity, operating in anything like the same degree of international flux. The post-war wave is also the only one which comes close to the post-communist in scale and longevity of international involvement. Ideological and security agendas—to capitalize on the collapse of communism and stabilize the security environment—have combined to fuel high international engagement in post-communist transitions.

Such international 'pull' is complemented by a domestic 'push' towards the industrialized West more widespread and intense than in other recent democratization waves. Most immediately, this push towards the West was a flight from the East, from subordination to a Soviet system typically seen as undermining national sovereignty. The West also stands as a pole of attraction because many East Europeans, especially the elites, wish to identify with what they see as the heartland of European civilization. Less conscious, though no less important a factor pushing East Europeans towards the West, is a historically conditioned tendency to look beyond their borders for solutions. Long centuries of subordination to imperial rule exposed these states to high levels of external penetration. This experience accustomed domestic elites to cope with external constraints by a combination of adjustment and resistance. Both these strategies fostered an elite preoccupation with external factors which remains evident in current concern to engage outside involvement in their economic and political development.

The simultaneity of democratization and marketization is a distinctive feature of East European transition more often noted than explored. Its implications are as far-reaching for those seeking to promote change from the outside as they are for those seeking to do so from within. The task of transforming both the economy and polity often involves sequencing choices for external as well as domestic actors. External actors tend to give priority to promoting the market, claiming that this will strengthen democratization as well as secure ties with the West. In practice, this strategy helps to 'economize' democratization. Domestic leaders, on the other hand, are concerned first and foremost with building power and tend to 'politicize' economic reforms. For the citizens of these states, the close interplay of marketization and democratization makes both vulnerable to the weakness of either set of changes. Such mutual vulnerability makes the whole process of change and its international connections more likely to attract popular criticism.

While the above traits make the post-communist wave of democratization distinctive, it is important to be aware of the diversity among East European states themselves. It is precisely because of the diversity of post-communist transition that this volume embraces Eastern Europe in its broadest geographical definition and considers developments in as wide a range of states as possible. The canopy of communist party rule covered a collection of states and societies which always differed in fundamental respects. As transition has proceeded, so these differences have become more pronounced.

Four differences or sets of characteristics matter particularly for any analysis of the role played by external factors in domestic regime change. The first is proximity to core, in essence West European, values and traditions. Historical affinity with Europe, whether in the form of close political, economic, and cultural ties or inclusion within European empires, continues to resonate. So does historical distance from Europe, particularly the membership of non-European centred empires. One does not have to subscribe to theories of civilizational conflict to notice that historical and cultural legacies in Eastern Europe seem remarkably resilient. More recent historical experience provides the second set of distinguishing characteristics: the relationship between nationalism and communism. Here the main distinction is between those states (Russia, Serbia) where communism took significant root in national soil and those (notably Poland, Hungary, and the Baltic states) where communism was sharply counterposed to national identity and interest. The third distinguishing feature concerns the ethnic composition of the state and its qualities of 'stateness'.[2] The division here lies between those states based on ethnically homogeneous historical nations and

---

[2] Juan J. Linz and Alfred Stepan, *Problems of Democratic Transition and Consolidation: Southern Europe, South America and Post-communist Europe* (Baltimore: Johns Hopkins University Press, 1996), 26–33.

those with fragile national identities and ethnically fragmented populations. In the latter group, state and nation building figure prominently in the process of transition.

The stage reached in democratic transition is the fourth and final distinguishing characteristic. Nearly all the states covered in this volume fall into the broad category of democratic consolidation. Definitions of democratic consolidation centre around the institutionalization and legitimization of democratic processes. As Schedler argues, the term democratic consolidation has been stretched to cover both conditions which prevent regression and those which complete and deepen democracy from its electoral minimum to its full liberal form.[3] Conditions that establish institutional anchoring and recognition of the democratic rules of the political game sufficient to stop slippage into authoritarianism may be seen as creating low levels of democratic consolidation. High levels of democratic consolidation are associated with conditions which enable democratic institutions, processes, and culture to take deep root. Few of the states under review qualify as highly consolidated democracies, even if Poland, Hungary, the Czech Republic, and Slovenia are well on their way towards that end of the democratic consolidation spectrum. At the middle of the range lie Bulgaria, Romania, Slovakia, Latvia, and Lithuania, where electoral democracy exists though without the extensive underpinning essential to a high level of consolidation. Towards the lower end of the spectrum comes Ukraine Russia where electoral democracy remains illiberal and so fragile that it hardly merits the term consolidated. Serbia under Milošević and Belarus under Hukashenka are off the scale; in the former transition from authoritarianism has scarcely began, while the latter has seen regression and de-democratization.

When combined, the four distinguishing features just sketched delineate some fairly clear clusters of states. Poland, Hungary, Czech Republic, and Slovenia stand out as the cluster with the most consistent profile, at one end of the scale in all four categories and also at the top of any league table of susceptibility to Western promotion of reform. At the other end of the scale come Russia and Serbia, whose transitions have proved among the most difficult, especially as far as international influences are concerned. Between these two polar clusters lie states, ranging from Lithuania to Bosnia, which typically possess mixed characteristics. This schematic categorization lays no claims to providing the key to the varying interplay

---

[3] Andreas Schedler, 'What is Democratic Consolidation?', *Journal of Democracy*, 9 (Apr. 1998), 4.

between international factors and democratization; it merely draws attention to some dimensions of diversity among the states covered in this volume.

Because post-communist transition has been so varied we have tried to cover a fairly comprehensive range of states. All too often analyses concentrate on the leading East Central European trio, Poland, Hungary, and the Czech Republic, as these are the most advanced in their domestic transition and their Western engagement. States such as Romania and Slovakia, where democratization has proved more difficult and international involvement has fared less well, are just as important for any exploration of the connections between democratization and external factors. Each of the country chapters (six deal with single states, four cover two or more) considers aspects of democratization and democratic consolidation that best illustrate how international and transnational factors bear on those processes. Those factors are treated thematically in the first part of the volume. By taking a thematic as well as a country-focused view, we seek to provide a rounded picture of the complex nexus between the domestic and international dimensions of democratization and democratic consolidation.

The complexity of this nexus is frustrating for those pursuing parsimonious theory. We have far more modest aspirations and have not tried to force contributors into any Procrustean framework of analysis. Rather, we take heed of the wise counsel offered by Gabriel Almond, to take 'an eclectic, dynamic and indeterminist approach to the interaction of economy, society, polity and international system . . .'[4] If the connection between the international and the domestic has long been recognized, its operation remains poorly understood. Analysis of what Hintze called 'the constant collaboration of the inner and outer world'[5] has suffered from the lack of cooperation between students of politics and specialists on international relations, few in either group daring to cross the caste-like divide between sub-disciplines. Some might argue that such is the complexity and singularity of what many social scientists regard as no man's land that they would prefer to leave the subject to historians. Historical analysis, of immense value here as elsewhere, should be complemented by other approaches. Those social scientists bold enough to venture into no man's land, and apply insights from both Comparative Politics and International Relations, have

[4] Gabriel A. Almond, 'Review Article: The International-National Connection', *British Journal of Political Science*, 19 (July 1989), 237–59, esp. 252.
[5] Ibid. 241.

done most to advance our understanding of the interface between democratization and the international.

Having straddled the disciplinary divide, the problem one then faces, ironically enough, is how to separate the domestic from the international sufficiently to be able to analyse their interaction. As the international and transnational impinge more on national developments, so the boundaries between the two spheres obviously become more permeable and indistinct. So blurred do the boundaries appear to some analysts trying to assess democratization in states acceding to the European Union that they find it 'unhelpful' to classify Brussels' inducements as either external or internal.[6] The fact that such inducements interact with domestic factors at various levels complicates classification of their effects rather than obliterates their provenance. Similarly, complex structural change, such as the collapse of communist rule in Eastern Europe, makes separating out the external and internal very difficult rather than, as some have argued, 'arbitrary and artificial'.[7] All analysis of complex change involves an element of artificiality and simplification, acceptable as long as its use is explicit and furthers understanding. For analytical purposes we have to try and trace international factors as they cross borders and enter the domestic atmosphere. As they travel, these factors often remain identifiable even if their impact on anything that happens within the state is naturally mediated by the domestic environment. Where we have been able to identify external and internal factors, we should not be concerned primarily with counterposing them so as to pass judgement on which is dominant in a given situation.[8] In the rare cases where we have sufficiently good information on how policy is made, we might comment on the approximate weight of the two sets of factors in shaping a particular decision. In as complicated a process as democratization and democratic consolidation, a more realistic approach, and one taken in this volume, is to try and illuminate the role international factors have played, where and how they have interacted with domestic factors, which remain the ultimate determinants of developments within states.

[6] Laurence Whitehead, 'Democracy by Convergence: Southern Europe', in Laurence Whitehead (ed.), *The International Dimensions of Democratization: Europe and the Americas* (Oxford: Oxford University Press, 1996), 272.

[7] Laurence Whitehead (ed.), 'Democracy and Decolonization: East-Centre Europe', in Whitehead, *International Dimensions*, 388.

[8] Basilios Tsingos, 'Underwriting Democracy: The European Community and Greece', in Whitehead, *International Dimensions*, 315–55.

External Factors

The wide range of factors in this category may be divided into transnational phenomena, regionalism, non-governmental organizations, and state as well as international institutional actors. The diffusion of ideas across frontiers has always been a feature of the international system. In recent years, and especially since the end of the Cold War, ideas associated with liberal democracy and the market have travelled effectively and widely. The pervasive if diffuse influence of these Western ideas and norms on East European elites and publics is probably the most important kind of international effect on the development of democratization. The vehicles carrying these ideas range from cultural events and the mass media to specialist seminars and conferences. Transnational meetings and exchanges between specialists before the end of communism had profound effects on the thinking of historians, philosophers, and economists who came to play key advisory and political roles in transition. The proliferation of such meetings in the last decade has been supported by Western non-governmental organizations as well as states. The transport of ideas and values also comes in the form of the mass movement of peoples across frontiers, whether for purposes of leisure, business, or migration (see Chapter 6). The explosion of tourism has given East Europeans a more realistic view of the West, of both its democratic and material achievements and their social consequences. Short tourist stays rarely have a serious impact on popular attitudes towards democratization. The longer exposure to life in the West involved in business travel, and especially in migration, might be expected to foster commitment to democratic norms, as happened a century ago. Interestingly, Ewa Morawska finds the opposite to be the case. Stays in the West, now typically of shorter duration, tend to reinforce undemocratic attitudes and habits, as traders and migrants find that informal methods get things done abroad as well as at home. Even the highly skilled international travellers, who generally support democracy, tend to help strengthen rather than undermine the growth of cronyism and corrupt practice.

Some of these travellers form part of the transnational criminal networks which Leslie Holmes discusses in Chapter 7. As he shows, the sharp rise in the visible incidence of organized crime is associated in most post-communist states with greater openness to the outside world. More porous borders have opened up new territories for international criminal groups and provided their domestic partners with easier access to a wealth of facilities. These facilities have made it easier to salt away proceeds from the corrupt deals popularly associated with privatization. Growing crime and corruption have caused considerable public concern and had a doubly corrosive effect on democratization. They sully the cause of reform and undermine the credibility of politicians and government. They tend also to increase support for a strong state using even anti-democratic methods to combat illegal and illicit activities. International help for states engaged in this combat has proved rather limited. To prevent crime and corruption from seriously undermining democratic consolidation, more is needed in the way of Western aid and regional cooperation.

Much of the flow of crime and migration involves states within the region. Regional influences played a prominent part in the beginning of transition from communist rule, when changes in the Soviet Union and throughout Eastern Europe had a strong 'contagion' effect. In the wake of the collapse of the old regimes, regional groupings, such as Visegrad, have proved weak and vulnerable to defection (see Chapter 2). Moves to join the West turned out to be more competitive than cooperative. One can see some regional spillover and demonstration effects in the area of economic reform, far less so in that of democratization. As Iver Neumann notes, regional organizations such as Visegrad and the Baltic Council have democratic potential. States more advanced along the path to democratic consolidation and Western club membership may try to help lagging partners even if altruism is mixed with concern to ease their own situation. Czech support after mid-1998 for early Slovak accession to the EU reflected not simply sympathy with the new government but concern to relieve Prague's southern border problems. These are likely to become considerable as Prague, as part of its accession process, has to comply with Schengen regulations. Such restrictions on transnational flows will increase divisions and tensions within geographic, economic, and cultural regions separated by alignments with the main Western clubs. The need to assert national identities within the new context of alignment with the West helps to explain the remarkable weakness to date of regionalism and regional influence.

On the Western side (our definition of the West includes Japan), the main categories of international actors are non-governmental organizations, states, and intergovernmental bodies. A variety of non-governmental organizations, including political parties and private foundations, are involved in democracy promotion and protection. Foundations have spent somewhat more than the US government in efforts to these ends (see Chapter 1). Governments themselves have taken an active role in promoting democracy through their own Foundations and, mainly, by developing economic and political relations with democratizing states.

Bilateral relations perhaps play a more important role than appears to be the case in a landscape seemingly dominated by multilateralism. Individual states have often pursued distinct agendas, giving priority to those transition countries traditionally close to their national interests. The Scandinavians have concentrated on the Baltic states, the French have taken a particular interest in Poland and Romania, the Germans in the Czech Republic, Hungary, and Croatia. Different policy priorities have on occasion had negative effects on the process of democratization. Such was the case with German championing of Croat independence, a move that encouraged Hungarian support for Zagreb and, as László Valki notes in Chapter 10, perhaps strengthened revisionist aspirations in Budapest. Of all state actors it is the USA which has perhaps made the greatest single external impact on democratic transition in the region. Washington has vigorously promoted the institutional, constitutional, and legal dimensions of democracy. American diplomacy and US forces have taken the lead in interventionist efforts to stabilize areas of conflict, notably in former Yugoslavia. In American policy, stability, order, and a free market have figured as much as or more prominently than the promotion of democracy. Viewed by the USA and other Western states as part of a transition package, these elements have remained central in the activity of leading international organizations such as the IMF, World Bank, and NATO.

International Organizations

The major international organizations dealing with Eastern Europe (G7, G24, IMF, NATO, OSCE, EU) share a common if loose set of stated objectives: to help promote democracy and marketization as well as stability and security. The thrust of what Karen Smith calls the Western project seems clearer than its priorities and motives. There are idealistic as well as tough pragmatic threads in the rationale of democracy promotion in post-communist Eastern Europe. The idealistic, even ideological, commitment to furthering democratic values typically takes rhetorical pride of place. There is a missionary element in these organizations' efforts to advance the spread and consolidation of liberal democracy in the wake of the collapse of communism. Less to the fore in the post-communist context are the security concerns which underpinned much of the support given to democratization in southern Europe in the 1970s when countering communism was a major preoccupation of the West. Now security policy is about preventing instability. Security concerns are seen as complementary to the promotion of democratic values as these supposedly provide the best guarantee of long-term stability within states and peace between them. The real strength of Western concern for stability has come through in support for leaders, such as Berisha, Yeltsin or Putin, who have been closely associated with market reform even if they have failed to observe the niceties of political democracy.

Western promotion of free market capitalism also reflects a mix of idealism and pragmatism. International financial institutions have shown an almost missionary attachment to the neo-classical free market paradigm; they see transition as imitation.[9] Sceptics might point to pragmatic considerations of the economic gains the creation of free markets in Eastern Europe brings the advanced industrial West. As well as opening up opportunities to win assets and trade, marketization leads to the expansion of economic systems compatible with those of the West. As with marketization so with democratization, the ultimate benefit and rationale lies in enlarging the sphere of compatible, Western-like, systems. Compatibility and likeness promise to deliver freedom and security as well as plenty. In the Western project, these are components of a single model. In the minds of many Western policy makers, especially those in Washington, the free market and liberal democracy are twin pillars of a single structure, symbiotic parts of an organic whole. In practice, the relationship between marketization and democratization is full of tensions and hard choices. When Western organizations have to choose between the two, they often concentrate on the economic rather than political side of the project. They frequently do so more for reasons of practicality than principle. It seems far simpler to export market capitalism. There is more confidence that the capitalist model can travel across borders; after all, globalization is more advanced in economics than in politics. International organizations think they have more effective levers in the economic realm than in the political.

---

[9] David Stark and László Bruszt, *Postsocialist Pathways: transforming politics and property in East Central Europe* (Cambridge: Cambridge University Press, 1998), 5.

Whatever the degree of basic agreement on Western aims in helping transition states, the practical support from international organizations has been far from consistent or coordinated. On the democratization front, the West, as Karen Smith notes, has found it difficult to develop a coherent and collective strategy. Rather than establishing a special framework to support transition, the G7 left the responsibility to existing international organizations which have worked along parallel and overlapping rather than coordinated lines. They have sent out inconsistent policy signals and made far from the most effective use of the limited resources at their disposal. As a result, the whole exercise of democracy promotion often amounts to less than the sum of its parts.

A leading role in this exercise has been taken by the World Bank and the IMF. Both disburse funds on the basis of economic criteria and conditionality. The IMF has in practice often taken political factors into account, in some cases to the benefit of democratization and in others to its detriment. In Romania, for instance, the IMF suspended a loan in 1995 because of the political misuse of previous credits (see Chapter 14). Such niceties do not seem to have troubled the IMF in Russia where concern for stability has ensured support for politicians who have repeatedly misappropriated funds. In the Russian case, as in others, it is assumed that extending economic support to governments committed to democratic and marketizing reforms, even when their conduct falls short of Western standards of probity, is preferable to withdrawing support and risking the accession to power of less pro-Western and pro-market leaders. This assumption, and the argument that promoting the economic dimension of the Western project will ensure that developments on balance favour democracy, strongly reflect American thinking.

American priorities have also made themselves felt in the part NATO plays in democracy promotion. NATO has the potential to help strengthen democratic government, especially in the area of civil–military relations. It has considerable leverage here on those East European states keen to meet requirements for joining an organization which offers them access to a key Western power centre, as well as to relatively cheap security (see Chapter 4). Formally committed to furthering democracy, NATO has a track record of considerable tolerance of authoritarian regimes as long as these have served its security interests. So far the Alliance has placed little emphasis on the direct promotion of democratic governance in Eastern Europe, concentrating instead on making indirect contributions by establishing a broad network of partnerships

with states varying widely in their democratic credentials. NATO
can use the accession process to foster improvement in democratic
performance; all the states which joined NATO in 1999 scored well
on this front.

NATO's main contribution to democratization and democratic consolidation has been the indirect one of encouraging neighbouring
states troubled by ethnic conflicts to come to terms. The most direct
and intensive NATO efforts to help resolve ethnic disputes have
focused on former Yugoslavia, where the Alliance has sought, with
mixed results, to improve the security environment for democratic
transition in the whole of south-eastern Europe (see Chapter 16).
As the centre of security gravity in Europe has shifted increasingly
to domestic ethnic conflicts (see Chapter 5), so NATO has moved
into areas of peacekeeping traditionally associated with the UN and
the OSCE. Far more directly concerned than NATO with sustaining democratization, the OSCE has nonetheless failed to use political conditionality in its accession process. Its predecessor, the CSCE,
missed a major opportunity to influence democratization in the
new states of the former Soviet Union when it admitted them *en
masse* without political conditions. A weak organization with few
resources, the OSCE has done a good deal, often in very difficult
circumstances. It has tended to concentrate on monitoring elections
and scrutinizing observance of individual and minority rights.

The European Union, by contrast, has the most powerful and integrated set of resources for promoting democracy of any Western
organization. As the embodiment of West European economic and
political success, the EU has become the main pole of attraction
for most democratizing states. For them there is little real alternative. The attraction derives from the costs of being left outside EU
borders perhaps even more than from the benefits of inclusion. Small
states on the outside find it costly to exist alongside a highly protectionist regional organization and difficult to negotiate economic
and political problems with large states on a bilateral basis. Once
inside the Union, they have protection and access to net budgetary
inflows as well as the opportunity to punch above their weight in
decision-making councils.

Democracy figures more centrally in the EU's constitutional
order than in its enlargement strategy. Giving the promotion of
democracy top priority would have involved a more visionary and
proactive policy towards the states emerging from communism.
Instead of political vision, Brussels has often displayed considerable bureaucratic and technical myopia. Political conditionality
has played a part in the accession process, though by no means an

overriding one. Economic criteria and political support from member states proved decisive in the selection of the first group of entrants. The failure to satisfy the Europe Agreement requirements on minority rights was given as the reason for initially excluding Slovakia from the first tranche of prospective members (see Chapter 14). Meciar's violation of his own constitution did not help the Slovak case. Yet the fact that Estonia, which scarcely fared better in minority rights terms, was initially included in the first group of applicants highlighted the importance of economic criteria and political support from EU members, both areas in which Estonia was better placed than Slovakia.

Economic performance and administrative capacity, rather than political democracy, emerged as the most important areas of concern in the Commission's 1997 *avis* assessing applicants' progress. This in part reflects the greater practical difficulty in setting democratization criteria and evaluating political performance. Political targets are typically qualitative and hard to define as precisely as economic goals. The economic and administrative emphasis also reflects the Commission's cautious approach to enlargement which seeks to minimize the disruption this process will bring to the Union of Fifteen. From this perspective, it is vital that accessor states have economies compatible with the Community and administrative machinery capable of absorbing the *acquis* and working with Brussels. Democracy remains a very important objective, its achievement perhaps less urgent a matter. The Community and Union can live with democratic deficits more easily than with budgetary and administrative ones. In any case, it is assumed that the road to EU membership is also the road to the market and democracy. While the twinning of democratization and marketization is conceived in a more sophisticated fashion in Brussels than in Washington, the relationship is still seen as a very close one.

This Brussels view of transition is reflected in the EU's programme of support for democratization. As Karen Smith notes, the Union assigns relatively meagre resources to promoting democracy. The EBRD, which has far larger funds at its disposal, formally takes account of political factors when extending support yet is naturally concerned primarily with the economic viability of projects.

Political criteria, along with all conditions for entry, are the product of unilateral decisions within the EU rather than the result of discussions with aspiring entrants. The Structured Dialogue failed to give the East Europeans democratic participation in the accession process. It remains to be seen whether the Europe Conference will do this. Without an enhanced East European role and greater attention to the specific circumstances in the accessor states, the promotion of democracy will continue to run two kinds of risks. The first is that inadequate feel for the political and psychological climate in these states can mean poor communication and signalling of intentions. The Slovak government under Meĕiar chose to ignore the EU's political requirements partly because it simply did not believe that Brussels took them very seriously (see Chapter 13). The greater risk is one of overload.[10] Just as the inflexibility of economic requirements may burden development, so rigid political conditionality and insufficient sensitivity to the stage of development and local conditions may damage and retard the course of democratization. Promoting the kind of 'regulatory state' found in the EU may well be inappropriate for states trying to build market democracies.[11] Loading a fragile administrative system with a huge *acquis* will result in ineffective absorption and may help institutionalize inefficiencies. Far from all the aspiring entrants benefiting from political shock therapy, it can lead to cosmetic constitutional conformity. Beneath superficial democratic adjustment, undemocratic practices may persist and prove more resilient, especially if Brussels' technocratic approach to policy reinforces local bureaucratic practices.[12] These risks in no way invalidate the very considerable positive influence which the EU has on democratization. They may, however, make the process of democracy promotion itself less democratic and less effective.

States and international organizations have an armoury of instruments they can use to promote reform in Eastern Europe. These range from 'hard' resources such as material aid and military intervention to 'soft' ones like training and education programmes. This array of measures and methods can be ranked on a scale of intensity, power, and intrusiveness. Standing as an example and offering a model for democratic development comes at the low end of this scale as the signal transmitted is diffuse even if the long-term impact may be considerable. Next comes the giving of advice, approbation, and criticism. Somewhat higher up the scale, as more precisely targeted and intrusive, is the provision of material aid to support policy preferences. At its most active and intrusive, this takes the form of actual intervention to help with

---

[10] Giovanni Sartori, 'How Far Can Free Government Travel?', *Journal of Democracy*, 6 (July 1995), 105.

[11] Heather Grabbe, 'A Partnership for Accession? The Nature, Scope and Implications of Emerging EU Conditionality for Central and East European Applicants', *EUI Working Paper* (1999), 5–6.

[12] Ibid. 31.

economic, social, or political problems. Intervention, and more generally aid, gains leverage and comes further up our scale, especially when it forms part of a package wrapped in conditionality. The more wide-reaching and integrated the conditionality package, and the more tightly linked to membership of an attractive club, the greater its likely leverage and power.

Where and how International Factors Impinge on Democratic Consolidation

How conditionality, or any set of instruments lower in the scale, affects democratic consolidation depends of course not simply on the properties of the external factors. As we are dealing with an interactive process rather than a one-way export of influence, the domestic dimension is critical. However powerful external signals and levers may be, it is where and how they are received internally that proves decisive. International and transnational factors may condition, constrain, catalyse, and induce developments in the course of democratic consolidation; they rarely if ever ultimately determine them. It is far easier to generalize about the overall importance of the international context than to show particular influences.[13] Three variables, wholly or predominantly in the domestic realm, affect how the international bears on democratization and democratic consolidation: issue area; the international position of the state; and the domestic political context.

Issue areas

When considering different areas of domestic developments two variables are of particular interest. One is internationalization, the exposure and susceptibility of a particular area to international influence and leverage. The other is democratic salience, how centrally an area connects to the process of democratic consolidation. There is no necessary or even typical correlation between these two variables and it is important to understand that low susceptibility to international factors can often be associated with high centrality of the issue area to democratization and vice versa. What is an area of core or primary importance for democratic consolidation may be one of relatively low or secondary exposure to

---

[13] Andrew Hurrell, 'The International Dimensions of Democratization in Latin America: the Case of Brazil', in Whitehead, *International Dimensions*, 146–7.

international factors. Only in a few cases do the two variables coincide either to marginalize areas or, at the high end of both axes, to produce arterial links which can bring international factors to the heart of democratic consolidation. To identify areas as providing arterial links or secondary ones is not to make any judgement about the degree to which international factors affect the development of consolidation in particular spheres. Even where arterial links exist, the international influences they convey may ultimately make a small impact. By contrast, diffuse flows of international traffic into secondary areas, such as economic reform, may ultimately have a very great indirect and conditioning effect on democratic consolidation.

1. Democratic institutions, rules, and values

First let us consider two areas which house arterial links: elections and civil rights and liberties. Elections stand out as most clearly qualified to be called an arterial link. They lie at the heart of democratization, contributing as they do, to both Sartori's fundamental elements of democracy, to 'demo-power', through participation in the political process and to 'demo-protection', by way of accountability.[14] Holding free and fair elections is seen by the international community as the minimal requirement for recognition of any state as democratic. Many analysts make changes of government through free elections the most important criterion of democratic consolidation. To help promote fair and free elections, states and international organizations have offered advice and sent observers to monitor the election process throughout Eastern Europe (see Chapter 1). Elections have properties that make them particularly amenable to this kind of exercise. The authorities in democratizing states claim to conduct elections according to international democratic practice, the whole process is concentrated in time and relatively open to scrutiny. True, there is a temptation to assess the whole on the basis of its visible parts, underrating less easily observable elements such as candidate selection and campaign finance. Still, elections remain the most obvious, regular litmus test of democratic consolidation and election certification remains one of the most salient and potentially powerful forms of international leverage over the course of democratization.[15]

---

[14] Sartori, 'How Far Can Free Government Travel?', 102.
[15] G. O'Donnell, 'Illusions about Consolidation', *Journal of Democracy*, 7 (Apr. 1996), 34–51, esp. 45.

The other area which provides an arterial link are civil rights and liberties and the operation of a legal system that ensures their observance. All agree that the rule of law is a necessary condition for building and preserving a democratic state and society. The whole sphere of law and civic rights comes high on the agenda of international organizations seeking to promote and protect democracy. The EU has made compliance with international norms in this area one of the conditions for moving towards accession. Both the Council of Europe and the OSCE have taken an active part in trying to improve individual and minority rights. The OSCE has sent long-term missions to monitor the observance of minority rights where these are weakly established in local law and often violated. Where disputes have arisen, the OSCE and its Human Rights Commissioner have on occasion played a mediating role. It is through their vigilance in the area of civil rights that international bodies have probably made their main contribution to improving the wider legal system.

The rule of law and the effective operation of an independent judiciary is central to democratic consolidation. Yet it is less accessible to external influence than the more discrete area of civil rights. International engagement here is more diffuse and fragmented, scrutiny more difficult. A large number of actors, many nongovernmental, give advice and training on technical matters. They comment on performance here, as in the whole field of public administration. In both fields, external assessments of progress are sometimes reinforced by being parts of larger conditionality packages. In many cases, though, underlying problems, whether to do with the efficiency and political neutrality of civil servants or of judges, remain largely beyond their reach, let alone their grasp.

Similar generalizations apply to the broader institutional infrastructure of political and civil society, such as political parties and issue groups of various kinds. Parties frequently receive aid from fraternal organizations, especially if they become active in international movements. Comparable, if less well-funded, international links support the activities of trade unionists, journalists, and other professionals who play key roles in the democratization process. In the case of journalists, external organizations are concerned less with professionalism than with fostering vigorous media debate in a climate of free speech.

Freedom of expression is just one of the core values necessary for the construction of a sustainable democracy. Without embedded democratic values even the most perfect institutional framework of elections, parliaments, and parties remains a fragile and empty shell. It is the culture of democratic politics that lends political systems and societies a self-sustaining capacity. Instilling beliefs in political pluralism, negotiation, and compromise is of course an exceedingly long and complex process, not susceptible to any quick-fix formulaic approach. Values and ideas may be transmitted across state borders through like-minded groups of professionals acting as epistemic communities. Through these and other more diffuse, fine-veined channels, successful foreign models and examples may well make some impact, however gradual and indirect.

2. Security issues

If all elements in the institutional and procedural values cluster just considered are central to democratic consolidation, international linkages vary. These from the arterial to the fine-veined. By contrast, security issues bear less directly on democratization and are considerably more internationalized. While indispensable for any successful consolidation of democracy, security factors condition rather than drive the process. This relationship of indirect conditioning applies of course more to matters of external security than to problems of internal security which often directly affect the course of democratization.

A secure international environment benefits democracy building in at least two ways. It may allow the release of economic resources from defence to sectors which address domestic social and political problems. By no means all improvements in external security yield this kind of dividend immediately. NATO membership involves higher defence expenditure by the accessor states, though feelings of insecurity engendered by staying outside the Alliance might well produce even higher spending on the military. The second and political dividend of a more secure climate is that it narrows the scope for leaders, whether civilian or military, to justify authoritarian measures by reference to external threats. Where the reality or image of threat to national interests exists, democratization fares badly. Serbia under Milošević is a graphic case in point. For most East European states the international climate since the end of the Cold War has proved benign and worked to help democratization in terms of institution building as well as general stabilization.

Accession to NATO requires East European aspirants to establish effective civilian control over the armed forces (see Chapter 4), so helping to ensure that the military continue to play the non-political role so characteristic of the region in the past. NATO has also used its conditionality leverage and influence to encourage states such as Hungary and Romania to improve and stabilize relations with their neighbours (see Chapters 10 and 14). Settling outstanding disputes over territorial and minority rights questions, helps to relieve tensions within these states which might otherwise hamper democratic consolidation.

International organizations are also involved directly in trying to help tackle such tensions. As Neil MacFarlane shows in Chapter 5, the EU, Council of Europe, and most notably the CSCE/OSCE, have used a mix of more or less intrusive methods to prevent, manage, and even try to resolve ethnic-related disputes and conflicts. Some of the more intrusive, interventionist moves may produce resentment among majority groups and complicate the political situation. On the other hand, since ethnic divisions often fuel the kind of nationalist politics that undermine democratization, anything external actors can do to alleviate tensions on this front makes a useful contribution to democratic consolidation. The actions of international organizations may not only help stabilize the domestic environment in immediate terms. By giving greater voice to minority views they may help engage potentially disruptive groups more constructively in the democratization process. Ethnic minority rights can act as a multiplier of international influence, increasing the impact on democratic consolidation of what is often very limited external involvement in the area of internal security.

3. Economic issues

The economy is a highly internationalized area which has a pervasive, if largely indirect, bearing on democratic consolidation. The high degree of internationalization flows from the failure of the native command systems, the West's active promotion of market capitalism, and the strength of globalization. Because the bankruptcy of the command economy was so evident by the end of the communist regimes, nearly all members of the East European political elite looked for new formulas to achieve growth and build their own power. Those who found themselves in power after 1989–90 for the most part actively solicited external help and advice which was equally eagerly given. That advice has drawn enormous strength from the unchallenged material and intellectual primacy of market capitalism, transmitted and magnified by globalization. Sheer economic success impressed East European politicians and their advisers; they typically also saw market capitalism as offering the only way forward. The 'scientific', law-like quality of its prescriptions was scarcely questioned, even by those who thought they would be extremely difficult to follow. Aid, trade, and investment have added further power to the force of liberal market models and policies. Their penetration of Eastern Europe has come through state as well as commercial channels. It is in the economic sphere that states and international organizations have deployed some of their most effective sticks and carrots of conditionality and linked these with private sector investment and involvement in the region. It is in the economy, far more extensively than in the polity, that external factors enter everyday life. The economic traffic is thick and flows at all levels, ranging from IMF-to-government exchanges to transnational criminal transactions.

These flows of economic traffic impinge on democratic consolidation in very significant if indirect ways. It is often taken as axiomatic that marketization fosters economic competition and growth, both seen as being conducive to democratization. Insofar as competition strengthens pluralism and choice it clearly benefits democratization; where it creates extreme inequalities and large numbers of losers, competition may well have less positive political effects. How economic growth relates to democracy is a very complicated question.[16] There are no simple correlations between democracy and patterns of economic development, though it is plausible to contend that rapid falls in economic performance weaken the basis for democratic consolidation.[17] Given the mutual vulnerability of marketization and democratization, sudden failures in one sphere tend to disrupt the other, creating downward spirals. Similarly, good performance in one area can cushion against destabilization produced by adverse developments in the other.

When trying to map the interactions between external economic factors and democratic consolidation, it might be useful to distinguish between those located at the 'macro' level of general state policy and popular response, and those operating in 'micro' areas of the real economy. Even if it is extremely difficult to generalize about the overall role of the international dimension in economic policy, in some decisions, such as adoption of the Balcerowicz Plan, external factors played a key part (see Chapter 11). As László Valki notes in Chapter 10, pressures from the IMF were crucial in moving the Horn government to introduce austerity measures in 1995. In both instances, the moves associated with external influence formed part of generally successful economic strategies. Economic

[16] J. M. Maravall, *Regimes, Politics and Markets: Democratization and Economic Change in Southern and Eastern Europe* (Oxford: Oxford University Press, 1997); A. Przeworski et al., 'What Makes Democracies Endure?', *Journal of Democracy*, 7 (Jan. 1996), 39–55.

[17] Jon Elster et al., *Institutional Design in Post-communist Societies: Rebuilding the Ship at Sea* (Cambridge: Cambridge University Press, 1998), 307.

success in turn had positive rather than negative consequences for democratic consolidation. Where economic strategies have repeatedly ended in tears, as in the case of Russia, those failures have weakened the credibility of Western advice and the liberal market capitalist path. There may be some damaging spillover to the image of Western democratic models. In the East Central European states, a Western imprimatur seems to have lent reform measures greater credibility particularly among elites. The material support often tied to reform measures can help governments cushion against adverse consequences; and the fact that taking reform steps may boost the chances of joining a prosperous club can further enhance their popularity. In many cases, East European leaders have been able to use external pressures to help sell tough measures or at least make them more palatable. To the extent that this has strengthened political stability through periods of disruptive economic change, external factors have eased the course of democratization, quite apart from foreign aid and support helping to alleviate some of the social pain involved in rapid marketization.

The 'micro' dimension of economic reform reaches more directly and deeply into areas bearing on democratization. It is through connections with changes in the real economy that Western factors have most palpably affected democratic consolidation. Privatization is a case in point. A central plank in the Western economic reform project, privatization was actively promoted by international agencies as well as state-funded non-government bodies, like the Harvard Institute for International Development. By depriving state bureaucracies of their control over large tracts of the economy, privatization may have weakened groups with a vested interest in opposing both economic and political reform and so helped ease the course of democratization. Voucher-based privatization, pioneered in Czechoslovakia by Klaus, was meant to act as a democratizing agent by giving all citizens a stake in the new economic system. Despite some initial success here, the scheme eventually fostered corporate pluralism, as most of the vouchers were purchased by large investment funds. Privatization has typically had a limited democratizing effect, since in many post-communist states it has been viewed as a process of selling valuable state property at artificially low prices to members of the old and new elite. The cronyism, corruption, and crime surrounding privatization has damaged the image of market capitalism and underlined the weakness of the state. The withdrawal of the state from the economy, encouraged by Western actors, has in some states, such as Russia and Ukraine, associated external advice and influence with lawless, disorderly, and even anarchic change. The process of economic liberalization offers Western actors a large number of avenues through which they have exercised what have proved to be problematic as well as beneficial influences on democratization.

International position

The network of avenues available in any issue area depends in part on the international location of the state, on its relations with the major external actors. Positional factors may be as important as chronological ones in conditioning the overall impact of the international context. Philippe Schmitter has proposed that 'the significance of the international context increases over time in the course of a "wave of democratization" . . .'[18] In the East European 'wave' this appears to be valid only if one holds constant reasonably good relations with the West. The proposal best fits Poland, Hungary, and the Czech Republic which have seen a fairly steady thickening of relations with major Western institutions. Many other states, especially those further east, have experienced volatility and regression in their relations. Even in the cases that fit best, it is very difficult to show that the overall significance of the international context has grown over time. Major shifts in Soviet foreign policy allowed transition from communism to begin. During the transition stage, enthusiasm for Western models reached heights never equalled in later consolidation phases. In any event, it is difficult to gauge and compare the significance of very different phenomena: the volcanic international explosions affecting early transition and the channelled flows of international influence bearing on consolidation. Rather than seeking to find increases over time in the significance of the international context, it may be more realistic to look for variations in its role in states at different stages[19] and in different positions vis-à-vis major international institutions. The international category in which an East European state finds itself affects the kind of external signals transmitted and the way they are received and thus how they impinge on democratization.

The states covered in this study fall into three broad positional categories defined by degree of inclusion in the international

---

[18] Schmitter, 'Transitions from Authoritarian Rule', 47.

[19] Geoffrey Pridham, 'The International Dimension of Democratisation: Theory, Practice and Inter-regional Comparisons', in Geoffrey Pridham, Eric Herring, and George Sanford (eds.), *Building Democracy? The International Dimension of Democratisation in Eastern Europe* (London: Leicester University Press, 1997), 18–20.

community. The most important practical yardstick here is the position of states in queues for membership of the main Western clubs—NATO and the EU—or at least for association with these organizations. In the first category are the 'insiders', those states with secure prospects of early membership of NATO and/or the EU. The core, or 'double insiders', are Poland, Hungary, and the Czech Republic, who joined NATO in 1999 and are in line for early accession to the EU.[20] The other 'insiders', Slovakia and Estonia, are generally considered to be in line for the first wave of accession to the EU but in the second for NATO. The second category is queuing states, such as Slovakia, Bulgaria, Romania, and Croatia, reckoned to be in line for club entry though in the distant and rather uncertain future. Located beyond these queues are the 'outsiders': states which, at the most, have loose and semi-detached associations with NATO and the EU and little or no prospect of ever becoming full members. Ukraine is the 'outsider' closest to the end of the queues, while Russia lies some distance from them. Serbia under Milošević and Belarus qualify as extreme 'outsiders', ostracized by the international community.

The 'insiders' are obviously the states most deeply engaged with Western institutions and under closest general scrutiny. Yet this does not mean that international factors have necessarily made more of a difference so far to democratic consolidation in 'insider' than in 'queueing' states. Brussels has paid greater attention to conformity with economic and administrative requirements than to progress in democratic consolidation. In the 'core' states, acceptable performance on the democratization front has long been taken almost for granted. Since the decisions in principle were taken to admit the 'insiders', conditionality has arguably in practice applied mostly to technical areas. The 'insiders' have responded by concentrating attention on these areas, basically confident that they will gain accession as long as they conform to most of the technical requirements. As a result, democratic consolidation could become an area of relatively low external leverage and little internal response.

In 'queueing' states, both leverage and response tend to be higher if more sporadic. Western attention to democratic deficiencies may be higher as political shortfalls are typically greater and often exercise tighter constraints on economic reform. Where political conditionality is used to relegate states to queueing status,

[20] Heather Grabbe and Kirsty Hughes, *Enlarging the EU Eastwards* (London: Royal Institute of International Affairs, 1998), 112.

as happened with Slovakia in 1997, this can have mixed effects on democratization. Leaders may try to strengthen the nationalist basis of their support through more authoritarian and sustained defiance of international criticism. In other circumstances, international pressure may indeed aid the replacement of authoritarian governments by more democratic ones. For it is in 'queueing' states that public support for Western involvement tends to be greatest (see Chapter 8). The balance of effects depends partly on the length and nature of the queue. The power of conditionality tends to vary with perceived prospects of progress towards accession. In 1999 the EU and NATO had considerable potential leverage over political actors in Slovakia, Bulgaria, and Romania, striving to be part of an early second wave of accessions. By 2005, the gap separating the 'queueing' from the 'insider' states, several of which are likely to have joined both clubs, may have widened enough to dampen expectations and weaken leverage among those at the back of the line.

The distance dividing the 'outsiders' from prospects of anything more than loose association with the key clubs narrows international leverage to selective material incentives and sanctions. International sway over 'outsider' states with 'pariah regimes', as in Serbia under Milošević or Belarus under Lukashenka, becomes tenuous and the exercise of positive influence on democratization a very lengthy and difficult process.[21] Even in less extreme cases, such as Russia, external influence over democratization diminished in the late 1990s as the failure of radical market reforms prompted growing distrust of Western advice and suspicion of the West (see Chapter 19). Such inward-looking tendencies can lead to a downward spiral of marginalization, with national leaders championing self-reliance and the West writing off the state as a permanent 'outsider', relations with which should pursue security rather than democracy.

Domestic political context

While international positional factors may condition external flows and their reception, it is the domestic context which ultimately determines the effects on democratic consolidation. Domestic contexts in Eastern Europe may be seen as ranging over a spectrum from the liberal democratic to the illiberal, minimally democratized,

---

[21] Laurence Whitehead, 'Democratic Regions, Ostracism, and Pariahs', in Whitehead, *International Dimensions*, 406–10.

verging on the authoritarian. These contexts can be plotted on the kind of scale of democratization we noted earlier.

International promotion of democracy obviously fares well in liberal contexts and operates with considerable difficulty in illiberal and authoritarian ones. A key factor distinguishing the two kinds of political context is ethnic nationalism.[22] It is notable by its absence in the politics of the more liberal democratically advanced East Central European states. Where ethnic nationalism is strongly present, it makes politics more resistant to both external influence and liberal democratic consolidation. This has been patently clear in Serbia and was evident for periods in Romania and Slovakia. Milošević, Iliescu, and Mečiar used nationalist defiance to mobilize support for what amounted to traditional authoritarian rule. In other states, where ethnic nationalism has figured importantly if not as dominantly, it has had less predictably negative effects on the fortunes of international promotion of democracy. Sensitivity to ethnic questions made it more complicated for the governments of Latvia and Estonia to respond positively to Western requirements on minority rights. In neither case did the political salience of ethnic nationalism filter out external promotion of liberal democracy. The filtering effects depend on the specific role played by ethnic nationalism and its interaction with other domestic political factors. It is these other factors, such as mass and elite attitudes and the calculations of leaders, that largely explain the weakly liberal or illiberal nature of democratizing states in the former Soviet Union. In all former communist states it is these factors which ultimately determine the impact of the promotion of democratization from outside.

The general openness of the elites to international influences, and particularly to the Western project, distinguishes the more liberal states. It is self-evident that the Western orientation of most of the Polish, Czech, and Hungarian political class has made them receptive to the democracy promotion project. Members of the sub-class of experts and advisers in these states are especially attracted to foreign models for democratization and marketization, some by a general identification with things Western, others by the absence of viable alternatives and the appeal of what seems modern, progressive, and fashionable. In the less liberal states, these specialists, and the political class in general, have been more warily

---

[22] Milada Vachudova and Tim Snyder, 'Are Transitions Transitory? Two Types of Political Change in Eastern Europe since 1989', *East European Politics and Society*, 11 (Winter 1997), 1–35.

favourable, approving Western models in principle while insisting on the need to adjust them to national conditions.

How the political class stands on Western ideas conditions the response of political leaders to international signals. The generally pro-Western climate of opinion in Hungary helped to account for the toning down of nationalist elements within Antall's positions and the improvement in relations with Slovakia and Romania (Chapter 10). Some politicians have tried to lead from the front on questions of external involvement. In Klaus's case this meant taking neo-Western positions; in Mečiar's, it entailed a far more critical stance. For both, positions adopted on the question of international involvement brought gains in domestic standing. All leaders view the issue of external help and advice in terms of its repercussions not just within the political class but in their own party and among actual or potential coalition partners. Political expediency in relation to elite reaction figures prominently in calculations on how to respond to international signals.

Calculations of expediency extend to how external involvement may play with the public, particularly in connection with elections. There is a widespread assumption that elections typically amplify external signals bearing positively on democratic consolidation. This reasoning is based on the supposition that public opinion, freely expressed, will favour both democracy and close involvement with the West. Some evidence from Ukraine (Chapter 17) suggests a significant association between support for democratization and Western orientation. Over the region as a whole, however, patterns of popular attitudes seem to be more complex. According to Stephen Whitefield and Geoff Evans's data (Chapter 8), there is a connection between approval of markets and of the West. The link between support for democracy and favourable attitudes to Western involvement turns out to be a far weaker one.

Western involvement emerges from the data as less salient a popular issue than other internationally linked ones, such as national identity, sovereignty, and patriotism. These seem to be defined largely in relation to neighbouring states rather than to the West as a whole. So electoral support for Mečiar or Iliescu may not denote widespread anti-Westernism as much as ethnic nationalist sentiment. These leaders doubtless reckoned that taking an independent, even defiant, stance on international requests to do with minority rights would enhance their popular electoral appeal. Their defiantly nationalist stance probably helped them win elections in the early 1990s. It may be tempting to interpret their later electoral defeats in part as a reaction against their independent stance, as a victory for pro-Western and pro-democratic opinion. In all likelihood, economic shortfalls, always at the top of voters' grievances, figured more importantly than international and democratic deficits in shaping the outcome. If their defiance of international opinion played a role it was probably by dint of its association, highlighted by opposition groups in Romania and Slovakia, with poor economic performance.

How leaders and governments respond to external signals relating to democratization depends not just on political calculations of elite and public reactions. Decisive in such calculations is the overall compatibility of domestic leaders' policy priorities with those advocated by external actors. In the more liberal states there has been extensive overlap between domestic and Western preferences. It may therefore be easy to overstate the importance and impact of the Western project, to mistake policy confluence for policy influence. Equally, the basic tensions between Western policy priorities and those of authoritarian leaders might lead one to underestimate external influence in less obviously stable and liberal states. Where the domestic political climate is fragile, international factors may still make a significant contribution to democratization. In the sensitive context of ethnic policy in Estonia and Latvia, international agency officials have had to tread delicately but have certainly helped to create safeguards for minority rights (Chapter 9). In the difficult circumstances of Romania in the early 1990s, international non-governmental organizations made what Gallagher (Chapter 14) describes as a crucial contribution in supporting democratic values. In some ways, then, external contributions to democratization can be more critical in hard (illiberal) cases than in easy (liberal) ones. This should not be taken too far. In hard cases, contributions may be more palpable yet they tend to be less wide-reaching, less consistent, and less cumulative in their effects. The more advanced the process of democratic consolidation and the more compatible with Western approaches, norms and requirements, the more likely it is that international factors will have a positive, long-term impact.

This introductory review of how international factors bear on democratic consolidation in Eastern Europe has sought to convey the sheer complexity of the configurations and interactions involved. The multiplicity of external actors, the confusion of mixed signals, and the range of domestic contexts make analysis as challenging as it is interesting. The chapters that follow range widely in examining both international factors and domestic settings to try and shed light on the complex and often shadowy interplay between democratization and its external environment.

Comparative Perspectives

Part 1

Comparative Perspectives

1

Western Actors and the Promotion of Democracy

Karen E. Smith

This chapter examines the particular role of 'the West' in strengthening the process of democratic consolidation in Eastern Europe. Western actors have played an unprecedented, active role in promoting democracy in Eastern Europe, using a variety of instruments. These actors include Western governments, multilateral organizations, non-governmental organizations (NGOs), and foundations. The emphasis in this analysis will be on the policies and activities of governments and multinational organizations. These activities can be described as a 'Western project' to encourage democracy in Eastern Europe. The term implies a collective strategy, which has not thus far been articulated, and more coordination among the actors than has actually been the case. But it is accurate in that the Western actors involved agree on the ultimate aim of consolidating democracy in the region and, to a greater or lesser extent, on the instruments and means that should be used to do so. The East Europeans certainly have perceived the activities of the Western actors as a collective project.

The Western actors discussed here are individual Western states and primarily European multilateral organizations: the European Union (EU), the Organization for Security and Cooperation in Europe (OSCE), the Council of Europe, and NATO.[1] Other international

I would like to thank Margot Light, Jan Zielonka, Alex Pravda, Andrzej Korbonski, and the participants of the EUI workshop on democratic consolidation for their helpful comments on this chapter.

  [1] Until 1993, the European Union was generally known as the 'European Community' (with 'European Political Cooperation' the mechanism for coordinating foreign policies of the member states); until 1994 the OSCE was the 'Conference on Security and Cooperation in Europe' (CSCE).

organizations (the International Monetary Fund, World Bank, and European Bank for Reconstruction and Development (EBRD)) have also been involved in Eastern Europe, but mainly in helping the economic transformation; their activities are discussed in the chapter by Susan Senior Nello.

To a striking extent, Western states have worked collectively through multilateral European organizations to support democratic consolidation in Eastern Europe. Sceptical observers might view collective action as a 'cover' for national action. But this view is too simplistic: collective action is seen as potentially more effective, and more legitimate, than national efforts. European organizations can also wield instruments that individual states cannot: most notably, they can extend membership to the East European countries.

Although Germany has been the primary trading partner for many of the East European countries considered here, one of the largest sources of investment in Eastern Europe, and the largest single donor of aid to the region, it has sought to 'multilateralize' Western policy towards Eastern Europe.[2] Germany has not wanted to be left on its own with the responsibility for supporting Eastern Europe's transformation or for dealing with security problems in the region. Several Western states have also pushed for multilateral action, as a way of balancing Germany's potential role in the region.[3] Germany championed enlargement (most notably in the case of the EU), but it has not been the only state to do so: the UK, Denmark, and now even France strongly support EU enlargement; the USA has pushed for NATO enlargement (to the Czech Republic, Hungary, and Poland, at least); the Scandinavian countries would like the EU to embrace the Baltic states; Italy has supported Slovenia's membership in the EU and NATO; and France has supported the Council of Europe's enlargement.

---

[2] Germany's relations with several of its neighbours (particularly the Czech Republic and Poland) are not problem free, and it needs to act within a multilateral context or risk alienating them. See Hans Stark, 'L'Est de l'Europe et l'Allemagne: des rapports complexes', *Politique étrangère*, 4 (1991); Lothar Gutjhar, *German Foreign and Defence Policy after Unification* (London: Pinter, 1994); and Reinhardt Rummel, 'The German Debate on International Security Institutions', in Marco Carnovale (ed.), *European Security and International Institutions after the Cold War* (New York: St Martin's, 1995).

[3] France, in particular, has supported a strong EU role in Eastern Europe, closer ties between the WEU and East European countries, and a strengthened Council of Europe. See Jean-Christopher Romer and Thomas Schreiber, 'La France et l'Europe Centrale', *Politique étrangère*, 4 (1995).

The new East European regimes themselves declared that their first foreign policy priority was to 'rejoin Europe', meaning those organizations that seemed to have ensured security, democracy, and prosperity in Western Europe: the EU and NATO. Western states cannot escape from the fact that these organizations have become the focus of East European foreign policies; this has necessarily over-shadowed their bilateral relations with the countries of the region.

The first section of this chapter analyses the West's objectives with respect to Eastern Europe. Promoting democracy is not the only Western aim, nor is it even the primary one. Western actors have paid considerably more attention to aiding the economic transformation, and in certain countries, to maintaining stability. The second section discusses the instruments that the West has used to promote democratic consolidation—from aid to the conditional offer of membership in European organizations. The third and final section evaluates the impact that the West has had on democratic consolidation in Eastern Europe. Western pressure and assistance have helped political reform, but the West's impact varies. In some cases, Western actors may even have had a negative impact on the process.

Western Objectives

There has been a consensus in the West that democratization in Eastern Europe should be supported and promoted, and that the final goal is that of consolidating democracy throughout the region. However, Western governments and multilateral organizations have not defined the components of 'democracy'. In fact, the implicit model of democracy that has guided Western assistance has varied from country to country—with each country touting its own model.[4] Nor have Western countries set out a strategy (individual or collective) on how they will try to reach the objective of democratic consolidation in specific East European countries. This lack of strategic direction has meant that the signals sent to Eastern Europe about democratization have sometimes been unclear. Furthermore, the objective of democratic consolidation in Eastern Europe has not always fitted with other objectives. The West has also sought to promote the market economy in Eastern Europe, prevent conflicts, implement a Balkan peace plan, and counter international criminal activities.

---

[4] See Thomas Carothers, 'Democracy Assistance: the question of strategy', *Democratization*, 4: 3 (1997), 120–2.

The East European case is unique in that political and economic systems must be transformed—an unprecedented situation compared with other cases of democratization. The West would like to see both the successful consolidation of democracy and the transformation to the market economy in the region. While, in the long term, stability and security depend on the success of both transformations, in the short term economic and political reforms may not be compatible or mutually reinforcing. Western actors have not clearly stated what their priorities are among these objectives.

In the immediate aftermath of the 'revolutions of 1989', it was more or less assumed that democracy would naturally accompany the economic transformation from communism. The new regimes also seemed willing to pursue democratic reforms, so less outside help for democratization seemed necessary. The East European countries have received much more assistance for economic reform, an indication of the emphasis given to aiding the economic transition.

Little attention has been paid to the political effects of economic reform programmes (and vice versa).[5] Economic liberalization can weaken the state, particularly if governments are forced to adopt certain reforms (as in structural adjustment programmes). Thus, economic reform may not be compatible with reforms aimed at establishing accountable and transparent government. Furthermore, economic reforms entail enormous costs for the population, notably in rising unemployment.

Observers are divided over the consequences of the economic transition for democratic consolidation. Peter Volten warned that economic assistance needed to take political factors into account, and that the 'democratizers should be left room for policy choices *vis-à-vis* their electorate'.[6] But Juan Linz and Alfred Stepan argued that in East Central Europe, democratic institutions, seen as legitimate, are insulated from the economic system.[7] In any event, a more comprehensive and consistent approach to supporting economic and political reforms would be desirable.

Several observers have suspected that the West's real aim has been to see market economies introduced in Eastern Europe (with

[5] As Thomas Carothers found in the case of US assistance to Romania. Thomas Carothers, *Assessing Democracy Assistance: The Case of Romania* (Washington: Carnegie Endowment for International Peace, 1996), 106–7.

[6] Peter Volten, 'Introduction and Assessment', in Peter Volten (ed.), *Bound to Change: Consolidating Democracy in East Central Europe* (New York: Institute for East West Studies, 1992), 23.

[7] Juan Linz and Alfred Stepan, 'Toward Consolidated Democracies', *Journal of Democracy*, 7: 2 (1996), 30.

the consequent increased opportunities for investment and trade), and that political reform is promoted only to the extent that it allows economic reformers some leeway.[8] In the most eastern countries of the region, the West has supported economic liberalizers who may not be so democratically minded (as in Russia), particularly where there has been interest in investment in natural resource sectors (such as gas and oil). There has been, though, support for promoting democracy as an end in and of itself: democracies make better neighbours, so democratic consolidation in Eastern Europe will ensure long-term security. In 1996, US Deputy Secretary of State Strobe Talbott wrote:

The larger and more close-knit the community of nations that choose democratic forms of government, the safer and more prosperous Americans will be, since democracies are demonstrably more likely to maintain their international commitments, less likely to engage in terrorism or wreak environmental damage, and less likely to make war on each other.[9]

The objectives of political and economic reform have, in several cases, been overtaken by that of stability. By the early 1990s, there were signs that the transformation process in Eastern Europe would not be a smooth one. Political liberalization unleashed destructive, nationalistic forces, tragically so in the case of Yugoslavia.[10] The imperatives of halting the Yugoslav conflict and preventing further outbreaks of violence have entailed Western tolerance of (or even support for) authoritarian leaders, in the Balkans in particular. Assisting political reforms has been seen as a way of preventing conflicts, but in the long term; in the short term, the objective of stability has won out over that of democratic consolidation. While this is understandable under the circumstances, the West has sent inconsistent signals about its objectives and priorities, which may undermine attempts to encourage democratization in these and other East European countries.

---

[8] Gordon Crawford suggested that the UK has tended to see political liberalization as a means to economic development rather than as an end in itself; see *Promoting Democracy, Human Rights and Good Governance through Development Aid: A Comparative Study of the Policies of Four Northern Donors*, Centre for Democratization Studies, Working Paper on Democratization no. 1 (Leeds: Leeds University Press, 1996), 6–9.

[9] Strobe Talbott, 'Democracy and the National Interest', *Foreign Affairs*, 75: 6 (1996), 48–9.

[10] The process of democratization can result in violent conflict, especially if politics come to be dominated by ethnically based political parties pursuing nationalist claims. See Renée de Nevers, 'Democratization and Ethnic Conflict', *Survival*, 35: 2 (1993).

There is also concern about the implications of the political transition for international crime (nuclear materials smuggling, drug trafficking, illegal immigration rings, and so on). A desire for a strong leadership better able to combat such activity may outweigh, at least in the short term, the West's objective of democracy. In addition, the West needs to secure the cooperation of the more important East European states—in particular Russia—in various areas of international affairs. Russian (tacit or explicit) support has been needed for United Nations Security Council resolutions on Iraq or Yugoslavia, for disarmament initiatives, for nuclear non-proliferation, and so on.[11] Pressuring Russia to carry out democratic reforms could endanger these other goals, particularly when an alternative (though democratically elected) leadership may be even less inclined to cooperate with the West.

Thus, the objective of supporting democratization in Eastern Europe has competed with other considerations and has not always come out on top. While it would be unrealistic to expect it to be otherwise in international relations, the signals that the West has sent to the East European countries have been quite confused. This could hinder Western influence on the democratic consolidation process.

Western Capabilities

The West has used numerous instruments to strengthen democratic consolidation in Eastern Europe, which reflect both 'top-down' and 'bottom-up' approaches. Top-down pressure for reform has been applied primarily through the use of political conditionality: the East European countries are supposed to meet certain political conditions to benefit from aid, loans, trade concessions, closer ties, and membership in key regional organizations. Other top-down instruments have been international observation of elections, to ensure they are conducted freely and fairly, and intrusive measures (such as fact-finding missions), which have been launched in cases where progress in political reform has been slow or specific help requested. These instruments have placed pressure on governments to carry out democratic reforms or follow democratic rules. The bottom-up approach has entailed giving aid to help build democratic institutions and practices, including the development of civil society.

---

[11] Granted, of course, Western countries themselves are not always united behind many of these goals.

The top-down approach has posed numerous problems. Joan Nelson argued against the use of conditionality as a means of promoting democratic consolidation: 'Other than to discourage backsliding, dialogue and support are generally more appropriate techniques than conditionality for promoting broadened participation and competitive politics.'[12] Mary Kaldor and Ivan Vejvoda argued, however, that 'international insistence on compliance with formal criteria is essential', and that emphasis must also be placed on 'substantive' aspects of democracy.[13] Assistance should be given to fostering bottom-up democratization, such as supporting community development. Both approaches can be effective, and should be combined.

The various instruments have not been used altogether consistently, nor has there has been enough emphasis on coordinating the instruments used by the different actors involved. There has been considerable overlap between organizations and governments carrying out similar activities. There was, for a time, even rivalry between the OSCE and the Council of Europe over responsibility for promoting democracy in Eastern Europe.[14]

The use of political conditionality

To encourage democratic reforms and the protection of human rights, the West has used political conditionality in its relations with East European countries. Political conditionality entails the linking, by a state or international organization, of perceived benefits to another state (such as aid, trade concessions, cooperation agreements, or international organization membership) to the fulfilment of conditions relating to the protection of human rights and the advancement of democratic principles.[15] Given the extent to which the East European countries want the benefits on offer from the West, the use of conditionality could provide a strong push towards democratization. But the East European countries have not all been offered the same benefits. Essentially two zones have

---

[12] Joan M. Nelson with Stephanie J. Eglinton, *Encouraging Democracy: What Role for Conditioned Aid?* (Washington: Overseas Development Council, 1992), 61.

[13] Mary Kaldor and Ivan Vejvoda, 'Democratization in Central and East European Countries', *International Affairs*, 73: 1 (1997), 82.

[14] See Victor-Yves Ghebali, *L'OSCE dans l'Europe post-communiste, 1990–1996: vers une identité paneuropéenne de sécurité* (Brussels: Bruylant, 1996), 548–65; and Neil Kritz, 'The CSCE in the New Era', *Journal of Democracy*, 4: 3 (1993), 24–7. France wanted to develop the Council of Europe's role, while the USA preferred the OSCE (not surprisingly, given that it is a member of the OSCE but not the Council of Europe).

[15] See Georg Sorensen, *Political Conditionality* (London: Frank Cass, 1993), 4.

developed. The first has been closely tied to the West and included in the queue for EU and NATO membership, while the second has been much less connected. Conditionality has more of an effect on 'recalcitrant' countries in the first zone, less on those in the second. It has also been inconsistently applied in the second zone to a greater degree than in the first.

Of the Western actors, the EU has gone the furthest in applying conditionality. Given the benefits it can offer, it could potentially wield a great deal of influence as a result. By and large, the East European countries have been eager to prove they meet the conditions, although some have been irritated by conditionality: Hungary once described it as 'patronizing', while Poland argued it was not necessary since it had already demonstrated its commitment to democracy.[16] While in some cases, conditionality may be largely superfluous (as the governments needed little outside pressure to undertake reforms), the EU conditions could have been influential where democratic reforms were more contested. Setting conditions has provided a guide for governments pursuing the rewards on offer, and given them an excuse for launching unpopular reforms.

From 1988, the European Community (EC) set conditions for the conclusion of trade and cooperation agreements with the East European states. These were not explicitly declared, but if a country contravened CSCE human rights provisions or did not make progress with political reforms, the EC withheld the prospect of an agreement. For example, trade and cooperation agreements with Bulgaria and Romania were held up in 1989 and 1990 over concerns about their treatment of minorities.

Explicit and stricter conditions were set for second-generation association ('Europe') agreements. Prospective associates would have to be committed to five conditions: the rule of law, human rights, a multi-party system, free and fair elections, and a market economy. There are now ten East European associates: Bulgaria, the Czech Republic, Estonia, Hungary, Latvia, Lithuania, Poland, Romania, Slovakia, and Slovenia. In some cases, Europe agreements seem to have been extended less as a result of a careful examination of whether a country met the conditions than because of geopolitical concerns: for example, agreements with Bulgaria and Romania were negotiated in the wake of the attempted coup in the Soviet Union in August 1991. It was considered important in this case to extend the Western 'sphere of influence' to these countries.

---

[16] See Giles Merritt, *Eastern Europe and the USSR: The Challenge of Freedom* (London: Kogan Page, 1991), 23–4.

EU relations with the former Soviet republics (with the exception of the Baltic states) have been less intense than those with the associates. They have been offered partnership and cooperation agreements (PCA), which are less far-reaching than the Europe agreements. These are to be concluded only with countries that have proceeded with economic reform and are politically stable. Almost all of the former Soviet republics have now concluded a PCA, even where their commitment to human rights and democratic principles is questionable.[17] But in September 1997, the EU decided not to conclude a PCA with Belarus because of that country's disregard for democratic principles and human rights.

The EU has had even more trouble deciding how to handle relations with Russia. It held up implementation of the PCA with Russia over the intervention in Chechnya in December 1994. But by June 1995, the European Council decided to proceed with the agreement: the view prevailed that building ties with Russia was more important than trying to pressure Russia to stop the fighting. With renewed warfare in Chechnya in 1999–2000, the Council decided to impose limited sanctions on Russia, but did not suspend the PCA. Once again, the fears of isolating Russia prevailed over the implementation of conditionality.

The EU has also set conditions for the conclusion of Stabilization and Association agreements (SAA) with the countries in southeastern Europe: Albania, Bosnia-Hercegovina, Croatia, Federal Republic of Yugoslavia, and the former Yugoslav Republic of Macedonia (FYROM). In addition to conditions regarding respect for democratic principles and human and minority rights, each country must be willing to develop relations with its neighbours and comply with obligations under the peace agreements (where applicable).[18] Only FYROM has thus far been considered eligible to negotiate an SAA; Croatia, following elections there in January–February 2000, will be the next in line.

Since May 1992, the EU has inserted a 'human rights clause' into its agreements with OSCE states. This permits the suspension of the agreements if human rights, democratic principles, and the principles of the market economy are not respected. But, such measures can be taken only after consultations have taken place,

---

[17] At the first meeting of the PCA cooperation council with Uzbekistan in September 1999, the EU delivered a strong message requesting that Uzbekistan improve its human rights and democratic record. *European Voice* (9–15 Sept. 1999).

[18] General Affairs Council, 'Council Conclusions on South-East Europe' (21–2 June 1999).

and priority is to be given to keeping the agreement operational wherever possible.[19] No agreement with an East European state has yet been suspended on the basis of the human rights clause.

In 1989, the West launched several aid programmes for Eastern Europe. In August 1989, the G24 (the twenty-four members of the OECD) agreed to coordinate their aid to Poland and Hungary, the two fastest reforming countries in Eastern Europe at the time (the programme is coordinated by the European Commission). At the same time, the EC set up its own aid programme, PHARE, initially also for Poland and Hungary. Both aid programmes set conditions for the extension of aid to other countries: commitment to the rule of law, respect for human rights, establishment of a multiparty system, the holding of free elections, and economic liberalization. Thus, G24 and PHARE aid was not extended to Romania until the beginning of 1991, because it did not fulfil the conditions. PHARE was not extended to Croatia or Serbia/Montenegro, and was limited to supporting the implementation of the peace agreement in Bosnia-Hercegovina. TACIS, the EU aid programme for the former Soviet republics (set up in 1991), is also conditional: action can be taken if human rights and democratic principles are not respected. In September 1997, the EU cut off technical assistance to Belarus.[20] In January 2000, the Council decided to channel TACIS funding to Russia into humanitarian projects.

In May 1990, the EBRD was established to provide loans to assist economic reform in Eastern Europe. It was the first multilateral organization obliged to link loans to political conditionality. Only countries that are committed to and applying the principles of multiparty democracy, pluralism, and market economics are eligible for loans.[21] EBRD operations in a country can be suspended or modified if it does not make progress towards democracy.

[19] See European Commission, 'On the Inclusion of Respect for Democratic Principles and Human Rights in Agreements between the Community and Third Countries', COM (95) 216 final (23 May 1995). Since 1995, the human rights clause has also been included in EU agreements with all third countries, but the clause does not include the principles of the market economy. This illustrates the uniqueness of the dual transition in Eastern Europe.

[20] Humanitarian projects, or those which support the democratization process directly, were exempt. In December 1997, the Council approved a programme (ECU 5 million over two years) to develop civil society in Belarus (OJ L 1, 3 Jan. 1998).

[21] According to Article 1 of the agreement establishing the EBRD. The EBRD compiled a list of factors that are relevant for judging the state of democracy in recipient countries, including free elections, independent judiciary, and freedom of speech. See European Bank for Reconstruction and Development, 'Political Aspects of the Mandate of the European Bank for Reconstruction and Development', London (no date).

No country has had its EBRD loans suspended because of political concerns, although the EBRD's Board of Directors has found that in a few countries, commitment to the three principles was inadequate.[22] The EBRD has not explicitly stated that its policy towards a country has changed as a result of political considerations, but loans have been granted to private enterprises rather than governments, as in the case of Belarus, and countries further behind in (economic and political) reforms are less attractive lending targets in any event. None the less, the EBRD's message regarding political conditionality is unclear.

Conditionality has been most manifestly used with respect to membership in European multilateral organizations. Because of the extent to which the East European countries want to join European organizations, the conditionality of membership has been the West's most powerful instrument for encouraging democratization.

Membership in the Council of Europe has been seen as the first step towards EU and NATO membership, as it would confirm the democratic credentials of the new East European regimes. Already in 1989, several East European countries applied for membership. In October 1993, the first summit of the Council of Europe set out the membership conditions (until then only implicit): the people's representatives must have been chosen by means of free and fair elections based on universal suffrage; freedom of expression and notably of the media must be guaranteed; the rights of national minorities must be protected; and the state must sign the European Convention on Human Rights and accept its supervisory machinery within a short period.[23]

No major questions arose regarding the democratic credentials of the first three countries admitted, Hungary, Czechoslovakia, and Poland. Other East European countries also joined, although there has been less consensus regarding their eligibility for membership (see Box 1.1). Belarus, however, has been given the cold shoulder: in January 1997, the Parliamentary Assembly suspended its guest status. The Parliamentary Assembly increasingly attached obligations to its opinions on the membership candidates (particularly with respect to the protection of national minorities), but the view prevailed that excluding them from membership would lead in the long run to a weakening of domestic democratic forces.[24]

---

[22] European Bank for Reconstruction and Development, *Annual Report 1995*, 7 and *Annual Report 1996*, 8. See also the *Annual Report 1998*.

[23] See Hans Winkler, 'Democracy and Human Rights in Europe: A Survey of the Admission Practice of the Council of Europe', *Austrian Journal of Public and International Law*, 47: 2–3 (1995), 155.

[24] Ibid. 158–67.

Box 1.1. *East European Membership in the Council of Europe*

Hungary (1990)
Czechoslovakia (1991)
Poland (1991)
Bulgaria (1992)
Czech Republic (1993)
Estonia (1993)
Lithuania (1993)
Romania (1993)
Slovakia (1993)
Slovenia (1993)
Albania (1995)
Latvia (1995)
Former Yugoslav Republic of Macedonia (1995)
Ukraine (1995)
Croatia (1996)
Russia (1996)
Georgia (1999)

The accessions of Russia and Croatia generated considerable controversy. In February 1995, the Parliamentary Assembly suspended its consideration of the Russian application over the intervention in Chechnya.[25] After peace talks began, the Parliamentary Assembly voted in September 1995 to reactivate the application; that decision was finalized in December, after Council of Europe observers declared that the Duma elections were fair and correct. In early 1996, several states (most notably Germany and France) came out strongly in support for Russian membership: not only would this boost President Yeltsin's chances of re-election in the June 1996 elections, but it would give Russia recognition as NATO moved closer to enlargement. As a result, even though a Council of Europe report acknowledged that Russia did not fulfil the conditions, Russia was admitted in January 1996.[26] It was too important an actor to exclude. As French Foreign Minister Hervé de Charette said, 'I believe it is preferable to let Russia sit at the table so that we can talk among ourselves.'[27]

---

[25] Evelyne Gelin, 'L'Adhésion de la Russie au Conseil de l'Europe à la lumière de la crise tchétchène', *Revue générale de droit international public*, 99: 3 (1995), 625.
[26] See Alister Doyle, 'Council of Europe Accepts Russia, Boosts Yeltsin', *Reuters* (26 Jan. 1996).
[27] Quoted in 'France Backs Russia to Join Council Europe', *Reuters* (25 Jan. 1996).

The exception made for Russia opened the way for Croatia to protest its exclusion: if Russia could join, why not Croatia? Consideration of the Croatian application was suspended and delayed several times in 1996, over concerns about minority rights, democracy, freedom of the press, and the Croatian role in the Bosnian peace process. In June 1996, Croatia was asked to meet five conditions before it could join, including cooperation with the International War Crimes Tribunal, support of free elections in Bosnia (particularly in the city of Mostar), return of Serb refugees to Croatia, and dropping prosecutions against the independent media. The Croatian government and opposition protested that Croatia was being asked to meet tougher standards than such member countries as Russia, Romania, or Albania.[28] In October 1996, the Council of Ministers voted to admit Croatia, having determined (perhaps prematurely) that the conditions had been met.

The prospective benefits of Council of Europe membership have evidently been considered to outweigh any potential leverage gained from excluding countries on the basis of conditionality. In this view, membership would initiate a process of familiarization with and socialization into Western democratic practices. But ensuring that new member countries fulfil the membership criteria and respect democratic principles and human rights may become problematic. Membership could be seen to have legitimized the regime and may not contribute to changing undemocratic practices. Croatia made little progress towards democracy before President Tudjman's death in December 1999. In May 1998, a Parliamentary Assembly committee noted that Russia had still not fulfilled several key obligations. As a last resort, of course, the Council of Europe can expel a country. There is a mixed record in this respect. Greece withdrew on its own accord in 1969, before being forced out. Turkey, however, was suspended from the Parliamentary Assembly's activities, but not from the Council of Europe, following the 1980 military coup. In April 2000, the Parliamentary Assembly considered suspending Russia over the violation of human rights in Chechnya. But the Committee of Ministers did not follow suit. Rather than press Russia, the Council of Europe chose not to alienate it, at a time when Russia's relations with the West were tense (as a result of issues such as NATO enlargement and Kosovo).

The West may have wasted leverage by hastily offering membership in the Council of Europe to so many East European countries.

---

[28] Open Media Research Institute, *Daily Digest* (17 May 1996).

EU and NATO enlargement has been envisaged only as a possibility for a limited number of East European states. Opening up at least one key organization may mitigate the effects of exclusion from others. But none the less, the signals sent by the West have been confused.

EU membership has been a top priority of the new regimes in Eastern Europe. In addition to generating prosperity, European Community membership helped to consolidate democracy in Greece, Spain, and Portugal (ineligible for membership until they embarked on a course of democratization), so it could be expected to do the same in Eastern Europe. But the member states were initially quite divided over the issue of enlargement. Germany, the UK, and Denmark actively favoured enlarging to East European countries, primarily because it would help spread stability and security eastwards. The other member states were much less positive, concerned about the implications of an eastern enlargement for the EU's institutions, decision-making procedures, and policies (such as the Common Agricultural Policy).

In June 1993, the European Council finally agreed that the East European countries that had concluded Europe agreements could join the EU, but would have to meet certain conditions first. Applicant states must have a functioning market economy with the capacity to cope with competitive pressures and market forces within the Community; they must have achieved stability of institutions guaranteeing democracy, the rule of law, human rights, and respect for and protection of minorities; and they must be able to take on the obligations of membership, including adherence to the aims of economic and political union.[29] All ten East European associates then applied to join (Bulgaria, the Czech Republic, Estonia, Hungary, Latvia, Lithuania, Poland, Romania, Slovakia, and Slovenia). The conditions do seem to have prompted most of these countries to undertake political reforms, and to take steps to improve relations with their neighbours (including guaranteeing minority rights).

In July 1997, the Commission published its opinions on the membership applications: it judged that several countries had problems in areas such as minority rights and the stability of institutions, but that only Slovakia did not meet the political criteria and so should be excluded from membership negotiations on that basis.[30]

[29] European Council in Copenhagen (21–2 June 1993), Conclusions of the Presidency, SN 180/93, 13.

[30] See European Commission, 'Agenda 2000: For a Stronger and Wider Union', *EU Bulletin, Supplement 5/97*. The EU has also taken steps to ensure that

The European Council in December 1997 decided to launch accession talks with the five East European countries that came closest to meeting the Copenhagen conditions: the Czech Republic, Estonia, Hungary, Poland, and Slovenia.

The decision was not entirely free of inconsistencies. Estonia was not that much further ahead in its fulfilment of the EU's membership conditions than its Baltic neighbours: its participation in the first round of enlargement talks seemed to reflect an attempt to mitigate the effects of exclusion from NATO (see below). Once more, then, considerations of stability clashed with the application of conditionality; the outcome again sent mixed signals to Eastern Europe about the West's objectives.

There was concern that exclusion from the first round of EU enlargement would have negative implications for the remaining applicant countries. Thus, in early 1998, special Accession Partnerships were concluded with all ten East European countries (including Slovakia), which contain a precise timetable for meeting the membership criteria and provide for additional EU aid. By the end of 1999, Latvia, Lithuania, and Slovakia (thanks to the election of a democratically minded government) had made considerable progress and the EU was ready to open talks. But this would have isolated Bulgaria and Romania at a time of great instability in south-eastern Europe. The Helsinki European Council in December 1999 decided to open talks with all five countries on the basis that all met the Copenhagen political conditions. This might have been jumping the gun again in the name of geopolitical stability, as well as conveniently allowing the EU to justify not opening talks with Turkey.

NATO has likewise agreed to enlarge to other European countries. Its September 1995 Study on Enlargement indicated that there was no rigid or fixed list of criteria—enlargement would be decided on a case-by-case basis. New member states will, however, be expected to conform to principles of democracy, individual liberty, and the rule of law.[31] Strategic considerations are none the less

---

sanctions against member states that 'regress' can be taken even after accession. The June 1997 Draft Amsterdam Treaty provides for the suspension of a member state that violates EU fundamental principles (liberty, democracy, respect for human rights and fundamental freedoms, and the rule of law). The EU would, thus, have a rather dramatic means of exercising leverage over member states whose democratic consolidation process reverses.

[31] NATO, 'Study on NATO Enlargement' (Brussels, 1995), chs. 1 and 5. See also NATO's Washington Summit Communique (24 Apr. 1999).

paramount: even if a country met the criteria, membership is not ensured. NATO's leverage for encouraging democracy is less signific-ant than the EU's.[32]

In June 1997, NATO agreed that it would enlarge first to the Czech Republic, Hungary, and Poland, leaving many disappointed East European states in the waiting room. While the Partner-ship for Peace programme was designed to be inclusive, there has remained a dramatic distinction between NATO members and out-siders, marked by a nuclear guarantee. This has made exclusion from NATO that much more potentially damaging, in addition to the negative implications it could have for the West's relations with Russia (and for undermining pro-Western reformers there). The divisive process of NATO enlargement may end up destabiliz-ing Eastern Europe—which would negatively affect democratic consolidation.

Election monitoring

International election observation has become one of the most popular instruments for promoting democracy. Its aim has been to deter electoral fraud and to ensure that elections are 'free and fair'. Of the European organizations, the OSCE has been the most active in this area and its Office of Democratic Institutions and Human Rights (ODIHR) has often coordinated Western electoral observation missions.[33] In 1998 alone, the ODIHR sent election observation missions to Armenia, Azerbaijan, Bosnia-Hercegovina, Czech Republic, FYROM, Hungary, Latvia, Moldova, Montenegro/ Federal Republic of Yugoslavia, Slovakia, and Ukraine.[34] The USA, Canada, West European countries, and the EU have sent observers (as have NGOs in North America and Western Europe).

Election observation may be useful in spotting irregularities, but there have been problems with the way it has been carried out.[35] Too many observers have been inexperienced, have spent very little time in the country holding elections, and have not coordinated

[32] This in addition to the consideration that NATO did not exclude Greek and Portuguese authoritarian regimes from membership, so that its democratic cre-dentials appear less firm.

[33] The ODIHR was initially (1990–2) called the Office of Free Elections.

[34] Organization for Security and Cooperation in Europe, *Annual Report 1998* (Vienna).

[35] Thomas Carothers, 'The Observers Observed', *Journal of Democracy*, 8:3 (1997), 19.

their activities with each other. Although the election itself may be conducted regularly, foreign election observers who are only present for a short period may miss aspects of the electoral process which are highly undemocratic (such as restricting the opposition's access to the media).[36] The ODIHR has been developing a more in-depth approach to election observance, with an Electoral Task Force formed for each major operation.[37] Technical assistance is also given to countries to help them prepare for elections.

Improvements to international election monitoring will mean little, however, if Western states are not prepared to take action in cases in which elections are not free and fair. Criticizing an election could be politically untenable (especially when the incumbent government is supported by Western countries) or could be seen as contributing to a country's isolation. There has been little agreement as to how severely new and fragile democracies should be judged. This inevitably has led to mixed signals about the West's stance on the importance of free and fair elections.

On several occasions, Western governments have been unwilling to criticize East European countries even though observers witnessed irregularities. After the first round of Albanian legislative elections in May 1996, the ODIHR denounced grave irregularities in the voting, including fraud and intimidation of voters. Its final evaluation called for a partial rerun of the elections, although other election observers (including the US diplomatic mission in Tirana) decided that the irregularities did not bring into question the legitimacy of the newly elected parliament.[38] Backed by Western states, Albanian President Sali Berisha agreed to hold new elections in only three constituencies. This may only have bottled up trouble, as the events of 1997 later illustrated. The OSCE also condemned Croatia's presidential election in June 1997 but this prompted little criticism by Western governments.[39]

---

[36] The EU observation mission in Russia, in December 1993, suffered from several of these problems. There were only 207 observers, dispatched in 66 teams throughout the country, and they did not stay long enough to witness irregularities in the counting and tabulation of votes. The EU mission was not coordinated with that of national and European parliamentarians, who refused to coordinate with the CFSP observers. Elsa Fenet, 'Joint Actions in the Field of Election Observation', *CFSP Forum*, Nos. 3 and 4 (1996).

[37] OSCE Office for Democratic Institutions and Human Rights, *Annual Report for 1996* (Warsaw, Poland), 7–8.

[38] Ghebali, *L'OSCE*, 623–6.

[39] 'Seeing that it's all fair and above board', *The Economist* (23 Aug. 1997).

Intrusive measures

More intrusive than election observance are other measures such as expert and fact-finding missions. Under the OSCE's Vienna Mechanism (agreed in 1989), every OSCE state can ask for information from another state on human dimension matters (such as human rights), and request a bilateral meeting to discuss a possible solution to the problem. In the first two years, the Vienna Mechanism was applied 100 times. In 1990, the mechanism was expanded to include expert missions and, in 1991, to rapporteur missions. Such missions can be sent without the invitation of the state concerned, although, in practice, it is difficult to see what the OSCE could do to force a state to accept a mission.[40] Serbia, for example, refused to authorize a mission on its territory in 1993. The OSCE's High Commissioner on National Minorities (a position established in 1992) is also supposed to be able to enter a state without its approval. The High Commission's task is to try to contain and ease tensions involving national minority issues, and to alert the OSCE when such tensions threaten to escalate.

These intrusive measures have been useful in helping governments, or parties to a dispute, that are willing, in the first instance, to try to resolve problems and in the second, to ask for outside assistance. Where these conditions do not hold, as in Serbia, such measures may prove considerably less effective.

Aid for consolidating democracy

In addition to the above instruments, the West has provided assistance specifically targeted at building democracy from the ground up. But compared to the resources devoted to assisting the economic reform process in Eastern Europe (which many have also criticized as insufficient), only a small amount of aid has been specifically targeted to supporting democratization.

Multilateral programmes

Three European organizations—the Council of Europe, OSCE, and EU—have launched assistance programmes to help consolidate democracy in Eastern Europe. While these programmes may indeed help to consolidate democracy, they have been hampered by

[40] The EU has also sent fact-finding missions to East European countries (such as Belarus in 1997), but these have the approval of the country concerned.

complex administrative procedures, which East European actors find confusing.

The earliest democracy assistance programmes were those of the Council of Europe, set up in 1989 for new and prospective member states: the Demosthenes, Themis, and Lode programmes. They have trained policy makers, judges, prosecutors, lawyers, elected officials, local leaders, and administrators, in fields such as legal cooperation, human rights, media, education, social affairs, local politics, and finance, through the use of East–West exchanges of experts, seminars, and training programmes. The 1996 budget for the programmes was French Francs (FF) 50 million (approximately ECU 7.5 million or $8.3 million).

The OSCE has provided aid for democratization, on a small scale, through the ODIHR. Because of its small budget (in 1999, it was 7.64 per cent of the total OSCE budget),[41] the ODIHR has concentrated on election monitoring, assisting in the building of civil societies, and providing legal support. Its activities have included long-term projects to implement new laws and establish human rights institutions, and to train judges, officials, and NGOs. Between 1992 and 1995, the ODIHR held ten seminars on issues such as tolerance, migration, free media, and local democracy. The seminars, however, were too general and not interactive enough—taking on the format of lectures to the new democracies. In 1994, the number of seminars was reduced to two a year, with an emphasis on regional seminars.[42] The reliance on conferences and seminars, by the OSCE and Council of Europe, has been criticized by East Europeans as too 'academic' (rather than practical) in nature.[43]

The EU's democracy programmes were set up only in 1992, after the European Parliament insisted that such assistance be given. The 1998 budget for assisting democracy in the ten associates and the south-east European countries was ECU 15 million; the budget for the former Soviet republics and Mongolia was ECU 8 million. This amounts to less than 1 per cent of the total aid budget for those regions. The democracy programmes have provided aid to develop parliamentary practices, improve the transparency of public administration, promote and monitor human and minority rights, build awareness of democracy, establish an independent media, encourage local democracy, and strengthen

---

[41] The total budget was approximately ATS 1.5 billion.
[42] Ghebali, *L'OSCE*, 478–9.
[43] Carothers, 'Democracy Assistance: The Question of Strategy', 120–3.

NGOs. The EU has funded primarily macro projects, which involved local and EU-based NGOs in PHARE and TACIS countries, and micro projects, involving only local NGOs mainly in the PHARE countries.[44]

Clearly these three European organizations have funded similar projects; this may have a desired multiplier effect, but it also entails a risk that efforts are unnecessarily duplicated. Coordination is now increasing. The Council of Europe and European Commission together support several joint programmes, in Albania, the three Baltic republics, Russia, and Ukraine. These provide mainly for the training of judges and lawyers, and assist with constitutional and legislative reform. There is also a joint programme on minorities in Central European countries (providing for study visits, training of professionals, and seminars), and a joint 'Octopus' project to assist in the fight against corruption and organized crime. Total 1996 funding for the joint programmes was FF 40.5 million (approximately ECU 6 million or $6.6 million).

The EU's democracy programmes have been highly praised. A 1997 evaluation report concluded that they have:

been of considerable value for the development of democracy and civil society in Central and Eastern Europe. [They have] contributed to the growth of an NGO sector in the countries of Central and Eastern Europe which plays a crucial role in the process of democratisation.[45]

The PHARE democracy programme has been more successful than the TACIS democracy programme: more money has been spent in the PHARE countries, where the emphasis has been much more on micro projects (which have been a big success); in the TACIS countries, the local partners were weak, and assistance mainly involved partnerships with Western NGOs which dominated the local NGOs.[46]

---

[44] The EU has also launched initiatives to aid NGOs: the Partnership and Institution Building Programme develops partnerships among NGOs across Europe, in sectors such as local and regional government, community development, and worker and consumer interests, while the Link Inter-European NGO Programme supports NGO initiatives to provide social safety nets in East European countries.

[45] *Final Report: Evaluation of the PHARE and TACIS Democracy Programme 1992–1997*, prepared by ISA Consult, Sussex University European Institute, and GJW Europe (Sept. 1997), at v. Support for the NGO sector in Romania probably contributed to the positive results of the November 1996 elections, which were won by a reformist government.

[46] Ibid. 88.

Bilateral programmes

Western states also have their own bilateral programmes to support democratic consolidation in Eastern Europe. The most important donors have been Germany (through the party foundations) and the USA. There has been little, if any, formal attempt to coordinate the aid programmes of the USA, West European governments, and European organizations. Exact figures for assistance are hard to come by. According to the European Commission's G24 Coordination Unit, between 1990 and 1996, the OECD countries and the EU gave a total of ECU 148.89 million for civil society and democratization to the East European countries (excluding the countries of the former Soviet Union, but including the three Baltic states).[47]

Since 1989, the US government has strongly supported democratization around the world.[48] Between 1989 and 1994, under the Support for Eastern European Democracy Program, the USA gave $110 million to democracy-related programmes in the Central and East European countries (out of a total of $1.69 billion in aid). In addition, in the same period, the National Endowment for Democracy (government-funded, but semi-autonomous) provided $17.8 million of democracy-related assistance to the region.[49] Thomas Carothers, however, argued that the USA has focused 'far too much on formal institutions as the essential elements of democratization at the expense of underlying values and processes'.[50] US aid also has tended to be highly partisan, mainly supporting parties opposing former communists.[51] In contrast, the West Europeans have given considerable assistance to developing political parties along the lines of the West European democratic spectrum.

German political aid has been channelled through the political foundations (*Stiftungen*) set up by the four major political parties (Christian Democrat, Social Democrat, Free Democrat, and Christian

[47] G24 Scoreboard (9 Sept. 1997).

[48] As Gordon Crawford points out, the US government during the 1980s had launched a 'crusade for democracy', but this did not prevent it from supporting anti-communist authoritarian regimes: *Promoting Democracy*, 20.

[49] Carothers, *Assessing Democracy Assistance: The Case of Romania*, 2.

[50] Thomas Carothers, 'Democracy Promotion under Clinton', *Washington Quarterly*, 18: 4 (1995), 23. US programmes also make little use of local expertise; they are instead staffed with young, inexperienced Americans with little knowledge of the language or country. Carothers, *Assessing Democracy Assistance: The Case of Romania*, 108–9.

[51] Ibid. 94.

Social Union). Since the late 1980s, they have opened offices throughout Eastern Europe.[52] Between 1989 and 1994, the Konrad Adenauer, Friedrich Ebert, Friedrich Naumann, and Hanns Seidel Foundations gave $52.1 million to Central Europe (Hungary, Poland, the Czech Republic, and Slovakia).[53]

The UK's Know How Fund has focused on mainly the economic transition process in Eastern Europe, but has also provided for democracy projects, including legal reform and training of journalists. The Westminster Fund for Democracy, a political foundation set up in 1992, has mostly financed trips by East European party politicians who wish to observe British electoral and parliamentary practices.[54] Both of these funds were relatively small (between 1992 and 1994, the Westminster Fund gave $1.57 million to the four Central European countries).[55]

Independent foundations have also provided a great deal of assistance for democratization in Eastern Europe, greater even than that provided by many governments and European organizations. The Soros Foundations, in particular, have been extremely active in supporting democratization projects—and the Foundations are highly praised for disbursing funds quickly and involving local people in decision-making.[56] They gave approximately $122.3 million between 1989 and 1994 to Central Europe (Hungary, Poland, Czech Republic, Slovakia, and regional projects).[57]

Western assistance for democracy has had some impact: it has contributed to the growth of NGOs, for example, and indirectly to democratization. However, there have been problems with the way official assistance programmes have been run. Generally, they have been too bureaucratic and centralized, undifferentiated according to country, and not coordinated with programmes to assist economic reform. One observer noted: 'If we have learned anything since 1989, it is that assistance should be more recipient-driven with informed and significant oversight from donors.'[58] While foundation

[52] See Michael Pinto-Duschinsky, 'Foreign Political Aid: The German Political Foundations and their U.S. Counterparts', *International Affairs*, 67: 1 (1991).

[53] These figures, however, are not complete for all years. From Kevin F. F. Quigley, *For Democracy's Sake: Foundations and Democracy Assistance in Central Europe* (Washington: Woodrow Wilson Center Press, 1997), table A.1, 122–3.

[54] Michael Lee and Steven Curtis, *British Aid to Overseas Legislatures*, Birkbeck College Department of Politics and Sociology Research Paper, no. 5 (London, 1993), 44–5.

[55] Quigley, *For Democracy's Sake*, table A.1, 123.

[56] Ibid., ch. 7.   [57] Ibid., table A.1, 122–3.

[58] Janine R. Wedel, 'U.S. Aid to Central and Eastern Europe; Results and Recommendations', *Problems of Post-Communism* (May/June 1995), 50.

assistance may be less plagued by these sorts of problems, there have been shortcomings there too—little attention has been paid to 'sustainability', that is, to whether partner organizations in Eastern Europe would be able to continue programmes in the absence of outside funding.[59]

Most problematic of all, however, was that the democracy assistance given (by governments, multilateral organizations, and foundations) has been but a drop in the ocean relative to the scale of the task—particularly in countries that have never experienced democracy. If the West expected to be able to show better results for its efforts, then this reflects highly unrealistic expectations of what a small amount of aid could accomplish.

The West's Impact on Democratic Consolidation

The extent to which the West has had—or can have—an impact on democratic consolidation in Eastern Europe has varied from case to case. The West's influence has been both indirectly and directly wielded, and to greater or lesser extent, depending on the country in consideration. Indirect influence has arisen simply from the West's 'example'. Direct influence has resulted from the use of the policy instruments discussed above.

As a group of observers noted: 'Western democracies have offered a model to be emulated at least in some degree. Moreover, the new ruling elites are, in general, concerned about how their country is perceived internationally and this influences their behaviour.'[60] Thomas Carothers found that, in the case of Romania, the influence of the Western 'model' was profound in and of itself, but this was coupled with the effects of conditionality:

The attractive model of Western democracy and capitalism is a driving force behind the whole project of post-communist transition in Romania and other countries of the region. And since 1989, Romania's leaders have shaped their domestic political agendas and undertakings with an almost constant eye on how the West will perceive and judge their actions.[61]

Western influence depends on both internal factors (the extent to which the country is sensitive to Western pressure and seeks the rewards on offer) and on external factors (what the West can agree to offer or to impose as sanctions). Laurence Whitehead argued

---

[59] Quigley, *For Democracy's Sake*, 107–10.
[60] *Evaluation of the PHARE and TACIS Democracy Programme*, 27.
[61] Carothers, *Assessing Democracy Assistance: The Case of Romania*, 90.

that the international impact on democratization in Eastern Europe will largely

depend upon whether the main international actors can remain united in their support for democratic consolidation in the region, whether their attention becomes distracted by crises elsewhere and whether the objective of democracy promotion remains harmonious with other externally desired objectives (the restoration of capitalism; the control of international crime; the avoidance of warfare; etc.).[62]

However, even if the West remains united in support of democratic consolidation, there are still areas where it can have little impact. With a few exceptions, the extent of Western influence can be mapped out geographically. Those East European countries closest to Western Europe have been those where the 'pull of the West' has been strongest; countries further away have been much less susceptible to Western influence on democratic consolidation.

The emphasis which most East European countries have given to joining European multilateral institutions has provided a powerful imperative for continuing with democratization so that they can meet the membership conditions. While in several countries, this imperative has merely supplemented domestic forces, in others, it has had more of an impact. As Bruce Parrot noted: 'In Eastern Europe, a desire to be admitted to NATO and the European Union has tempered the political conduct even of lagging states such as Romania.'[63] However, membership may be such a long-term prospect that states become disillusioned and less susceptible to outside pressure to proceed with political (and economic) reforms. Steps have been taken to reassure the East European countries that enlargement remains very much a possibility—particularly by opening membership talks with all the Central and East European applicant countries.

EU and NATO membership, however, has not been offered to all the East European countries considered in this book. Where there is little or no possibility that countries will be allowed to join the most exclusive organizations, the West may not be so influential because it cannot and will not hold out the most significant carrots. This has been the case of Russia, Ukraine, Belarus, and (for the

---

[62] Laurence Whitehead, 'East-Central Europe in Comparative Perspective', in Geoffrey Pridham, Eric Herring, and George Sanford (eds.), *Building Democracy? The International Dimension of Democratisation in Eastern Europe* (London: Leicester University Press, 1994), 52.

[63] Bruce Parrot, 'Perspectives on Postcommunist Democratization', in Karen Dawisha and Bruce Parrot (eds.), *The Consolidation of Democracy in East-Central Europe* (Cambridge: Cambridge University Press, 1997), 9.

foreseeable future) the remaining states of the former Yugoslavia and Albania.

In addition, Western influence in many countries—in the former Soviet Union and the Balkans, for example—has been less important than other, primarily domestic, considerations. These have been areas where concerns for (political and economic) stability and security predominate, or where authoritarian leaders have proved heartily resistant to Western pressure. Top-down approaches have thus been considerably less effective in strengthening the process of democratic consolidation.

Western influence has also been limited by problems inherent in the use of conditionality. Conditionality is supposed to encourage states to proceed with democratic reforms, but also necessarily entails punishing those states that do not make the grade. The consequences of sanctions for political and economic stability within the country concerned (and, therefore, also for its relations with its neighbours) could be quite negative. Applying conditionality could end up isolating those states in the 'slow lane', which may need trade relations, aid, and ties with the West the most. Reforms may proceed slowly in some countries because they are starting the process from further behind, and have to overcome much stronger 'legacies of the past'.[64] Keeping such countries in the slow lane, by applying conditionality and refusing to proceed with agreements, for example, would only make matters worse.

This dilemma of using conditionality has been exacerbated, however, by the inconsistent signals that the West has sent. The West has been unwilling to endanger relations with Russia, and so has refrained from applying conditionality. Yet, other states have then demanded similar treatment: Croatia's demand for Council of Europe membership, following Russia's accession, was a case in point. If there are rewards for countries that do not appear to be meeting the conditions, then there will be less motivation elsewhere to fulfil them.

There have been areas where Western influence has actually been negative. Greek hostility towards FYROM was not effectively

[64] Beverly Crawford and Arend Lijphart note that there are two competing explanations of the dominant conditions underlying regime change: the 'legacies of the past' approach, in which the past (the period of Soviet domination, communist government, and so on) shapes the environment in which democratization is attempted; and the 'imperatives of liberalization', which stresses that the negative influences of the past can be overcome. In 'Explaining Political and Economic Change in Post-Communist Eastern Europe: Old Legacies, New Institutions, Hegemonic Norms, and International Pressures', *Comparative Political Studies*, 28: 2 (1995), 172.

balanced by other Western countries; democratization, as a result, did not proceed in a particularly propitious environment. In the name of the Bosnian peace process, the West tolerated authoritarianism in Croatia. It completely misjudged the situation in Albania (until the collapse of the pyramid savings schemes, Albania was seen as a promising partner), and thus failed to take action earlier that might have altered the course of events.

The West, but particularly the USA, has tended 'to equate a particular leader with democracy and to assume that steadfast support for that leader is the best means of promoting democracy'.[65] The 'Great Leader approach' has been most evident in Russia, where USA and West European support for Boris Yeltsin entailed tolerating several undemocratic practices, such as the shelling of the Russian parliament in October 1993. Yeltsin was also seen as the only leader who could deliver economic reforms. The West was quite attached to former Albanian president Sali Berisha, which inhibited criticism of his government. While rewarding stability in the form of strong (autocratic) leadership may appear to be the best policy in the short term, in the longer term, pent-up domestic opposition could erupt, resulting in a far less stable situation. Certainly, there are other concerns for Western policies—peace, combating international crime, stability—but there may be a long-term cost to pay for backing authoritarian leaders.

The increasingly restrictive immigration stance of the EU may also impair the process of democratic consolidation in Eastern Europe.[66] The EU's stricter policy on asylum seekers has essentially shifted the burden of accepting asylum seekers to the East European countries—which can hardly be considered a priority there. Those East European countries at the front of the EU membership queue have had to follow the EU lead and adopt stricter immigration policies themselves. New restrictions in the Czech Republic and Poland, for example, apply to Russians, Ukrainians, and Belarusians. This has contributed to tensions between EU 'insiders' and 'outsiders' and could negatively affect democratic consolidation. Pro-democracy activists in Belarus have expressed concern that the restrictive measures could leave them even more isolated.[67]

[65] Carothers, 'Democracy Promotion under Clinton', 23.

[66] See Sandra Lavenex, 'Asylum, Immigration and Central-Eastern Europe: Challenges to EU Enlargement', *European Foreign Affairs Review*, 3: 2 (1998). Visa restrictions, for example, remain even for countries that are included in the EU enlargement process (Bulgaria and Romania).

[67] Ian Traynor, 'Fortress Europe Shuts Window to the East', *Guardian* (9 Feb. 1998).

Conclusions

The Western project to help consolidate democracy in Eastern Europe has been at least partially successful. By 2000, those countries closest to EU membership were certainly on their way to consolidating their new democracies. Of course, this was not primarily the result of Western direct influence—domestic conditions favoured democratic consolidation. But, even in countries that were most strongly oriented towards the West, and where domestic democratic forces were strong, the Western model of democracy, pressure for reforms, and aid for democracy projects had a positive, contributing effect. Where the domestic context was more troubled, Western influence was even greater, as, for example, in Bulgaria and Romania. The prospect of joining 'Europe'—in the form of EU and NATO membership—has been, to a significant extent, the reason why the West has been so influential.

The Western project in the remaining countries has been much less effective, due not only to the weakness of domestic democratic forces but also to limitations of the project itself: less democracy assistance has been given, EU and NATO membership is not on offer, and the signals sent have been extremely inconsistent. Strengthening domestic democratic forces, by extending much greater assistance for bottom-up democracy projects, should now be the focus of the Western project. Although top-down pressure is less likely to be effective in these regions, Western signals sent primarily through the use of conditionality should be much more consistent. The rhetoric of promoting democracy must be matched with action.

2

Regionalization and Democratic Consolidation

Iver B. Neumann

One would expect that the development of regionalization between states or parts of states will have some bearing on democratization since it is a prerequisite for democracy that there exist more nodes of power than one, and also that there exists some kind of an arena on which politics may play itself out. Yet, the relationship between democracy and regionalization is very far from clear. The problem may be stated simply. Within the parameters set by the Western political canon, in order for there to be democracy, there must first be a particular *demos*—a people. Where the delineation of the people is unclear, and more than one human collective is seen to have overlapping rights and obligations that make for overlapping loyalties and identities, it is hard to conceive of democratic politics. Since regionalization is a phenomenon involving more than one state, and various parts of one state, it does not lend itself immediately to the perspectives offered by the literature on democracy.

Robert Dahl's lauded attempt to think of democracy in terms of, what he calls, polyarchy may serve as an example. A polyarchy has seven attributes: elected officials, free and fair elections, inclusive suffrage, the right to run for office, freedom of expression, alternative information, and associational autonomy.[1] In order to determine whether or not a political entity may be called a polyarchy, that entity must be clearly delineated and ready to stage an exclusive game of representational politics, played out with clearly defined

I would like to thank Alyson Bailes, Arne Olav Brundtland, Marius Dirdal, Geir Flikke, Karsten Friis, Jakub Godzimirski, Jan Zielonka, and, particularly, Alex Pravda for comments on earlier drafts.

[1] Robert Dahl, *Democracy and Its Critics* (New Haven: Yale University Press, 1989), 221.

rules and resources. If the political entity is, on the other hand, enmeshed in a web of other entities, and seen as coming into its own only in certain political contexts, then the question of whether it may be called a polyarchy becomes moot. The literature on democracy is preoccupied with the ancient Greeks and the states of the Westphalian system. It is mostly concerned with those exceptional political periods and places where there existed clear political entities about which to theorize.[2]

This is not to say that democratic theory has shied away from theorizing about democracy as a phenomenon that goes further than the individual state. However, when it has done so, the problem is treated as a question of how states interact, that which, following Jeremy Bentham, we call an international problem. The volume entitled *The International Dimensions of Democratization* is an apt demonstration of this logic.[3] It poses the questions of how and why democracy spreads from certain sets of states to others, whether democracy is a 'virus' which speeds by nature, whether it is a 'vaccine' or 'transplant' administered by certain states to other states, and how, in this terminology, the patients react to these injections.[4] Thus, the question of global democratization is reduced to the one of how to make the internal structures of more and more states similar to the internal structures of the democratically pioneering states.

The problem in this context is not the extent to which such a perspective becomes deterministic.[5] It is, rather, the explicitly state-centred point of departure of the exercise. Whitehead has maintained that 'a peaceful international system needs to generate consent (both within and between nations) for a precisely agreed pattern of interstate boundaries and security alignments,' and that democratic states may simply be superior when it comes to generating such consent.[6] Thus, the question of regionalization and democracy becomes one of 'the construction of democratic regional communities of states, and the transmission of liberal democratic practices and institutions from state to state within a region'.[7]

---

[2] Adam Watson, *The Evolution of International Societies: A Comparative Historical Analysis* (London: Routledge, 1992).

[3] Laurence Whitehead, *The International Dimensions of Democratization: Europe and the Americas* (Oxford: Oxford University Press, 1996).

[4] Ibid. 8–9.

[5] See also Guillermo O'Donnell, 'Illusions about Consolidation', *Journal of Democracy*, 7: 2 (1996), 34–51.

[6] Whitehead, *International Dimensions of Democratization*, 17–18.

[7] Ibid. 395.

We may call this the international democratic problematique of regionalization. It is, indeed, a very important one. It allows us to ask the first of the two questions posed in this chapter, namely how regionalization in Eastern Europe is connected to what Whitehead calls the construction of a democratic regional community of states in this part of the world, namely the European Union (EU). 'Regions' are spoken into existence; therefore, they lie where politicians want them to lie. This opens up a whole range of possibilities that have already been tapped to some extent. There is, however, still ample scope for exploring more of what may be called region building.[8] Of course, however free statesmen and women are to go about their region building activity to start with, the question of limitations will arise. This question will arise as an integral part of the wider question of the contemporary plight of the state itself. The system of states sets down certain parameters for the kind of region building in which states may engage. The strength of societal groups may also be a limitation on the plans of the states. A legitimate starting point for a discussion of regionalization in Eastern Europe, therefore, is the European system of states.

This chapter also addresses another problematique, referred to here as the global democratic problematique of regionalization. This is concerned with the question of how regionalization may not only confirm, but also challenge, the present state-centric political order in Europe. By starting from the premiss that democracy is something which plays itself out inside an already defined political entity, and by reducing global politics to what happens between states, Whitehead occludes this second problematique.

It is, however, present in two major attempts at rethinking the idea of democracy in a global era, namely those of David Held and Andrew Linklater. Their common point of departure is that the relativization of the state as an arena for political life requires an exploration of the possibilities which exist for democratic politics in other arenas, and in social practices other than those which involve us as citizens of a particular state. For both of them, regionalization represents such a practice. For Held, the EU is not only the project of the states involved, but also a direct responsibility for democrats:

In the context of regional and global interconnectedness, however, people's equal interest in autonomy can only be adequately protected by a commitment from all those communities whose actions, policies and laws

[8] See Iver B. Neumann, 'A Region-Building Approach to Northern Europe', *Review of International Studies*, 20: 1 (1994), 53–74.

are interrelated and intertwined. For democratic law to be effective it must be internationalized. Thus, the implementation of a cosmopolitan democratic law and the establishment of a cosmopolitan community—a community of all democratic communities—must become an obligation for democrats, an obligation to build a transnational, common structure of political action which alone, ultimately, can support the politics of self-determination.[9]

Furthermore, and this is where the global problematique becomes tangible, such a process cannot fail to relativize the role of states. As Held puts it,

While such a system requires an overarching set of institutions to nurture the entrenchment and application of basic law, it could be composed of a diverse range of decision-making centers which are autonomous; that is, which act within their own sphere of competence subject only to meeting requirements of democratic law. Such 'centers' could clearly be nation states, but they need not only be states. Networks of states, that is, regions, could in principle assume this form, on the one hand, while sub-national entities or transnational communities, organizations or agencies might do so, on the other. Thus, sovereignty can be stripped away from the idea of fixed borders and territories and thought of as, in principle, malleable time-space clusters.[10]

Thus, Held points in the direction of the question posed in this chapter about the interconnectedness between regionalization in Eastern Europe and the existence of the EU. Held also argues that regions may be interesting from a democratic point of view in their own right, as possible arenas for a democratic politics which is more that a state-derived phenomenon. Andrew Linklater concurs with this argument. In his view, the EU and West European regionalization alike are social practices which may be read as harbingers of post-Westphalian political communities.[11] Whereas in the Westphalian state-centric system, there was strong tension between the two roles of 'state citizen' and 'human being', the post-Westphalian order extends a promise that humans may be able to engage in multiple political practices, which are simply better at handling the clash of obligations we experience as members of particular political communities on the one hand, and members of the human species on the other. To Linklater, regionalization relativizes the question

---

[9] David Held, *Democracy and the Global Order: From the Modern State to Cosmopolitan Governance* (Cambridge: Polity Press, 1995), 231–2.

[10] Ibid. 234.

[11] Andrew Linklater, *The Transformation of Political Community: Towards a Post-Westphalian Order* (Cambridge: Polity Press, 1998).

of 'us' and 'them' by establishing a set of political contexts in which this is not a question of citizenship. Inasmuch as these practices are more inclusive when it comes to building political communities, they are more democratic, because they open up new possibilities for political practice. This represents one way in which the democratic process may be conceived in a global and more inclusive fashion than the international perspective offered by Whitehead.

One need look no further than the Cold War examples of the Warsaw Treaty Organization (WTO) or the Council of Mutual Economic Aid (CMEA) to conclude that there is nothing inherently democratic either about the *raison d'être* of regional organizations, or in the way regional organizations are run. However, in a rather abstract manner, Held and Linklater suggest the second question addressed in this chapter: to what degree can the global democratic promise they see in Western European regionalization also be seen in Eastern European regionalization.

Eastern Regionalization and the Western Project

It is my contention that region building in East Central Europe after the end of the Cold War has been almost exclusively a reactive phenomenon. This phenomenon has been reactive, first and foremost, to the expectations of 'the West' generally, and to the existence of the EU and the North Atlantic Treaty Organization (NATO) specifically, that is, to what Karen Smith refers to in Chapter 1 as 'the Western project'. These two organizations have acted as the institutional template upon which 'the West' has drawn up its specifications of how a normal, European nation-state should look in the 1990s.[12] The EU's formal so-called Copenhagen criteria specified that a normal, European state has the institutional capacity to deal with EU membership, as well as no outstanding border issues with neighbouring states. One of the ways in which an applicant state can show that it lives up to these two criteria has been to engage in effective regional institutional cooperation with its neighbours.

Of course, not all regionalization can be viewed as part of a process of preparing for integration with 'the West' generally and EU and NATO membership specifically. In every state, nationalist forces have been against a Westernizing policy, and foreign policy-

---

[12] Iver B. Neumann, 'European Identity, EU Expansion and the Integration/ Exclusion Nexus', *Alternatives* 23: 3 (1998), 397–416.

making has revolved around the question of 'Westernization' as a general orientation in the overarching policy of 'transition' to the political model of democracy and the economic model of the market. To the extent that a policy of regional cooperation has been predicated on such an overall foreign policy orientation, it has been domestically contested. In at least four states, namely Serbia, Croatia, Belarus, and Russia, joining the EU and NATO is not on the immediate political agenda. These states did not immediately acknowledge the hegemonic pull of NATO and the EU.

The former Soviet Union

Of these four states, Russia has stood out. Whereas the other three have simply chosen not to top their foreign policy agenda with a thrust towards NATO and EU membership, Russia has been the only one which attempted something which may be interpreted as a counter-hegemonic policy. The attempt at building the Commonwealth of Independent States (CIS) has been a regional project, which can also be seen as a response (but so far aborted because too traditionalist) to the existence of NATO and the EU.

With the Warsaw Pact and its former allies gone, and the possibilities for refashioning a new security community around itself in the CIS frustrated by Ukrainian opposition, Russia was left with two options, both of which involved setting itself up as an actor distinct from Europe. The first option was to continue to insist that the Conference for Security and Cooperation in Europe (CSCE, since 1994, OSCE) be the central agency for security policy in Europe. This organization was the only one of which Russia was a full member, and the only one set up in order to facilitate the participation of Moscow as a great power. The second option was to fashion a new relationship with NATO. Russia availed itself of both opportunities, by foregrounding the CSCE/OSCE in its European policy, and by insisting on a central role in NATO's Partnership for Peace (PfP). Russia insisted, when PfP was introduced, that it would not let itself be treated as a country on a par with other non-members of NATO, and required qualitatively different agreement from those offered to the other countries involved. This strategy has been partially successful, inasmuch as there now exists a NATO-Russia elaborate cooperation mechanism. However, the Russian search for a unique relationship with NATO has been partly frustrated by the simultaneous creation of a Ukraine-NATO Charter.

It is very hard to see how the CIS should have any democratic potential whatsoever. First, whereas most other regional organiztions in Eastern Europe have made democracy a prerequisite of membership, this precondition is conspicuously absent in the CIS Charter that was adopted in January 1993.[13] Secondly, at least two of the organization's members, Azerbaijan and Georgia, cannot be said to have joined entirely of their own volition. Thirdly, and related to the second point, every important initiative in the organization's development has come from one and the same member state, namely Russia. Rather than being an organization with multiple membership, the CIS has been dominated by Russia. Furthermore, as can be seen in the decision-making procedure involved in making Russian businessman Boris Berezovsky responsible for CIS affairs, the CIS is dependent not only on Russia as such, but directly on its president, Boris Yeltsin. Berezovsky's predecessor Oleg Rybakov's summary of the first five years of the CIS's existence is relevant:

The realization of large and multi-planned work on the development of integration between Russia and other CIS states demands a qualitatively new level of work by Russian ministries and departments involved in this sphere of activity. And such work develops in accordance with the Russian Federation's strategic course in regard to CIS states, affirmed by President Yeltsin on 14 September, 1995.[14]

This anchoring of the organization in the Russian executive rather than in the parliaments of the member states is, of course, not at all unique for an international organization. However, where the issue under consideration is democratic potential, this fact is significant.

In March 1996, Russia, Belarus, Kazakhstan, and Kyrgyzstan signed an intentional agreement to establish a Council of Integrating States, which was supposed to include a Customs Union. This new Council does not seem to offer any additional democratic potential. Perhaps in partial reaction to this move, as well as to developments in the bilateral relationship Belarus-Russia, one must note the emergence in November 1997 of the so-called GUAM group, composed of Georgia, Ukraine, Azerbaijan, and Moldova. Uzbekistan joined two years later, making it the GUUAM. GUUAM may be understood more generally as a response to Russian pressure to follow a CIS-centred foreign policy. If the CIS may be seen as an anti-hegemonic project directed against the EU and NATO, the GUUAM group has represented an anti-CIS project in favour

[13] Ann Sheehy, 'The CIS Charter', RFE/RL Research Report 2, No. 12 (1993), 23–7.

[14] Oleg Rybakov, 'CIS: Five years of Existence', *International Affairs* (Moscow), 5: 6 (1996), 104.

of the EU and NATO.[15] To the extent that GUUAM has amplified voices in European politics which may be in danger of being drowned out by Russia's CIS policy, it has presented some anti-hegemonic potential. As it has found itself at the interface of NATO and EU-oriented states on the one hand, and Russia on the other, GUUAM may be seen also as one of the institutional arrangements which serve to make for a fuzzy boundary between Russia and the Brussels-based European order. In the wider sense in which democracy was discussed in the introduction to this chapter, GUUAM holds out the promise of becoming what the CIS does not, namely a regional association consisting of aspiring democratic states. As such, it may offer another arena for the orderly settling of international affairs. In terms of global governance, however, the organization does not seem to have a democratic potential at the present juncture.

Characteristically, the GUUAM group has been at its most effective inside the OSCE, on such questions as which organizations should be given a mandate to carry out peace operations on behalf of the OSCE (and also of the United Nations). On this question, the GUUAM group argued that only the EU, the Western European Union (WEU), and NATO should be given such a mandate. By implication, such a mandate should not be given to the CIS. This policy runs counter to Russia's bid to maintain the OSCE as an organization which may overarch both the CIS and NATO, with the CIS being if not on a par with NATO, then, at least, of preponderant regional standing. As witnessed by the activities of the GUUAM group, however, this policy seems to find little support outside Russia and Belarus. The CIS, thus, seems to be an organization devoid of democratic potential. Furthermore, its logic does not seem to fit into the present mould of mainstream European politics.

East Central Europe

Whereas the CIS may be characterized as counter-hegemonic to the Western Project, the common denominator of regionalization in East Central Europe has been a wish to link up with NATO and the EU. Regionalization is considered a normal activity in 'the West',

---

[15] This point should, however, not be overemphasized, as demonstrated not least by Uzbekistan's membership of the GUAM group. The same goes for the drawing of a border between the CIS area at large and Central Europe: after all, after its June 1996 enlargement, the Central European Initiative now encompasses 16 states, including *both* Belarus and NATO countries such as Italy. It thus explodes all the categories of regions used in this chapter.

and there exists in the West an expectation that regionalization will spread to Eastern Europe. As such, if a state intends to join the EU and NATO, one of the ways of demonstrating this intention and its bona fide credentials has been to engage in regionalization.

The goal of 'full inclusion into the European political, economic, security and legislation system' was set forth explicitly by the leaders of Poland, Czechoslovakia, and Hungary when they launched the Visegrad group in February 1991. The initiative was followed by the founding of the Central European Free Trade Association (CEFTA) in October 1991. These measures were predicated on the phenomenal success of what may be called the discourse on Central Europe itself. These two institutions were part of a wider effort to present 'Central Europe' as the obvious front runner for inclusion into European structures. The discourse on Central Europe was a very productive one, in the sense that the term 'Central Europe' was very soon adopted also by Western politicians. In record time, the idea became widely accepted that Central Europe had a self-evident place at the head of the queue for EU and NATO membership. This turn in the debate was so swift and decisive that it soon obscured the fact that the Czech Republic, Poland, and Hungary had with equal certainty been known as parts of 'Eastern Europe' only a few years before. As this success played itself out, new states across the former Eastern Europe, and also in certain parts of the former Soviet Union, raced to have their country subsumed also under the term 'Central Europe'.

One reason for these efforts was a perceived need to partake of the success of the Central European enterprise of the 1980s. After 1990, the concept of 'Central Europe' established a distinction not only with Russia, but also with that other half of the old 'Eastern Europe', namely the Balkans. The Balkans has become a new 'other' to Central Europe, 'sometimes alongside with, sometimes indistinguishable from' Russia.[16] Maria Todorova produces, as convincing discursive evidence for this, a citation from the debate about the pacing of NATO enlargement, where it was argued that NATO

cannot suddenly open its doors to anyone at all . . . the contiguous and stable Central European belt borders both on the traditionally agitated

---

[16] Maria N. Todorova, *Imagining the Balkans* (New York: Oxford University Press, 1997), 160. This chapter lays itself open to an attack along similar lines by having deemed Balkan developments such as the Royaumont Initiative and the Southeast European Cooperative Initiative to fall outside its purview, but see pp. 245–52 in Renata Dwan (ed.), *Building Security in Europe's New Borderlands: Subregional Cooperation in the Wider Europe* (Armonk, NY: M. E. Sharpe, 1999).

Balkans and the great Eurasian area, where democracy and market economics are only slowly and painfully breaking away toward their fulfilment. In short, it is a key area for European security.[17]

As pointed out in Milada Vachudová's chapter, there was at least one person in the area which saw the Visegrad Group and the entire regionalization effort as an instrumental ploy, namely Czech Prime Minister Václav Klaus. In Klaus's view, once the Czech republic had joined the EU, there would be no further point in maintaining the Visegrad Group or the CEFTA. Such thinking may undermine the democratic potential of these two organizations. Furthermore, this kind of thinking is not 'Western', as regionalization has become part and parcel of European politics at large, and considered 'normal'. To dissolve Visegrad and CEFTA, therefore, would show that one has not bought into this particular part of the Western project. This could prove counter-productive, inasmuch as the efforts to integrate into the European structures would be a huge leap forward, but would certainly not be complete with the simple fact of accession.

The Visegrad Group has had democratic potential in two very tangible ways. First, it could complement the efforts which the EU has made, as detailed in the preamble of its Europe agreement with Slovakia in particular, to discourage any return to authoritarian political practices. The member states shared a Cold War heritage which make the Visegrad Group an appropriate forum in which to address concretely specific issues.

Secondly, as can be seen from the entire range of regional initiatives throughout the European Union, EU membership does not put an end to, but rather enhances the need for complementing organizations, mediating between the nation-state and the EU itself. A number of problems—for example those to do with waterways—are more easily solved in such organizations. The Visegrad Group played a role in the settlement of the Hungarian–Slovakian problem of the Gabcikovo Nagymaros dam. Such problems are certain to arise again. The Visegrad Group, to recall David Held's argument, could be one of a diverse range of centres of autonomous decision-making inside the Union. Klaus's assessment of the relationship between the Visegrad group and the EU, or indeed between Central Europe and Western Europe, may simply prove erroneous. As the Czech Republic and other states become parts of 'Western Europe', their need to maintain their acquired identity

---

[17] Václav Havel, *New York Times* (17 Oct. 1993), 17; quoted in Todorova, *Imagining the Balkans*, 156.

as 'Central Europe' will not disappear. These two identities are complementary to one another. A parallel may be drawn to the way Denmark, Finland, and Sweden maintain their Nordic identity, and, indeed, use it actively inside the EU, even since becoming members and hence card-carrying 'Westerners'. As such, the Visegrad Group has both international and global democratic potential, which it would be a shame to squander.

A similar argument can be made for the Baltic Council, which was set up by Estonia, Latvia, and Lithuania in June 1994. This initiative emerged out of the Baltic Assembly, which was formed as early as November 1991. In an area which has somewhat neglected parliamentary cooperation, the Baltic Assembly has stood out as a particularly promising forum in terms of democracy building, although the order in which these two organizations were formed seems to owe more to the need for finding a low key cooperation mechanism in the last days of the Soviet Union and before restoration of state sovereignty, than to any deliberate allocation of priority to parliaments over executives.

In any case, this parliamentary cooperation is Europe-compatible, as can be seen already from the ease with which the Baltic Assembly has established cooperation with the parliamentary cooperative organs of the Nordic Council and the Benelux. Much as in the case of the Visegrad Group, Baltic cooperation owed its inception to the expectations of 'the West' and Baltic eagerness to oblige.[18] In an area where there was little cooperation—indeed little interaction at all—before the end of the 1980s, the international democratic potential of the regional organizations are great. With Estonia among the front runners for EU membership, in the longer term, there also seems to be global democratic potential.

Zipping the Old East–West Divide

In due course, the Visegrad Group offers the possibility of maintaining contacts between the new EU members of the Czech Republic, Poland, and Hungary on the one hand, and Slovakia on the other. The Baltic Council may perform a similar function should Estonia join the EU before Latvia and Lithuania. Thus, regional formations may act as zips which may ease the new divisions, which will be created by the EU's gradual enlargement.

[18] Ole Wæver, 'The Baltic Sea: A Region after Post-Modernity', in Pertti Joenniemi (ed.), *Neo-nationalism or Regionality? The Re-structuring of Political Space around the Baltic Rim* (Stockholm: NordRefo, 1997).

A discussion of regionalization in Eastern Europe must include also those regional organizations which have already played and are still playing such a role with regard to the old East–West divide of the Cold War. Taken from north to south, these are the Barents Euro-Arctic Council, the Council of Baltic Sea States, and the Black Sea Economic Cooperation Zone.[19]

Sverre Jervell, sometime acting director of the Planning Division and an adviser to the former Norwegian foreign minister Thorvald Stoltenberg, described how the leadership of the Norwegian state launched what was to become the Barents Euro-Arctic Council: 'It is possible to draw a circle on a map and define this circle as a new region and await the events. . . . We invented a region, and a bit to our surprise, it became a reality.'[20] This statement on the initial steps to this creative act of invention is of interest. Clearly, Jervell and the other inventors of the Barents region took their cue from what was going on around the Baltic Sea, where the Council of Baltic Sea States was about to take shape as the institutionalization of loose region-building ideas. The formation of the Barents region was directly inspired by the experience of fashioning the Baltic Sea region. However, as there are a number of other regions in this area, the region-building process in Europe cannot be explained only in terms of direct inspiration between the various region-building projects. Something more is at stake. If we can determine what this 'something' is, then we should be able to say more about the prospects for building regions.

Could it be that the regions before us constitute the zip, by dint of which the East and West of a once-divided Europe will come together, and that the driving force behind the region-building projects is the search to overcome the East–West divide? It is undeniable that the invention of these regions coincides with the end of the Cold War. It also seems undeniable that one of the key reasons for their political appeal was that there was more than a whiff of newness about projects which straddled the old bloc divide. If we accept this explanation, however, it has immediate effects

---

[19] Tor Bukkvoll, 'The Black Sea Region', in E. Hansen (ed.), *Cooperation in the Baltic Sea Region, the Barents Region and the Black Sea Region: A Documentation Report* (Oslo: Fafo-paper, 1997), 4; Lassi Heininen, 'The Barents Region', in Harald Baldersheim and Krister Ståhlberg (eds.), *Nordic Region-Building in a European Perspective* (Aldershot: Ashgate, 1999), 99–110.

[20] Sverre Jervell, 'Top-down or bottom-up Region Building: Some Notes on the Barents Cooperation', paper presented to the IEWS Conference on 'Multi-Layered Integration: The Sub-Regional Dimension' (Bucharest: Oct. 1996).

on our assessment of the prospects for these regions prospering. If straddling the East–West divide is the main reason why these regions developed, then the prospects for developing new regions along the same lines are limited, and the prospects for deepening regionalization are limited. Thankfully, however, we would restrict the prospects for new regions to emerge and existing regions to deepen unnecessarily, if we kept our gaze fixed on the old East–West divide. These regions must be understood not only as East–West zips, but also as a subdivision of a much wider phenomenon, namely the European border regions.

In order to say something about the prospects for these regions, one has to speculate about why regions are becoming part of the organization of Europe. A functionalist response is immediately obvious. Because the economic organization of the continent has blown the roof off the nation-state, political organization has to follow, and one of the axes along which this happens is in the formation of border regions. This argument seems fine as far as it goes, but it cannot be applied mechanically. Let us simply consider the fact that border regions do not necessarily materialize where flows of goods, capital, and services are most intense, and when they do, they are not necessarily the most potent of political forces. If they were, then the 'four motors for Europe' region should have been a resounding success. As things stand, few have heard about it outside Catalonia.

What of a culturalist explanation? Is it not because areas are somehow culturally similar that they end up sharing regions, or indeed, states? Anyone who has even the most remote knowledge of Croatian and Serbian culture will immediately cry foul: except for organized religion, which was not very popular in these areas, the cultural differences between the Serbs and the Croats hardly seem enormous. Their intermarriage rate, moreover, used to be the highest in Europe between any two ethnic groups. All this notwithstanding, their contribution to political life in Europe in the 1990s is not noted for its region- and community-building quality. By extension, the culturalist arguments for region building stand exposed as lacking in explanatory power.

We are left with the political as a partly autonomous sphere. There is something about the way in which the political field is constituted in contemporary Europe which invites region building. The question is what this 'something' could be. Region building is about nothing, if it is not about devolving certain powers away from what for the last 350 years or so has been the central matrix of the political field in Europe, namely the state. It stands to reason, then, that the relativization of the state invites region building.[21] The states in the area could have chosen, and indeed do choose, other preparatory strategies for EU and NATO membership also. Still, at the very least, one may argue that the shape which NATO and particularly EU politics take at the present juncture is eminently compatible with the forging of border area regions. When these have taken off along the old East–West divide, and not in other places where region building has been attempted such as in the Carpathians and in the Narva region on the Estonian–Russian border, it may simply be because 'Western' states still have more experience with and hence a larger capacity for multi-level governance than do the states under democratic consolidation.

However, there has been a lot of rather slippery thinking about how the link between the state level and the regional level is constituted. It seems to me that the key error has been to cast a 'Europe of the regions' in the role of *alternative* to the Europe of nation-states. This definitely makes too clear an issue of a rather murky development. One notes immediately, for example, that regions are somehow *derivative* of nation-states in the sense that the rhetoric in which their invention and maintenance are cast has been highly reminiscent of the rhetoric used about nations. For this exact reason, however, the rhetoric has been also less efficient: the political power which goes into sustaining nation-states as imagined communities is spent first on that, and only then and always derivatively, on regions. The day when even the most well-established region—the Benelux or the Nordic Council—is cast as an alternative focus of political identification, loyalty and efficiency does not seem near. Regions are derivative and, in a number of key respects, even isomorphic of states, and so are not real contenders as an alternative matrix for politics. As is clear from the example of the Barents region, furthermore, the 'we' which invented it was, indeed, a state, in cooperation with other states.

To sum up this section, regions are invented by political actors as a political programme, they are not simply lying around waiting to be discovered. But when they are invented, stories about how 'natural' it is that just these regions and no others exist are invariably told—history is shorn of all alternative stories which could have been told, and the story of the particular region is allowed to reign supreme. In the case of the Barents Euro-Arctic Region, for

---

[21] Pertti Joenniemi, 'The Barents Euro-Arctic Region: On the Restructuring of Northernmost Europe', paper presented to the IEWS Conference on 'Multi-Layered Integration: The Sub-Regional Dimension' (Bucharest: Oct. 1996).

example, stories are told about the natural flow of trade in these parts, and how these flows gave rise to 'natural' political sentiments. This line of argument is, of course, wholly spurious, inasmuch as the economic and political history of the areas which are suddenly and unsuspectingly being called 'the Barents Region' was not only one of cooperation, but also, and perhaps foremost, one of conflict. But this is put to one side. The reason why these particular inventions—regions—come into being, is that they are nation-states *manqués*; bits of territory with bits of administration and people who are being told, and sometimes even tell one another, that they have a common identity. Because they are states *manqués*, it is easy for states to regulate their invention, and to put them in the service of state foreign policy. It is, furthermore, easy to demonstrate how politicians are extremely voluntaristic when it comes to imagining regions, how they try to place the cities and countries, to which they give voice, at the hub of the regions they imagine, and how, at least in the three cases before us, they have actually been able to bring it off.

Lastly, this section has suggested that the driving force behind politicians' perception of region building as a positive idea is an all-European, and not an East–West one. This drive is concerned with trying to tackle growing interdependence in world politics by devolving certain functional political issues to arenas where they are somehow out of the way, but where a veto can still be waged against them. If this had been a *Festschrift* to regions, I could have concluded that they are one of the major embodiments in contemporary European democratic politics of the dictum that one should think globally and act locally.

Conclusions

Just like any other political entity, regions are dependent on local relevance and attention to lay claim to any more than a fleeting existence. State politicians may lend their symbolic capital to the establishment of regions, but without regional backing, regions will die. In the longer term, participation, that old chestnut of democratization, is not only ornamental but also vital. It is easy to find territories which, at some earlier historical point, were put forward as politically relevant regions but then went on to disappear. The same thing may happen—and happen quickly—to the regions under discussion. Without measures being taken, the Visegrad project may follow this path.

In order to prevent this, one must, but not necessarily, make these regions 'functional' in the sense that they serve some material purpose, and also, again not necessarily, inculcate a feeling of cultural homogeneity among the region's inhabitants. It may be enough to ensure that stories are being told about the region, locally and in as many other locales as possible. There is always some local activity occurring which can be made into 'CEFTA activity', or 'Baltic activity' and 'Black Sea activity'—witness the plethora of educational facilities and programmes, business fora, exchange programmes, and environmental workshops which have shot up where none were before. If, and when, these activities gain a partially self-sustaining character, then stories about them will also be stories about the regions in which they were engendered and in which they unfold. As such, they will contribute to sustaining not only themselves, but also the region in which they are lodged. The decisive shift occurs when local activity is presented not as having been fashioned by states, but as 'spontaneous', 'bottom up', 'local', and 'grassroots based'. For states, it does not even necessarily matter if they are made into the antithesis of what the region is all about, which may be happening in the Barents region, where the region's state-driven genesis is now fast being forgotten and the region is presented as being 'the people's own'. There is no reason whatsoever why the states involved should not be able to afford such representations to exist, provided, of course, that states remain self-assured enough of their own overall relevance and do not begin to view regions as contenders. As already noted, this definitely would be historically premature.

For states, then, relations to regions bear a number of similarities not only to relations with other parts of the state apparatus, but also to relations with civil society. There are definite advantages in having them around, but, at some level, one has to secure a veto against activity which may directly threaten the state. They may be nudged into existence, but if their entire mode of operation is state run and directly dependent on state subsidies, they lose their *raison d'être*. They may generate useful activity, or they may also be a nuisance, and it is hard to foresee the mix of the two in advance.

In terms of limitations, then, it is obvious that states need to be rather strong, in the sense that they are already present in a number of different local arenas, for them to be able to abdicate from the local region-building work to the extent necessary. Furthermore, there needs to be people locally, with enough political skills and room for manœuvre, to undertake relevant activities, and mediate these activities *vis-à-vis* the state. In countries where entire swathes of territory harbour people who are expert in extracting subsidies from the state, this is not difficult. In countries whose recent regime-types have tended to bar such activity, it may be less easy to bring this kind of personnel to the fore. As the standard Polish joke went a few years ago, it is easy to make fish soup of an aquarium, but rather more difficult to make an aquarium out of fish soup. That goes for regional aquariums as much as it goes for civil society aquariums.

A final limitation resides in the shape of the system of states as such. It is an old saw of liberalism that institutions may modify the anarchical situation in which states find themselves by offering an arena for norm building, which will dampen the tendency for states to avail themselves of self-help. Regions are certainly institutions of this type. However, at the present stage, they are hardly amongst the most sturdy of such institutions. One may put a convincing case that the existence of an institution such as the European Union minimizes the chances that its members will use their recourse to self-help: the chances that EU member states may go to war with one another are minimal, if not non-existent. However, this function of the EU is hardly existent in the regions under discussion. These institutions may, at best, alleviate the chances that their member states will avail themselves of the self-help option in relation to one another. However, no one can argue that they will rule out this possibility altogether. If the formation of these regions must be seen in the light of the all-European transformation of politics and the relativization of the role of the state, then it is also the case that the limited role of these regions in the field of security must be seen as complementary to the transformational agency of the integration process centred on the EU. In this sense, these regions are fair weather and derivative institutions.

That does not lessen their appeal, or make short shift of their prospects for prospering. In opening up political space in which civil society-like activity can prosper, and in furnishing states with other mediating arenas, these regions are among the numberless indications that politics is still a state-centred affair. However, they also highlight that we have entered an era in Europe where the contours of a multidimensional political order can be discerned.

To sum up this chapter, the CIS does not seem to have democratic potential. The GUUAM group, however, has developed international democratic potential, in that it may contribute to settling interstate problems between its participants. The same may be said about the Black Sea initiative. The international democratic potential has already started to be realized by the Visegrad Group, the Baltic Council, and two of the zips across Europe's old East–West divide, the Barents Euro-Arctic Council and the Council of Baltic Sea States. In addition to their international democratic potential, all of these regional initiatives have what we have called a global democratic potential. That is, in contemporary Europe, where the EU encourages regionalization, this phenomenon has a democratic potential that complements that of nation-states. Held's and Linklater's argument that regions are one of the system-transforming traits of a post-Westphalian order, therefore, cannot be dismissed. We must conclude, however, that these are very early days for regionalization in Eastern Europe. It is easy to argue that regionalization is part of the accommodation to the Western project that most of these states seek to join. However, there is no guarantee that these regions will develop along the same line as the Benelux or a border region such as 'four motors for Europe'. The central task of regionalization may be to counteract the new divisions which will inevitably arise once certain states join the Union and others remain outside. In such a situation, the more fuzzy the boundary between the inside and the outside of the Union, the better. Regionalization in Eastern Europe has, so far, been a by-product of the membership applications to the EU. It is potentially important, but definitely not a key aspect of democratic consolidation.

3

The Impact of External Economic Factors: The Role of the IMF

Susan Senior Nello

The unprecedented nature of transformation from 1989 in the Central-East European countries (CEECs) and after 1991 in most of the New Independent States of the former Soviet Union (NIS) meant that governments in those countries faced difficult choices concerning how (or, in some cases, whether)[1] to introduce democracy and market-oriented economies. In the literature there seems a certain consensus that the international dimension played an important role in influencing these choices. However, the emphasis tends to be on political rather than economic factors, though the two cannot always be separated. The aim here is to examine how external economic influences may affect democratic consolidation and the introduction of market forces in the post-communist countries.

The term 'external economic factors' covers a wide range of very different influences. A first distinction can be made between external shocks and developments on the one hand, and external actors on the other. External shocks and developments include the attempted reform and break-up of the Soviet Union, the collapse of the Council for Mutual Economic Assistance and the Warsaw Pact, disintegration and war in Yugoslavia and the subsequent embargo, the split of Czechoslovakia, and the recession in West Europe at the beginning of the 1990s. There also seem to have been strong interconnections between the transition of various post-communist

---

[1] As the EBRD (European Bank for Reconstruction and Development) *Transition Reports* describe, not all these countries undertook transition. Turkmenistan, Belarus, and Uzbekistan, for example, maintained many of the features of the traditional Soviet-type system.

countries, with changes in one country influencing what happens in others.[2]

The main external actors in the economic field are the EU (European Community/Union),[3] the IFIs (International Financial Institutions), and national governments, banks, and enterprises. The IFIs include the IMF (International Monetary Fund), the World Bank (IBRD)[4] the European Bank for Reconstruction and Development (EBRD), and the European Investment Bank (EIB). The Council of Europe, NATO, and the OSCE (Organization for Security and Cooperation in Europe) will not be considered here as their activities are predominantly political.

As there is already a substantial literature on the impact of external shocks on transition,[5] the analysis will concentrate on the role played by external economic actors, taking as a case study the IMF. Discussion of the EU (which is the main external economic actor in many of the transition countries) is limited here to comparing its role with that of the IMF.[6]

Difficulties may arise in distinguishing between external and internal influences on transition, in particular, because external factors influence internal ones and vice versa. Often (but by no means always) the policies proposed by the main external actors in the economic context (the IMF and the EU) would probably have been introduced anyway, and the fact that these policy recommendations came from

[2] There has been much discussion of the phenomenon of 'transition by contagion' whereby change in one country influences events in others in a kind of domino reaction. See Laurence Whitehead (ed.), *The International Dimensions of Democratization* (Oxford: Oxford University Press, 1996). As will be shown, there were strong links between the transition process in different countries (for instance, the 1990 Polish Balcerowicz Plan was copied elsewhere), but this account leaves open the question of why some groups of countries undertook more rapid transformation (or transformation *tout court*) and not others.

[3] For simplicity the term 'EC' will generally be used when referring to the period before the creation of the European Union, and 'EU' otherwise.

[4] International Bank for Reconstruction and Development.

[5] See, for example: Anders Åslund, *Gorbachev's Struggle for Economic Reform* (London: Pinter Publishers, 1989). Michael Ellman, Egor T. Gaidar, and Grzegorz W. Kolodko, with P. H. Admiraal (eds.), *Economic Transition in Eastern Europe* (Oxford: Blackwell, 1993); John Flemming and J. M. C. Rollo (eds.), *Trade, Payments and Adjustment in Central and Eastern Europe* (London: Royal Institute of International Affairs, 1992); Milica Uvalic, Jochen Lorentzen, and Efisio Espa (eds.), *Impediments to the Transition in Eastern Europe* (Florence: European University Institute, 1993).

[6] The influence of the EU and the EBRD on democratic consolidation in the CEECs is covered by the contribution by Karen E. Smith in this volume.

outside provided domestic politicians with a scapegoat, rendering unpopular measures more palatable.

The IFIs and EU provide financial and technical assistance to facilitate the political and economic transition process. They also furnish policy advice, and act as catalysts to obtain financial support from other sources. However, their assistance is generally based on the principle of conditionality.

Since 1989 the EC has always applied political as well as economic conditionality in its dealings with the post-communist countries. This was the case for the various trade and aid measures aimed at facilitating the transformation process, and also for the 'pre-accession strategy' designed to help CEECs to prepare for eventual EU membership.[7] Among the conditions for enlargement laid down by the 1993 Copenhagen European Council, the applicant country was specifically required to have achieved *stability of institutions guaranteeing democracy, the rule of law, human rights and respect for and protection of minorities*.[8] It was also stipulated that the applicant countries are able to take on the 'obligations of membership', which is generally taken to mean their ability to adopt the *acquis communautaire*.[9] The applicant countries are also required to ensure effective implementation of the *acquis* and this will entail substantial changes in their administrative and judicial capacities.[10]

The term *conditionality* emerged chiefly in the context of IMF and World Bank[11] assistance to developing countries in the 1980s

[7] Of the CEECs, Bulgaria, the Czech Republic, Estonia, Hungary, Latvia, Lithuania, Poland, Romania, Slovakia, and Slovenia have all applied for EU membership.

[8] In addition, the Copenhagen Summit stipulated the so-called 'economic criteria', which entail that the applicant country has a functioning market economy and the capacity to cope with competitive pressures and market forces within the Community.

[9] The *acquis communautaire* is the body of EU legislation, practices, principles, and objectives accepted by the member states. It is composed of the Treaties (and, most importantly, the Treaties of Rome, the Single European Act, the Maastricht Treaty, and the Amsterdam Treaty); legislation enacted at the EU level and judgments of the European Court of Justice; Justice and Home Affairs; Foreign and Security Policy and Treaties of the EU with third countries. The *acquis* has been accumulating over the years and now amounts to some 12,000 legislative acts.

[10] *Agenda 2000* (at 45) presents a framework for this task which entails implementing the provisions of the Europe Agreements, adopting the programme for regulatory alignment with the Single European Market set out in the Commission's 1995 White Paper, and taking on other aspects of the *acquis* in areas such as agriculture and the environment.

[11] In contrast with the IMF, the institutional mandate of the World Bank requires it to place greater emphasis on promoting growth and the process of

where it referred to the various economic policies that a country was requested to implement in order to gain access to financial resources.[12] However, over time the role of the IMF has been changed, and so too have the type of conditions imposed.[13]

The initial aim of the IMF was to assist the functioning of the fixed exchange rate system established at Bretton Woods. When this system collapsed in 1971, the activities of the IMF became increasingly focused on financial support for developing countries, in particular, after the debt crisis in Mexico and other Latin American countries. With its involvement in the transition countries after 1989, the role of the IMF again altered, and the IMF began to provide advice on a far wider range of issues than previously. These issues included privatization, financial systems, taxation, and so on. The transition countries needed advice and were offered it from many sources, though the credits offered by the IMF generally ensured a particularly favourable hearing for its suggestions. Having established this precedent, when the IMF became involved in the East Asian countries from 1997 it continued with this expanded agenda, insisting on a wide range of changes in institutional structures as well as in economic policies as a condition for its financial assistance.[14]

From the 1990s political conditionality has been increasingly applied by the multilateral organizations. As it became evident that many developing countries were not making significant economic progress, the idea that there was a symbiosis between democracy and development began to gain ground. In particular, the World

catching up. The Bank encourages structural policies, which, in the case of the transition economies, includes the liberalization of prices and trade, and facilitating privatization, competition, and restructuring, as Wallich describes: C. I. Wallich, 'What's Right and Wrong with World Bank Involvement in Eastern Europe', *Journal of Comparative Economics*, 20 (1995), 57–94. It makes loans to finance specific projects, and generally will only make a loan if it is satisfied that the return is sufficient to ensure interest payments and repayment of the original sum lent. The Bank works in close collaboration with the IMF, and frequently applies cross-conditionality, requiring that agreement is also reached with the IMF before funds are disbursed.

[12] Policy conditionality was not envisaged in the constitutions of the IMF and World Bank when they were established at Bretton Woods in 1944.

[13] The term 'Washington consensus' coined by Williamson in the early 1980s is frequently used. However, relationships between the two Bretton Woods Institutions have evolved over time, and in 1999 seemed somewhat tense, in particular, in view of the criticisms of the IMF by Stiglitz, then chief economist at the World Bank.

[14] For a description of this changing role of the IMF, see, for example, M. Feldstein, 'Refocusing the IMF', *Foreign Affairs* (Mar./Apr. 1998), 20–33.

Bank increasingly insisted on measures to promote 'good governance' and observation of human rights which would establish a framework in which development to take place. In some cases the IMF also applied explicitly political conditionality.[15]

However, even where the IMF restricts its conditionality to questions relating to introduction of a market-oriented economy, this has implications for the process of democratic consolidation in the transition economies. In order to show how this is the case the second section (below) will describe the activities of the IMF in transition countries, the third discusses links between a market-oriented economy and democratization at a general, theoretical level, while the fourth indicates how tensions may arise between the two in the specific case of transition countries.

Conditionality implies a loss of sovereignty, and a central question which arises concerns how free a country is to accept or reject the conditions imposed from outside. The freedom of a country to reject the conditions will depend on the needs, objectives, and characteristics of the country itself, its ability to bargain with the international organization in question, and the international economic and political environment. In order to address this question, the fifth section discusses IMF conditionality as applied to the transition countries.

Following its intervention in East Asia, Russia, and Brazil the IMF has come heavily under attack, and there have been growing calls for its reform.[16] In East Asia, at least initially, the IMF failed to understand the scale of the crisis, and so recommended excessively tight fiscal and monetary policies, which further contributed to the economic slowdown.[17] The Fund's opposition to capital restrictions for so long came in for criticism as the risks of liberalizing international capital movements in countries with underdeveloped financial sectors became increasingly evident. The legitimacy of the IMF in pushing for far-reaching structural and institutional

---

[15] As Polak described, South Africa, China, and Vietnam were denied financial assistance by the IMF on political grounds during the late 1980s. However, he argues that in general disregard for human rights was not considered 'a bar to access to the Fund, as was evident from the Fund's active financial relations with repressive regimes in countries such as Chile, Zaire, Uganda, Liberia or Romania': Jaques J. Polak, *The Changing Nature of IMF Conditionality*, Essays in International Finance, No. 184, Department of Economics (Princeton: Princeton University Press, 1991).

[16] See, for example, the attacks by Stiglitz *inter alia* in the *Financial Times* (3 Dec. 1998), and Sachs in the *Financial Times* (22 Jan. 1999).

[17] In many cases the IMF subsequently relaxed the conditions imposed on these countries.

measures in East Asia was questioned, especially as the prescriptions were modelled so closely on the Anglo-American institutional model.[18] The IMF was also criticized for encouraging Russia and Brazil to defend overvalued exchange rates for too long.

Another major question which arises is therefore how appropriate the policy prescriptions of the IMF were for economies in transition and this is addressed in the sixth section. The seventh section deals with the proposals for IMF reform, before conclusions are drawn in the final section.

The Activities of the IMF in Transition Countries

According to Article 1 of its constitutive document, the aims of the IMF include: encouraging international monetary cooperation, facilitating the expansion and balanced growth of world trade, promoting rate exchange stability, and assisting the establishment of an international system of payments. In order to further these aims, the Fund may make its resources temporarily available to its members under adequate safeguards to provide them with an opportunity to correct balance of payments disequilibrium.

What was initially intended primarily as short-term balance of payments support for industrialized countries (as, for instance in the famous stand-by arrangement[19] with Belgium of 1952) gradually became increasingly focused on financial support (including assistance for structural adjustment) for developing countries and subsequently for economies in transition.[20]

Support for the former communist countries has come through the traditional stand-by arrangements (typically of 12–15 months);[21]

---

[18] See, for example, Feldstein, 'Refocusing the IMF'.

[19] Initially conditionality was imposed on any drawing that exceeded 25% of a member's quota with the IMF. The introduction of the stand-by arrangement in 1952 facilitated access to IMF credit as it allowed countries which did not have immediate balance of payments problems future access to Fund resources.

[20] Czechoslovakia and Poland were founding members of the IMF, but subsequently abandoned it, rejoining again in 1986 and 1990 respectively. Romania has been a member since 1972, Hungary since 1982, and Bulgaria since 1990. See Santaella for a discussion of the changes in the way in which IMF financial assistance has operated. J. A. Santaella, 'Stylized Facts before IMF-supported Macroeconomic Adjustment', *IMF Staff Papers*, 43: 3 (1996), 502–44, esp. 502–3.

[21] When a country joins the IMF it is assigned a quota which determines, among other things, its potential access to Fund resources. The size of the quota reflects the relative economic position of the member and the level of world trade. Initial

TABLE 3.1. *Assistance to the CEECs*

	1996 PHARE assistance (ECU million)	Cumulative total of PHARE assistance 1990–6 (ECU million)	% PHARE assistance 1990–6	Total official development assistance 1997 ($ per capita)	Total official development assistance 1997 (% GDP)
Albania	53	385	5.8	51	6.7
Bulgaria	63	539	8.1	25	2.2
Czech Rep.	54	284	4.3	10	0.2
Slovakia	5	131	2.0	13	0.3
Estonia	62	130	2.0	44	1.4
Hungary	101	684	10.3	16	0.4
Latvia	37	132	2.0	33	1.5
Lithuania	53	179	2.7	27	1.1
Poland	203	1,389	20.9	17	0.5
Romania	119	726	10.9	9	0.6
Slovenia	22	91	3.4	49	0.5
Total	1,223	6,636	100		

Source: Alan Mayhew, *Recreating Europe: The European Union's Policy towards Central and Eastern Europe* (Cambridge: Cambridge University Press, 1998); World Development Report.

extended arrangements involving a country's commitment to medium-term adjustment;[22] compensation for export shortfalls (the Compensatory and Contingency Financing Facility or CCFF); the concessional facility for low-income countries (Enhanced Structural Adjustment Facility or ESAF), and the system transformation facility (STF) created in 1993. The STF was created as a temporary mechanism to assist IMF member states in dealing with the disruptions arising in the process of adjusting to multilateral market-based trade. Tables 3.1 and 3.2 provide an indication

subscriptions and increases in quotas are usually paid in the member country's own currency with a smaller portion (not more than 25%) in reserve assets (SDRs (special drawing rights) or other members' currencies). The principal way in which the IMF makes its resources available to members is to sell them currencies of other members or SDRs in exchange for their own currencies. The credit tranche policy is often referred to as the IMF's basic financing policy. Credit under this policy is available in tranches, each tranche being equal to 25% of quota. Credit tranches are granted outright or on a stand-by basis.

[22] The Extended Fund Facility was established in 1974 to make resources available for longer periods and in larger amounts than under the credit tranche policies to members that are experiencing balance of payments difficulties because of structural imbalances in production, trade, or prices.

TABLE 3.2. *Total IMF credit and loans outstanding (millions of Special Drawing Rights, situation at 30 June 1998)*

	Total IMF credit and loans outstanding	CCFF	STF	Stand-by/ credit tranche	Other borrowed resources	ESAF trust resources
Albania	45.8			8.8		36.9
Belarus	184.4		134.4	50.0		
Bulgaria	781.6	107.6	116.2	557.8		
Croatia	169.4		130.8	9.8	28.8	
Czech Rep.	—					
Estonia	32.9		22.3	10.6		
FYR Macedonia	74.4		24.8	22.3		27.3
Hungary	—					
Latvia	52.0		43.8	8.2		
Lithuania	187.1		49.6	2.9	134.6	
Moldova	151.8	9.2	41.3	63.9	37.5	
Poland	—					
Romania	436.9		188.5	248.3		
Russia	10,716		2,066.7	4,313.1	4,336.3	
Slovakia	155.6		123.3	27.2	5.0	
Slovenia	—					
Ukraine	1,816		489.7	1,318.2		

Key: Compensatory and Contingency Financing Facility (CCFF), Enhanced Structural Adjustment Facility (ESAF), system transformation facility (STF). See text or IMF International Financial Statistics for explanation.

Source: IMF International Financial Statistics.

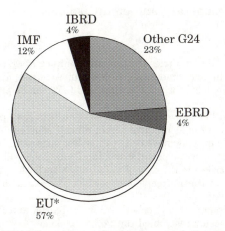

FIG. 3.1. *G24 PHARE assistance by donor, cumulative total 1990–1996*
* includes bilateral aid from EU member state
Source: Mayhew, Recreating Europe

of the scale of financial assistance given to some of the transition countries,[23] including that given by the IMF.

Given the size and number of post-communist economies, and the cost of transition, it was inevitable that the role played by external financial assistance would be relatively modest.[24] It could be argued that the restricted scale of these transfers limits the dependency of the transitional countries on the West (leaving aside the case of CEECs applying for EU membership). However, at times external assistance played a valuable role because it arrived at a crucial, vulnerable time.[25] For instance, in 1997 the run on the lev and the drastic reduction in Bulgarian reserves lent urgency to the need to reach an agreement with the IMF.

The credit from the IMF is conditional on reaching agreement with the Fund on macroeconomic stabilization measures and on realizing certain performance targets. In general, extensive negotiations take place between the donor and the recipient in order to draw up the programme. Once agreed, the financial assistance is typically divided into tranches, and the release of each tranche is conditional on the performance of the recipient country and on strict observation of the timetable for reforms.

The model for IMF-agreed stabilization programmes in the transition economies was the Polish Balcerowicz Plan that came into effect from 1 January 1990.[26] Subsequently other transition countries introduced similar packages. The main elements of these programmes were:[27]

- rapid and almost complete price liberalization
- restrictive monetary and credit policies

[23] In some of the NIS countries the amount of financial assistance as a share of GDP in 1994 was higher, amounting to 9.8% in Armenia, 7.5% in Georgia, but only 0.6% for Russia, 0.3% for the Ukraine, and 0.5% for Belarus (World Development Report, 1997).

[24] However, as will be shown below, the EU and IFIs have played an important role in attracting additional financing from official sources, including debt relief through the Paris Club. They have been rather less successful in attracting complementary private financing or private (London Club) debt relief.

[25] As Drábek describes in the case of the former Czechoslovakia: Z. Drábek, 'IMF and IRBD Policies in the Former Czechoslovakia', *Journal of Comparative Economics*, 20 (1995), 235–64.

[26] At the beginning of 1991 Czechoslovakia, Bulgaria, and Romania introduced programmes that closely resembled the Polish package.

[27] See Bruno for a comparison of these programmes: Michael Bruno, 'Stabilisation and Reform in Eastern Europe: A Preliminary Evaluation', *IMF Working Paper*, 92/30 (1992).

- tight fiscal discipline, and the wide-scale elimination of price subsidies
- substantial trade liberalization
- incomes policies[28]
- privatization
- the reform of the banking and financial systems

The IMF generally expressed a preference for fixed nominal exchange rates as a nominal anchor for inflation in the transition economies. However, in the event these countries opted for a wide range of exchange rate regimes, reflecting diverging views among economists and policy makers with regard to which was the most 'appropriate' exchange rate regime to adopt, but also the differing macroeconomic conditions at the start of transition.[29] The availability of reserves was an important factor, and was a major reason behind the initial decision of Bulgaria and Romania to float.

The Links between Market Economies and Democracies

The policy prescriptions of international organizations often tend to assume that the introduction of democracy and market economies go hand in hand. This tendency to link the two probably reflects prevailing economic and political doctrines in North America and Western Europe, but the connection is perhaps not as obvious as is sometimes assumed. A more critical stance generally tends to be adopted in the literature, with, for instance, Schmitter and Karl arguing that in the long run democracy and market economies are 'not incompatible',[30] or Milton and Rose Friedman maintaining that economic freedom to engage in market transactions is a necessary but not sufficient condition for political freedom.[31]

According to Schumpeter, competition is a common element of democracy and markets. Democracy is defined as an institutional arrangement for arriving at political decisions in which individuals

---

[28] In Poland, Hungary, and Romania, tax-based incomes policies were introduced, while in Bulgaria real wages were cut by 35% and ceilings on wage bills were introduced.

[29] Pál Gáspár, 'Exchange Rates in Economies in Transition', *Hungarian Academy of Sciences Working Paper*, 56 (1995).

[30] Philippe C. Schmitter and T. L. Karl, 'What Democracy is . . . and is Not', *Journal of Democracy*, 2: 3 (Summer 1991), 75–88.

[31] Milton Friedman, *Capitalism and Freedom* (Chicago: University of Chicago Press, 1982).

acquire the power to decide as a result of a competitive struggle for the vote.[32] It could, however, be argued that competition is a necessary but not sufficient condition for democracy, as political competition is compatible with a very restricted franchise. Authors such as Schmitter and Karl (p. 78) accept the role of competition in the democratic process, but argue against confining democracy's operations to competitive interest maximization, maintaining that other activities such as cooperation play an important role.

Bearing these qualifications in mind, the 'working definition' of Vanhanen is useful: democratization takes place under conditions in which power resources have become so widely distributed that no group is any longer able to suppress its competitors or to maintain its hegemony.[33]

Von Hayek provides an interesting explanation of why democracy and the market might not always go together:

Competition is, after all, always a process in which a small number makes it necessary for larger numbers to do what they do not like, be it to work harder, to change habits or to devote a degree of attention, continuous application or regularity to their work which without competition would not be needed.

If in a society in which the spirit of enterprise has not yet spread, the majority has the power to prohibit whatever it dislikes, it is most unlikely that it will allow competition to arise. I doubt whether a functioning market has ever newly arisen under an unlimited democracy, and it seems at least likely that unlimited democracy will destroy it where it has grown up.[34]

However the analysis between market economies and democracy at this general level is complicated by the fact that competition does not work 'perfectly' in either field. Economic textbooks explain cases of market failure (or impossibility of establishing a market) such as public goods, economies of scale, externalities and information failures, while the shortcomings of political competition have long been documented.[35] Partly as a result, there are numerous models

---

[32] Joseph A. Schumpeter, *Capitalism, Socialism and Democracy* (London: George Allen & Unwin, 1943).

[33] As reported in Geoffrey Pridham and Tatu Vanhanen, *Democratization in Eastern Europe: Domestic and International Perspectives* (London: Routledge, 1994).

[34] Friedrich A. von Hayek, *Law, Legislation and Liberty,* vol. ii (London: Routledge & Kegan Paul, 1973–9), 77.

[35] *Inter alia* by writers such as Alexis de Tocqueville and John Stuart Mill.

of both democracy and of the market economy, complicating the analysis of links between the two.[36]

Shifting the emphasis from a 'market economy' to development, a vast literature has emerged following the seminal work by Lipset that found a correlation between development and democracy.[37] There have been numerous empirical studies,[38] but, as Maravall points out, even where these appear to confirm the Lipset result, in general they simply argue that if development occurs, the probability that there will be democratization increases. Huntington[39] maintains that the prospects for democratization increase when a certain minimum threshold of development is reached. Other authors argue that the causality between development and democracy runs indirectly through other variables,[40] and that as an economy develops and becomes more complex, it becomes harder to manage under an authoritarian government.[41]

One of the main problems in analysing the links between democracy and development is that of defining and measuring the two. In general 'indices' of democracy are used, and numerous indices have been developed.[42] Probably the earliest attempt to measure democracy systematically is that of Bollen[43] which is based on six indicators: fairness of elections; methods of legislative and executive selection; freedom of the press and of group opposition; and government sanctions. The Gurr index covers the 1800–1986 period

[36] See, for example, Robert Alan Dahl, *Polyarchy: Participation and Opposition* (New Haven: Yale University Press, 1971); or K. A. Bollen, 'Political Democracy: Conceptual and Measurement Traps', *Studies in Comparative International Development*, 25 (1990), 7–24.

[37] Seymour Martin Lipset, 'Some Social Requisites of Democracy: Economic Development and Political Legitimacy', *American Political Science Review*, 53: 1 (1959), 69–105.

[38] See José Mária Maravall, *Regimes, Politics and Markets: Democratization and Economic Change in Southern and Eastern Europe* (Oxford: Oxford University Press, 1997); or S. M. Lipset, K. R. Seong, and J. C. Torres, 'A Comparative Analysis of the Social Requisites of Democracy', *International Social Science Journal*, 45: 2 (1993), 155–75, for a list of these studies.

[39] Samuel P. Huntington, *The Third Wave: Democratization in the Late Twentieth Century* (Norman: University of Oklahoma Press, 1991).

[40] See, for example, Dahl, *Polyarchy*.

[41] The arguments advanced are frequently redolent of those of the economic calculation debate of the 1920s and 1930s between von Mises, and von Hayek on one side, and Lange on the other.

[42] For a list of these various indices see Svante Ersson and Jan-Erik Lane, 'Democracy and Development: A Statistical Exploration', in Adrian Leftwich (ed.), *Democracy and Development: Theory and Practice* (Cambridge: Polity Press, 1996).

[43] K. A. Bollen, 'Issues in the Comparative Measurement of Political Democracy', *American Sociological Review*, 44 (1980), 572–87.

and provides two indicators for measuring democracy, institution-alized autocracy, and institionalized democracy.[44] The Freedom House Index is based on thirteen indicators, and takes into account political rights and civil liberties.[45] Clearly, comparison of results based on the use of different indices is not appropriate.

A first distinction to make in the case of development is between the level of development and its rate of change. Although some authors consider GDP per capita as a proxy for the level of development, in general various social and economic indicators are also taken into account. This broader concept is sometimes referred to as 'human development'. Also here numerous indices have emerged. For example, the UN Human Development Index is based on an adjusted estimate of GDP per capita, infant mortality, life expectancy, and adult literacy. Other indices also include measures of poverty and income inequality. Clearly, the level of apparent development will vary according to the variables included and weights given to each, and the results of empirical analysis using different indicators will not be compatible.

A further difficulty is that some of the variables appearing in the indices for human development can be altered by redistributive policies, spending on health care and education, and so on. The picture that emerges is therefore complex, and it is impossible to assert that development is either a necessary or sufficient cause of democratization. According to Maravall, all that emerges from the numerous empirical studies is a 'weak and rough correlation' between democracy and development.[46]

Further complications arise from the fact that the relationship is two-way, with democratization having implications for development. For instance, on the basis of a comparative study of international patterns of growth, Sachs and Werner argue that the rule of law promotes growth,[47] with corruption, government breach of contract, expropriation of property, and inefficiency in public administration all being found to have a negative impact on growth. Ersson and Lane find a robust relation between democracy and

---

[44] As described in Ersson and Lane, 'Democracy and Development'.

[45] See Lipset, Seong and Torres, 'Social Requisites of Democracy', for a description of this index.

[46] Maravall, *Regimes, Politics, and Markets*.

[47] Jeffrey D. Sachs and A. M. Warner, 'Achieving Rapid Growth in the Transition Economies of Central Europe', *Development Discussion Paper* No. 544 (Harvard Institute for International Development, 1996). Similar results for an extended version of this approach carried out for the Asian Development Bank's *Emerging Asia* were presented in *The Economist* (14 June 1997).

human development, though they do not find evidence for a stable relation between democracy and economic growth.[48]

The literature on the political business cycle could offer another approach to examining 'democracy and the market' insofar as it analyses the links between economic performance and political popularity or electoral results.[49] However, the results of this type of approach are rather disappointing, and various difficulties are encountered: elections or the popularity of governments depend on a wide number of issues; it is not clear which economic variables ought to be taken into consideration[50] or what their relative importance is; certain variables may be outside government control,[51] and it seems likely that the reactions of the population may change over time and in any case take place after a time lag. However, the limitations of these studies are probably a reflection of the broad, aggregative macroeconomic framework underlying most of the analysis, and it seems likely that more interesting results could be obtained with a more disaggregated approach.

A more promising approach to the question might therefore be to identify ways in which tensions might arise between the creation of a market economy and democratization in the specific case of the transition countries, and this is attempted in the next section.

Links between Economic Transition and Democratic Consolidation in the Transition Countries

Economic transition inevitably gives rise to economic and social costs. This is true of the three main elements of economic transition:

[48] Ersson and Lane, 'Democracy and Development'.

[49] See, for example, the work by Bruno S. Frey and F. Schneider, 'On the Modelling of Politico-Economic Interdependence', *European Journal of Political Research*, 3 (Dec. 1975), 339–60.

[50] Although the early work in this field by, for example, Frey, concentrated on the impact of the level of unemployment on government popularity, it could be argued that the electorate is more concerned with changes in unemployment than its level. See Bruno S. Frey, 'A Politico-Economic Model of the United Kingdom', *Economic Journal*, 88 (June 1978), 243–53. Stigler maintained that because the unemployed are few in number and uninfluential, income distribution is the variable to consider in this context. George J. Stigler, 'General Economic Conditions and Natural Elections', *American Economic Review*, 63 (May 1973), 160–7.

[51] This goes to the heart of the debate on economic theory, with, for instance, the New Classical Macroeconomic argument that government intervention will be ineffective as economic agents will use all available information to offset the impact of government action.

macroeconomic stabilization, structural adjustment and privatization, and systemic change. During the early years of transition most countries displayed an urgent need for macroeconomic stabilization in order to limit inflationary pressures and produce external balance, and IMF-agreed packages were implemented in all these countries, with the sole exception of Turkmenistan. Though external discipline and borrowed credibility[52] can play a useful role in post-communist countries where fiscal deficits are too high, reduced government spending has had negative repercussions for services such as health, pensions, and education. As a result, there may be greater hardship for the weaker groups in society, including the old, large families, and the unemployed. Higher interest rates associated with restrictive monetary policies, and increased taxation and its improved collection may render the survival of small, new private firms precarious. Structural adjustment is costly, and at least initially involves falls in output and unemployment as resources are reallocated. Systemic change involves evolving a role of the state appropriate to a modern market-oriented economy. This involves laying off employees in state enterprises, and expenditure to develop administrative and judicial capacity and to establish a well-regulated financial sector. These economic and social costs will affect society as a whole, but will also affect some groups more than others.

As Przeworski describes, economic transition is therefore 'socially costly and politically risky'.[53] If it hurts large social groups and evokes opposition from important political parties, according to Przeworski, 'democracy may be undermined, or reforms abandoned, or both'.

---

[52] If governments take advantage of the temporary trade-off between inflation and unemployment and raise inflation to reduce unemployment, agents will come to expect them to do so and will predict a higher level of inflation. What is needed is a way of making commitment to lower inflation credible so that the inflation-prone country may 'borrow' credibility.

[53] Adam Przeworski, *Democracy and the Market: Political and Economic Reforms in Eastern Europe and Latin America* (Cambridge: Cambridge University Press, 1991), 136. China offers an interesting case study on this point. As Nuti describes, China is an authoritarian gerontocracy 'still subject to the political monopoly of the Communist Party, which together with the military is deeply and directly involved in the economy, creaming off a significant share of national profits'. Domenico Mario Nuti, 'Comparative Economics after the Transition', paper presented at the AISSEC-EACES Round Table Discussion, 'La Sapienza' (University of Rome, 25–6 Sept. 1997), 2. Although the state sector remained dominant, and privatization was very limited, in September 1997 the 15th Party Congress appeared to endorse the restructuring and privatization of state enterprises. If this takes place, it is an open question whether the resulting bankruptcies and unemployment will undermine control by the Communist Party.

What is perhaps surprising is that in most transition countries reforms have not been abandoned, even though electoral backlash has been experienced at times. Even where reformed communist parties have come to power, as the EBRD 1999 *Transition Report* describes, the fear that they would try to limit or reverse reforms appears only partially warranted. In countries such as Hungary, Lithuania, and Poland governments led by reformed communists have been active in sustaining reform, though this is partly to be explained by the priority given to the task of preparing for accession to the EU.

However, even without abandoning transition its speed may vary. The EBRD argues that in countries where change was particularly slow, such as some former Soviet Republics and certain Balkan countries, reform was often managed by leaders who already held office under the previous regime.[54] In contrast, where there has been a changeover in the political élite, new governments may favour reform also as a means of limiting the power of bureaucrats and employees in state-owned enterprises who retained their position from the previous regime. Moreover, a high degree of consensus within society over the main goals of transition tends to ease the implementation of reform and reduce the likelihood of policy reversals.

In indicating how economic transformation may influence the process of democratic consolidation, distinction can be made between four elements:[55]

- the impact of changes in overall macroeconomic variables such as growth, unemployment, and inflation;
- increases in income disparities and individual uncertainty;
- corruption, and, in particular, perceived injustices in the privatization process, and scandals arising from incomplete transformation of the financial sector, and
- mistakes in policies.

In all the post-communist countries, economic transition was associated with substantial initial declines in output, and though these declines have been reversed in most of the CEECs (though not the NIS), in 1998 only Poland, Slovenia, and Slovakia had recovered their 1989 level of output (see Table 3.3).

[54] EBRD *Transition Report* (1999).

[55] This distinction is a somewhat modified form of that made by Roland in his explanation of electoral backlash in transition countries. G. Roland, 'Political Constraints and the Transition Experience', in Salvatore Zecchini (ed.), *Lessons from the Economic Transition: Central and Eastern Europe in the 1990s* (Dordrecht: OECD, Kluwer Publishers, 1997).

TABLE 3.3. *Growth in the transition economies*

	1990	1991	1992	1998	1999 estimate	1998 GDP relative to 1989
Albania	−10.0	−27.7	−7.2	8.0	8.0	86
Belarus	−3.0	−1.2	−9.6	0.1	1.5	78
Bulgaria	−9.1	−11.7	−7.3	3.5	0.0	66
Croatia	−6.9	−20.0	−11.0	2.3	−0.5	78
Czech Rep.	−0.4	−14.2	−6.4	−2.3	0.0	95
Estonia	−8.1	−7.9	−14.2	4.0	0.0	76
FYR Macedonia	−9.9	−12.1	−21.1	2.9	0.0	72
Hungary	−3.5	−11.9	−3.1	5.1	3.0	95
Latvia	2.9	−8.3	−35.0	3.6	1.5	59
Lithuania	−5.0	−13.4	−37.7	5.2	0.0	65
Moldova	−2.4	−17.5	−29.0	−8.6	−5.0	32
Poland	−11.6	−7.0	2.6	4.8	0.0	117
Romania	−5.6	−12.9	−8.8	−7.3	−4.0	76
Russia	−4.0	−13.0	−14.5	−4.6	0.0	55
Slovakia	−2.5	−14.6	−6.5	4.4	1.8	100
Slovenia	−4.7	−8.1	−5.4	3.9	3.5	104
Ukraine	−3.4	−9.0	−10.0	−2.5	−2.5	37

Source: EBRD.

Explanations advanced for the initial larger than expected fall in output include the monopoly behaviour of public enterprises (which restricted output and raised prices) and the slow growth of the emerging private sector and/or the failure of official statistics to reflect the growth of that sector adequately. Bruno also argues that reduced output was the result of a 'comprehensive management shock' with the policy disorientation of public enterprises after the collapse of central planning, and the tendency to adopt a 'wait and see' attitude.[56] Output statistics in the former centrally planned system were exaggerated, and part of the subsequent registered fall in output also reflected a cut in wasteful (if not negative value-added) production. The previous system gave priority to heavy industry and the defence sector, and with transition these priorities were reversed, so substantial falls in production were

[56] Bruno, 'Stabilisation and Reform in Eastern Europe'. After 1989 enterprise managers who were used to operating in a command economy, where their market was assured, and financing was accommodative, had to adapt to a transformed and very uncertain environment.

to be expected in these sectors. Under the former system, which was characterized by shortage, both enterprises and households held excessive levels of inventories. It was therefore to be expected that there would be a substantial cut in orders for new inputs on the part of firms, and precautionary purchases by households in the early stages of transition.[57]

In a regression carried out on twenty-six transition countries Fischer et al. find that stabilization packages are generally followed by an improvement in growth and lower inflation.[58] Recovery appears to occur sooner in those countries where reform began earlier and where macroeconomic control was maintained most effectively under control. However, caution should be used in interpreting the results as the problems of establishing counterfactual evidence create difficulties for ascribing success to the IMF-agreed policies.

There has been much debate about how far the fall in output in early years may have contributed to the electoral backlash which took place in some of the transition countries.[59] As discussed in the previous section, Maravall refers to a 'weak and rough correlation' rather than a mechanical, deterministic relationship between development/growth and democracy. If the correlation also holds in this case, the higher growth found by Fisher et al. to follow IMF stabilization packages might be accompanied by an increased probability that democratic consolidation takes place.

As shown in Table 3.4, inflation has proved unexpectedly persistent in all the transition countries. Economic transformation may contribute to inflationary pressures in a number of ways: through price liberalization, devaluation, the monopoly pricing of (former) state enterprises if privatization is not accompanied by demonopolization, and increased pressure for public spending on infrastructure and unemployment benefits, wage indexation, and, in some countries, servicing of the public debt. When the formerly closed and inefficient centrally planned economies were opened up to market forces a process of catching up with rapid gains in productivity occurred. If the productivity gains are faster in the

[57] Jan Winiecki, 'The Applicability of Standard Reform Packages to Eastern Europe', *Journal of Comparative Economics*, 20 (1995), 347–67.

[58] S. Fischer, R. Sahay, and C. A. Végh, 'From Transition to Market: Evidence and Growth Prospects', in Zecchini, *Lessons from the Economic Transition*.

[59] Sachs contests the extent of the output fall, and argues that in some countries, such as Poland, where electoral backlash occurred, welfare was actually increasing. His explanation for the return of former communists is that they were backed by pensioners and other groups calling for an improvement in welfare entitlements. Jeffrey D. Sachs, 'Postcommunist Parties and the Politics of Entitlement', *Transition Newsletter* (World Bank), 6: 3 (1995), 1–4.

TABLE 3.4. *Inflation in transition economies*

	1996	1997	1998 estimate	1999 projection
Albania	17.4	42.1	8.7	2.0
Belarus	39.2	63.4	181.7	155.0
Bulgaria	310.8	578.6	1.0	2.0
Croatia	3.4	3.8	5.4	4.0
Czech Rep.	8.6	10.0	6.8	3.5
Estonia	15.0	12.5	4.4	3.1
FYR Macedonia	0.2	2.6	−3.1	2.0
Hungary	19.8	18.4	10.3	8.0
Latvia	13.1	7.0	2.8	2.1
Lithuania	13.1	8.5	2.4	2.5
Moldova	15.1	11.2	18.2	30.0
Poland	18.5	13.2	8.6	6.5
Romania	56.9	151.4	40.6	40.0
Russia	21.8	10.9	84.5	45.0
Slovakia	5.4	6.4	5.6	14.5
Slovenia	8.8	8.8	6.5	6.5
Ukraine	39.7	10.1	20.0	17.0

Source: EBRD, *Transition Report*, 1999.

traded than in the non-traded sector, this could also generate inflation.[60] As a result there may be increased inflationary expectations and these could prove self-fulfilling.

The impact of inflation is to erode the purchasing power of the savings and incomes of large segments of the population, and times of hyperinflation are generally associated with increases in poverty.

Table 3.5 sets out statistics for unemployment in the transition economies. A low level of unemployment is an ambiguous indicator in transition countries since it may reflect the slow pace of adjustment, or may be a positive indicator of the ability to create new

[60] This phenomenon is called the Balassa–Samuelson effect. When a small economy opens to international trade its export prices are set at the world level. If the country is on its production possibility frontier, increased productivity in traded goods leads to increased wages in the traded-goods sector. However, if wages are equalized between the traded and non-traded goods sectors, and the non-traded goods sector has lower productivity, inflation will increase. Grafe and Wyplosz stand this argument on its head, arguing that in transition economies the real appreciation determines real wages and hence the pace at which workers will leave the state sector, and join the new traded and non-traded sectors. See C. Grafe and Charles Wyplosz, 'The Real Exchange Rate in Transition Economies', *CEPR Discussion Paper* No. 1773 (London, 1997).

TABLE 3.5. *Unemployment in transition economies*

	Unemployment %, ILO definition			1998 est.
	1995	1996	1997	
Albania	16.9	12.4	14.9	17.7
Belarus	2.7	3.9	2.8	2.3
Bulgaria	11.1	12.5	13.7	12.2
Croatia	14.5	16.4	17.5	17.2
Czech Republic	2.9	3.5	5.2	7.5
Estonia	9.7	10.0	9.7	9.6
FYR Macedonia	37.7	31.9	36.0	34.5
Hungary	10.4	10.5	10.4	9.1
Latvia	18.1	19.4	14.8	13.8
Lithuania	6.2	7.0	5.9	6.4
Moldova	1.4	1.8	1.6	n.a.
Poland	14.9	13.2	10.5	10.4
Romania	9.5	6.6	8.9	10.3
Russia	8.3	9.2	10.9	12.4
Slovakia	13.1	11.1	11.6	11.9
Slovenia	7.4	7.3	7.4	7.9
Ukraine	0.5	1.3	2.3	1.7

Source: EBRD, *Transition Report*, 1999.

jobs. Higher rates of unemployment have been accompanied by increased unemployment risk at a time when social safety nets have been worsening. As Roland argues, even if the unemployed are not pivotal in elections, state workers probably are, and 'It is state workers facing the prospect of restructuring who are the natural constituency of the former communist parties, hoping for a reduction in the unemployment risk.'[61]

All transition countries have experienced increases in income disparities and poverty, and in the Baltic States and many members of the CIS life expectancy has declined.[62] Roland notes a link between increased income inequality and poverty and declining reform support in Russia and Bulgaria.[63]

[61] Roland, 'Political Restraints and the Transition Experience'.
[62] EBRD *Transition Report* (1998). For a discussion of increasing income disparities and poverty in the transition economies see also World Bank, 'Changes in the Wage Structure during Economic Transition in Central and Eastern Europe', *Technical Paper* No. 340 (Washington DC, 1996).
[63] Roland, 'Political Restraints and the Transition Experience', 180.

Corruption may destroy confidence in government and in political processes, and may undermine the political support which is necessary if reforms are to continue. In Russia, in particular, the interconnections between politics, industry, finance, and the media are placing strains both on economic performance and on the process of democratization.

If on the one hand the privatization process may be popular in giving away assets to the population (in the case of mass or voucher privatization), on the other it provides major opportunities for corruption. This can lead to popular resentment, as the EBRD Transition Report describes:

While large parts of the population lost significant fractions of their accumulated assets, some smaller groups have seen their wealth vastly increased. Moreover, at least a fraction of the large gains obtained by some groups have been made in ways which have caused resentment and disenchantment with the transition process. These include certain types of privatization to management insiders, particularly in the natural resource sector, crime and mafia-related activities.[64]

In some countries slow progress in privatization and restructuring of the financial sector has had such negative repercussions that doubts about the resilience and non-reversibility of the transition process have arisen. Though various countries (including Romania) have experienced turbulent developments, the transition process seemed particularly at risk during the financial crises in Bulgaria, and the fraudulent investment schemes leading to political and social disintegration in Albania. As the UN/ECE describes:

In both cases the crisis started with large-scale market failures leading to a more general deterioration of the economic situation and to serious political crises. Whereas a peaceful political solution leading to early parliamentary elections was found in Bulgaria, the unrest in Albania went out of control and led to a virtual disintegration of some basic state institutions.[65]

Although economic and social costs are an intrinsic element of economic transformation, the aim of governments should be to ensure that they are small and as short-lived as possible. Policy mistakes (see below) are likely to speed up the process of eroding the 'window of opportunity' offered by the early reform euphoria which followed the collapse of communism.

---

[64] EBRD *Transition Report* (1996), 29.
[65] *Economic Survey of Europe* (1996–7), 64.

In the initial years of transition there was much debate about the relative merits of shock therapy or gradual measures. In the event this turned out to be largely a false dichotomy. Privatization is inevitably a slow process, and, as Andreff describes, despite the prescriptions of the IMF, after a few years of transition there was a convergence among all the CEECs toward a 'rather mild austerity policy'.[66] Over time the more restrictive stabilization policies in the CEECs were relaxed as austerity shocks are not socially bearable by the population for more than one or two years. At first Poland was presented as a shock therapy country, but by 1992 wage regulation was being loosened, and after 1994 stabilization aimed at curbing inflation was combined with 'a slight Keynesian recovery programme'.[67] Moreover, the privatization process in Poland was relatively slow. Hungary is generally taken as the model of gradualism, but in 1995 introduced a severe stabilization package to curb the fiscal and foreign deficits.[68]

Some countries (such as Romania) missed the opportunity of introducing necessary stabilization packages during what Balcerowicz referred to as the period of 'extraordinary politics' when society's willingness to accept far-reaching change, including painful policies, increased substantially.[69] Over time reform fatigue sets in and the use of austerity measures which are unpopular with the electorate may run the risk of undermining government support, and causing a political backlash. As Daianu describes for Romania: 'if the population at large loses further patience with reform policies that do not bring sufficiently tangible results, social and political stability will suffer, and scarcely any politician or party will be able to keep things under control.'[70]

[66] Wladimir Andreff, 'Nominal, Real, Structural and Institutional Convergence: Is the Convergence of Central Eastern European Countries with the European Union "Systematic?"', Paper presented at the AISSEC Conference 'Convergence and Divergence of Economic Systems, La Sapienza' (Rome, 25–6 Sept. 1997).

[67] Ibid. 6.

[68] Csaba argues that the description of the Hungarian strategy as gradualist is not only a myth, but was 'by and large contrary to what happened'. Laszlo Csaba, 'A Decade of Transformation in Hungarian Economic Policy: Dynamics, Constraints and Prospects', *Europa-Asia Studies*, 50: 8 (1998), 1381–91.

[69] L. Balcerowicz, 'Common Fallacies in the Debate on the Economic Transition in Central and East European Countries', *EBRD Discussion Paper* (London, 1993).

[70] D. Daianu, 'Economic Policy in Public Debate: A Romanian Perspective', in Crawford D. Goodwin and Michael Nacht, *Beyond Government: Extending the Public Debate in Emerging Democracies* (Boulder, Colo.: Westview Press, 1995), 227–48, see esp. 243.

IMF Conditionality

Conditionality by its nature involves a degree of coercion, and a crucial question that arises concerns how free a country is to accept the policy prescriptions of the IMF. Given the institutional mandate of the IMF, balance of payments disequilibrium is a necessary prerequisite for IMF intervention. The balance of payments need for financial resources as reflected in low holdings of foreign reserves, high external indebtedness, and/or a deficit in the overall balance of payments or its major components (see Table 3.6) could therefore be regarded as a first proxy for the 'dependency' of a country on the IMF.

However, in their analysis of the demand and supply of IMF arrangements Knight and Santaella carry out a survey of earlier empirical work in order to identify the variables entering in the demand for IMF financing.[71] As well as the need for balance of payments financing, these authors find that domestic factors, such as slow growth or high inflation may also play a role. It also seems more probable that low-income countries seek assistance as their access to private capital markets may be more limited, and they may require technical assistance. If a country has received IMF financing in the past, it is also more likely to seek an arrangement again as it will be familiar with IMF modes of operating.

The question of whether a country is likely to seek IMF assistance is not, however, the same as 'dependency' and, as will be shown below, the bargaining capacity of a particular government may play a central role in determining how far it is obliged to implement IMF prescriptions.

The conditionality applied by the IMF is reinforced by the widespread practice of *cross-conditionality*. This entails that the assistance of other international organizations such as the World Bank or EU may only be forthcoming if an agreement is reached with the IMF. Many commercial banks and other international financial organizations regard an agreement with the IMF as a sort of 'seal of approval' of the ability and willingness of a country to repay loans.[72] IMF surveillance[73] of the economy of a country is also seen

---

[71] Michael Knight and J. A. Santaella, 'Economic Determinants of IMF Financial Arrangements', *Journal of Development Economics*, 54 (1997), 405–36.

[72] Bilateral aid from other major donors may also be cut off quite suddenly if a country fails to implement IMF or World Bank conditions.

[73] The IMF role of *surveillance* is partly the consequence of conditionality in the use of the Fund's resources and the consequent need for supervision. It also arose

TABLE 3.6. *The external balance in transition economies*

	Current account balance 1997 ($ million)	Current account balance as % 1997 GDP	Current account balance as % 1998 GDP	Current account balance as % 1999 GDP	Total external debt 1997 ($ million)	Total external debt as % 1997 GDP
Albania	−272	−12.2	−6.3	−12.8	706	22
Belarus	−789	−23.7	−33.1	−27.2	1,162	5
Bulgaria	427	4.3	−2.3	−5.7	9,858	96
Croatia	−2,434	−4.4	−12.0	−7.1	6,842	36
Czech Rep.	−3,271	−6.1	−1.9	−1.1	21,456	40
Estonia	−562	−12.1	−9.2	−6.3	658	14
FYR Macedonia	−275	−7.4	−9.0	−8.8	1,542	75
Hungary	−982	−2.1	−4.8	−5.4	24,373	52
Latvia	−345	−6.1	−11.1	−8.0	503	8
Lithuania	−981	−10.2	−12.1	−11.3	1,540	15
Moldova	−267	−13.5	−19.7	−20.3	1,040	52
Poland	−5,744	−3.1	−4.5	−5.5	39,889	27
Romania	−2,338	−6.2	−7.9	−7.0	10,422	29
Russia	2,569	0.7	0.9	5.5	125,645	27
Slovakia	−1,359	−10.0	−10.1	−5.2	9,989	48
Slovenia	88	0.2	0.0	−0.7	879[a]	7[b]
Ukraine	−1,335	−3.0	−2.8	−1.3	1,901	21

[a] EBRD data.
[b] 1998.

Source: EBRD and World Development Report.

as a means of avoiding renewed financial crisis. The IMF may also play a pivotal role in obtaining debt rescheduling for a country. As a result, a country's chances of obtaining financial support from other sources may also depend on it reaching an agreement (and accepting the conditions) of the IMF.[74]

The conditionality applied to financial support operations of the IMF has always been contentious. However, what is controversial

because the Fund had to investigate domestic economic policies in order to carry out its role of encouraging consultation and collaboration of international monetary problems effectively. H. James, 'The Historical Development of the Principle of Surveillance', *IMF Staff Papers*, 42: 4 (1995), 762–93.

[74] For instance, at the 1989 Strasbourg Summit of the European Community it was agreed to introduce a stabilization fund, conditional on Poland reaching an agreement with the IMF, and a World Bank structural loan was also conditional on that agreement.

is probably less the existence of conditionality (all creditors impose conditions) than the nature and impact of IMF policy prescriptions.

Rather than being technocratic and apolitic the underlying philosophy of the IMF is accused of being rooted in the neo-classical economic paradigm, with a strong commitment to the free market, integration into the international economy, and macroeconomic stability.[75] The ideology favoured by the IMF therefore coincided closely with that of the early post-communist governments in the CEECs. In the first years of its transition the Czech Republic proved a model pupil in this context, and at times surpassed even the expectations of the IMF as, for example, in the size of its fiscal surplus and below-target growth of credit.[76]

Bruno argues that many of the measures proposed by the IMF for the transition countries would probably have been introduced anyway:

It is important to point out that unlike many past cases, IMF programs in Eastern European economies thus far have typically been self-imposed, drastic adjustment programs, to which the IMF has given its blessing rather than having been the primary initiator.[77]

However, the application of the standard package, and the limited ability of the recipient countries to avoid the conditions imposed, sometimes gave rise to resentment, as Daianu describes for the case of Romania:

economic policy has somehow slipped into a kind of straightjacket master-tailored by the IMF and World Bank, along the prevailing pattern of conventional wisdom . . . most of Central and Eastern Europe is economically at the mercy of regional and continental dynamics. Individual countries may find themselves unable to accomplish desired reforms for at least partly external reasons.[78]

IMF-agreed packages are also accused of being negotiated in a 'very narrow financially-oriented framework'[79] which fails to take adequate account of the implications of the programmes for agriculture, industry, health, welfare, and other aspects of the economy.

---

[75] See, for example, Marc Williams, *International Economic Organisations and the Third World* (New York: Harvester Wheatsheaf, 1994). See esp. 70–1 for a discussion of this issue.

[76] The Czech government even decided not to make the last two drawings and to make repayments contractually agreed before in its third IMF stand-by arrangement of 1993.

[77] Bruno, 'Stabilisation and Reform in Eastern Europe', 743.

[78] Daianu, 'Economic Policy in Public Debate', 243.

[79] H. W. Singer, 'Aid Conditionality', *Institute of Development Studies, Brighton, Discussion Paper* No. 346 (1994), 1–18.

Sachs refers to the IMF as an 'anti-inflation zealot' that is prepared to accept deep recessions if it thinks these will cut inflation by a few percentage points.[80] The IMF is also criticized for attaching too little attention to objectives such as the reduction of poverty, income inequality, and employment.

It is argued that the recommendations of the IMF carry so much weight not only because they offer the prospect of financial resources, but also because they are backed by powerful sponsors such as the USA.[81] In recent years there has also been increasing reference to a Wall Street–Treasury complex which stands to gain from some of the IMF policy prescriptions, and, in particular, from the combination of fixed exchange rates and freedom of capital movements which, until recently, was generally advocated by the Fund.[82] Bhagwati maintains that the interest of this complex 'ties in with the IMF's own desires, which is to act as a lender of last resort.[83] They see themselves as the apex body which will manage this whole system. So the IMF finally gets a role for itself, which is underpinned by maintaining complete freedom on the capital account.'

A further question raised by conditionality is that of 'ownership' of programmes. If a programme is imposed against the wishes of the recipient country, there will be less incentive for the government of that country to persevere with its implementation and fulfil all the conditions. According to Singer this occurs frequently, because many governments are under pressure when negotiating conditions with the IMF.[84] The IMF maintains that governments should come to the Fund at an earlier stage, before they are in extreme pressure, but if countries are not under pressure, there is no need for them to resort to the IMF. If ownership of programmes is a question, recipient countries may blame policy failure on mistaken IMF policy prescriptions, while the IMF may accuse the country in question of lack of political will or competence. Nobody will accept responsibility. This comes back to the question of coercion: if the country perceived the policy prescription in its

---

[80] In the *Financial Times* (22 Jan. 1999).

[81] For instance, in the 1998 Brazilian crisis distinction between US and IMF initiatives became extremely blurred.

[82] Sachs in the *Financial Times* (22 Jan. 1999) refers to US investors wanting to get their money out of Brazil and Russia without devaluation losses, and the problem of the IMF and US Treasury listening too much to 'Wall Street importunings'.

[83] Interview in *Times of India* (31 July 1998), reported in R. Wade, 'The Asian Debt- and Development Crisis of 1997–?: Causes and Consequences', *World Development*, 26: 8 (1998), 1535–53.

[84] Singer, 'Aid Conditionality'.

own best interest there would be no need to insist on conditionality unless external discipline and the intervention of a scapegoat were seen as the only method of ensuring effective implementation of the policy.

In a historical account of the 'cordial discord' between the IMF and Hungary both before and after 1989, Csaba provides an interesting description of the limits on the ability of the IMF and World Bank to impose their policies on a country.[85] These limits became only too apparent in 1993 when the Hungarian government proposed a budget deficit of double the level suggested by the IMF, and the latter suspended the three-year stand-by arrangement with Hungary.

In general Hungary has tended to resort to the IMF as late as possible, when the request for external assistance was unavoidable. As soon as the situation improved, successive Hungarian governments have revealed themselves vulnerable to pressure group requests, postponing institutional reforms, and introducing populist measures. Csaba describes a 1994 speech of the Minister of Finance, Szabó, who argued that after forty years of socialist dogmatism, Hungary did not need anti-socialist free market dogmatism, and that growth and social consensus were more important than fiscal cuts and anti-inflationary concerns.[86]

None the less, in general the IMF has granted favourable treatment to Hungary, and in times of real difficulty such as 1982 and 1990 it was quick to grant assistance. Csaba offers various reasons for this tolerance: the commitment of Hungary to the market economy and the reluctance to ask for assistance for the foreign debt.[87] Moreover, Hungarian governments tended to accept the underlying philosophy of the IMF, even though they frequently declared its proposals untimely or ignored them for fear of social resistance.

Criticisms of the IMF-agreed Programmes in the Transition Economies

In principle, the standard stabilization package proposed by the IMF is applicable to any economic system since its main aim is to ensure

---

[85] Laszlo Csaba, 'Hungary and the IMF: The Experience of a Cordial Discord', *Journal of Comparative Economics*, 20 (1995), 211–34.
[86] Ibid. 226.   [87] Ibid. 231.

consistency in the evolution of the main macroeconomic variables in order to achieve the aims of low inflation, fiscal restraint, and a sustainability of the balance of payments position.[88] Where controversy arises is in the applicability of this model to economies in transition. The slow progress in microeconomic restructuring and institutional change has profound implications for macroeconomic policy and as a result some aspects of the standard IMF reform package have acquired perverse implications when applied in this context. In part this reflected the uncharted and incredibly complicated nature of the transition process, and the IMF has generally demonstrated a flexibility and willingness to correct its mistakes.

The criticism of failing to understand the system-specific features of transition economies falls into a more general attack against the IMF, by which it is accused of failing to make sufficient allowance of the different circumstances, political situations, cultures, and objectives of the recipient country.[89] In particular, IMF officials are accused of spending too much time in Washington and with each other, and too little time in the country concerned.

Various ways in which IMF prescriptions appear inappropriate to transition economies can be indicated:

1. Both the IMF and the World Bank made large errors in forecasting growth, investment, and inflation in the early years of transition, partly because inadequate account was taken of the systemic features of these economies.

2. The IMF generally expressed a preference for fixed nominal exchange rates (reserves permitting). However, in the case of the transition countries the risk is that this might not allow sufficient flexibility to meet the problems arising from real appreciation of the exchange rate, and capital inflows.

Various studies confirm that transition economies have generally followed a pattern of significant initial undervaluation of the

---

[88] For a more detailed discussion of the standard IMF package as applied in the CEEC context see Stanislaw Gomulka, 'The IMF-Supported Programmes of Poland and Russia, 1990–1994: Principles, Errors and Results', *Journal of Comparative Economics*, 20 (1995), 316–46; and Salvatore Zecchini, 'The Role of International Financial Institutions in the Transition Process', in Zecchini, *Lessons from the Economic Transition*.

[89] Ironically, another major attack against the IMF is that it tends to be too country-specific in elaborating its policy prescriptions. For example, individual East Asian countries were urged to introduce restrictive measures, underestimating their impact on real contagion in the form of a slowdown in growth. This is an example of the fallacy of composition.

exchange rate followed by real appreciation.[90] This real appreciation can be explained by the productivity gains associated with the catching-up process and the inflationary pressures intrinsic to transition.[91] As Halpern and Wyplosz argue, real appreciation is the 'equilibrium outcome of successful transition.'[92]

3. Most of the CEECs furthest advanced in economic transition (such as the Czech Republic, Poland, and Hungary) have, on occasion, experienced difficulties as a result of large-scale capital inflows.[93] These were encouraged by the relatively high interest rates implied by the macroeconomic stabilization programmes in transition economies at a time when interest rates in Western Europe and the USA were relatively low.

Capital inflows may create difficulties for the recipient country in a number of ways.[94] Sudden surges in capital inflows may lead to rapid monetary expansion, inflationary pressures, real exchange rate appreciation, and widening current account deficits. The inflow of foreign capital may also lead to speculative bubbles, with sharp

[90] See for instance László Halpern and Charles Wyplosz, 'Equilibrium Exchange Rates in Transition Economies', *IMF Staff Papers*, 44: 4 (Dec. 1997), 430–61, esp. 459); or Nuti, 'Comparative Economics after the Transition'.

[91] The Czech case proves a good example of the difficulty of attempting to peg the nominal exchange rate in a transition economy. A currency basket peg was first introduced in 1991. The composition of the basket was changed in 1992, and again in 1993 when the koruna's exchange rate was based on a basket made up of the dollar (35%) and D-mark (65%). Full convertibility of the koruna was implemented from 1 Oct. 1995. The fluctuation band of +/–0.5% was increased to +/–7.5% in February 1996. Initially the magnitude of the devaluation prevented the exchange rate from acting as an effective anchor. Subsequently, nominal currency stability and a higher rate of inflation than in OECD countries undermined the cushion which an undervalued exchange rate provided in the early years of transition. The real appreciation of the exchange rate was not matched by increases in productivity, and Czech firms began to lose competitiveness. Strong speculative pressure emerged and the Czech Central Bank attempted to fight the speculative attacks using foreign exchange intervention and an increase of interest rates. It is estimated that some $2 billion in reserves was spent in an attempt to maintain the fixed exchange rate system: *Financial Times* (1 Dec. 1997). However, in May 1997 it was forced to switch to a managed float based on a target rate of 17–19.5 koruna per D-Mark.

[92] Halpern and Wyplosz, 'Equilibrium Exchange Rates'.

[93] As Gabrisch explains, the difficulties experienced by certain CEECs as a result of capital inflows could be repeated after enlargement as a consequence of transfers to these countries from the Common Agricultural Policy and Structural Funds. H. Gabrisch, 'Eastern Enlargement of the European Union: Macroeconomic Effects in New Member States', *Europe-Asia Studies*, 49: 4 (1997), 577–80.

[94] As Calvo et al. explain for the case of developing countries: Guillermo Calvo, Leonardo Leiderman, and C. Reinhart, 'Inflows of Capital to Developing Countries in the 1990s', *Journal of Economic Perspectives*, 10: 2 (1996).

increases in prices of property and on the stock exchange. A major fear is that, given the volatility of international capital movements, substantial capital inflows may be followed by capital flight. As sterilization may be difficult to implement and costly in transition economies, an alternative solution could be more a flexible exchange rate arrangement.

For many years the IMF put pressure on various governments to liberalize their capital accounts, and only recently has there been a recognition that controls on capital movements and prudential financial regulation can help to contain financial fragility. The experience of Slovenia has been rather positive in this respect. The Slovenian tolar has displayed relatively little nominal volatility, partly as a result of regular intervention by the Central Bank, but also because of the relatively restrictive stance adopted with regard to capital movements.[95]

4. The IMF should have given more priority to transforming the financial sector and the need to develop prudential regulation and effective supervision, a lesson that the East Asian crisis again underlined.

The slow progress in reforming the financial sector in the transition economies created difficulties for the operation of monetary instruments. For instance, distortions arose as the result of the widespread diffusion of 'bad debts' of state enterprises which obtained credit from banks and each other (in the form of arrears) in order to continue operating and avoid, or at least postpone, bankruptcy.[96] These enterprises were backed by government guarantees and were not very sensitive to the price of credit. As Zecchini describes, tightening of monetary policy did not prevent the banks supporting these enterprises, or the rapid growth of inter-enterprise credit.[97] Substantial increases in the price of credit often failed to limit credit expansion and frequently meant that

---

[95] Slovenia completed liberalization of current account transactions in 1995, and though there was some liberalization of capital account transactions, capital controls were reintroduced in 1995 and 1997. Most CEECs liberalized current account transactions and capital flows associated with FDI (foreign direct investment) fairly early. The Baltic States opted for a relatively high degree of openness with regard to capital flows, while the Czech Republic, Hungary, and Poland have been easing restrictions on capital movements also with an eye to their commitments as OECD members.

[96] Vito Tanzi, 'The Budget Deficit in Transition: A Cautionary Note', *IMF Staff Papers* (1993), 697–707.

[97] See Zecchini, 'The Role of International Financial Institutions in the Transition Process'.

small private firms were crowded out as an increasing share of credit went to the large state enterprises.

5. At times privatization was pushed too fast and insufficient attention was paid to creating an effective regulatory framework, strengthening the rule of law and building institutions such as courts.[98]

6. The IMF has always placed great emphasis on fiscal discipline, but excessive concern for budgetary constraint may hinder transition.[99] All these countries face pressure for additional government spending from a number of sources. Improvements in infrastructure are urgently required, and in most cases bad debts remain a problem. The task of taking on the *acquis* in CEECs preparing to join the EU also calls for budgetary expenditure, in particular, in areas such as the environment, the modernization of administration, and improvement in judicial capacity. The transition countries have to undertake fundamental reform of their pension systems, health care, and education.[100]

There are also other ways in which too much concern for the budget deficit might slow down transition. For instance, if state enterprises lay off workers, government spending on unemployment benefits is likely to rise. To avoid this increase in spending, governments might encourage firms to continue hoarding workers, and this could render restructuring and privatization more difficult. If a country devalues its exchange rate, its interest payments on foreign debt measured in domestic currency will rise, adding to government expenditure. If the foreign debt is large, a rigid limit on the budget deficit might cause the government to delay exchange rate adjustment.

In Russia and the Ukraine budgetary deficits have been contained simply by withholding payment for government purchases and for public sector wages and pensions.[101] According to Nuti, this occurred

---

[98] This was one of the main criticisms of Stiglitz. See, for example, *The Economist* (19 Sept. 1999).

[99] See also Tanzi, 'Budget Deficit', for a discussion of these issues.

[100] A further difficulty could arise from the high share of budgetary redistribution in GDP. According to Palankai this amounted to 60% for Hungary in 1993, compared with 40–5% in Western Europe, and 46% for the Czech Republic: T. Palankai, 'Hungary and Meeting the Membership Criteria—Capacity to Cope with Competitive Pressures and Market Forces with a View to Targeted EU Development', in Ferenc Mádl (ed.), *On the State of the EU Integration Process: Enlargement and Institutional Reforms*. Acts of an International ECSA Conference in Budapest (Budapest, 6–10 Nov. 1996).

[101] Even on conservative estimates in 1996 the total stock of payment arrears in Russia amounted to almost twice the stock of domestic currency: *UN/ECE Economic Survey of Europe in 1996/1997*, 72.

with 'the unbelievable complicity and support of international financial institutions such as the IMF'.[102]

7. The difficulties of reform of the tax system were also underestimated, and the growth of a new, greenfield private sector was accompanied by widespread tax evasion. However, attempts to clamp down on this evasion are likely to force many new small firms into bankruptcy.

The IMF in a New International Financial Architecture

Following the East Asian, Brazilian, and Russian crises, the debate about the need for a new international financial architecture, with a changed role for the IMF gained a new urgency. Numerous blueprints have been advanced, and the discussion here does not pretend to be comprehensive.

The resources of the IMF are proving increasingly inadequate and in 1998 were only one-third as big relative to world output as they were in 1945.[103] In view of the expanding world economy, the vast increase in international financial transactions, and the scale of the bail-outs necessary in 1997 and 1998, the IMF is overstretched, and its resources need replenishing. Keynes envisaged IMF resources equivalent to the value of 50 per cent of world imports, but in 1998 they only amounted to about 1 per cent.[104] However, the difficulty of getting the $18 billion IMF quota passed through the US Congress in 1998 does not augur well for substantial increases in IMF resources.

There has been considerable debate as to whether the IMF should streamline its activities and return to its original agenda. For example, the US Treasury secretary, Larry Summers, has called for the IMF to move out of longer-term assistance for developing countries, and to concentrate more on preventing and managing financial crises.[105] In this way there would be less blurring of responsibility between the IMF and World Bank. Summers did, however, favour a continuing role for the IMF in poverty reduction, also because it was an important actor in the initiative to reduce debt for the highly indebted developing countries (HIDCs). Others

---

[102] Nuti, 'Comparative Economics after the Transition', 3.

[103] As presented in a speech by Stanley Fischer reported in the *Financial Times* (11 Jan. 1999).

[104] As reported in *The Times* (19 Aug. 1998).

[105] See *Financial Times* (15 Dec. 1999).

such as Michel Camdessus, outgoing director of the IMF, maintained that such emphasis on crisis prevention and emergency support would be too limiting, and that continued IMF support would be necessary for countries not poor enough to attract concessional financing, but unable to attract sizeable capital inflows.[106]

It is generally argued that the IMF should be more accountable as its officials are, after all, unelected technocrats without a direct democratic political mandate. A related issue is that of transparency and increased openness about the prospects and policies of the country concerned. The inscrutable IMF reaction to this was that the 'IMF should adopt a presumption in favour of release of information except where this might compromise confidentiality'.[107] Steps have, however, been taken to improve data dissemination and place more emphasis on public relations.

IMF assistance is always *ex-post*, after the crisis has occurred, so it has been maintained that a pre-emptive facility should be introduced, which would allow rapid deployment of cash for countries with appropriate policies and who qualify for access. However, it is difficult to see what criteria should be used in deciding which countries qualify for using this facility. The proposal would also seem to require supervision before the intervention of the IMF, laying the IMF even more open to the claim of eroding national sovereignty and undermining political legitimacy. It also seems likely that the risk of moral hazard would increase, and that the IMF would be permitted considerable political discretion in deciding whom to help and when. Moreover, if a country off the list were refused assistance, the result may be to precipitate crisis.

It is frequently claimed that IMF officials have too little familiarity with the specific social, cultural, and institutional features of the country concerned, so a proposed solution is to co-opt more local experts and/or to insist that IMF officials spend more time at the country level.

It has also been proposed to increase the role of regional organizations, such as regional development banks (the EBRD in Europe) or regional integration blocs such as the EU. It is argued that this would help to overcome the alleged failure of the IMF to take sufficient account of the specific characteristics of countries, since, presumably, regional neighbours understand each others' needs better. One of the criticisms of this proposal is that it would exacerbate existing problems of duplication and lack of coordination

---

[106] *Financial Times* (2 Feb. 2000).
[107] IMF, *World Economic Outlook* (1998).

between the various international organizations. In general, however, the policy prescriptions of the EU have been consistent with those of the IMF, and sometimes too much so.[108]

In the case of Europe, this proposal has *de facto* already been implemented. The policy prescriptions of the EU are generally in line with those of the IMF, but EU intervention to promote political and economic transition, in particular, in those countries which have applied for EU membership, is far more pervasive than that of the IMF. CEECs wanting the benefits of peace and prosperity which EU membership is expected to bring simply have to meet the accession criteria, and adopt and implement the *acquis communautaire*. It is a situation of 'take it or leave it'. The CEECs had virtually no say in the process of defining those criteria, nor in the way in which they were interpreted. The economic situation of these countries means that the Swiss or Norwegian option is not viable, and the Slovakian experience suggested that the only alternative appeared to be strengthening the links eastwards.

The conditionality applied by the EU is probably at its strongest while these countries are waiting to join. None the less, once these countries become members, they will be enmeshed in a wide range of social, political, and economic interdependencies and it is hoped that these will be used by the EU to ensure that the process of democratic consolidation continues.

Aside from the continuation of this enhanced regional role for the EU, and agreement on debt relief for the highly indebted developing countries, it seems likely that few changes will be introduced by what the G7 governments called the 'strengthened financial architecture for the global marketplace of the millennium'.[109] There are too many differences of opinion concerning what form that architecture should take, and too little financing is forthcoming. Nonetheless much might be achieved by concrete, more modest-seeming measures such as increased IMF transparency and accountability; a more open position on capital controls and exchange rates; increased emphasis on growth, employment, poverty, etc., and a concerted effort to improve prudential and supervisory standards of the financial system.

---

[108] For instance, the conditionality applied in granting assistance for macroeconomic stabilization to the CEECs is closely modelled on that of the IMF. Assistance operations generally take the form of loans which are disbursed in tranches conditional on the fulfilment of certain macroeconomic performance and structural adjustment criteria. These criteria generally relate to the economic programmes of the beneficiary country as agreed in an arrangement with the IMF.

[109] In November 1998.

Conclusions

There has been much debate about the role of the IMF in the transition countries after 1989, but the real controversy exploded later as a consequence of IMF intervention in East Asia, Russia, and Brazil. The record of the IMF in the other transition countries was more positive, but not without errors.

Austerity measures, the most unpopular IMF recommendation, were necessary in the face of the high and (with the benefit of hindsight) persistent inflation in the transition countries. Moreover, when the collapse in output turned to growth in the early 1990s in most of these countries, the IMF macroeconomic prescriptions appeared vindicated, and became more politically acceptable. According to Fischer et al., macroeconomic stabilization in the transition countries was generally followed by improved growth performance, and Maravall maintains that various empirical studies suggest that when economic development/growth occurs, the probability of democratization will increase.

However, austerity measures impose economic and social costs that can undermine political support and lead to electoral backlash. Cuts in spending on services such as health care, pensions, and unemployment benefits have increased income disparities and poverty in the transition economies, while higher interest rates have added to the difficulties of new private firms.

A reduced role for the state was undoubtedly necessary in the former centrally planned countries, but mistakes were made in the privatization process, and the scandals and corruption which resulted in all the transition economies have, at times, led to popular resentment. Increased unemployment and uncertainty hits state workers particularly and in some cases these have proved the natural constituents of former communist parties. Where these parties have returned to power in most cases (with some notable exceptions such as Belarus) they remain committed to the process of transition, but at times they have been associated with its slower implementation.

In applying its conditionality, the IMF failed to insist sufficiently on progress in transforming the financial sector. The Czech crisis of 1997, like that of the East Asian countries, clearly illustrated the need for sound, competitive, well-regulated, and adequately supervised financial sectors. In their absence countries may be vulnerable to financial scandals which threaten the process of democratic consolidation (as occurred in Albania), and to the risks of volatile short-term capital movements. If capital flight occurs it may force painful adjustment of the current account, and slower (or negative) growth, placing strains on the political system.

The IMF has been accused of undermining the sovereignty and political legitimacy of beneficiary countries. These countries are said to have little choice but to accept the unpopular measures forced upon them by the IMF. It is true that at times when the external situation of a country deteriorated rapidly, with balance of payments disequilibrium, loss of reserves, and, in some cases, difficulty in servicing foreign debt, transition countries have been heavily dependent on the IMF for assistance (in particular, because of the application of cross-conditionality). However, over time the bargaining power of the recipient country may play an important role, and all the transition countries have proved unwilling or unable to protract the application of austerity measures for more than a year or two.

Given the claims of mistaken policies, undue interference, and lack of transparency against the IMF on the one hand, and the increasing volatility of the international financial system on the other, the debate about reform of the international financial architecture has acquired a new urgency. In the case of Europe one of the main reforms proposed, i.e. an increased role for regional integration blocs, has *de facto* already been implemented. At least in the countries that have applied for membership, the EU is the main external actor, and applies a more far-reaching and stringent economic and political conditionality than was ever the case for the IMF. It is only to be hoped that the application of that conditionality will render the interlinked processes of economic transition and democratic consolidation as swift and as painless as possible.

4

International Security and Democracy Building

Reimund Seidelmann

The transition and democratic consolidation process in Eastern Europe has been primarily a matter of politics and economics. Although security issues have played only a secondary role in democratization and civil society building, they should not be neglected. In particular in areas like the Balkans, the interrelation between security, peace, and democracy has dominated the political agenda.[1] The link between security and democratic consolidation in Eastern Europe must be seen as a process, in which specific national and regional constellations have interrelated with general patterns and dynamics of security and democracy building. This analysis combines a systematic approach of hypothesis building with an empirically based discussion, in order to contribute to the general process of theory building and to place developments in Eastern Europe into a wider analytical framework.[2]

The following research is based on work conducted within the framework of the project entitled 'Security Policies of East Central European Nations and the Development of a New European Security Architecture' (1995–7) funded by the Volkswagen Foundation. The author takes full responsibility for the views expressed in this article.

[1] It should be noted that the civil society approach defines democratization not only as a matter of institutional reform but as the establishment of a broadly and deeply participating set of non-governmental actors in the political, socio-cultural, and economic decision-making process. For further details, see Jean-Michel de Waele, 'Les Théories de la transition à l'épreuve de la démocratisation en Europe centrale et orientale', in Pascal Delwit and Jean-Michel de Wael (eds.), *La Démocratisation en Europe centrale* (Paris: Éditions Complexes, 1998), 29–58.

[2] It has to be underlined that both are understood not as static but dynamic concepts, open both for progress and regression.

The Interrelation between Security and Democratic Consolidation

Both security and democracy studies have seen the interrelation between security and democracy less a matter of a direct causal link and more one of conditioning relations.[3] While security is defined as a necessary but not sufficient condition for the development of democracy, democratic structures, identities, and policies condition the means and the objectives of security policies. Authoritarian policies often use a perceived security threat as a justification—as witnessed in the case of the Yugoslav conflict. Transition theories have implied that economic and political development may reinforce each other, as economic growth may stabilize democratization processes in Eastern Europe, and socio-economic problems have been the prime danger to democratic consolidation. The link between security and democracy has been more complicated, less direct, and may be of high political relevance.

This link has foreign and domestic dimensions, each with different political logics and raising different problems. The external dimension results from the fact that although the provision of security is an essential function of the state, it constitutes a political objective related primarily to neighbouring countries, the surrounding region, and the wider international system. States have to respond to the security dilemma in the absence of a global government which could guarantee peace.[4] While the need to use force to provide national security and defence is the logical answer to this security dilemma, it leads to three further dilemmas, which are well known in general European history and can be seen in the Balkans today.

The first dilemma is in that the military instrumentalization of security policy may lead to further insecurity and politically unacceptable risks—as modern conventional, chemical, and nuclear

---

[3] Consider, for example, Emil Kirchner, and Kevin Wright (eds.), *Security and Democracy in Transition Societies*, Conference Proceedings (Essex, 1998).

[4] For a detailed discussion, see Philipp Borinski, 'European Security: The Realist View', in Eric Remacle and Reimund Seidelmann (eds.), *Pan-European Security Redefined* (Baden-Baden: Nomos Verlagsgesellschaft, 1998), 51–74. See also Reimund Seidelmann, 'Weltsystem, Weltgesellschaft, Weltstaat: Zugänge zur Theorie internationaler Beziehungen', in Franz Neumann (ed.), *Handbuch politische Theorien und Ideologien*, vol. ii (Opladen: Leske & Budrich, 2000), 445–80.

warfare may threaten the very existence of the state.[5] Even medium and low-intensity conflicts, such as in the former Yugoslavia, have highlighted the enormous financial, human, and political costs for the societies and economies involved.[6] The second dilemma is in that the cumulating costs of such a security policy can threaten the stability of government, ruling elites, regime, and the political system.[7] Third, the schizophrenic approach to physical force—with the legitimization of the use of force outside states and its criminalization within states—creates a permanent problem of political credibility and acceptance.[8] These dilemmas explain why Eastern European states have been so eager to achieve additional security through NATO and EU membership. The contemporary European security system promises a concept of security for Eastern Europe in which these dilemmas will be reduced and politically controlled and the conditions for political participation improved.

The second dimension of the link between security and democracy results from both historical development and 'issue logic'. Historically, foreign and security policy in Europe has been characterized by the primacy of the executive and significantly lesser public participation than domestic policy.[9] It has been a mistake so far to allow the new governments in Eastern Europe to limit democratic participation and control in these areas. Excluding these policy areas from democratization has allowed these governments to pursue foreign and security policies which contradict democratic values, and to use force against democratic movements outside and inside the state. However, democratization in these policy areas requires strong political will. Such reforms are constrained by the

[5] One has to remember that a full-scale Soviet conventional attack against Germany, followed by a Western military response, would have caused the loss of roughly one-third of its population, infrastructure, and industrial capacities within days. Even limited or selective nuclear escalation in Central Europe would have led to devastating and long-lasting destruction.

[6] For an updated data collection, see Thomas Rabehl, *Das Kriegsgeschehen 1997: Daten und Tende zen der Kreige und bewaffneten Konflikte* (Opladen: Leske und Budrich, 1998), 22.

[7] Although even today it is still difficult to come up with precise data of Soviet defence expenditures, estimates between 15 and 25% of GNP underline the magnitude of such 'non-productive' expenditures.

[8] See, for example, the arguments of the peace movements in the early 1980s. For communist parties in Eastern Europe, domestic militarization and peace rhetoric constituted a special credibility problem.

[9] This varies between European states but shows the same general pattern. And it is not by chance that both Maastricht's and Amsterdam's understanding of the CFSP show little involvement of the European Parliament—integration is defined primarily as an intergovernmental and executive affair.

specific logic of security.[10] Effective security and military policies need to be fully integrated, hierarchical, and speedy structures. Modern war fighting and conflict prevention clashes with the democratic concepts of checks and balance and an inclusive participatory process. In a system defined by the security dilemma, it may be necessary to compromise between the democratic ideal and the necessities of state security. These circumstances add a further double conditionality to the relationship between security and the democratic process. In the case of Eastern Europe, democratization and the modernization of the military have reinforced each other and created a situation where political elites have been able to organize support for their programme of structural change.

Such an understanding of the relationship between security and democracy combines Realist and Idealist elements. This understanding also defines security as 'negative peace', characterized by the absence of open conflict. As such, security is a necessary but not sufficient condition for general peace. At the same time, it is the first step in the process of achieving a better peace. In Realist terms, power and security resulted for Eastern Europe in a negative conditionality during the Cold War. The end of the Cold War led to the emergence of a positive link, or conditionality.[11] In Idealist terms, the link between democracy and international peace was blocked during the Cold War. Only in its aftermath was this link re-established.[12] Kant's ideal to build 'eternal' peace through a community of democratic nations implies that democracies are more peace oriented than non-democratic societies.[13] Both the European Union (EU) and the North Atlantic Treaty Organization (NATO) have defined themselves as democratic value-communities.

---

[10] For an overview of the European aspects of democracy, see Mario Telo (ed.), *Démocratie et construction européenne* (Brussels: Éditions de l'Université de Bruxelles, 1995).

[11] For the recent debate on realism and European security, see Philipp Borinski, 'Realism and the Analysis of European Security', *Journal of European Integration*, 2–3 (1997), 131–52.

[12] Consider Martin Kahl, 'European Integration, European Security, and the Transformation in Central Eastern Europe', *Journal of European Integration*, 2–3 (1997), 153–85.

[13] See Martin Kahl, 'Security Effects of the Transition Process in Eastern Europe', in Remacle and Seidelmann, *Pan-European Security Redefined*, 137–80. And, at 177, Kahl states: 'Stable democracies do not, or rarely, go to war against each other, and the farther and faster democratization goes ahead in Eastern Europe the better the prospects that conflicts will be settled without resort to military force.' For a more cautious view, see Ernst-Otto Czempiel, 'Are Democracies Peaceful? Not quite yet', *PRIF Report*, 37 (Frankfurt, 1995).

These organizations are based on the assumptions that only democratic societies can engage in common and cooperative security,
and that integration may overcome the security dilemma. Linking
these two assumptions has meant first demanding that Eastern
Europe continues democratization, and second offering them in
exchange a form of security which they never experienced during
the Cold War. This discussion about the interrelation between
democracy and security shows that, in the case of Eastern European transitions, a combination of both Realist and Idealist approaches is valuable—in order to promote democratization and
security, and to create a positive and constructive dynamic between
the two.[14]

Four aspects of the interrelation between security and democracy should be noted. First, this relationship is characterized by
mutual conditionality: security is a precondition for any democratic
development, while the democratic process within a state sets
specific conditions for its foreign and security policy. Second, this
relationship has a foreign and a domestic dimension each with a
specific logic and set of problems. The external dimension is characterized by three basic dilemmas of traditional security policies,
which may delay democratic development. The domestic dimension
poses an additional challenge to democratization and consolidation.
Third, specific problems such as nuclear war, escalating threat perceptions, and military intervention in domestic affairs constitute
a permanent problem for the democratic agenda. Fourth, only a
combination of Realist and Idealist approaches in understanding
this interrelation will optimize security while improving conditions
for democratic development; in more idealistic terms, optimizing
democracy enables a state to achieve significant security gains.

The End to the Cold War and the Downgrading of Military Security

For Eastern Europe, the end of the Cold War led to major structural
changes in their security policies, which had been long sought
by reformists and nationalists alike, and were actively supported
by them during the transition period.[15] This affected Eastern

---

[14] Security was defined not only as territorial integrity but as the preservation
of the nation's political identity and its self-fulfilment.

[15] The term 'Eastern Europe' allows us to understand a set of nations and/or
societies as a region, which can be defined both in geographical as well as political-

European security in three ways: first, in terms of the end of the military-political threats posed by the East–West conflict; second, in terms of the opportunity to join Western structures; finally, in terms of the resurgence of the potential for conflict in the region and in particular in the Balkans.

For Western Europe and the Atlantic Alliance, the end of the Cold War opened the opportunity to realize the political-economic transformation of the Eastern European societies, to extend Western political, economic, and military influence towards the former USSR, and to reorganize the European state system on the Western model. Although Eastern European and Western interests were not identical, they proved compatible. Countries like Poland, the Czech Republic, and Hungary—due to their long and intensive exposure to the West—have had only minor difficulties in adapting to new circumstances and in pursuing these compatible interests. Other countries faced more difficulties. Bulgaria and Romania have lagged behind due to the problems in their transformation as well as limited Western interests. For the group of newly independent Eastern European countries like Slovakia and the former Soviet republics, the challenges of nation building, professionalization of new elites, management of socio-economic crisis, and the redefinition of national identity have run parallel with limited Western interest—so delaying their adaptation to new circumstances. This often produced political confusion, contradictory policies, and counter-productive strategies, as witnessed in the Slovak case. For Russia, the severe decline of power further complicated its transformation and 'Westernization'.[16] In general, while these processes have varied from country to country, democratization and the search for security have been linked to a policy of integration in and cooperation with Western structures.

In terms of the political dimension of security, the collapse of the WTO and the fundamental change in Soviet and Russian policies

geographic terms. This has the advantage of allowing us to generalize about the problems of these countries. However, even the most systematic comparison of these countries shows that the term 'Eastern Europe' implies a homogeneity or comparability that exists more as a general projection than an empirical reality. Structures, problems, and policies in these countries differ considerably; and these countries' foreign and regional policies lead to the conclusion that there is only limited common interest, which would allow us to treat them as a group of countries. While still employing the term here, this methodological reservation has to be underlined.

[16] See Jens Fischer, *Eurasismus: Eine Option russischer Außenpolitik* (Berlin: Berlin-Verl, 1998).

towards Eastern Europe allowed the Eastern European countries and former Soviet republics to renationalize their foreign and security policy. It has allowed these states to redefine their geopolitical position—that is, to realize their hidden Western orientation —and to restructure both the surrounding sub-regional and the pan-European system.[17] However, the end of Soviet political-military power projection in Eastern Europe also created new security needs.[18]

These needs resulted from three sources. First, historical experience with Soviet power projection played an important part in a heated security debate, which demanded from the Soviet Union and then the Russian Federation a complete abandonment of any hegemonic intentions. Again, the nature of this debate has varied across the region. Bulgaria has not expressed such concerns because of its traditionally friendly relations with the USSR. However, President Wałęsa made the 'Soviet/Russian threat' a major point in the Polish foreign and domestic political agenda. While Slovakia continued military cooperation with Russia and saw its geopolitical position as a bridge between East and West, the former Soviet republics viewed Russian coercive policies as one of the main obstacles to CIS cooperation.[19] Second, Eastern European consolidation sometimes reinforced and even produced Soviet/Russian political-military threats, which served to secure Western close support, to integrate divergent domestic forces through a strategy of foreign conflict, and to define a new national identity in opposition to the USSR/Russia. For example, the Ukrainian-Russian disputes over the Black Sea Fleet and Crimea showed an interactive

---

[17] Various Eastern European national views on European security can be found in *Un défi pour la Communauté Européenne: les bouleversements à l'est et au centre du continent* (Brussels: Éditions de l'Université de Bruxelles, 1991); Mario Telo (ed.), *Vers une nouvelle Europe?* (Brussels: Éditions de l'Université de Bruxelles, 1992); Klaus Gottstein, *Tomorrow's Europe: The Views of Those Concerned* (Frankfurt: Campus Verlag, 1995); Remacle and Seidelmann, *Pan-European Security Redefined*; The Olaf Palme International Center (ed.), *Visions of European Security: Focal Point Sweden and Northern Europe* (Stockholm: Olaf Palme Centre, 1996); Christoph Bluth, 'The View from the East', in Christoph Bluth, et al. (eds.), *The Future of European Security* (Aldershot: Dartmouth, 1992), 205–28.

[18] Consider Thomas Meyer, 'Nations et nationalisme dans l'Europe post-communiste', in Mario Telo (ed.), *De la nation à l'Europe: paradoxes et dilemmes de la social-démocratie* (Brussels: Bruylant, 1993), 99–112.

[19] See Ivo Samson, *Die Sicherheitspolitik der Slowakei in den ersten Jahren der Selbständigkeit: zu den sicherheitspolitischen Voraussetzungen der Integration der Slowakischen Republik in die euroatlantischen Verteidigungsstrukturen* (Baden-Baden: in print for Nomos-Verlag, 1998).

pattern, and played an important role in nation building. Third, Eastern European military capacities are still no match for Russian military power. Although Russian power projection capabilities have been limited to neighbouring countries, its military power nevertheless has created concerns and security needs for the whole region.

With regard to such security interests, Eastern European states faced three options. First, these states could pursue a policy of neutrality and bridge building between the West and the new Russia. This option, which was favoured by Slovakia, proved not only anachronistic but was not accepted by the main actors.[20] The second option was to create sub-regional security alliances or systems within the OSCE framework. In fact, the various Eastern European sub-regional projects, of which the Visegrad Group was the most promising, have not materialized or led to 'common' policies.[21] The CIS project has been plagued by the problem of Russian hegemonic policies.[22] The third option was to seek membership in the Western structures. This option seemed most attractive in terms of historical experience, cost–benefit calculations, and political-military perspectives. Although membership in the EU and NATO signified a loss of sovereignty, it appeared for all Eastern European states as the most desirable way to achieve greater and cheaper security.

In terms of the military dimension of security, the end of the Cold War meant a fundamental downgrading of the military security issue. The collapse of the WTO and the USSR as well as the domestic problems facing the new Russian Federation reduced the former Soviet military threat towards Eastern Europe to a minimum.[23] In present circumstances, the political will and military ability of Russia to pose even a limited military threat to Eastern Europe

[20] See Ivo Samson, 'The Security Position of Slovakia: Reality and Perspectives in the Mid-nineties', in Remacle and Seidelmann, *Pan-European Security Redefined*, 235–49; Ivo Samson, 'Transformation and Structural Change in Central Eastern Europe: Slovakia's Adjustment to New Security Challenges', *Journal of European Integration*, 2–3 (1997), 187–200; Samson, *Sicherheitspolitik der Slowakei*; Sona Szomolanyi and John A. Gould (eds.), *Slovakia: Problems of Democratic Consolidation and the Struggle for the Rules of the Game* (Bratislava: Slovak Political Science Association, 1997).

[21] To a certain degree, this resulted from decades of Soviet power politics, which cultivated intra-bloc conflicts in order to consolidate Soviet rule.

[22] For details, see Günter Trautmann, 'Russia and the Euro-Atlantic Community', *Journal of European Integration*, 2–3 (1997), 201–32.

[23] Russian military activities in the Chechen conflict proved the deplorable state of the Russian armed forces.

are limited.[24] The Russian Federation may still pose a threat to its neighbours. However, this threat is limited due to weak offensive capabilities and the Russian government's apparent willingness to seek political solutions to disputes. Bilateral and multilateral ways of 'pacifying' Russian foreign and security policies have been complemented by the creation of the new NATO–Russia special relationship, which added an important institutional element to a cooperative pan-European security system.[25] If military security threats are defined as military capability times political will to use these capabilities, the Russian threat to its close neighbours in Eastern Europe has been more a problem of political psychology than military reality. Whatever role the Russian threat has played and will play in Eastern European politics, in objective terms it has not constituted a structural problem for Eastern European security.[26]

Moreover, the threat posed by aggressive neighbours within Eastern Europe has also been limited. Yugoslavia's neighbours had to consider the possibility of military spillover from the violation of borders to systematic subversive activities from Serbia.[27] As a result, containing military developments in Bosnia and Kosovo became an important security issue for these states. Linked with this objective, NATO membership and Western guarantees also became critical policy objectives. The military capabilities of the states of former Yugoslavia were extremely limited. However, potential military aggressors like Serbia and Croatia were not about to be integrated in EU and/or NATO—these states showed a limited willingness to respond to OSCE and Western initiatives. While these states seem 'uncontrollable' within former Yugoslav borders, they carefully prevented any horizontal escalation beyond these

[24] See Christoph Lotter, 'The Nature of the Threats to Western Europe from the East', in Christoph Lotter and Susanne Peters (eds.), *The Changing European Security Environment* (Weimar: Boehlan Verlag, 1996), 83–105.

[25] See, for example, the German and US role in managing the Baltic–Soviet/ Russian and the Ukrainian–Soviet/Russian conflicts.

[26] The argument that Russia could rebuild its military power as well as revitalize the old Soviet policies of military threats is correct in principle. But while political will can change relatively quickly it would take 10–15 years and major resources to rebuild military capacities to such an extent. Concerning nuclear threat options, already the Soviet Union had learnt that such options are ineffective instruments of policy.

[27] See Pal Dunay, 'The Security Policy of Hungary' in Remacle and Seidelmann, *Pan-European Security Redefined*, 203–34. And, at 210, Dunay states: 'The second most important identifiable source of threat (for Hungary) lay in the developments related to the dissolution of Yugoslavia.'

former borders in order to limit the West's willingness to intervene with full-scale force. In other words, existing military capacities and these political calculations limit the threat posed by aggressive neighbours in Eastern Europe.

Thus, the military security environment in Eastern Europe has become 'demilitarized'. Compared with the Cold War period, all the structural political, economic, and military dilemmas of the European security system have become marginalized or simply disappeared. Even the interim period, between the collapse of the Soviet bloc and membership in the NATO system, has provided more military security for Eastern Europe than the old bloc system ever could.

Finally, the transformation of the socio-economic and political system in Eastern Europe has affected both the political will to pose military threats as well as the military ability to make such threats credible. The demilitarization of Eastern European societies has led to a structural downgrading of the political relevance of the military. Doubts about the loyalty of the armed forces in these states have now eased, which has reinforced this downgrading.[28] If one defines the democratization process not only as the establishment of effective democratic control of the military, but also as the development of a civil society in terms of domestic and foreign behaviour, the democratization of Eastern European security policies was the result not only of historical experiences and cost–benefit rationality. It also resulted from changes in the domestic patterns, goals, and structures of Eastern Europe as well as the policies of Western European states and organizations that are engaged in the region. The emergence of an alliance between democratic modernizers in Eastern Europe and in Western Europe, the EU, and NATO was not only a matter of rational choice but also reflected explicit normative change, based on the assumption that only democratic societies are able and willing to establish a peaceful regional order.

It is notable that Eastern European military elites have supported the democratization process and a Western orientation—in effect, they have joined this alliance. Although the transformation process has meant far-reaching political and military change, there has been no attempted *coup d'état* as witnessed in the USSR. While extremist forces in Eastern Europe may 'count upon the military in their far-reaching future plans', this does not as yet constitute

---

[28] It has to be kept in mind that in some cases political change and nation building relied on militias and not the military.

a major threat to transformation.[29] Support from the military has been less norm-oriented, resulting mainly from the traditional primacy of the civilian leadership—a legacy of the communist system. It also resulted from awareness among the military elites of the structural dilemmas that arose from the Cold War and the belief that a military regime could not solve the structural crises. The attractiveness of political cooperation with the West and the military's hopes to receive benefits in return for its loyalty has been another important reason.

Patterns of civilian-military interaction have varied across the region. In the Polish case, a traditionally more nationally oriented military did not pose any problems for the transformation, democratization, and modernization of the military because these processes was perceived as serving Polish interests. In Hungary, where the military traditionally played a very marginal role, transformation and Westernization was fully supported by the military because it meant modernization, access to NATO, and a new role in peacekeeping.[30] Despite more problematic loyalty in Bulgaria and Romania, the military remained neutral towards political change and accepted political and military reorganization as the necessary price to pay for cooperation with the West. In the Czech and Slovak case, separation opened new opportunities as well as problems of political loyalty.[31] The Baltic states and Ukraine faced similar problems with greater intensity. For their military high commands, the creation of national military systems was viewed as an issue of nation building; thus, transformation and separatism constituted opportunities which secured military loyalty towards the new elites.

These developments shaped Eastern Europe's transition and created a new constellation in the relation between security and democratic consolidation. These developments confirmed the idea that the foreign and domestic dimension of the interrelation of secur-

---

[29] See Anatoly S. Grytsenko, 'Civil–Military Relations in Ukraine: A System Emerging from Chaos', *Harmony Papers* (Groningen, 1997), 54.

[30] See Wolfgang Zellner and Pal Dunay, *Ungarns Außenpolitik 1990–1997* (Baden-Baden: Nomos Verlagsanstalt, 1998); Dunay, 'The Security Policy of Hungary', 203–34.

[31] The developments, which excluded the Slovak Republic from the first round of NATO enlargement, were primarily political ones and in the hands of the political elites. While the military accepted continued cooperation with Russia—including imports of Russian weaponry—it nevertheless was highly interested in NATO membership. See Martin Bútora and Thomas W. Skladony (eds.), *Slovakia 1996–1997* (Bratislava: Friedrich-Ebert-Stiftung, 1998), 96–7.

ity and democracy are linked, as well as the hypothesis of double conditionality. As in the Cold War period, security and the political system condition each other. During the Cold War, the mechanisms of military security were used to repress political change, national independence, and democratization. Moreover, the intra-bloc and the domestic power rationale conditioned a security policy aimed at maintaining the status quo.[32] During the Cold War, this link represented a negative dynamic, in that security policies prevented democratic change. Since the end of the Cold War, this link has become positive. The changes in the security arena have created favourable conditions for transformation and democratization; and the democratization process has created equally favourable conditions for new security concepts and policies.

NATO and EU Enlargement and Democratic Consolidation

Eastern European interests and policies

The collapse of the Cold War in Europe left East European states with no alternative but to seek cooperation with and integration into Western structures, mainly the EU and NATO.[33] Cooperation with the USSR/Russia had been discredited. Sub-regionalization within Eastern Europe appeared far less cost-effective than joining Western structures.

The new elites in Eastern Europe pursued a set of political objectives: at a minimum, to seek Western assistance; and at a maximum, to seek full participation as equals in the Western European political, economic, and security architecture. Even if Eastern European states had not underestimated the price of participation in the political organization of Western Europe—in terms of a loss of national sovereignty—they would still have

[32] Although détente played a decisive role in preparing for the end of the East–West conflict it constituted a reformist strategy, which did not call existing structures into question, but sought to gradually reduce their costs and risks.

[33] It is an open question whether the collapse of Soviet power projection and continued communist party rule would have led to developments similar to membership in the EU and NATO. Continued communist party rule, however, would not have been possible without major change in the political and economic system and the renationalization of foreign and security policies. In order to optimize national interests and system stability, this would have led to a rapprochement with NATO and close association—if not membership—in the EU.

continued this policy because of an expectation that the overall advantage outweighed even such a political price.[34] Membership in the EU and NATO was not only a matter of concrete advantages but also a symbolic step for these states in their 'return to Europe'. In this view, the Realist understanding of membership, as a security guarantee, power multiplier, and external democracy-stabilizer was juxtaposed with the Idealist view of membership as a decisive step towards 'Europeanization' and democratization. Given the obstacles to rapid membership in the EU, NATO membership emerged as a prime objective in the foreign and security policies of Eastern European states. The fact that NATO selected only three Eastern European countries in its first round of enlargement did not lessen this priority; in fact, it will lead to additional efforts to attain this objective from the other states.[35]

In security terms, association with and membership in the EU and NATO is seen by the political and military elites in Eastern Europe as bringing with it four basic advantages. First, the direct and indirect security guarantees of NATO and the EU are seen as deterrence against any Russian or regional military threat.[36] While

[34] A more rational debate about the advantages and disadvantages began as late as in the mid-1990s, when the policy of seeking membership had become already irreversible. Before that, knowledge about the general costs of membership and the mechanisms, procedures, and political patterns of organizations like NATO and the EU was limited. Various Eastern European political leaders viewed membership in the EU and NATO as issues of a political nature that could be decided very rapidly. On the issue of sovereignty, Eastern European elites had never been exposed to the specific type of Western European integration. WTO and COMECON on the one hand and CSCE and international organizations on the other did not provide any experience in the sort of supranationalization to which Western European elites and societies have become accustomed.

[35] The fact that NATO limited enlargement to three candidates resulted from NATO policies (see Reimund Seidelmann, 'EU's and NATO's Enlargement towards the East: Constructive Reinforcement or Competitive Conflict?', in Mario Telo and Eric Remacle (eds.), *L'Union européenne après Amsterdam: adaptations institutionelles, enjeux de la différenciation et de l'élargissement* (Brussels: Rapport remis à la Fondation Paul-Henri Spaak, 1998), 98–118; Reimund Seidelmann, 'Amsterdam e la sicurezza europea: un' opportunità nuova o perduta', *Europa Europe*, 1 (1998), 66–86. It also resulted, at least for Slovakia and Slovenia, from these states' political mistakes, misperceptions, and shortcomings in approaching NATO. Slovakia is a perfect example of such shortcomings in underestimating Western conditionality and political messages. See also Samson, *Sicherheitspolitik der Slowakei.*

[36] It has been one of the major political shortcomings in Eastern European integration policies to underestimate the WEU. Despite its political and military shortcomings, the WEU nevertheless constitutes—together with Eurocorps and the project of a Common European Armament Market—an interesting development

this was of minor relevance for the Czech Republic, Hungary, and Bulgaria, this aspect has played a major role in Baltic, Polish, and Ukrainian policies, where NATO membership or special relations with NATO have been seen as the best and cheapest reassurance against any Russian military threat or political blackmail.[37] As in Western Europe after 1945, contemporary Eastern European policies have demonstrated a mixture of multilateralism, bilateralism, and supranationalism. Hungary's engagement in the OSCE, EU, and NATO, and bilateral activities with its neighbours were notable examples of such complex policies.[38] It has been clearly understood that even the most extensive national arms build-up programme would drain resources desperately needed for economic reconstruction and social stabilization, and could not provide equivalent security guarantees. The EU and NATO have also been seen as organizations providing political reassurance against a potentially dominant Germany.[39] Although this has not been a primary objective, it has played an additional role for Germany's eastern neighbours Poland and the Czech Republic.

Second, the EU and NATO's conflict management mechanisms can provide assistance, support, and even action to stabilize intraregional relations.[40] These Western organizations have acted as sub-

---

for a future security dimension of the EU. In addition, it carries certain advantages in comparison to NATO. The WEU treaty contains an automatic defence promise to all members. When Russia threatened to respond to NATO enlargement with disruptive policies, membership in the WEU, which was acceptable for Russia, would have indirectly led to *de facto* membership in NATO because of the close political relation between NATO and the WEU after the introduction of the concept of interlocking institutions. See Christoph Lotter, *Die parlamentarische Versammlung der westeuropäischen Union* (Baden-Baden: Nomos Verlagsgesellschaft, 1997).

[37] See Wojciech Multan, 'The security policy of Poland', in Remacle and Seidelmann, *Pan-European Security Redefined*, 181–202; Lubomir W. Zyblikiewicz, 'The Role of Germany in European Crises Policies', in Reimund Seidelmann, *Crises Policies in Eastern Europe* (Baden-Baden: Nomos Verlagsanstalt, 1996), 293–302; Oleg Strekal, *Nationale Sicherheit der unabhängigen Ukraine (1991–1995): zur Analyse der Sicherheitslage und der Grundlagen der Sicherheitspolitik eines neu entstandenen Staates* (Baden-Baden: in print for Nomos-Verlag, 1998); Siegfried Bock and Manfred Schünemann (eds.), *Die Ukraine in der europäischen Sicherheitsar-chitektur* (Baden-Baden: Nomos Verlagsanstalt, 1997). See, for example, Algis Krupavicius, 'Lithuania's Security Dilemma in the Transforming Europe', in Remacle and Seidelmann, *Pan-European Security Redefined*, 249–86.

[38] See Zellner and Dunay, *Ungarns Außenpolitik 1990–1997*.

[39] For a Polish, French, and German view on Germany's role in Europe, see Seidelmann, *Crises Policies in Eastern Europe*.

[40] For a detailed discussion of conflict and crises policies of various European institutions, see *Seidelmann, Crises Policies in Eastern Europe*.

regional stability multipliers. They have also allowed governments to exploit conflicts with their neighbours in domestic politics without risking such rhetoric leading to open external conflict. In other words, two-tier tactics have emerged in the region between neighbours over sensitive issues: in this, these conflicts have been verbally escalated for domestic political purposes while the EU, NATO, and OSCE have been used to promote cooperation at the regional level. In this process, domestic criticism can be neutralized by governments' referring to the fact that EU and NATO had forced them into cooperation. Even in traditionally cooperative Hungary, the first transition governments made reference to historical myths to display national grandeur and power towards its neighbours—not in order to escalate conflicts with these neighbours but for the purposes of national identity building and as strategies to legitimize the coalition government.

Third, integration into the EU and NATO has required modernization and reform, which otherwise would have been difficult to sustain and legitimize. Defining disputed transformation and modernization measures as necessary preconditions for widely accepted membership policies allowed governments in Eastern Europe to blame the EU and NATO for shortcomings and claim any successful results as their own, thereby creating a win-win situation. In the case of the military, NATO integration has been seen as a way to secure the West's technical, military, and financial assistance in the modernization and reform of the military.[41] Only membership is seen to allow these states access to the latest Western military technology. Thus, in terms of security, participation in the EU and NATO has promised cost-effective security and provided additional legitimization for necessary reform.[42]

Finally, NATO's new role in peacekeeping has promised Eastern Europe's military systems a new functional legitimacy, justifying

---

[41] While, due to the political dispute between the USA and Europe about sharing the burden of NATO's enlargement towards the East, major financial support for the new Eastern European members of NATO seems less feasible, one can assume that financial transfers will occur as soon as the dispute has calmed down. For details of the burden sharing dispute, see Reimund Seidelmann, 'EU's and NATO's Enlargement Towards the East', 98–118; and Reimund Seidelmann, 'Costs, Risks, and Benefits of a Global Military Capability for the European Union', *Defence and Peace Economics*, 8: 1 (1997), 23–143.

[42] It is not by chance that even the USA has supported the doctrine, linking EU with NATO enlargement. For a typical political statement in this direction see Howard Baker Jr, et al., 'Enlarge the European Union before NATO', *International Herald Tribune* (6 Feb. 1998), 8.

demands for additional funds and modernization.[43] Furthermore, access to NATO infrastructure has been viewed as a cost-effective multiplier of national peacekeeping capabilities, which therefore will be able play a more active role in such activities.

Although rational-choice calculations played an important role —in particular for the military elites—they were only of secondary relevance. The primary motivation for seeking membership in the EU and NATO has been of a political nature. Membership and institutionalized cooperation with the EU and NATO have become essential parts of a common Eastern European grand strategy. In contrast to the economic dimension, where the aim of EU membership has played an essential role in Eastern European policies of socio-economic stabilization, the advantages of membership for improving national security were important but not essential. Objective military threats have been limited in general, and could not fully justify the costs entailed by membership.[44] Moreover, the restructuring of the military could have been pursued even without the promise of membership. Any security guarantees from the EU could be at best only indirect and with limited relevance for hard deterrence. Also, NATO security guarantees have been clearly limited and—after the creation of a special NATO–Russia relationship—subject not only to intra-NATO but also to NATO–Russia bargaining. Finally, the PfP could have substituted for full membership in pressing for military modernization and restructuring.[45]

Thus, the most important factor explaining Eastern European integration policies results neither from security interests nor from the need to seek assistance in downgrading the military. It results mainly from political logic. These states have viewed NATO and the EU—and not the OSCE, Council of Europe, or the WEU—as the principal European actors, constituting the main pan-European structures after the end of the Cold War. As NATO has developed a special relationship with Russia and the EU remains committed

[43] Although hopes and demands of US armament industries to transfer considerable funds to support broad-scale modernization of the armed forces of Eastern candidates for NATO membership were scaled down, Eastern Europeans still expect major financial and other support for military modernization from NATO as such or from important NATO members like the USA and Germany.

[44] The Baltic countries as well as the Ukraine constituted exceptions due to political geography, historical development, and their problems with Russian minorities.

[45] For a more detailed study of Russian foreign policy and its cooperative aspects see Günter Trautmann, 'Russia and the Euro-Atlantic Community', *Journal of European Integration*, 2–3 (1997), 201–32.

to further integration, these two actors became even more relevant.[46] As a result, Eastern European states have only two options—either to remain isolated and subject to these organizations' policies or to seek membership in order to participate in their decision-making.[47] The Eastern European states pursued integration policies even after it became clear that membership meant at best only marginal Eastern European influence.[48] These states view even limited influence as important given the possible participation in these organizations' policy-making process.

Dual integration policies have been important for these states for three reasons. First, as the EU has represented an economic centre and NATO a military power, it has made sense for these states to seek to become members of both in order to influence the main centres of military and the economic decision-making in Europe. Second, the EU and NATO constitute two different models of power: the EU pursues European objectives while NATO is a transatlantic structure with a Russian link. Despite attempts to complement the EU with a security dimension, it is questionable whether the EU will emerge as the dominant model. Participating in both structures has been seen by these states as a path that allows them, to a certain degree, to play one organization against the other in order to optimize their own interests. Furthermore, full participation within EU and NATO guarantees formal and informal access to major actors like the USA, Germany, and France, which would be difficult to create and maintain without membership.

Moreover, as stated above, the attractiveness of the EU, and to a lesser degree NATO, resulted from its performance in generating and enhancing democratic stability, wealth, welfare, as well as security. In light of Europe's tumultuous past, the Eastern Europe states agreed that integration has proved beneficial not only in terms of optimizing national interests but in terms of power as well. With regard to the EU underlying power formula, which gives 'small' powers a proportionally greater influence in EU policy-making,

---

[46] EMU is not only regarded as the creation of a monetary union but as a major political move in integration and power projection.

[47] A third option of orientation towards Russia, which has been propagated in Slovak foreign policies, seems to be only a 'lose-lose' option. For more details, see Ivo Samson, 'Transformation and Structural Change in Central Eastern Europe: Slovakia's Adjustment to New Security Challenges', *Journal of European Integration*, 2–3 (1997), 187–200.

[48] Such as forming an Eastern European bloc within these organizations, creating an Eastern European-German axis or triangle models like the one of the 'triangle of Weimar' between Poland, France, and Germany.

Eastern Europeans expect that membership will increase their overall power position. As a result, these states perceived that the transfer of sovereignty involved in membership will be compensated by an increase in their power through participation in a supranational power organization.[49]

Thus, in addition to the economic, military, and political benefits to be gained from integration, membership has promised a net advantage in absolute and relative power for these states. The more unstable the domestic or sub-regional situation has been and the more the new ruling elites have had to experience domestic or foreign constraints in their policy-making, the more these states have been inclined to follow the Western European model. From an Eastern European view, dual membership has been primarily a matter of power politics, and only secondarily one of net advantage in terms of security building and democratic consolidation.

Western interests and policies

Western interests in the enlargement of the EU and NATO towards Eastern Europe have been complementary to Eastern European interests but have had different priorities. Western enlargement policies resulted from a double cost–benefit calculation. First, membership was regarded as the most cost-effective way to secure political stabilization and economic recovery in Eastern Europe. Second, enlargement sought to expand the EU and NATO power formulas and types of order towards the East.[50] Both organizations had to set conditions in order to optimize the cost-benefit equation of enlargement. As such, enlargement was not to change the identity, basic structures, and political power formulas of EU and NATO. Cost-effectiveness meant that enlargement had to occur at the lowest possible costs and risks.

These basic guidelines for enlargement dictated a selective, gradual, and conditioned process aiming at domestic change and democratic consolidation in Eastern Europe.[51] Western gradualism has two strategic dimensions. First, it has translated into a strategy

---

[49] Consider for example the rotating presidency, the distribution of votes and seats in the Council of Ministers and the European Parliament.

[50] Consider Reimund Seidelmann, 'NATO's Enlargement as a Policy of Lost Opportunities', *Journal of European Integration*, 2–3 (1997), 233–45.

[51] As it is detailed in Reimund Seidelmann, 'EU's and NATO's Enlargement Towards the East', 98–118, formal enlargement timetables of EU and NATO differ but the real adjustment of Eastern countries will take place in similar time horizons.

of political timing, which used existing and new institutions of cooperation to maximize conditionality and minimize risks for the
West. Second, it led to a strategy of prioritizing Western interests.
In general, the West has pursued wide-ranging objectives such as
more regional security and increased democratization. However, it
has tailored specific objectives to the circumstances of each state.
For those countries closest geographically to the EU and NATO,
such as Poland, the Czech Republic, and Hungary, enlargement is
regarded primarily as a means to secure and stabilize the eastern
glacis—in particular for countries like Germany, which was a driving force behind enlargement, and Austria. For more countries such
as the Baltic states, the Slovak Republic, and the south-eastern
European countries, direct military security concerns were of lesser
significance. Western objectives towards these states lay primarily
in general stability, in order to prevent the emergence of situations in which the West would be asked or would feel obliged to
intervene, such as in the cases of political-economic collapse in
Romania, civil wars in the region, or Russian intervention in the
Baltic states.[52]

NATO's gradual enlargement resulted not only from internal dissent and Russian opposition but constituted a coherent strategy of
incremental change. The four institutional steps taken by NATO
reflected a policy seeking the lowest-possible risks and highest-
possibility conditionality, targeting both the military and political
dimensions of security. First, the North Atlantic Cooperation
Council (NACC) was designed to secure disarmament and arms
control after the dismantling of WTO and the USSR. It was also
to provide limited political access to NATO without real participation.
NACC's impact as a forum for political-military cooperation between
East and West as well as within Eastern Europe in the critical years
of the mid-1980s should not be underestimated.[53]

The subsequent creation of PfP raised the vague political promise for eventual future membership—again without allowing real

[52] In the West, three scenarios were discussed: (1) political-economic collapse,
(2) collapse plus 'Balkanization', that is, civil, ethnic, and separatist warfare, and
(3) collapse plus 'Balkanization' plus Soviet military intervention. The first scenario
would demand major economic assistance, the second would mean a second
Yugoslav scenario under severe conditions, and the third would create a major
political-military dispute and would confront the West with either toleration or
unacceptable and risky military intervention.

[53] Solving the problems of the distribution, control, and dismantling of the Soviet
nuclear military capabilities was primarily a matter of direct US-Soviet/Russian
negotiations. Cooperation within the NACC, however, eased acceptance and
implementation.

participation in NATO's political and military decision-making. The programme underlined that the peaceful solution of conflicts was an essential condition for future membership, and introduced far-reaching military confidence building measures and steps towards the democratic reorganization of security and military policy. PfP not only widened and deepened this role of the NACC but added a significant military dimension. By offering the Eastern European military limited access to NATO structures and direct participation in joint military activities, PfP proved instrumental in reinforcing the process of democratization in these states' security and military policies. PfP also helped to secure political support from these military elites and strengthen the processes of sub-regional and neighbour-to-neighbour military confidence building.[54] An example of the constructive role of the PfP can be found in the Baltic states' active involvement, which has eased both the formation of a democratically controlled military in these states and has contributed to the resolution of Baltic-Russian conflicts.

The creation of agencies between NATO and specific countries which are not regarded as potential candidates for enlargement has been the third component of NATO's eastern strategy. The NATO–Russia and the NATO–Ukraine special relationships, together with specific military, political, and economic cooperation schemes, emerged as reasonable counterbalances for states which have not been considered for membership.

The final aspect was in the offers of NATO membership to Poland, the Czech Republic, and Hungary, and the vague option of future rounds of enlargement, which confirmed the willingness of NATO to widen membership as well as its determination not to compromise the political and military conditions for membership. Slovakia's exclusion from the first round resulted not only from its internal and external problems but also from NATO's desire to signal to Eastern Europe its firmness on the terms of conditionality.[55] In addition, this exclusion reflected German interests and priorities, which played a major role in promoting enlargement. Germany's primary security interests focused on its

---

[54] See, for example, the effects of visitor programmes, and Eastern European participation in higher military education such as in the NATO College/Rome.

[55] Two other reasons have to be taken into consideration. First, the exclusion of Slovakia could, in addition, be sold to NATO and EU member states as its willingness to compromise between those member states which supported enlargement and those which preferred a more cautious approach. Second, Slovakia's geographic position made it less attractive for the first round, which concentrated on the consolidation of NATO's eastern neighbours.

close neighbours; Slovakia does not belong to this group nor has it had special relations with Germany as has Hungary.[56]

Despite wide grounds of consensus, the specific priorities set by Eastern European aspiring members and EU/NATO have differed. The EU and NATO have established strict political conditions for membership, which have had direct impact on Eastern European foreign and security policies and their democratic domestic performance. Given the asymmetric relationship between EU/NATO and aspiring members, these states have had little choice but to accept those conditions. In analysing the link between security and democratic consolidation, three conditions have been relevant: first, the resolution of external and internal conflicts; second, the consolidation of democracy; and third, the restructuring of the military and arms industries.[57]

EU and NATO interest in giving membership only to countries with a low domestic and foreign conflict potential resulted from a desire not to burden their political agenda with problems which would entail high risks and costs for the West European states. These organizations' experience in the Bosnian conflict gave this objective a high priority. Despite this constraint on their national sovereignty, Eastern European states accepted that foreign and domestic conflicts would also delay and obstruct nation building, the resolution of socio-economic crises, and their regime consolidation.[58] Nevertheless the selective approach of the EU and NATO, which threatened to postpone membership for those countries who did not fulfil such conditions, reinforced the national will in these countries to do so and gave the fulfilment of these conditions a higher priority on the internal agenda. Again, this was acceptable because it meant a double win-win situation for these organizations: the

[56] Special German–Hungarian relations date to the détente period and advanced significantly before and during Germany's '2+4' negotiations. Political elites in Germany traditionally welcomed Hungary's domestic political reforms and peaceful and cooperative foreign policy and were impressed by Hungary's policy to tolerate mass migration through Hungarian territory in the autumn of 1989.

[57] Joining integrated structures means, with the exception of Russia, limited survival for the few remaining Eastern European armament industries. Given the developments in USA and Western European arms industries, like mergers and the potential for a Common European Armament Market for the EU, these arms industries can only survive if they combine their niche role with a policy of association or merger with dominant US and/or Western European industries. Integration is therefore a necessary condition for the survival of these industries.

[58] In a number of cases this view has not prevented governments and ruling elites from doing the opposite; compare, for example, the policies of Yugoslavia's conflicting parties, the policies of the Slovak Republic towards its Hungarian minority, and the reluctance of the Baltic States to resolve the Russian minority problem.

resolution of foreign conflicts and domestic political conflicts in these countries meant their increasing consolidation; it would also give additional legitimization to the new democratic regimes in Eastern Europe as well as to the EU and NATO.[59]

In principle, NATO objectives of democratic consolidation, military-political control of Eastern Europe through participatory integration, and the widening of the Western security order to the East could have been pursued without the democratic reorganization of security, defence, and military policies and the modernization of the armed forces in Eastern Europe. In the past, NATO allowed for a variety of forms of organization in members' security and military policy. In this regard, the case of Turkey is often noted. During the détente period, NATO explicitly decoupled the demand for democracy from the pursuit of its security interests in cooperation with Eastern Europe. While power and security motives have had clear priority, contemporary political circumstances allowed NATO to focus on these specific demands for 'democratic' security and military policies. This was the case not only because the Eastern European states were willing to accept such supplementary conditions but also because an enlarged NATO would be easier to manage if political structures, defence postures, and military modernization concepts were compatible. While NATO demands to democratize security and military policies have played an important role in Eastern European democratic consolidation, it must be remembered that in terms of NATO's specific interests, such demands have assumed only a secondary role. It must be underlined again that the reorganization of the European security order has been not only a matter of concrete policies but also of perspectives, ideals, and myths. Thus, while democracy has played only a secondary role in NATO's concrete initiatives towards the East, the equation of 'more democracy' and 'more peace' has been essential for the process of Eastern Europe's transformation, its orientation towards the West, and its participation in the EU and NATO.

A New Security Problem: The Balkans

While the end of the Cold War allowed for the transformation, Westernization, and structural reorganization of the European

[59] NATO enlargement and the Madrid Summit in 1997, which linked enlargement with the creation of the NATO–Russia special relationship, have been part of NATO's relegitimization drive, in which NATO portrayed itself as the willing and capable pan-European security provider.

security system, it also permitted conflicts in Eastern Europe to emerge and escalate. In the case of Yugoslavia, unresolved border, minority, ethnic, religious, socio-economic, and historical conflicts were exploited as means to pursue independence, nation building, and power formation.

Although this potential for conflict exists throughout Eastern Europe, the wider situation has differed from Yugoslavia in two aspects. First, the Yugoslav conflicts had a cumulative dynamic not replicated elsewhere. Second, in other areas nation building and power formation made only partial use of such conflict potential and states have used mainly non-military measures—partly because of these other states' ongoing democratization and partly because of a recognition of the high political, economic, and military costs involved in following the Yugoslav precedent. As the situation in the Bosnian conflict became worse, Western conditions for enlargement, association, and cooperation became increasingly highlighted. These conflicts demonstrated the negative relationship both between the absence of democratization and remilitarization and between identity/nation building and the exploitation and militarization of foreign conflicts. In addition, it created a new distinction within Eastern Europe between regressive nation building and conflict-prone states and Western-oriented national and sub-regional development.

From a phenomenological perspective, the range of conflicts that have emerged in the Balkans region constitute the main problem of European security. Singer and Vildavsky identified a new division in Europe between a zone of peace and prosperity and a zone of war and instability. The present political-military agenda of NATO, EU/WEU, and the OSCE has been dominated by the challenges of managing, resolving, and preventing conflicts of this type. However, an empirical analysis would show a much more complex picture of overlapping zones with different levels of security, stability, and political-economic progress. Moreover, a structure-oriented analysis would highlight a fundamental difference between the security and stability problems in Eastern Europe, which have been discussed above, and the problems posed by the conflicts in the Balkan region. The end to the military-political threats posed by the Cold War and the gradual involvement of Eastern Europe into Western structures represent the fundamental structural change in the European security system. In this light, the ethnic, nation-building, and power-formation conflicts in Yugoslavia must be seen as having only limited structural relevance.

There are two reasons for such a conclusion. First, equally controversial conflicts in other parts of Eastern Europe have not led to military clashes. The break-up of Czechoslovakia, the consolidation of Ukraine, and the numerous ethnic-minority conflicts in south-eastern Europe did not follow the Yugoslav pattern. In fact, these conflicts proved that strategies that sought political solutions with the assistance of European organizations opened genuine possibilities for cooperative conflict resolution.[60] Second, a closer look at the dynamic of the Yugoslav conflicts reveals that these could have been managed and prevented within the existing European security structures—if these structures had been adequately modernized and if a common political will and ability had existed.[61] In other words, such security challenges do not pose structural dilemmas.[62] As such, the Yugoslav security and democracy problem constitutes an aberration from the structural dynamic in the overall security-democracy link in Eastern Europe.

Summary and Outlook

This analysis confirms the assumption of a relationship between security and democracy building in Eastern Europe, based on the concept of dual conditionality, in which security conditions democratic development as much as democratic consolidation conditions regional security and positive peace building. While this conditionality was negative during the Cold War, it has become positive, not only because of post-Cold War structures but also because of political experiences in the past and the political promise of the project of 'Europeanization'.

While the hypothesis of dual conditionality has been confirmed, three general caveats must be noted. First, conditionality does not mean a direct and unidimensional causal relationship. Security does not guarantee democratic development; it only conditions it, which means that other factors, such as patterns of domestic and regional socio-economic development, play an even more important role. The EU and NATO enlargement policies have been important

---

[60] For details and the political relevance of Hungarian minorities in neighbouring countries see Zellner and Dunay, *Ungarns Außenpolitik 1990–1997*; Pal Dunay, 'The Security Policy of Hungary', 203–34.

[61] See, for example, Eric Remacle, 'Lessons from the Yugoslav Crises for the European Union', in Remacle and Seidelmann, *Pan-European Security Redefined*, 391–410.

[62] Structure should not be confused with organization, that is the European Security architecture, which has to be fundamentally reorganized. For more details see Reimund Seidelmann, 'EU's and NATO's Enlargement towards the East', 98–118; Reimund Seidelmann, 'Amsterdam e la sicurezza europea: un' opportunità nuova o perduta', *Europa Europe*, 1 (1998), 66–86.

factors in Eastern European transformation and pacification. Democratic development favours but does not determine peaceful regional structures, which means that the establishment of a stable regional order is caused primarily by other factors.[63]

Second, well-established academic approaches which assume that realism and idealism are fundamentally contradictory and that democracies are inherently peaceful have proved to be of limited explanatory value in an evaluation of the interrelation between security and democratic consolidation in Eastern Europe.

Third, the specifics of this relationship have depended strongly on the historical setting. The Cold War and contemporary European circumstances differ fundamentally when it comes to security and its impact on the regional order, national policy formation, and the domestic and European political agendas. In contrast to the past, where the management of security was an essential condition for any political development and a vital political priority on the regional and national agenda, security has become a politically marginal factor, as military threats between European states have dissipated. The relationship between security and democracy has changed, as security has lost its political relevance. The Yugoslav conflict has not constituted a structural contradiction but only an exception to this conclusion. The problems in this region in terms of democracy and security could have been controlled and prevented within the existing structures if the political will and ability to act had existed.

Additional caveats also emerge from a more detailed analysis of contemporary Eastern Europe. First, Eastern Europe cannot be treated as a sub-regional entity but at most as a group of states

---

[63] For the specific interrelation between security and democracy in Eastern Europe, the general debate about the peaceful character of democracies is not very helpful. For example, see Martin Kahl, 'European Integration, European Security, and the Transformation in Central Eastern Europe', *Journal of European Integration*, 2–3 (1997), 153–85, and Remacle and Seidelmann, *Pan-European Security Redefined*. While the idealistic view that democracies are more peaceful than other political systems seems attractive, which can be found already in the political philosophy of Immanuel Kant, empirical testing has led to contradictory results, which place this hypothesis in doubt. Thus the more cautious view of Czempiel, 'Are Democracies Peaceful?', seems more appropriate. In addition, the general simplification, which is implied by this hypothesis, seems counter-productive, when it comes to empirical analysis as in this case. In other words, the equation 'democracies equal peace', which means that democratic consolidation in Eastern Europe—including Russia—would automatically secure peaceful foreign policies, has to be replaced by a more differentiated approach like that of a dual conditionality, which means that peace policies are the product of a complex set of interrelated factors, structures, and dynamics and not of a simplistic unidimensional equation.

at different stages of transformation. This group has a general orientation towards 'Europeanization' but also showed different particular conditions and opportunities to participate in this process, and different relations between the new political elites and the military. Second, Eastern European policies seeking participation and membership in the EU and NATO resulted from a desire to participate in the general Europeanization of power formation and power stabilization. These policies were only secondarily a matter of political modernization strategies and of particular military security policies.

Third, Eastern European policies and the objectives of EU and NATO enlargement have joined in a specific political equation, where compatible interests from both sides reinforced each other and created a 'no alternative' dynamic, which dominated the relation between Eastern and Western Europe and between security and democratic consolidation in Eastern Europe. The EU/NATO and Eastern Europe have different priorities. Eastern Europe has sought membership primarily in order to participate in the new European power formation process. On the one hand, this is the result of a realistically oriented cost–benefit analysis. It also reflected the impact of the experience of the socialist past and the belief in the idea of the Western European model as a democratic growth and peace community. On the other hand, this reflected the new political-military situation in Europe and in Eastern Europe in particular where for the foreseeable future the possibility of major military threats is marginal and can be managed within the present structures—in other words, even without membership in the EU and/or NATO. The EU and NATO has sought enlargement primarily in order to expand stability, to supplement their power base, and to establish better political, economic, and military control of Eastern Europe in order to further enhance the Western European community model.

These different priorities have met in the process of democratic consolidation. The EU and NATO have established democratic consolidation and related measures in security policies as preconditions for membership; Eastern European elites have used the argument of democratic consolidation as political measures to ease membership and to improve their opportunities for participation.

Despite this double downgrading of security—first, by the marginalization of military threats and second, by the Eastern European focus on general participation and modernization—there is a substantial regional advantage in terms of the European order and its military security services. This results both from the changes in Eastern Europe as a result of the end of the Cold War and the enlargement process. The conflicts in Yugoslavia, the Caucasus, and Chechnya highlighted the shortcomings of the post-Cold War European order. Moreover, the concept of enlarging the European democratic growth and peace community has been to a considerable degree a myth related to a new European power formula. Despite these facts, the overall chances of the regional system to establish a stable order, which combines democratic development in Eastern Europe with the resolution of intra-regional conflicts and a fairer power sharing formula, have significantly improved. These circumstances also significantly improved the overall performance of the regional order with regard to democratization and security, which in turn led to an improvement of the 'external' conditioning of democratic developments in some East European states.

5

The Internationalization of Ethnic Strife

S. Neil MacFarlane

Introduction

The 1990s put paid to the proposition that the end of bipolarity would produce an era of peace and stability in the European regional subsystem.[1] With the removal of strategic overlay, a series of active sub-state conflicts in south-eastern and Eastern Europe replaced the frozen hostility of the Cold War. Many of these conflicts involved ethnicity and interethnic struggles for power and resources. They carried significant implications for European security and evoked an array of international responses. These responses raised important questions about the boundary between the civil and the international, about the changing meaning of sovereignty in international politics, and about the capacity of external actors to regulate internal disputes.[2] They have posed profound challenges to a Western Europe seeking to spread liberal values through the European space. As Dominique Moïsi noted as early as 1991: 'The euphoria of 1989, with its rejoicing over European unity, seems light years away. Today in the West, Euro-pessimism is back in fashion where Eastern Europe is concerned.'[3]

One might add, however, that, at least as regards ethnic disputes, the pessimistic swing of the pendulum perhaps went too far. At the beginning of the 1990s, ethnic disputes appeared to be a serious

[1] Stephen Van Evera, 'Primed for Peace: Europe after the Cold War', *International Security,* 15: 3 (Winter 1990–1), 7–56.

[2] For a good early treatment of this general subject, see Manus I. Midlarsky (ed.), *The Internationalization of Communal Strife* (London: Routledge, 1992).

[3] As cited in Adrian G. V. Hyde-Price, 'Democratization in Eastern Europe: The External Dimension', in Geoffrey Pridham and Tatu Vanhanen, *Democratization in Eastern Europe: Domestic and International Perspectives* (London: Routledge, 1994), 221.

threat to regional stability. People conceived of the entire region of Central and Eastern Europe as a roiling sea of intercommunal violence. As it turns out, however, in their severe form, they have been rather isolated, in both their intrastate and interstate types. In the first place, the region is not uniformly heterogeneous in ethnic terms. A number of its states are either quite homogeneous (Poland, Hungary, Armenia) or have minority populations so small that—in the absence of foreign interference—neither majorities nor minorities are likely to see any particular utility in ethnic civil war (Bulgaria, the Czech and Slovak Republics). The foyers of ethnic disputes have been highly concentrated in two sub-regions—the Balkans and the Caucasus. There is little evidence of their proliferation to other parts of the European regional system. The fact that they have been isolated has meant that they have on the whole had little impact on the broader life of Europe. That is in part why the international response to them has been, on the whole, diffident. The Bosnian war lasted more than three years before a decisive NATO intervention. The Kosovo crisis lasted seven years before the dramatic escalation that provoked a NATO military response. There have been no significant multilateral engagements in the conflicts of the southern Caucasus.

In this chapter, I examine the internationalization of ethnic strife. I begin with a discussion of the nature of ethnicity and ethnic conflict and of the parameters of internationalization and its relationship to democratization. I then proceed to an analysis of the record of efforts by international actors to control this post-Cold War problem in European security. I conclude with a number of observations regarding the effectiveness of these responses and their meaning for the development of the European system.

Ethnic Disputes

By dispute, I mean a politically significant confrontation between two groups. This covers a wide range of intensity from, for example, inter-party competition through political challenges to the state (such as campaigns for autonomy or for separation) to military conflict. Given the focus on internationalization, it is the latter end of the spectrum that draws our attention. However, to the extent that we are interested in conflict prevention, we are interested also in early warning and early response, both of which draw our attention to inter-group dynamics that have not yet attained the level of open civil conflict.

Second, what do we mean by 'ethnic' disputes? The definition of 'ethnic dispute' seems at first glance to be rather straightforward— it is conflict involving two or more ethnic communities. By 'ethnic', I refer to groups who define themselves and/or who are defined by others in terms of a sense of cultural, linguistic, or customary unity that distinguishes them from other groups.[4] The critical element is a sense of valued difference shared within the group and an analogous shared sense on the part of those outside the group that the group is meaningfully distinct.

Employment of the category 'ethnic conflict' presumes that it has analytical utility. It implies first of all that ethnic division has some causal relevance to the conflict, and that the characteristics of ethnic conflict serve to distinguish it from other types of conflict in ways that are significant for conflict resolution. With regard to cause, it is worth noting that most ethnic groups in diverse communities within the borders of single states live in peace one with another most of the time.[5] This draws into question the Kaplanesque explanation of ethnic conflict in terms of ancient historical hatreds and suggests that ethnic difference by itself has little utility in the explanation of moments of conflict.

If such conflicts are not caused by ethnic difference *per se*, this draws the utility of the category into some question. In methodological terms, this problem underlies the argument frequently encountered in Central and Eastern Europe that conflicts are not 'ethnic', but 'political'. That is to say, they are the products of manipulations by political entrepreneurs or by foreign forces seeking to take advantage of ethnic difference to weaken and destabilize the state. One particularly influential version of this argument is that of Mansfield and Snyder who relate ethnic nationalism and consequent conflict to the needs of political elites in conditions of rapid (democratizing) transition.[6]

There are several difficulties with this line of argument. First, when deployed by a party to such a conflict, it obviously reflects motivated bias. To the extent, for example, that the Georgians are able to convince others that the Abkhaz problem is not a product

---

[4] For discussion of the meaning of ethnicity, see Anthony D. Smith, *Theories of Nationalism* (New York: Holmes & Meier, 1983), 180–91, and also *The Ethnic Origins of Nations* (Oxford: Blackwells, 1986); Donald Horowitz, *Ethnic Groups in Conflict* (Berkeley and Los Angeles: University of California Press, 1985), 57–91.

[5] David Lake and Donald Rothchild, 'The Origins and Management of Ethnic Conflict', *International Security*, 21: 2 (Fall 1996), 43.

[6] Edward Mansfield and Jack Snyder, 'Democratization and the Danger of War', *International Security*, 20: 1 (Summer 1995), 5–39.

of the insecurity of a rather small ethnic community within Georgia in the face of the assertion of majoritarian national identity, but is instead a reflection of a combination of treason and external political manipulation, then they need not recognize the legitimacy (from a minority rights perspective) of the claims of this community, they can avoid serious consideration of major structural change in the distribution of state power within Georgia and they can deny international organizations the right to become involved in the dispute on minority rights grounds. That is to say, defining the conflict as political rather than ethnic suits the agenda of a majoritarian nationalism that seeks to deny the relevance of diversity within the state.

Second, the causal interpretation is incomplete in its own right. It is not sufficient to account for ethnic disputes purely in terms of the machinations of unprincipled political entrepreneurs deploying ethno-chauvinism as a means of gaining power and sidelining their adversaries.[7] One also has to ask why they choose this particular strategy and why people respond to it. In part, it is the existence of ethnic diversity within a state that makes the choice attractive. For people to respond, the categories deployed in ethnochauvinist discourse have to have some resonance with them. In this sense, a sense of ethnic difference provides the raw material —the precondition—for the entrepreneurial manipulation of the symbols and fears associated with ethnic identity.[8]

With regard to characteristics, the fact that the origins of an ethnic conflict may lie, for example, in the competition for political power during a period of structural transition makes it no less ethnic with regard to the descriptive characteristics of the dispute (i.e. that it proceeds along lines defined by ethnic identity). From the perspective of the challengers of the status quo, the objectives they pursue may include a quest for greater autonomy and wider rights within an existing structure of state power, the effort to separate a section of a state from the whole (either to unite it with a neighbouring state or to create an independent entity), or—in a variant rarely encountered in Europe but more common in Africa —the effort to secure control over the central state and the resources it has at its command. From the perspective of the 'titular' nationality, strategies range along a spectrum of options from placation

---

[7] See V. P. Gagnon, 'Ethnic Nationalism and International Conflict: The Case of Serbia', *International Security*, 19: 34 (Winter 1994–5).

[8] On this point, see S. Neil MacFarlane, 'Democratization, Nationalism and Regional Security in the Southern Caucasus', *Government and Opposition*, 32: 3 (Summer 1997), 413–15.

through compromise (Canada), to co-option and submergence of minorities into a larger community through assimilation (the USA for much of its history), to their physical removal (Serbian Bosnia), and, in the extreme, their elimination (Rwanda).

Violent ethnic conflicts have specific qualities that distinguish them in unfortunate ways from other types of civil war. Ethnic conflicts are particularly vicious and resistant to settlement for several reasons. Since the definition of community political identity in terms of ethnicity means that those not sharing the identity are not part of the community, the objectives of ethnic groups involved in such conflict are served in essence not by compromise with the adversary, but by the latter's removal. In this respect, ethnic conflict blurs the principle of discrimination between belligerent and non-belligerent populations. The adversary's community as a whole, civilian and military, is the target. In short, ethnic conflict contains a predisposition to 'ethnic cleansing', if not to genocide.

In its assault not merely on that minority of the population engaged in military activities, but on defenceless civilians, ethnic conflict has an important subjective impact on participants. The indiscriminate quality of violence multiplies the personal grievances of individuals within the affected communities. In the process of settlement, one is dealing not only with redistribution of resources, but with the necessity of righting a legion of personal wrongs.[9]

For all of these reasons, conflict of this type is likely to be particularly extreme and intractable, and to require rather more complex modalities of resolution than are conflicts where this dimension is absent. In the context of internationalization, these are rough waters for organizations such as the United Nations (UN), whose capacities for effective action in internal conflicts are limited, and when such capacities depend so strongly on the inconstant commitments of major member states, a number of which are deeply sensitive to the prospect of taking casualties in such operations.[10]

---

[9] S. Neil MacFarlane, 'The Role of the United Nations in World Politics', Inaugural Lecture of the Lester B. Pearson Professorship of International Relations (Oxford University, 1997), 7–8. Charles King also notes the role of conflict itself in exacerbating grievances of those involved, in Charles King, *Ending Civil Wars* (Adelphi Paper 308) (London: IISS, 1997), 37. See, finally, Midlarsky, *Communal Strife*, xii.

[10] See, for example, Art. 2(7) of the United Nations Charter: 'Nothing contained in the present Charter shall authorize the United Nations to intervene in matters which are essentially within the domestic jurisdiction of any state or shall require the Members to submit such matters to settlement under the present Charter; but this principle shall not prejudice the application of enforcement procedures under Chapter VII.'

In addition, these conflicts pose specific problems in the context of the international agenda of democratization. Beyond the generic problems of creating democratic constitutions and institutions in post-communist societies, there are the further challenges of restoring trust between profoundly alienated communities, creating constitutional structures that foster such trust and reduce insecurity, ensuring an adequate ethnic balance of power in political institutions, and fostering the development of multiethnic social and political identities. Given the weakness of state structures in societies having experienced ethnic disputes, this may require a prolonged international monitoring role.

Parameters of Internationalization

The international impacts of ethnic disputes

There are three principal aspects to the internationalization of ethnic disputes. The first is the nature of the impact of ethnic disputes on international relations. The key point here concerns spillover from civil conflict. This can take several forms. An ethnic dispute within a state may involve a group that dominates a neighbouring state, for example Hungarians in Transylvania, Vojvodina, and southern Slovakia. This may attract the neighbouring state into the civil conflict.[11] Ethnic disputes frequently generate large flows of migration across state boundaries (see the conflict in Bosnia), creating significant resource problems for neighbours and for international agencies responsible for the care and support of refugees. Newly arrived populations may compete for resources with the host population, creating the possibility of violence. They may also threaten the societal values of the host state with consequent increases in instability. Those who migrate may use their sanctuary in the neighbouring state in order to continue their struggle. This constitutes a threat to the security of the state of origin. Such action may result in military retaliation across state frontiers, posing a security threat to the recipient state. The results of the two factors in combination may be a higher probability of interstate war between host and recipient states. Moreover, a migrant population can be an instrument in the hands of the host state and directed at the state from which it came.

[11] For an interesting account of the relations between 'homeland states' and their neighbours having substantial minorities from the former, see Rogers Brubaker, *Nationalism Reframed: Nationhood and the National Question in the New Europe* (Cambridge: Cambridge University Press, 1996).

Security/stability effects of migration are not necessarily localized in the immediate vicinity of the ethnic dispute. Refugee flows may spread farther afield causing analogous problems in other states, as occurred, for example, with the rise of xenophobia in Germany in the early years of this decade and that of the far right in Switzerland and Austria as a result of anti-migrant sentiment. Disaffected refugees may transport their grievances to their new home, creating potentially serious problems of terrorism, as Canada learned with its Sikh population.

As Myron Weiner has pointed out, the extent to which conflict-related migration results in tension and further security problems depends on a number of factors, including the economic absorptive capacity of recipient states, the volume of the flow, and the existence or absence of ethnic affinity between migrants and the host population.[12] To these one might add the nature of relations between host states and states of origin, and the extent to which international organizations are willing to lighten the burden of migration on host states.

Second, the concern of international actors to limit migration across borders for all of the above reasons may invoke various forms of intervention in the attempt to ensure that people stay where they are. This pattern of behaviour became increasingly common as states' commitments to the international refugee regime have weakened in the face of dramatic increases in the level of forced migration. This weakening was evident, for example, in changes to Germany's asylum laws and in the tightening of entry procedures throughout the European Union (EU) and North America.[13] If states are no longer willing to accept large flows of people as refugees, then they are motivated to protect victims of conflict at or near their normal places of residence. Hence, for example, the ill-starred effort of the United Nations to establish and then protect safe areas in Bosnia.[14]

[12] Myron Weiner, 'Security, Stability and International Migration', *International Security*, 17: 3 (Winter–Spring 1992–3), as reprinted in Sean Lynn-Jones and Steven Miller (eds.), *Global Dangers: Changing Dimensions of International Security* (Cambridge, Mass.: MIT Press, 1995), 196–7.

[13] For a compelling account of the erosion of European and North American commitment to the refugee regime, see Philip Rudge, 'Reconciling State Interests with International Responsibilities: Asylum in North America and Western Europe', *International Journal of Refugee Law* 10: 1/2 (1998), 7–20.

[14] For a substantial and useful account of current trends in international approaches to forced migration, see Kathleen Newland, 'The Soul of a New Regime: Progress and Regress in the Evolution of Humanitarian Response', Paper prepared for the conference on 'The Evolution of International Humanitarian Responses in the 1990s', (23–6 Apr. 1998) at the White Oaks Plantation, Yulee, Florida.

Patterns of engagement

External involvement in ethnic disputes may be unilateral or multilateral. In the first instance, outside states may foster tension and conflict out of the raw material of ethnic diversity in pursuit of unilateral hegemonic or other interests. Examples of this possibility are Russian incitement of conflict between ethnic groups in Georgia, the use of the Russian diaspora question in Russia's relations with Latvia, Estonia, and Kazakhstan, and the Serb use of Serbian minorities in Croatia and Bosnia as instruments in the effort to retain dominance over the former Yugoslav space and to construct a 'Greater Serbia'.

Unilateral great power intervention is generally seen as corrosive of international norms and stability. However, this may not be the case. Through their efforts to accumulate power and to build influence, such states may contribute to international order.[15] Hegemonic stability theory produces the same conclusion. It is the self-interested use of hegemonic power that produces the public goods of stability and cooperation in the absence of strong multilateral or supranational institutions.[16]

More concretely, one might argue (as many do) that Russian interventionism in the southern Caucasus and in Central Asia may contribute to stability in otherwise anarchic regions that produce negative externalities (crime, migration, spillover of instability) for the system as a whole. Likewise, it is plausible that Russian pressure on Latvia and Estonia on behalf of the Russophone minorities in those two countries—to the extent that it results in a more liberal and tolerant approach to minority rights—may reduce the probability that the tensions associated with these countries' approaches to their minorities will produce civil violence, ethnic cleansing, and Russian intervention.

Likewise, to some extent, it is credible to argue that Russian-mediated ceasefires and Russian peacekeeping—although they flow from a Russian calculus of regional hegemony—have produced a degree of stability greater than would have been present without them.[17] However, in this instance the argument is weakened by the

[15] On this point, see Hedley Bull, *The Anarchical Society* (New York: Columbia University Press, 1977).

[16] See Robert Gilpin, *War and Change in World Politics* (Cambridge: Cambridge University Press, 1981).

[17] For further discussion of this point, see S. Neil MacFarlane, 'On the Front Lines in the Near Abroad: The CIS and the OSCE in Georgia's Civil Wars', in Thomas Weiss, *Beyond UN Subcontracting* (London: Macmillan, 1998), 129–33.

strong empirical evidence of Russian involvement in the instigation of the conflicts they subsequently sought to control.[18] Moreover, it is not clear how far Russia can go with the transition from the freezing of conflicts to their resolution. It is the freezing that makes affected societies dependent on Russia and that produces the influence the policy is intended to provide. Full resolution of these conflicts would remove a considerable amount of leverage and would, therefore, weaken the Russian position. Consequently, one might argue that the Russian interest in normalization is only partial. Moreover, even if the interest were genuine, the transition to peace requires substantial material investment that Russia would find it difficult to make on its own.

Finally, reliance on hegemonic power as a strategy for enhancing regional stability has a price. Order is presumably not the only objective of international society. This particular approach to order has important implications for justice, since it permits the construction of inequitable and exploitative relations between the hegemon and the lesser states that are left to its mercies. This carries costs in terms of the norms of equality, sovereignty, and democracy to which the European community purportedly subscribes.

There are numerous other types of unilateral intervention in ethnic disputes. These may reflect strategic objectives. In the Bosnian case, for example, US military assistance to Croatia was a key element in shifting the military balance against the Serbs. This had a significant role in promoting the Dayton compromise. The Serbs could see the military balance shifting against them and so had an incentive to lock in their gains.

Unilateral engagement may also result from domestic political factors little related to systemic power-political considerations. The policies of the United States towards the Karabakh conflict have reflected the domestic political influence of Armenian Americans. The United States has rendered full Azerbaijani access to US public assistance conditional upon the ending of Azerbaijan's blockade of Nagorno Karabakh and Armenia.[19] Similarly, Turkey blockaded Armenia in 1993 in response to Armenian victories in the territory surrounding Nagorno Karabakh essentially in response to domestic pressure to do something about the defeat and humiliation of Azerbaijan. In both instances, these unilateral policies significantly

---

[18] Thomas Goltz, 'The Hidden Russian Hand', *Foreign Policy*, 92 (Fall 1993), 92–116.

[19] For discussion of this aspect of US policy, see S. Neil MacFarlane and Larry Minear, *Humanitarian Action and Politics: The Case of Nagorno-Karabakh* (Providence, RI: Watson Institute Occasional Paper No. 25, 1997), 52–4.

complicated multilateral humanitarian response. Finally, domestic pressure in favour of self-determination for the former Yugoslav republics was one factor among several leading Germany to pressure its European partners into precipitate recognition of Slovenia and Croatia.[20] This recognition in turn played a significant—though probably not determining—role in the outbreak of civil war in Bosnia.

Turning to multilateral engagement, the activity of international organizations in internal ethnic disputes—and more broadly with regard to intervention in general—is to an important extent circumscribed by norms regarding sovereignty, domestic jurisdiction, and consent. However, these norms have been weakened in some respects by three factors. First, although Article 2(7) of the UN Charter embeds non-intervention as a fundamental principle of the United Nations, the article specifically exempts international action under Chapter VII (enforcement measures) from this norm. Action under Chapter VII of the Charter is justified as a response to threats to international peace and security. This concept is not clearly defined in the Charter and is susceptible to varying interpretation. In practice, the parameters of such threats have expanded to include humanitarian crisis and substantial displacement of populations. The case of UN-sanctioned intervention in Haiti in 1994 suggests, moreover, halting movement towards the possibility of UN intervention in the cause of democracy-restoration. Arguably, the understanding of sovereignty underlying protection of states against intervention in internal affairs is coming to reflect standards of performance in state–society relations (including treatment of minorities) rather than resting on traditional measures of territorial control and recognition. This resulted (at least in the early 1990s) in a qualified reduction in the importance of consent as a prerequisite for UN action.[21] To the extent that this is so, the purview of internationalization of internal ethnic disputes is substantially broadened.

Second, and specifically in the European context, the capacity of international organizations to become actively seized of domestic violations of minority rights has been broadened by the acceptance

---

[20] James Gow, *Triumph of the Lack of Will: International Diplomacy and the Yugoslav War* (London: Hurst, 1997), 8, 49.

[21] See Adam Roberts, 'The Crisis in UN Peacekeeping', in C. Crocker and F. Hampson with P. Aall (eds.), *Managing Global Chaos: Sources of and Responses to International Conflict* (Washington: US IP Press, 1996), 303. Roberts rightly stresses a number of dangers associated with the exploration of this uncharted territory.

of the member states of the Organization of Security and Cooperation in Europe (OSCE) states of its Human Dimension, reflecting
their agreement that:

Human rights and fundamental freedoms, the rule of law and democratic
institutions are the foundations of peace and security, representing a
crucial contribution to conflict prevention, within a comprehensive concept of security. The protection of human rights, including the rights of
persons belonging to national minorities, is an essential foundation of
democratic civil society.[22]

As one observer pointed out, 'the commitments contained in this
dimension are based in part on the view that ethnic conflict is less
likely to occur in democratic multiethnic societies where the rights
of minorities are legislated and respected.'[23]

Although compliance with the Human Dimension has been
spotty—and not only in the east—the norms embodied within it
provide an important justification for the insertion of the OSCE
into what are traditionally considered matters of domestic jurisdiction, as well as providing an international standard against which
the domestic performance of members can be judged.

This normative development has been accompanied by an increasing use of conditionality (on membership, association, and assistance)
by both multilateral entities and states in the effort to address the
potential for ethnic violence and to contribute to the resolution of
such conflict where it occurs. Here, the principle of non-intervention
does not obviously apply. International actors are under no legal
obligation to provide these goods and are at liberty to define a price
for their provision.

The involvement of international organizations in ethnic disputes
may occur in any of three phases: prevention, management, and
resolution. In the area of prevention, one major vehicle has been
to tie recognition and access to valued resources to responsible behaviour in coping with ethnic and national questions. One could cite
here the incentives provided by the European Union, for example,
as a means of changing parties' calculus of cost, benefit, and risk.
There is substantial reason to believe, for example, that the desire
of both parties for close relations with, if not membership in, the

---

[22] CSCE, 'Budapest Document 1994: Towards a Genuine Partnership in a New
Era,' (Vienna: OSCE, 1994), 27.
[23] Natalie Mychajlyszyn, 'The OSCE and Conflict Prevention: The Case of
Ukraine', in S. Neil MacFarlane and Oliver Thränert (eds.), *Balancing Hegemony:
The OSCE in the CIS* (Kingston, Ont.: Queen's University Centre for Interna-
tional Relations, 1997), 145.

European Community gave Western Europe leverage in assuring a peaceful separation of the Czech and Slovak Republics.[24] One might also cite here the incentive provided by the possibility of membership in North Atlantic Treaty Organization (NATO) for Hungary to sort out its residual problems in relations with Romania and Slovakia over territorial delineation and minority rights. The same factor played a significant role in Romania's settlement of its territorial claims with respect to Ukraine.

A more proactive form of conflict prevention is identification and active mediation of incipient conflicts, as occurs in the efforts of the OSCE Conflict Prevention Centre (CPC) and the High Commissioner on National Minorities (HCNM). The latter has played a particularly active role in Latvia and Estonia in pushing these states towards a more pluralistic view of citizenship and language rights. The High Commissioner has also played an active and reasonably effective role in the dispute between Crimean and central Ukrainian authorities.

Beyond conflict prevention is multilateral management of conflicts that have not been prevented. Here, the focus is on efforts to bring active hostilities to an end and to create an environment that is conducive to conflict resolution, through the provision of peacekeeping forces and active mediation between the parties, as well as through the provision of assistance to deal with the humanitarian consequences of conflict. This may involve not only neutral intervention, but also pressure on one or more of the parties to compromise. There is a wide spectrum of instruments for such pressure, starting at the sharp end with the use of force under Chapter VII of the United Nations Charter in response to situations that the Security Council deems threatening to international peace and security, through sanctions, to aid conditionality. The obvious example of the use of force in this sense was the NATO bombing of targets in Serb-controlled Bosnia in the summer and autumn of 1995 in order to bring the Serbs to the negotiating table at Dayton. Bosnia also provides a prominent example of the use of sanctions in the embargo on arms to the parties in the conflict.

Management shades into resolution, a third modality of external involvement in ethnic disputes. This has included not merely good offices in the production of a final settlement (as, for example, in the role of the OSCE Minsk Group with regard to Nagorno Karabakh, and that of the EU and the UN regarding the former

---

[24] Robert Young, *The Breakup of Czecho-Slovakia* (Kingston, Ont.: Queen's University Institute of Intergovernmental Relations, 1994), 51.

Yugoslav conflicts), but also assistance to the affected society in making the settlement stick. This aspect of internationalization has many dimensions. In the first place it may involve the deployment of military forces in order to deter any resumption of hostilities, as in the case of IFOR in Bosnia. A second area of engagement is assistance in resettlement of returning displaced persons, and assistance in reconstruction. Again, multilateral and bilateral efforts in Bosnia come to mind.

Third, multilateral organizations and states have used conditionalities on assistance to ensure compliance with peace agreements. In the case of Bosnia, for example, in October 1996, Momcilo Krajisnik, the newly elected Serbian member of the collective presidency threatened to refuse to attend the presidential swearing-in ceremony in Sarajevo. This risked a serious delegitimation of the institution of the presidency. Representatives of the EU, the World Bank, the European Bank for Reconstruction and Development (EBRD), and the United States jointly visited Pale to inform him that if he did not attend, Serb areas of the republic would receive no reconstruction assistance. Four days later, Krajisnik arrived in Sarajevo for the ceremony.[25] In the extreme, international actors have assumed sovereign responsibilities within affected states, as is evident in the gradually escalating involvement of the High Representative in Bosnia in matters of domestic jurisdiction since the Dayton Accord and in the evolving international administration of the Kosovo region in 1999–2000.

The unilateral (hegemonic) and the multilateral strands of internationalization are not necessarily alternatives. The two kinds of activity may complement each other. The stabilization goal is shared to some extent at both levels. Although a regional hegemonic actor can bring major force to bear as part of an effort to manage an ethnic dispute (and is indeed the actor most likely to do so, because its interests are more directly affected by the externalities of the conflict), other international actors may bring additional resources to bear in areas where the hegemon is lacking. Moreover, their presence may temper the excesses of the hegemon.

This is the theory behind the involvement of the UN and the OSCE in the management of conflicts where the lead is taken by the Russian Federation (in Georgia and Moldova). In these instances, the Russians provide the major peacekeeping capability and have

---

[25] James K. Boyce and Manuel Pastor, 'Aid for Peace: Can International Financial Institutions Help Prevent Conflict?', *World Policy Journal* (Summer 1998), 42.

taken the lead on mediation, while the international agencies enhance transparency, provide humanitarian and economic assistance associated with efforts at stabilization, contribute to establishing the political conditions for durable resolution, and provide a degree of protection for the target state in the face of the hegemonic objectives of the regional power.

Democratization and ethnic conflict

This raises the issue of the relationship between democratization and ethnic disputes rather clearly. By democratization, I mean a transition from authoritarian forms of governance to more open and inclusive ones. This may be measured in terms of wider respect for individual rights, an environment in which the expression and dissemination of ideas is less subject to political constraint, and in which the exercise of individual political choice (consent) matters to political elites.[26]

It is conventionally taken as a given that the transition to democracy may discourage ethnic disputes. To the extent that there are constitutional means for the pursuit of group objectives, then the option of extra-systemic challenges to the constitutional order is less likely to be exercised. It is true that certain forms of democratic structure (for example, unambiguously majoritarian systems) may not adequately protect minority rights (particularly when majorities and minorities define their political activities along ethnic lines). But there are recognized mechanisms (such as federalism) by which to mitigate this danger.

More recently, a reasonably powerful critique of this line of reasoning has developed. Mansfield and Snyder among others argue that, although all of this may be true of mature democratic systems, the opposite may be true of the process of transition from authoritarian to democratic governance. This is so, because in such transitions the growth of popular participation in politics outruns institutional adaptation. This in turn creates threats to established elites, and the instrumental manipulation of ethnic nationalism is one promising means of responding to these threats in the effort to maintain power and position.[27] Likewise, the appropriation of ethnic nationalism may serve as a useful means for aspiring elites to challenge the positions of established ones. In short, the process of democratization may contribute to, rather than

---

[26] For a more elaborate discussion of the content of democratization, see Mansfield and Snyder, 'Democratization and the Danger of War', passim.

[27] Ibid., 7.

mitigate, interethnic tensions.[28] From the perspectives of the international community, this creates a degree of tension between the agenda of promotion of democracy and that of preventing or managing ethnic disputes. For example, where a free press is used to promote exclusive ethno-national objectives in diverse societies, a concern for conflict prevention might lead one to the conclusion that a degree of limitation on press freedom is desirable.

This problem is linked to the issue of the state in transitional societies. Arguably, processes of democratizing transition in weak states are more likely to produce ethnic disputes than are similar processes in strong ones. The contrast here between Georgia and South Africa is compelling. This is because one essential function of the state in diverse societies is to adjudicate disputes between communities. For this to work, the state has to be widely seen to be legitimate, and it must possess a credible capacity to make adjudication stick.[29] The parties to potential disputes must see the state to be a credible defender of their position. Where the state is weak (as it clearly was and is in many societies where ethnic disputes have emerged), it lacks legitimacy and credibility. The situation with respect to intercommunal relations comes to resemble anarchy in the international system. Communities consequently turn to self-help.[30]

This suggests that in their approach to political development in diverse societies, international actors need to address not merely the problem of democratic transition, but also that of state building. The problem here again is that there is some tension between the two. The effort to build a 'usable' state in conditions of considerable social disorder and intercommunal tension may require sacrifices in the area of civil rights and democratic development as the state consolidates power and establishes credibility. On the other hand, without this reconstruction, it is difficult to proceed with the entrenchment of democratic governance.

As with other elements of the international response to ethnic tension, democracy support may be targeted on prevention, management, and resolution. In the first instance, the idea, presumably, is that one can prevent conflict between ethnic communities through the design of political structures that ensure that no specific group can be excluded from political decision-making. The development of representative democratic institutions in this sense strengthens

---

[28] See V. P. Gagnon's account of conflict in the former Yugoslavia, 'Ethnic Nationalism and International Conflict'.

[29] Lake and Rothchild, 'Origins and Management of Ethnic Conflict', 43.

[30] Barry Posen, 'The Security Dilemma and Ethnic Conflict,' *Survival*, 35: 1 (Spring 1993), 27–47.

the credibility and legitimacy of the state and, thereby, its capacity to play an effective mediating role between groups. Various
European institutions and states have been heavily involved in
the effort to strengthen state capacity and credibility in societies
threatened by ethnic conflict. Activities range from OSCE advice
on constitutional legal, and human rights issues, the OSCE Office
of Democratic Institutions and Human Rights' (ODIHR) training
and support of electoral commissions and monitoring of elections,
the Council of Europe's (COE) legal capacity-building programmes,
and OSCE and EU sponsored training of judges and police officials, to NATO-Partnership for Peace training in democratic civil–
military relations.

Summary

Before assessing the impact of internationalization on ethnic
disputes, it is worthwhile identifying the principal objectives of
international actors more specifically. With regard to unilateral
actions by states, their behaviour is determined largely by self-
interested calculation of strategic interest. The primary example
(particularly in the former Soviet region) is the Russian Federation.
The principal rationale for Russian involvement in ethnic disputes
in the former Soviet 'space' has been to retain and to reconstruct
influence in what it perceived to be its back yard. An additional
significant stated aim has been the protection of the language and
civil and political rights of Russophone minorities in this 'space'.
The principal methods employed have been covert intervention
(Georgia and Karabakh), overt intervention (Moldova), arms transfers (Karabakh), mediation and good offices (Georgia, Tajikistan,
Moldova, and Karabakh), the insertion of peacekeeping forces,
either on its own initiative (South Ossetia) or within the framework
of the Commonwealth of Independent States (CIS) (Abkhazia and
Tajikistan), and the manipulation of Russian minority politics
(Latvia, Estonia, Kazakhstan, and Ukraine).

The second category could be loosely termed the international
community in its European (the EU, the OSCE, the COE, the
Western European Union), transatlantic (NATO), and universal (UN)
dimensions. International civil society organizations also play an
important role in this context.[31] The principal proximate objectives

---

[31] It is often unclear, however, to what extent these should be considered
autonomous non-state actors, since the bulk of the funding of their activities in
the countries of south-eastern Europe and the newly independent states comes from
governmental or intergovernmental sources.

of these interventions have been the prevention of conflict and its associated negative externalities (for example, the Czech and Slovak Republics, and Macedonia), assistance to the victims of ongoing conflict (the role of UNPROFOR and associated humanitarian intergovernmental and non-governmental organizations), obtaining ceasefires and durable settlements to such conflict, and the reconstruction of societies in the aftermath of conflict. The underlying motivations are presumably twofold. The Western European states in particular seek to contain migration and other negative externalities associated with instability to their east. They seek in a general sense to implant Western democratic and human rights norms in these regions in the belief that democratic governance leads to stability, as well as facilitating the westward integration of post-communist economies and societies.

The major methods employed include preventive diplomacy (for example, the HCNM in the Baltic states), preventive deployment (Macedonia), humanitarian action (Bosnia, Georgia, Azerbaijan), mediation, and good offices in the effort to obtain ceasefires and durable political settlements, and post-conflict reconstruction assistance (often rendered conditional on the constructive behaviour of the parties).

At a deeper level, there has been heavy use of democratization and state-building initiatives in both the preventive and post-conflict phases of ethnic disputes. These include elections support and observation, constitutional and judicial reform, and capacity building in civil society.

The Record

A major instance of internationalization in the realm of prevention is the Czech and Slovak case, where the European Union and Germany in particular went to considerable lengths—using conditionality on assistance and prospects for membership in Western institutions—to ensure that the divorce would be at the very least peaceful, if not amicable. The odds for a deterioration into intercommunal violence were quite low in any case, since there were no historical irredenta, proportions of Czechs living compactly in Slovakia and vice versa were very low, and there was no profound historical enmity between the two groups.[32]

---

[32] For a much earlier and similar set of observations, see Jan Zielonka, *Security in Central Europe* (Adelphi Paper No. 272) (London: Brassey's for the IISS, 1992), 12. See also Carol Skalnik Leff, *The Czech and Slovak Republics: Nation versus State* (Boulder, Colo.: Westview, 1997), 141.

A second example is provided by the Baltic states of Latvia and Estonia, where the Conference on Security and Cooperation in Europe (CSCE) and then OSCE (notably through the High Commissioner on National Minorities) have been heavily involved in seeking ways to normalize relations between the titular nations and their Russian minorities. The early CSCE intervention in Estonia in 1992 (a six-month mission to investigate the situation of the Russian minority at the request of the Russian government under the Moscow mechanism[33]) had an important effect, in the words of one observer, in 'giving local Russian leaders a voice in the West, and of reassuring them they had not been forgotten'.[34] The later activities of the HCNM in the region have been accompanied by clear movement in both countries towards liberalization of language and citizenship law.

A third has been the role of the OSCE Mission of Long-Term Duration and the HCNM in Ukraine in the effort to find a solution to the Crimea question and the related issue of Tatar return and civil and political rights for this minority, as well as in the broader question of the rights of that country's substantial Russian minority.[35] A fourth, and one that has received a great deal of positive attention, is the preventive UN military deployment (UNPREDEP) in Macedonia, beginning in November 1992 and joined by a US contingent in July 1993. One author judged the operation as follows:

Given troop movements on the Serbian side of the border in 1993 and the repeated Serbian armed provocations along the Macedonian border in 1994, including several armed incursions across the border, the stationing of this force . . . seemed to offer some reassurance.[36]

One might add that the presence of US ground troops in the force probably had a deterrent effect on the Serbs.[37] This international military effort was coupled with the efforts of the OSCE mission

---

[33] See CSCE, 'Document of the Moscow Meeting of the Conference on the Human Dimension of the CSCE' (Moscow: CSCE, 1991).

[34] Anatol Lieven, *The Baltic Revolution: Estonia, Latvia, Lithuania and the Path to Independence* (New Haven: Yale University Press, 1993), 378.

[35] For a full discussion, see Mychajlyszyn, 'The OSCE and Conflict Prevention', 152–60.

[36] Sabrina Ramet, *Balkan Babel: The Disintegration of Yugoslavia from the Death of Tito to Ethnic War* (Boulder, Colo.: Westview, 1996), 233. UNPREDEP is a significant moment in the history of UN peace support operations, since it was the UN's first preventive force deployment and the first armed UN operation that included US troops under non-US command.

[37] Gow, *Triumph of the Lack of Will*, 120.

in Skopje to assist the Macedonian government in defining a constitutional dispensation for that country's various minorities and notably the Albanians in the hope of preventing exacerbation of interethnic relations within the country.

Turning to conflict management, we see a mix of hegemonic and multilateral efforts. In Georgia, the Russian Federation and the OSCE have cooperated in the effort to sustain the ceasefire in South Ossetia while attempts are made to achieve a durable settlement. Russia provides a contingent to a mixed Osset/Georgian/Russian force, while the OSCE Mission of Long-Term Duration established in Georgia in 1992 monitors the performance of the peacekeepers as well as the general security situation in the conflict zone.

In Abkhazia, a similar collaboration developed in 1993–4 between Russia and the UN. The Russian Federation, ostensibly under the auspices of the Commonwealth of Independent States, deployed a peacekeeping force along a security and weapons exclusion zone dividing the parties. They have been joined by a force of up to 136 UN military observers (the UN Observer Mission in Georgia—UNOMIG). The UN—with Russian facilitation and now in cooperation with Friends of the Secretary General for Georgia —is responsible for mediation of a settlement through a special representative of the secretary general for Georgia, currently Ambassador Dieter Boden.[38]

In the case of Chechnya, the OSCE was invited by the Russian Federation to dispatch a mission to assist in mediation between Chechen and Russian authorities. The level of internationalization of the Chechen dispute has been, however, quite limited, given the residual power and political importance of the Russian Federation, its jealousy with regard to domestic jurisdiction, and the concern of other states not to jeopardize their wider agendas in relations with Russia through an intrusive approach to the question.

The most substantial venue for internationalized conflict management has been the former Yugoslavia, where in various guises at various times, the EU, the OSCE, the UN, NATO, and the WEU and numerous state actors have all had a crack at management of the conflict and creating conditions conducive to conflict resolution in Croatia and Bosnia-Hercegovina.[39]

With regard to conflict resolution, again one sees a mix of state-centred and multilateral efforts to achieve a resolution of

[38] The Georgian cases are covered in detail in S. Neil MacFarlane, 'On the Front Lines of the Near Abroad'.

[39] For a comprehensive, if depressing account of this extremely complex engagement, see Gow, *Triumph of the Lack of Will*.

the relevant disputes. In the case of Karabakh, there has been Iranian, Turkish, Russian, American, and French mediation, along with the multilateral *encadrement* of the OSCE Minsk group, which has been motoring along without obvious effects since 1992. Of the various endeavours in this case, the Russian ones have clearly been the most effective in producing a ceasefire, if not a resolution of the dispute, in May 1994.

In the case of South Ossetia, the OSCE and Russia are leading a process of negotiation that may produce a positive outcome in the fairly near future, although the Ossets appear to be delaying until they see what kind of deal the Abkhaz get. As for Abkhazia, the United Nations, in the person of the personal representative of the secretary general, has taken the lead here since 1992, with Russian 'facilitation'. With the passage of time, they have been joined by the Friends of the Secretary General for Georgia. In both the Abkhaz and Karabakh cases, the Russians have frequently pursued a parallel direct track in mediation, in addition to cooperating more or less sincerely with the multilateral efforts of the OSCE and the UN.[40] UN agencies and the OSCE (in South Ossetia) have supplemented these diplomatic efforts with an innovative use of conditionality on reconstruction assistance to bring the parties closer to reconciliation.

In the Yugoslav case, a variety of regional organizations tried their hands at conflict resolution before the mantle settled on the United Nations and the EU operating in tandem with one mediator from each group. Several years of frustration followed, culminating in a dramatic increase in the willingness to use force multilaterally to induce compliance of the parties on a compromise settlement drafted finally at Dayton and sponsored by the USA. As noted, agreement was also facilitated by deliberate state-centred efforts through military assistance to alter the military balance to the disfavour of the Serb party. This produced the deployment of IFOR and subsequently SFOR and a modest stabilization of the situation on the ground in Bosnia-Hercegovina. There remain significant difficulties in stabilizing the settlement, however. Notably, for much of the IFOR/SFOR period, there has been a clear disconnection between the military tasks of stabilization

---

[40] On this point, see Elizabeth Fuller, 'The Karabakh Mediation Process: Grachev versus the CSCE?', *RFE/RL Research Report*, 3: 23 (10 June 1994), 13–17. For an informed and insightful account of the mediation process in Karabakh, see John Maresca, 'Resolving the Conflict over Nagorno-Karabakh: Lost Opportunities for International Conflict Resolution', in Crocker and Hampson, *Managing Global Chaos*, 255–73.

and deterrence and the civil tasks of state building and strengthening law and order, refugee return,[41] and prosecution of alleged war criminals. The fact that military forces deployed to Bosnia have fairly steadily avoided significant support of civil tasks has made it very difficult to implement Dayton provisions on return. Moreover, civilian entities are not in a position to restore a reliable system of law and order. And without the arrest of war criminals, the construction of envisaged integrated governmental structures is at best problematic.[42]

Conclusions

Rather than go into greater detail about these cases, I should like to discuss what general lessons we might take away from them with regard to the internationalization of ethnic disputes. First, it is striking that—despite the power available to the various intervenors—the record of their interventions has been very spotty. Arguably, although by definition not demonstrably, the greatest positive impacts have been felt in the area of conflict prevention. There is good reason to believe that international constraints contributed to the peaceful character of Czecho-Slovakia's divorce and that the discreet interventions of the HCNM in incipient conflicts in the former Soviet Union reduced the likelihood of serious outbreaks of conflict in a number of instances. Likewise, there is reason to believe that the preventive deployment of Nordic and American troops in Macedonia in what became UNPREDEP contributed to a stabilization of the situation in that country and, in conjunction with OSCE efforts in the area of political development, reduced the likelihood of an eruption of ethnic conflict in that republic. Finally, the OSCE long-term mission in Ukraine played a significant, if ancillary role, in the mediation of the Crimea dispute and in the construction of legislation that would mollify the Russian minority elsewhere in the country. These multilateral responses were supplemented by state policies that favoured the

---

[41] Writing in 1998, Jane Sharp noted that during 1996–7 of the 2.3 million persons displaced by the war, only some 381,000 had returned home, mostly to areas where they were part of an ethnic majority. See 'Prospects for Peace in Bosnia: The Role of Britain', in Marie-Janine Calic et al., *The Issues Raised by Bosnia and the Transatlantic Debate* (Chaillot Paper 32) (Paris: Western European Union, May 1998), 39.

[42] On these points, see Nicole Gnesotto, 'Prospects for Bosnia after SFOR', in Calic, *Bosnia and the Transatlantic Debate*, 30–1.

same outcome. Although it is difficult to sort out the relative causal weight of multilateral as opposed to state forms of engagement, there seems little reason to doubt that the overall impact of internationalization was constructive.

The record of conflict management has been more mixed and less ambiguous. In the southern Caucasus, Russian intervention did produce an end to open hostilities in Abkhazia and South Ossetia. In Moldova, the record has been also reasonably positive—the intervention of Russia's 14th Army and the subsequent creation and deployment of a mixed peacekeeping force did force an end to hostilities in the agreement of 21 July 1992. In contrast, there has been little evidence of success in Karabakh. The ceasefire there has been stable largely because the military balance is stable, and not because of any serious peacekeeping effort. In Croatia and Bosnia-Hercegovina, it is probable that UNPROFOR contributed to a modest stabilization and, despite Srebrenica, it assisted in avoiding an even more serious humanitarian catastrophe. But UNPROFOR faced serious operational difficulties associated with the inadequacy of its mandate and of the resources deployed to implement that mandate.

The ultimate measure of the lack of success in the UNPROFOR phase of the internationalization of the Bosnian dispute lies in the fact that ultimately UNPROFOR was pulled out of the way in the context of serious escalation in the international use of force and in preparation for the deployment of a large heavy ground force (IFOR). Stabilization in the Bosnian instance was achieved not through the classic techniques of peacekeeping or through more limited forms of enforcement, but through state-centred efforts to alter the military balance against the Serbs (with the arming and training of the Croats and—less obviously—the Muslims), as well as the use of massive air power against Serb targets and the insertion of equally massive ground forces.

Where the record is least impressive is in the area of conflict resolution. This is perhaps the most important dimension, since it is next to impossible to construct stable, prosperous, democratic societies around unreconciled but frozen internal conflicts. Here the most obvious problem cases have been Bosnia, Georgia, and Azerbaijan. In the first case, despite massive international involvement and agreement by the parties on a structure for normalization, progress towards implementing Dayton has been very spotty in a number of areas—notably the return of Internally Displaced Persons, apprehending individuals indicted by the War Crimes Tribunal, and the establishment of effective integrated state structures, including credible and impartial law enforcement capacity. This led to the return of talk about partition as the most effective solution—which it may well be.

All of this suggests a number of conclusions. First, international response to ethnic disputes is most likely to be effective if it occurs before open hostilities begin—before the rupture and discrediting of the state and before the grievances associated with ethnic conflict accumulate and destroy whatever residual trust between communities that remains. The irony, of course, is that conflict prevention is arguably the most difficult response to generate. It is hard to generate interest in a substantial response to something that has yet to happen.

The key difficulty with both hegemonic and multilateral efforts to deal with active ethnic disputes is the transition from management to political settlement. There are a number of reasons for this. Dealing first with the hegemonic side, there is in part a problem of motivation. In the case of Russia and the CIS, the hegemon's influence has been rooted largely in the persistence of abnormality. As such, its interest in normalization has been limited. Russia has been aware that time and economic forces are working against it in the southern Caucasus and Moldova. The leverage it retained has been associated largely with its role in peacekeeping and mediation.

This is related to a second problem—Russia, although stronger than the others, was weak. It has had little other than its residual military power as a basis for the influence many Russians desire along its southern periphery. This favoured a reliance on military instrumentalities on Russia's part and reduced Russia's attractiveness as a regional leader for the others. Ultimately, this problem may diminish in significance if Russia gradually shifts from a power-oriented agenda to a welfare and profit-oriented one, a prospect that appears to be diminishing given the political changes in the Russian Federation in the summer of 1998 and more so since the renewal of the war in Chechnya in the autumn of 1999.

Turning to the multilateral level, despite the earlier comments on normative development, international responses have been hampered in general by a degree of normative dissonance. Both in the UN and the OSCE contexts, international responses have reflected a tension between norms regarding sovereignty, territoriality, and domestic jurisdiction on the one hand and those concerning self-determination on the other. It is worth stressing that these are not inherently incompatible one with another, since there are—in theory and in practice—ways in which the aspirations of distinct minority communities can be addressed within the context of a defence of territorial integrity.[43] On the other hand, this requires that the state be perceived as legitimate and as capable of effectively and fairly mediating between communities. Presumably this is the central purpose of democratization in divided societies. However, the process requires trust and that is exactly what is destroyed in ethnic conflict.

One final problem is that of asymmetrical motivation. For the participants, the issues involved in ethnic disputes are matters of survival. Moreover, they generate distorted structures of political economy and associated interests that profit significantly from the continuation of war. This often renders local positions on conflict resolution quite intractable.[44] Such situations demand a willingness on the part of outsiders to commit substantial resources and take large risks to create a stable framework for intercommunal discourse. For outsiders, however, such conflicts are on the whole peripheral inconveniences. The externalities may be painful. The lack of progress may be embarrassing. But they are, in the final analysis, tolerable. In such circumstances, it has been extremely difficult for disinterested outsiders to develop sufficient credibility to have a decisive impact on the process. Ultimately, it may be the exhaustion of the parties or decisive shifts in the political/military balance—both of which are largely factors internal to the process of conflict—that produce settlement, and not the more or less well-intentioned, more or less disinterested activities of external actors.

[43] For a recent treatment of this issue, see Ruth Lapidoth, *Autonomy: Flexible Solutions to Ethnic Conflicts* (Washington: USIP Press, 1996).

[44] For an expansion of this point, with particular attention to secessionist elites, see Charles King, *Ending Civil Wars* (Adelphi Paper No. 308) (London: Oxford University Press for the IISS, 1997), 30–54.

6

International Migration and the Consolidation of Democracy

Ewa Morawska

This chapter examines the relationship between westbound international migrations and the consolidation of democracy in contemporary East Central Europe (ECE). Both processes play an important role in the incorporation of ECE societies into the capitalist/democratic world, and each of them has attracted a large volume of studies. However, their interrelation has remained outside the purview of either democratic transition/consolidation or international migrations analyses.[1]

An examination of the impact of the movement of residents of ECE to and from the West on the consolidation of democracy in that region is worthwhile for two reasons. One is the apparently 'natural' affinity of these phenomena. The destination of the vast majority of contemporary international migrants are Western societies, which are also the source of the ideas and practical models of democracy for ECE. It should be reasonable to expect that migrants' Western travels provide an opportunity for 'participant observation' of the everyday operation of democratic societies; an

---

[1] In the former group see the recent studies of Geoffrey Pridham, Eric Herring, and George Sanford (eds.), *Building Democracy? The International Dimension of Democratisation in Eastern Europe* (London: Leicester University Press, 1997); Juan Linz and Alfred Stepan, *Problems of Democratic Transition and Consolidation* (Baltimore: Johns Hopkins University Press, 1996); Laurence Whitehead (ed.), *The International Dimensions of Democratization* (Oxford: Oxford University Press, 1996). For the latter, see Solon Ardittis (ed.), *The Politics of East–West Migration* (London: St Martin's Press, 1994); Tomas Frejka (ed.), *International Migration in Central and Eastern Europe and the Commonwealth of Independent States* (New York: UN Economic Commission for Europe, 1996); Heinz Fassmann and Rainer Münz (eds.), *European Migration in the Late Twentieth Century* (Aldershot: Edward Elgar, 1994).

experience which these migrants transplant upon return to their home countries.

The second reason is comparative and historical. Observers of westbound travels from that region during the period of mass economic migrations one century ago (1880–1914) documented the active role of the (e)migrants and the returnees in the development of democratic ideas and practices in their home countries. This raises questions pertinent to contemporary circumstances. Has a more dense interconnection of parts of the world in the 1990s enhanced the relationship between international migrations and democratic developments in the sending societies? Or have the political, socio-economic, and cultural contexts of these processes changed in ways that modify this impact?

In what follows I argue that, paradoxically in view of the rapidly expanding connection of ECE with the West, the relationship between westbound travels of a vast majority of migrants and demo-cratization processes in their home countries has weakened. What remains of it has become considerably more complex in compar-ison to the situation at the turn of the twentieth century. An examination of the present situation against the background of the positive impact of turn-of-the-last-century ECE (e)migrants and returnees on the democratic processes in their home countries constitutes the main part of this chapter. To make the assessment more complete, I consider also the actual and potential influence of the emerging elite or 'brain exchange' international travellers.

Two basic concepts inform this discussion: 'international migra-tion' and 'consolidation of democracy'. The former is understood as travel across state borders for purposes other than exclusively tourism, regardless of the duration of sojourn abroad. This encom-passing definition of international migration has been dictated by the specificity of cross-state travels of the residents of post-communist Europe and, in particular, the relatively short-distance or borderland nature of most of these migrations which are aimed mainly at generating income.

The consolidation of democracy involves 'substantial attitudinal support for and behavioral compliance with the democratic insti-tutions and the "rules of the game" which they establish'.[2] Box 6.1

---

[2] Juan Linz, Alfred Stepan, and Richard Gunther, 'Democratic Transition and Consolidation in Southern Europe, with Reflections on Latin America and Eastern Europe', in Richard Gunther, Nikiforos Diamandouros, and Hans-Jurgen Puhle (eds.), *The Politics of Democratic Consolidations* (Baltimore: Johns Hopkins University Press, 1995), 77–123. See also Linz and Stepan, *Problems of Democratic Trans-ition and Consolidation*.

Box 6.1. *Constitutive elements of democracy*

I. Democracy as a political system:

1. Government is elected by citizens and is responsive to them;
2. Government operates by parliamentary and majoritarian or consensual rules;
3. Separation of judiciary, executive, and legislative powers;
4. Government delegates and supervises the carrying out of its 'collective good functions';
5. System of laws/regulatory frameworks guarantees (1), (2), (3), and (4) and protects civil liberties of citizens (freedom of speech, press, and assembly, and protection of individual and group rights against arbitrary state action) and the fundamentals of the 'Democratic Creed' [(8)(9)(10)]).

II. Democracy as a form of community:

6. Existence of civil society or the plurality institutions and associations that operate independently from the state;
7. Participation based on inclusion rather than exclusion and deriving from civic-universalist rather than ethnonationalist-particularistic criteria.

III. Democracy as a culture (set of normatively binding concepts that inform social-political institutions and popular orientations):

8. Individualism, holding that the primary task of the government is to enable each individual to achieve the highest potential development;
9. Liberty, which allows each individual the greatest amount of freedom consistent with order, and
9a. Postulating that individuals will cooperate in creating a wholesome society through the execution of their rights and duties through participation in civic-political affairs;
10. Equality, maintaining that all people are created with equal rights and opportunities;
11. Deliberative-negotiatory (rather than zero-sum confrontational) manner of resolving conflicts and building consensus;
12. Respect for the institutions and processes of political life and for their outcomes—laws, regulations, policies, and election returns—even if they are disliked.

Sources: S. M. Lipset (ed.), *The Encyclopedia of Democracy* (Washington: Congressional Quarterly Inc., 1995); R. Dahl, *Democracy and its Critics* (New Haven: Yale University Press, 1989); B. Turner and P. Hamilton (eds.), *Citizenship: Critical Concepts* (London: Routledge, 1994); J. Linz and A. Stepan, *Problems of Democratic Transition and Consolidation* (Baltimore: Johns Hopkins University Press, 1996); A. Przeworski, *Sustainable Democracy* (Cambridge: Cambridge University Press, 1995); A. Lijphart, 'Democratic Political Systems: Types, Cases, Causes and Consequences', *Journal of Theoretical Politics*, 1 (1989), 33–48.

specifies the democratic institutions and 'rules' that require the support of political elites and significant segments of citizenry. The constitutive elements of democracy specified in Box 6.1 involve legal-political, social-communal, and cultural-normative aspects in their macro and micro dimensions and represent an extensive interpretation of the concept, combining procedural (conflict management and resolution) and deliberative-participatory (shared effort toward the common good) elements.[3] This broad definition of democracy and its consolidation is dictated by the subject matter of this analysis. Spaces most readily accessible to migrants' potential influence are primarily located at mezzo-to-micro levels of the democratization processes. These areas include civil society (conceived as a normative principle, a style of organization, and a form of participation), economic society (seen as a set of socio-politically crafted rules and institutions that mediate between state and market), and levels of the political society (including political parties and legislative bodies).[4]

This chapter focuses on East Central Europe including Poland, the Czech Republic, and Hungary. All three countries received ratings above the minimal threshold of democratic practices on the Freedom House Scale of Political Rights and Civil Liberties,[5] and have entered a phase of democratic consolidation. Their pending incorporation into the European Union (EU) moderates and accelerates this process, at least in its legal/procedural-institutional aspect. The primary destination of international migrations from those countries has been Western Europe and North America, which are also the main models of democratic ideas and practices. Elsewhere in the region, these flows have been mostly internal (CIS, excepting Jews and German *Aussiedlers*) or directed at ECE (Poland, the Czech Republic, and Hungary) which has attained the most advanced transformation. These three countries have also attracted the largest numbers of highly skilled Westerners employed as facilitators of the transformation. This discussion focuses on the

[3] On these two projects of democracy, see Ralph Dahrendorf, 'Citizenship and Beyond: The Social Dynamics of an Idea', *Social Research*, 41: 4 (1974), 673–701; T. H. Marshall, *Citizenship and Social Class* (Cambridge, Mass.: Harvard University Press, 1950); Bryan Turner and Peter Hamilton (eds.), *Citizenship: Critical Concept* (London: Routledge, 1994); Michael Walzer (ed.), *Toward a Global Civil Society* (Oxford: Berghahn Books, 1995).

[4] After Linz and Stepan, *Problems of Democratic Transition and Consolidation*, 7–14.

[5] Raymond Gastil (ed.), *Freedom in the World: Political Rights and Civil Liberties, 1993–1994* (New York: Freedom House, 1994), 677–8.

Box 6.2. *Major factors influencing the relationship of migration-democratization**

I. The sending societies:
—economic structure and developmental dynamics;
—political (state) independence and form of government;
—prevailing orientation(s), laws and policies regarding state-national membership: civic-universalist *versus* ethnonationalist-particularist;
—official and popular civic-political culture/practice regarding, in particular:
    (i) respect for the law
    (ii) trust in public institutions and their functionaries
    (iii) negotiatory versus confrontational approach to conflict resolution.

II. The receiving societies:
—economic structure and dynamics;
—'health' and vitality of the democratic system;
—immigration policies;
—degree of socio-political isolation/integration from/into mainstream society of (im)migrants and availability to the latter of models of democratic procedures and organization.

III. International relations:
—international power-politics, pressures and conflicts/disagreements, especially involving home countries/region of (im)migrants;
—involvement of (im)migrants' home countries/region in international agreements and institutions regulating/monitoring trans-statal population flows to and from these countries/region on the one hand, and, on the other, the compliance with the democratic requirements.

IV. Characteristics of (im)migrants:
—economic status/location in the sending and the receiving society;
—political status in the receiving society;
—duration of stay abroad;
—scope and nature of contacts with natives;
—intra-group organization of (im)migrants;
—accustomed orientations regarding
    (i) collective self/other perceptions
    (ii) authority (especially state and law)
    (iii) civic-political involvement
    (iv) resolution of interpersonal and intergroup differences/conflicts.

* All factors specified here are conceived not as fixed conditions but, in accord with the structuration approach, as inherently changeable situations.

Box 6.3. *ECE migrations in a historical perspective:*
20th–21st versus 19th–20th Centuries

1. Average Ratios of ECE/NW (West Europe and USA combined) per capita
   GNP and Monthly Wages:
   —ECE/NW per capita GNP:
         1913: 42 per cent
         1995: 33 per cent
   —monthly wages:
         1913: 1:3 to 6
         1994: 1:5 to 10

2. Volumes, Frequency, and Destinations of ECE International
   Migrations:
   —Estimations of volume:
         1870–1914: 25–30 million westbound 'comings' and 'goings';
         1990s: 20–5 million annually
   —Frequency:
         1890–1910: average 1–2 annual trips per migrant
         1990s: 5–6
   —Most common destinations:
         1870–1914: Germany, USA, Austria
         1990s: Germany, Austria, Scandinavia, Italy, USA

3. ECE Migrants' Occupational and Gender Distribution:
   —Occupational distribution:
         1880–1914: 95 per cent in agricultural occupations (Jews—
         80 per cent in small trade and handicrafts);
         1990s: around 65 per cent in manufacturing/construction and
         services around
         15 per cent in professions (Jews—around 65 per cent in
         professions)
   —Gender distribution:
         1880–1914: proportion of women 25 to 40 per cent (Jews—
         around 50 per cent);
         1990s: proportion of women 40 to 70 per cent

4. Most Common Migration Types:
         1880–1914: middle-to-longer length duration or permanent
         income-seeking/economic type (Jews: political-economic);
         1990s: short-to-middle length duration (Jews: permanent)
   —tourism combined with trade or undocumented employment;
   —family/friends visiting combined with undocumented employment;
         'pendel' trade and/or employment

common features of the migration–democracy relationship in East Central Europe. Within the limited scope of this chapter, relevant differences between its component parts are also noted.

Informed by the conceptualization of different arenas of social life: the economy, politics, social relations, material and symbolic culture, not as separate structures but as criss-crossing reciprocal constructions, each structured by and structuring the other through human action and its intended and unintended consequences, the proposed comparative-historical configurational approach demonstrates one mode of such getting together that is compatible with the recent appreciation among 'consolidologists' of the contingency of democratization processes in time- and space-specific circumstances and their resulting diversity and underdeterminacy.[6]

The major circumstances that have shaped the relationship between types of contemporary westbound migrations and democratization processes in ECE are listed in Box 6.2. The discussion of these configurations and their influence on the migration/democracy relationship has been set against the comparative background of turn-of-the-century mass migrations (Box 6.3 presents summary data on the economic backgrounds and selected sociodemographic characteristics of the 20th–21st and 19th–20th centuries international migrations of East Central Europeans in all categories combined).

ECE Arbeitstouristen and Handelstouristen

The largest category of post-1989 ECE international migrants, the income-seeking *Arbeitstouristen* and *Handelstouristen*, has been directed primarily to Western Europe (85 per cent) and North America (15 per cent). Because a large proportion of those quasi-tourists engage in work abroad without appropriate immigration documents or circumvent customs regulations by hiding the

---

[6] On the structuration model of society, see Anthony Giddens, *The Constitution of Society* (Berkeley and Los Angeles: University of California Press, 1984); William Sewell, 'A Theory of Structure: Duality, Agency, and Transformation', *American Journal of Sociology*, 98: 1 (1992), 1–29. On the configurational analysis in comparative-historical sociology, see Theda Skocpol, 'Emergent Agendas and Recurrent Strategies in Historical Sociology', in Theda Skocpol (ed.), *Vision and Method in Historical Sociology* (New York: Cambridge University Press, 1984), 368–91; Charles Ragin, *The Comparative Method: Moving beyond Qualitative and Quantitative Strategies* (Berkeley and Los Angeles: University of California Press, 1987).

quantity of merchandise they smuggle, only estimates of their numbers are available. The volume of contemporary economic migrations from ECE has increased enormously compared to similar flows of a century ago. In 1995 alone, the volume of income-seeking travels of East Central Europeans was estimated at 25–30 million 'crossings', equalling the mass international migration *za chlebem* (after bread) from that region during the thirty years preceding the First World War. (In comparison, the number of legal or contract ECE migrant workers reported in the West totalled 400,000–450,000 in 1995.) Proportionately, Poles have engaged in much more *indocumentado* work and trade during their travels than have the Czechs and Hungarians.[7]

Available data reveal the following socio-demographic characteristics of income/work-seeking migrants (differences between countries have not been significant). Most of them (more than 70 per cent) are urban residents. Men are more numerous than women (about 60 per cent). In both gender groups, most migrants

I have used a variety of sources. Regional and individual country studies of democratization and international migration in ECE have been used to provide broader explanatory contexts for the presence (or absence), arenas, and forms of relationship between these two processes. Also, I have examined numerous social surveys and ethnographic studies conducted during the 1990s in ECE and Western destination countries, drawing also from my own ongoing comparative study of East European migrants' social microenvironments in Berlin and Philadelphia. In these studies, I noted all information about actual and potential travellers' purposes of westbound migration, reasons for their preferences for particular destination countries, pre-migration expectations and after-return evaluations of the specific gains and losses from sojourns abroad for individual migrants and their families, and for their local communities and for the country at large. In addition, I have inspected ECE press reports and secondary analyses on transnational population movements, in particular the influx of repatriate members of diasporas and Western personnel. I also examined available statistical data on (registered) joint business/industrial ventures involving ECE and Western partners. As a considerable number of these sources have few references to the question of democracy /democratization, the discussion also draws upon informal interviews conducted with 23 authors of these and other relevant studies.

[7] For the estimates of contemporary international migrations of East Central Europeans, see Frejka, *International Migration*; *Trends in International Migration* (Paris: OECD/SOPEMI, 1996); *Tourism in Central and Eastern Europe* (Geneva: World Tourism Organization, 1995); Mirjana Morokvasic and Hedwig Rudolph (eds.), *Migrants: les nouvelles mobilités en Europe* (Paris: Éditions L'Harmattan, 1996). On contemporary versus 19th/20th-century flows, see Ewa Morawska, 'Structuring Migration in a Historical Perspective: The Case of Travelling East Europeans', EUI Working Paper-Forum No. 98/3 (Florence: European University Institute, 1998).

are between 30 to 40 years of age. A majority (52–8 per cent) have middle-level education, and a considerable proportion (15–25 per cent) were unemployed at the time of migration.[8]

Asked about motives for their travel abroad, between 85 and 95 per cent of migrants point solely to economic reasons. 'Learning about the world' as an accompanying motive is mentioned by 7–15 per cent of respondents.[9] Not surprisingly, considering the dominant purpose of migrants' travel abroad, their images of the West and particular destination countries focus on affluence, high standards of living, and opportunities to earn money. (The 1995 GNP ratio if East Central European and West European/North American countries was 1 : 3, and that of average official ECE wages and

---

[8] Compiled from Heinz Fassmann, Joseph Kohlbacher, and Ursula Reeger, 'Les Étrangers et l'emploi: analyse de la recherche d'emploi en Autriche', in Morokvasic and Rudolph, *Migrants*, 187–210. Jarmila Maresova, 'Czech Republic' and Judit Juhasz, 'Hungary' in Frejka, *International Migration*, 49–56 and 69–80; Mirjana Morokvasic, 'Entre l'Est et l'Ouest des migrations pendulaires', in Morokvasic and Rudoph, *Migrants*, 19–58; Marek Okolski, 'Poland' in Frejka, *International Migration*, 95–110; Krystyna Slany (ed.), *Orientacje Emigracyjne Polakow* (Cracow: Uniwersytet Jagiellonski, Instytut Socjologii, 1997); Zsuzsa Berencsi and Endre Sik, 'Intentions to Emigrate and to Work Abroad in Hungary in 1993–1994', in Maryellen Fullerton, Endre Sik, and Judit Toth (eds.), *Refugees and Migrants: Hungary at a Crossroads* (Budapest: Institute for Political Science of the Hungarian Academy of Sciences, 1995), 129–42. The proportions of female migrants shown in Box 6.3 (40% to 55%) represent the ratio for all contemporary ECE migrants rather than just the worker and trade tourist categories combined.

[9] These and the following data pertain mostly to short- and middle-term tourist-workers, including those who planned trips at the time of the survey/interview; compiled from: Frejka, *International Migration*; Barbara Cieslinska's communication to the author (1 Mar. 1998); Ewa Jazwinska and Marek Okolski, *Causes and Consequences of Migration in Central and Eastern Europe* (Warsaw: Institute for Social Studies/University of Warsaw, 1996), 18; Bożena Karpiuk, 'Emigracje Zarobkowe Mieszkancow Siemiatycz do Brukseli', Ph.D. dissertation (Filia Uniwersytetu Warszawskiego w Bialymstoku, 1997); Beata Siewiera, 'Les Immigrés polonais sans documents', in Johan Leman (ed.), *Sans documents: les immigrés de l'ombre* (DeBoeck Université, 1995), 71–112; Berencsi and Sik, 'Intentions to Emigrate'; Norbert Cyrus, 'In Deutschland arbeiten und in Polen leben: was die neuen WanderarbeiterInnen aus Polen bewegt', in Buro Arbeitschwerpunkt Rassismus und Fluchtlings politik (ed.), *Zwischen Flucht und Arbeit: neue Migration und Legalisierungs debatte* (Hamburg: Verlag Libertore Assoziation. Poplawski, Tadeusz, 1995); Rajmund Mydel and Heinz Fassmann, *Strategie Migracyjne i Sieci Powiazan* (unpublished manuscript, 1997); Rajmund Mydel and Heinz Fassmann, *Nielegalni Robotnicy Cudzoziemscy i Czarny Rynek Pracy* (Cracow: Institute of Geography of the Jagiellonian University, 1997); Ewa Morawska, *Recent East–West European Migrants and Their Social Micro-Environments in a Comparative-Historical Perspective* (study in progress).

average migrant income in Western informal economy 1 : 10.[10]) With no significant between-country differences, references to Western democratic politics and culture or the rule of law as the appealing features appear, if at all, in no more than 1–3 per cent of answers in both closed (preset categories) and open-ended questions.

Ethnographic and ethno-survey studies of westbound travels of East Central Europeans have also inquired about migrants' experience during their travels and the effects of such migrations on their own and families' lives and local communities. Migrants' answers reflect, again, the primarily economic character of their sojourns. Occasionally, Western 'lack of spiritual values' (contrasted with migrants' national culture) and the 'brutality' of life are mentioned, but more constructive encounters with Western democratic ideas or institutions are largely missing from these migrants' perceptions.

The gains from international migration for the respondents' families and local communities are perceived in almost exclusively economic/material terms. For individual families, migration permits consumer purchases (house/apartment, car, household amenities) and, thus, the elevation of their social status. Between 10 and 15 per cent of the returnees found business enterprises—an investment that may in the future make them active supporters of democracy, thereby making migration an influential factor (see the next section on this category of migrants). Local communities also gain from migration of their residents. Most responses point to the influx of money and increase of economic affluence and/or decrease of unemployment. The possible effects on local democracy are hardly mentioned at all. The question about the effects of (outward) temporary migrations for the respective ECE countries posed in public opinion surveys elicited similar evaluations. The nearly exclusive economic focus and the absence of income-seeking migrants' impact on democracy in their home countries are confirmed in press reports and analyses.

Because social survey and ethnographic studies of migration make minimal reference to democracy, I talked to those who have done participatory research. Their comments by and large support my conclusion. Westbound migration may have helped to deflate possible protests 'from below' against the traumas of economic transformation by providing subsidiary work and income abroad (in itself a negligible facilitator of democratic consolidation). The minority

[10] On ECE's economic performance in comparison with the Western world, from the turn of the 20th century until the 1990s, see Ivan Berend, *Central and Eastern Europe, 1944–1993: Detour from the Periphery to the Periphery* (Cambridge: Cambridge University Press, 1996).

of migrants who invest their savings in businesses might have contributed to creating potential 'democratic investment' for the future. This apart, the largest contingent of contemporary west-bound migrants has had minimal or no impact on the consolidation of democracy in post-communist East Central Europe.

This conclusion is interesting in two ways. First, it suggests that rather than acting as a facilitator of democratic consolidation, migration towards the West has had inconsequential or, as I argue below, possibly even negative effects on this process. Second, it stands in sharp contrast to the historical experience of democratic involvement, both in the destination country and, after return, the home societies of the turn-of-the-century ECE income-seeking travellers, and, especially, *Amerikanci* or peasant-migrants to the United States. The Amerikanci constituted about one-third of the total westbound population movements from that region between the 1880s and 1914. No less than 30–40 per cent eventually returned to their home countries.[11]

The democratic initiatives of these migrants were neither forceful enough nor sufficiently embedded in the social forms and political institutions of East Central Europe still waste-deep in the remnants of the feudal past to really transform them. Two devastating world wars, separated by the Great Depression of the 1930s and followed by the communist takeover in 1945 eradicated these nascent developments. However, they were visible enough to be recorded by contemporaries. These activities involved several elements of democratization at local and national levels, including the creation of People's Houses and agricultural cooperatives in villages, active participation in urban labour unions, the formation of peasant and working-class political parties, and (an important 'demonstration effect' for migrants' countrymen only one or two generations removed from serfdom) a newly acquired sense of individuality.[12]

[11] East European Jews, whose emigration was permanent, were the exception and have been excluded from this discussion. On 1880–1914 ECE international population movements, see Dirk Hoerder and Leslie Moch (eds.), *European Migrants: Global and Local Perspectives* (Boston: Northwestern University Press, 1996); Klaus Bade, *Deutsche im Ausland—Fremde in Deutschland: Migration in Geschichte und Gegenwart* (Munich: Verlag C. H. Beck, 1992); David Berger (ed.), *The Legacy of Jewish Migration: 1881 and Its Impact* (New York: Columbia University Press, 1983).

[12] Feudal serfdom was abolished in 1848 in the Austrian-Hungarian Monarchy and 1861–4 in Russia. On the democratic activities of turn-of-the-century ECE peasant migrants in their home countries, see Emily Balch, *Our Slavic Fellow Citizens* (New York: Charities Publication Committee, 1910; repr. New York: Arno Press, 1969); Franciszek Bujak, *Zmiaca: Wies Powiatu Limanowskiego*

The macro-structural and local circumstances that induced turn-of-the century migrants' participation in democratic activities differed significantly from contemporary conditions which actually diminish or even corrupt the 'democratic impulse' among migrants.

A combination of several factors 'opened up' turn-of-the-century international migrants to democratic influences. Of primary importance on the sending (ECE) side was the multiple *state of becoming* or transition from feudal corporatism and ascription-based sense of selfhood and social organization to modern civic-political and sociocultural commitments and identities among East Central European rural populations. This situation of loosened old forms and unsettled new ones combined with those income-seeking peasant-travellers' genuine curiosity about the faraway world into which they could and had ventured for the first time, facilitated their absorption of new ideas and practices.

On the receiving side, three factors were important. First, as unskilled industrial labourers (95 per cent of non-Jewish foreign-born East Central Europeans in American cities were so employed in 1910), (im)migrants found themselves at the bottom but right within one of the main sectors of the host society's economic structure. In several branches of industry, these migrants participated in labour union activities as early as the 1900s, learning the democratic skills of worker interest representation.[13]

Second, although middle-class native-born Americans perceived new (im)migrants from South-Eastern Europe as culturally inferior, the spirit of Progressive Reform dictated that they assist them in embracing civic-political ideals and the American way of

(Cracow: Gebethner, 1903); Franciszek Bujak, *Limanowa: Miasteczko Powiatu Rzeszowskieg* (Cracow: Gebethner, 1902); Jan Slomka, *From Serfdom to Self-Government: Memoirs of a Polish Village Mayor, 1842–1927* (London: Minerva Publishing Company, 1941); Wincenty Witos, *Moje Wspomnienia*, 2 vols. (Paris: Kultura, 1964); Mark Wyman, *Round-Trip to America: The Immigrants Return to Europe, 1880–1930* (Ithaca, NY: Cornell University Press, 1993); Julianna Puskas, *From Hungary to the United States, 1880–1914* (Budapest: Historical Institute of the Hungarian Academy of Sciences, 1982); Marek Drozdowski (ed.), *Pamietniki Emigrantow* 2 vols. (Warsaw: Ksiazka i Wiedza, 1977).

[13] This discussion has been compiled from: Robert Park, *The Immigrant Press and Its Control* (New York: Harper & Bros., 1922), 51; Victor Greene, *For God and Country. The Rise of Polish and Lithuanian Consciousness in America* (Madison: State Historical Society of Wisconsin, 1975); Christiane Harzig and Dirk Hoerder (eds.), *The Press of Labor Migrants in Europe and North America, 1880s–1930s* (Bremen: Bremen University Press, 1985); Puskas, *From Hungary to the United States*; Mark Stolarik, *Slovak Migration from Europe to North America, 1870–1917* (Cleveland: Cleveland Historical Society, 1980).

life.[14] Through so-called Settlement Houses established in foreign neighbourhoods in most cities, (im)migrants were taught the principles of the 'American creed', the rights and duties of citizenship, and the procedures of democratic laws and government. In these neighbourhoods, they also experienced the workings of political democracy in local and national elections. Although motivated primarily by the desire to augment their electorate, local representatives of the political parties combed (im)migrant neighbourhoods, soliciting their residents to fill out naturalization papers to become citizens and—a revolutionary idea for peasant migrants— 'influence the affairs of America'.

Third, East Central European peasant-(im)migrants organized themselves into various associations. Among the sociocultural institutions they created, those promoting national consciousness and symbolic attachments to 'imagined communities' as Poles, Czechs, Hungarians, and so on, were particularly innovative. The Lithuanians referred to the United States as 'the second birthplace of the[ir] nationality' and the same may be said of others as well.[15] For their fellow ethnic groups in their home countries, however, acculturation into larger national communities occurred under political oppression by Russia, Germany, and Austria, making a zero-sum opposition of 'us' versus 'them' a central theme in their emerging identities. Even though it unavoidably contained home-country motives of struggles against enemies, the nationalization process of the *Amerikanci* took place in a democratic environment and in a democratic manner.

None of the conditions that induced the democratic involvement of turn-of-the-century ECE international travellers is present today and replacement facilitators do not exist. On the contrary, multiple obstacles to such engagement have emerged. On the sending side, the major obstacles have been the following. In comparison with their predecessors, who also were set in motion by large-scale socio-economic transformations but for whom the notions of democracy encountered during their Western sojourns represented an exciting idea, contemporary migrants arrive at their destinations encumbered by undemocratic preconceptions and embedded habits. One of them has been the understanding of democracy prevalent in ECE. During the communist era and by

<hr />

[14] J. H. Timberlake, *Prohibition and the Progressive Movement, 1900–1920* (Cambridge, Mass.: Harvard University Press, 1966); Maureen Greenwald and Margo Anderson (eds.), *Pittsburgh Surveyed: Social Science and Social Reform in the Early Twentieth Century* (Pittsburgh: Pittsburgh University Press, 1996).

[15] Park, *Immigrant Press*, 51.

way of opposition to that politically authoritarian and economically inefficient regime, a largely implicit popular understanding of democracy emerged composed of three elements: freedom from state controls (understood as the elimination of the communist regime), economic affluence for all, and the return of genuine sovereignty to the states of the 'socialist family'.[16] The collapse of the Soviet-dominated communist order was viewed as equivalent to the establishment of the Western capitalist-democratic one.

The experience of 'real democracy' and increased contacts with the Western world are gradually bringing this understanding closer to reality. However, two components of this perception—democracy understood as 'negative freedom' from state legal and political-institutional constraints and as a system that cares for the disadvantaged while assuring economic affluence for everybody—have endured in popular understanding. Absent from these common representations have thus far been the constitutive elements of 'positive freedom' (elements II/7, III/9a, 11, 12 in Box 6.1) as necessary contributors to the construction of a stable funtional democracy.[17]

The regaining of national sovereignty by ECE states has not eliminated the preconceptions that are incompatible with the principles of a democratic community and a democratic culture and involve, in particular, national orientations informed by ethnic-particularist rather than civic-universalist principles. (The latter component has been more prevalent among the Czechs than the Poles and Hungarians.)[18]

---

[16] Whitehead, *International Dimensions of Democratization*, 386; Adam Przeworski, *Sustainable Democracy* (Cambridge: Cambridge University Press, 1995).

[17] See Laszlo Bruszt and Janos Simon, 'Political Culture, Political and Economical Orientations in Central and Eastern Europe during the Transition to Democracy', unpublished manuscript (Budapest: Erasmus Foundation for Democracy, 1992); Renata Siemienska, 'The Changing World of Ideological Conceptions in Central and Eastern Europe', *International Review of Sociology*, 7: 3 (1997), 461–84; Ronald Ingelhart, *Modernization and Postmodernization: Cultural, Economic and Political Change in 43 Societies* (Princeton: Princeton University Press, 1996); Szonja Szelenyi, Ivan Szelenyi, and Winifred Poster, 'Interests and Symbols in Post-Communist Political Culture: The Case of Hungary', *American Sociological Review*, 61: 3 (1996), 466–77; Andre Liebich and Daniel Warner (eds.), *Citizenship East and West* (London: Kegan Paul International, 1995).

[18] On these two traditions of nationalism, see Hans Kohn, *The Idea of Nationalism* (New York: Macmillan, 1960); Walker Connor, *Ethnonationalism: The Quest for Understanding* (Princeton: Princeton University Press, 1994); Liah Greenfeld, *Nationalism: Five Roads to Modernity* (Cambridge, Mass.: Harvard University Press, 1992). On the Czech democratic national tradition, see Jaroslav Krejčí and Pavel Machonín, *Czechoslovakia, 1918–1992* (Oxford: Macmillan, 1994); Ernest Gellner, *Nations and Nationalism* (Oxford: Basil Blackwell, 1983).

Unresolved problems with ethnic minorities inside and outside these three countries contribute to the persistence of exclusive nationalist orientations in the region. Hungary has a large (1.6 million) and discontented minority in Romania and contains itself sizeable and equally dissatisfied populations of Slovaks and Romanians (more than 0.5 million combined). As a result, it is more encumbered by undemocratic popular attitudes than are Poland or the Czech Republic, which have homogeneous ethnic/national compositions and no significant conflicts over minorities with neighbouring countries.[19]

Moreover, the recent influx into those countries of immigrants and refugees from non-European parts of the former Soviet Union, Asia, and Africa has had undemocratic repercussions on residents' perceptions. This influx has been limited: excluding illegal worker-tourists and repatriate nationals from CIS, in 1993 about 10,000 such [im]migrants entered the Czech Republic, 15,000 in Poland, and 15,000 in Hungary; the latter has also received considerably larger inflows of Romanian and Yugoslav refugees. But the appearance of these 'visible aliens' on the streets—a new sight to locals—combined with depictions of refugee camps in the media and discussions about the necessity to feed and house their residents from taxpayer money, have evoked expressions of antipathy and occasional overt aggression against those newcomers in all three ECE countries.[20]

Perhaps the greatest obstacle to the consolidation of democracy 'from below' has been the enduring syndrome of practices that were survival strategies in the communist period. In particular, three related elements of this *homo sovieticus* syndrome—habits of coping with the previous system—are now a hindrance to the construction of a functional democratic order: a popular distrust of public institutions, especially the state, its organs, and functionaries combined with widespread civic apathy, and the pervasive corruption that has made 'beating the system' and 'going

[19] Janusz Bugajski, 'The Fate of Minorities in Eastern Europe', in Larry Diamond and Marc Plattner (eds.), *Nationalism, Ethnic Conflict, and Democracy* (Baltimore: Johns Hopkins University Press, 1994), 102–17; Dusan Sidjanski, 'Is the Re-Emerging Nation-State in Central and Eastern Europe Compatible with the European Union?', in Pierre Allan and Jan Skaloud (eds.), *The Making of Democracy* (Prague: Czech Political Science Association, 1997), 107–20; Maryellen Fullerton, Endre Sik, and Judit Toth (eds.), *From Improvisation toward Awareness? Contemporary Migration Politics in Hungary* (Budapest: Institute for Political Science of the Hungarian Academy of Sciences, 1997).

[20] Frejka, *International Migration.*

around the law' into widely accepted social norms. Whereas the anti-state orientation in Poland had the longest pre-communist history and the broadest social reach during the communist era, these features were also deeply embedded in the other two countries.[21]

After a short period of popular mobilization following the collapse of state-socialist regimes, the deeply rooted habits formed under communist rule combined with the hardships of economic transformation to produce widespread civic anomie or cynicism toward government and a mass withdrawal from political involvement. Social surveys conducted in Poland and Hungary in 1993–4 showed more than 70 per cent of young citizens, including the highly educated, reporting a lack of interest in politics. About three-quarters believed that their influence on public affairs was very limited and that politicians are more interested in retaining power than the good of the country.[22] Perhaps because of the presence of very popular leaders in top political positions, the Czechs in 1994 scored considerably higher than their two ECE neighbours on 'trust in the government': more than 50 per cent of affirmative answers compared to a little more than 20 per cent in Poland and Hungary. In the wake of the corruption scandal involving Prime Minister Vaclav Klaus in 1997, those ratings dropped to levels approaching Poland and Hungary.[23]

Another enduring component of the *homo sovieticus* syndrome has been widespread corruption and nepotism. Ubiquitous under

[21] Vladimir Tismanyanu, *Reinventing Politics: Eastern Europe from Stalin to Havel* (New York: Free Press, 1992); George Schöpflin, *Politics in Eastern Europe, 1945–1992* (Oxford: Blackwell, 1995).

[22] K. Roberts and B. Jung, *Poland's First Post-Communist Generation* (Aldershot: Avebury, 1995); Arpad Szakolczai, 'Re-Building the Polity: A Comparative Study of Mayors in the Hungarian, Czech, and Slovakian Republics', *EUI Working Paper SPS 93/8* (Florence: European University Institute, 1993); 'Podmiotowość Obywatelska Polakow: Poczucie Wplywu na Życie Publiczne' (Centrum Badania Opinii Spolecznej [CBOS], Nov. 1997); 'Nowe Przepisy o Ruchu Granicznym: Pierwsze Reakcje i Oceny' (Centrum Badania Opinii Spolecznej [CBOS], Mar. 1998); Krzysztof Jasiewicz, 'Citizenship in Post-Communist Poland: Civil Society or *Das Volk?*', in Liebich and Warner, *Citizenship East and West*, 79–100; Paul Lewis, 'Democracy and Its Future' in David Held (ed.), *Prospects for Democracy: North, South, East, West* (Cambridge: Polity Press, 1993); Szelenyi, Szelenyi, and Poster, 'Interests and Symbols'; Lena Kolarska-Bobinska, 'Nasza Mala Stabilizacja', *Polityka* (21 Feb. 1998), 30–4.

[23] Richard Rose and Christian Haerpfer, 'New Democracies Barometer III: Learning from What is Happening', *Studies in Public Policy*, 230 (1995), 320–36; Martin Palouš, 'Questions of Czech Citizenship', in Liebich and Warner, *Citizenship East and West*, 141–59; Gabor Toka, 'Political Support in East-Central Europe', in Hans-Dieter Klingemann and Dieter Fuchs (eds.), *Citizens and the State* (Oxford: Oxford University Press, 1995), 355–82.

communist rule, the 'privatization of the public sphere' has persisted into the new era. This has been sustained by the embedded orientation of 'working the system' and a reliance on informal connections and illegitimate means.[24] Current losses to the state treasury in each of ECE countries from unreported earnings in home or Western informal economies, as well as unpaid taxes, have been estimated at billions of dollars annually. (This disrespect for the law and the ensuing losses to the state are even much greater in the more eastern former Soviet republics.[25])

The combination of economic deprivations and frequent changes in the laws regarding taxes, private property, and investment act as an impediment to active popular interest in and involvement on behalf of the consolidation of democracy. The ECE migrants' experience during their sojourns in the West not only does not teach them democratic habits or modify the undemocratic ones to which they are accustomed, but, on the contrary, enhances some of these habits, either by making them useful for migrants' purposes, or through a 'demonstration effect' that shows Western democratic practices as similar to the practices prevalent in migrants' home countries.

The overall politicization of contemporary international migration has made the determination of who can enter, how long they can stay, and what activities they can undertake, entangled in politics and ideology that are negotiated at the national and international levels, well above the heads of the migrants who are

[24] On corruption and nepotism in the communist system, see Zvi Gitelman, 'Working the Soviet System: Citizens and Urban Bureaucracies', in Henry Morton and Robert Stuart (eds.), *The Contemporary Soviet City* (Armonk, NY: M. E. Sharpe, 1984), 221–43; Maria Los, *The Second Economy in Marxist States* (London: Macmillan, 1990); Kenneth Jowitt, *New World Disorder: The Leninist Extinction* (Berkeley and Los Angeles: University of California Press, 1992). On post-communist ECE, see Oleg Kharkhordin, 'The Soviet Individual: Genealogy of a Dissimulating Animal', in Mike Featherstone et al. (eds.), *Global Modernities* (London: Sage, 1994), 209–26; Krejci and Machonin, *Czechoslovakia, 1918–1992*; Endre Sik, 'Network Capital in Capitalist, Communist and Post-communist Societies', *International Contributions to Labor Studies*, 4 (1994), 73–93; Endre Sik, 'The Size of Unregistered Economy in Post-Communist Transformation', unpublished manuscript (1994); *Szara Gospodarka w Polsce: Rozmiary, Przyczyny, Konsekwencje* (Warsaw: Studia i Prace Zaklady Badan Statust.-Ekonom, GUS i PAN, zeszyt, 1996), 233.

[25] Sik, 'Network Capital' and 'Unregistered Economy'; Okolski, 'Poland', 95–110; Marek Grabowski, *Ukryte Dochody i Nierejestrowany Rynek Pracy w Polsce* (Gdansk-Warsaw: Instytut Badan nad Gospodarka Rynkowa, 1994). Stephen Handelman, *Comrade Criminal* (New Haven: Yale University Press, 1995); Karen Dawisha and Bruce Parrott (eds.), *Democratic Changes and Authoritarian Reactions in Russia, Ukraine, Belarus and Moldova* (New York: Cambridge University Press, 1997).

subject to these decisions. At the turn of the twentieth century, these decisions were by and large the prerogative of the migrants themselves, their families, and local communities.[26] Contemporary ECE migrants' subjection to receiver-country limitations on stay duration and work has created a large army of marginalized 'illegal' migrants.

Moreover, the profound economic restructuring of Western countries has produced two processes relevant for the position of ECE migrants. First, the shift towards services-driven economies has been accompanied by a shift towards short-term and flexible production based on versatile companies. Related to it has been a rapid growth of the informal ('third') economic sector, offering variable, usually substandard, wages and no employment security, and largely 'detached' from mainstream advancement/integration opportunities and from the fiscal and welfare systems.[27]

Migrants involved in *Arbeitstourismus* or *Handelstourismus* make up the largest category of ECE travellers to the West. Whereas their predecessors one century ago found themselves at the lowest echelons but within mainstream political and economic

---

[26] Guy Goodwin-Gill, 'International Law and Human Rights: Trends Concerning Migrants and Refugees', in Bruce Mazlish and Ralph Buultjens (eds.), *Conceptualizing Global History* (Boulder, Colo.: Westview Press, 1993), 526–46; Wayne Cornelius, Philip Martin, and James Hollifield (eds.), *Controlling Immigration: A Global Perspective* (Stanford, Calif.: Stanford University Press, 1994); Myron Weiner, *The Global Migration Crisis: Challenge to States and to Human Rights* (Cambridge, Mass.: MIT Press, 1995). At the turn of the century, the entry selection on the part of the receiver societies was based on the arrivals' individual characteristics (e.g. their age, healthy appearance, or criminal record). A precursor of the 'etatization' of international migrations was the German government, which intervened in migratory movements to a considerable extent by limiting the length of stay of the migrant sojourners, particularly those from Eastern Europe. On the sending side, the Russian government imposed, too, (e)migration controls by withholding exit passports for the petitioners from ethnic-national groups or political circles considered 'untrustworthy'. Regarding the relatively open immigration policies of the receiving societies, especially the United States, it should be noted that throughout the entire period of turn-of-the-century mass immigration from South-Eastern Europe there was a heated public debate about the threats posed by those 'culturally inferior' entrants and the means to control their influx until the latter was instituted in the 1920s. See John Higham, *Send These to Me: Jews and Other Immigrants in Urban America* (New York: Atheneum, 1975).

[27] On the emergence of the post-industrial economy and its major features, see Ronald Kent Shelp, *Beyond Industrialization: Ascendancy of the Global Service Economy* (New York: Praeger, 1981); Manuel Castells, *The Informational City: Information Technology, Economic Restructuring, and the Urban-Regional Process* (Oxford: Blackwell, 1988); Saskia Sassen, *The Global City* (Princeton: Princeton University Press, 1991).

structures of the receiving societies, which facilitated their direct experience with democratic practices, contemporary migrants' position as undocumented informal-sector workers or 'grey' or 'black' market traders marginalizes and isolates them from everyday contacts with host country institutions and their representatives.[28]

Contacts that exist are limited. For migrants engaged in illegal work, they involve subordinate relations with native employers and with workers whose employment conditions are better than their own, and with immigration officers combing foreign neighbourhoods and work sites for indocumentados. These contacts are not appropriate for learning the principles of democratic society and culture (elements 6, 7, 10, 11, 12 in Box 6.1). Western employers' search for cheap foreign workers and the eagerness of 'mini-transnational' business enterprises to deal in contraband merchandise reinforce migrants' accustomed undemocratic perceptions. Returnees then reimplant these 're-energized' undemocratic orientations into their home-country economic societies.

ECE migrants' Western experience has contributed to the reinforcement of such preconceptions in yet another way. Long since gone among the dominant sociocultural strata of Western societies is the 'spirit of Progressive Reform' (or its contemporary European social- and Christian-democratic equivalents) that led members of turn-of-the-twentieth-century elites to immigrant neighbourhoods to educate their residents in the practical rights and duties of citizenship. Today, moral philosophers and social scientists deplore the increasing cynicism regarding the principles of the 'democratic creed', growing political distrust and disillusionment, and the dwindling of civic participation.[29]

The media are flooded with Western advertisements and entertainment programmes followed avidly by East Central Europeans at home and during their sojourns in the West. The 'good works' of democracy are scarcely represented, at least not in a way

---

[28] On migrants' isolation from mainstream host societies, see Siewiera, 'Les Immigrés polonais', 71–112; Norbert Cyrus, *Polnische Pendler/innen in Berlin* unpublished manuscript (1995); Norbert Cyrus, 'In Deutschland arbeiten und in Polen leben. Was die neuen WanderarbeiterInnen aus Polen bewegt'; Wladyslaw Misiak, 'Losy i Aktywnosc Polakow w Berlinie (Analiza Wynikow Badan 1994r)', *Słowo*, Special issue on Poles in Berlin (Berlin: Polskie Duszpasterstwo Katolickie, 1995), 23–65; Mydel and Fassmann, *Nielegalni Robotnicy*.

[29] Hans Koechler (ed.), *The Crisis of Representational Democracy* (Frankfurt: Lang, 1987); Robert Entman, *Democracy without Citizens: Media and the Decay of American Politics* (Oxford: Oxford University Press, 1989); Carl Boggs, 'The Great Retreat: Decline of the Public Sphere in the Late Twentieth-Century America', *Theory and Society*, 26: 4 (1997), 741–80.

understandable to foreign viewers without linguistic skills and familiarity with the intricacies of Western politics. These representations
confirm migrants' preconception of democracy as the freedom to mind
one's own business and enjoy ever-proliferating consumer goods.
According to one observer, the 'democratic attitudes' commonly displayed by successful returned migrants express the view that 'what
is important is not that the roads (in their countries) are in a bad
state, but the fact that (they) drive on them in (their) Mercedes'.[30]

Two other factors in the situation of contemporary ECE migrants
during their Western sojourns diminish their opportunities to
become acquainted with the (good) works of democracy and sustain instead their home-bred orientations and behavioural habits:
the-back-and-forth or *pendel* (shuttling) nature of their travels;
and the reluctance of the migrants to organize themselves. In these
regards, too, contemporary migrants differ from their predecessors.
The average duration of turn-of-the-century non-permanent ECE
sojourns to America was three to five years. Visits of their contemporary successors have been of a much shorter duration, ranging
from a couple of days (traders) to a few months to one year (undocumented workers). A significantly increased presence of women
among migrants (they average about 40 per cent of the total as compared with 25 per cent century ago), many of whom are married and
have under-age children at home, has also shortened the duration
of work abroad.

In this situation contemporary migrants' lives during their
sojourns abroad remain immersed in their home-country outlooks
and concerns. Considering that the primary purpose of their travels
is the improvement of the material standards and social status of
their families, not much space is left in the existence of these
migrants to become acquainted with and to absorb new democratic
ideas and practices.

Contemporary ECE migrants' reluctance to organize themselves
—a communist legacy of non-involvement resulting from a gen-
eralized distrust of public institutions—may be understandable.
Undocumented worker migrants prefer to keep a low profile for fear
of being deported (this attitude, however, has been displayed also
by those with legal status). But it not only alienates them further
from opportunities to acquire knowledge of civil society, but also
cuts them off from sources of legal advice and defence, as well as
umbrella organizations, such as the European Union Migrants'

---

[30] Stefan Abner, 'Wizyta w Warszawie', *Kultura* (Dec. 1997), 82–5, esp. 83.

Forum (EUMF) that represent migrants at the national and international levels.[31]

Business and 'Brain Exchange' Re-/Expatriates: The Promise of Democratization?

With the removal of passport and tourist visa restrictions after the collapse of communist regimes in East Central Europe, another kind of international traveller has been emerging 'at the top' of that region's social structures. Provided the stabilization of the democratic legal-institutional structures in ECE, these new travellers – highly skilled resident and émigré/expatriate ECEs and visiting Western managers, businesspeople, professional consultants, and so on—with (considerable) time might, if not replace the now prevalent types, at least overcome or neutralize their contrary effects through repercussions from their 'good works'.

These new international migrants can be classified into four categories: (1) a minority of *Handels-* and *Arbeitstouristen* who became owners of small to medium-size enterprises; (2) highly skilled ECE migrants, including business executives, managers, and scientists who have made regular professional trips to the West; (3) highly skilled ECE émigrés from the post-war period who have repatriated or, as is more common, 'shuttle' to and from their native countries; and (4) 'expat' Western specialists, consultants, managers of international companies, researchers, and others who have gone to ECE for professional purposes.

The professional activities pursued by these travellers, and their secure positions both in the sending and the receiving societies, make these migrants into 'natural allies' of the democratic order. However, their different social-institutional locations, life experiences, and habits, as well as the purposes of their activities, affect their relationship with the democratization process in ECE in different ways: 10–15 per cent of ECE tourist-workers and tourist-traders have invested the money they earned in the West to fund their own businesses, often (registered) joint ventures with Western partners, in their local communities. They have thus acquired legal status and moved into the formal sector of the

---

[31] Jurgen Fijalkowski, 'Solidarités intra-communautaires et formations d'associations au sein de la population étrangère d'Allemagne', *Revue européenne des migrations internationales*, 10: 1 (1994), 33–51; Mydel and Fassmann, *Nielegalni Robotnicy*; Misiak, 'Losy i Aktywnosc'; Siewiera, 'Les Immigrér polonais'.

economy. For these fledgling businesses to prosper, a consolidated and stable legal-institutional democratic environment is needed. The limited evidence that exists suggests that these migrants support the consolidation of democracy not only in their home countries in general but also in their local communities.[32] However, democracy may lose the support of this emerging group if its representatives opt for larger revenues from illegal big business. The slower the democratic consolidation in the upper layers of the ECE political and economic societies, the greater is the likelihood that smaller-to-middle local establishments will move into that avenue. Conversely, although with a more gradual impact, the greater the number of local-level supporters of democracy among new businessmen, including international migrants, the greater the chance that the upper-state echelons will contribute to the consolidation of democracy.

Highly skilled international travellers, the second group considered here, constituted about 12–14 per cent of the total number of temporary westbound migrants (excluding 'pure' tourists) from each of the three countries by the mid-1990s.[33] These are managers of successful private businesses, service and production centres, including those owned by joint-venture and multinational companies that employ increasing numbers of highly skilled native workers competent in foreign languages, scientists, and researchers, including graduate and postgraduate students on Western fellowships.[34]

---

[32] Barbara Cieślinśka, *Male miasto w procesie przemian w latach 1988–1994: Monografia socjologiczna Moniek* (Bialystok: Wydawnictwo FUW, 1997), and personal communication to this author (28 Feb. 1998); Misiak, 'Losy i Aktywnosc', and personal communication to this author (3 Mar. 1998).

[33] Christopher Ulrich, 'The Price of Freedom: The Criminal Threat in Russia, Eastern Europe and the Baltic Region', Working Paper in the Conflict Series published by the Research Institute for the Study of Conflict and Terrorism (1–30 Oct. 1994). *Briefing on Crime and Corruption in Russia* (Washington, DC: Commission on Security and Cooperation in Europe, 10 June 1994).

[34] Estimates of highly skilled migrants compiled from: Berencsi and Sik, 'Intentions to Emigrate'; Juhasz, 'Hungary'; Vladimir Cermak, 'Talents in Migration Process', Paper presented at the International Conference 'Central and Eastern Europe New Migration Space', Pultusk, Poland (11–13 Dec. 1997); Slany, *Orientacje Emigracyjne Polakow*. See also D. Hottbrugge, *Personalbeschaffung in Mittel- und Osteuropa: Ergebnisse einer empirischen Untersuchung*, Universität Dortmund, Arbeitspapiere des Lehrstuhls für Unternehmensfuhrung, No. 17 (1994); D. Redor, 'Les Migrations de spécialistes hautement qualifiés entre l'Europe centrale et l'Union Européenne: analyse et perspective', *Revue d'études comparatives Est–Ouest* (3 Sept. 1994), 161–78; Felicitas Hillmann and Hedwig Rudolph, 'Au-delà de la "fuite des cervaux": la mobilité des personnes hautement qualifiés de l'ouest vers la Pologne', *Revue européenne des migrations internationales*, 13 (1997), 71–92; Cermak, 'Talents in Migration Process'.

The socio-demographic profile of these migrants—most are under 35 years of age with graduate or postgraduate education, professional occupation, and residents of large urban centres—locates them in a social group that is better informed than others about public affairs, and more likely to identify with an idea of inclusive civic-political participation (element II/7 in Box 6.1), and to support rules of democratic governance (I/1–5, III 9, 11, 12).[35] These migrants' professional activities, and their participation in international institutional and social networks informed by democratic practices, enhance these orientations and provide a 'training ground' to turn preferences into habitual behavioural patterns.

Two actual and two potential problems exist regarding the impact of these ECE migrants on democratic consolidation in their home countries. One of the actual problems has been the persistence of 'brain drain' emigration. Although it has significantly diminished since the early 1990s, it continues to deplete members of the youngest cohorts, namely, graduate and postgraduate students. The other problem has been the reported reliance by these new ECE managers and businessmen on informal 'crony' rather than legal-institutional avenues to manage their professional affairs.[36] The more effective democratic consolidation in ECE becomes, the more likely are its international migrants to rely on legal-institutional channels. And, in turn, increases in the number of such migrants making their native countries the permanent or semi-permanent bases of their professional activities and playing by the (institutional) rules favour the consolidation of democracy.

Two potential problems exist. First, the transnational professional activities and institutional networks, and also the lifestyles of international travellers, locate them in what Robert Dahl (1989), has called the third, global stage of democracy, which evolved from lower-level historical formations, the (premodern) local community and the (modern) nation-state.[37] Eastern Europe has already had an unfortunate experience with 'jumping stages' (the Marxian

---

[35] Gerd Meyer (ed.), *Die politischen Kulturen Ostmitteleuropas im Umbruch* (Tübingen: Francke Verlag, 1993); Liebich and Warner, *Citizenship East and West*.

[36] Janusz Hryniewicz, Bogdan Jalowiecki, and Andrzej Mync, *Ucieczka Mozgow z Nauki i Szkolnictwa Wyzszego w Polsce w latach 1992–1993* (Warsaw: Studia Regionalne i Lokalne UW, 1994); Cermak, 'Talents in Migration Process'; Slany, *Orientacje Emigracyjne Polakow*; Kazimierz Frieske, 'Instytucjonalny Pluralizm czy Personalne Wpływy?', Working paper (Warsaw: Friedrich Ebert Stiftung, 1997); Janina Wedel, 'The Unintended Consequences of Western Aid to Post-Communist Europe', *Telos* (Summer 1992), 131–8.

[37] Walzer, *Toward a Global Ciril Society*.

'iron model' of historical development wherein communism was to issue from mature capitalism but not from the post-feudal/ proto-capitalist socio-economic order). Could this work this time? Could local- and national-level democracy develop 'from above' or from a global democratic order? There are, of course, no ready answers to these questions, except perhaps the recognition that the greatly increased interconnectedness of different parts and 'levels' may facilitate such a development to a greater extent than in the past.

Second, these migrants' involvement with democracy in their professional activities is limited to its procedural aspects, leaving out the participatory dimension (elements II/6 and III/9a in Box 6.1). A civil society whose members support not only the negative freedom from oppression but also the positive freedom to participate in public affairs and contribute to the common good is a *sine qua non* for democratic consolidation. This orientation-cum-practice is very much missing in post-communist ECE societies where civic apathy is widespread. In this context, the nearly exclusive emphasis on procedural democracy and the neglect of its participatory dimension in the experience of highly skilled ECE international migrants appears overly restricted in regard to the broader-scope needs of their societies as they build whole new democratic orders.

Returned ECE émigrés from the communist era are the third category of migrants whose professional activities are likely to contribute to the consolidation of democracy in that region. More than 3 million citizens of Poland, Hungary, and Czechoslovakia combined (Poles making up more than a half of that number) either stayed on in the West as displaced persons (DPs) after the conclusion of the Second World War and the imposition of communist rule in East Central Europe or left during the fifty years it endured. The proportion of college educated professionals among those émigrés was high, around 25–30 per cent.[38] After 1989–90, encouraged by post-communist governments eager to establish links with potential allies abroad to negotiate reintegration with the West, considerable numbers of these émigrés repatriated or returned to their native countries on long professional sojourns. Estimates in the mid-1990s

---

[38] Estimates, excluding German *Aussiedlers*, compiled from Okolski, 'Poland'; Juhasz, 'Hungary'; Maresova, 'Czech Republic'; Krejci and Machonin, *Czechoslovakia, 1918–1992*; Zoltan Dovenyi and Gabriella Vukovich, 'Ungarn und die Internationale Migration', in Fassmann and Munz, *European Migration*, 263–84; Slany, *Orientacje Emigracyjne Polakow*.

of these two categories combined ranged from 10,000–15,000 in the Czech Republic to 20,000–5,000 in Poland and Hungary.[39]

These repatriates hold multiple residences, citizenships, and memberships in professional organizations in several countries. They represent a wide variety of specialists from investors of capital, (co)owners of production and service establishments, to financial consultants, privatization experts, consultants of the market economy and management, international lawyers, political scientists, and organizational sociologists.[40] Their professional expertise and simultaneous involvement with Western (sending) companies and organizations and with ECE (receiver) institutions and people allow those specialists to demonstrate and teach the latter 'hands on' the rules and procedures of functional democracy in their respective economic and political societies. In particular, they teach the art of 'democratic craftsmanship' or the deliberative-negotiatory methods of solving conflicts and formulating consensus and respect for democratically implemented laws and policies of public institutions, even if they are disliked (elements I/5 and III/11 and 12 in Box 6.1). Unlike representatives of the second category of international migrants, whose democratizing activities concentrate predominantly in the largest urban centres, repatriates have also based themselves in provincial centres and small communities.[41] As a result, the effects of their activities have had a broader social reach.

The democratic effects of repatriates' activities have been limited, however, by their almost exclusively procedural character. Another constraint has been the undemocratic impact of the 'diaspora legacy' imported by some re-émigré activists engaged in the

[39] Estimates compiled from Juhasz, 'Hungary; Maria Redei, 'Internal Brain Drain', in Fullerton, Sik, and Toth, *Refugees and Migrants*, 105–18; Marešová, 'Czech Republic'; Okolski, 'Poland'; Ewa Wilk, 'Najazd Ekspatow', *Polityka* (9 Aug. 1997), 3–8. Also author's communications with Judit Juhasz and Hedwig Rudolph (7–16 Mar. 1998).

[40] See Geoffrey Pridham and Tatu Vanhanen (eds.), *Democratization in Eastern Europe* (London: Routledge, 1994); Michael Kennedy and Pauline Gianoplus, 'Entrepreneurs and Expertise: A Cultural Encounter in the Making of Post-Communist Capitalism in Poland', *East European Politics and Societies*, 8: 1 (1994), 58–93; Juhasz, 'Hungary'; Hillmann and Rudolph, 'Au-delà de la "fuite des cervaux"'; Misiak, 'Losy i Aktywność', and Misiak's communication to the author (3 Mar. 1998); Okolski, 'Poland'; Cermak, 'Talents in Migration Process'.

[41] Morawska, *Recent East–West European Migrants and Their Social Micro-Environments in a Comparative-Historical Perspective*; Misiak, 'Losy i Aktywnosc', and Misiak's communication to the author (3 Mar. 1998); Leszek Goldyka et al. (eds.), *Transgranicznosc w Perspektywie Socjologicznej* (Zielona Gora: Poligrafia Politechniki Zielonogorskiej, 1997); Cieślinśka, *Małe miasto w procesie przemian w latach 1988–1994*, and Cieślinśka's communication to the author (1 Mar. 1998).

political arena. This has included the 'totalizing antitotalitarianism', on the one hand, and belligerent nationalism (enemies of the democratic consolidation elements 7, 9 and 11 in Box 6.1) on the other.[42]

The last group to be considered are highly skilled Western expatriates who come to ECE in business and professional capacities similar (although usually in higher positions within their organizations) to those of the majority of ECE re-emigrants. This has been a rapidly growing population: the 1995 estimates of college-educated longer-term work permit holders of non-ECE backgrounds from Western Europe and North America were more than double the figures three years prior, standing at about 25,000 to 30,000 in each of the three countries. The number of short-term Western business visitors has been much larger. The average age of these expatriate migrant experts is 40–5, and the largest proportions of them are from Germany, the United States, Austria, Great Britain, and France.[43]

The skills brought into the ECE institutions by such Western professionals are similar to those noted in the discussion of highly trained re-emigrants and the emerging stratum of ECE business and professional globetrotters. Studies of ECE employees' performance in Western/international firms and organizations suggest that on the job they learn democratic procedures, elements of political culture (III/11 and 12 in Box 6.1), as well as active responsibility for 'the whole' (III/9a), in this case, the employer-institution.[44]

Two potential problems related to the proliferation of Western/multinational companies should be noted. A decade of experience with nascent capitalist democracy has significantly undermined its popular representation in ECE as the paradise system of economic affluence for all. The 'velvet revolution' period of 1989–90, when 'us' meant the united people and 'them' the collapsing communist regime, gave way to a perception of 'us' as struggling citizens versus 'them' comprising the new political and economic elites. ECE

---

[42] There existed, of course, important exceptions. A polyvalent civic-cultural and universalist national orientation has been consistently represented, for example, by the Polish émigré journal *Kultura* published in Paris since 1947; see Krzysztof Pomian, *Rozmowy z Jerzym Giedroyciem* (Warsaw, 1997).

[43] Estimates compiled from: Juhasz, 'Hungary'; Wilk, 'Najazd Ekspatow'; Redei, 'Internal Brain Drain'; Hillmann and Rudolph, 'Au-delà de la "fuite des cervaux"'; Krystyna Iglicka, 'Recent Immigration into Poland', Paper presented at the International Conference 'Central and Eastern Europe—New Migration Space', Pultusk, Poland (11–13 Dec. 1997); Maresova, 'Czech Republic', and personal communications from the authors (6–20 Mar. 1998).

[44] Wilk, 'Najazed Ekspatow'; Hillmann and Rudolph, 'Au-delà de la "fuite des cervaux"'; Kennedy and Gianoplus, 'Entrepreneurs and Expertise'.

employees of international firms, paid four to eight times more than average local wages, have been viewed as an integral part of the new 'them'. Could training for the incorporation of top skilled ECEs into world elite global commuters, rather than broadening the base for the trickle down of democratic patterns to their societies at large, contribute instead to the kind of hardening of the division between super- (educated, earning, and interconnected) and underclasses familiar in highly developed post-industrial societies?

Should a development in this direction actually take place, it could be still more complicated. ECE employees of multinational companies usually occupy lower-level positions in these firms, earning two to three times less, and with lower ceilings on their promotion opportunities than their Western colleagues. The ECE employees themselves talk about their Western co-workers living in 'their own [separate] world' because of the 'contents of their wallets'.[45] This situation may well be temporary. With the passage of time, as Poland, Hungary, and the Czech Republic join the European Union and as long as their economic transformations progress successfully, the positions and prospects of talented natives may well come to equal those of their Western peers. But this may not happen, in which case East Central Europe together with its highly skilled international-firm employees will remain 'poor partners' in the antechambers of world democratic capitalism dominated by its Western 'core'.

Conclusion

The purpose of this discussion has been to initiate a conversation between specialists in transnational migration and experts in democratization. Both of these processes have been shaped by international events, and their conditioning factors and outcomes have partially overlapped. I have argued that the ways in which they are linked have been far from straightforward, which makes the investigation of the relationship between contemporary transnational migrations and democratization processes more complex and interesting.

This examination of the impact of contemporary migration on democratic consolidation has produced two main conclusions. First, the contribution to the democratization process of the vast

---

[45] Hillmann and Rudolph, 'Au-delà de la "fuite des cervaux"'; Hottbrugge, *Personalbeschaffung*; Redei, 'Internal Brain Drain'; Wilk, 'Najazd Ekspatow', 5–6.

majority of contemporary ECE migrants to the West, *Handels-* and *Arbeitstouristen*, has been practically non-existent. If anything, their impact has been negative, sustaining rather than diminishing accustomed undemocratic ways in their home societies. In explaining this phenomenon, I have identified several macro- and micro-level factors in the sending (ECE) and receiving (WE/USA) environments of migration that have had a cumulative effect on making this experience irrelevant or even damaging to the consolidation of democracy in migrants' native societies. To bring into sharper relief the relationship between contemporary ECE migrations and the democratization processes in their home countries, I have set this discussion against a contrasting pattern of the migration-democracy connection that obtained one century ago during the period (1880–1914) or mass rural migrations from East Central Europe to America.

Second, the 1990s have seen the emergence of a heterogeneous group of highly skilled international travellers to and from ECE. Their structural location in the sending and receiving countries, and their professional activities in ECE, have provided them with opportunities to contribute to the implantation of the 'hard' and 'soft' skills needed to operate in democratic economic and political societies. However, their contributions have had serious limitations. Given the widespread persistence in post-communist ECE societies of the *ancien régime* legacy of civic apathy it is regrettable that the highly skilled migrants have been involved almost exclusively with the procedural aspects of democracy to the neglect of its participatory dimension. With their primarily big-city, narrow-elite contacts they are able to influence the top echelons of the restructuring East Central European societies but barely, if at all, penetrate their larger segments.

More specifically focused investigations of the effects of international migrations on democratization processes in the turn-of-the-twenty-first-century world are obviously needed for a better-grounded assessment of this relationship. This chapter has shown that taking into account transnational migrations reveals the impact of the international contexts on democratic consolidation as much more problematic than some consolidologists have claimed. Using evidence from migration studies to access the impact of international movements on democratic consolidation makes such studies more relevant to those interested in democratization. This initial exercise has, hopefully, demonstrated the epistemic and possible policy gains which can result from the rapprochement of these two fields of inquiry.

Appendix

Contacted ECE migration and democratization specialists, and authors of studies who provided additional information for this article (in alphabetical order):

Vladimir Čermak, Barbara Cieślinśka, Norbert Cyrus, Jeroen Doomernik, Heinz Fassmann, Tomas Frejka, Leszek Gołdyka, Adam Grzeszak, Krystyna Iglicka, Judit Juhasz, Mirosława Marody, Silvia Mihalikova, Władysław Misiak, Jana Reschova, Hedwig Rudolph, Andrzej Sadowski, Renata Siemieńska, Beata Siewiera, Endre Sik, Krystyna Slany, Wisła Surazska, Victor Susak, Eva Uhlirova.

7

Crime, Corruption, and Politics: Transnational Factors

Leslie Holmes

According to a 1998 article in the London *Times*, a two-year study on organized crime in Russia conducted by an agency close to the CIA concluded that such activity 'constitutes a direct threat to the national security interest of the United States by fostering instability in a nuclear-armed power'.[1] Another analyst summarized the significance of the rise of Russian organized crime as follows: 'The emergence of the Russian mafia is the major development in transnational organized crime in the 1990s.'[2] While such assessments might appear sensationalist, they are only two of numerous similar ones that have been published in the West in recent years.[3]

I wish to thank Alex Pravda and Yves Mény, in particular, for their constructive comments on an earlier version of this paper. All interpretations and errors remain my responsibility, of course.

[1] J. Lloyd, 'Red Alert', *The Times* (magazine) (31 Jan. 1998), 24–31 at 27. Although Lloyd's article does not specify the full details of his source, it is in fact William H. Webster (ed.), *Russian Organized Crime: Global Organized Crime Project* (Washington: Center for Strategic and International Studies, 1997); the sections on the nuclear threat can be found at 19–22 and 61–3.

[2] Guy Dunn, 'Major Mafia Gangs in Russia', in Phil Williams, *Russian Organized Crime* (London: Cass, 1997), 63.

[3] Perhaps the best-known and most readily accessible sensationalist analysis of the threat to the West of post-communist criminality is Claire Sterling, *Crime without Frontiers: The Worldwide Expansion of Organized Crime and the Pax Mafiosa* (London: Warner, 1995). See also B. Freemantle, *The Octopus* (London: Orion, 1995); one of the more bizarre forms of crime in which organized gangs have become involved in recent years, and on which Freemantle focuses (see 146–55), is trade in human body parts. In marked contrast to these sensationalist approaches is J. Bäckman's study, *The Inflation of Crime in Russia* (Helsinki: National Research Institute of Legal Policy, 1998). Bäckman suggests that the West's focus on post-communist (especially Russian) criminality and its internationalization is a

Moreover, even if such assessments overdramatize the situation—and whether they do or not is a matter of judgement rather than fact—there is no doubting that crime rates in Central and Eastern Europe (hereafter CEE) and the Former Soviet Union (the FSU) have increased, in many cases substantially, since the collapse of communist power, and that the ramifications of criminality in many of these countries extend far beyond national boundaries.

The rise and internationalization of crime and corruption, in which the formerly communist states are clearly playing a significant role, has serious implications for both established democracies and democratizing countries. Several of the various forms this threat assumes will emerge in the course of this chapter; at their most extreme, substantial rises in the proportion of illegality in international economic activity can destabilize national economies, which in turn can engender serious social and political problems and instability. At this juncture, the fundamental point to be made is that the dangers are even greater in democratizing or transitional states, since they are more fragile. Since the cultures of both liberal democracy and the rule of law are less internalized in these countries, they are less secure; this is particularly true if citizens in post-communist countries associate criminality with the democratization and marketization projects.

Unfortunately, detailed survey data on this issue of mass perceptions in CEE and FSU states of a linkage between criminality and democratization are still scarce. However, a recent analysis of post-communist states by Richard Rose and others, based on John Reed's 1995 assessment of levels of corruption, drew the following conclusion:

The presence or absence of the rule of law, as measured by the corruption index, shows a significant correlation with regime support. The higher the level of corruption in a new democracy, the less likely individuals are to

---

function of the ending of the Cold War; in an ideological void, the West needs a new 'threat' from a new 'other'. While Bäckman's deconstructionist argument is interesting and for the most part well made, it goes too far; the increase in crime in most post-communist countries, and the internationalization of such crime, *is* a legitimate cause for concern, even if it is important to keep the situation in perspective. For a scholarly analysis and interpretation of both the sensationalist and the overly sanguine approaches to post-communist organized crime, at least with respect to Russia, see Phil Williams, 'Introduction: How Serious a Threat is Russian Organized Crime?', in Williams, *Russian Organized Crime*, 1–27. One other useful—if often more polemical—source on Russian organized crime is part 5 of P. Ryan and G. Rush (eds.), *Understanding Organized Crime in Global Perspective* (Thousand Oaks, Calif.: Sage, 1997), 149–200.

support the new regime (–.24) and the higher the current level of corruption, the less likely individuals are to reject undemocratic alternatives (–.21).[4]

Moreover, there is abundant evidence that many CEE and FSU citizens link democratization (i.e. a political process) and market reforms (an economic process), treating them as two dimensions of a single phenomenon even though there is no *necessary* connection between them. Unfortunately, the problems of early post-communism have meant that democratization and market reforms often conflict with each other; criminality can thrive in such a contradictory situation.

It is hypothesized here that the post-communist regimes have experienced legitimacy problems because of popular perceptions that the new putatively democratizing systems are in many cases at least too tolerant of the new criminality, and in some cases directly involved with and benefiting from it. This association in the public's mind between increased criminality on the one hand, and the democratization and marketization/privatization projects on the other, is a complex one. Recent research conducted by a team based at the University of Glasgow suggests that many citizens in at least some post-communist states still support the abstract concepts of democracy and the market economy, but mistrust the actual politicians and state officials who are charged with implementing the transition to these.[5] Acknowledging these research findings, this chapter argues that—perhaps counter-intuitively—this distinction between theory and practice makes the whole democratization and marketization project more difficult and fragile. Too prolonged a serious disjuncture between the abstract concepts and perceived reality could undermine public support for the former.

Unfortunately, the democratization process in CEE and FSU has been rendered even more problematical by the frequently low-key or ambivalent responses of the international community towards post-communist criminality. Despite the increase in crime in the post-communist world and its internationalization, the West's

---

[4] Richard Rose, William Mishler, and Christian Haerpfer, *Democracy and its Alternatives* (Cambridge: Polity, 1998), 188; see too ibid. 221–3. The corruption index used by Rose et al. is J. Reed's, in his 'The Great Growth Race', *Central European Economic Review* (Dec. 1995), 9–11; Reed's evaluation of the relative level of corruption in various post-communist states is broadly in line with Transparency International's—see text accompanying n. 84 below.

[5] Åse Grødeland, T. Koshechkina, and William Miller, '"In theory correct, but in practice . . .": Public Attitudes to Really Existing Democracy in Ukraine, Bulgaria, Slovakia and the Czech Republic', *Journal of Communist Studies and Transition Politics*, 14: 3 (1998), 1–23.

attitude towards this phenomenon has often been confused and confusing. On the one hand, influential actors such as David Veness, head of the organized crime unit at London's Scotland Yard, have publicly warned that the primary threat to inner cities in the UK by the late 1990s will be from criminals originating from CEE and Russia.[6] On the other hand, although the situation has improved recently, with states, transnational organizations, and TNCs (transnational corporations) all now adopting a more critical stance towards international corruption and organized crime, there is a danger of this being a case of 'too little, too late'.

Such mixed responses have understandably led some citizens in the transition states to wonder if they are observing a new version of 1938; while the West proclaims its commitment to democracy and the rule of law, it has seemed reluctant to take as firm a stand on transgressions of these as many in the post-communist countries would prefer. Sometimes, its primary concern appears to some to be marketization and privatization at almost any cost, with the consolidation of democracy and the fight against crime only a secondary objective.

Yet many CEE and FSU citizens appear to *want* the West to play a greater role in combating criminality, especially among state officials. This point has been strongly suggested by the Glasgow team's findings in four post-communist states that a clear majority of respondents in all these countries would consider international pressure (for example, in the form of withholding aid or investment) to be a 'good way' of forcing their own governments to tackle corruption; the percentages supporting this position range from 59 per cent in Slovakia to 78 per cent in Bulgaria, with the Czech Republic and Ukraine both at 68 per cent.[7]

As already indicated, there have been signs that the international community has now woken up to the threat posed to it by the criminality of the post-communist world. One analyst has argued that it is the rapidly growing awareness of corruption precisely in the *transition* economies that has led international agencies such as the IMF and the World Bank to focus on this problem in the 1990s.[8]

---

[6] Cited in Stephen Handelman, *Comrade Criminal* (London: Michael Joseph, 1994), 244.

[7] William Miller, Åse Grødeland, and T. Koshechkina, 'What is to be Done about Corrupt Officials? Public Opinion and Reform Strategies in Postcommunist Europe', *International Review of Administrative Sciences*, forthcoming in 65: 2 (1999), 8 in original manuscript (kindly provided by Prof. William Miller).

[8] M.-C. Bonzom, 'IMF: Anti-corruption Champion?', *African Business* (Nov. 1997) (downloaded from http://www.africaria.com/icpubs/ab/nov97/abis1101.htm).

It can only be hoped that this new-found commitment to fighting crime is genuine and will prove effective.

Yet while the international community's (especially the West's) role is very important in bringing post-communist criminality under control, ultimately it is these countries themselves that must bear the primary responsibility. Unless they do, the viability of both the marketization and democratization projects will be jeopardized.

The objectives of this chapter are fourfold, and correspond approximately with its main sections. The first is to provide a brief overview of the crime situation in the region, highlighting changes in rates of crime, and what kinds of crimes are increasing most. Given the scale and nature of a chapter like this, only a broad brush stroke picture can be drawn. But it will be possible on the basis of the available information and analyses to contrast countries in which crime is clearly playing a significant role in disrupting both domestic and international security with those in which, while being a problem, the overall international significance of crime should not be exaggerated.

The second and third parts of the chapter are concerned with the second objective, namely to explain the phenomena identified in the first in terms of both domestic and international/transnational factors, and the interplay of these. In the fourth section, the implications of the rise in crime for the whole democratization and transition project are assessed. Following this, the fifth section provides an overview of international responses to crime in CEE and FSU states. The conclusions to the chapter locate the criminalization issue in the broader one of the problems of post-communist transition, particularly democratic consolidation.

Crime in the CEE and FSU States

One of the many areas in which the situation has improved in comparison with the communist era is in the provision of official statistics on crime. This has been a function of two developments. The first has resided in the moves towards greater state transparency that is rightly seen by most post-communist politicians and officials as a necessary component of the democratization process. Second, the break-up of the USSR, the SFRY, and Czechoslovakia has meant that many statistics that were previously provided only in aggregated form for a whole federation are now provided for each of the successor states.

TABLE 7.1. *Registered crime rates in selected post-communist and Western states (official rates per 100,000 population)*

	1985	1989	1990	1991	1992	1993	1994	1995	1996	1997
Belarus	586	655	741	792	937	998	1161	1276	1236	1251
Bulgaria			702	2,081	2,544	2,912	2,532	2,340		
Czech R.		1,175	2,517	2,748	3,450	3,854	3,604	3,636	3,820	3,916
Estonia	969	1,217	1,504	2,007	2,670	2,450	2,360	2,653		
Georgia		327		402	443	406	325	290	267	255
Hung.	1,556	2,129	3,287	4,017	4,065	3,889	3,789	4,885		
Latvia	972	1,107	1,291		2,350	2,437	2,360			
Lith.		844	995	1,202	1,513	1,619	1,576	1,637	1,835	1,143
Mold.		942	987	1,021	1,113	1,094	1,094	1,112	1,028	
Poland	1,463	1,442	2,306	2,261	2,293	2,217	2,351	2,527	2,325	2,568
Roman.		210	276	612	636	964	1,039	1,305		
Russia	990	1,099	1,243	1,459	1,857	1,885	1,775	1,860	1,777	1,629
Slovak.			1,000+	1,670		2,743	2,571	2,134		
Sloven.				2,139	2,739	2,242	2,210	1,933		
Ukraine		625	717	780	921	1,034	1,102	1,246	1,208	1,162
Germany		7,031	7,046		7,837	8,316	8,030	8,166		
UK[a]		7,654	8,949	10,349	10,924	10,760	10,194	9,862	9,684	
USA	5,207	5,741	5,820	5,898	5,660	5,483	5,374	5,278		

[a] England and Wales only.

Sources: See n. 9.

The data[9] suggest that there was a noticeable increase in crime at the beginning of the 1990s; the rate more or less doubled very rapidly in some countries, approximately tripled in Bulgaria (between 1990 and 1991) and Hungary (cf. the 1985 and 1995 figures), and increased more than sixfold in Romania between 1989 and 1995. However, the official statistics indicate that the rate of increase of recorded crimes had slowed down perceptibly, or even been slightly reversed, in most countries by the mid-1990s.[10] The data also suggest that there was a marked increase in criminality in the earliest days of post-communism compared with the late communist period. While this *might* have been the case, two points need to be borne in mind. The first is that communist authorities in many countries used to massage data for political purposes. This point was made explicitly by the then head of the Soviet Statistical Office, V. Kirichenko, when he wrote in 1990 that:

In truth, for decades the prevailing stance has been to demonstrate successes and advantages, to keep silent about difficulties and negative features in the development of the country and its regions. Statistics, as well as theory, were assigned a perverted ideological function of forming the

[9] Data are mostly either taken directly from national official statistical year-books of the respective countries, or else calculated by the author on the basis of other data contained in those yearbooks (primarily the total number of recorded crimes and the total population figures); most of the data from CIS countries are from the 1997 or 1998 CIS *Statisticheskii Spravochnik*. Other sources used include K. Engelbrekt, 'Toward the Rule of Law: Bulgaria', *RFE/RL Research Report*, 1: 27 (1992), 4–9; Jiri Pehe, 'Crime Rises in Czechoslovakia', *RFE/RL Research Report*, 1: 14 (1992), 55–9; S. Girnius, 'Crime Rate in Lithuania Rises Sharply', *RFE/RL Research Report*, 2: 31 (1993), 50–3; S. Girnius, 'Lithuania Makes Modest Progress in Fight against Crime', *RFE/RL Research Report*, 3: 7 (1994), 24–8; Jiri Pehe, 'Czech Republic's Crime Rate Slows Down', *RFE/RL Research Report*, 3: 8 (1994), 43–8; R. Lotspeich, 'Crime in the Transition Economies', *Europe-Asia Studies*, 47: 4 (1995), 555–89; A. Muth (ed.), *Statistical Abstract of the World* (Detroit: Gale, 1997); J. Burianek, 'Democratization, Crime, Punishment and Public Attitudes in the Czech Republic', *Crime, Law and Social Change*, 28: 3–4 (1997–8), 213–22; The *Statesman's Year-Book* (various years); and the *International Crime Statistics* yearbooks produced by Interpol. I have used the last of these only as a last resort, since the figures are exclusively police statistics, not judicial statistics; this said, a comparison of them with the statistics reproduced in or generated from national statistical yearbooks reveals that the figures are either identical (as in Hungary or Russia), or else so similar that the difference is of marginal significance—especially in light of the argument here about not over-fetishizing the data.

[10] For a reasonably up-to-date table comparing the growth or decline in reported crime rates in all CIS countries between 1996 and 1997 see *SNG Statisticheskii Byulleten*, 17 (Sept. 1997), 36. This revealed a decline of nearly 10 per cent in Russia, while the CIS country with the highest growth rate in reported crime was Moldova.

illusion of the well-being and infallibility of the command-administrative system.[11]

Since high crime rates could have been interpreted as reflecting badly on the effectiveness of the communist state, there was clear justification for being sceptical about crime statistics from the communist era.

The second reason has been that citizens may have become more willing to report crime in the early post-communist era, given changed attitudes towards the state. Unfortunately, this factor can operate in radically different ways. Thus, the apparent slowdown in the growth of criminality in many countries by the mid-1990s *could* be partly a function of growing cynicism about the state and its agents. If people trust the state less than they did—whether in the sense that they see it as being less effective than they had previously believed, or in the more sinister sense that its own officers are perceived to be colluding with criminals—they might report crime less.[12]

One other point to emerge clearly from the table is that, assuming the data are not *too* inaccurate, crime rates in the post-communist states have remained considerably below those of many leading Western states. However, there has been a popular perception that there is a much higher proportion of serious—often very violent—organized crime in many post-communist states.[13] Some idea of why this perception has gained ground is provided by the statistics on organized crime. For instance, according to a Russian source cited by Bäckman, the number of registered crimes

[11] Cited in Secretariat of the Economic Commission for Europe, *Economic Survey of Europe in 1989–90* (New York: United Nations, 1990), 82.

[12] For survey results on levels of trust in CEE states see William Mishler and Richard Rose, 'Trust, Distrust and Skepticism about Institutions of Civil Society', *Studies in Public Policy*, 252 (Glasgow: CSPP at the University of Strathclyde, 1995). For survey evidence suggesting that Polish citizens were opposed in the early to mid-1990s to private sponsorship of various state agencies, largely because this could lead to collusion and corruption, see Centrum Badania Opinii Społecznej, *Sponsorowanie Instytucji Państwowych a Korupcja i Łapownictwo* (Warsaw: CBOS, Mar. 1994).

[13] Unfortunately, as with so many aspects of this research area, there is no systematic set of cross-polity longitudinal survey data to 'prove' this point. But one indication of the problem is the fact that over-time survey analysis conducted by the respected Polish organization CBOS during the mid-1990s indicated that 'the feeling of being threatened by rising crime and the activities of various mafias has clearly increased (up by 22 percentage points)'; in fact, by February 1996, it was clearly the biggest concern for Poles, according to a survey of 1,205 respondents conducted in that month—ahead of poverty, health, unemployment, etc. See CBOS, *Polish Public Opinion* (Feb. 1996), 3.

committed by organized crime groups in Russia in 1995 was 19,604; this represented a substantial increase on the 1990 figure of 3,515.[14] There has also been a marked increase in bombing in countries that were long considered to be relatively peaceful. According to the *Baltic Independent*, there were no fewer than 150 bombings reported in Lithuania in 1993, of which 31 were in the capital (Vilnius),[15] while in the first eleven months of 1995, 17 large bombs were exploded in the Estonian capital of Tallinn;[16] in both cases, the bombings were attributed primarily to protectionism and turf wars associated with organized crime.

Such activity has implications for the legitimacy of transitional regimes, since it can intensify public perceptions that the state is weak and ineffective. It also discourages foreign investment,[17] and hence renders economic recovery and eventually growth more difficult. Both of these factors—low levels of legitimacy and of foreign investment—can negatively affect the democratization project.[18]

Hence, the total number of crimes might not be as politically and economically significant as either the rapid increase in criminality or the proportion of serious crimes and corruption. In several countries, these latter have risen even faster than overall crime rates, and have often continued to rise when the overall rate has largely flattened out.[19] Four further points need to be made. First,

---

[14] Bäckman, *Inflation of Crime*, 99 (Appendix 3).

[15] Cited in Richard J. Krickus, 'Democratization in Lithuania', in Karen Dawisha and Bruce Parrott (eds.), *The Consolidation of Democracy in East-Central Europe* (Cambridge: Cambridge University Press, 1997), 317.

[16] Toivo U. Raun, 'Democratization and Political Development in Estonia, 1987–96', ibid. 366.

[17] This is not only because investors may fear for their own safety or that of their employees, but also because they, too, may perceive the substantial increase in violent crime as reflective of an ineffectual state. If the state is ineffective in this area, it probably is in others that directly affect the investment climate.

[18] This said, recent discourse analysis based on focus group research and Q-methodology confirms the findings cited in n. 5 that just because particular regimes claiming to be building democracy do not enjoy high levels of legitimacy does not of itself mean that citizens will lose faith in the abstract concept of democracy; this appears to hold true even if the economy is not performing particularly well. See John S. Dryzek and Leslie Holmes, 'The Real World of Civic Republicanism: Making Democracy Work in Poland and the Czech Republic', paper presented at the Conference on Communist and Post-Communist Studies (Melbourne, July 1998; amended version in *Europe-Asia Studies*, 52: 6 (2000), 1043–68). The long-term implications of such a disjuncture remain a concern, however.

[19] The sources on which the statement about serious (including violent) crimes is based are as for n. 9. The data on corruption in CEE and the FSU are patchy and unreliable; for what they are worth, however, see e.g. Leslie Holmes, 'Corruption in Post-Communist Countries, with Particular Reference to Poland',

much of the violent crime has been conducted within the criminal 'fraternity', and has often not been reported to the authorities. Second, corruption by its very nature has often gone unreported. Third, the prosecution rates of those who *are* accused of corruption has in many cases been extraordinarily low. In Poland, for instance, only *four* public officials were prosecuted for corruption between the beginning of 1990 and the end of 1996.[20] The Russian situation is better; yet even there, the number of criminal cases of corruption initiated but not actually brought to trial had by the mid-1990s exceeded those that did reach the courtroom, while the number of prosecutions for official corruption between the mid-1980s and the mid-1990s was only one-eleventh of the number of cases of official corruption registered.[21] Finally, clear-up rates of serious crime have in many cases been very low. For instance, only seven of the sixty contract murders reported in Moscow during 1995 had been solved by January 1996—although this rate was marginally better than that for the pan-Russian detection rate for such murders, which was a mere 10 per cent.[22] Given all this, the limited value of the official aggregate statistics, especially in terms of providing evidence on public perceptions of criminality and the state's handling of it, becomes even more obvious.[23]

In sum, while it is of interest to gather and compare crime statistics, they should not be fetishized; where possible, efforts should be made to disaggregate aggregated data.[24] At most, the crime

in Leslie T. Holmes and Wojciech Roszkowski (eds.), *Changing Rules: Polish Political and Economic Transformation in Comparative Perspective* (Warsaw: Institute of Political Studies, Polish Academy of Sciences, 1997), 145–8; V. Luneev, 'Korruptsiya, Uchtennaya i Fakticheskaya', *Gosudarstvo i Pravo* 8 (1996), esp. 87; and B. Panev, 'Economic Reforms and Corruption', in N. Genov (ed.), *Human Development Report—Bulgaria 1997* (Sofia: United Nations Development Program, 1997), 24–6.

[20] Information provided to the author verbally by the Polish Ministry of Justice (24 Feb. 1997).

[21] Abstract of *Prestupnost' v Rossii v devianostykh godakh i nekotorye aspekty zakonnosti bor'by s nei* (Moscow: Russian Criminological Association, 1995) in *Trends in Organized Crime*, 1: 4 (1996), 84–5; Luneev, 'Korruptsiya', 86.

[22] Williams, *Russian Organized Crime*, 235.

[23] The Georgian statistics suggest particularly low levels of crime. While they *might* reflect the real situation, it is likely they can be explained partly by Georgian clan traditions, whereby many people prefer to 'resolve' conflicts with others directly, rather than by recourse to the state.

[24] For a refreshing, if probably overstated, counterweight to the usual gloomy statistics from and interpretations of the general—not specifically crime-related—situation in Russia see V. Voronkov, 'The Corruption of Statistics', *Transitions*, 5: 3 (1998), 40–5.

statistics can act as one very rough guideline—to be used in conjunction with more qualitative data and common sense—to what is actually happening in societies. If it is accepted that public *perceptions* of whether crime have increased or not is at least as important as the actuality of the situation, then the fact that statistics are published matters greatly, since it is reasonable to infer that public attitudes are influenced by such publication. A limited amount of survey and focus group data on attitudes towards crime (especially corruption), plus references to further sources of such data, are provided in the fourth part of this chapter. For now, it is assumed that crime rates really have increased in recent years, even though their growth may have slowed down. Some of the major factors affecting these rates are briefly outlined in the next two sections. Here, the point should be made that rises in criminality in states such as Russia and Ukraine have had more of an impact internationally than the increased criminality in Latvia or Bulgaria.

Straightforward geographical logic has meant that Italians and Greeks might be more affected by an increase in car-theft by Bulgarians or Macedonians than are Germans or Danes (who are more affected by Polish car thieves). However, the point made at the beginning of this chapter about crime relating to the nuclear weapons status of Russia (and Ukraine) has meant that the potential effects of some Russian and Ukrainian criminality could be global and devastating. Although there have been fewer reports of this lately, there was serious concern in Western countries such as Germany, Austria, and France, and in other post-communist states such as Poland and Bulgaria, in the period 1992–4, as it emerged that nuclear material suitable for weapons use had been smuggled from Russia and Ukraine.[25]

While the nuclear issue is the one of greatest *potential* threat to the rest of the world, it is the international implications of post-communist organized crime in other areas that have caused serious problems for so many countries. Anyone who has visited Helsinki in recent years, for instance, will be aware of the perception there of a substantial increase in prostitution, drug-dealing, and to a lesser extent protectionism as a result of the activities of, primarily, Russian gangs.[26] The same could be said of many cities

[25] On this issue see J. Ford, 'Nuclear Smuggling: How Serious a Threat?', *National Defense University Strategic Forum*, 59 (Jan. 1996); and Rensselaer Lee, 'Recent Trends in Nuclear Smuggling', in Williams, *Russian Organized Crime*, 109–21.

[26] See Bäckman, *Inflation of Crime*, esp. 20–30. Bäckman notes (at 23) that official statistics suggest remarkably *low* levels of Russian criminality in Finland.

in both the West and other post-communist countries.[27] Such activities often involve violence, including gangland killings, the scale of which has apparently increased substantially in recent years.[28]

Domestic Influences on Changing Crime Rates

Numerous factors explain criminality in the post-communist states, just as they do in other kinds of state. In an earlier study of just one type of criminal and/or anti-social behaviour in the communist states, corruption, the present author identified three broad categories of explanation (cultural; psychological; system-related); each of these had several subsections, so that more than sixty individual factors were isolated—and that list was doubtless incomplete.[29] This helps to explain why it would be impossible in a chapter of this scale to analyse all or even most of the factors that might account for the full gamut of criminality in the CEE and FSU states. Since the interest here is only in forms of criminality that might affect the democratization project in these countries and/or their relations with other countries, our principal focus is on corruption and organized crime.

While the concepts and practice of corruption and organized crime frequently overlap and interact, especially in post-communist states, they are conceptually distinct.[30] In the way most specialists understand the term, corruption is restricted to officials—of various kinds—of the state, whereas organized crime need not directly involve officials at all. Moreover, corruption can be engaged in by

However, he also acknowledges that much crime is hidden, and that, since prostitution is not illegal in Finland, public concern about this is a social issue, not something to be addressed by legal agencies.

[27] See Sterling, *Crime without Frontiers*; Freemantle, *Octopus*; and James Finckenauer and Elin Waring, 'Russian Émigré Crime in the United States: Organized Crime or Crime that is Organized?', in Williams, *Russian Organized Crime*, 139–55.

[28] For colourful if sickening popular analyses of the violence of some Russian criminal gangs, albeit mainly within Russia, see A. Konstantinov et al., *Korrumpirovannyi Peterburg* (St Petersburg: Folio, 1997); N. Modestov, *Moskva Banditskaya* (Moscow: Tsentrpoligraf, 1997); and F. Razzakov, *Bandity Vremen Kapitalizma* (Moscow: EKSMO, 1997).

[29] See Leslie Holmes, *The End of Communist Power* (Cambridge: Polity, 1993), esp. 157–201.

[30] For two recent collections of articles on corruption and organized crime in the post-communist states see *East European Constitutional Review*, 6: 4 (1997) and *Transitions*, 5: 3 (1998).

individuals working alone, and need not involve collective behaviour. In contrast, organized crime is necessarily a form of group behaviour. Having made these points, it must be emphasized that, both in practice and in the public's perception, the two concepts are often closely linked and at times essentially indistinguishable. For instance, it is clear that many ordinary Russian citizens believe that organized crime has only managed to become as salient a feature of contemporary Russian life as it has because of the complicity of both politicians and the police.[31]

There are a number of factors that are, if not in all cases unique to post-communist states, at least far more salient in them than in most other kinds of system. Despite the claims of some comparative transitologists, the first *is* unique to the post-communist world. This is the implications of the *multiple and simultaneous transition*. The CEE and FSU countries have been engaged not only in political, economic, and boundary/identity transitions (identified by Claus Offe as the 'triple transition'),[32] but also in radical changes to their legal and educational systems, ideologies, international allegiances, and social class structures.

The necessarily simultaneous attempts at multiple transitions, plus the absence of a true bourgeoisie that *inter alia* acts as a control on the state, can be combined to form a partial explanation of the problem of criminality in post-communist countries.

One aspect of the complexity of the transition relates to the context of path-dependency from the communist past. The lack of a tradition of compromise in politics and of institutional arrangements that will ensure strong but non-dictatorial leadership has meant that it has often been difficult to secure any agreement among leading politicians on the optimal way forward, with the 'shock therapists' and the gradualists arguing among themselves while their countries deteriorate. Unfortunately, this can lead to and/or be used to justify quasi-dictatorship, as in Belarus and arguably Slovakia (at least until Mečiar's fall in September 1998); or it can be a major reason for leadership drift (as in Russia under Yeltsin).

---

[31] For a scholarly recent analysis of organized crime and corruption in Russia see T. Frisby, 'The Rise of Organized Crime in Russia: Its Roots and Social Significance', *Europe-Asia Studies*, 50: 1 (1998), 27–49. For a typical example of evidence that some citizens perceive a connection between organized crime and state officials see 'By the Grace of God', *Business Central Europe*, 6: 50 (1998), 12; this brief article is incorporated in a longer one on Slovak corruption—see F. Harris, 'Can Cronyism Work?', ibid. 11–13.

[32] Claus Offe, 'Capitalism by Design? Democratic Theory Facing the Triple Transition in Eastern Europe', *Social Research*, 58: 4 (1991), 865–92.

The moves towards both dictatorship and leadership drift can encourage a rise in criminality. The reasons for this are perhaps more obvious in the latter case than the former. A weak state renders it that much easier to get away with crime than does the presence of a strong state determined to combat illegal behaviour. The reason that quasi-dictatorial (or dictatorial) states can encourage crime is that, in practice, these often set a bad example to the population. Nepotism, cronyism, and various other forms of corruption are usually a feature of such systems, and the limitations on the mass media that are typical of them mean that one of the potentially most powerful instruments of civil society for controlling the misdemeanours of political actors is severely blunted. Nevertheless, citizens 'discover', often through rumour, what is happening in the state; if the state sets a bad example, then why should citizens abide by unclear rules? This question becomes even more acute when the ethical vacuum and the economic hardships of early post-communism are borne in mind.

Most early post-communist governments sought rapid and extensive privatization. They did so in societies lacking extensive and established bourgeoisies. Yet, in most cases, they initially preferred not to transfer too much of the economy into foreign ownership and control; having just thrown off one foreign yoke, they were unwilling to submit themselves to another. Given the shortage of *legitimate* private domestic wealth, at least two of the responses were conducive to, and perhaps even encouraged, criminality. The first was to encourage investment without enquiring about the origins of often abnormally high investment sums from domestic sources; Hungary is a good example of a country that engaged in this.[33] The second is a major explanatory factor for the apparent rise in official corruption. Many post-communist politicians and state officials who played a direct role in the privatization process took advantage of their position. In some cases, they sold off state property at unrealistically low prices, in return for kickbacks. In other cases, they were able to borrow funds themselves, and became co-owners or even principal owners of newly-privatized enterprises which, once again, were sold off much cheaper than would have been the case had market forces (notably including foreign investment) been permitted free rein.

The willingness of many state officials to tolerate corruption—often because of their own involvement—exacerbates the general

---

[33] For evidence of the current Bulgarian government thinking along these lines see E. Veleva, 'Legalise It?', *Insider Special Issue* (Jan. 1998), 54–5.

weakness of the state in combatting this type of illicit and often illegal behaviour. These circumstances help to explain the link between corruption and organized crime that is so much a feature of some countries in the region, and also the link between criminality and the weak state. The sheer scale of transition being attempted (or even intended) in all post-communist states, plus the absence of a culture of compromise, has meant that the legislative process has frequently been severely delayed. Often, laws from the communist era have been either implicitly or explicitly, and formally or informally, revoked before substitute laws have been adopted. This has opened the way for people to take advantage of ambiguity and confusion; some will do this consciously, while many others will do so because of their own uncertainty as to what is and is not legal. This *legislative lag* is yet another component of the explanation of crime that relates to the specific qualities of post-communist transition.

Apart from the state,[34] the only other potential domestic source for fighting corruption is civil society. Unfortunately, civil society has remained frail in most parts of the post-communist world, to no small extent because citizens have in recent years been more concerned with survival and accommodating to a radically different system. There is one branch of civil society that could and sometimes does play an important role in highlighting and even exposing crime, including corruption, namely the mass media. Unfortunately, the media in many post-communist states are all too often working for particular political parties. While this might be understandable at this stage, it has meant that particular newspapers and magazines often highlight the corruption of political actors from other parties, and cover up (including through deliberate omission) that of their own. Moreover, some parties have become better linked with particular media outlets than others, so that there is no 'level playing field'.

Moreover, in the partisan point-scoring that has been so much a feature of post-communist politics, allegations have often been made on the basis of very little evidence. The principal effect of a constant barrage of unsubstantiated allegations of corruption has been to undermine public confidence in *all* agencies of the state, including political parties generally. The cumulative effect of an onslaught of allegations has thus been counter-productive even to

[34] In a somewhat disheartening way, Huntington has argued that the very transition from authoritarian to democratic systems can encourage corruption and anomic behaviour by weakening the state and undermining traditional values—see Samuel Huntington, 'Democracy for the long haul', *Journal of Democracy*, 7: 2 (1996), 3–13.

the political parties and their newspapers that make the allegations. In addition, if media are seen to be closely linked to particular political organizations, they will also be perceived by many to
be in some sense part of the state. Hence, the linkage has not only
been detrimental to the popular image of the *state*, but has also
meant that what should be a key element of *civil society* has often
not developed in the optimal way.[35]

International and Transnational Factors

The focus in the previous section was on domestic factors affecting changing crime rates; it is now appropriate to consider international and transnational factors. At this stage, only negative (that
encourage crime) factors will be considered, while positive ones that
seek to reduce rates are considered in the fifth section.

Unfortunately, the revolutions of 1989–91 coincided with a
recession in the West. The economic problems of the nascent post-
communist states were unquestionably exacerbated by this. Some
of the rise in criminality and corruption in these can be explained
in terms of desperation on the part of both citizens and officials.
While this aspect of the international economic climate has often
been noted, there is another vitally important dimension of this
general economic climate that has been overlooked—the birth
of post-communism coincided with the dramatic rise of neo-liberal
(economic rationalist) ideology in most of the West.

In its cruder forms, economic rationalism can encourage corruption.
The reasons for this include both the greater job insecurity for public officials and an increase in the number of opportunities associated with out-sourcing and privatization. To the extent that some
post-communist countries—notably Poland and Russia in the early
1990s, several others more recently—were deeply influenced by this
ideology, the difference between the old system and the intended
new one was greater than would have been the case had the
dominant capitalist model been what was known as the Nordic or
Rhineland model (a more social democratic model). The attempt to
jump from the former communist model of a planned economy and
'cradle to grave' welfare to a radically neo-liberal model thus
constituted even more of a shock to both officials and citizens. If

[35] On the role of the media in CEE and the FSU see the various articles
in *Transition*, 1: 18 (1995) and 2: 8 (1996), 5–45; S. Splichal, *Media beyond Socialism*
(Boulder, Colo.: Westview, 1994); and Patrick H. O'Neil (ed.), *Post-Communism and
the Media in Eastern Europe* (London: Cass, 1997).

economic rationalism has been one important factor explaining the apparent rise in corruption in the West since the 1980s,[36] it seems reasonable to assume that it has been a factor encouraging official corruption in post-communist states.[37] And if public officials have set a poor example of abiding by the law in a time of confusion and collapsing values, then an increasing number of citizens are also likely to engage in criminal activity.

In addition to these general factors, a number of more specific international factors need to be incorporated into any analysis of rising and diversifying criminality among CEE/FSU officials and citizens. The fall of the Berlin Wall, in both literal and figurative senses, granted much greater freedom to travel for people from many parts of the formerly communist world. But the collapse of communist power was also accompanied by the redrawing of boundaries in many parts of CEE and the FSU, some of which was achieved through warfare. As a result of both the greater freedom to travel in general and the substantial growth in the numbers of Europeans seeking refugee status because of wars, the possibilities for crime to cross borders, and in some cases to stay there, increased. Once within the EU, the early implications of the 1985 Schengen Convention between many of the continental member states of the EU may have rendered it easier for criminals to move from country to country in the West.[38]

Having reached the West, it is clear that many criminal gangs have started to interact with long-established groups to form new criminal conglomerates; these groups include the Italian Mafia, Colombian drug cartels, the Chinese Triads, and the Japanese Yakuza.[39] Hence, post-communist organized crime has been assisted

[36] For an argument along these lines see Donatella Della Porta and Yves Mény, 'Conclusion: Democracy and Corruption: Towards a Comparative Analysis', in Donatella Della Porta and Yves Mény (eds.), *Democracy and Corruption in Europe* (London: Pinter, 1997), 166–80.

[37] The present author has explored some of the possible connections between corruption and neo-liberalism in Leslie Holmes, 'Corruption, Economic Rationalism and the Crisis of the State' in *La Trobe Forum*, 12 (1998), 14–15; there will be a much fuller analysis in his forthcoming book, provisionally entitled *The Irresponsible State: Corruption, Transition and Neo-Liberalism*.

[38] Although the Schengen Convention did not become operational until 1995— a decade after it had been signed—some liberalization of movement occurred between the signatory states in the intervening period.

[39] For a very brief but up-to-date analysis of the international connections and division of labour between the five most significant crime syndicates globally (the four named in the text plus the Russian 'mafia') see F. Bresler, 'When co-operation is a dirty word', *High Life* (London: British Airways), (Apr. 1998), 86–91.

by existing organized crime groups beyond CEE and the FSU. It should be noted that CEE and FSU criminal groups have not been the only ones to have travelled further afield in the 1990s; the first confirmed example of Yakuza activity in Europe was in 1993.[40] Nevertheless, the spread of post-communist criminal influence has been particularly rapid and recent.

At the same time, the 1990s explosion in access to global information technology has rendered communication between the most powerful and significant organized crime gangs much easier. Some CEE and FSU gangs and corrupt officials have made considerable use of sophisticated computer technology to assist them in their nefarious activities.[41] Moreover, and although there appears to be little hard evidence on this, it is widely assumed that CEE and FSU criminal gangs have played a major role in the Internet pornography industry. The worldwide explosion in the use of 'the net' in the 1990s has added to the list of potential sources of illegal or questionable revenue for organized crime.

Once criminals—whether gangsters or corrupt officials—have acquired illicit funds, the opaque and traditionally unquestioning (misleadingly described by some as 'discreet') banking traditions in countries such as Cyprus, Switzerland, and Luxembourg have made it relatively easy to hide these in a secure location. Many of the often ingenious money-laundering methods used by criminals involve banks *within* the post-communist world, which liaise in an outwardly 'normal' (legal) way with banks in other countries; the fact that some of these banks in CEE and the FSU, particularly in Russia, appear to be owned and/or managed by organized crime has made the whole process easier for gangs to transfer money internationally.[42] Gangs have also created offshore companies and joint ventures with foreign firms as a way of facilitating the international transfer of funds in ways that appear 'above board'.

Some officials have argued that the introduction of the Euro may make money-laundering even easier in future for organized crime than it has already become. This point was made by the Belgian Finance Minister, Philippe Maystadt, at the second meeting of the international Financial Action Task Force (FATF—of which

[40] Freemantle, Octopus, 73–4.

[41] Computer technology has been used by criminals from the post-communist world not only to defraud banks, but even to destroy police files—see Webster, *Russian Organized Crime*, 36–7.

[42] For a scholarly analysis of the transfer of funds, both legal and questionable, from Russia during the 1990s, see Vladimir Tikhomirov, 'Capital Flight from Post-Soviet Russia', *Europe-Asia Studies*, 49: 4 (1997), 591–615.

Maystadt is the Chair) in Paris in April 1998. The reason given was that the highest denomination Euro will be worth considerably more than the highest denomination US dollar, so that—for those criminals who prefer simpler ways of transferring their gains than via the establishment of joint ventures—it will in future be possible to transport large sums of money in much smaller containers. Maystadt announced that several ministers at the FATF meeting had specifically mentioned CEE as a major centre of money-laundering operations.[43]

A familiar form of criminality in Europe in the early and mid-1990s was the substantial growth in car theft in the West as a result of gangs smuggling stolen cars from the West to the CEE and FSU countries. As with many areas of criminality, this was one in which corruption and organized crime often went hand in hand; the problem of car smuggling would not have been as great had there been far fewer border guards and customs officials prepared to turn a blind eye to suspicious movement of motor cars in return for bribes and other forms of kickback.[44] It might be assumed that 'the West' was invariably hostile to this development. This was not always the case. Interviews conducted in Berlin in January 1997 suggested to this author that many Germans who had their cars stolen were pleased—assuming their car was fully insured—since they would then be able to purchase a newer model. Moreover, common sense suggests that Western car manufacturers could also benefit from this 'redistribution', as victims of car theft replaced their stolen vehicles.

Becoming involved in questionable joint ventures and 'turning a blind eye' to car theft have not been the only ways in which some Western companies and governments have played a role in encouraging international economic crime. Although this situation looks set to change (see below), many non-US corporations have until now been legitimately able to claim tax write-offs for bribes ('inducements') they have paid in connection with overseas tendering. There was, thus, an incentive for them to encourage the acceptance of bribes among post-communist officials with whom they were negotiating.

It is not possible to determine whether domestic or foreign factors have been more influential in the internationalization

---

[43] M. Atkinson, 'Race on to keep euro away from criminals', *Guardian* (30 Apr. 1998).

[44] See e.g. J. Nikolov, 'Organized Crime in Bulgaria', *East European Constitutional Review*, 6: 4 (1997), 80. The provisional government appointed in Bulgaria in Feb. 1997 considered the customs service so corrupt that it transferred the control of border crossings to the military.

and transnationalization of post-communist criminal activity. Both organized crime and corruption rates appear to have been on the increase in most parts of the world in the 1990s, and both kinds of activity have become more transnational. This said, the rise appears to have been more marked in CEE and FSU than in most other parts of the world,[45] and the increase in other countries is in some cases related to the growing influence of post-communist activity. This suggests that domestic factors are more significant, but that they are connected with, and boosted by, the opportunities afforded by the world beyond CEE and the FSU. Domestic and transnational factors explaining the rise of East European organized crime and corruption in the 1990s are closely linked.

Implications for Transition

The significance of corruption and organized crime to the democratization project in post-communist states should not be underestimated. While there are no detailed and directly comparable survey data across the post-communist countries, and very few time-series data for individual countries, a comparison of opinion polls and focus group research from several states unambiguously suggests that citizens consider economic crime to be a serious problem, and sometimes that they associate it with the privatization and transition processes.[46]

---

[45] This inference is based on the author's comparison of the cross-polity time-series data provided by the annual Interpol *International Crime Statistics*. The reader is reminded that data on Germany, the UK, and the USA are included in Table 7.1 above.

[46] I am unaware of any major survey that *directly* invites respondents to identify the principal causes of crime and corruption; most surveys elicit views on how serious the problem is, which groups are most involved, whether or not respondents have been personally affected, etc. Such surveys, plus one-on-one interviews, letters to the press, etc. provide a great deal of circumstantial evidence of the correlation being suggested here. For instance, the research being conducted by the Glasgow team reveals that at least 40% of respondents in Bulgaria, Czech Republic, Slovakia, and Ukraine believe that most politicians behave worse now than during the communist era; this figure reaches 87% in Ukraine (William Miller, Åse Grødeland, and T. Koshechkina, 'Are the People Victims or Accomplices? The Use of Presents and Bribes to Influence Officials in Eastern Europe', *Crime, Law and Social Change*, 29: 4 (1998), 273–312—here at table 4 and accompanying text). The percentages who believe local officials behave worse now than in the late communist era is even higher, the lowest figure being 45% in Bulgaria, the highest 89% in Ukraine, ibid.

Some indication of just how widespread has been the impression that organized crime has *political* power was suggested by an August 1997 Russian survey. In response to the question 'Who do you believe is running Russia?' 52 per cent of respondents opted for 'the mafia, organized crime', compared with just 21 per cent for 'the state apparatus', and 14 per cent for 'the president'.[47] Having already provided an overview of surveys relating to corruption in a 1997 publication,[48] I shall not repeat the exercise in full here. But recent Bulgarian studies, which were not cited in the earlier analysis, are fairly typical, if more detailed than most. They provide some indication of how widespread concern is, and of which groups Bulgarians believe are most prone to corruption. The overview of these surveys will then be compared with abbreviated versions of some of the findings on other countries recently summarized and published.

The Bulgarian studies were conducted by Vitosha Research, the survey research unit of the Centre for the Study of Democracy (CSD); they comprised three separate surveys over a ten-month period, and were very much focused on attitudes towards corruption.[49] The first was conducted in March 1997, and involved 1,185 respondents; the second was conducted in September 1997, and involved 1,032 respondents; while the third was conducted in December 1997 and January 1998, and involved 1,519 respondents.

They revealed, first, that Bulgarians were critical of all forms of corruption among elected officials—though, unsurprisingly, much less so the acceptance of free meals than free holidays, money, or gifts. Second, respondents tended to be somewhat more critical of corruption among civil servants than among elected officials, though the difference was not substantial. Third, the results indicated that official campaigns against corruption can increase popular indignation, but perhaps only on a short-term basis. Thus, the new government that came to power following the April 1997 elections made the fight against corruption a top priority, and sought to raise public awareness and disapproval of it. That it succeeded

[47] The survey appeared in *Moskovskii Komsomolets* (5 Sept. 1997), and is cited in Peter Rutland and N. Kogan, 'The Russian Mafia: Between Hype and Reality', *Transitions*, 5: 3 (Mar. 1998), 26.

[48] Leslie Holmes, 'Corruption in Post-Communist Countries, with Particular Reference to Poland', esp. 151–2; surveys are cited from the Czech Republic, Slovakia, Poland, Russia, and Ukraine.

[49] The results of the project have been published in Bulgarian as *Mnenieto na bulgarite za koruptsiyata: mart 1997—yanuari 1998* (Sofia: Vitosha Research, 1998). I am indebted to the Director of Vitosha Research, Aleksandr Stoyanov, for having kindly provided me with this report (as well as that cited in n. 53) during a visit I made to Bulgaria in February 1998.

in this objective was reflected in the uniformly higher levels of condemnation in the September survey compared with the March responses. However, the January 1998 results were remarkably similar to the March 1997 data. Interviews conducted by this author in Sofia in February 1998 indicated that the campaign had lost little impetus by then; given this and the survey results, it would appear that the public was becoming immune or indifferent to government exhortations.[50]

The third of the Bulgarian surveys was conducted by CSD as part of an international project being conducted by the Glasgow-based team referred to in the introduction (W. Miller, T. Koshechkina, and Å. Grødeland), and uses that team's questions.[51] It was concerned with popular attitudes towards state officials, and provides further evidence of how widespread Bulgarians consider corruption to be.[52] The survey, of people aged 18 and over interviewed on a face-to-face basis, revealed that 84.5 per cent of respondents considered it either 'bad' (53.5 per cent) or 'bad, but unavoidable' (31 per cent) that one might have to give money, presents or do favours in

[50] Another possible explanation is that the government fight against corruption was already being so effective that public concern about the problem had declined. While the government was clearly making a real effort to combat corruption, this explanation seems either far-fetched or, more charitably, premature.

[51] The Glasgow project was funded jointly by the Overseas Development Administration (now the Department of International Development) and the (British) Economic and Social Research Council.

[52] *Attitudes of Citizens towards Public Administration* (Sofia: Vitosha Research, 1998). It should be noted that the results are very close but not identical to those for Bulgaria cited in various analyses that have been produced by the Glasgow team—see esp. Miller, Grødeland, and Koshechkina, 'Are the People Victims or Accomplices?' and Miller, Grødeland, and Koshechkina, 'What is to be Done about Corrupt Officials?'. Neither of these articles was available in Australia at the time of writing the present chapter, and I am extremely indebted to Prof. William Miller for providing me with the manuscripts of both and permitting me to cite them; the analytical figures contained in them have considerably enriched the present study. The slight discrepancy between the Vitosha figures and those provided in the two articles just cited are insignificant in terms of the argument here; they appear to have arisen primarily because the Glasgow team has usually calculated percentages after omitting all mixed and 'it depends' responses, whereas the Vitosha team has sometimes included mixed responses (and have indicated this where they do). Given my own preference for *including* indefinite responses (since this provides a fuller picture of attitudes, even though it is 'messier'), plus the facts that I had access to the Bulgarian results first and went to the length of translating the Bulgarian-language over-time ones referred to in n. 49, I have opted to use those for this part of the analysis. However, I have used Miller et al.'s figures for the summary of Czech, Slovak, and Ukrainian attitudes that follows the Bulgarian analysis.

order to influence public administrators.[53] The survey also provided some evidence on which groups of public officials are considered most and least corrupt. Respondents were asked the question, 'Imagine a person who needs something that he (*sic*) is *entitled to by law*. Is it *likely* that this person would have to offer money, a present or a favour to get help from each of the following groups of officials?' (emphasis in original). Far and away the most 'corrupt' group are 'doctors in hospitals'; no less than 85.9 per cent or interviewees responded that 'it is likely' they would have to offer a bribe of some kind. However, since most comparative analyses of corruption would not include doctors as state officials, they will be discounted for the purposes of the present analysis.[54] After doctors, the next most corruptible groups were seen as customs officials (73.6 per cent of respondents believed they would have to offer a bribe), court officials (62.9 per cent), municipal officials (61.5 per cent), and police officers (56 per cent). Elected officials were considered to be somewhat less susceptible to corruption, with members of parliament scoring 48.2 per cent on this question, and elected municipal councillors 45.7 per cent.

But, in line with findings in some other post-communist states,[55] the Bulgarian data suggest that popular perceptions of levels of

[53] The Vitosha percentages for this question are based exclusively on respondents who provided a definite answer (i.e. all 'neither' and 'don't know' responses were excluded).

[54] This decision becomes even more justifiable when it is borne in mind that Bulgaria is currently introducing a very controversial reform of the health services, one aspect of which is to be widespread privatization of the sector.

[55] See e.g. the results of focus group research on Bulgaria, Czech Republic, Slovakia, and Ukraine in T. Koshechkina, Åse Grødeland, and William Miller, 'Different Perspectives on Coping with Officialdom in Four Postcommunist Countries: A Focus Group Approach', paper presented at the annual conference of the British Association for Slavonic and East European Studies (Cambridge, Apr. 1997); and primarily in Ukraine and Czechia—but also Hungary, Russia, and Slovakia— in William Miller, T. Koshechkina, and Åse Grødeland, 'How Citizens Cope with Postcommunist Officials: Evidence from Focus Group Discussions in Ukraine and the Czech Republic', *Political Studies*, 45: 3 (1997), 597–625. An abbreviated version of some of these findings, comparing Bulgaria, Czech Republic, Slovakia, and Ukraine, can be found in Åse Grødeland, T. Koshechkina, and William Miller, 'In-depth Interviews on the Everyday Use of Bribes in Postcommunist Europe', *ecpr News*, 9: 2 (1998), 7–9. The research of the Glasgow-based team indicates that, while many Ukrainians actually have had direct experience of low-level corrupt officialdom, many Czechs believe there is a great deal of corruption but have not personally experienced it (for further details, see text below). For Polish survey data that produces rather similar results to these Czech findings see Centrum Badania Opinii Społecznej, *Nieuczciwość i przekupstwo w instytucjach wymiaru sprawiedliwości* (Warsaw: CBOS, June 1994), 2; while most respondents in the

corruption *might* be exaggerated in comparison with actual levels. To the question, 'In the last few years, did it ever happen to you that you contacted a public official who . . .', only 6.5 per cent of interviewees replied that the official had 'asked for money or a present'—although it must be acknowledged that a further 34.2 per cent replied that the official 'showed he was expecting something'. On the other hand, nearly half the respondents (48.3 per cent) had not been aware of any such demands or expectations, while a surprisingly high 11.1 per cent 'did not know'.

Whether or not popular perceptions have exaggerated the scale of corruption in Bulgaria, it is clear that many citizens were irritated by the phenomenon. It is also clear that far more citizens were annoyed by corruption 'at the top' than at lower levels of the political system. In response to the question, 'Which annoys you more—corruption amongst . . .', 47.9 per cent answered 'top public officials', and 20.7 per cent answered 'lower-ranking public officials'; most of the other respondents answered 'it depends' or 'don't know'.

As indicated earlier, surveys and focus group research have suggested that corruption has been seen as a major problem in most parts of the post-communist world.[56] A brief overview of a few of the findings proves this point. Thus, Slovak opinion polls conducted in the mid-1990s consistently identified corruption as one of the three most significant concerns of citizens.[57] When asked in May 1992 if they agreed with the statement that 'corruption represents a serious threat to our society', 74.2 per cent of the 2,032 Russians surveyed responded that they either 'fully agreed' (53.4 per cent) or 'tended to agree' (20.8 per cent). Time-series data conducted in Russia between 1994 and 1997 reveal that although only approximately one-quarter of respondents (rising to almost 30 per cent in January 1997) considered corruption one of the most serious threats to them personally, crime more generally was consistently perceived as either the second or the third greatest threat, after inflation and, sometimes, unemployment.[58] A February 1995

June 1994 Polish survey reported in this source were concerned about corruption, only 15% had ever had direct personal experience of it or knew someone who had; 82% had never either experienced corruption or known anyone who had.

[56] It is almost certainly of concern in the remaining parts, too, but there is insufficient quantitative evidence on this at present.

[57] Transparency International, *Report of the Mission of Transparency International to the Slovak Republic and Romania 20–29 May 1996* (Berlin: Transparency International), 9.

[58] Russian data kindly provided to the author by Yurii Levada, Director of the well-regarded VTsIOM, in Moscow (25 Apr. 1997). More readily available Russian

survey conducted by one of Poland's most respected opinion polling organizations revealed that only 2 per cent of respondents believed their politicians and senior public servants were completely uncorrupted, whereas 51 per cent believed that 'many' politicians and senior appointed government officials were somewhat corrupt, and a further 36 per cent believed that 'some' were.[59] But is this concern about corruption sufficient to undermine the transition process? Is there a connection in people's minds between democratization, privatization, and corruption/economic crime?

It is not possible on the basis of the existing data to provide authoritative answers to these questions.[60] Moreover, the answers will not necessarily be the same in all countries. Certainly, there is survey evidence to suggest that citizens in Kazakhstan and Uzbekistan have been ambivalent towards democratization and economic reform because of the belief that these processes are associated with corruption and organized crime;[61] as pointed out earlier, other survey and other types of evidence, including some of that just cited, tends to endorse this image of a common correlation in the public mind between radical economic reform (privatization and marketization) and crime.[62] For those enthusiastic about promoting political and

data on attitudes towards crime generally and corruption specifically can be found in the 'Informatsiya: Resul'taty Oprosov' section of VTsIOM's bi-monthly publication *Ekonomicheskie i Sotsial'nye Peremeny: Monitoring Obshchestvennogo Mneniya*.

[59] Centrum Badania Opinii Społecznej, *Czy politicy są uczciwi?* (Warsaw: CBOS, Feb. 1995), esp. 1–14. I wish to thank Prof. Lena Kolarska-Bobińska for providing me with these survey results, and Mr Oliver Freeman for assistance in translating them from Polish.

[60] It is worth noting that one of the most significant cross-polity surveys of the level of trust citizens in CEE and the FSU have towards political and civil institutions does not directly address the issue of crime and corruption—see Mishler and Rose, 'Trust, Distrust and Skepticism'. All too often until recently, studies of 'formal' or institutional politics on the one hand, and crime and corruption on the other, in post-communist states have been conducted more or less in isolation from each other. This situation is clearly inappropriate, and is now gradually being rectified—including by Mishler and Rose who, with co-author Christian Haerpfer, conclude in a 1998 book that 'The chief shortcoming of post-Communist new democracies is their inability to enforce the rule of law (. . .) today the biggest problem is corruption': Rose, Mishler, and Haerpfer, *Democracy and Its Alternatives*, 222.

[61] N. Lubin, *Central Asians Take Stock* (Washington, DC: United States Institute of Peace, 1995), as abstracted in *Trends in Organized Crime*, 1: 4 (1996), 84. The Kazakh government is clearly very concerned about corruption, having recently (late 1998) established a ministerial-level agency and adopted a two-year 'programme' to fight it—see 'O gosudarstvennoi programme bor'by s korruptsiei na 1999–2000 gody,' *Kazakhstanskaya Pravda* (9 Dec. 1998).

[62] Though the reader is reminded of the distinction Miller et al. draw between the theory and practice of marketization and privatization—see n. 5 and accompanying text above.

economic reforms in the post-communist world, this is of concern. However, let us consider the Bulgarian case once again, since it suggests that there might be a more optimistic way of interpreting the recent surveys than might appear to be the case on the basis of the findings reported so far. The tentative conclusions drawn about the Bulgarian case might apply to other countries in the region.

The first point is that many Bulgarians appeared to have mixed feelings about corruption. While condemning it on one level, many have also adopted a pragmatic approach to it. Thus, in response to the question, 'Imagine a person *gave money or a present* to a public official and got what he/she wanted. How is it most likely for the person to feel?' (emphasis in original), 41.2 per cent of interviewees responded 'happy', while another 19.7 per cent answered 'mixed feelings'. Only 7.9 per cent of respondents described their feeling as anger, while 6.9 per cent would feel ashamed and 6.6 per cent worried.

Second, when asked what sort of system a respondent would personally prefer, 27.8 per cent of respondents claimed they would prefer one in which public officials 'sometimes accept money or presents', while a further 18.6 per cent answered that 'it depends'; only 40.0 per cent stated unambiguously that they would prefer a system in which public officials would 'never accept money or presents'. Clearly, there is a grey area here.

Third, to the question mentioned above concerning the groups among which corruption is found to be most annoying, only 11.9 per cent answered 'influential businessmen' (*sic*); while it is questionable whether or not businesspeople should have been included in a survey of attitudes on corruption (in that they are not usually public officials), this finding does suggest that the Bulgarian public may be prepared to accept more 'questionable' ethical behaviour in the private sector than in the public.[63] On one level, at least, this surely bodes well for the move away from a state-run economy.

On another level, however, the survey could also be interpreted as indicating that many Bulgarians still look to a strong state for dealing with the problem of corruption, rather than greater democratization or, as a corollary, a greater role for civil society. This inference can be drawn from the responses to a question about the best methods to be adopted for ensuring public officials treat

---

[63] In Bulgaria, as in many other post-communist countries, the communist legacy of merging the state and the economy means that many citizens continue to draw only a hazy distinction between the two. This said, recent economic rationalist approaches in the West mean that the distinctions are increasingly blurred here too.

citizens fairly; in the context of this survey, this clearly relates to the measures required for eradicating or reducing corruption. Having been asked to nominate just one method, the preferred method (29.2 per cent of respondents) was 'stricter control of officials'; just behind this was a factor that might bode well, in the sense of becoming more feasible as the economy picks up, 'higher salaries for officials' (at 28.1 per cent). In contrast, measures that might be seen as reflective of more democratization and transparency were considerably less favoured; these methods included 'more openness' (5.2 per cent), 'better appeal procedures for citizens' (4.8 per cent), 'notices with the rights of citizens' (2.6 per cent), and 'reporting to the public about deficiencies' (1.6 per cent). Similarly, a measure that might be seen as taking some of the emphasis off officials and placing more responsibility on citizens—'penalties for people who bribe officials'—appealed to only 3 per cent of respondents as the preferred method.

How do these Bulgarian figures compare with those on other post-communist countries? The limited data available, added to those from more general public attitudes towards political and economic institutions,[64] suggest that this particular case study might be fairly typical of several post-communist countries, although the particular mix and balance of attitudes is, of course, unique to each country. It is important, therefore, to consider in more detail some of the findings of the Glasgow team in their comparative analyses (involving interviews conducted between November 1997 and February 1998 of almost 5,000 citizens *in toto*) of Bulgaria, the Czech Republic, Slovakia, and Ukraine. The attitudes will be addressed in the same sequence as employed for the Bulgarian findings.

The percentages of interviewees in the Czech Republic, Slovakia, and Ukraine who considered it either 'bad' or 'bad but unavoidable' that citizens might have to use money, presents, favours, or contacts in order to influence officials were remarkably similar to the Bulgarian percentages, at 94 per cent, 88 per cent, and 89 per cent respectively. If medical personnel are excluded (for reasons given above) along with university staff (for the same reasons as medical personnel), the three groups considered most corrupt in the Czech Republic were officials in state ministries, members of parliament, and customs officials; in Slovakia, the top three were officials in state ministries, court officials, and members of parliament; while

---

[64] For instance, the numerous survey results published under the joint auspices of the Centre for the Study of Public Policy at the University of Strathclyde and the Paul Lazarsfeld Society in Vienna.

in Ukraine, the four most corrupt were seen as the police, officials in state ministries, court officials, and municipal officials.[65] Although the rankings differed somewhat from country to country, perhaps the most important point is that *all* groups of officials were considered corrupt by at least 40 per cent of citizens in all four countries, and by more than half of the citizens in all countries except the Czech Republic (with the highest average percentages occurring in Ukraine).[66]

As in Bulgaria, it appears that relatively few citizens in the other three post-communist states had been directly asked by officials for money or a present (ranging from 2 per cent in the Czech Republic to 11 per cent in Ukraine), although the percentage of respondents who claimed that an official had 'seemed to expect' an offering was *higher* in the other three countries, ranging from 44 per cent in the Czech Republic to 64 per cent in Slovakia. There was a remarkably high level of agreement in all four countries that corruption among top-level government officials made citizens more angry than corruption among lower-level officials; the percentages ranged from 59 per cent in Slovakia to 71 per cent in Ukraine.[67] And like their Bulgarian counterparts, considerably more Czech, Slovak, and Ukrainian interviewees believed that a citizen who offered an official a bribe of some description and thereby secured their objective would feel 'happy' than that they would feel angry, worried, or ashamed.[68] Hence, the ambiguities of public attitudes towards corruption already identified in Bulgaria are replicated in other CEE and FSU states.

One area in which there were fairly substantial differences between the Bulgarian respondents and their counterparts in

[65] Data for this paragraph are from Miller, Grødeland, and Koshechkina, 'Are the People Victims or Accomplices?', tables 10 and 6 and accompanying text. The reason the top four Ukrainian positions are included here is because the latter three listed scored the same (87%).

[66] The observant reader will note that this statement *appears* to conflict with some of the percentages I have already provided for Bulgaria. The reason is that, for this comparative summary, I am using the figures on Bulgaria provided by Prof. Miller and his colleagues rather than the Vitosha reports. As already indicated, the latter are very similar but not identical to the Glasgow project figures, for reasons explained in n. 52.

[67] Miller, Grødeland, and Koshechkina, 'Are the People Victims or Accomplices?', tables 15 and 21 and accompanying text. The Bulgarian percentage cited by the Glasgow team in connection with attitudes towards corruption among higher- or lower-ranking officials is somewhat higher than that cited in the Vitosha report, at 60%.

[68] Miller, Grødeland, and Koshechkina, 'Are the People Victims or Accomplices?', table 23 (question 103) and accompanying text.

some of the other countries was in terms of their preferred system (i.e. one in which officials sometimes accepted presents and in return did favours for people, or one in which officials never accepted presents and never did favours); while the Ukrainians were close to the Bulgarians on this answer, a much higher proportion of Czechs and Slovaks preferred a 'clean' state, in which officials never accepted bribes or equivalents. Nevertheless, there was still a majority in both Ukraine and Bulgaria who preferred a corruption-free system, so that the differences were not as great as they initially appear.[69]

The Bulgarian response towards 'corruption' among top businesspeople was more in line with the other three countries. Using the Miller et al. methodology, some 15 per cent of Bulgarians found this more annoying than corruption among either top government officials or local officials, compared with 17 per cent in the Czech Republic, 16 per cent in Slovakia, and a rather lower 5 per cent in Ukraine.[70] It seems reasonably safe to infer from this that many of the moves away from the state-run economy have been widely accepted in many post-communist states.

The final area for comparison concerns citizens' beliefs about the optimal methods for combating corruption. Yet again, the Bulgarian responses were for the most part very similar to those in the other three countries. Thus, the most favoured method in Bulgaria (stricter controls or penalties for officials) was also the most favoured method in both the Czech Republic and Ukraine; it was the second most favoured method in Slovakia, after better training for officials. The second most favoured method in Bulgaria (higher salaries for officials) was also the second most favoured method in Ukraine, and the third most favoured in Slovakia; Czechs were an exception on this variable. The Bulgarians' disinclination to advocate measures that place less onus on the state and more on citizens or civil society was remarkably similar to the attitudes in all of the other three states.[71]

---

[69] Miller, Grødeland, and Koshechkina, 'Are the People Victims or Accomplices?', table 11 and accompanying text. It should be noted that this is one table in which the exclusion of the 'mixed' responses from the Miller et al. analyses appears to produce a rather different picture from the Vitosha figures. Closer inspection again reveals, however, that the differences are not as significant as they initially seem; even in the Vitosha figures cited above, far more interviewees prefer a system in which officials never accept gifts than one in which they sometimes do.

[70] Ibid., table 21 and accompanying text.

[71] Miller, Grødeland, and Koshechkina, 'What is to be done about corrupt officials?', table 3 and accompanying text.

The above survey (interview-based) data suggest that, in four different post-communist states, public attitudes towards corruption, at least, have been remarkably similar. It is to be hoped that detailed survey results from many more post-communist states, and concerning many more forms of criminality (especially organized crime), will become available in the coming years. But before concluding this section, and given the interest here in perceptions of the interaction between domestic and international factors in post-communist criminality, it is worth noting one further finding of the Glasgow team. Their research indicated clearly that very few citizens in the four countries they investigated believe that 'foreigners' either have been benefiting most, or are likely to benefit most, from moves towards a market economy. In terms of who has *already* benefited most, the respondents citing 'foreigners' range from a very low 3 per cent of the total in Slovakia to a not much higher 7 per cent in Ukraine. Whilst the figures about assumed future profiteering are somewhat higher, ranging from 5 per cent in Slovakia to 14 per cent in the Czech Republic, they still fall far below the proportion of interviewees who believe that 'politicians and officials' or 'the mafia' have been and will continue to be the major beneficiaries of market reform.[72] Of course, these figures do not relate *directly* to crime and corruption; yet it seems reasonable to infer from them that many post-communist citizens are blaming their own political and criminal elites far more than external agencies for improprieties in their systems.

International Responses to Post-communist Criminality

This section examines the constructive measures taken by the international community to counter the influence of post-communist organized crime and corruption, particularly when these spread beyond the borders of CEE and the FSU. Having considered many of the measures adopted, it will be argued that there is scope for a much more concerted effort than even the very recent intensification of counter-crime strategies. It is also suggested that the often half-hearted approach of foreign, international, and transnational agencies has reflected a mixture of ambivalence towards, and inadequate appreciation of the seriousness of, the problem of crime.

[72] Miller, Grødeland, and Koshechkina, 'Are the People Victims or Accomplices?', tables 2 and 3 and accompanying text.

In analysing the responses to post-communist criminality from the international community—here meaning primarily the West— it is appropriate to distinguish between at least four kinds of agency. The first is the individual nation-state and its agencies (national police forces). The second resides in international and supranational agencies that are in essence established by groups of nation-states. This group has included organizations such as Interpol, the EU, the IMF, and the World Bank. The third kind of agency exists primarily to analyse corruption, and to assist government agencies bent on reducing this. Such an agency is independent of both governments and supranational agencies, even though it often cooperates with them. There is only one such agency—Transparency International; its nature and role will be explored below. Finally, no analysis would be complete without some consideration of the role of transnational business.

A few Western countries have become so concerned about the spread of criminality beyond the borders of certain post-communist states that they have established formal links with policing agencies in the latter. The best-known example of this is the Federal Bureau of Investigation (FBI), which has established offices in Moscow and Warsaw. The Metropolitan Police of London also have a formal link with their Moscow equivalents. In addition, the USA established an International Police Academy in Budapest in 1996 at which police from CEE and FSU countries could be trained in combating crime. It should be noted that the involvement of Western police agencies has typically been requested by post-communist countries. Even countries that have in recent years developed a reputation for wanting to solve their own problems with minimal foreign involvement have recently turned to the West for assistance. A prime example has been the Czech Republic, which sought FBI advice in dealing with the banking scandal that emerged in 1996 and involved a considerable amount of corruption.

In the fight against post-communist criminality, more common than the establishment of branches of Western agencies within the CEE and FSU countries themselves has been the creation of special divisions of such organizations within Western states. These new bodies have focused on gangs from Russia and elsewhere that have relocated to these countries. The best-known examples have been created in the USA, and relate to Russian criminals; they include the Tri-State Joint Soviet-Émigré Organized Crime Project (established in March 1992, and combining police efforts in New

York State, New Jersey, and Pennsylvania),[73] and the FBI unit established in New York in 1994 explicitly to deal with Russian criminals.[74]

Although it was initially believed by many that the Schengen Convention would render it easier for organized crime to cross frontiers once in the area of the EU covered by it, the awareness of this among the signatory states has made it much more difficult since its formal implementation for non-EU citizens not only to enter this area in the first place, but even to be 'free' of state interest in them once inside. In terms of the former, when Austria agreed in July 1997 to implement the Convention from April 1998, concern was expressed that the country's 1,300-kilometre border with CEE states would constitute a security threat. Austria acknowledged its awareness of this problem, and agreed to upgrade its border controls *vis-à-vis* its non-Schengen neighbours. Regarding the situation for 'outsiders' once inside the Schengen area, police powers and resources have been upgraded recently in a bid to counter the potential effects of highly mobile organized crime. Much of this upgrade was formalized and legitimized by the 1997 Amsterdam Treaty.

Until now, and as mentioned above, one of the ways in which organized crime and corruption in CEE and FSU states has been 'assisted' by the West has been through non-transparent banking practices in countries such as Luxembourg and Switzerland. This has rendered it relatively easy for criminals to hide their ill-gotten gains. It is, therefore, encouraging that Switzerland has now adopted a law, effective 1 April 1998, that requires banks to declare any suspicious deposits and other transactions in future.[75] Although it is likely that there will be problems in implementing this law, its adoption is of real significance symbolically. This decision sent a message to the post-communist criminal world that Western institutions are serious about clamping down on economic crime.

There has been a dramatic increase since the mid-1990s in the amount of attention supra- and transnational organizations have paid to criminality, especially corruption and organized crime, in the post-communist countries. Only a few examples will be cited here. One of the most significant has been the Council of Europe's

---

[73] For documentation on this project, see Williams, *Russian Organized Crime*, 177–226.

[74] Handelman, *Comrade Criminal*, 244.

[75] *Euronews* (television), Sofia (6 Feb. 1998).

'Octopus' project. This was established in June 1996 with the express purpose of combating corruption and organized crime in the CEE and FSU countries; no less than sixteen countries from the region agreed to participate in the project.[76] The project was to run for eighteen months, and involved *inter alia* harmonizing the legislation of cooperating states, increasing information exchanges, and establishing proper monitoring services. A conference to assess the success of the scheme was held in Strasbourg in December 1997, and recommended a number of specific measures that could be taken by individual post-communist states.[77]

In addition to projects such as 'Octopus' that specifically target the CEE and FSU countries, these states are also being affected by more global projects of supranational organizations that are designed to reduce economic crime everywhere. One example was the mid-1996 ruling of the World Bank that any evidence of official corruption in the implementation of investment and aid projects in which it is involved will result in immediate cancellation of that project. Some CEE/FSU states have also been refused loans, usually on a temporary basis, by the IMF *inter alia* on the grounds that they are doing too little to combat corruption; Ukraine was 'punished' in this way in 1997.[78]

But it is only very recently that supranational and international organizations have begun to focus on the problem of corruption and, in particular, its international implications. Various factors explain this. One is that there has been a knock-on effect from the OECD. In May 1994, this organization issued a set of 'Recommendations on Bribery in International Business Transactions', which has been described as 'the first multilateral agreement among governments to combat the bribery of foreign officials'.[79] A major impetus for these OECD guidelines was the USA, which has become increasingly concerned that it has been losing international business because of corruption. In 1977, in the wake of the Lockheed corruption scandal, the USA passed legislation making

[76] The 16 countries were Albania, Bulgaria, Croatia, Czech Republic, Estonia, Hungary, Latvia, Lithuania, Republic of Macedonia, Moldova, Poland, Romania, Russia, Slovakia, Slovenia, and Ukraine. Octopus II ran 1999–2000.

[77] The Council of Europe has recently made clear that it perceives the problem of corruption to be a pan-European one. Its Committee of Ministers adopted a Criminal Law Convention on Corruption in November 1998, which was signed by its Parliamentary Assembly in May 1999. Its implementation is monitored by 'GRECO' (Group of States Against Corruption).

[78] 'Ukraine', *Business Central Europe: The Annual 1997/98* (Dec. 1997), 53.

[79] Transparency International, *Sharpening the Responses against Global Corruption* (Berlin: Transparency International, 1996), 15.

it a crime for American companies to use bribes to secure overseas contracts. However, and as mentioned above, many other Western countries—including Australia, Austria, France, Germany, and the Netherlands—have not only not forbidden their companies from offering bribes in countries in which this is perceived to be 'normal' business practice but, just to add insult to American injury, have permitted their companies to claim such bribes as a tax write-off. All this has become intolerable to the USA, which has pressured international organizations such as the IMF, the World Bank and the OECD to introduce rules that would outlaw such behaviour. This has resulted in numerous declarations and guidelines, including the UN's 'Declaration against Corruption and Bribery in International Commercial Transactions' (December 1996),[80] the World Bank's anti-corruption guidelines of August 1997,[81] and the OECD's own more recent 'Convention on Combating Bribery of Foreign Public Officials in International Business Transactions' (signed by all twenty-nine members of the OECD and five non-member countries in December 1997, following recommendations adopted by the OECD's Council in May 1997). It remains to be seen how effective these prove to be in practice.

Another factor explaining the growing awareness of the problem in recent years has resided in the activity of an organization that was founded only in 1993, but which has already exerted a significant influence on international organizations, governments, and the business community. That organization is the Berlin-based Transparency International (hereafter TI). Founded and headed by a man who used to work for the World Bank, Peter Eigen, TI is dedicated to exposing and combating corruption, primarily as this impacts upon business. Since 1995, and with the cooperation of Dr Johann Graf Lambsdorff of Göttingen University, TI has published an annual 'corruption perception index'. Based on several surveys per country, this index provides a guide to how corrupt individual countries are perceived to be by businesspeople. The survey does not cover all countries, and is targeted very much at the kinds of corruption foreign businesspeople are most likely to encounter. Thus, for instance, it is doubtful that the kinds of experiences and knowledge many ordinary citizens in post-communist countries have

---

[80] For a collection of essays on the UN's growing concern about transnational organized crime and its strategies for dealing with this see Phil Williams and Ernesto U. Savona (eds.), *The United Nations and Transnational Organized Crime* (London: Cass, 1996).

[81] The current President of the World Bank, James Wolfensohn, has made the fight against corruption a top priority since he assumed office in 1995.

of police or military corruption would be reflected in this index. However, in terms of foreign investment, for instance, the index has the potential to be highly influential. In this connection, a recent survey conducted on behalf of the World Bank 'confirms earlier studies that corruption (as perceived by businesspeople) is negatively correlated with both investment and growth'.[82] Certainly, some post-communist governments have taken the potential influence of the TI index very much to heart. Hungary is one example; a September 1996 interview the present author conducted with a very senior official charged with combating corruption in Hungary revealed that his government was adopting various measures, on one level precisely because of the index and its influence over investment.

Government agencies themselves cannot join TI, which seeks to encourage civil society to fight corruption. Hence, it has established 'national chapters' in individual countries, run by locals who are concerned about corruption. Although there were such chapters in only eight post-communist countries by early 2,000 (Bulgaria, the Czech Republic, Hungary, Latvia, Poland, Romania, Slovakia, and Ukraine), several others (Estonia, Georgia, and Russia) were in the process of establishing them, while a third group (Albania, Bosnia-Hercegovina, Croatia, Lithuania, Republic of Macedonia, Moldova, Slovenia, and Yugoslavia) had national contacts.

In the first (1995) TI corruption perception index, only one post-communist state, Hungary, was among the 41 countries surveyed; it was ranked at number 28, where number one (New Zealand) was considered the 'cleanest' country, and number 41 (Indonesia) the most corrupt.[83] But the 1996 index included four post-communist states among its total of 54. Of these four, Poland was perceived as the cleanest (at position number 24 overall), just ahead of the Czech Republic (number 25); Hungary ranked at number 31, while Russia, unsurprisingly, performed worst, at number 47. Although the 1997 index was slightly smaller than the 1996 one, in that it covered only fifty-two countries, it added Romania to the existing four post-communist countries. The three Visegrad countries were

---

[82] 'Reducing Corruption', *World Bank Policy and Research Bulletin*, 8: 3 (1997), 2. Details of the survey methodology, plus a number of interesting regression analysis results, are provided in the article (1–4).

[83] The table was downloaded from the Transparency International homepage. It should be noted that China was also included in the first survey. This is a post-communist state in the economic sphere, but still communist in the political sphere. Given this, and the even more relevant point that this book is about CEE and the FSU, consideration of China is beyond the scope of the present study.

all perceived as having very similar levels of corruption, with the Czech Republic ranking number 27, Hungary 28, and Poland 29; Romania was some way behind, at position number 37, while Russia was even closer to the bottom of the overall list, at number 49 (ahead only of Colombia, Bolivia, and Nigeria, which was considered the most corrupt country of those surveyed).

The 1998 index was more comprehensive than the first three, surveying a total of 85 countries. In addition to the five post-communist states covered in the 1997 index, a further seven CEE and FSU countries (Belarus, Bulgaria, Estonia, Latvia, Slovakia, Ukraine, and Yugoslavia) were included in the later survey. As in the previous year, Hungary, the Czech Republic, and Poland received very similar rankings, at positions 33, 37, and 39 respectively, while Romania fared worse (at position 61), and Russia was again perceived to be the most corrupt of the post-communist states analysed, in 76th position. One of the new additions, Estonia, emerged as the least corrupt CEE state, in 26th position,[84] while Belarus and Slovakia came in at equal 47th, Yugoslavia was ranked equal with Romania (i.e. position 61), Bulgaria was in position 66, and Ukraine was ranked 69th. Counter-intuitively, it was another Baltic state, Latvia, that came second only to Russia as 'most corrupt' of the post-communist states,[85] being ranked in 71st place.[86]

In 1999, the index expanded to ninety-nine countries and covered another eleven CEE and FSU countries (Albania, Armenia, Azerbaijan, Croatia, Georgia, Kazakhstan, Kyrgyzstan, Lithuania, Macedonia, Moldova, and Uzbekistan). Estonia continued to lead the post-communist states in 27th position, followed by Hungary, the Czech Republic, and Poland, at positions 31, 39, and 44 respectively. The first of the newly surveyed countries, Lithuania, was ranked 50th. Latvia's position, in joint 58th position with Belarus, was an improvement on its 1998 performance, as was Russia's 82nd

[84] It is worth noting here that the then Estonian prime minister, Tiit Vahi, was obliged to resign in February 1997 following allegations of corruption, including that his daughter had benefited from a privatization deal.

[85] Like Estonia, Latvia lost a prime minister in 1997. Andris Šķéle's resignation in July did not relate to any alleged corruption by him, but primarily to differences between him and much of the rest of the ruling coalition over the implementation of Latvia's strict anti-corruption law. For further details see the entry on Latvia in *East European Constitutional Review*, 6: 4 (1997), 22–3.

[86] Given the amount of space that can be devoted here to TI, the analysis of the corruption perception indices has been very cursory. For a fuller analysis by the present author see Holmes, 'Corruption in Post-Communist Countries, with Particular Reference to Poland', 154–5. For a full analysis of the Graf Lambsdorff and TI methodology, see *TI Newsletter* (Sept. 1996), 5–8.

position, in comparison to Albania, Georgia, and Kazakhstan (all three at 84), Kyrgyzstan (87), Yugoslavia (90), Uzbekistan (94), and lastly Azerbaijan (96). In the centre group, Belarus continued to score surprisingly high at 58th rank, just below Slovakia (53), but above Bulgaria, Macedonia, and Romania (joint 63), Croatia (74), Moldova and Ukraine (joint 75), and Armenia (80).

Given the growing attention being paid to the TI index globally, and the point made earlier about foreign investment and corruption, post-communist governments will ignore the index at their peril. It constitutes one more way in which the international community can bring pressure to bear on post-communist states to 'clean up their act'.

The final area to consider has been the role of foreign companies, including TNCs. Such companies can on one level be seen as part of international civil society. At present, however, much of their activity in this area is being dictated by the international and supranational agencies mentioned above, and it remains to be seen whether or not they will play a distinctive 'good citizen' role in their own right. Certainly, some TNCs do appear to be taking economic crime and bribery more seriously. Shell Oil, for instance, has dismissed workers and cancelled contracts with contractors where the offering or soliciting of bribes has been proven. While this is not targeted specifically at CEE or FSU countries, its impact will be felt in that part of the world as elsewhere.[87] Unfortunately, such activity by TNCs does not currently appear to be nearly as common as it needs to be if the fight against bribery and corruption is to be effective. Moreover, the track record of TNCs in promoting better environmental awareness in the post-communist world would make observers sceptical that most will play a particularly worthy role unless forced to.

Conclusions

Crime rates do not have to keep increasing. One reason for the anomic behaviour that has become more salient a feature of so many CEE and FSU countries has been the sheer confusion—the scope of transition—of recent years. Recently, the situation has been in the process of calming down somewhat. While it is still too early to speak of true party *systems* in any of these countries, the

---

[87] See *Daily Telegraph*, London (22 Apr. 1998), 27.

situation has begun to crystallize in some.[88] Many governments and parliaments have started to catch up with their legislative backlog. As the privatization process continues, many of those who sought to take advantage of the confusion of early post-communism have begun to seek legitimacy for their economic position; they have become more enthusiastic than they were for laws that will protect their ownership. The application of computer technology to the control of crime has spread in the region. And as economies begin to pick up—and most are, if at a slower pace than had been hoped and anticipated—so the pressure to engage in crime, particularly the economic crime that was often seen in the early and mid-1990s both as a survival instinct and as a legacy of the communist system, will ease off. These are all encouraging factors.

But it would be naïve to assume that the dynamism of the current situation should necessarily encourage optimism about the future. Russia is still experiencing acute identity problems after having lost an empire. While the situation has been different and less acute in the other post-communist countries, there are still identity problems in all of them, as an inevitable result of the collapse of a totalizing system. This identity problem helps to explain the attraction of nationalism in many post-communist countries. But even nationalism is a quasi-ideology, and, as such, does not attract as many citizens as might be expected in the circumstances. It is still a belief system, and requires a basic faith that something can be done. In short, it requires a peculiar type of 'optimism'. The feelings of either despair or apathy throughout much of the region in recent years have been too deep to permit much optimism.

One method by which several post-communist countries have been seeking to strengthen their identity and legitimacy, and to raise domestic optimism, is through international recognition and acceptance. The most significant way in which they have been doing this is through their applications to join NATO and, more importantly in terms of encouraging more positive attitudes among the citizenry, the EU. In countries such as Hungary and Bulgaria, admission to the EU has almost become a new *telos* for some. For reasons that sometimes related more to unresolved issues within the EU itself than to its attitudes towards the CEE and FSU states *per se*, Brussels (or Strasbourg) was slow and cautious in beginning

---

[88] See Gabor Tóka, 'Political Parties and Democratic Consolidation in East Central Europe', *Studies in Public Policy*, 279 (Glasgow: CSPP at the University of Strathclyde, 1997) and Leslie Holmes, 'Towards a Stabilization of Party Systems in the Post-communist Countries?', *European Review*, 6: 2 (1998), 233–48.

negotiations with the ten post-communist applicants. The July 1997 EU decision to commence negotiations with five of the ten was on balance a positive move for those five—but possibly a negative development for the five 'laggards'. Negotiations between Brussels and those five (Bulgaria, Latvia, Lithuania, Romania, and Slovakia) finally began in February 2000, which should help to prevent them from turning inwards again, and away from democracy. This would have serious negative ramifications for both criminality and—by definition—democratic consolidation in those countries. Given the internationalization of crime outlined in this chapter, higher levels of alienation and criminality in these countries would inevitably mean more problems for their Western neighbours, and even for other parts of the world.

It has been argued that the West in general has been slower than it should have been, even in terms of its own vested interests, in recognizing and addressing the problems of organized crime and corruption in the post-communist world. It has further been suggested that the West, especially Western Europe, can do much to keep the democratization project in CEE and FSU countries on track by assisting in the fight against organized crime and corruption. It would be absurd not to recognize that the international context has been and remains extremely important to these countries; indeed, post-communism is as much a set of circumstances and a context as it is an identifiable phenomenon. Yet, ultimately, the problem of crime and corruption (and indeed democratic consolidation) within CEE and FSU states will have to be solved by those states and societies themselves. Post-communist governments that continue to permit overt conflicts of interest and even close ties between politicians, bureaucrats, and organized crime cannot expect the international community to respect them or treat them seriously. If the EU is to continue breaking down its internal barriers, countries that seek to join it must demonstrate a clear commitment to the consolidation of both democracy and legitimate—not *black*—market economics. Their attitudes and actions *vis-à-vis* crime and corruption will be one major indicator of this commitment. While some post-communist officials understand this, too many still do not. The ball is in their court.

8

Attitudes towards the West, Democracy, and the Market

Stephen Whitefield and Geoffrey Evans

Introduction

In both governmental and non-governmental arenas the West is generally considered to have played an important part in the process of democratization in Eastern Europe.[1] Most usually, the role of the West is seen operating at the elite level via the policies of Western governments towards the Eastern bloc and particularly the Soviet Union in the mid to late 1980s as it began to unravel,[2] or via the desire of emerging new East European political and economic elites to enter more fully into a global environment.[3] Considerable controversy, of course, has surrounded the issue of the extent to which Western involvement and influence in these senses counted in the transformation as against internal and domestic forces.[4] And discussion has also taken place on the extent to which elite views of the West—and their commitment to transition—have

Responsibility for this chapter is held equally by the two authors; order of authorship is rotated. This research was undertaken as part of the British Economic and Social Research Council's East–West Research Programme, Phase II (Grant no. Y 309 25 3025 'Emerging Forms of Political Representation and Participation in Eastern Europe').

[1] Laurence Whitehead, *The International Dimensions of Democratization: Europe and the Americas* (Oxford: Oxford University Press, 1996); Geoffrey Pridham and Tatu Vanhanen (eds.), *Democratization in Eastern Europe: Domestic and International Perspectives* (London: Routledge, 1994).

[2] Karen Dawisha and Bruce Parrott (eds.), *The Consolidation of Democracy in East-Central Europe* (Cambridge: Cambridge University Press, 1997).

[3] David S. Lane, *The Rise and Fall of State Socialism* (Oxford: Blackwells, 1996).

[4] Graeme Gill, 'The Sources of Political Reform in the Soviet Union', *Studies in Comparative Communism*, 24 (1991), 235–58.

persisted in the face of transition experience itself, including the success or failure of markets, the integration of post-communist states in Western economic and military structures (especially the European Union and NATO).[5] Many of these issues are explored in other chapters in this volume.

This chapter, however, concentrates on the stance taken by the mass publics of Eastern Europe, and in particular on their attitudes towards key aspects of the transition and how these may connect to their views of Western involvement. While there has been considerable work on mass attitudes towards democracy and the market,[6] attitudes of the public towards the West have received much less attention, at least with respect to systematic empirical analysis. None the less, a number of assumptions underlie much of the thinking on the relationship between views of the West at the mass level and support for the transition and it is these that we investigate here.

The reasoning behind these assumptions is as follows. Support for transition from communism came as an *ideological package* of mutually supporting elements, by which is meant a set of interlocking tenets that are organized into a political programme appealing to supporters and which structure their political attitudes and behaviour.[7] As such, the ideology of reform may be expected to be relatively stable over time, though subject of course to erosion with

[5] Richard Rose and Christian Haerpfer, 'Democracy and Enlarging the European Union Eastwards', *Journal of Common Market Studies*, 33: 4 (1995), 427–50; Leslie Holmes, *Post-Communism* (Oxford: Polity, 1997), 304–24.

[6] Ada W. Finifter and Ellen Mickiewicz, 'Redefining the Political System of the USSR: Mass Support for Political Change', *American Political Science Review*, 86: 4 (1992), 857–74; James L. Gibson, Raymond M. Duch, and Kent L. Tedin, 'Democratic Values and the Transformation of the Soviet Union', *Journal of Politics*, 54: 2 (1992), 329–71; Raymond M. Duch, 'Tolerating Economic Reform: Popular Support for Transition to a Free Market in the Former Soviet Union', *American Political Science Review*, 87: 3 (1993), 590–608; Arthur Miller, et al., 'Reassessing Mass Support for Political and Economic Change in the Former USSR', *American Political Science Review*, 88: 2 (1994), 399–411; Geoffrey Evans, 'Mass Political Attitudes and the Development of Market Democracy in Eastern Europe', *Centre for European Studies Discussion Paper*, no. 39 (Nuffield College: Oxford, 1995); Geoffrey Evans and Stephen Whitefield 'The Politics and Economics of Democratic Commitment: Support for Democracy in Transition Societies', *British Journal of Political Science*, 25 (1995), 485–514; David Mason, 'Attitudes towards the Market and Political Participation in the Postcommunist States', *Slavic Review*, 54: 2 (1995), 385–406; William Mishler and Richard Rose, 'Trajectories of Fear and Hope: Support for Democracy in Post-communist Europe', *Comparative Political Studies*, 28: 4 (1996), 553–81.

[7] Herbert Kitschelt, 'The Formation of Party Systems in East Central Europe', *Politics and Society*, 20: 1 (1992), 7–50.

changing circumstances. The relationships among the various components of the reform ideology, however, are historically and geographically bounded and contingent and in other reform contexts, particularly in earlier 'waves' of democratization,[8] the elements that are held to have cohered in Eastern Europe were less clearly associated. For example, in the so-called 'first' wave in which the thrust to democratization at the mass level came from the demands of the working class for enfranchisement, the relationship between support for democracy and the market were much weaker. Similarly, in the democratic movements of parts of Latin America and Southern Africa in the 'third wave', intercorrelation of democracy and both support for the market and for the West, conceived as the developed capitalist world, were also relatively absent.[9]

In Eastern Europe, by contrast, the conditions in which democracy was sought, the comparitors against which existing regimes were judged, and the main bearers of democratic support at the social level, all combined to make likely a distinct constellation of ideological elements. As Adrian Hyde-Price has written, citing Timothy Garton-Ash, 'if the revolutions of 1989 were inspired by anything, it was by the ideology of liberal-democracy, and by the "model" of Western Europe'.[10] First, and most obviously, democratization as an exit from communism made it highly likely that the economic correlate would be the market rather than state economic control; and vice versa, with marketization as an exit from communism it was more likely that the political correlate would be democracy rather than authoritarianism—though the latter variant, at least in some countries discussed below, was arguably less strongly grounded than the former. Second, the geographical location of the communist bloc and the nature of its political, strategic, and economic rivalries made it likely that the exit from communism would entail a shift to the West,[11] towards a resolution of the Cold War and the arms race, an ending of the division of Europe, and an attempt to catch up with the West by joining it rather than competing with it by other economic means. Third, those most in

[8] Samuel Huntingdon, *The Third Wave: Democratization in the Late Twentieth Century* (Norman: University of Oklahoma Press, 1991).

[9] Dietrich Rueschemeyer, Evelyne Huber Stephens, and John D. Stephens, *Capitalist Development and Democracy* (Cambridge: Polity, 1992).

[10] Adrian Hyde-Price, 'Democratization in Eastern Europe: The External Dimension', in Pridham and Vanhanen, *Democratization in Eastern Europe*, 225; Timothy Garton-Ash, 'Refolution: The Springtime of Two Nations', *New York Review of Books*, 36 (1989), 3–10.

[11] Adam Przeworksi, *Democracy and the Market* (Cambridge: Cambridge University Press, 1991).

favour of transition and most opposed to the communist order were more likely to wish to be included in the culture and benefits of the West and its democratic and market structures. Support for reform was most prevalent among the young, who were highly influenced by the dominant Western music, clothing, etc.; the educated, who may be seen to be advantaged under conditions of markets, who in general are more supportive of democratic norms, and who were most knowledgeable about the conditions in Western societies (from language training and access to foreign transmissions and materials etc.); and, of course, by entrepreneurs (or those with the potential and desire to become them), for whom markets and access to the West were essential and who saw democracy as the best way to undermine communist opposition.[12] This is not to say that only these groups shared an ideology of support for markets, democracy, and the West. As has been argued about other 'bourgeois revolutions', the success of the break from communism lay in the ability of the main proponents of change to build alliances with many other popular sectors on the basis that the ideology would lead to a general improvement in living standards.[13]

These arguments can be summarized as the following testable hypotheses:

Hypothesis 1: Support for the West, democracy, and the market is strong across the region.

Hypothesis 2: Support for the West is strongest where support for democracy and for the market is strongest.

Hypothesis 3: The countries where support for the West, the market, and democracy are at their greatest are those of Central East Europe; further East, levels of support for all three drop.

Hypothesis 4: Attitudes towards the West are strongly and positively correlated with support for democracy and the market across the region.

Hypothesis 5: Western support is most strongly correlated where democracy and the market are most strongly correlated.

Hypothesis 6: The countries in which the correlations between the market, democracy, and the West are at their greatest are those of Central East Europe; further East, the correlations among these items are weaker.

---

[12] Kitschelt, 'Formation of Party Systems'.

[13] Susan Eckstein, 'How Consequential are Revolutions? The Latin American Experience', in Dankwart A. Rustow and Kenneth Paul Erickson (eds.), *Comparative Political Dynamics* (London: HarperCollins, 1991), 309–51.

Hypotheses 3 and 6 need some further elaboration. As noted above, accounts of the region rightly point to the existence of diversity in responses and in the character of the transitions. Those countries, for example, with greater historic connections to the West, which are geographically closest, with strong cultural similarities (i.e. Catholicism versus Orthodoxy), which in strategic terms are least linked to Russia (as Russia itself is geo-strategically Eurasian), might be expected to be more committed to closer links with the West[14] and, as a consequence, to see the transition to democracy and the market as more strongly tied to the project of building relationships with the West, as compared to countries in the East (and arguably the South), whose economic, political, and cultural foci lie elsewhere and for whom the West remains a challenge to their security and identity.[15] Thus, the Czech Republic, Hungary, Poland, and Slovakia might be expected to be clearly more pro-West—and show stronger links between attitudes to the West and other dimensions of reform—while Russia, Ukraine, Bulgaria, and Belarus would be at the other end of the spectrum, with countries like Estonia, Lithuania, and Romania lying somewhere between the two extremes.

The rest of this chapter tests these hypotheses using data from national probability samples of the populations of Belarus, Bulgaria, Czech Republic, Estonia, Hungary, Lithuania, Poland, Romania, Russia, Slovakia, and Ukraine. Fieldwork was conducted in the summer of 1993 or spring of 1994. Further information on the timing, sampling, response rates, and Ns of these surveys is given in the Appendix. The surveys were based on a common questionnaire designed by the authors. The timing of the fieldwork at a point somewhat after the immediate transition and the establishment of democratic competition and the market means that some caution must be used in interpretation of data, particularly with respect to the extent to which given states had moved beyond the communist legacy at this time. None the less, given that the assumptions and arguments outlined above concern the formation of a *political ideology*, and not merely ephemeral responses, we should expect considerable stability in associations between various its various

---

[14] Attila Ágh, *The Politics of Central Europe* (London: Sage, 1998).

[15] Vladimir Shlapentokh, ' "Old", "New" and "Post" Liberal Attitudes towards the West: From Love to Hate', *Communist and Post-Communist Studies*, 31 (1998), 199–216; William Zimmerman, 'Markets, Democracy and Russian Foreign Policy', *Post-Soviet Affairs*, 10: 2 (1994), 103–26.

components and, therefore, continued evidence for the pattern of hypothesized relationships.[16]

Support for Democracy, the Market, and the West in Post-communist Eastern Europe

The first set of questions to approach relates to the level and extent of support for democracy, the market, and the West across post-communist states. How strong is support or opposition, and does it vary in ways which match some of the expectations outlined above? We consider these issues on the basis of responses to four questions put in each of the states.

First, respondents were asked what they thought about 'the aim of building democracy, conceived of as a system in which political parties competed for power'. Responses to this question are shown in Table 8.1.[17]

The results overall (bottom row) show a majority of support (55 per cent) for democratic norms in the region as against only relatively weak opposition (16 per cent). In this sense, democracy appears to be the 'only game in town' at the mass level, in terms at least of the public's views of how political competition should

[16] Elsewhere we have examined the stability of various aspects of political attitude structures and found considerable robustness in their patterns over time as well as some predictable and systematic evolution in their forms. See, for example, Geoffrey Evans and Stephen Whitefield, 'Cleavage Formation in Transition Societies: Russia, Ukraine and Estonia compared, 1993–95', Paper presented at the 92nd annual meeting of the American Political Science Association, San Francisco (Aug. 1996); Stephen Whitefield and Geoffrey Evans, 'Support for Democracy and Political Opposition in Russia, 1993–95', *Post-Soviet Affairs*, 12 (1996), 218–42; Stephen Whitefield and Geoffrey Evans, 'The Emerging Structure of Partisan Divisions in Russian Politics', in Matthew Wyman, Stephen White, and Sarah Oates (eds.), *Elections and Voters in Post-Communist Russia* (London: Edward Elgar, 1998), 68–99; Geoffrey Evans, 'Ethnic Schism and the Consolidation of Post-communist Democracies: The Case of Estonia', *Communist and Post-Communist Studies*, 31: 1 (1998), 57–74.

[17] Responses to this question were given on a conventional five-point scale which included the following options: Strongly support, Support, Neither support nor oppose, Oppose, Strongly oppose. The proportions of respondents who support and oppose democracy shown in Table 8.1 were calculated by aggregating supporters and strong supporters on the one hand, and opponents and strong opponents on the other. Similar scales and similar aggregation procedures were used for all of the other questions examined in this chapter when examining levels of support/approval. In the correlational analyses shown later the scale responses are not aggregated. They are simply scored from 1 through to 5 and coded so that a high score always represents a pro-West, or pro-reform, answer.

TABLE 8.1. *Support for democracy (%)*

	Support	Oppose
Belarus (n=1,200)	45	25
Bulgaria (n=1,932)	56	21
Czech Republic (n=1,520)	73	6
Estonia (n=2,029)	50	16
Hungary (n=1,314)	54	13
Lithuania (n=2,000)	57	18
Poland (n=1,729)	49	12
Romania (n=1,621)	81	10
Russia (n=2,030)	49	21
Slovakia (n=1,511)	59	15
Ukraine (n=2,537)	40	20
Overall (n=19,413)	55	16

be organized. Within this overall result, however, we can see very considerable variation between countries. At one extreme, with a preponderance of supporters over opponents of democracy at 66 per cent and 71 per cent, we find Czech Republic and Romania, respectively, with Slovakia and Hungary displaying the next highest levels of support for democratic norms. At the other extreme, however, we find Russia (28 per cent more supporters than opponents), Belarus (20 per cent), and Ukraine (20 per cent). There appears, therefore, to be some support for the expectations in hypothesis 3 about the relative distribution of support for democracy from West to East, although the case of Romania is somewhat anomalous. As we have argued elsewhere in this respect,[18] the explanation for the high levels of support for democratic norms in Romania—which is not matched by similarly high estimates (at least comparatively) of democracy in practice—may stem from the effects of the legacy of Ceauşescu which left Romania the most oppressed society among those in the study at the end of communism, and the relatively weak nature of the democratic transition from communism at the time the surveys were conducted which leaves a high residual level of desire to make the transition.

Table 8.2 shows the results of a similar question about the aim of creating 'a market economy with private property and freedom

---

[18] Evans and Whitefield, 'The Politics and Economics of Democratic Commitment: Support for Democracy in Transition Societies', 485–514.

TABLE 8.2. *Support for markets (%)*

	Support	Oppose
Belarus	56	25
Bulgaria	59	17
Czech Republic	73	6
Estonia	79	5
Hungary	62	9
Lithuania	70	12
Poland	59	14
Romania	78	12
Russia	62	22
Slovakia	61	14
Ukraine	50	23
Overall	64	15

of enterprise'. As with support for democracy, attitudes towards the market show overwhelming support across the region as a whole, with 64 per cent indicating support as against only 15 per cent opposition. As before, however, there are major differences between states, and once again we find the weakest levels of support—though even these remain quite powerfully in favour—for the market among the 'countries of the East': Belarus, with only 31 per cent excess of supporters over opponents; Bulgaria with an excess of 42 per cent; Russia, at 40 per cent; and Ukraine with only 27 per cent more supporters than opponents. These countries show relatively weak levels of support by comparison with others in Central Europe: Czech Republic (67 per cent), Hungary (53 per cent), Poland (45 per cent), and Slovakia (47 per cent). However, to a greater degree than was the case with democracy, support for the market outside Russia, Ukraine, and Belarus does not neatly fit with the geographical expectations of hypothesis 4: once again, Romania shows a very high level of support (excess of 66 per cent of supporters over opponents); but Estonia shows the highest levels of support of all (74 per cent excess), and Lithuania also appears more supportive than Hungary or Slovakia (58 per cent).

How, then, did the mass publics of Eastern Europe relate to the West? The first and most direct measure of this is shown in Table 8.3. Respondents were asked whether they thought that the West had been helpful to the (respondent's) country in making the transition or whether it had acted to take advantage of the country's

TABLE 8.3. *Approval of Western involvement (%)*

	Support	Oppose
Belarus	47	28
Bulgaria	46	20
Czech Republic	38	31
Estonia	20	46
Hungary	36	22
Lithuania	22	48
Poland	50	24
Romania	35	31
Russia	54	29
Slovakia	47	23
Ukraine	41	28
Overall	39	31

problems for its own benefit. Overall, as the bottom row indicates, attitudes towards the West are far less positive than those concerning democracy and the market, with only 39 per cent of respondents viewing the West favourably as against 31 per cent who see the West as taking advantage of their country's problems.

A second question concerns whether the major variations in levels of approval of the West follow the same patterns as those for support for democracy and the market. In this respect also, attitudes towards the West appear to be quite different from responses to questions about democracy and the market: *among those countries with the highest levels of support for the democratic and market transitions, we find some of the lowest levels of support for Western involvement.* In the Czech Republic, for example, the gap between approval of the West versus disapproval is only +7 per cent, and in Romania, where support for democracy and the market was particularly high, the gap is only +4 per cent. In the Eastern countries, however, approval of Western involvement is surprisingly high in absolute and relative terms: in Belarus, 47 per cent approve as opposed to only 28 per cent taking a negative view (a gap of 19 per cent); in Bulgaria, the approval gap is among the highest at 26 per cent and in Russia we find the highest approval rating of Western involvement among any of the states in the analysis—at 54 per cent, compared with only 29 per cent expressing negative views. These figures compare well with Poland—a 25 per cent approval gap—Slovakia, with 24 per cent, and Hungary with

TABLE 8.4. *Support for foreign ownership (%)*

	Support	Oppose
Belarus	32	48
Bulgaria	34	37
Czech Republic	28	50
Estonia	28	49
Hungary	49	24
Lithuania	18	64
Poland	35	48
Romania	38	38
Russia	39	47
Slovakia	25	54
Ukraine	31	43
Overall	32	46

only 14 per cent. Most intriguing of all the results in Table 8.3, finally, are those for the two Baltic states where there are very high levels of *negative* assessment of Western involvement: in both Estonia and Lithuania the approval gap is 26 per cent, with only 20 and 22 per cent approving, respectively. There appears to be little relationship therefore, between a country's rank ordering on approval of Western involvement and its rank in terms of support for democracy and the market; and levels of approval in the East appear surprisingly high.

To further check this intriguing finding we also examined another measure of support for foreign involvement, though in this case the question does not directly mention the West. (The analysis in the next section, however, indicates the extent to which responses to this measure are in fact associated with attitudes towards Western involvement.) Respondents were asked whether they favoured foreign ownership if it improved the state of the economy or if they opposed it *even if* it meant that the country would need to endure economic hardship. The question wording is thus weighted in favour of support for foreign ownership, while a negative response would indicate strong opposition. Again, however, responses to this measure correspond only moderately with support for market reform and very weakly indeed with support for democracy.

In the Czech Republic, for example, opponents of foreign ownership amount to 50 per cent of respondents as against only 28 per cent supporters, a deficit of 22 per cent; in Poland, the deficit is

13 per cent; in Slovakia it is 29 per cent; and in Lithuania, it is as high as 46 per cent—with only 18 per cent supporting foreign ownership as opposed to 64 per cent against! In Romania, where support for democracy and the market was surprisingly high, there are as many opponents of the foreign ownership as supporters. By comparison, some countries where support for the democracy and the market had been relatively weak show relatively high levels of support for foreign ownership. Russia, for example, has a deficit of Western supporters to opponents of only 8 per cent; Ukraine only 12 per cent; and Bulgaria only 3 per cent. Even Belarus, with a deficit of 16 per cent remains low by comparison with Czech Republic, Estonia, Lithuania, and Slovakia. The only country of Central Europe, in fact, which appears to confirm the direction of expected support for the West is Hungary, with a surplus of supporters over opponents of 25 per cent.

The findings so far, therefore, offer only relatively weak support for the first three hypotheses outlined in the introduction: there does appear to be strong support for democracy and the markets across the region as a whole, and the strongest levels of support do appear to be in Central East Europe with support declining the further East; however, approval of Western involvement and foreign ownership is much less positive. More importantly from the point of view of this chapter, the relative strength of aggregate approval across countries does not appear to parallel that for democracy and the market. To investigate further whether the sorts of relationships among democratic support, markets, and attitudes towards the West predicted by hypotheses 4–6 are in evidence, the next section analyses the relationships between responses to the various measures just examined.

The Relationship between Support for Democracy and the Market, and Approval of the West and Foreign Ownership

The second set of hypotheses (4–6) outlined in the introduction concerned the expected relationships among support for the democracy, the market, and the West. The underlying assumptions of these hypotheses, to recap briefly, were that the ideology of reform that emerged across Eastern Europe connected together democracy, the market, and the West; that where support for the West was strongest so these various dimensions of the reform ideology were most strongly connected; and, finally, that the strength of association between democracy, the market, and the West was most powerful in Central East Europe and declined to the East.

To test the validity of these claims, we now look at the relationships among the four items discussed above. To what extent are the relationships predicted present across the region? Are the correlations strongest where support for democracy, the market, and the West are strongest? And do the correlations decline to the East? The results are presented in Table 8.5.

(i) Democracy, markets, and the West

As the figures in the first column of Table 8.5 indicate, the relationship between support for democracy and support for the market is strong throughout Eastern Europe. For the region as a whole, the correlation is 0.43, and for each of the countries in the study, the correlation is highly significant, ranging between 0.28 at the lowest and a high figure (for survey studies of mass political attitudes) of 0.52. The data clearly indicate that, perhaps unlike other historical transitions, the two concepts comprise a reasonably closely bound package of pro- versus anti-reform beliefs in post-communist states.

This relationship, however, does not extend to a similarly powerful connection of democracy and the market to attitudes towards the West, as columns 2 and 3 indicate. The level of correlation across the region as a whole is much weaker at only 0.18 for markets and 0.10 for democracy. It is notable that the connection of approval of the West to support for democracy is particularly weak. In three states the correlation between the two measures fails even to reach statistical significance—quite a feat given the relatively large sample sizes on which the statistical calculations are based. While all of the relationships between the West and the market are statistically significant, in no state does the correlation rise above 0.24, in other words less than the weakest level of association between democracy and the market. On this evidence, it is difficult to conclude that attitudes towards the West are central to reform ideology—they are particularly distinct from attitudes towards democracy itself.

Unsurprisingly, attitudes towards the West are more strongly connected to the issue of foreign ownership. As the figures in column 4 show, the relationship between approval of Western involvement and the question of foreign ownership is more or less as strong as the relationship between support for democracy and markets. Overall, the level of association across the region is 0.37 and, once again, the weakest correlation in any of the states is higher than that of any relationship between the West and markets or democracy.

TABLE 8.5. *Correlations among attitudes towards various aspects of the transition*

	Democracy/Markets	West/Markets	West/Democracy	West/Foreign owners	Foreign owners/Markets	Foreign owners/Democracy
Belarus	0.45	0.24	0.10	0.39	0.29	0.15
Bulgaria	0.49	0.16	0.13	0.40	0.26	0.18
Czech Republic	0.44	0.24	0.23	0.42	0.29	0.19
Estonia	0.28	0.22	0.11	0.31	0.21	0.17
Hungary	0.37	0.12	0.09	0.33	0.20	0.13
Lithuania	0.28	0.14	0.00^{ns}	0.43	0.23	0.05^{ns}
Poland	0.38	0.16	0.06^{ns}	0.30	0.25	0.16
Romania	0.52	0.11	0.11	0.42	0.23	0.20
Russia	0.46	0.20	0.17	0.40	0.24	0.11
Slovakia	0.46	0.10	0.06^{ns}	0.26	0.20	0.10
Ukraine	0.41	0.12	0.06	0.34	0.21	0.12
All countries	0.43	0.18	0.10	0.37	0.23	0.13

Note: All correlations are statistically significant @ $P<0.01$ except those indicated otherwise; ns = not significant.

The final two columns show that as could be expected, the level of correlation between attitudes towards foreign ownership and support for democracy and the market parallels that of Western involvement and these aspects of reform beliefs.

We can conclude, therefore, that there is little evidence to support the strong claim made in hypothesis 4 about the existence of a reform ideology across the region comprising attitudes towards the West, democracy, and the market. While there is some evidence of a link between market support and approval of the West and foreign involvement in respondent's country's affairs, there is more or less no relationship between the latter two attitudes and support for democracy. Any popular concern over the involvement of the West does not imply such concern with respect to democratic reform more generally.

(ii) Western support is most strongly correlated where democracy and the market are most strongly correlated

(iii) Correlations are strongest in Central Europe and weaker in the East

A further possibility, however, is that the expected relationship of approval of the West with reform attitudes is present only in those countries in which markets and democracy are most strongly connected; and that these countries are mainly found in the area of Central Eastern Europe rather than the East. As outlined in the introduction, this possibility arises from the geographical, cultural, and strategic conditions of the transformation in some countries that make *both* the West *and* the whole interconnected reform package more viable for popular support. Where the conditions for pro-Western attitudes are lacking, so too may the reform ideology itself be relatively weak.

We noted from Tables 8.1–8.4 that support for the West, democracy, and the market were notably weaker in the East than among other states, especially in Russia, Ukraine, Belarus, and Bulgaria. However, differences among the other states did not appear to support the view that Central East Europe would consistently exhibit the highest levels of support. Similarly, from Table 8.5 we can consider whether more Eastern states show the weakest levels of correlation among the reform items, and whether the order of strength of correlations relates meaningfully to the extent of support for the West.

Again, however, the findings do not appear to confirm either of hypotheses 5 or 6. Taking first the relationship between democracy and the markets, which comprise a core element of reform beliefs, we can see no clear connection between countries of the East and a weakened strength of correlation: Romania shows the highest correlation, but Russia, Belarus, and Bulgaria each have as strong a correlation on these items as do the Czech Republic and Slovakia; even in Ukraine, the correlation is higher than in Poland and Hungary. Notably, Estonia and Lithuania have clearly weaker levels of association between responses to these two questions than the other states, a fact which we have explained elsewhere[19] in terms of the cross-cutting effects of ethnicity in these two newly established and insecure states in which members of the titular nationality who support markets appear concerned about the implications of extending democracy to Russians living within the states' borders. Conversely, Russian-speakers who tend to oppose markets understandably seek to extend democratic and citizenship rights to include themselves—in surveys conducted in both 1993 and 1995 around 70 per cent of Russian respondents reported that they were not entitled to vote in Estonian elections.[20]

At the same time, there does not appear to be a strong difference between Eastern and East Central states with respect to the level of correlation between approval of the West and support for democracy or markets. The correlation between approval of the West and support for markets, for example, is no higher in the Czech Republic than in Belarus; there is a stronger connection between these issues among Russians than among Poles or Hungarians; Bulgarians are somewhere in the middle of the range; and even among Ukrainians, where these issues are not very strongly correlated, the levels are higher than among Slovaks. Similar points may be made with respect to the relationship between approval of the West and support for democracy, where the correlations are, as observed above, at most very weak. While the Czech Republic is clearly strongest in this regard, Russia is next followed by Bulgaria and, after Estonia, Belarus. The correlations observed in Hungary, Poland, and Slovakia are among the lowest in the region.

Is Nationalism a Source of Opposition to the West?

Given the relatively weak relationships obtained between attitudes towards the West and attitudes towards reform, particularly

[19] Ibid.
[20] Evans, 'Ethnic Schism and the Consolidation of Post-communist Democracies: The Case of Estonia'.

democratic reform, it is important to examine whether there are other motivations and linked beliefs that either influence or are influenced by approval of the West in Eastern Europe. The most obvious such motivation is nationalism. National identities and concerns about national independence, supposedly the source of much political and social division in Eastern Europe generally[21] and evidently so in certain areas such as the Balkans, would appear to be prime candidates for interpreting why people approve or do not approve of the West's involvement in the affairs of their countries. Whilst a phenomenon as complex as nationalism is not easily indexed in our surveys, we do have a question that taps into attitudes towards national independence and another that attempts to capture the more emotive aspect of national pride and patriotism: 'Can you tell me how much you agree with the following statements about your country: *[respondent's country]* should cooperate with other countries even if it means giving up some independence.' 'People in *[respondent's country]* are too ready to criticize their country.'

Table 8.6 shows the correlations between the answers to these questions and those on the West and foreign investment.

TABLE 8.6. *Correlations between attitudes towards national independence and approval of the West and foreign ownership*

	West/Nat. independence	West/ Nat. pride	Foreign owers/Nat. independence	Foreign owners/ Nat. pride
Belarus	0.04^{ns}	0.08	0.02^{ns}	0.05^{ns}
Bulgaria	0.16	0.04^{ns}	0.08	−0.04^{ns}
Czech Republic	0.19	−0.04^{ns}	0.16	−0.05^{ns}
Estonia	−0.04^{ns}	0.04^{ns}	0.10	0.07
Hungary	0.02^{ns}	0.02^{ns}	0.08	0.00^{ns}
Lithuania	−0.08	0.01^{ns}	−0.08	0.00^{ns}
Poland	0.15	0.05^{ns}	0.03^{ns}	0.00^{ns}
Romania	0.13	0.18	0.09	0.13
Russia	0.18	0.07	0.09	0.03^{ns}
Slovakia	0.10	0.05^{ns}	0.07	0.00^{ns}
Ukraine	0.03^{ns}	−0.01^{ns}	0.03^{ns}	−0.08
All countries	0.10	0.08	0.06	−0.03

Note: All correlations are statistically significant @ P<0.01 except those indicated otherwise; ns = not significant.

[21] Kenneth Jowitt, *New World Disorder: The Leninist Extinction* (Berkeley and Los Angeles: University of California Press, 1992).

The overriding picture presented by this analysis is that issues concerning national independence and national pride are at most very weakly related to attitudes towards the West or any of the other issues examined here. The highest correlation observed anywhere is less than 0.20. Over half of the country-level correlations are non-significant even at the 5 per cent significance level, and some are even negative—indicating that there is a slightly *more* receptive attitude to the West and foreign ownership amongst those who express concern about lack of independence or lack of patriotism in their country! We can conclude that on this evidence approval of the West and foreign investment is effectively unrelated to opinions on national independence or national pride and patriotism.[22]

Conclusions

The discussion above has focused on the issue of the relative strength and connectedness of components of reform across Eastern Europe. Support for democracy and the market does appear to have been strong across the region and attitudes towards these two aspects of reform also appear to be related to one another in ways that suggest that they comprise a single reform ideology. Against expectations, however, attitudes towards the West work in a different way. Approval of the West is much less positive than is support for democracy and the market, and cross-nationally its aggregate level does not follow the patterns observed with support democracy and the market. Although Eastern states appear to be less strongly pro-democracy and market than others, they do not seem to be any less strongly pro-West. Moreover, at the individual level also there appears to be little or no relationship between approval of the West and support for democracy; and this does not differ in Central East Europe by comparison with countries further East. The case for the idea of a popular reform ideology which includes support for the West or for some states being more advanced in this regard than others, therefore, does not appear to be supported on our evidence. Also, attitudes towards the West appear to be effectively unrelated to attitudes towards national independence, thus indicating that these do not combine to form a separate axis of popular orientations that cross-cut those concerning

---

[22] Further analysis available from the authors also shows that opinions on national independence or national pride and patriotism are also effectively unrelated to support for democracy and marketization.

democratic reform. The only links that we have found at the individual level concern those between support for marketization and attitudes towards the West and foreign investment. Again, these are not strong, but they are not negligible.

These conclusions are of considerable importance to our understanding of the relationship between the West and the transition in Eastern Europe in a number of related ways. First, at least at the mass level, there appears little reason for believing that support for the democratic elements of the reform were significantly affected by views of the West. As a factor in a reform ideology, therefore, the role of the West may have been much less important than other influences affecting popular support for democracy and these elements, in turn, appear to be much less driven and connected to reactions to the West than some accounts have suggested. The corollary of this, of course, is that democracy itself may not depend on Western support or perceptions of the West's role. While there are no doubt good reasons for the West to be involved in supporting the transition in the region, including geopolitical stability and economic advantage, building democracy may be a less central consequence.

Secondly, the eastern parts of Eastern Europe, particularly the 'core' Slavic states of the former Soviet Union, do not appear to be different from other states in the ways in which the West impacts on their transitions. It does appear to be true that support for transition *per se* is weaker in these states than elsewhere in the region, and this is a matter for concern. However, support for Western involvement was not lower than other states and greater than many countries which were have been regarded as more Eurocentric in their international relations. The case for Russia, Ukraine, and Belarus as essentially anti-Western countries at the mass level does not appear to have been made on the evidence above. However, the corollary again of the analysis above is that the West may have less influence on building support for democracy in Russia and other states where it is relatively weak than other factors to do with the democratic process itself in these countries.

Thirdly, at the mass level approval of the West does not appear to be motivated by concerns about national independence. This weakens the possibility that nationalist movements in Eastern Europe can mobilize mass support against the West on such a basis. If concerns about national independence and patriotism are related to anything, it is more likely to be the near neighbours of countries within Eastern and East Central Europe with their long-running disputes and ethno-national antagonisms. So we have seen elsewhere that nationalist attitudes in Hungary are focused on the fate of ethnic Hungarians and former Hungarian territory in abutting states,[23] Estonian nationalism is more concerned about relations with Russia and Russian-speakers in Estonia,[24] and Slovaks about the territorial integrity of their new state especially in relation to the geographically concentrated (and on the Southern border) Hungarian-speaking minority and its connections with Hungary itself.[25]

Fourthly, our finding that a negative attitude towards the West and foreign investment in general is connected to a moderate degree with scepticism about the desirability of market practices provides some evidence of the incorporation of orientations towards the West into conventional democratic politics. Many East European states have seen the election of social democratic style governments in recent years as substantial proportions of their electorates have come to realize that they have a lot to lose in the unfettered free market. Such understandable reactions—exactly what might be expected on the basis of economic self-interest in a market environment[26] —do not appear to have resulted in an increased rejection of democracy itself over time.[27] Indeed, they have formed an axis of democratic political competition that can be argued to be an important element of stabilized electoral politics.[28] In a similar vein, we might expect negative views of the West to form part of this electoral competition, and not to imply a rejection of the Western model of democracy.

[23] Geoffrey Evans and Stephen Whitefield, 'Social and Ideological Cleavage Formation in Post-communist Hungary', *Europe-Asia Studies*, 42 (1995), 1177–204.

[24] Evans, 'Ethnic Schism and the Consolidation of Post-communist Democracies: The Case of Estonia'.

[25] Geoffrey Evans and Stephen Whitefield, 'The Structuring of Political Cleavages in Post-communist Societies: The Case of the Czech and Slovak Republics', *Political Studies*, 46 (1998), 115–39.

[26] For an exposition of this argument, see Geoffrey Evans and Stephen Whitefield, 'Identifying the Bases of Party Competition in Eastern Europe', *British Journal of Political Science*, 23 (1993), 521–48.

[27] For evidence on this see Evans and Whitefield, 'Social and Ideological Cleavage Formation in Post-communist Hungary'; Whitefield and Evans, 'Support for Democracy and Political Opposition in Russia, 1993–95'.

[28] Elsewhere we have conducted extensive assessments of the ideological basis of political partisanship and party competition which has provided cross-national (Evans and Whitefield, 'Social and Ideological Cleavage Formation in Post-communist Hungary'; Evans and Whitefield, 'The Structuring of Political Cleavages in Post-communist Societies: The Case of the Czech and Slovak Republics'), and over time (Whitefield and Evans, 'The Emerging Structure of Partisan Divisions in Russian Politics') support for this proposition.

Finally, we can infer from our evidence that differences in *state* responses to the West from the beginning of the transition do not appear to be grounded in differences in *mass* attitudes at least at the point in the transition captured in the surveys discussed here. As with many issues to do with the post-communist transformation, elite responses[29]—both in the East and the West—may have a substantial impact on policies adopted, whether this might be NATO or EU expansion. Over time, these policy choices may also have an effect on mass attitudes (though data available to the authors from subsequent surveys in Russia in 1995, 1996, and 1998 indicate that the shift in public opinion towards the West has not been enormous). But, at least for the period analysed here, there is little reason to believe that mass constraints to building support for the West in Eastern Europe have been powerful ones.

Appendix: The surveys

Sampling frames and stratification procedures varied between countries: in some countries census information was considered more reliable; in others electoral records were preferred; in other random route procedures were adopted with a Kish grid being used for final respondent selection. Each of these strategies was considered to be the most effective approach within the countries in which it was adopted.

Response rates were generally high despite a number of non-contacts in some countries. As far as can be told, given the fallibilities of official data, non-response biases are predictably like those in the West. Compared to Census data non-respondents tend to be older and to have lower levels of education. Non-response resulted mainly from non-contacts and refusals. Table 8.A1 summarizes the main characteristics of the surveys.

---

[29] Cf. Stephen Whitefield and Geoffrey Evans 'Support for Democracy and Political Opposition in Russia, 1993–95', *Post-Soviet Affairs*, 12 (1996), 218–42; Stephen Whitefield and Geoffrey Evans, 'The Emerging Structure of Partisan Divisions in Russian Politics', in Wyman, White, and Oates, *Elections and Voters in Post-Communist Russia*, 68–99; Geoffrey Evans, 'Ethnic Schism and the Consolidation of Post-communist Democracies: The Case of Estonia', *Communist and Post-communist Studies*, 31: 1 (1998), 57–74. (Evans and Whitefield, 'Cleavage Formation in Transition Societies: Russia, Ukraine and Estonia Compared, 1993–95'; Evans and Whitefield, 'The Structuring of Political Cleavages in Post-communist Societies: The Case of the Czech and Slovak Republics'; Whitefield and Evans, 'Support for Democracy and Political Opposition in Russia, 1993–95'; Whitefield and Evans, 'The Emerging Structure of Partisan Divisions in Russian Politics'; Evans, 'Ethnic Schism and the Consolidation of Post-communist Democracies: The Case of Estonia').

TABLE 8.A1. *The surveys*

	Sampling frame	Sampling	Response rate
Belarus Summer 1993	adult pop. (18+) Housing Offices' residence list of individuals	1. 7 regions 2. 26 settlements 3. local councils 4. individuals from residence lists randomly	names issued: 1,300+650 achieved sample: 1,200
Bulgaria Summer 1993	adult pop. (18+) 1992 census of households	two-step cluster 1. 211 census districts (from 42,000) 2. random: 12 households from each	names issued: 2,532 achieved sample: 1,932
Czech Republic Spring 1994	adult pop. (18+) list of voters from 1992 in sampled localities	1. 8 regions 2. 182 sampling points (localities) from 13,410 3. 2,104 addresses, of which: 1,681 random list sampling (electoral register): 423 random route + 111 quota	names issued: 2,104 achieved sample: 1,409+111
Estonia Summer 1993	adult pop. (18+) 1989 census of households	1. 5 regions 2. 15 counties 3. 321 sampling points 4. random-route/household 5. Kish matrix/respondent	names issued: 2,285 achieved sample: 2,029
Hungary Spring 1994	adult pop. (20+) Central Register of Population (1992)	1. 12 counties representing regions 2. 78 sampling points 3. random selection of individuals	names issued: 1,703 achieved sample: 1,314
Lithuania Summer 1993	adult pop. (18+) random route (rural) Register Office address lists (urban)	1. 5 regions 2. 180 sampling points 3. rural—random route urban—address list	names issued: 2,982 achieved sample: 2,000

TABLE 8.A1. (*cont'd*)

	Sampling frame	Sampling	Response rate
Poland Summer 1993	adult pop. (18+) Central Register of Individuals	1. 8 regions 2. 4 types of settlements	names issued: 2,040 achieved sample: 1,729
Romania Summer 1993	adult pop. (18+) Electoral Records	1. 4 provinces 2. 4 types of settlements 3. electoral constituencies (126 from 51 settlements)	names issued: 2,000 achieved sample: 1,621
Russia Summer 1993	adult pop. (18+) lists of 'privatization vouchers'	1. 10 regions 2. 56 settlements 3. indiv. from list of vouchers	names issued: 2,420 achieved sample: 2,030
Slovakia Spring 1994	adult pop. (18+) list of voters from 1992 in sampled localities	1. 4 regions 2. 215 sampling points (localities) from 4,191 3. 2,014 addresses of which: 1,100 first wave; 914 second wave. Random list sampling (electoral register) + 68 quota	names issued: 2,014 achieved sample: 1,443+68
Ukraine Summer 1993	adult pop. (18+) Housing Offices' residence list of individuals	1. 70 urban+50 rural settlements 2. 7 types (only urban)—selection proportional to size of pop. in each type	names issued: 2,984 achieved sample: 2,537

The questionnaires contained approximately 300 items developed over several months with extensive back-translation procedures. They were pilot-tested on 50 or more respondents in each country prior to being finalized for use in the survey. All interviews were conducted face-to-face in the respondents' homes. Checks on the interviewers were carried out by local area supervisors. Quality was also checked in most countries with a follow-up study of 10% of the respondents to the initial survey, who were randomly selected and re-interviewed a few weeks later.

The fieldwork in Belarus was directed by Dr A. Vardomatsky, of NOVAK, Minsk; in Bulgaria by Dr V. Topalova, Institute of Sociology, Bulgarian Academy of Sciences, Sofia; in the Czech Republic and Slovakia by L. Rezler and Professor J. Hartl of STEM; in Estonia and Lithuania by Dr R. Alisauskene, Baltic Surveys, Department of Sociology, University of Vilnius; in Hungary by Dr P. Robert, TARKI, Budapest; in Poland by Professor M. Ziolkowski, University of Poznan; in Romania by Dr I. Marginean, Institute of the Quality of Life, Bucharest; in Russia by Professor V. Yadov, director of the Institute of Sociology of the Russian Academy of Sciences; and in Ukraine by Dr N. Churilov, Director, Institute of Sociology, Ukrainian Academy of Sciences, Kiev.

PART II

National Perspectives

9

Estonia and Latvia: International Influences on Citizenship and Minority Integration

Vello Pettai

In 1986, Laurence Whitehead argued that external actors generally contribute more to consolidating democratizing regimes than
they do to initiating the transition process itself.[1] This statement
implied that any democratizing country was likely to follow its own
dynamic of exit from authoritarian rule (depending in part on the
type of non-democratic regime), while during the subsequent stages
of consolidation and integration with the rest of the democratic world,
international factors could play a more determining role. Yet such
a pattern of events, however, is complicated by the extent to which
particular pathways from authoritarian rule during the first stage
of transition may create dependent conditions for democratic consolidation and international influence during the second. During
the 1970s and early 1980s, Whitehead noted that democratic
transition in Central and Latin America often resulted in a surge
of left-wing politics, which later proved difficult for international
actors such as the United States to support.[2] During the 1990s wave
of democratic transition in Eastern Europe, the main challenge for
securing democratic consolidation through international influence
was the widespread rise of nationalism and ethno-political tension.

This chapter will argue that the Baltic states, and in particular
Estonia and Latvia, represent examples of this complicated sequence of endogenously derived transition and exogenously influenced

---

[1] Laurence Whitehead, 'International Aspects of Democratization', in Guillermo
O'Donnell, Philippe C. Schmitter, and Laurence Whitehead (eds.), *Transitions from
Authoritarian Rule: Comparative Perspectives* (Baltimore: Johns Hopkins Univer-
sity Press, 1986), 20.

[2] Ibid. 24–5.

consolidation. These two states were at the forefront of democratization and reform during the perestroika era of the Soviet Union. This impetus for change was deeply rooted and long-lasting enough to sustain the two republics through a four-year struggle for independence from Moscow. After the failed Soviet coup of August 1991, this progressive spirit further buttressed a rapid transition to procedural democracy, including the installation of new constitutional structures in all three states within a period of fourteen months. Yet, these democratic transitions also set certain parameters for their subsequent democratic consolidation. In particular, Estonia and Latvia opted for a nationalist, 'legal restorationist' view of their independence, which insisted that the two states had not seceded from the Soviet Union nor emerged as successor countries from its ruins, but had rather restored their legal statehood at the conclusion of a fifty-year illegal occupation and annexation by the Soviet Union.

This particular interpretation of transition represented a somewhat problematic combination of two paths toward redemocratization—paths which, based on Alfred Stepan's typology, could be described as 'society-led regime termination' and 'internal restoration after external reconquest'.[3] The first section of this chapter examines this apparent contradiction. Using the second approach ('internal restoration after external conquest') both countries drew certain unsettling conclusions regarding citizenship rights, which entailed a decision to deny automatic citizenship to over 1.2 million mostly Russian Soviet-era immigrants to the two republics (the argument being that these people had entered the countries during an illegal occupation). While these controversies never led to direct confrontation or violence, they did create important challenges for both democratic consolidation in Estonia and Latvia and the ability of international actors to influence this process. The nexus of international influence and democratic consolidation in the Baltic cases emerged most saliently in this respect. The second part of this chapter will examine the Estonian and Latvian cases at large, with a discussion of the major international actors involved in these transitions, their particular mechanisms of engagement, as well as their results to early 2000. In conclusion, it is argued that international influences (in particular, from the European Union) have increased as the two countries integrate more with the West. To be sure, the problems of citizenship and minority integration remained long-term,

---

[3] Alfred Stepan, 'Paths toward Redemocratization: Theoretical and Comparative Perspectives', ibid. 62–84.

requiring at least another decade to resolve. However, the strength of Western democratic organizations to provide that support both politically and financially had also so far proved substantial.

Paths of Democratic Transition

The process of democratic transition in the Baltic states during the late 1980s and early 1990s has already been widely documented.[4] These accounts tell the tale of three small peoples who pushed the liberalizing policies of Mikhail Gorbachev to the limit and helped bring an end to communism and the Soviet Union. Yet, to date, there has been little analysis of the transitions as set against one of the best known typologies of democratic transitions developed by Alfred Stepan in the mid-1980s. Placed in this context, the Baltic picture is no longer so clear. In fact, an interesting split emerges between two different models. This split has had important consequences for democratic consolidation in Estonia and Latvia.

Stepan's categorization of paths toward redemocratization was drawn from the wide range of countries in Southern Europe and Latin America that underwent the transition process either after the Second World War or during the 1970s. From this comparative perspective, Stepan identified three basic categories of transition, which focused on whether the transition was driven by (1) warfare and/or foreign conquest, (2) the relinquishment of power by the authoritarian rulers themselves, or (3) the successful efforts of opposition forces to restore democracy.

In his analysis, Stepan rightly stressed that 'any empirical case of redemocratization may well—and almost certainly does—contain features of more than one category'. 'In fact,' he added, 'successful

---

[4] Among the most comprehensive studies, see Rein Taagepera, *Estonia: Return to Independence* (Boulder, Colo.: Westview Press, 1993); Andrejs Plakans, *The Latvians: A Short History* (Stanford, Calif: Hoover Institution Press, 1995); Juris Dreifelds, *Latvia in Transition* (Cambridge: Cambridge University Press, 1996); Rasma Karklins, *Ethnopolitics and Transition to Democracy: The Collapse of the USSR and Latvia* (Baltimore: Johns Hopkins University Press, 1994); Alfred Erich Senn, *Lithuania Awakening* (Berkeley and Los Angeles: University of California Press, 1990); V. Stanley Vardys and Judith Sedaitis, *Lithuania: The Rebel Nation* (Boulder, Colo.: Westview Press, 1997); Ole Norgaard, Dan Hindsgaul, Lars Johannsen, and Helle Willumsen, *The Baltic States after Independence* (Cheltenham: Edward Elgar, 1996); Walter Iwaskiw (ed.), *Estonia, Latvia, Lithuania: Country Studies* (Washington: Federal Research Division, Library of Congress, 1996); Graham Smith (ed.), *The Baltic States: The National Self-Determination of Estonia, Latvia, and Lithuania* (London: Macmillan Press, 1994).

redemocratization, given the built-in limitations of certain paths taken by themselves, may well require the simultaneous pursuit of several paths.'[5] Yet, while this conclusion seems beyond doubt, it raises important questions about the possible consequences of such mixed-path transitions for further democratic consolidation and the influence that foreign actors may have on the consolidation process.

In the case of the Baltic states, two possible models emerge from Stepan's typology. The first echoes the widespread scholarly interpretation of Baltic redemocratization as having been a case of 'society-led regime termination'. Under this scenario, authoritarian rule was brought to an end by popular forces either through grassroots movements, spontaneous but effective public protest, or a general end to popular tolerance of the regime. In the Baltic states, these elements were all present after Mikhail Gorbachev's policy of perestroika unleashed a torrent of popular mobilization and led to the creation of opposition popular fronts in all three republics. These movements, in turn, spearheaded the toppling of the communist leaderships in each republic during 1988 and set the stage for democratic elections to take place in early 1990. The spirit of this path toward democracy was very much society based. It was epitomized by the 23 August 1989 Baltic chain, which stretched from Tallinn to Vilnius and involved up to 2 million people in a protest to mark the fiftieth anniversary of the Molotov–Ribbentrop pact, which ceded the Baltic states to the Soviet Union on the eve of the Second World War.

As Stepan noted, the final transition to democracy under such a society-driven model is usually carried out by moderate leaders of the authoritarian regime, who assent to holding elections and have the opportunity to set the new rules of the game. That is, the path usually switches to one where the authoritarian regime seizes the initiative, since popular protests or actions can exert pressure or initiate the process, but are rarely sufficient to take over actual government.[6] The society-based model may not be enough in itself to achieve full transition.

In the Baltic cases, the reform communist leaders who assumed power in 1988 sought to guide the transition once it had been started by the people.[7] The results were mixed depending on the country.

[5] Stepan, 'Paths toward Redemocratization', 64.

[6] Unless a dictator physically flees from the country, such as Ferdinand Marcos or Mobutu Sese Seko.

[7] These leaders were Vaino Väljas in Estonia, Anatolijs Gorbunovs in Latvia, and Algirdas Brazauskas in Lithuania.

As a result, these leaders also had a role to play in determining the modalities of transition. Still, the Baltic transitions have generally gone down in history as the 'Singing Revolution', where the Baltic peoples themselves drove the movement toward democracy and freedom through massive concerts and rallies during 1987 and 1988.

Yet, during this mobilization period, the references that were made to historical events such as the Molotov–Ribbentrop Pact and the Soviet takeover of the Baltic states in 1940 led to a second conception of transition in the Baltic states, which more closely resembled Stepan's first-category model of 'internal restoration after external reconquest'. In this scenario, 'redemocratization takes place when a functioning democracy that has been conquered in war restores democracy after the conqueror is defeated by external force.'[8]

At first sight, the Baltic cases do not appear to fit this model at all. None of the three states was a democracy before the introduction of Soviet rule in 1940; they had each already succumbed to authoritarian rule during the 1920s and 1930s. Nor is it possible to state that Soviet rule was defeated by 'external force' or 'reconquest'; rather, it simply collapsed. However, for a sizeable number of Baltic residents and politicians, redemocratization involved precisely the restoration of a previously legitimate state and regime, once the Soviet 'conqueror' had been vanquished. In all three countries, there were (in addition to the popular fronts) strong movements in favour of rejecting any recognition or participation of the existing communist rulers (whether reformist or not) in the process of redemocratization precisely because Soviet rule itself was deemed to have been an illegal conquest and therefore illegitimate *ipso facto*. The only way to come out of such a situation, it was argued, was to restore the pre-war regime, much as had been done in Norway, Holland, Denmark, or elsewhere after the Nazi German occupations of 1940–4. Although in the Baltic case the Soviet conquest had admittedly lasted fifty years, this did not diminish the historical fact that the three states had been illegally occupied and annexed by Stalin. Therefore, it was maintained that the process of redemocratization had to begin from that earlier, interrupted point in time. In fact, many believed there was even an element of 'external force' in the Baltic democratic restoration process to the extent that a majority of Western nations had never *de jure* recognized the incorporation of the Baltic states into the Soviet Union and therefore

[8] Stepan, 'Paths toward Redemocratization', 66.

were formally in favour of the restoration of the three states' independence and democracy. Although the West would never help reconquer Baltic democracy by force, it did provide important external moral and political support to Baltic leaders and thereby placed pressure on Moscow.

In Estonia and Latvia, in particular, this model was the one maintained and asserted by the 'Citizens Committees' movements.[9] Although initially based more on rhetoric and radicalism, these two movements went on to organize special 'citizens congresses' or quasi-parliaments elected on the basis of each country's pre-war citizenry and the principle of state restoration. The movements claimed in turn that only these congresses had the legal right to decide each country's mode of transition and restoration of independence from the Soviet occupying power.

Although neither of these movements was able to challenge the strength of the Estonian and Latvian popular fronts, they were nevertheless able to have a large part of their ideology put into practice. For example, both countries' 1990 independence proclamations (on 30 March and 3 May respectively) stressed the fact that in 1940 these states had been illegally occupied and annexed by the Soviet Union and that therefore the two peoples had a right to restore their statehood from that moment in time. For Estonia and Latvia, these statements represented clear declarations of 'internal restoration' after the 'reconquest' of power from Moscow, and not simply authoritarian collapse.

Yet, while this transition pathway proved to be relatively effective in terms of gaining exit from the Soviet Union, the consequences of this choice have been more ambiguous for democratic consolidation. In the scholarly literature, the concept of democratic consolidation has long been differentiated from that of democratic transition. Mainwaring, O'Donnell, and Valenzuela,[10] and also more recently Linz and Stepan,[11] have sought to understand the challenges of securing long-term democratic stability and development, once the basic transition to democracy has been completed. Beyond the holding of free and fair inaugural elections or even the establishment of procedural democracy, democratic consolidation has been defined as relating to more fundamental elements of change, such

---

[9] As well as the Freedom League in Lithuania.

[10] Scott Mainwaring, Guillermo O'Donnell, and J. Samuel Valenzuela (eds.), *Issues in Democratic Consolidation: The New South American Democracies in Comparative Perspective* (Notre Dame, Ind.: University of Notre Dame Press, 1992).

[11] Juan J. Linz and Alfred Stepan, *Problems of Democratic Transition and Consolidation: Southern Europe, South America, and Post-Communist Europe* (Baltimore: Johns Hopkins University Press, 1996).

as the development of sound constitutionalism, the maturation of effective party systems, the strengthening of civil society, the safeguarding of minority rights, and the execution of necessary economic reforms.[12] Clearly, these tasks take years, if not decades to achieve in any country. However, they are essential for guaranteeing the longevity of democracy as well as for improving the quality of democratic governance over time.

For the purposes of this chapter, it is important to note two points. First, in most cases, the path of democratic transition will have a great impact on (*a*) the particular challenges facing democratic consolidation and (*b*) its general prospects for success. Both the political or social forces who carry out the democratic transition, as well as the ideologies or understandings that they bring to the process, will determine the parameters for the second-stage process of democratic consolidation. In addition, the particular non-democratic regime type also matters (whether authoritarian, totalitarian, sultanistic, or other), as does the manner in which the constituent actors of such regimes conceive of their interests and imperatives. Hence, the question of democratic consolidation is in many ways path-dependent on the specifics of democratic transition.

Second, the challenges of democratic consolidation are such that no single democratizing country will be likely to cope with all of them alone. By definition, these problems will necessitate assistance from or cooperation with the international democratic community. Indeed, these challenges are likely to open up the international angle of democratic change; they both engage and expose a country to international democratic influences. Still, the extent of this influence remains to be seen precisely.

In sum, these circumstances reflect a nexus between an endogenously derived transition and an exogenously influenced consolidation. The Baltic cases present two contrasting paths of transition that were evident during 1988–91. We now turn more closely to the consequences of these paths for democratic consolidation.

The Baltic Test Case: Citizenship and Minority Integration

The victory of the restorationist path to democracy in Estonia and Latvia has led to a number of complications for democratic consolidation, in particular as regards the areas of citizenship and

[12] Ibid. 62–4; see also Guillermo O'Donnell, 'Transitions, Continuities, and Paradoxes', in Mainwaring, O'Donnell, and Valenzuela, *Issues in Democratic Consolidation*, 17–56.

minority rights. Such rights go to the heart of democratic politics. They are a precondition for social harmony and political development. At the same time, they are among the elements of democracy that often take the longest time to build and effectively institutionalize. Thus, this discussion will focus on them as a case study of international influences on democratic transition and consolidation in the Baltic states. We will see that the issue of citizenship and minority rights has been one of the more difficult areas for foreign actors to influence.

During the late 1980s, the idea of restoring pre-war statehood had been very positive from the standpoint of giving all three Baltic states the confidence to demand independence from Moscow. The legalistic arguments of Soviet occupation and annexation allowed a very clear case to be made that the only solution to the conflict with Moscow was independence. However, after 1991, the principle that Soviet rule had been illegal led to more problematic political practice.

In Estonia and Latvia, the restorationist thesis was applied additionally to the question of defining the status and rights of all Soviet-era immigrants to these two republics once independence was restored. If Soviet rule had been illegal, Estonian and Latvian politicians argued, then these immigrants (including their children) were also technically illegal. Even if they had lived in the republics for forty-five years or had even been born there, they had still entered the republics under an illegal occupation. Thus, it was considered impossible to now grant them automatic citizenship rights. Instead, they could at best hope to become naturalized citizens, and only after appropriate laws and procedures had been adopted, including the passage of a language exam as well as certain residency requirements.

In October and November of 1991, the Latvian and Estonian parliaments respectively adopted resolutions laying down these citizenship policies. More detailed legislation governing the precise naturalization procedures was passed later. Nevertheless, these decisions affected an estimated 450,000 people in Estonia and 750,000 in Latvia out of respective populations of 1.5 million and 2.6 million. With such a high percentage of people suddenly shut out of the political process, the question of whether these countries even continued to be democracies quickly surfaced.

The imperative to adopt such restrictive citizenship policies in both countries came largely from the sheer numbers of these mostly Russian immigrants. Soviet policy had encouraged Russian and other Slavic migration to Estonia and Latvia, ostensibly because of a shortage of labour for industrial development. Most Estonians and Latvians viewed this, however, as a veiled attempt to Russify the two republics, since the waves of immigrants came on top of large-scale deportations of native Estonians and Latvians during the late 1940s. In 1945, Estonia was over 95 per cent Estonian, and Latvia well over 80 per cent Latvian. By 1989, these figures had dropped to just 61.5 per cent and 52 per cent respectively. The idea of excluding all of these immigrants from automatic citizenship on the basis of legal restorationism seemed for many Estonians and Latvians a just measure of compensation for their own suffering and sense of injustice during the Soviet era. Their republics had been so profoundly altered ethno-demographically by Soviet rule that it seemed only right that a certain degree of prerogative be restored to the eponymous peoples, even if through such a drastic measure as citizenship. Such an approach also had the advantage that it was not based on ethnic criteria. On the contrary, many thousands of ethnic Russians in both countries also qualified for citizenship, since they or their descendants had lived in Estonia or Latvia before 1940, while some Estonians and Latvians, who had lived all their lives in Russia, did not qualify. None the less, the result of the new citizenship policy was that some 90 per cent of the citizens in Estonia were now Estonian, and roughly 78 per cent of the citizens in Latvia were Latvian—a much larger proportion than existed in the actual population of either country. After new parliamentary elections were held in each country during September 1992 and June 1993 respectively, the takeover of ethnopolitical power was complete: all 101 deputies in the new Estonian parliament (the Riigikogu) were ethnic Estonian, some 90 per cent of the deputies in the Latvian parliament (the Saiema) were ethnic Latvian.

The Challenge of International Influence: Players and Mechanisms

During the tumult of perestroika and the break-up of the Soviet Union, the international community had been largely ineffectual in influencing the course of democratic transition in the Soviet republics. With these countries now free and aspiring to democratic consolidation, however, the room for interaction and positive influence has become much greater. The desire on the part of most post-communist countries to join Western political organizations and to establish trade relations and economic cooperation seemed to augur well for encouraging democratic development in these new nations. In the case of the Baltic states, the prospects seemed particularly good, since a 'return to the West' had been the leitmotif of the entire democratic transition process beginning as early as 1987.[13] The Baltic states, thus, seemed especially open to international influence.

Still, the Baltic path toward democracy took them in some unexpected directions. In Estonia and Latvia, the legal restorationist ideology created major distortions in the democratic process through exclusionary citizenship policies. Confronted with this situation, the West had to see how much of this could be corrected or moderated through political engagement and gentle persuasion. The main lever of influence that the West was able to exert was conditioning the admission of Estonia and Latvia into major international organizations as well as monitoring their compliance with international norms once they became members. The key players in this process were thus the Organization for Security and Cooperation in Europe (OSCE), the Council of Europe (COE), and the European Union (EU).

The OSCE

The Baltic states' relations with the OSCE became one of the first cases of international influence on Estonia's and Latvia's democratic processes. For the Baltic states, the OSCE was important as a forum from where they could demand the speedy withdrawal of ex-Soviet troops from their territories. The OSCE helped the three states by drafting a resolution at the July 1992 Helsinki summit calling on Russia to remove its forces as soon as possible. However, the OSCE was equally concerned about the situation of ethnic minorities in the Baltic states, and in particular in Estonia and Latvia. By 1992, the outbreak of ethnic conflict in the former Yugoslavia, Moldova, Georgia, and Nagorno Karabakh had prompted the OSCE to develop diplomatic mechanisms to help mediate such hostilities.[14]

---

[13] Marju Lauristin et al., *Return to the Western World: Cultural and Political Perspectives on the Estonian Post-Communist Transition* (Tartu: Tartu University Press, 1997).

[14] For an overview of the OSCE's involvement in ethnic conflicts, see Diana Chigas et al., 'Preventive Diplomacy and the Organization for Security and Cooperation in Europe: Creating Incentives for Dialogue and Cooperation', in Abram Chayes and Antonia Handler Chayes (eds.), *Preventing Conflict in the Post-communist World: Mobilizing International and Regional Organizations* (Washington: Brookings Institution, 1996), 25–97.

In the case of the Baltic states, where no direct conflict had erupted, the issue involved developing 'preventive diplomacy', to prevent low-level ethnic tensions in the Baltics from escalating beyond control. This goal was given special impetus by the establishment of a High Commissioner on National Minorities also at the OSCE's July 1992 summit in Helsinki. The former Dutch Foreign Minister, Max van der Stoel, was assigned to the position. In the spring of 1993, van der Stoel visited all three Baltic states to assess the situation of ethnic minorities. Subsequently he wrote letters to all three Baltic foreign ministers, detailing his impressions and offering relevant suggestions to each country in order to improve ethnic relations.[15] In Lithuania, van der Stoel did not note any serious problems nor did he make any radical suggestions for change.[16] In Estonia and Latvia, however, van der Stoel was faced with the task of assessing the fairness of the two country's citizenship laws as well as other possible human rights concerns. At the conclusion of his trips to Estonia and Latvia, the High Commissioner was careful to stress the lack of any 'systematic' violation of human rights in either country. He did not explicitly comment on the two countries' legal restorationist policies on citizenship. However, he did emphasize the need to maintain a dialogue between citizens and non-citizens, including the possible creation of a national commissioner or ombudsperson for ethnic minorities in each country. Both Estonia and Latvia politely welcomed van der Stoel's suggestions. However, in practice, they generally adhered to their legalistic interpretation of the citizenship issue, which in accordance with international law was viewed as the sovereign right of each country.

Still, growing international scrutiny of Estonia and Latvia in the area of minority rights prompted Estonia to invite the OSCE in late 1992 to establish a Long-Term Mission to the country in order to monitor the local situation. The practice of setting up such missions had begun in the former Yugoslavia in mid-1992. However, Estonia was the first country to volunteer for such a presence. The formal decision was taken at a meeting of the OSCE's Committee of Senior Officials in December 1992, and the seven-member mission started its work in February 1993.[17] In its Terms of Reference, the

[15] For the complete collection of Max van der Stoel's communications with the Baltic states, see the website of the Minelres discussion list, http://www.riga.lv/minelres/index.htm.

[16] Indeed, this was the High Commissioner's only subsequent contact with Lithuania as of the beginning of 1998.

[17] For more on the work of the OSCE Mission to Estonia, see Vello Pettai, 'Developing Preventive Diplomacy and Ethnic Conflict Resolution: The OSCE

mission was charged with monitoring the situation in the areas of 'citizenship, migration, language questions, social services and employment' as well as 'to further promote integration and better understanding between the communities in Estonia'. In October 1993, a similar OSCE mission was established in Latvia. As their main task, the missions were to work with local Estonian and Latvian officials as well as with representatives of the non-Estonian, non-Latvian, and non-citizen communities to enhance dialogue between them. The missions were required to submit regular reports to the OSCE secretariat, in order to provide objective information on the exact state of ethnic tensions in each country. This aspect of the mission's work was very favourable for Estonia and Latvia, since it provided continuous proof of the fact that human rights were not being systematically violated in either country, as the Russian Federation frequently charged. Nevertheless, the missions were also part of an international oversight mechanism.

In 1994, the scope of the two missions was expanded to include the task of assisting in the implementation of Baltic-Russian Federation accords, which led to the final withdrawal of ex-Soviet troops from the region. This job included helping to monitor the dismantling of the former Soviet radar base in Skrunda, Latvia (a process which was completed in 1999), and the granting of residency permits to retired former Soviet military personnel in both Baltic states. Although the missions were officially accredited to each country for a limited six-month period, in practice their mandates were consistently renewed by the Estonian and Latvian governments. In the late 1990s there were signs that Estonia was ready to terminate the work of the OSCE mission by refusing to prolong its mandate. However, a consensus among Western countries that the mission should continue kept Tallinn from forcing the issue.

The Council of Europe

A second source of international influence on Estonia and Latvia was the Council of Europe (COE), the continent's premier organization for the defence of democratic norms and human rights. At the end of the Cold War, the Council faced a dilemma with the emergence of so many new democracies in Central and Eastern

Mission to Estonia', in Sarah Mendelson (ed.), *Evaluating NGO Strategies for Democratization and Conflict Prevention in the Formerly Communist States* (New York: Carnegie Endowment for International Peace, 2000).

Europe.[18] While wishing to contribute to the further democratization of these countries, the COE had to be careful about immediately admitting any or all of them without tangible evidence that democracy had taken root. This issue was often addressed individually with regard to each applicant country. In the Baltic states, the COE had to confront the citizenship issues in Estonia and Latvia as well as the more standard issues of capital punishment and prison reform in all three Baltic countries.

In 1991–2, the Council dispatched various teams of rapporteurs to each Baltic state to assess each country's level of democratization and suitability for membership. The main criterion was the holding of free and fair parliamentary elections, which the COE also helped to monitor on behalf of the international community. Estonia and Lithuania were the first to fulfil this requirement in September 1992 and November 1992, respectively. From then on, the road was clear for their admission on 14 May 1993. In Latvia, fresh parliamentary elections did not take place until June 1993. Thereafter, the COE continued to hold out until the country had adopted a formal citizenship law to flesh out the original restorationist declaration from October 1991. This did not happen until July 1994. As a result, Latvia's final admission was delayed until 10 February 1995.

The European Union

After their independence in 1991, the Baltic states did not expect to gain very early admission to the EU. Their economic condition and level of political institutionalization was simply not sufficient for any of them to join such an advanced international community immediately. Still, the Union itself maintained a positive attitude toward all of the new democracies of Central and Eastern Europe by providing millions of ECUs (later euros) in assistance for infrastructural projects, administrative capacity building, educational programmes, and political integration. Relations between the EU and the Baltic states were established in August 1991 immediately after independence. Thereafter throughout 1997, Brussels maintained a balanced approach toward the three states, always negotiating and signing all agreements with Tallinn, Riga, and Vilnius simultaneously. For example, on 11 May 1992 the EU concluded an

[18] For a discussion of the Council of Europe in the post-Cold War era, see Jean Manas, 'The Council of Europe's Democracy Ideal and the Challenge of Ethno-National Strife', in Chayes and Chayes, *Preventing Conflict in the Post-communist World*, 99–144.

Agreement on Trade and Commercial and Economic Cooperation with each of the Baltic states. This agreement provided for 'most favoured nation' trade status between the EU and the Baltic states. On 18 July 1994, an Agreement on Free Trade was signed between Brussels and the Baltic states, which went into effect on 1 January 1995. This agreement was significant in that it solidified the three countries' intention to join the Union in the future. Finally, on 12 June 1995 the three states signed Association Agreements with the EU, which was the last stage of cooperation before negotiating membership.

In the autumn of 1995, all three Baltic states formally applied to join the EU.[19] With this, they became eligible to participate in the process of accession which the European Commission worked out its 1995 White Paper on enlargement to Central and Eastern Europe. In April 1996, the three Baltic states were handed the EU's questionnaire on political and economic reform, which each applicant country was asked to fill out. On the basis of this, a preliminary decision was to be made by the Commission about the suitability of each state for beginning official membership negotiations. In July 1996, the Balts submitted their information to the Commission and together with the rest of the eleven candidate countries they began a year of anxious waiting to see which of them would be accepted into the first round of enlargement talks.

According to various reports from Brussels and the other EU capitals, the debate over whether to include any of the Baltic states in the first round was fairly contentious. While many EU member states (in particular, the Mediterranean countries and France) were cautious about rapid enlargement, the Nordic states generally supported Baltic inclusion. The European Commission itself was split over the exact number of states that should be given the initial nod. On 10 July the decision was taken in favour of Cyprus, Poland, Hungary, the Czech Republic, Slovenia, and ultimately Estonia. Despite previously having treated the Baltic states as a single whole, the Commission now decided to include Estonia separately. On the one hand, the acceptance of all three Baltic countries in the first round would have been too much to handle at once. On the other, many commissioners were keen to give a signal of the EU's intention to expand into the Baltic area. Meanwhile, Estonia for its part had the longest history of economic reform among the Baltic states. Also, in the six months prior to the EU's decision Tallinn had mounted a vigorous lobbying campaign among EU states

---

[19] Estonia on 28 Nov., Latvia on 27 Oct., and Lithuania on 8 Dec.

touting its readiness to begin accession talks. This combination paid off for Estonia, while in Latvia and Lithuania it led to great disappointment. At the Luxembourg EU summit in December 1997, the EU heads of government formally approved the Commission's selection of first-round candidates. Official negotiations began with Estonia on 30 March 1998.

International Influences on Estonian and Latvian Ethno-politics

The institutional links which the OSCE, the COE, and the European Union developed with Estonia and Latvia in 1992–3 proved their worth in subsequent years. However, the new citizenship policies caused shifts in Estonian and Latvian politics and gave rise to challenges in building truly integrated and democratic societies for the future. In the initial term, the West was more often forced to respond to political crises than it was able to focus on achieving long-term reconciliation and societal harmony.

Both Estonia and Latvia had always agreed to offer non-citizens the opportunity to become naturalized citizens. However, the question was now in terms of how favourable these procedures would be in order to promote the reintegration of these people into the political system. Would the citizenship divide be a temporary one, through which the Estonians and Latvians would achieve a symbolic recognition of their suffering during the Soviet era, but which thereafter would be quickly overcome through an acceptance of these non-citizens back into the body politic? Or would the divide stagnate over time, with naturalization requirements set too high and most non-citizens prevented from becoming citizens in the near future? These were the basic questions facing the OSCE, the COE, and the European Union in seeking to advance democratic consolidation in the region.

Estonia was the first country to face these pressures. Following its November 1991 decision to restrict automatic citizenship to pre-war citizens and their descendants, the Estonian parliament formally reinstated the country's 1938 citizenship law in February 1992 as its framework for naturalizing the new non-citizens. While, in principle, the terms were fairly liberal,[20] the law suffered delays before it was enforced. For example, there were delays in determining the

---

[20] These included a two-year residency requirement, the passage of a minimal language proficiency exam, and an additional year-long wait for processing.

exact specifications of the language exam, including the level of proficiency required as well as those people who might be exempted from the test because of disability or age. Also, the law allowed for citizenship to be passed on only along the paternal line of descent. In the process of negotiating Estonia's entry into the COE during early 1993, Strasbourg demanded the Estonian parliament amend these particular paragraphs in the law.[21]

Despite this positive beginning, a second controversy arose shortly before Estonia's final accession to the COE in May 1993. Under the country's 1992 constitution (Art. 156), non-citizens were given the special right to vote in municipal elections in order to allow them to participate in the political process at least on the local level. The provision did not, however, include the option to stand for office. During the final visit of Estonia's delegation to Strasbourg in May 1993, the COE (led by the chairman of the COE Parliamentary Assembly Miguel Ángel Martinez) sought to prompt Estonia to grant the right to run for local office to non-citizens. The pressure generated fierce debates in Tallinn as the Estonian parliament was precisely in the midst of discussing the law on local elections. Ultimately, however, Estonia (together with Lithuania) was admitted to the COE on 14 May 1993 and five days later, when the Riigikogu in Tallinn approved the local election legislation, an amendment to grant both electoral rights to non-citizens was overturned by nationalist deputies. In the end, only the voting rights were passed.[22]

This outcome soured Estonia's early relations with the COE. However, this was only the beginning of what became a fairly turbulent summer for Estonian ethno-politics and Western international organizations. Little more than a month after the local election controversy, both the OSCE and the Council of Europe faced one of the most serious tests of preventive diplomacy, when Estonia adopted a highly controversial Law on Aliens. The law as originally passed by the Riigikogu on 21 June required all non-citizens to apply for new residency permits within one year in order to maintain their legal status in Estonia. Moreover, there were no guarantees given that even long-standing residents of Estonia would be granted a new residency permit. This insecurity prompted widespread protests among the leaders of Estonia's non-citizen population, who viewed the measure as a veiled attempt to force

---

[21] These changes allowed citizenship to be passed on along the maternal line, and exempted people born before 1930 from the language exam.

[22] *Postimees* (20 May 1993).

non-citizens out of Estonia. Small demonstrations took place in the north-eastern towns of Sillamäe and Narva, where many non-citizens live. The controversy soon led to a special visit to Estonia by Max van der Stoel, who encouraged Estonian President Lennart Meri to veto the law while urging non-citizen leaders to avoid any rash responses.

Eventually, Meri vetoed the law and accepted an offer to have a team of legal experts from the Council of Europe review the legislation. This was one of the first instances where the COE was requested to share its considerable experience in legislative matters. Indeed, it created a useful precedent for resolving other minority rights issues in the Baltics. On 8 July, the Riigikogu amended several sections of the measure to include a guarantee that current legal residents in Estonia would receive new residency permits. Although the OSCE was unsuccessful in discouraging the local leaders in Narva and Sillamäe from holding controversial referendums in July on territorial autonomy for their two cities, the organization did win a pledge from the town leaders that they would respect a ruling by Estonia's Supreme Court on the legality of their move. In August, the Court declared the referendums unconstitutional and with that the crisis subsided.

The Aliens Law controversy in Estonia was an early success in the international community's efforts to mediate political tensions in the Baltics. However, it also underscored the degree to which monitoring efforts would still have to go in order to hope for long-term normalization of the citizenship issue. If controversy had already erupted over the simple issue of establishing legal residency rights for non-citizens, then the chances for promoting more rapid integration of these societies were limited at best.

This type of crisis alleviation reoccurred during the summer of 1994, when the Latvian parliament began its own debate on a naturalization law for non-citizens. Spurred on by radical nationalist deputies, the Saeima's first draft provoked considerable controversy by including a strict limit on the number of people, who could be naturalized in one year.[23] Again, the OSCE mission, as well as Max van der Stoel, encouraged Latvian President Guntis Ulmanis to veto the law. They argued that such restrictions would be undemocratic since they could potentially prevent some people from being naturalized simply because the quota for any given year

---

[23] The figure was 0.1% of the total number of citizens during the particular year in question, which in turn would have meant a total of only around 1,600 naturalizations per year.

had been filled. The Council of Europe also made recommendations regarding the citizenship law. This combined pressure eventually proved effective, as on 22 July the Saeima agreed to abandon the quotas. Instead, the parliament opted for a staggered (or so-called 'windows') system of naturalization, whereby different categories of non-citizens would gradually become eligible to apply for naturalization depending on the length of their residency in Latvia.[24] This compromise, although not ideal, relieved some of the tension surrounding the issue and allowed the process to continue.

Positive Integration Takes Hold

Only in 1996–7 did the first signs of a shift in ethnic policy become evident. In Latvia, work began in early 1996 on a National Programme for Latvian Language Training. This was one of the first initiatives taken in order to encourage a long-term improvement in the ethnic climate. Sponsored by the United Nations Development Programme and other foreign donors, the ten-year plan was designed to provide Latvian language training for students and teachers of all ages. During 1997, the programme developed new Latvian language textbooks and teaching methodologies. It also held several cycles of language courses across the country. The aim was to improve the Latvian language skills of average Russian-speakers in Latvia, so that they would be better able to integrate into Latvian society, both on a daily and professional level. The idea proved so successful that in 1996 work began on a similar programme in Estonia. The European Union agreed to allocate an impressive 1.4 million euros to finance the Estonian programme. However, a language strategy for teaching Estonian was not completed until early 1998. As a result, work did not begin on implementing the programme until the middle of the year. Still, by 2000 the programme was running as extensively as in Latvia.

In Estonia, progress in promoting openness was made also with the creation of a special ministerial post for ethnic affairs in May 1997, held by Andra Veidemann, the leader of the small Progressive Party. While this was in part a political move by Prime

[24] For example, those born in Latvia and aged 16–20 would become eligible already in 1996. In 1997, the circle would widen to include non-citizens born in Latvia and aged 21–5. Thereafter, more 'windows' would be opened each year until all non-citizens would become eligible by the year 2003. Still, this meant that, for instance, those people who were born outside Latvia and had moved to the republic after the age of 30 would become eligible to apply only in the year 2002.

Minister Mart Siimann to gain the support of the Progressive Party in parliament, Veidemann took her appointment very seriously. Within two months, she had formed a high-level commission in order to work out an official minority integration policy for Estonia as a blueprint for the future. Although the four-page document which was completed in early 1998 was vague, it did call explicitly for 'a significant reduction in the number of persons with undetermined citizenship' (i.e. non-citizens), as well as 'a substantial breakthrough in the teaching of the Estonian language and the real participation of non-Estonians in Estonian society'.[25] In February, it was adopted by the government as official policy; in June, it was also endorsed by the Estonian parliament. Subsequently, a more detailed programme of action was drafted, which included the creation of a special Integration Foundation to fund various non-governmental organizations and other projects related to minority integration. For 1998–2000 the Foundation was given roughly 6 million Estonian kroons (about $425,000) annually from the state budget. In 2000, the government was preparing a comprehensive integration programme totalling over 50 million kroons ($3 million).

These positive steps in both countries provided encouragement that international influences were working. However, an important reason for this success was that during 1997–8 both countries had significantly improved their prospects for joining the European Union within the next decade. More than any other single mechanism of influence, the EU made most Estonian and Latvian politicians realize that improving the citizenship issue was critically important. While the European Commission's July 1997 reports on Estonia and Latvia had been generally positive, both noted the serious need 'to accelerate naturalization of Russian-speaking non-citizens, to enable them to become better integrated' into Estonian and Latvian society.[26] While it was unlikely that the EU would condition Estonian or Latvian membership on a radical reversal in policy and the granting of easy citizenship to non-citizens, it was clear that the EU viewed the citizenship issue as a problem, especially if the rate of naturalization were to stagnate

[25] 'The Integration of Non-Estonians into Estonian Society: The Bases of Estonia's National Integration Policy', Document adopted at the 10 Feb. 1998 session of the Government of the Republic of Estonia. For later versions of the Estonian integration program, see http://www.riik.ee/saks/ikomisjon/programme.htm.

[26] See 'Summary and Conclusion' in *Agenda 2000—Commission Opinion on Estonia's Application for Membership of the European Union*, as well as *Agenda 2000—Commission Opinion on Latvia's Application for Membership of the European Union*.

and non-citizens in the two countries were to become a permanent underclass.

In order to prevent such a development, the OSCE High Commissioner Max van der Stoel began to stress in 1997 the need to make at least one important change to the two countries' citizenship laws. This involved granting automatic citizenship to children born to non-citizen parents, particularly if the child would otherwise be stateless. This was a principle accepted by all other OSCE member states, but had yet to be incorporated into Estonian and Latvian legislation. Each year some 1,000 or more stateless children were born in each country, meaning that, at this level, Estonia and Latvia were actually perpetuating their citizenship divide.

In both countries, legislation was drafted in order to rectify this situation. However, getting the bills through parliament proved to be a difficult endeavour. Estonia was the first to draw up its bill, which the government submitted to parliament in December 1997. The Riigikogu, however, did not take up the bill until March 1998. Thereafter, the bill languished, as the minority government led by Mart Siimann became too consumed with other political crises to risk forcing the delicate citizenship issue. In June, the parliament briefly discussed the law again (partly at the behest of President Meri). However, thereafter the discussion was adjourned until December, at which point the bill was finally passed—quite pointedly just in time for another EU summit.

In Latvia, a minority government also struggled for survival. It was caught in an even more serious bind, since Prime Minister Guntars Krasts was leader of the nationalist 'For Fatherland and Freedom' party, which opposed any changes in the citizenship law that did not *tighten* naturalization procedures. Moreover, when the six-member government coalition was formed in July 1997, their agreement included an explicit statement that changes to the citizenship law could take place only if all the parties agreed. As a result, the government and parliament were largely paralysed on the issue. Only President Guntis Ulmanis was free to act. Since late 1996 he had been calling for a liberalization of the citizenship law, and in particular, for the abolition of the 'windows' system. His calls, however, fell on deaf ears. In early 1998, the result was another political crisis requiring international mediation and influence.

On 3 March 1998 a demonstration by some 1,000 mostly Russian pensioners took place outside the Riga city council building. The pensioners were protesting against price increases for heating in the city as well as the miserly level of pensions in Latvia, which fell below even the government's estimate of a minimum subsistence income. The unauthorized meeting, however, led to disruptions in street traffic and a confrontation with police trying to regulate the crowds. In the ensuing chaos, television cameras captured the police beating a number of pensioners. The footage was soon broadcast around Europe, prompting a major political crisis. The Russian government immediately charged Latvia with gross human rights violations and calls were made in the Russian parliament to impose economic sanctions on Latvia. Tensions increased on 16 March when approximately 400 Latvian war veterans from the Nazi German army held an annual gathering in Riga. The veterans were all old men. However, they included many who had served in the infamous Waffen-SS. Although the Latvian government had banned its top officials from attending the gathering, both the commander of the Latvian army as well as the deputy chairman of parliament took part. A few days later the army chief was forced to resign by President Ulmanis. However, on 1 April a bomb was planted at the Jewish synagogue in downtown Riga causing heavy damage. Five days later a similar small device exploded near the Russian embassy.

In the midst of this political instability, attention coalesced on demands to amend the Latvian citizenship law. Both Max van der Stoel and the European Union tried to steer Latvia toward this point of compromise, in order to relieve the crisis. In April, the Latvian government drafted a series of amendments based on recommendations van der Stoel had made several months beforehand. These steps included abolishing the 'windows' system, granting citizenship to stateless children, and easing language requirements from citizenship applicants over 65. Controversy arose repeatedly around the second requirement, as many Latvian parliamentarians favoured granting citizenship to stateless children only at the age of 16 and only if they had attended a Latvian school and passed the state education exam in Latvian language.[27] Van der Stoel, however, strongly opposed these moves, arguing that they would render that particular amendment meaningless. The European Union also put pressure on Latvia to pursue a genuine liberalization of the law, mainly through statements by the United Kingdom, which held the EU presidency at the time.

Again, the West was forced to play a delicate balancing act between prompting compromise from Latvia on citizenship and

---

[27] Similar attempts to water down the citizenship law amendments were made in Estonia during the June 1998 debate in parliament. However, these amendments were defeated by the government coalition.

appeasing the vociferous complaints of the Russian Federation. On the one hand, increasing economic and political instability in Russia itself had made it more tempting for Russian politicians to assail problems in neighbouring countries as a way of deflecting attention from domestic travails. Calls to protect the rights of Russian compatriots in the former Soviet republics have been a popular nationalist slogan since 1992. However, Latvia had painted itself into a corner by resisting changes to its citizenship law, even after it became evident in 1997 that the 'windows' system was not working and that it was doing more harm than good to the minority integration process.[28] The result was that Latvia was forced to make amendments to its law under direct pressure from Moscow and the West, instead of on its own terms. This added strain led to a split in the Latvian government. On 8 April, the largest party in the coalition, the Democratic Party-Saimnieks (DP-S) abruptly left the government, claiming that Prime Minister Krasts had failed in his handling of the political crisis. The DP-S clearly hoped to force a general collapse of the government, after which it could potentially take over the reins of government. However, Prime Minister Krasts survived a subsequent series of no-confidence votes and eventually shored up a government majority.

On 22 June, the Latvian Saiema finally adopted the three amendments to the citizenship law, as van der Stoel and the European Union had recommended. This move brought commendations from the West and even a certain amount of recognition from Moscow. However, the issue was not fully resolved. The law was suspended for two months, after thirty-four deputies in parliament used a special clause in the Constitution to force a delay in its implementation. During this time, a signature campaign was started in order to put the law to a national referendum. Although the effort succeeded, the referendum itself failed to pass and in October the law went into effect.

The 1998 crisis in Latvia was certainly a setback for Western efforts to finally turn the ethno-political corner and begin promoting the positive integration of non-citizens and minorities into

---

[28] For example, by July 1997, only 5,000 people had been naturalized under the existing system, even though some 124,000 non-citizens had become eligible. Studies showed that while a majority of non-citizens were interested in applying for citizenship, they often felt they would not be able to pass the necessary language or civics exams; see 'National Integration and Social Cohesion', in *Latvia: Human Development Report 1997* (Riga: UNDP, 1997), 54–5. Many non-citizens had also been simply demoralized by all the political controversies, so that they no longer felt motivated even to try.

Latvian society. With the EU also now stressing minority integration and the accession of Latvia to the Union, Western pressure
seemed to be increasing. However, in late 1998, the issue of the
adoption of a new, tougher Latvian language law remained open.
The Latvian parliament had drawn up this law in 1996, but its
passage had been halted by criticism from the Council of Europe
and the OSCE.[29] The COE, in particular, had organized an expert
legal analysis of the draft (just as it had done with the Estonian
Aliens Law in 1993), which had pointed to several questionable provisions within it. While some of these critiques were accepted, many
were not, and finally the law was simply passed by the parliament
in July 1999. The result was a new crisis with the West, which
forced the newly elected president of Latvia, Vaira Vike-Freiberga
to make a tough choice in vetoing the legislation. This move again
forced the Saeima to back down in December and remove objec-
tionable provisions in the law. Yet, with each instance of crisis, the
same scenario appeared to be repeating itself.

Still, one promising development was the formation in May 1998
of a government commission to draft an official policy on minority
integration, similar to the one adopted earlier in the year by
Estonia. The commission again was very much the result of the
European Union, which had pressured the Krasts government into
approving the idea. However, its members included a wide spectrum of moderate as well as radical Latvian officials with only a few
non-Latvians. Moreover, the parliamentary elections of October 1998
meant that the implementation of any integration policy would be
delayed until a new governing coalition had been formed. Indeed,
this highlighted another important precondition for progress: the
formation of a strong and capable government to lead the integration
process into the future. By 2000, the programme had gone through
a wide-ranging public discussion, but it still awaited a complete
set of policy tasks and funding allocations.

Conclusions

This case study of Estonia and Latvia has argued, on the one
hand, that the specific path a country chooses toward democratic

---

[29] The draft law stipulated that all documents, correspondence, and business
meetings in private firms would henceforth have to be in Latvian. It also man-
dated that all public gatherings and demonstrations should be conducted only in
Latvian. Both points drew criticism from the COE and the OSCE for violating the
rights of private business as well as the right to public assembly.

transition is likely to create certain path-dependent problems that it (and the rest of the democratic community) will ultimately have to face during democratic consolidation. In Estonia and Latvia the choice of state restorationism during 1990–1 led to the emergence of a significant divide in both societies on the basis of citizenship. It was a legacy which would take years to resolve, not only in terms of simple naturalization, but also in terms of improving social integration. Still, the strength of the Western 'pole of attraction' for the Baltic states meant that, at many key moments in time, the West played a crucial role in returning Estonia and Latvia to an even keel. The OSCE and the Council of Europe were the first players in this process, while starting in 1997–8 the European Union became the central actor, as it represented the most advanced level of democratic integration that the Baltics could aspire to, and it therefore possessed the most leverage in terms of setting particular political demands.

By early 2000, Estonia and Latvia showed signs of modifying their ethno-political policies in order to encourage the positive integration of minorities and overcome the policy of political exclusion. International influence on this process would no doubt continue. Still, the story of the Baltic transition had been one largely of struggling towards consolidation, out of the hole that had been dug by 'legal restorationism'. Many would argue that this hole had originally been dug by the Soviet Union and its policy of Russification in the Baltic states. On this score, these arguments are certainly right. However, with the Soviet Union gone and the Baltic states looking to rejoin the West, the minority question was one that only the Estonians and Latvians themselves could resolve and for which only they would ultimately be responsible.

10

Hungary: Understanding
Western Messages

László Valki

Democratic consolidation has proceeded more easily in Hungary than in most East European countries. In 1989 the Hungarian political and economic elite was relatively well prepared to establish democratic political institutions and to introduce a market economy. The reform government and the existing political parties reached an agreement on free elections, on the details of a pluralistic parliamentary system, on abolishing the command economy, and on attracting foreign capital to Hungary.

Hungary's development between the 1960s and 1989 in many ways paved the way for the new system as reforms brought greater openness and exposure of the political and economic elite to influences from the West. Economic reforms were introduced in the mid-1960s, and a kind of—as they called it—'social compromise' reached between the political leadership and the nation. The political institutions did not change, but the scope for freedom of thought and action widened to some extent. The standard of living rose, limited travel to the West became possible; freedom in scientific and cultural life was one that Honecker's or Ceauşescu's subjects never enjoyed. As a result, an intellectual elite emerged that knew much about the democratic institutions of the West.

This elite included those who were part of the political establishment—they were later called 'reform communists'. Another part of the elite did not join the establishment; it was confident that the communist system would sooner or later vanish. The latter gathered in opposition groups. János Kádár tried to restrict their activity by using various police measures, but that was all he could do. Kádár had to show considerable tolerance toward the opposition. By the 1980s the regime had become considerably dependent on the West. This was due first and foremost to the increasing deficit in Hungary's balance of payments, primarily as a delayed consequence of the oil crisis. Since Kádár wanted to maintain the standard of living, he had no choice but to obtain Western loans. As a result, Hungary became increasingly dependent on Western political decision makers, who used this opportunity to apply the policy of conditionality. The West compelled Kádár to refrain from implementing drastic suppressive measures against the opposition. Conditionality could be maintained continuously since decisions on extending loans had to be taken in short intervals. Kádár could only impede, but not stop the opposition in its activity.

The third group in the elite consisted mainly of the representatives of an older generation which had opposed the communist regime from the beginning, though—with some exceptions—did not fight against it. This group upheld the *Weltanschauung* of the 1930s characterized among others by opposition to the 1920 Trianon Peace Treaty which had deprived Hungary of two-thirds of its territory and one-third of its population. This group looked back on the foreign policy of governor Horthy during the inter-war period with some sympathy, particularly on his attempts to regain possession of territories inhabited by Hungarians. This group began to play an increasingly important role in the opposition movement which emerged in the second half of the 1980s, and was joined by many of the younger generation, for whom Trianon and the border question did not carry much significance, but who condemned Ceauşescu's and Husák's suppressive, nationalist ethnic policy and would have liked to help their compatriots beyond Hungary's borders. This group described itself as having 'national sentiments' as opposed to the 'liberals' who were allegedly indifferent to the fate of ethnic Hungarians in Romania or Czechoslovakia. Since this whole *Weltanschauung* was rooted in the Horthy era, it could never get away from its legacy of nationalism. Thus concern about the fate of ethnic Hungarians in the neighbouring countries became linked with concern for Hungarians living in Hungary. Many claimed that the 'liberals' also pushed 'genuine Hungarians' into the background. Inevitably, 'reform communists' were rated among the liberals though they were neither communists, nor liberals (maybe social democrats). All in all, in the second half of the 1980s, this rather heterogeneous Hungarian intellectual elite was ready to establish a Western-type pluralistic democracy.

This introduction has tried to clarify the nature of a special conflict that characterized this period of democratic consolidation in Hungary. While there was complete agreement with regard to the essential aspects of the establishment of the democratic institutions, debates on the 'nationalist agenda' were disproportionately intensive. Foreign policy conflicts directly became domestic policy conflicts, dominating in many ways the period between 1988 and 1998. Thus, the need for direct intervention in Hungary's democratic consolidation on the part of the international environment arose relatively few times where domestic political development was concerned, and rather often where Hungary's actions in international relations—mostly with neighbouring countries—were concerned.

Establishing Democracy

The 'social compromise' between the communist leadership and the nation started to dissolve rapidly from the mid-1980s. Between 1985 and 1987, the first free and open intellectual gatherings took place, the most important meeting of which was held in Lakitelek in autumn 1986 and was attended by both 'reform-communists' and members of the 'national' and 'liberal' opposition. The congress of the Worker's Party held in May 1988 ended the Kádár era. Kádár himself was dismissed from the Politburo and replaced by a more liberal communist leader. These months marked the first phase of the transition to a pluralistic political system. The recent leading parties were established at that time. In March 1988 the Federation of Young Democrats was founded, in September the Hungarian Democratic Forum, in November the Alliance of Free Democrats, the Smallholders' Party, the National Peasants' Party, and the Hungarian Social-Democratic Party.[1] The government became increasingly independent of the Workers' Party, the reformer Miklós Németh became prime minister, and a few months later Gyula Horn was appointed foreign minister.

In November 1988, the parliament discussed the 'democracy package' submitted by Imre Pozsgay. After its acceptance, the parliament commenced the preparation of the most important laws serving the establishment of political pluralism. The laws on the creation of the Constitutional Court, on the right of association, including the right to establish a party, the right of assembly, the right to strike, and on plebiscite were passed in the spring of 1989. Codification of institutional elements of the new democratic system posed no real difficulties. Exhaustive work had been carried out for years at universities and in research institutes, in the course of which the experts became acquainted with the operation of

---

[1] Soon the Peasant's Party and the Social Democratic Party disappeared from the political scene. Their members mostly joined other parties.

Western institutional systems. These experts spent months in leading democratic countries studying the advantages and disadvantages of various constitutional and legal models. For historical reasons, the German model, whose electoral system is characterized by a combination of proportional and individual constituency, as well as by a strong prime ministry and a powerful Constitutional Court, was the most influential in developing the Hungarian constitutional structure.[2] The question of introducing the American or French presidential system did not even arise since they had no roots in Hungarian constitutional and legal culture.

The process of development of democratic institutions was interrupted by an unexpected turn. In June 1989, the Workers' Party commenced negotiations in the framework of a 'Roundtable' with the opposition parties concerning the institutions of the new political system.[3] There was nothing to compel the party leaders to do so. There were no demonstrations, opposition parties did not exert special pressure on the Workers' Party, and more or less everyone was satisfied with the course of events. According to some observers the Workers' Party might have wanted to come to an agreement with the emerging opposition parties in the hope that a coalition government could be set up under socialist leadership. This would have meant a modelling of the Polish pattern. At similar roundtable negotiations in the spring of 1989, the Polish Workers' Party made an agreement with Solidarity to the effect that it would have a 'reserved' two-thirds majority in parliament. Some say that the leaders of the Hungarian Workers' Party would not have considered the Polish model attractive enough even had negotiations ended differently in Warsaw.[4] However, such a proposition was never on the agenda in Hungary. The negotiators—putting aside the democracy package—came to an agreement in September 1989 with regard to all essential issues. The government had no choice but to pledge an obligation to submit bills to parliament in accordance with the agreement.

Many explain this with reference to the direct pressure applied by Western governments, which closely followed the course of events at the time, and played an important role in having the Németh government consent to holding these negotiations. Primarily American politicians and diplomats, together with the British and

---

[2] Since Hungary was part of the Habsburg Monarchy, both the German language and the German legal and political culture dominated the Hungarian legal research.

[3] 'National Roundtable' (13 June 1989).

[4] Rudolf Tőkés, *Hungary's Negotiated Revolution* (Cambridge: Cambridge University Press, 1996), 307.

the Germans, played a decisive role. At the time, these diplomats were in daily contact with the members of the government, as well as with the representatives of every significant political group. President Bush's visit in July 1989 may have also had an impact on the outcome of the Roundtable. Bush supported the standpoint of the opposition, and he insisted publicly on meeting with the leaders of the opposition parties. Otherwise, according to Rudolf Tőkés, the Workers' Party hard-liners 'might have been tempted to terminate the regime's dialogue with the Hungarian "insurgents" in July 1989'.[5]

More generally, the July 1989 G7 summit in Paris may have also contributed to the creation of more favourable conditions for Central European changes. The summit declared Poland, Czechoslovakia, and Hungary as the 'countries with the best chances of success in effecting peaceful transitions to a postcommunist world'. According to Tőkés, in doing so the Western political community made an explicit bid to become active participants in the areawide process of Central Europe's forthcoming realignment.[6] The West— particularly the United States—did much to also reassure the leading politicians: 'Washington extended explicit guarantees to the incumbents of their personal immunity during and after the political transition.'[7] If this is true, then the West made a vital contribution to peaceful transition in Central Europe.

This, however, offers only a partial explanation for ensuing events. The reformers made many independent decisions of crucial importance. In July 1989, the government ordered the removal of the technical alarm system from the Austro-Hungarian border. In August, Németh and Horn decided that East German refugees would be allowed to leave Hungary in a few weeks' time. No doubt, their intention was to hasten the collapse of the East German regime. The government renounced the secret bilateral cooperation agreement with the KGB, and the last Soviet liaison officers were removed from the Interior and the Defence Ministries. In October, the Workers' Militia, the paramilitary organization of the Workers' Party, was disbanded. At the beginning of October, the Workers' Party itself was disbanded, and the Hungarian Socialist Party was founded. The 23rd of October, the anniversary of the 1956 revolution, was declared a national memorial day and the 'Republic of Hungary' was proclaimed.[8] In March 1990, the Németh government signed an agreement with the Soviet Union on the withdrawal of

---

[5] Ibid.   [6] Ibid. 435.   [7] Ibid. 437.
[8] Replacing the 'Hungarian People's Republic'.

Russian troops from the country. The last Soviet soldier left Hungary on 16 June 1991, two weeks before the deadline set by the agreement.

However, the Németh government was disappointed by Western policy. It believed that the West, specifically the IMF, would save the Hungarian economy which was teetering on the brink of bankruptcy. In the spring of 1989, the IMF delegation proposed that the Hungarian government implement strict austerity measures in exchange for loans, but the government considered this step very dangerous, and the delegation left without reaching an agreement. The government then turned to the European Community, but was also rejected. In November 1989, Jacques Delors explicitly told the Hungarian prime minister that the Community would refuse to extend any assistance unless an agreement was reached with the IMF. Germany did not give assistance either. In December, Chancellor Kohl visited Budapest, expressed his gratitude to Németh and Horn, but did not promise anything. In other words, the international community wanted to achieve Central Europe's peaceful transformation rather cheaply.

According to the compromise reached at the Roundtable, the first free general elections took place in May 1990, and were won by a coalition of three opposition parties. The right-wing Hungarian Democratic Forum obtained 25 per cent of the votes, the Smallholders 12 per cent, and the Christian-Democrats 6 per cent. The prime minister became the chairman of the Forum, József Antall. In fact, the second largest party at the time, with 21 per cent of the votes, was the liberal Alliance of Free Democrats. The Socialists obtained only 11 per cent. They both remained in the opposition with the (then) liberal Federation of Young Democrats which received 9 per cent of the votes.

The second free elections, held in 1994, rearranged the allotment of the seats in parliament entirely. The Socialists won 33 per cent of the votes but, due to special rules of the elections that favoured the winners, they gained 54 per cent of the seats in parliament. This party could have formed government alone but it decided to govern in a coalition with the Free Democrats, who obtained 20 per cent of the votes. Consequently this government had a comfortable, 72 per cent majority in the parliament. The Democratic Forum obtained only 12 per cent and the Young Democrats 7 per cent. The prime minister became the chairman of the Socialist Party, Gyula Horn.

After 1994, the Federation of the Young Democrats abandoned its liberal position and turned conservative, successfully trying to create an alliance of right-wing parties. As a result, when the third election took place in 1998, it was won by the Federation of Young Democrats by 30 per cent of the votes, the Smallholders by 13 per cent, and the Democratic Forum by 2.8 per cent.[9] The prime minister became the chairman of the Young Democrats, Viktor Orbán. The Socialists received 33 per cent of the votes but had to go to the opposition.

The democratic consolidation in Hungary was more or less completed between the second and the third elections.

Economic Reform and Consolidation

Economic survival was a question of life or death for the new democratic state. Following the changes in 1989–90, the economic situation in Hungary became extremely difficult, like in the other Central and East European countries. Due to the sudden collapse of the command economy and the disintegration of the Comecon market, Hungarian economy faced a crisis. Between 1989 and 1992, GDP declined by 18 per cent. Although consumption did not decline at the same rate since the population began to exhaust its savings, the standard of living fell considerably, by about 10 per cent, and 20 per cent of the population already lived below subsistence level.[10] Hungary reached its lowest point in 1991 when, compared to the previous year, GDP declined by 11.9 per cent, inflation rose to 35 per cent, and 7.8 per cent of the labour force became unemployed in a country where there had been virtually no unemployment since the Second World War. In 1991, the per capita gross external debt was highest in Hungary among the CEE countries (2,192 USD).[11]

In Budapest both the government and business circles looked to external assistance. Some talked about the necessity for a new Marshall Plan. The well-known economist, Iván T. Berend stated that all the countries of the region were incapable of pulling themselves out of their own crisis.[12] Antall was aware of the gravity of the situation even before the elections. He assumed that unless he

[9] The Forum did not reach the 5% threshold but had enough directly elected representatives to join the new coalition. Between the first and the third elections the Forum lost most of its supporters and also its ballast, the extreme right wing of the party and the leadership of an old generation. Now the Forum is a moderate conservative party.

[10] László Csaba, 'A rendszerváltás gazdaságpolitikájának egy évtizede' ('A Decade of Transformation in Economic Policy'), *Beszélő*, 3: 5 (May 1998), 16.

[11] *CESTAT Statistical Bulletin*, 1977, No. 6.

[12] Iván T. Berend, 'Új Marshall-tervre lenne szükség' (There is a Need for a New Marshall Plan), *Népszabadság* (11 Jan. 1991).

managed to obtain foreign assistance for the post-election period, economic collapse would ensue. He therefore began negotiations with the IMF, the bankers of G7 countries, and with some heads of state, among them Helmut Kohl. Antall thought that, in order to assist 'well-behaved' Hungary, the West would cancel a considerable part of the debts, or at least reschedule them. He was proved wrong. As in case of the Németh government in 1989, the IMF refused to extend any extraordinary assistance, furthermore, it was not prepared to support either cancellation or rescheduling of debts. The country's currency reserves at the time of Antall's election amounted merely 650 million USD. Nevertheless, the West expected Hungary to service its debts.

As in the case of other CEE countries, the European Community made no special effort to assist the East European countries, including Hungary. In accordance with the resolution of the Dublin summit in April 1990, negotiations on association commenced between the Community and Hungary. The text of the so-called Europe Agreement was finalized and signed by the end of 1991. Thereafter it took two whole years for the member states to ratify the agreements; thus it entered into force in February 1994. The Hungarian participants reported that the negotiations were difficult, the EC remaining firm in representing the interests of its member states. Brussels primarily wanted guarantees that the Hungarian markets, companies, banks, etc. would be accessible to its member states. Earlier, it achieved this aim by admitting new members and compensating them with aid paid from various funds, but the association agreements contained nothing about compensation. Hungary—like the other CEE associate countries—were compelled to accept the conditions of an industrial free trade without membership rights, although their economy could not be prepared in such a short time. Furthermore, free trade did not include the agricultural export of Hungary into the Community, which represented a significantly greater volume than their agricultural imports. The Community continued to pursue a protectionist policy. Hungary gave unilaterally greater benefits to the Community than it received through the Europe Agreement. The liberalization of trade and services had similar consequences. True, prior to these negotiations, the Community did make a gesture toward Hungary. As of 1 January 1990, it unilaterally rescinded its quantitative import restrictions, extended its general system of preferences (GSP) to Hungary, and launched the PHARE aid programme.[13] Subsequently, due to

---

[13] Initially, the PHARE assistance was offered to Hungary and Poland but later nearly all CEE states were involved in the project.

the protraction of ratification by Western states, an Interim Agreement was concluded between the Community and Hungary according to which the regulations governing trade and trade-related issues of the agreements became effective as early as 1 March 1992.

However, the association agreement did not stop the economic recession in Hungary. At that time, the average rate of the Community's external industrial tariffs was around 4 per cent. More than half of these were immediately rescinded when the agreement entered into force. However, all tariffs on textile and steel products considered 'sensitive'—which constituted 25 per cent of Hungarian exports—were rescinded only in 2000. Obviously, rescinding such low tariffs contributed very little to the economic development of the beneficiary country, especially, since they involved commodities that were exported into the Community in very limited quantities. The Community's caution in granting these benefits was hard to understand anyway, since total CEE exports constituted barely 2 per cent of the Community's imports. It may well be that—as some western experts asserted—'the Europe Agreements [were] the EU's most far reaching response to the changes in Central and Eastern Europe,'[14] but this response, in fact, did not reach very far.

Thus the international environment exerted a special influence on Hungary by forcing it to carry out fundamental reforms. Budapest was to some extent prepared for these reforms. Since the economic reforms of the 1960s, market-oriented thinking was gaining ground. By trading with Western companies, and by participating in international economic organizations, the economic elite acquired wide-ranging international experience. Hungary had been a member of GATT since 1973, and of the IMF and the World Bank since 1982. Handling the debt problems of the Kádár era created a particularly well-trained banking elite. Many legal experts were proficient in Western economic law, thus they knew what legal institutions needed for creating a market economy. As early as in 1988, company law was adopted, then in 1992 the laws on the independent National Bank, the commercial banks, national accounting, and bankruptcy. The German legal culture played a major role in this sphere as well, but some elements were borrowed also from American legal practice.

Yet, carrying out the reforms was extraordinary difficult, and that was further aggravated by some mistakes. The Antall government

---

[14] Barbara Lippert and Heinrich Schneider, 'Association and Beyond: The European Union and the Visegrád States', in Barbara Lippert and Heinrich Schneider (eds.), *Monitoring Association and beyond: The European Union and the Visegrád States* (Bonn: Europa Union Verlag, 1995), 25.

was trying to create a 'Christian Hungarian middle class' but it impeded privatization. The government favoured primarily the leading figures and clients of the Democratic Forum rather than foreign investors. At the initiative of the Smallholders' Party the Antall administration began large-scale compensation by giving coupons to those whose property had been nationalized after 1945. These coupons could be used to buy state-owned land, industrial property, or stores. It was a morally understandable measure, but there was no guarantee that those who had been deprived of their property—or their heirs—would actually make good entrepreneurs or shopkeepers.[15] Moreover, some businessmen bought a considerable part of these coupons below nominal value and used them to obtain valuable property, gaining big profits. Big enterprises and banks were unsuited or not prepared adequately for such privatization. The Antall government sold the supermarket chains to Western investors who bought products from their traditional Western suppliers. As a result, Hungarian farmers and the food industry were unable to sell their own products, and Hungarian consumers were compelled to buy expensive Western goods. This measure did not have a beneficial effect on the balance of payments either.

Hungary proved, on the other hand, to be more attractive to Western investors. During the first three years nearly 6 billion dollars were invested, primarily by American businessmen. Among the CEE countries, Hungary had the highest per capita foreign direct investment.

As a result, while according to some indicators the Hungarian economy was beginning to revive, others showed further grave problems. State administration expenses were growing unchecked. The share of state expenditure in GDP rose to 62 per cent by the end of the term of the Antall government, and the balance of payments deficit continued to grow, thus the rate of indebtedness also grew. It reached its peak level of 35 billion dollars in 1995, and the share of debt servicing in the same year rose to 49 per cent of GDP. Due to these unfavourable economic indicators, the IMF suspended its three-year agreement with Hungary as early as 1992, and the planned 1994 loan agreement was not signed either.[16]

---

[15] Zoltán Farkas, Az Antall-kormány politikája a gazdasággal (The Economic Policy of the Antall Government), in Kormány a mérlegen 1990–1994 (Government in the Balance 1990–1994) (Korridor: Budapest, 1994), 168.

[16] László Csaba, 'A nemzetközi pénzügyi szervezetek és a kelet-európai rendszerátalakító politika' (International Monetary Organizations and the East-European Transformation Policy), *Közgazdasági Szemle*, 42: 2 (Feb. 1995), 117.

After the 1994 elections, Horn's finance minister László Békesi saw clearly that another economic crisis was looming. But in the first nine months of his term Horn was reluctant to implement austerity measures; instead he had his finance minister resign. The IMF also recommended austerity measures, which Horn disregarded, in spite of the fact that the coalition government had more than a two-thirds majority in parliament, and could have easily adopted even an unpopular programme.

The IMF continuously expressed its disapproval and hinted that Hungary may not be in a position to negotiate if it did not implement immediately effective austerity measures and did not appoint appropriate persons to head the Ministry of Finances and the National Bank. The prime minister thought that these measures could be postponed. He relied on Germany's and the EU's assistance.[17] However, Germany was busy in assisting its eastern provinces, and firmly opposed economic growth based on inflation and indebtedness in the other countries. The Union also declined to help on the basis of the Maastricht principles, stressing the necessity of maintaining economic balance. Thus Hungary had to overcome the economic difficulties by its own measures. Allegedly, this opinion was expressed by Richard Holbrooke with unusual clarity during a visit to Budapest.

Under increasing foreign and domestic pressure, Horn gave in. He found financial experts who were ready to carry through the austerity package in the parliament, and to introduce strict fiscal policy in the National Bank. Lajos Bokros was appointed finance minister and György Surányi the president of the National Bank. By March 1995, the so-called 'Bokros package' was presented to the parliament. It proposed the introduction of an 8.5 per cent temporary import surcharge tax, a crawling peg (regular devaluation of the forint), and a number of restrictive budgetary measures. The package, published a day before the arrival of the IMF delegation, created a huge uproar. Two ministers resigned, many civil organizations and the press criticized the government for the negative social consequences of the package. Nevertheless, it was accepted by parliament. That was a turning point in the post-1989 history of the country. Hungary essentially successfully managed the economic crisis. The immediate benefits were derived not so much from the measures themselves as from the re-established credibility

---

[17] László Lengyel, Egérfogó (Mousetrap), in Kérdőjelek: a magyar kormány 1994–1995 (Question Marks: The Hungarian Government 1994–1995) (Korridor: Budapest, 1995), 43.

of the government and the acceptance of austerity measures by the people. After this change in policy was carried through, the IMF concluded the loan agreement with Budapest. The amount of foreign direct investment remained continuously at a high level. Between 1990 and 1999 up to 20 billion dollars were invested in Hungary, successfully compensating the permanent trade deficit. The investment of big companies brought modern technologies to the country.

Since the last quarter of 1996 constant economic growth has been experienced in Hungary. In 1997, the growth in GDP amounted to 4.6 per cent, in 1998 to 4.9 per cent, and in 1999 to 4.4 per cent.[18] Foreign direct investment grew and the balance of payments deficit declined. The growth in exports was 20 per cent in 1996 and 30 per cent in 1997. (Interestingly enough, it approached the value of Russia's total foreign trade.)[19] The inflation rate declined to 20 per cent in 1997 and to 10 per cent in 1999.[20] After the Bokros package, the government carried out an extensive privatization programme. It used the payments for assets sold to foreign investors for repaying its foreign debts. As a result in a couple of years it was no longer compelled to draw on loans by the IMF. Gross foreign debt declined to $27.6 billion in 1996 and to $26 billion in 1999, and debt service ratio declined to 18 per cent of GDP. In the meantime the National Bank accumulated considerable reserves, so net debt did not exceed $12 billion at the beginning of 1999.[21] It was already manageable. The temporary import surcharge was abolished, and the percentage of the crawling peg declined over time. This represented a major change in the economic situation. For the first time since the 1960s, Hungarian economic development was not impeded by a huge deficit in the balance of payments.[22] Simultaneously, the rate of state expenditure declined to 45 per cent, unemployment to 6.6 per cent, and the annual growth in GDP reached 4.4 per cent.[23] This development is probably sustainable notwithstanding the fact that privatization is virtually at an end and, therefore, external sources are no longer available.

[18] *Magyar statisztikai évkönyv* (Hungarian Statistical Yearbook) (Budapest, 1997, 1998, 1999). For 1999 figures see www.ksh.hu.

[19] In 1997, total Hungarian imports made up $20.6 million, compared with Russia's $33 billion. See Csaba, 'A rendszerváltás gazdaságpolitikájának egy évtizede', 21.

[20] See www.ksh.hu.   [21] See www.ksh.hu.

[22] Csaba, 'A rendszerváltás gazdaságpolitikájának egy évtizede', 21.

[23] *Magyar statisztikai évkönyv*, 1999.

Crime, Public Security, and Politics

One of the undesired consequences of the systemic changes was the rapidly rising crime rate. In 1987, the total number of reported crimes amounted to 188,397. In 1997, this figure was as much as 514,403, thus in ten years the public experienced an increase of 273 per cent.[24] The number of burglaries, thefts, and other offences against property (including theft of cars) rose even more rapidly, by 337 per cent. With a share of 75 per cent, they became the dominant form of crime.[25] The rate of violent crime rose during these ten years by about 10 per cent only, although there was a greater increase in murder cases (from 203 and to 289).[26] Although the rise of the crime rate seemed to come to a halt after 1997, the threat perception of the public continued to grow. The explanation lies in the fact that while in the late 1970s and 1980s violent crime was associated with rural areas, by the 1990s it had become a feature of urban life. Conventionally, violent crimes were committed in passion and the victims belonged to the immediate environment of the offenders. Now anybody can be a victim of urban violence.

Thus, in a relatively short period of time, the public was confronted with crime as a problem which at the beginning appeared as an unmanageable threat. More and more people were exposed to various offences, from time to time mafia wars broke out in Budapest, shots and even detonations shook the belief in public security. Measures were taken against organized crime, without much success. Many foreign offenders were registered, 37 per cent of them in 1998 holding Romanian, 16 per cent Yugoslav, 9 per cent Ukrainian-Russian, 6 per cent German passports.[27] Since the most conspicuous crimes tend to be committed by professional foreign offenders hired to liquidate Hungarian 'businessmen', and the media covered these stories extensively, xenophobia began to grow in some parts of the society. People talked about the Russian and Ukrainian and Arab mafia and demanded more resolute measures against foreigners. Taking into consideration that the borders are open (about 35 million travellers cross the Hungarian frontiers annually) this task was rather difficult to accomplish. Experts suggested that

---

[24] *Tájékoztató a bűnözésről* (Bulletin on Crime). Published by the Advocate General of the Republic of Hungary (1999).

[25] Ibid.   [26] Ibid.

[27] *Külföldi állampolgárok és a bűnözők kapcsolata Magyarországon az 1996–1998. években* (Foreign Citizens and Crime in Hungary in 1996–1998). Published by the Advocate General of the Republic of Hungary (1999).

only covert operations and intensified international cooperation could bring about some result.

However, the rising crime rate did not endanger democratic consolidation, perhaps with one exception. Since the beginning of the 1990s, the spread of corruption in administration and in business constituted a rather serious problem. There is no country in the world where privatization has not been accompanied by corruption, but both foreign and Hungarian public opinion rank Hungary among the leading countries in this respect. The problem already existed during Antall's term of office. Political scientist László Lengyel said in public as early as 1993 that in the state administration everyone had a price up to the level of heads of department. In a move characteristic of the period, the prime minister filed a criminal suit for slander against Lengyel, though he did not name anyone. He was of course acquitted, but the case strengthened the suspicion that corruption was rapidly growing. The Horn government made no serious effort to put an end to corruption either, and there was a rumour that his party collected considerable sums for the party budget. The nature of the question meant there were no exposures, with one noteworthy exception: in 1996 the government agency in charge of privatization paid a lawyer the equivalent of $4 million for work actually not done. Presumably, the agency intended the money to be paid into the party budget, but it never arrived there due to the exposure. Even the dismissal of the minister in charge of privatization and of the entire board of directors of the agency failed to impress on public opinion that henceforth the policy of 'clean hands' would prevail. The Socialist Party lost the 1998 elections due among other factors to the public belief that many in the prime minister's entourage were corrupt.

The Federation of Young Democrats, which won the 1998 elections, also had to face charges by the press of illegally obtaining money for party purposes when the party had been in opposition. The director of the national tax authority who was held most responsible for these illegal acts had to resign after a year of heavy political fighting but has never been indicted. At the same time the new government fired the whole leadership of the state-owned 'Postabank' which had been deeply involved in corruption since the beginning of the 1990s.

The Role of New Democratic Institutions

The most important legal institution that contributed to democratic consolidation was probably the Constitutional Court, established in

1989, following the model of the German *Bundesver-fassungsgericht*. At the Roundtable the participants agreed to confer rather broad powers on the Court. The Court has the jurisdiction to interpret the constitution in actual cases and to declare null and void any legal norm made by the government, or even one made by the parliament if it was found unconstitutional. In fact, in some cases the Court went beyond its codified powers and, indirectly, created new laws. The chairman of the Court referred to an 'invisible' constitution and said that it was one of the functions of the Court to help establish a coherent legal democratic order. In 1990, for example, the Court abolished capital punishment, even though this should have been the function of the parliament, since Hungary had joined the Council of Europe. In its first ten years, the Court took essential decisions on questions including freedom of the media and freedom of 'communication', the conditions of the 'rule of law', the legal powers of the president of the republic (who is, according to the constitution, also the commander-in-chief of the army), the admissibility of the referendum, relations between the local self-governments and the national government, and guarantees of the independence of judges.

In 1993, another important democratic institution was set up: the office of parliamentary commissioners for human rights. The first Hungarian ombudsmen were elected by parliament in 1995.[28] In defining the powers of the commissioners, the legislators clearly used the Scandinavian pattern of *ombudsman*, and in the following years the European ombudsmen shared their experiences with their Hungarian colleagues. The commissioners may investigate any individual complaint by citizens concerning the infringement of their human rights. Without previous notice, the commissioners may enter, at any time, any office or site of government or local authorities, including those of the police, the prison, or the army; they may ask any question and may read any document. All officials have to give an answer to the questions and have to provide all documents requested. The results of the investigations are formulated in recommendations, which might or might not be accepted by the respective authorities. However, in the latter case the ombudsmen may report directly to the parliament, which would take a final decision. Apart from that, the commissioners prepare a yearly report on the state of human rights in Hungary, which is discussed by the

[28] Four persons were elected by two-thirds majority: the parliamentary commissioner for [general] human rights and her deputy, the commissioner for data protection, and the commissioner for minority rights.

respective committees and by the plenary session of the parliament. On average, 20,000 complaints a year have been submitted to the commissioners. The overwhelming majority of these recommendations were accepted by the authorities. The commissioners contributed to democratic consolidation especially where courts did not have the power to resolve cases. However, neither the commissioner for minority rights nor other politicians were able to achieve representation in parliament for the ethnic minorities living in Hungary. Even if these minorities do not feel oppressed by the authorities, their lack of representation remains one of the major shortcomings of democratic consolidation.

Hungary and Its Neighbours: An Issue of Domestic Politics

The winner of the first elections, the Hungarian Democratic Forum, consisted at the time of those segments of the elite who upheld the *Weltanschaaung* of the 1930s. As early as in his speech celebrating Hungary's national day on 20 August 1990, prime minister Antall spoke about the injustice of the Trianon Treaty, and called some successor states of the Habsburg monarchy 'artificial political formations'.[29] In September, a state secretary of the Ministry of Defence suggested the restoration of a memorial built in the 1930s 'in memory' of the Trianon Treaty.[30] Antall stated several times that he wished to be 'in spirit' the prime minister of 15 million Hungarians.[31] Since Hungary had a population of only 10.5 million, this statement was interpreted both by neighbouring countries and the West as Hungary's intention to extend its influence beyond the borders.[32] The reference to 15 million Hungarians was not a slip of the tongue. Antall and the Forum's politicians believed that the landslide that began in 1989 would not stop with the fundamental changes in the political system, but would somehow lead to the redrawing of the borders in Central and Eastern Europe. The members of the Forum hoped that the historical processes would lead to the development of a new peace system in a relatively short time by way of closing the Cold War period. Foreign minister Jeszenszky expressed this hope in a speech delivered at the 1992

---

[29] *Népszabadság* (21 Aug. 1990).   [30] *Népszabadság* (21 Sept. 1990).

[31] See e.g. Antall's interview in *Newsweek* ('Hungary in the Middle', 4 Nov. 1991).

[32] Antall gave an incorrect figure. The total number of Hungarians in the region did not exceed 13.5 million.

Helsinki meeting of the CSCE. He advocated 'reshaping Europe as the Vienna Congress had to do in 1814–1815, or the Paris peace conference in 1919. The present settlement must be better than those two were: it should be genuinely democratic, respecting and satisfying the interests of all. It must function smoothly and remain stable for a long time.'[33] The opposition parties heavily criticized this attitude. They maintained that the West would not support any change of borders whatsoever, and that Antall's policy would create grave conflicts with the neighbouring countries.

The 2+4 conference that ended in July 1990 and which created the conditions for the rapid unification of the two Germanies made a deep impression on Antall. He counted on the help that a unified Germany would be able to give in solving Hungary's national question. 'Let us be fair,' political scientist László Lengyel wrote, 'German policy made these conclusions possible at the time. Partly for election reasons and partly under the influence of political euphoria, the German Christian-Democratic government, with the chancellor in the lead, presented itself in the role of a new great power, playing the arbitrator in Eastern Europe and, indeed, in Europe, subordinating its economic decisions to this role.'[34]

Antall assumed that historical considerations—more exactly, a guilty conscience—would lead the West to support Hungarian aspirations for a European peace settlement. He believed that the West would admit that it had made a mistake in Trianon in 1920, in Paris in 1947, and also in 1956 when it had failed to assist the Hungarian revolution. Presumably, the verbal encouragement by German politicians also gave grounds for this belief. The Germans had no idea at the time that the integration of eastern territories would tie up so much of their political and economic capacities that active support of the Hungarian case would be out of question. In any event, members of the Antall government took every opportunity to meet with Western politicians to talk about the tragic events in Hungarian history and the discriminatory minority policy of the neighbouring countries.

Hungary acted accordingly, and began to actively assist Croatian separatist aspirations. At the end of 1990, Hungary sold 10,000 Kalashnikovs to Croatia. In January 1991, Belgrade television

[33] Géza Jeszenszky, 'What We Need under the Present Circumstances is a Completely Different CSCE', Speech of the Hungarian Foreign Minister (24 Mar. 1992), *Current Policy*, No. 4 (1992). Ministry of Foreign Affairs.

[34] László Lengyel, *Külpolitika vagy nemzetpolitika, in Kormány a mérlegen 1990–1994* (Foreign Policy or Nation Policy, in Government in the Balance 1990–1994) (Korridor: Budapest, 1994), 351–2.

reported the deal. First the Hungarian Foreign Ministry denied the deal. Two weeks later the government admitted that the weapons had in fact been sold to Croatia, but added that Hungary did not want to intervene in Yugoslavia's internal affairs. The Serbian government and the Belgrade press repeatedly accused Hungary of supporting forces which were at war with the Serbs. The deal also led to a sharp protest by the Hungarian opposition parties.

Another source of conflict with neighbouring countries was the question of borders. In 1991, the government suggested the inclusion of a paragraph in the basic treaty to be concluded between Hungary and Romania. According to it Hungary would recognize its existing borders, which could be changed only by 'peaceful means'. The government added that Hungary would not pursue any changes of frontiers by using force. This was rather dubious in the light of another basic treaty negotiated at the same time between Hungary and Ukraine, in which Hungary was to recognize the borders without any preconditions.[35] In the other two cases, however, Hungarian politicians referred to the formula of the Helsinki Final Act which allowed peaceful changes 'in accordance with international law'.[36] Thus the 'Helsinki formula' conveyed the message that the Hungarian government left the door open for 'negotiated' settlements in the distant future with those countries with Hungarian minorities, except for its strongest neighbour, Ukraine. Antall announced in 1993, during the ratification of the bilateral treaty with Ukraine, that the provision excluding any changes of the border between the two countries would not constitute a precedent for other cases, i.e. the basic treaty to be concluded with Romania and Slovakia.[37] Finally, parliament managed to ratify this treaty with the votes of the opposition parties, the Socialists and the Free Democrats.

Another conflict arose from a statement Antall made during his talks with Francesco Cossiga in July 1991.[38] Antall said that Vojvodina did not belong to Serbia, because the 1920 peace treaties had annexed Vojvodina—a former Hungarian territory—to the

[35] The basic treaty with Ukraine was signed on 5 Dec. 1991. It contained the following provision: 'The Parties recognize each other's territorial integrity. They do not, and will not have in the future, any territorial claims against each other.'

[36] This formula had been included in the Final Act in 1975 at the request of West Germany, who did not want to exclude a possible peaceful unification of Germany in the future.

[37] *Országgyűlési Napló* (Transcripts of the Sessions of the Parliament) (11 May 1993), 26685–6.

[38] The meeting took place on 6 July 1991. *Népszabadság* (7 July 1991).

newly created, non-federal Kingdom of Serbs, Croats, and Slovenes, and not to Serbia, which did not exist at that time. Vojvodina became a part of Serbia only when the unitary state became a federation, but this was a domestic and not an international decision. The announcement gave ground for one interpretation only: if Vojvodina was originally not a territory under the sovereignty of Serbia, after the collapse it could belong to *any* country, including Croatia or even Hungary. The statement triggered off sharp reactions in Belgrade. The Yugoslav government stated that Hungary made an intervention into its domestic affairs and is pursuing a revisionist policy.[39]

Political reaction in the neighbouring countries to Hungarian foreign policy was very negative. Interestingly enough, Western reaction was not strong, much less effective. Western governments at that time let the Hungarian government know through diplomatic channels that they did not favour references to the Trianon Treaty, but they did so too carefully, and the inexperienced politicians of the Forum did not see any reason to change their policy. At the same time the basic goals of Hungarian foreign policy became the Number One domestic political issue, causing grave political disputes among the coalition and opposition parties. The Socialists and the Free Democrats sharply attacked both the essence and the rhetoric of the Antall government. According to the Free Democrats, 'Hungary has to declare that . . . it has no territorial claim against either of the neighbouring states'. Whatever the considerations with regard to the improvement of the living conditions of the Hungarian minorities, Hungary could, under no circumstances, reckon on any changes of the borders. These changes would not contribute to a solution of the problem of minorities, since they would lead only to a change in the subject (i.e. instead of having a large Hungarian minority in Romania, there would be a large Romanian minority in Hungary).[40] Former deputy state secretary of the Foreign Ministry Dávid Meiszter wrote that 'we have to declare first very clearly that we do not have territorial claims against any of our neighbouring states whatsoever, irrespective of the fact whether they do have such a claim against third countries [e.g. Romania against Moldavia] or not.' Second, that we do not want

---

[39] *Népszabadság* (16 July 1991). The Hungarian state secretary of foreign affairs announced that Hungary did not want to intervene in the domestic affairs of Yugoslavia. *Népszabadság* (18 July 1991).

[40] *A szabaddemokraták külpolitikája* (The Foreign Policy of the Free Democrats), Draft Programme (Sept. 1992).

to change our borders 'neither by using force, nor peacefully, in other words, not even by negotiations'.[41]

Other statements went beyond direct criticism of Antall's foreign policy aims, putting the border question and the policy toward Hungary's neighbours in a wider context. Many contended that in many respects these were also domestic policy issues. Péter Tiszay, for instance, wrote that the Antall cabinet 'uses foreign policy as a tool legitimising its domestic policy. In wake of increasing domestic political and economic difficulties the government identified foreign policy as the area where the Antall cabinet attained general international recognition.'[42] Pál Dunay perceived a similarity in the domestic policy of the Hungarian, Romanian, and Czechoslovak governments. According to him, 'generally, the new political leadership [in the neighbouring countries] is not comprised of patriots or enlightened liberals with an understanding for the problems of the minorities, but of nationalists who . . . have arrived at the conclusion that the exclusion of the minorities from the concept of nation, the restriction of their rights strengthens social cohesion, stabilizes their power. . . . [In Hungary,] the exaggerated concern for ethnic Hungarians beyond the borders . . . serve similar purposes, i.e., the diversion of attention from other, vital problems. The two [sides] . . . are doing each other good services.'[43]

Both authors were right. It was not only conviction, but also tactical domestic reasons that determined Antall's minority policy. First, putting the minority issue in the forefront of attention seemed easier than entering into debate with the opposition about the state of the economy or environment. Second, Antall presumed that the 10 million Hungarians in Hungary were greatly interested in the fate of ethnic Hungarians living beyond the borders, therefore, this policy would gain many supporters in the constituencies. The critics of this policy could then justifiably be called 'non-national-minded', pointing out that they were wrong about the ethnic issue, thus they could not be right in other disputed questions either, because they represented interests 'alien' to the Hungarian people. Third, Antall probably thought that the nationalism represented by Mečiar and Iliescu, their measures taken against ethnic Hungarians would strengthen solidarity among the Hungarians, and

[41] Dávid Meiszter, 'A határkérdés határai' (The Frontiers of Border Questions), *Népszabadság* (19 Aug. 1992).

[42] Péter Tiszay, 'A sikerpolitika kudarca' (The Failure of a Successful Policy), *Népszabadság* (18 Mar. 1994).

[43] Pál Dunay, 'Lesz-e még biztonság Közép-Európában?' (Will there be any security in Central Europe?), *Európai Szemle*, No. 4 (1992), 35.

this solidarity would increase the government's authority at home. As will be shown later, Antall misjudged the situation in every respect. He was unable to divert attention from the fundamental economic problems, the overwhelming majority of the voters either remained indifferent to the situation of the minorities, or did not consider it a decisive factor in judging the performance of the government.

The Antall cabinet can be given credit for just one, if very important, point. Throughout its four-year term it engaged only in a rhetorical war with the neighbouring countries, which, with the exception of the Kalashnikov case, was never accompanied by militant measures. The government did not proclaim any armament programme, on the contrary, it kept its military expenditure at a distinctly low level. During the Yugoslav war it did not take any military action against the troops and fighters that penetrated Hungarian territory, it did not order mobilization of the Hungarian army, it did not send even a single tank in the direction of the border; and it did not encourage ethnic Hungarians in the neighbouring countries to use force in fighting for their rights. In other words, the Antall government really did what it promised to do: it tried to change the status quo by peaceful means.

Nationalism and Racism

However, from the point of view of democratic consolidation, Antall's minority policy had other, extremely unfavourable consequences: it also created scope for the development of nationalism at home. Nationalism and revisionism in the Horthy era went hand in hand with racism, and it seems the two became inseparably linked in this case as well.

During those years some members of the Democratic Forum made more and more openly racist statements. They alleged that the state administration and, especially, the media employed many 'non-Hungarian' elements. Some hinted that such elements could be found among the Free Democrats in particularly large numbers. This type of nationalism simply painted over the conflicts between the parties. Hence, the political actors did not merely dispute the prevailing issue, they looked for other motives behind every remark or action. The leaders of the Forum tried to disassociate themselves from anti-Semitism and complained about the oversensitivity of the Jews. The Antall government faced a very serious challenge: the majority of the mostly liberal media was extremely critical of every single step the government took.

This led to the so-called media war. In keeping with its customarily inept pattern, the government launched an attack against many journalists in the media, primarily in the state television and radio. The Minister of the Interior declared that he would like to see on the screen 'country boys and girls who speak pure Hungarian' and did everything to have the liberal, 'urban' reporters removed, for they obviously did not speak this kind of language. Between 1992 and 1993, the government put an end to the independent operation of the television and radio, thereby seriously obstructing democratic consolidation. In 1993, the heads of both media resigned, and the new leaders quickly dismissed those whom the government did not favour. They were unable to do the same in the case of the daily press because it had been privatized and was fully independent. The government also proclaimed that it aimed to create a 'Christian Hungarian middle class' in the course of the otherwise sluggish privatization. 'In Hungary everybody who is not a Jew belongs to this class,' the columnist of *Népszabadság*—owned by Bertelsmann —wrote in his commentary.[44]

Anti-Semitism did not have broad popular support in Hungary. Any return to the anti-Semitism of the 1930s or 1940s had no real chance, because the socio-political conditions were fundamentally different. The coalition misinterpreted the attitude of the great majority of the voters. As has been said before, there were fewer people interested in solving the problems of Hungarian national minorities than the government believed. Similarly, few people regarded the task of making the media 'more Hungarian' as the most immediate one for the government, and few people thought that the country had to adopt pre-war symbols, traditions, and political patterns. They were more interested in other questions such as who was going to solve the economic problems, to contain inflation, and carry out privatization.[45]

The most prominent extreme right-wing figure was the vice-chairman of the Democratic Forum, István Csurka, who wrote controversial articles in his *Magyar Fórum*. His most striking, published in August 1992, stated that 'in 1995, the Treaty of Yalta expires [*sic*]. Until that time, the life of all successor states around us will develop in another setting . . . The fundamental question is whether there will be a new Hungarian generation around that can

---

[44] László Zappe, 'Az új középosztály' (The New Middle Class), *Népszabadság* (13 Oct. 1992).

[45] László Lengyel, 'Az elit nem válaszol' (The Elite does not Respond'), *Magyar Nemzet* (23 Dec. 1990).

cope with the new dangers, and can live with the new opportunities creating a new Hungarian *Lebensraum* . . .' Criticizing the behaviour of the president of the Republic, Árpád Göncz, he complained that Göncz was receiving 'orders from those who stand behind him: the communists, the reform communists, members of the liberal and radical "nomenklatura", the liaison people of Paris, New York and Tel Aviv'. Two forces were at war in domestic policy, the 'national centre' and the 'left wing bloc'. He added that the latter, which included the Jews, successfully maintained the continuity of its power since 1945. He complained about the activity of the IMF and the troubles with some genetic deformations of a social layer in the country.[46] The article aroused an outcry even within the Democratic Forum. One of the party members called Csurka's views 'racist, anti-democratic . . . and anti-Semitic', which fully 'correspond to a Nazi ideology'.[47] 'It is very difficult to negotiate with the IMF,' said the minister Iván Szabó, 'if the Vice Chairman of the leading coalition party describes the IMF as the strike force of World Jewry'.[48] The presidium of the Forum had a long discussion about the article, but it did not condemn it openly. Antall remained silent. He thought that a considerable number of extreme right-wing party members backed Csurka, and he did not want to take the risk of alienating them.

The Csurka article was probably the turning point in Western reaction, both in domestic and foreign policy. After its publication Antall and Jeszenszky received an increasing number of serious warnings via official and informal channels.[49] They could reject criticism by neighbouring countries, but could not disregard the standpoint of their future allies. Antall once said indignantly that he had had enough of always having to explain, wherever he went abroad, who Csurka was and what it was he published in a journal.[50] It was due mostly to Western pressure that the Democratic Forum dismissed Csurka from the presidium, subsequently from the

[46] István Csurka, 'Néhány gondolat a rendszerváltozás első két esztendeje és az MDF új programja kapcsán' (Some Thoughts in Connection with the First Two Years after the System Changes and the New Programme of the HDF), *Magyar Fórum* (20 Aug. 1992), emphasis added.

[47] 'József Debreczeni, Nyílt levél Csurka Istvánhoz' (Open Letter to István Csurka), *Népszabadság* (27 Aug. 1992).

[48] *Népszabadság* (27 Aug. 1992).

[49] Of course, they cannot be documented, except for some news in the press. e.g. US Congressman Tom Lantos heavily criticized Csurka's views in Budapest, saying that he would raise the problem at the Capitolium, in *Népszabadság* (2 Sept. 1992).

[50] Television interview (13 Jan. 1993).

party.[51] Following this, Csurka founded an extreme right-wing party which won 1.5 per cent of the votes in the 1994 elections.[52] However, even after Csurka's removal there was no fundamental change in the domestic policy of the coalition. The 'media war' continued, and culminated in the dismissal of 139 prominent journalists from the Radio in the spring of 1994. The policy of the government proved to be fully counter-productive and resulted in a protest vote against the Democratic Forum at the elections of 1994 which brought about the landslide victory of the Socialist Party.

The Basic Treaties

The Democratic Forum failed to take appropriate steps toward normalizing relations with the neighbouring countries.[53] It maintained the position that Romania, Serbia, and Slovakia must improve the situation of their Hungarian minorities before any progress could be made in other spheres of interstate relations. Antall did not really see that Hungary could improve the living conditions of minority groups only by cooperating with the governments of the neighbouring countries. 'The road can lead only through Bucharest and Bratislava,' as two Hungarian critics of government policy observed.[54] Although the Antall government approached both countries, it was unable to negotiate a sensible compromise with either—among others because of the border question. After the split of Czechoslovakia, Hungary's attempt to veto Slovakia's accession to CSCE also had an unfavourable effect on its relationship with these countries. This step evoked strong diplomatic protest on the part of the Western member states of CSCE. Hungarian foreign policy makers failed to realize that Western interests lay clearly in maintaining good relations among the countries in the region, and definitely not in the isolation of one CEE country by another

[51] First the position of vice-chairman of the Forum was abolished in December 1992, which was followed by Csurka's dismissal in June 1993.

[52] 'Hungarian Party of Justice and Life'. However, at the 1998 elections István Csurka's extreme right-wing party passed the 5% threshold and got into parliament. Its representatives were seated among the opposition parties but in most cases they supported the government.

[53] On the development of bilateral relations with Romania and Slovakia, see Wolfgang Zellner and Pál Dunay, *Zwischen Integration, Nachbarschafts- und Minderheitenpolitik: Ungarns Aussenpolitik 1990–1997* (Baden-Baden: Nomos Verlagsgesellschaft, 1998), 244–344.

[54] Dávid Meiszter and Pál Dunay, 'Sikerek és kudarcok között' (Between Successes and Failures) *Társadalmi Szemle*, 49: 8–9, 38.

in the international arena. The conflict came to an end when Budapest issued a memorandum calling on Slovakia to respect the obligations stipulated in the Helsinki Final Act.[55] Hungarian diplomacy did not learn from the Western protests. In June 1993 it again threatened to impose a veto, this time against the admission of Slovakia to the Council of Europe. Hungary referred to the Slovak non-compliance with the norms of the Council of Europe on ethnic minorities. Many member states, including Germany, protested resolutely against Hungarian behaviour. Slovakia declared that it would observe the rights of ethnic minorities. Finally, with Hungarian abstention, Slovakia was admitted to the Council. The diplomatic protest at least had the effect that Hungary ceased trying to prevent Romania's admission to the Council of Europe, though it did try to make it conditional on respect for minority rights. Some of the Hungarian demands were accepted by a Romanian declaration. So, with the abstention of Hungary, Romania also became a member of the Council of Europe.

The Balladur Plan initially seemed to offer some prospects of reducing such tensions.[56] Launched in 1993, the Plan—the first Joint Action of the European Union's Common Foreign and Security Policy—was based on the philosophy of preventive diplomacy. The French government proposed the convocation of a general conference for the purpose of signing a Stability Pact and further bilateral agreements on minority problems which would improve relations among the Central and East European countries.

Bilateral agreements became an important issue during the term of office of the next government led by Gyula Horn. This government promised a considerably more progressive policy than its predecessor. It sharply rejected all forms of nationalism and racism in its domestic and foreign policy. It started out from the concept that the living conditions of Hungarian ethnic minorities could be improved only if intergovernmental relations were normalized first. This corresponded with Western interests, and with the interests of the neighbouring countries at least as far as bilateral relations were concerned.

After May 1994, the authors of the Balladur Plan as well as the leading Western states urged the new Hungarian government to

---

[55] Statement by the Minister for Foreign Affairs of the Republic of Hungary in the CSCE Council of Ministers, Stockholm (15 Dec. 1992). Press Release of the Ministry of Foreign Affairs of the Republic of Hungary.

[56] See Pál Dunay and Wolfgang Zellner, 'The Pact on Stability in Europe: A Diplomatic Solution or a Lasting Success?', *OSCE Yearbook 1995/1996* (Baden-Baden: Nomos Verlagsgesellschaft, 1997), 297–312.

sign basic treaties with its neighbours. In the 'Study on NATO Enlargement', prepared in September 1995, they clearly concluded: 'States which have ethnic disputes or external territorial disputes, including irredentist claims, . . . must settle those disputes by peaceful means in accordance with OSCE principles. Resolution of such disputes would be a factor in determining whether to invite a state to join the Alliance.'[57] Naturally, the study made no reference to the concept of a basic treaty, but that was also what it actually meant.

The government was prepared to sign such a treaty, though it foresaw the difficulties involved. Before beginning negotiations, it laid down demonstratively that it had no territorial claims against its neighbours, nor would it make such claims in the future; furthermore, that it was prepared to include a provision to this effect in the treaty without any conditions. After this only the 'details' were left to negotiate. But these were rather complicated details, since neither Slovakia nor Romania wished to grant overly extensive rights to the Hungarian minorities. In fact, Hungary faced quite awkward nationalist governments in Slovakia and Romania. The incorporation of Recommendation 1201 of the Parliamentary Assembly of the Council of Europe offered the solution to this problem, first in the case of Slovakia. This otherwise non-binding document on the rights of minorities was made legally binding in the basic treaty between the two countries. Thus, both parties reached a compromise, though when it came to signing the treaty in Paris in March 1995, Slovakia handed over a note declaring that according to its interpretation, the recommendation did not refer to collective rights nor any autonomy. All in all, the Hungarian–Slovak treaty was the one tangible result of the Balladur Plan.[58] After Balladur lost the elections at home the whole plan was forgotten. According to one analysis, 'the reason why the Central European countries went along with this project even though almost all of them viewed it sceptically at the beginning is because they wanted to join the EU and regarded work on the Stability Pact as a condition of that'.[59]

While the conclusion of the Hungarian–Slovak basic treaty was motivated by aspirations to join the EU, the possibility of accession to NATO played a greater part in the conclusion of the treaty with Romania. At first Bucharest did not seem to have much

[57] Para 6.

[58] 'Treaty of the Republic of Hungary and the Slovak Republic on Good Neighbourliness and Friendly Cooperation', signed in Paris (19 Mar. 1995).

[59] Dunay and Zellner, 'Pact on Stability', 310.

interest but later it became attracted by the possibility of joining NATO. After nearly two years of prolonged negotiations the parties signed the basic treaty in September 1996. In this case, Recommendation 1201 was mentioned only in a footnote, nevertheless it became as legally binding as in Slovakia's case. The Western diplomatic pressure put on Romania was decisive in the conclusion of the treaty.

In Hungary, the Democratic Forum and the other opposition parties concerned with the 'national cause' sharply criticized the content of both treaties. They alleged that the socialist-liberal coalition had betrayed the minorities and had given in unreservedly to Western demands, especially when it had accepted the note containing the Slovak government's peculiar interpretation of the text. They maintained first, that the treaty did not contain more guarantees for the minorities than the national laws of the two countries; second, that, in order to protect the minorities, the government should have included in the treaty the recognition of the autonomy and collective rights of Hungarians; third, that these countries would not comply with the treaty anyway. However, the opposition had already randomly criticized the government for renouncing 'peaceful' border changes. In what marked an important domestic political step forward Hungary, by signing the treaties, virtually put the Trianon syndrome behind it. Since then, only the extreme right parties have referred publicly to the Trianon issue. As a result, the threat perceptions of Hungary in neighbouring countries have also diminished.

Had Hungary not signed the two treaties, it would have never made it into the first circle in NATO and EU enlargement negotiations. Never has Hungarian foreign policy received so much recognition from the international community as it did in connection with the conclusion of the treaties. This time the West finally believed that Hungary did not represent a potential source of conflict in the region any longer, and that it was really prepared to do anything to solve its disputes, and that it would not be Hungary's fault should it fail to reach an agreement with its neighbours. As a result, Hungary became a member of NATO in 1999.

The Gabcíkovo-Nagymaros Dam Dispute

The conflict with Slovakia over the Gabcíkovo-Nagymaros Dam Project turned out to be the most serious international conflict for Hungary since 1989, and also became a domestic political issue.

The treaty on the construction of the project was signed in 1977 and was then applauded as a 'socialist achievement'. In the second half of the 1980s it was heavily criticized by the opposition in Hungary for both economic and environmental reasons, and became a symbol of the gigantomanic socialist constructions and a target of the attacks of the opposition. As a consequence, in 1989, the Németh government made a political decision: it decided first to suspend and later to discontinue work. However, the continuation of the construction of the project became one of the priorities of the Slovak government. At that time the Slovak section at Gabcíkovo was already close to completion. The project became a political symbol of independent Slovakia.

In 1991, intergovernmental negotiations took place without any result. The Slovak government never entered into any discussion about the issue itself. It merely kept repeating that the project would have to be finished. For that reason, work commenced in 1990 in order to divert the Danube below Bratislava to Slovak territory. Responding to this activity Hungary terminated the 1977 treaty in May 1992. The Antall government counted on Western Europe's and primarily Germany's diplomatic and political support but that was a mistake. Antall—as in other cases—believed that after the Trianon and Paris treaties the West would 'not allow' another severe injury to Hungarian interests. But, aside from statements by a few German politicians, nothing happened. At Hungary's request, in April 1992 the European Commission offered professional mediatory assistance on condition that all unilateral action would be suspended during the joint investigation. The Slovak party did not accept this condition, and diverted the Danube in October 1992. After the diversion, due to the mediation of the European Commission, the two parties agreed to bring the case before the International Court of Justice. Without this mediation Slovakia would have never gone before the Court.

The Court delivered its judgment in September 1997. It found both parties responsible for breach of international law, one for the termination of the 1977 treaty, the other for the diversion of the Danube. It formally restored the validity of the 1977 treaty. However, it did not recommend that the parties construct what, against the treaty, had not been constructed earlier (the Nagymaros dam) and destroy what had been illegally constructed (the new dam at Cunovo that diverted the Danube). Much to the surprise of the Hungarian public, it became known that during the Court proceedings Prime Minister Horn's aides had conducted secret bilateral negotiations with the Slovaks and had accepted every Slovak demand, including the construction of the Nagymaros dam, although the Court did not ultimately prescribe this. In addition, Horn openly misinterpreted the judgment by saying that Hungary had lost the case completely. This arbitrary move brought about a public outcry. In the end, due to strong protest from the Free Democrats, the opposition parties, and his own foreign minister, Horn did not sign the initialled final agreement. The solution of the dispute was thus postponed until after the 1998 elections. However, the arbitrary behaviour of the prime minister contributed to a large extent to his party's electoral defeat.

Conclusions

This chapter has focused primarily on problems and conflicts. Nevertheless, the historically unprecedented task of the consolidation of democracy in Hungary was carried out rather successfully between 1988 and 1998.

After the first free elections, parliamentary democracy worked without a hitch. Parties disbanded or became marginalized, and administrations were replaced after each election, but, unlike in other CEE states, no government crises occurred and no early elections were held. With the single exception of a taxi drivers' protest in 1990[60] there were no riots, illegal strikes, or massive street demonstrations to disturb public order. Contrary to the expectations of many, the democratic parties that came into power did not embark on a witch hunt of the leading politicians of the Kádár regime. The coalition government elected in 1998 took over a working democracy and a prosperous economy.

The international environment played an important part in helping democratic consolidation. The West provided the Hungarian political and economic elite with an attractive democratic pattern as early as the 1980s. The German legal system, numerous elements of which were later taken over by the Hungarian constitutional system, played a particularly important part. Western diplomacy and some international organizations also played a part in this process. Leading Western powers occasionally put direct and effective pressure on the Hungarian government when they saw that nationalist and populist elements were gaining ground in its domestic and foreign policy. NATO and the European Union

---

[60] Protesting against rising gasoline prices, taxi-drivers blocked the major roads of Budapest for some days in October 1990.

successfully urged Hungary to reconcile itself with its neighbours by signing the basic treaties. As far as economic consolidation was concerned, the Western policy showed little altruism. The West actually compelled Hungary to carry out its own austerity programme without foreign assistance. In the final analysis, however, this may also have contributed to democratic consolidation.

Poland: Compatibility of External and Internal Democratic Designs

Antoni Z. Kamiński

Poland has made remarkable progress in its transition to market capitalism and liberal democracy. That progress has owed much to support from Western governments and international institutions. The success Poland has enjoyed in attracting international backing and in dealing with the problems of transition has reflected the country's historical compatibility with the Euro-Atlantic liberal-democratic political and economic order. Poland scores well, by comparison with other post-communist states, in any ranking of what may be called 'European compatibility potential'. Geographical proximity and easy access to Western Europe has fostered a deep familiarity with democratic culture. Ever since Poland became part of European civilization in what historians call the 'long tenth century', its people have had a close cultural affinity with Western Europe. They have shared traditions of self-government, the separation of Church and state, law, and a belief in the dignity of the individual. These European values, central to Polish national identity, sustained resistance through four decades of communist rule. Of all the Soviet satellites, Poland proved the most troublesome, with a record number of rebellions: three major ones in 1956, 1970, and 1980–1, and two minor ones, in 1968 and 1976.

Characteristically, Poland led the way in 1989 by electing the first non-communist prime minister in Eastern Europe since the imposition of Soviet rule. The victory of Solidarity in the June 1989 elections marked the start of a complex political transition. The decision to hold presidential elections in late 1990, well ahead of parliamentary ones, represented a 'perverse sequencing in regime building', producing the uneasy combination of Lech Wałęsa and a quasi-communist legislature.[1] The Polish population had to wait until the end of 1991, two years longer than the Hungarians, Czechs, and Slovaks, to vote in truly democratic parliamentary elections. Wałęsa paid little regard to either the parliament or the constitution, concentrating his efforts on building a strong presidency. While his efforts to do so failed, he succeeded in weakening the state.

Despite such problems and the general weaknesses of constitutional design, Poland made impressive progress in consolidating democracy. Between 1989 and 1998, the country underwent three parliamentary elections and was ruled by four different political coalitions. In each case, power changed hands smoothly, without any intervention from the military or the security forces. On the economic front, stabilization and privatization programmes have successfully gone forward. Strong institutional foundations have been laid for local self-government. These institutional changes have all contributed to the consolidation of democracy. In order to assess the role of international factors in these developments, this chapter examines four areas of change in the years following the breakthrough of 1989: the economic stabilization programme; Poland's foreign policy reorientation; the issue of civilian control over the military; and the reorganization of the Polish state. All four changes have been of interest to international actors, although this interest varied in intensity between these four areas.

Economic Stabilization

The economic stabilization programme was known as the 'Balcerowicz programme,' after the name of its executor, or as 'shock therapy'. The latter term is not quite appropriate for, as much as a 'shock therapy' is indispensable under conditions of a deep structural change, the economic stabilization programme affected the policy environment of the economy, rather than its institutional structure. In order to give a proper account of circumstances under which it was implemented, one must remember that, at the end of the 1980s, and to be more precise, since the end of the 1970s, Poland was practically a bankrupt state and, therefore, highly vulnerable to external influences. This left Poland little room for manœuvre: an alternative to success being a national catastrophe. Under rampant inflation and a stagnant economy, only stringent measures could

---

[1] Antoni Z. Kamiński and Agnieszka Gogolewska, 'Civil Control of the Russian Military since 1991', *European Security*, 5: 4 (Winter 1996), 589.

produce a change. These measures were also indispensable if external support from the IMF, the World Bank, the governments of major creditor countries, and private banks was to be forthcoming. The logic of the situation was such that only decisive policy measures could both boost the confidence of external creditors, and reinforce this confidence by producing quick results, and convince the electorate that the government meant business. There is no doubt that the impact of external factors was significant in this respect: without a clear change, Poland could not count on external assistance, nor inspire confidence among potential private investors. Thus, radical change coincided with the broadly accepted Polish *raison d'état*—no other option existed to provide conditions for a quick revival of the economy.

The last proposition may give rise to some objections. The Polish economy was in an exceptionally desperate state. However, Hungary's foreign debt per capita was larger than Poland's, and yet its post-communist governments did not even consider tough austerity measures like those adopted in Poland. In reality, these similarities were only superficial. Under communism, the two countries followed very different political and economic strategies.[2] In Hungary, the strategy consisted in politically co-opting the professional elites within the framework of 'economic reform'. From the very beginning, the project of reform was crippled, because its logic had to be reconciled with existing political constraints: the nature of the political system and property relations. However, this reform did enhance overall economic rationality and improve economic efficiency. The Hungarian economy remained communist, but came to represent a slightly more rational brand of it. Such reform also helped to establish a positive image of Hungary abroad and enhanced trust in its ability to meet its financial obligations. Thus, the feeling of urgency prevalent in Warsaw was less apparent in Budapest. From the viewpoint of 1998, there can be no doubt that much of the Hungarian reform was an exercise in self-delusion in which the communist leadership duped professionals to believe that they mattered, and professionals fooled their party patrons by maintaining that communism was reformable.

The party leadership in Poland had great difficulty in controlling an unruly population. External loans and credits obtained during the 1970s were used in large part to finance consumption and to support the military effort of the USSR. No serious attempt

---

[2] Antoni Z. Kamiński, *An Institutional Theory of Communist Regimes: Design, Function and Breakdown* (San Francisco: ICS Press, 1992).

to reform the economy was made. The authorities felt too insecure to risk it; economic decisions were a matter of political expediency. By the mid-1970s, communist Poland had become insolvent and its reputation as a reliable debtor destroyed. The first post-communist government of Mazowiecki pledged to honour the debts of its predecessors. However, it was immediately forced to start negotiations for the rescheduling and reductions of these debts. Rescheduling and reduction would be possible only if the new government demonstrated the will to put its house in order. The Balcerowicz programme did just that. The programme was announced at the beginning of January 1990, after which protracted negotiations, first with public creditors (the Paris Club) and later with private banks (the London Club) started.

The World Bank and the IMF were consulted in the planning phase of this programme. Suggestions from these institutions were treated very seriously by the Polish government, for international financial acceptance was seen as crucial for the success of the programme. In another sign of support, Western governments created a foreign currency reserve to back the internal convertibility of the zloty. These governments also provided assistance to the privatization programme through expert advice and the training of the Polish professionals (most notably by the USA, Germany, Great Britain, and France).

Western actors were not always able to influence the content of policies carried out by the Polish government. For instance, World Bank experts had initially been critical of the *popiwek* tax imposed as part of the economic stabilization package on companies that introduced unjustified wage increases. The World Bank changed its position only in 1992, subsequently recommending similar measures to other reforming post-communist economies.[3]

Even assuming that there was little alternative to reform, one may wonder whether, without the external stick (the prospect that creditors would become intractable) and carrot (foreign financial support for the programme and the promise of a better future), the policy change, and the risks it implied, would have been so easily accepted by the Polish political class and the society. At the very least, external factors were among the most important forces generating the change. No other post-communist country, at that moment, was in greater political and economic disarray than Poland. As such, Poland's internal conditions were receptive to such

[3] Private communication from Mr Jerzy Osiatyński, former minister of finance to one of the post-communist governments.

external forces. No organized internal interests existed at that time to hamper the reform programme.

Once the Polish economy started to grow, as of 1992, at a pace of 5–7 per cent of GNP a year, the constraints required by the market economy became easier to accept by the population.[4] External recognition of this success, followed by foreign investment, fortified the will of the Polish political class to respect fiscal discipline, and continue privatization. Moreover, association with the European Union (EU) and the prospect of accession forced the government to open the economy to foreign competition, despite heavy protectionist pressures exercised by some sectors of the Polish economy.

Foreign Policy Changes

The disintegration of the Soviet system and the Soviet Union itself required a reorientation of the foreign policy of the former Soviet satellite states. Without changes in Poland's foreign policy, it would not have received Western support on the scale that it did. The demise of communist party monopoly power in June 1989 and the disintegration of the communist bloc produced deep changes in Poland's foreign policy. For the first time since the Second World War, Poland had a government whose legitimacy was internally derived. Moreover, between the June 1989 elections in Poland and the demise of the USSR in December 1991, the international environment in Europe changed dramatically. The former satellite countries discovered that part of their recovered sovereignty involved the freedom to rebuild broken ties with Europe.

The situation of Poland was unique because, as a result of agreements after the Second World War, the country had moved several hundred kilometres west. Poland lost Vilnius to Lithuania, and western parts of Belarus and Ukraine. The collapse of the Soviet system, and the reunification of Germany, revived the problem of the Polish–German border. It also potentially revived the problem of the Poland's eastern frontiers. The situation was aggravated in 1989 by Helmut Kohl's electoral courtship of the right-wing Republican Party, which led Kohl to avoid definite statements on Germany's eastern borders. This inspired the Polish government to take measures which subsequently complicated the withdrawal

---

[4] See: Marek Ziółkowski (ed.), *Polacy wobec ładu monocentrycznego* (Warsaw: Institute of Political Studies, Polish Academy of Sciences, 1993); Anita Miszalska, *Reakcje społeczne na przemiany ustrojowe: Postawy, zachowania i samopoczucie Polaków w początkach lat dziewięćdziesiątych* (University of Łódź Press, 1996).

of Soviet/Russian troops from Polish territory. Fortunately, Bonn quickly recognized the importance of the problem. Negotiations on the border issue and bilateral cooperation were soon concluded. These negotiations resulted in the Border Treaty (signed on 14 November 1990) and the Treaty on Good Neighbourly and Friendly Cooperation (signed on 17 June 1991). The latter contained detailed clauses on national minority rights (Arts. 20–2), which have provided a standard for other such documents signed in Europe.

The two treaties were followed by a series of treaties and declarations with other Western states, expressing the Polish intention to join the EU and the North Atlantic Treaty Organization (NATO), and underlining Western support to these intentions. In 1990 negotiations started on the Association Agreements between Poland and the European Community. The crown to these efforts was Poland's admission to NATO in 1999, and to the EU in the beginning of the twenty-first century.

At the same time Poland developed contacts with her eastern neighbours. In 1991 Warsaw established quasi-diplomatic relations with all western republics of the USSR. These representations became full-fledged embassies as soon as these republics gained full independence. After 1991 negotiations started on treaties to regulate bilateral relations. The most important issues in these negotiations were border regulations and minority rights.

Successive Polish governments have demonstrated common sense and a businesslike approach to reorienting Poland's foreign policy. Again, Polish governments had very little freedom for manœuvre. A more revisionist foreign policy course with regard to its eastern borders would have provoked a backlash in Germany, with claims to the western areas of Poland. Faced with such a threat to stability in Europe, the West would have had to put all possible pressure on Poland. In addition, Russia would have exploited such Polish adventurism to its advantage. However, Poland could have been more intransigent in approaching its neighbours. This may have made its relations with the West more difficult, however, without producing a catastrophe. It is clear, therefore, that while the external factor was relevant, the benevolence of the Polish public opinion and the constructive attitude of its political elite were also very important in changing Polish foreign policy.

The USA has supported many Polish policy aims. It has often been argued that the positive attitude of Washington to these policies has reflected the size of the American electorate with Polish origins. However, the USA has also been driven by geopolitical concerns. For the USA, independent Poland has played an important role in assisting the new Russian Federation to become a 'normal' state with no designs on its neighbours. This interest has been shared with Polish governments. This shared interest in regional stabilization was the most important factor in securing US approval for Poland's accession to NATO.

Poland's foreign policy course, which has aimed to integrate into NATO and the EU while maintaining strong cooperation with its eastern neighbours including Russia, has had very strong popular support. According to a survey, conducted in 1995, close to 75 per cent of respondents supported Polish membership in NATO (6 per cent opposed membership). The proportions of those for/against membership in the EU were 76 to 5 per cent.[5]

Civil–Military Relations

The establishment of civilian control over the military involves many different institutional changes. In the Polish case, attempts to establish such civilian control had not produced a clear picture by 1998. The parliament remained ineffective in performing control functions. A weak presidency was endowed with surprising powers in military-related areas. Polish political parties remained weak, and public life highly partisan. Public administration was inefficient, corrupt, and permeated with partisan politics. Yet, despite an oversized and ineffective government, Poland has been one of the most stable post-communist states, and its economic and foreign policies have remained consistent during the transition.

Nothing has been more indicative of the particular characteristics of the Polish transition than the powers that were granted to the president. After the round table talks in April 1989, the position of the president was strengthened. Yet, the communist defeat was so complete that the formally strong President Wojciech Jaruzelski possessed little real power. At no point has there been a debate in Poland on the relative merits of parliamentary and presidential systems of government. The political elite has been indifferent to the strategic need to design an efficient political system. This indifference was illustrated by the comment made to the author in the spring of 1990 by a well-placed observer: 'Mr X knows he will not be president and he is for a weak presidency, Mr Y thinks he

---

[5] At the same time, over 60% of the respondents supported close cooperation with Russia, while 22% opposed it. See W. Adamski, 'Interes narodowy w procesach zmiany systemowej i integracji europejskiej', *Kultura i społeczeństwo*, 42: 1 (Jan./Mar. 1998).

will be president and favours a strong presidency, while Mr Z knows he will be president and shares this attitude.'

Lech Wałęsa struggled to promote a strong presidency along the lines of the French Fifth Republic. At the same time, Wałęsa's constitutional ideas remained closer to those of President Boris Yeltsin. Wałęsa and Yeltsin both favoured extensive presidential powers without full accountability.[6] Most of Wałęsa's demands were frustrated by the Seym. For one, Wałęsa never obtained the right to issue presidential decrees. Nonetheless, the Provisional Constitution of 1993 gave him some powers of supervision over the Ministries of Foreign Affairs, Internal Affairs, and Defence. Wałęsa concentrated on gaining control over the 'power ministries': the Ministry of Internal Affairs, and especially the Bureau of State Security within that ministry; and the Ministry of Defence, and especially its General Staff.[7] Lech Wałęsa was able to place trusted men in charge of the Ministry of Internal Affairs.

However, the situation with regard to the Ministry of Defence was different. Wałęsa held a personal interest in the army, and did not tolerate anybody placing themselves between him and 'his' generals. The most important condition all aspirants to NATO membership had to meet was the establishment of an effective mechanism of civilian control over the military.[8] On this basis, the opposition was able to challenge the cosy relationship that had developed between Wałęsa and the armed forces. The Provisional Constitution did not give the president vast formal powers, but his office remained outside effective popular control, and retained veto powers.[9] Under the former and present Constitution, the president is nominally the commander-in-chief of the armed forces in time

[6] In a paper written in 1994, the similarities were described as follows: 'There is hardly any difference between Boris Yeltsin and Lech Wałęsa in their intentions, *albeit* not in achievements. Both tried to monopolize control over the executive, and reduce the role of the legislative (. . .) while assigning broad legislative powers to their office, through the right to issue decrees that must not be accepted by the legislative; both felt uneasy with the Constitutional Tribunal as well as other autonomous public bodies, and dreamt about creating a National Guard under their direct orders. Both planned to subordinate the General Staff to themselves. The difference is that Mr Yeltsin has been, by far, the more successful of the two in implementing these desires.' See Kamiński and Gogolewska, 'Civil Control of the Russian Military', 589.

[7] Until the implementation of military reform in 1996, the chief of staff had been in command of the ground forces. The Constitution introduced, along with the navy and air force, a separate command for the ground forces.

[8] Jeffrey Simon, *Central European Civil-Military Relations and NATO Expansion*, McNair Paper 39 (Washington: National Defense University, 1995).

[9] In this respect, the Constitution adopted in 1997 is not much different.

of war, and also presides over the Council of National Defence. His active role in defence matters is reinforced by the existence of a National Security Office within the president's administration. Moreover, the president must be consulted before the nomination of the defence minister. However, the defence minister is responsible solely to the prime minister, and the president's consent is not required to revoke the defence minister.

In order to strengthen his grip over the military, Wałęsa encouraged conflicts between the General Staff and the minister of defence, supporting the former in this struggle.[10] This conflict, which touched the very essence of the question of civilian control over the military, was the only way through which Wałęsa could seek direct control over the armed forces. This presidential protection was exploited by the General Staff to constrain the powers of the minister of defence, and to ensure the General Staff's autonomy.

As chair of the parliamentary constitutional commission from autumn 1993 to autumn 1995, Kwaśniewski had struggled to restrict the prerogatives of the presidency. The post-communist coalition rejoiced in the idea of cutting Wałęsa down to size. However, as the presidential elections of 1995 approached, and the likelihood of Kwaśniewski's victory increased, his enthusiasm for restricting presidential prerogatives faded. Upon becoming president, Kwaśniewski's views on this issue became identical to those held previously by Wałęsa. Kwaśniewski's efforts to change the Constitution to increase the powers of the president, which, by that time, had already been agreed upon, came too late to be effective. Kwaśniewski succeeded only in obtaining the right to nominate the chief of staff, and the commanders of the ground and air forces and navy without need for consultation. Like Wałęsa, Kwaśniewski sided with the military, in defence of their privileges and professional discretion. This was clear in December 1997, when he vetoed a parliamentary bill which would have levelled the military's substantial privileges in the indexing of rents and retirement pensions. Governmental ineptitude allowed the president to present himself as the 'defender of national security' against 'politicians', keen on depriving the military of justly merited rewards.

Thus, despite external pressures from NATO, the establishment of civilian control over the military in Poland in 1998 still faced difficulties. True, there has been no danger of a military coup. However, circumstances in which civilian politicians compete for

[10] It was at Wałęsa's direct instigation that top generals twice refused to obey the minister of defence: first in August 1993, and again in 1994.

political support from the army have not contributed to political stability. Poland's membership in NATO may help to resolve this problem, but any long-term solution must be found internally. Jeffrey Simon's diagnosis in 1995 remained valid in 1998:

The civil-military crisis resulted from Poland's failure to delegate authority between the president and government, and of the Seym Defense (Commission and Committee's) inability to exercise effective oversight. It also demonstrated the inability of the civilian defense ministry to control the military; hence, the chief of staff and general staff remain independent of the defense minister, and the army remains popular and heavily politicized.[11]

State Reform

The questions of local self-government, and the need to decentralize the state, were a major area of controversy during the round table talks. Reform in this area started in early 1990, with legislation establishing effective self-government at the local (*gmina*) level. The reform was incomplete, in particular on the issue of financing, because of strong opposition from some segments of Mazowiecki's government. Solidarity's position was that stable democracy required a high level of participation. One way to achieve this was the decentralization of decision-making and the devolution of state power to the local self-government level. The initiative was purely internal—no reform of this type has been attempted either in the Czech Republic or in Hungary. Yet it received a sympathetic response from the West. The material support, needed to educate thousands of local self-government officials, came mainly from the American sponsored Endowment for Democracy. In order to understand the nature of this problem, it is necessary to examine the history of discussions of state reform.

Before the administrative reforms of 1975, the territory of Poland had been divided into seventeen *voyevodships* and 360 *powiat* (counties)—in what was a three-layer administrative hierarchy. The weakness of this system, as perceived by the communist leadership, resided in the role played by the voyevodship party secretaries, who were decisive in securing the ouster of Władysław Gomułka from the party leadership. Gomułka's successor, Edward Gierek, to make his position more secure increased the number of voyevodship to forty-nine, and reduced the number of layers to two,

---

[11] Simon, *Central European Civil-Military Relations*, 71–2.

by eliminating the powiats. This allowed him to strengthen the role of the centre with regard to the territorial units, but at the cost of losing some control over the functional divisions of state administration. As some observers commented at the time: 'a federation of ministries replaced the federation of voyevodship.'

When the post-communist transition began, it became immediately evident that one of the principal issues to be addressed was the problem of state administrative coordination. Governments have approached this problem in different ways. Some sought a solution in reorganizing central state power. One such programme was partly implemented by the SLD/PSL coalition government, although abandoned by its successor. The reform proposal, devised by the centre right coalition in 1998, involved the reintroduction of the third layer, the powiat, and a reduction in the number of voyevodships to twelve large regions.[12] In this plan, the local and powiat level would be self-governing, while most of the administration for a unitary state would reside at the level of the voyevodship. The unitary state would meet the needs for administration of self-government in a voyevodship seym, with its own administration. The prerogatives of these levels are formally delimited, with serious conflict to be adjudicated by the courts. The heads of the voyevodship will be state officials nominated by, and responsible to, the prime minister, represented in this case by the minister for administration. However, these heads will have to coexist with local self-government, which will possess its own administration and budget revenue. All top officials in local self-government will be selected through elections.

In 1998, the reform faced two forms of opposition. The officials in the voyevodship viewed this reform as a distinct threat to their positions. Also, the Peasant Party feared that its influence in the countryside, where the main body of its electorate resides, may be diminished. The second form of opposition resided in those circles supporting a highly centralized state. With regard to the impact of external factors, while the reform was supported by the European Commission, it was not initiated by this organization. From the point of view of future Polish membership in the EU, large self-reliant regions would be an advantage as they would ensure better access to structural funds. This argument appeared several times in discussions concerning the reform, but it never played an

[12] An agreement was reached in the middle of July 1998 between the governing coalition and the main opposition party, the SLD, to increase the number of voyevodships to sixteen.

important role—internal perspectives and partisan interests were much more important. Also, the European Commission agreed to support the reform from the PHARE funds as part, and subject to the conditionalities, of the Institution Building programme. Again, this argument was never used in debates about the merits of the programme within Poland. The sources of this reform were both ideological and pragmatic. The idea and blueprint for the reform were internally generated.

Conclusions

On the basis of the Polish example, it is possible to consider under which circumstances: (1) the impact of external factors is most effective; (2) policy makers take external factors into account and are careful to maintain some appearance of compliance, *albeit* perhaps without real adhesion; and (3) external expectations are entirely disregarded.

There are several determinants of internal responses to external factors. First, the number of relevant actors in the external environment must be limited enough to make a coordinated impact possible. Second, these external actors must share the same well-defined set of expectations, and have some understanding of the problems faced by internal political actors. Third, external actors must control resources crucial for the realization of priority interests of domestic political actors. Fourth, it is best that conformity with external expectations should be easy to monitor. An internal feeling of urgency helps external actors to make an impact. Sixth, it is of critical importance that domestic policy makers have enough sophistication to understand the nature of external expectations and be willing and able to adapt to these in a way that takes into account the logic of the internal situation. Related to this, the perceived impact of external reactions to policies of the government on the matrix of political and economic interests in the country should be favourable, mobilizing the political elite. Finally, domestic public opinion should be convinced of the legitimacy of external expectations.

The first two changes implemented in Poland, the policy of economic stabilization and shifts in foreign policy, can be assessed on the basis of well-defined criteria. The approval or disapproval of external agents could have had important long-term consequences for the country for a broad spectrum of the public opinion. Both the World Bank and the IMF act on the basis of an evolving economic paradigm that is widely accepted and provides a useful yardstick to measure the quality of a government's economic policies.[13] Yet it is important to note that although the relationship between a state undergoing transition and these institutions is highly asymmetrical, the learning process goes both ways: the IMF and the World Bank have shown an ability to adapt to contingencies which had not been foreseen. With regard to foreign policy changes, the West evaluated the activities of post-communist governments in terms of their impact on international stability. The most important of the West's foreign policy criteria was the acceptance of existing borders, and a willingness to respect the rights of minorities.

Poland's economic and political vulnerability stimulated the implementation of important policy changes. International actors knew what to require in Poland, and how to enforce policies conforming with their expectations. In Poland, external actors also had capable interlocutors in the government. It was relatively easy to control conformity, because concrete measures were required to achieve economic stability. The results of radical economic reform emerged quickly, which confirmed internal and external perceptions of the validity of Poland's reform choice. The feeling of urgency, and the ensuing readiness to accept sacrifice for the sake of national survival, was sufficiently widespread to render feasible measures which otherwise might have been unacceptable. Finally, when the economic stabilization programme was introduced the communist status quo had been already destroyed. No established interests, at that moment, could counteract it. Thus, Balcerowicz operated under conditions of minimal political friction, although the situation changed after only a few months.

The extension of external influence over internal developments during a transition faces great problems when external expectations threaten strong institutional interests and/or incite deep-seated anxieties. In Poland, corporate military interests have exploited an unclear constitutional situation by playing the president against the government and the parliament. Examples of subversion of external demands by established institutional groups have abounded in Poland. Such groups have ensured high-level monopolization in some sectors of industry and services, despite requests from the European Commission to demonopolize. Moreover, the problem of corruption has affected all levels of the state. Despite continued

[13] Harold James, *International Monetary Cooperation since the Bretton Woods Agreements* (New York: Oxford University Press, 1996).

external demands that decisive measures must be taken, no government has done much to remedy this situation.[14]

Whatever the role of particular interests in the Polish economic policy process, the professional integrity of the economists in charge of budgetary and financial policies has been high enough to keep these out of the realm of partisan quarrels. This has been an important factor in Poland's relative economic success. Similarly, the existence of a group of professionals with a strong ideological commitment to self-government, and the support this found among local and regional elites, were decisive factors in stimulating the drive toward the reform of the Polish state. The European Commission has supported this reform, by making it a condition for accession and by providing funds. International factors have only contributed to making this reform feasible.

By far the most important factor has been the relative openness of Poland to Western influence since 1956. Poles travelled abroad more than any other nation within the communist camp, and were able to acquire knowledge, albeit limited, of how the West operated. Polish scholars and students studied at Western academic institutions. Millions of émigrés in the West maintained close contacts with their families in Poland. Polish society was relatively well prepared for the change of regime. The fact that despite these propitious circumstances this task proved difficult highlights the complex nature of democratic transition under post-communist conditions.

[14] The Buzek government promised to take some steps in this direction. The results remain to be seen. Antoni Z. Kamiński, 'Corruption under the Post-Communist Transformation: The Case of Poland', *Polish Sociological Review*, 2: 118 (1997).

The Czech Republic: The Unexpected Force of Institutional Constraints

Milada Anna Vachudová

The Czech Republic provides an interesting study in the way that international institutions may shape democratic consolidation and economic reform in states that wish to join them. In Eastern Europe, since 1989, the prospect of membership in the European Union (EU) and in the North Atlantic Treaty organization (NATO) has provided a strong incentive to build liberal democratic states. Governments will implement difficult domestic reforms and modify their foreign policies in order to obtain the political, economic, and security benefits of membership. Yet for this dynamic to work, candidates must consider membership to be a realistic goal. They must believe that these institutions will expand, and that they can fulfil the requirements of membership. They must also believe that they are unprepared as yet for membership, that work remains to be done.[1] The Czech case demonstrates how this process depends on a certain tension between confidence in securing membership and fear of suffering rejection due to inadequate reform. An overabundance of assurance on the part of the Czech governments of Prime Minister Václav Klaus undermined the execution of comprehensive

My thanks to Dagmar Ašerová, Matthew Evangelista, Rick Fawn, Timothy Garton Ash, Jiří Pehe, Alex Pravda, Matthew Rhodes, Marek Škréta, Timothy Snyder, Jonathan Stein, Stephen Whitefield, and Kieran Williams for comments on an earlier draft. This chapter also benefited from conversations with officials of the European Commission and of the Czech Ministry of Foreign Affairs, including Jiří Havlík, Petr Lunák, Martin Palouš, and Pavel Telička. The research was funded by a NATO-National Science Foundation postdoctoral fellowship, and supported by the Prague centre of the East–West Institute.

[1] This argument draws on Milada Anna Vachudová, *Revolution, Democracy and Integration: East Central and South Eastern Europe since 1989* (Oxford: Oxford University Press, forthcoming).

domestic reforms and the design of rational foreign policy. The Commission's 1997 'Opinion' on the Czech Republic's application alluded to this attitude in a single laconic sentence: 'Confident of its progress towards meeting the obligations of EU membership, the Czech Republic has at times shown reluctance to acknowledge difficulties and seek a collaborative approach to resolving them.'[2]

The influence of international factors on the consolidation of Czech democracy since 1989 can be divided into four stages, corresponding roughly to the changes of government. In the first, from 1989 to 1992, the Czechoslovak government was led by former dissidents who sought to create a Western liberal democracy and return Czechoslovakia to Europe. The influence of the West, as a model and as a goal for the Czech political and economic transformation, was profound. Securing membership in the EU and NATO became fundamental goals, and the perceived requirements of membership shaped policy in the new state. This occurred well before either the EU or NATO had committed to eastern enlargement, much less set down specific requirements for membership. To the extent that the West did set down explicit conditions, for example on the treatment of ethnic minorities by the Council of Europe (COE) or on the liberalization of trade by the EU, these coincided with the liberal democratic agenda of the Czechoslovak government. Meanwhile, the speeches of Czechoslovak President Václav Havel during this period helped crystallize Western Europe's vague plans to integrate the post-communist east.

In the second stage, which will be the chief concern of this chapter, the centre-right coalition of Prime Minister Václav Klaus governed the Czech Republic from June 1992 until November 1997. Although the independent Czech Republic perceived itself, and was generally perceived by others, as among the most pro-Western states in Eastern Europe, the reform project was surprisingly insulated from international influences. Klaus had his own strategy—a personal mix of free market ideology and political pragmatism—for creating a 'Western' state, fit for membership in the EU and NATO. From 1993, Klaus and other Czech officials asserted that the transition was complete, and that the damage to society under communism had been reversed. Until 1997, supported by impressive macroeconomic indicators, they succeeded in projecting a very positive image of the Czech Republic. The influence of the West as

---

[2] 'Commission Opinion on the Czech Republic's Application for Membership in the European Union', A. Introduction. Commission documents are all at europa.eu.int/comm/enlargement/.

a model and as a goal remained during this stage, but was necessarily weakened by claims that the Czech Republic had already become part of the West. Indeed, Klaus's Czech Republic became so convinced of its virtues as the most advanced post-communist state with the most successful economy in Europe that basic reforms remained unfinished.

The conditions necessary for direct international influence on the policy choices of the Czech government did not emerge until the end of this second stage. For much of the 1990s, the criticisms and diplomatic initiatives of Western governments and international institutions were aimed at those post-communist governments who violated democratic standards and whose use of ethnic nationalism threatened the rights of ethnic minorities and peaceful relations with neighbouring states. This was not the case in the Czech Republic. Nor was the Czech Republic, with its low levels of debt and good macroeconomic indicators, under pressure from the International Monetary Fund (IMF) or the World Bank. Nevertheless, international censure did eventually force the Czech government to change a 1993 citizenship law which, by design, disadvantaged Roma applicants.

Over the course of the second stage, the EU gradually developed the tools to identify the problems plaguing democratic consolidation in the Czech Republic. After taking the necessary step of committing itself to eastern enlargement in 1992, the EU's expectations of the aspiring candidates became more concrete. It set out the general political and economic requirements of membership in 1993, and the extensive regulatory requirements of the internal market in 1995. In view of approaching negotiations, the European Commission examined Czech political and economic reform to write its Opinion on the Czech Republic's application, published in July 1997. This scrutiny revealed the reforms which had been neglected or unsuccessful, notably enterprise restructuring, bank privatization, and public administration reform.

As the Commission's Opinion was being written and the start of negotiations drew near, economic downturn and political instability in the Czech Republic announced the third stage in summer 1997. After the fall of the Klaus government in November 1997, an interim government led by Prime Minister Josef Tosovsky held power until the early elections of June 1998. By force of necessity but also of its political outlook, this government was more responsive to outside advice and more attentive to the conditionality inherent in the EU accession process.

The greatest international influence on the consolidation of Czech democracy would arise from an abiding desire of the Czech

Republic to gain entry into the EU. If the Czech Republic is to join in the first wave, the most direct and substantial influence will occur in the fourth stage: current and subsequent Czech governments must tend to the requirements of EU membership. The elections of June 1998 yielded a minority Social Democratic government led by Prime Minister Milos Zeman. Its reform efforts in 1998 and 1999 were dragged down by inexperience and opposition intransigence. After two negative progress reports from the Commission, however, reform showed signs of a revival. If the pursuit of reform does overcome the stultifying politics of 1997, 1998, and 1999, it will be thanks to the incentives of EU membership and the momentum inherent in the accession process.

NATO underwent an evolution similar to that of the EU, inviting the Czech Republic to begin membership negotiations in December 1997. However, the reforms NATO demanded concerned a much smaller part of state policy, and the political decision to admit the Czech Republic was largely divorced from how well these reforms were pursued. Perhaps qualifying for membership was too easy. Days after the Czech Republic entered NATO along with Poland and Hungary in March 1999, opposition to the airstrikes against the Federal Republic of Yugoslavia suggested the ambivalence of a considerable part of the Czech political class to the Czech Republic's newfound alliance commitments.

Dissidents 'Return to Europe': Czechoslovakia, 1990–1992

From 1989 to 1992, the Civic Forum governments of Czechoslovakia worked to create a Western liberal democracy and to return Czechoslovakia to Europe. Aside from the deepening imbroglio with the Slovaks in 1991 and 1992, the reform programme of successive Czech governments was essentially unchallenged by a post-communist right or left, as neither the defence of the Czech nation nor protection from the hardships of economic reform resonated strongly with the Czech electorate. The Civic Forum dominated political discourse during the formative years after 1989, and for all of its subsequent divisions, it was united, resolute, and successful in building the foundations of a liberal democracy.

The influence of the West—as a model and as a goal for the Czechoslovak transformation—was profound, yet the impetus for change came from within the Czech political class. Czechoslovak membership in the EU formed the cornerstone of the foreign policy programme of the Civic Forum from its inception in 1989. Securing membership in the EU and, from 1991, in NATO became goals of state policy, and the anticipated requirements of membership increasingly shaped policy choices in the new state. For their part, Western governments and international institutions looked on approvingly, while experimenting with a wide array of tools for supporting the transformation. Czechoslovak president Václav Havel enjoyed significant moral authority in the West, and his speeches during this period, calling on the West to integrate the East, made a strong impression on Western policy makers.[3]

The influence of the East initially was more concrete, as the Czechoslovak government had to extricate itself from the Warsaw Pact and from its close economic ties to the Soviet bloc. The dramatic collapse of trade among the CMEA (Council for Mutual Economic Assistance) members and the (successful) reorientation of Czechoslovak trade to the West demanded considerable effort. Meanwhile, the idealism of the post-dissident Czechoslovak government and its sympathy for the difficult domestic position of Mikhail Gorbachev led it to propose the simultaneous dissolution of the Warsaw Pact and NATO, accompanied by the creation of a collective security system embracing the whole of Europe based on the Conference on Security and Cooperation in Europe (CSCE, after 1994, OSCE).[4] Membership in NATO only became a declared goal of Czechoslovak foreign policy in 1991, by which time the CSCE proposal had faded under Western disapproval.[5]

Susceptibility to Western Influence, 1992–1997

Until the mid-1990s, the project of anchoring the Czech Republic firmly in the West and removing it decisively from the orbit of

[3] The strongest criticism of the Civic Forum's foreign policy, led by Foreign Minister Jiří Dienstbier, came from Klaus and others who held that Czechoslovak interests were being sacrificed to grand foreign policy initiatives with pretensions of changing the course of European integration. Pavel Seifter, 'Hic Europa, O Nesamozřejmosti Československých Národních Zájmů', *Mezinárodní Politika*, 6: 4 (Apr. 1992), 3; and Ústav Mezinárodních Vztahů et al., *České národní zájmy* (Prague: Ústav Mezinárodních Vztahů, 1993).

[4] For an overview, Jiří Sedivý, 'From Dreaming to Realism: Czechoslovak Security Policy Since 1989', *Perspectives* (Winter 1994/5), 61–71.

[5] NATO officials described the 1990 proposal as 'shocking'. Josef Vesely, 'Spolecné politické struktury jsou duležitější než společné ozbrojené síly', *Mladá Fronta Dnes* (17 Dec. 1991), 6.

Moscow was still underway. The Civic Forum governments of Czechoslovakia had prepared the way for the independent Czech Republic's stellar image in the West, and for the presupposition that subsequent governments would simply advance the democratic project. The overarching goal of the two ODS-led governments (June 1992–June 1996 and June 1996–November 1997) was to create a Western market democracy, crowned by EU and NATO membership. However, Klaus also wondered aloud whether these institutions were good enough for the Czechs, and needlessly irritated Western leaders by implying that the EU should join the Czech Republic, and not vice versa. The Klaus governments were successful in projecting a very positive image to the West, while fostering an 'ideology of Czech exceptionalism' at home.[6] Although they sought to emulate and even surpass Western economic success, the influence of Western actors on policy choices in the new state was minimal.

The European Union: a sleeping giant

From 1992 to 1997 the pro-EU comportment of the Czech government, necessary to keep the Czech Republic well within the 'first wave' of EU candidates, did not interfere with day-to-day policy-making. The general expectations of the EU in many areas coincided with the political and economic agenda of the Czech government. When they did not (as in reform of the state administration, protection of minority rights, and support of civil society), this remained largely hidden for lack of a systematic evaluation of Czech reforms. The Czech Republic was the darling of the West, a self-perpetuating status thanks to the shared impressions of Western policy makers and the (mostly) favourable, cross-referenced reports of international organizations.

The Europe Agreement governing trade liberalization between the Czech Republic and the EU came into force in early 1995, but most of its provisions were adopted with the earlier Interim Agreement of 1992. The agreement provided for a steady liberalization of trade over a ten-year period, with exceptions in agriculture and other 'sensitive' areas. For reasons of free market ideology, the Czech government called for an acceleration of the schedules for trade liberalization contained in the Europe Agreement. It was generally the protectionist measures of EU member states—not of the Czech

---

[6] Jiří Pehe, 'Souvislosti domácí a zahraniční politiky', *Mezinárodní Politika*, 12: 1 (Jan. 1998), 6–7.

Republic or of other associated states—which raised charges that the Europe Agreements were being violated. Instances of EU protectionism, such as the 1993 total ban on the import of livestock, meat, and dairy products from Eastern Europe, risked discrediting the EU among the Czech public.[7] Spates of EU protectionism strengthened Klaus's confident message of Czech economic superiority and helped limit the impact of other, more positive Western models of state interference in the economy.

Soon after the EU committed itself to enlargement, the so-called 'Copenhagen Requirements' for aspiring members were set out by the Copenhagen European Council in June 1993.[8] These requirements called for (1) the stability of democratic institutions including the protection of minority rights; (2) a functioning market economy able to cope with the competitive pressures within the EU; and (3) the ability to take on the obligations of membership. These requirements were very general, and therefore, by any account, the Czech Republic was making progress toward them in the mid-1990s. However, from 1993 onward the Czech government was criticized by many international actors for its treatment of the Roma minority (see below). While these criticisms eventually forced change, Czech officials were able to downplay the problem of racism in the state administration. In this period, the West's attention was generally directed at states where the treatment of ethnic minorities posed a much more obvious problem and democracy seemed much more tenuous than in the Czech Republic.[9]

In 1995, the Commission published the White Paper stipulating the requirements for integrating into the Single Market. Like the free trade provisions of the Europe Agreements, the White Paper measures on the free movement of goods, services, capital, and people corresponded with the Czech government's free market ideology. In fact, Klaus liked to equate the entirety of the EU's membership requirements with the White Paper. Meanwhile, the Government Committee on European Integration, chaired personally by the prime minister, was set up to coordinate the Czech drive for EU membership. The formal application was submitted in January 1996, by which time the Czechs had already made notable

---

[7] Jan Machácek, 'Nejsme protekcionisté', *Respekt*, 4: 15 (19 Apr. 1993), 15.

[8] On the EU's approach, Alan Mayhew, *Recreating Europe: The European Union's Policy towards Central and Eastern Europe* (Cambridge: Cambridge University Press, 1998).

[9] For benchmarks, Jacques Rupnik, 'The Postcommunist Divide', *Journal of Democracy*, 10: 1 (1999), 57–62.

progress in meeting the regulatory demands of the 1995 White Paper.[10]

Leading EU politicians regretted that the Czechs seemed to solicit EU membership purely for reasons of national interest.[11] Klaus lobbied for rapid membership in the EU, but he was also a vocal critic of the integration projects envisioned by the Maastricht process.[12] Klaus identified with the so-called Eurosceptics, portraying Czech independence and the Czech neoliberal economic project as being under threat from the 'socialist internationalism' of the Brussels bureaucracy. Criticism of the EU did not tarnish the Czech Republic's star status in the West, in part because the Czech foreign ministry worked overtime to smooth over Klaus's controversial statements. But it did limit the indirect influence of the EU on Czech politics. By claiming to be 'West' of the West Europeans, Klaus ensured that his administration, much of the media, and a good deal of public opinion retained a provincial confidence in Czech superiority, rather than opening the country to perhaps salutary influences. EU membership came to be understood as a reward for an economic job already well done.[13]

No federation, no cooperation: creating the perfect candidate?

Klaus relied upon his own calculations as to which 'foreign' policies would most help the Czech Republic become part of 'the West'. In 1992, he did not heed the advice of West European leaders to preserve the Czechoslovak federation and to pursue cooperation within the Visegrad Group of Czechoslovakia, Poland, and Hungary. While the West provided the motivation for government policies, Western actors had little if any say about their content.

In the case of the break-up of Czechoslovakia, the desire to emulate Western economic success played a critical role: Slovak politicians hindered the implementation of reform measures, and foreign investors were deterred from investing in Czechoslovakia

---

[10] The government reported that by early 1997 it had incorporated 417 out of 899 White Paper measures. Their correct application however required 'highly developed and effective regulatory, standardization, certification and supervisory authorities,' about whose existence the Commission had doubts. 'Commission Opinion', 4.2 Administrative Capacity to Apply the Acquis.

[11] Commission President Jacques Santer excerpted in 'Evropa rozumu a nadšení', *Respekt*, 7: 16 (15 Apr. 1996), 1.

[12] Martin Weiss, 'Evropská integrace a my', *Respekt*, 4: 3 (18 Jan. 1993), 3.

[13] 'Svoboda a Prosperita', ODS Party Program (Apr. 1996).

by the Czech-Slovak confrontation. An independent Czech Republic promised the Klaus government easier reform, greater prosperity, and a more westerly geopolitical position.[14] Although Western leaders called for the preservation of the federation,[15] Klaus reasoned that when it came time to evaluate candidates for EU and NATO membership, Czech political stability and economic success would more than compensate for the West's transient displeasure at the dissolution of Czechoslovakia.[16]

On the question of union with Slovakia, this view proved correct: the geostrategic position and economic health of an independent Czech Republic were better without Slovakia. More importantly, though less remarked upon, an independent Czech Republic was free of what could have been an enduring stalemate between Czech and Slovak politicians in a common Czechoslovak state. Such a stalemate could have proved another formidable obstacle to the consolidation of democracy. In any case, the West did not punish the Czechs for the split, which scarcely delayed integration with the West: the Czech Republic and Slovakia became separate members of the Council of Europe on 30 June 1993, and signed new association agreements with the EU on 4 October 1993.

Klaus treated cooperation within the Visegrad Group of Czechoslovakia, Poland, and Hungary much as he had the Slovaks: as an obstacle to the rapid Western transformation of the Czech Republic.[17] West European leaders supported Visegrad cooperation as a proving ground for East Central European states. Klaus,

---

[14] The agreement between the ODS and the Movement for a Democratic Slovakia (HZDS) of 20 June 1992 states that the HZDS wanted a confederation of two republics, but that the ODS refused, preferring the creation of two wholly independent states. 'Politická dohoda ODS a HZDS', *Lidové Noviny* (21 June 1992), 2.

[15] EU officials highlighted the costs of Czechoslovakia's dissolution, and EU parliamentarians reminded Czechs and Slovaks that no association agreement could enter into force without 260 votes in the European Parliament. Karel Gruber, 'ES versus Česká a Slovenská republika', *Mladá Fronta Dnes* (7 Aug. 1992), 5; and Josef Veselý, 'Znovu o postoji ES k dělení Československa', *Mladá Fronta Dnes* (11 Aug. 1992), 6.

[16] EU leaders only encouraged Klaus by warning that Czechoslovakia's association agreement would have to be renegotiated individually by the successor states with regard to the divergence of their 'economic performance'. See British Prime Minister John Major's remarks in 'Koncem dekády by ČSFR mohla vstoupit do Evropy', *Mladá Fronta Dnes* (28 May 1992), 4.

[17] Dienstbier and Havel believed that cooperation would strengthen the position of the East Central European states with regard to the EU. From the outset, they emphasized that the Visegrad Group constituted neither a military alliance nor an institution for economic integration.

however, reasoned that Visegrad cooperation would retard the Czech Republic's admission to the EU and NATO: these institutions might claim that East Central European states were, for now, best left to develop their own structures. They might also commit themselves to accepting all four states together, and then postpone their admission because of the political or economic problems of any one state. By 1993, Bulgaria, Romania, and even Ukraine were clamouring for membership in the Visegrad Group. This set the stage for the founding members to create their own membership requirements and occupy themselves with judging the political reforms of their post-communist neighbours, a questionable undertaking at best.

While these apprehensions may have been reasonable, Klaus overplayed the part of the 'Western' state by loudly severing ties with his purportedly backward neighbours. Visegrad cooperation including Slovakia would have faded of its own accord due to the anti-democratic behaviour of the Meciar governments (behaviour which in 1997 earned Slovakia its exclusion from membership negotiations with the EU and NATO). Klaus speculated publicly that the Czech image would suffer by association not only with Slovakia, but also with Poland and Hungary. (From the perspective of 1999, when the Czechs find themselves near the bottom of the Visegrad heap, ranked behind Hungary and Poland in the EU membership queue, this is amusing at best.) In the end, it was Klaus's widely criticized public stance against regional cooperation that damaged the Czech image.[18] Visegrad cooperation was limited to the Central European Free Trade Area (CEFTA); this was considered a success and admitted new members according to economic guidelines.

As relations with eastern neighbours were downgraded, those with the Czech Republic's powerful western neighbour were to be intensified: Germany was recognized by the Czech government in 1990 as the only West European state having real interests in the integration of the Czech Republic into NATO and the EU. The government hoped to create a special relationship with Germany by way of the political stability, the geostrategic position, and above all the economic success of the Czech Republic. Czechs miscalculated German interests in two ways. First, of greater concern to

---

[18] One colourful American report described Czech foreign policy as 'ethnocentric' and 'provincial, if not nationalist'. It concluded that 'Czech policy, although it professes integration with NATO and the EU, reflects a general renationalization of security policy that largely stems from an internal failure of vision.' Stephen Blank, *Prague, NATO, and European Security* (Carlisle Barracks, Pa.: Strategic Studies Institute, 1996).

Bonn than pushing the membership of the Czech Republic—because this would be an easy state for Western institutions to absorb— was the stability of the whole of East Central Europe. Diminished ties between the Czech Republic and its eastern neighbours were considered destabilizing, and met with displeasure. Second, the Czech government underestimated the strength of the Sudeten German lobby in German politics.

Once again, while the West provided the motivation for state policy, it could not shape its execution: the Czech government refused any discussion with organizations representing the 3 million ethnic Germans who were expelled from the Sudetenland by the Czechoslovak government just after the Second World War. The Czech government's dismissive stance toward these organizations increased support for their cause in Germany. The Sudeten problem made the Czech Republic an unlikely candidate for German favoritism, as Czechs and Germans were unable to undertake a reconciliation such as had occurred between Poles and Germans. The Czech–German declaration was finally signed by Klaus and Kohl on 21 January 1997, but a deeper reconciliation remained elusive.[19] Throughout this period, foreign policy was marked by Klaus's personal tendency to reduce relations to economic matters, disregarding the importance of history, diplomacy, culture, and security. This circumscribed the influence of western as well as eastern neighbours on the Czech polity.[20]

Western Influence on Domestic Reform, 1992–1997

Domestic reform was carried out according to Klaus's beliefs about how to create a Czech economic miracle, sure to please the public and the West. Between 1993 and 1997, there was no clear Western voice disputing his strategies. By 1997, when the shortcomings of the reforms had become clear, the damage to individual Czechs, to their belief in the value of the market and of reform, to Czech civil society, and thus to democratic consolidation, had already been done. In December 1997, Havel noted: 'if I criticize those who have resigned, it is not so much for any particular sin they may have committed, but far more for their indifference and outright hostility

[19] For a critical view, Andrew Stroehlein, 'Czechs and the Czech-German Declaration: The Failure of a New Approach to History', *Glasgow Papers*, 1 (1998).

[20] Rudolf Kučera, professor at Charles University and director of the Institute for Central European Culture and Politics, interview in Prague (May 1994).

to everything that may even slightly resemble a civil society or contribute to its creation.'[21]

An economist under the communists, once in power Klaus portrayed himself as a free market purist and navigated through the transformation using a macroeconomic compass. The Czech government adopted a strategy of privatization by which ownership, unhindered by law or state oversight, was to be sorted out by the higher laws of the market. However, pragmatism and political expediency clashed with market ideology: having pushed privatization in the early 1990s, Klaus put off key reforms in 1994 and 1995 in order to win re-election in June 1996. To forestall unemployment, the banks were not fully privatized, while rents and energy prices were not deregulated. This combination of rushed reform in some areas and gradualist back-peddling in others produced the Czech economic miracle, followed by the Czech economic mess.

The golden years

The dissolution of Czechoslovakia aside, the first four years of government by Klaus were marked by impressive political calm. After the June 1992 elections, Klaus's victorious Civic Democratic Party (ODS) formed a coalition with the Civic Democratic Alliance (ODA) and the Christian Democratic bloc (KDU-CSL). This coalition controlled 105 out of 200 seats, and held together until the elections of 1996. The popularity of all three coalition parties remained stable, and the ODS preserved the support of more than 30 per cent of respondents to opinion polls. During this period, Klaus's political power was not threatened by dissent within his own party or by the disintegration of his coalition. Klaus's power was also not checked by a strong, experienced opposition: the weak parties of the fragmented left were ineffective watchdogs. The media was likewise inexperienced and ineffectual. Havel was elected to the Czech presidency, but the powers of the president were restricted, and he was overshadowed by Klaus.[22]

[21] For the text of his landmark December 1997 address to parliament in English, Václav Havel, 'The State of the Republic', *New York Review of Books*, 45: 3 (5 Mar. 1998), 42–6.

[22] Klaus and Havel disagreed on many issues, most dramatically on the value of the Czechoslovak federation and of civil society. See Timothy Garton Ash, 'Prague: Intellectuals and Politicians', *New York Review of Books* (12 Jan. 1995), 34–41; Kieran Williams, 'National Myths in the New Czech Liberalism', in George Schöpflin and Geoffrey Hosking (eds.), *Myths and Nationhood* (London: Hurst, 1997), 79–89; and Martin Potůček, 'Havel versus Klaus: Public Policymaking in the Czech Republic', lecture at the Institute for Human Sciences (IWM), Vienna (27 Jan. 1998).

The ODS-led government, therefore, enjoyed remarkable political freedom. It augmented this freedom by neglecting to establish an independent civil service and by undermining poles of opinion outside the government, such as universities, non-governmental organizations, and interest groups. Dialogue with civic groups was avoided, and a legal framework for non-governmental organizations was delayed until 1995. No effort was made to foster public discussion and few public information campaigns were attempted. No freedom of information law was passed.[23] The International Helsinki Foundation observed that 'it was nearly impossible for individuals to obtain any information or documents from the government or other bodies of state administration.'[24] Perhaps most telling was Klaus's eagerness to be rid of the Central European University in Prague, which harboured Czech opposition intellectuals and formed part of George Soros's project to create civil society in post-communist Europe. All together, these practices stunted the Czech polity by impeding the creation of a vibrant civil society and a new class of Czech elites.[25]

For their part, those non-Czech actors (international institutions and foreign governments) who disagreed with Klaus were often ignored.[26] Out of fear of competition with Western-trained elites and scorn for their advice, the Klaus government also shunned Czechs who had been exiled abroad. Foreigners in general were regarded with suspicion, and significant obstacles were placed in the way of their legal residence.[27]

The Klaus government devoted itself to creating the image that market reform was 'complete' in the Czech Republic. It managed to preserve low inflation and very low unemployment, while balancing

[23] While the Charter of Fundamental Rights and Freedoms, of which the Czech Republic is a signatory, guarantees the right to information and obliges state bodies to provide information about their activities, the Czech parliament did not pass a freedom of information law until 1998.

[24] International Helsinki Federation for Human Rights, *The Czech Republic, Annual Report 1997*.

[25] On the impact of the Prague Spring of 1968 and of normalization on the Czech elite: Kieran Williams, *The Prague Spring and Its Aftermath: Czechoslovak Politics, 1968–1970* (Cambridge: Cambridge University Press, 1997); and Grzegorz Ekiert, *The State against Society: Political Crises and Their Aftermath in East Central Europe* (Princeton: Princeton University Press, 1996).

[26] Klaus often declared himself suspicious of West European 'socialist' economic practices, and had few contacts in West European governments and international institutions. However, he admired the United States and reportedly lent an ear to the advice of conservative American think tanks such as the CATO Institute.

[27] Jiří Pehe, 'Cizinci v Čechách, Češi v cizine', *Lidové Noviny* (15 June 1998), 10.

its budgets. The contraction of the economy was reversed in 1993, to be replaced by steady growth. Rapid privatization and a large-scale restitution of communist-confiscated property were hailed at home and abroad as dramatic successes. To Klaus's credit, a great deal of foreign investment found its way to the Czech Republic due to the strong performance of the economy and to the government's free market rhetoric. Moreover, the economic hardships of the transition experienced by the population were curbed as compared to other post-communist states. After much hard work, the Czech Republic became the first state of the former Soviet bloc to join the OECD. A triumphalist Klaus invited West European leaders to Prague for pointers on how to run their own national economies.

Positive macroeconomic indicators masked the shortcomings of the government's economic policies—these would come to light just as Klaus's political juggernaut began to lose steam in 1996 and 1997. Klaus's three-party coalition fell short of a parliamentary majority in the June 1996 elections. In the 200-seat parliament, the coalition won 99 seats, while the Social Democrat Party (CSSD) won 61, the Communists (KSCM) 22, and the Republicans (SPR-RSC) 18.[28] Improving dramatically on its modest 7 per cent showing in 1992, the CSSD received 26 per cent of the vote in 1996. From this point, Klaus led a minority government, which treaded water until it sank in November 1997.

Was it privatization?

Privatization, the crown jewel of Klaus's reforms and one argument for Czech economic superiority over its East Central European neighbours, began to seem less impressive in the late 1990s. Voucher privatization itself was a self-consciously 'Czech' undertaking, designed by Klaus's economic team with the advice of a handful of Western-trained Czech economists, but without the help of Western actors. Indeed, the IMF and the World Bank discouraged it—but without recommending a clear alternative. By 1996, serious problems were evident in the Czech economy, many of them

---

[28] The electoral results of June 1996 for the major Czech parties, with the results of June 1992 in parentheses, are as follows. Klaus's coalition: Civic Democratic Party (ODS) 29.6% (29.7%), Christian Democrats (KDU-CSL) 8.1% (6.3%), and Civic Democratic Alliance (ODA) 6.7% (6%). The opposition: Social Democratic Party (CSSD) 26.4% (6.6%), Communist Party (KSCM) 10.3% (14.1%), and Republican Party (SPR-RSC) 8% (6%).

related to the privatization process: voucher privatization had failed to restructure and to privatize enterprises, while government policy had stifled the creation of new enterprises and set the stage for corruption by insiders in the distribution of the firms inherited from communism.[29]

That the Klaus government only allowed the participation of Czech actors in voucher privatization was to the detriment of enterprise restructuring. The goal was a nationalist one: to keep Czech enterprises out of foreign (especially German) hands. The absence of foreign investors meant that 'privatized' enterprises received no influx of capital or know-how. As a result, most enterprises lacked the tools necessary to increase their competitiveness. In comparison, the enterprises privatized with the participation of foreign investors during the so-called small and large privatization were much more successful.[30]

Meanwhile, the financial structure of the Czech Republic became an opaque maze of interconnected banks, investment funds, and newly privatized firms. Many Czechs sold their vouchers to so-called investment funds, allowing such funds to gain control of most firms privatized using the voucher method. Most of these funds were in turn controlled by a handful of major banks and insurance companies, which were in their turn still partly owned by the state. The 'privatized' firms were by then greatly indebted to the banks, and the banks were often called upon by the government to decide which enterprises should receive state financing. State-dominated banks were at once the owners, the creditors, and sometimes the auditors of 'privatized' firms.

Voucher privatization not only failed to restructure and to privatize, it also created an investment climate distinctly unfavourable to new, legitimately private firms. To forestall the shocks of economic restructuring, Klaus's reform strategy offered communist-era managers advantageous loans and loan-forgiveness by way of the state-dominated banks. The banks, who could count on being bailed out by the state, were the indirect owners of old communist enterprises and therefore continued to loan them money. At great

[29] John Gould, 'Winners, Losers and the Institutional Effects of Privatization in the Czech and Slovak Republics', *EUI Working Papers*, RSC 99/11.

[30] For an overview, Ivka Kalus-Bystricky and Pedro Pick, 'The Reform Process in Czechoslovakia and the Czech Republic: A Progress Report and the Tale of One Company', in H. Shaughnessy (ed.), *Privatisation and Economic Development in Eastern Europe and the CIS* (London: John Wiley & Sons Ltd., 1994), 47–75; and Aureliusz Pedziwol, 'Kupónová privatizace: úspech, ale jaky?' *Střední Evropa*, 69: 4 (1997), 98–109.

expense to the taxpayer, the government in turn provided the banks with various forms of state aid to cover these bad loans. Of necessity, this choked the liquid capital available to new firms, and increased indebtedness to foreign creditors. New firms also had to face burdensome taxes which undermined the rise of a new middle class.

In addition to creating a good imitation of state socialism, voucher privatization led to massive corruption. Three mammoth deficiencies in the privatization process produced the conditions for a new financial operation dubbed 'tunneling': when the assets of investment funds, banks, and enterprises are transferred to other businesses owned by the same people who manage the 'tunnelled' entity. While these 'managers' enrich themselves, the legal owners —for example, the shareholders in an investment fund—are effectively robbed.

The first deficiency sprang from the desire to privatize as much and as rapidly as possible. This priority led to a disregard for the details of who got rich by what means, and an all-out assault on the rule of law. Some advisers close to Klaus advocated 'switching off the light': allowing initial property allocations to sort themselves out without a legal framework or state oversight. Secondly, loopholes in the legal code governing the capital market and the banking sector created the opportunity for managers to legally steal from owners.[31] As of 1998, there was still no law to effectively protect minority shareholders or members of cooperatives from tunnelling. Thirdly, even when confronted with persistent tunnelling, the government failed to use what instruments it had to staunch the flow of assets into foreign bank accounts. When attempted, state oversight in banking and the capital markets was hampered by a shortage of able and experienced staff.[32]

Millions of inexperienced shareholders could do nothing to protect their interests. Instead of building a society of shareholders, voucher privatization alienated the average citizen from an economic system increasingly seen as corrupt. A February 1998 poll found

[31] On tunnelling, 'Co nového prinesl česky kapitalismus světu', *Lidové Noviny* (7 Feb. 1998), 3. On corporate governance, Susan Senior Nello, 'The Economic Accession Criteria for EU Enlargement: Lessons from the Czech Experience', *EUI Working Paper*, 11 (Robert Schuman Centre, 1999).

[32] After the collapse of several Czech banks and the loss of hundreds of millions of dollars the government set up a special team to investigate bank fraud and other large-scale financial machinations in September 1996. Czech officials admitted that the country did not have enough domestic experts to understand and deal with the complexities of bank fraud.

that only 5 per cent of Czechs considered economic reform to have been 'rather successful', while 0 per cent believed it 'very successful'.[33] A central question is whether the architects and early observers of voucher privatization could have been ignorant of the consequences. Klaus himself was reportedly very surprised by the growing power of the investment funds, and by the financial crimes which they perpetrated. These crimes occurred in part because so many people, after forty years of communism, were accustomed to finding ways to steal. Did Czech officials not realize that this made state instruments to combat financial crime all the more necessary? Some say they did.[34] In any case, although by 1998 everyone was clamouring to criticize voucher privatization, not more than a handful of Western economists and investors familiar with the Czech market warned of its pitfalls before 1996.[35]

Economic misadventures

The Czech economy enjoyed the confidence of investors and of international financial institutions to 1996. It was only at the summit of the European Bank for Reconstruction and Development (EBRD) in April 1997 that the Czech Republic was heavily criticized by representatives of Western institutions.[36] The IMF, the World Bank, and the OECD had already been prodding the Czech Republic for some time about the slow pace of bank privatization. But Western criticism of economic reform, when it finally came, was a simple result of faltering macroeconomic indicators, just as Western praise had earlier reflected favourable ones. It is difficult, then, to speak of the influence of international factors on the character of Czech economic reform.

As evidence of financial crime mounted, the economy worsened, and corruption scandals loomed, the Klaus government began to

[33] Adam Drda, 'Transformační iluze', *Lidové Noviny* (5 Mar. 1998), 10; and 'Česká transformace: kde se staly chyby a kudy ven?' *Lidové Noviny* (21 Feb. 1998), *Orientace*, 1.

[34] For example, Tomáš Ježek, the self-appointed father of voucher privatization and the minister in charge of the National Property Fund in 1992, declared that he battled for the early creation of a Securities and Exchange Commission. 'Zlamání kuponové privatizace se ekonomové vůbec nediví', *Lidové Noviny* (7 May 1998), 17.

[35] On privatization, Pedro Pick, Patria Finance Tomáš Ješek, interview in Prague, June 1998.

[36] Piotr Maszczyk, 'Czeska lekcja', *Gazeta Wyborcza* (30 Jan. 1998), 16–17.

totter in the spring of 1997.[37] Growth fell to 1 per cent due to
weak export performance, a consequence of insufficient enterprise
restructuring and an overvalued currency. Weak tax revenue forced
the government to cut expenditures. Meanwhile, the trade deficit
increased due to strong household consumption fuelled by high wage
growth (exceeding gains in productivity). Lower exports combined
with high consumer spending on imports had resulted in a steady
increase of trade and current account deficits from 1995 to 1997.

To counter the rising trade deficit, the Czech government introduced an import deposit scheme in April. This was widely interpreted as a show of force by an embattled government, and not as
a serious economic instrument. The scheme required importers
to deposit in a Czech bank, at 0 per cent interest for 180 days, an
amount equal to 20 per cent of the value of the goods they wished
to import. The European Commission criticized the measure and
called for its rapid withdrawal. It violated the Europe Agreement
according to which 'exceptional' protectionist measures must be
targeted at a particular, distressed sector, not at the lion's share
of all imports. Moreover, the Europe Agreement called for consultation with the Association Council before the realization of any trade-
restrictive measures; the Czech government had implemented
the scheme unilaterally. An arbitration was scheduled within the
Association Council for September 1997.[38]

Pressure from the European Commission was reinforced by
criticism from EU member states, the IMF, and the World Trade
Organization (WTO). The Czech government suspended the import
deposit scheme in August 1997, citing a (questionable) reduction
in the trade deficit, not the censure of the EU. However, the scheme
was very likely withdrawn as a direct result of EU pressure, to which
even the Klaus government had to be increasingly sensitive as
negotiations drew nearer.[39] The scheme was particularly ill-timed,
as the Commission completed its Opinion on each candidate in the
spring of 1997: the Czech Opinion is, therefore, replete with references to this (in fact minor) instance of misbehaviour.

[37] On the political corruption and financial malfeasance that brought down Klaus,
Mitchell Orenstein, 'Václav Klaus: Revolutionary and Parliamentarian', *East European Constitutional Review*, 7: 1 (Winter 1998), 46–55.

[38] The Association Council, which oversees the Europe Agreement, is composed
of officials from the EU Council of Ministers, the European Commission, and the
Czech government. Carlo González, 'The Czech Republic's application for membership
in the EU', Report to the European Parliament, *Euro-East* 61 (Dec. 1997), xv–xvii.

[39] For this argument, Guido Dolara, 'The Impact of Prospective Membership
of the European Union on Czech Domestic Policy', thesis submitted for the degree
of M.Phil. (University of Oxford, Trinity Term 1998).

A New Era of EU Conditionality: The Tošovský and Zeman Governments, 1998–1999

The Klaus government was deposed in November 1997 by the ODS's coalition partners and a faction within the ODS itself. It emerged that money had flowed into the ODS and also the ODA party coffers in exchange for favours related to privatization and banking. As the Klaus government fell and stage three began, EU scrutiny of the Czech reform effort intensified in light of the upcoming negotiations. The Klaus strategy of projecting a positive image westward no longer sufficed.

In July 1997, the Commission published its 'Opinion' on the fitness of the Czech Republic for EU accession. The Opinion noted that many economic reforms had been neglected or mishandled, in particular reform of the banking sector, regulation of the capital markets, and enterprise restructuring. Without further reform, the Czech Republic could not be competitive in the internal market, nor could it be in compliance with internal market rules. The Opinion also highlighted the need to reform agriculture, improve the environment, and reinforce state borders.

The Opinion criticized the Czech Republic most emphatically for its failure to reform the public administration. It cited the lack of any coherent plan for public administration modernization as 'the single greatest cause for concern' regarding the administrative capacity to apply the *acquis communautaire* and qualified existing measures as 'thoroughly inadequate'. The judiciary and the civil service were judged in greatest disrepair. The Opinion predicted that 'a wide ranging reform process will need to be instigated and sustained if the Czech Republic is to establish a civil service of the overall quality, level of training, motivation and flexibility required on the country's path to further economic and social development, and membership in the EU.'[40] Preconditions for reform included an independent civil service statute and an increase in the salaries of civil servants. The judicial system was found to be remarkably slow and incompetent, exacerbating the Czech Republic's serious problems with financial crime and enterprise restructuring. A later report of EU judicial experts, even more

[40] 'Commission Opinion', B.4. Administrative Capacity to Apply the Acquis. For proposed reforms, 'Analyza veřejné správy České republiky' and 'Návrh strategie reformy veřejné správy České republiky', Národní vzdělávací fond (Aug. and Oct. 1998).

damning than the Opinion, found that the judiciary lacked independence from government control.[41]

Following on the Opinion, the Commission created the Accession Partnership in March 1998 which set out what the Commission believed should be the priorities of Czech reform. PHARE assistance became conditional on addressing these priorities, which included areas outside the 31 chapters of the *acquis*, such as the protection of ethnic minorities. After the Opinion brought the problems of the Czech judiciary to the fore, for example, they began to be addressed in 1998 thanks to financial assistance from the PHARE programme.[42] The twinning of institutions and administrations in the Czech Republic with relevant bodies in the EU member states provided an additional conduit for EU influence.

The Tosovsky interim government

In December 1997, Czech National Bank Governor Josef Tošovský formed a centre-right 'technocratic' government which included independents as well as members of the ODA, the KDU-CSL and the anti-Klaus wing of the ODS. This government secured the support of the Social Democrats by agreeing to early elections in June 1998. Many politicians left the ODS, which soon became a mere backdrop for its charismatic leader, Václav Klaus. A new right-wing party, the Freedom Union (US), was formed in January 1998 and collected departing ODS members and leaders of the disintegrating ODA. The Freedom Union rebuked the Klaus government for tolerating a market without rules, and called for a revival of civil society and the creation of reliable state institutions.

The Tošovský government gained legitimacy and coherence by presenting itself as a responsible political force whose policies would assist Czech integration into NATO and the EU and repair the damage of instability. Its energies were visibly oriented toward fulfilling the requirements of EU membership even in areas, such as bank privatization, where it lacked the time or the political mandate to carry them out.[43] Unlike the Klaus governments, it used the requirements as an argument for new legislation. Public opinion supported the drive towards EU membership. In January

---

[41] 'Commission Opinion', B.3.7 Judicial Cooperation.

[42] 'Rule of Law and Judicial Reform', Remarks by Otakar Motejl, President of the Supreme Court of the Czech Republic, at the conference 'Making the Czech Republic Ready for the EU Accession' (Prague, 20 Mar. 1998).

[43] For example, it prepared the extensive government paper 'Economic Strategy of Joining the European Union: Key Issues and Options for Policy-making' (June 1998).

1998, 61 per cent of Czechs polled favoured entry (as compared to 58 per cent in September 1997 and 42 per cent in March 1996).[44]

With an eye toward the West, the Tošovský government executed difficult reforms for which the Klaus government had lacked the courage, such as a steep increase in rent and energy prices. It also held to the austerity package adopted by the Klaus government in the spring of 1997, thus improving the trade balance and re-establishing macroeconomic stability. As recommended by the Association Partnership, the Tošovský government improved the regulation of the capital markets and adopted policies to attract Western investment.

Its record was not perfect. The Tošovský government also approved, in January 1998, a quota on the import of apples from the EU which violated the Europe Agreement and was implemented without consultation with the Commission. The stated aim was to allow domestic producers to sell last year's harvest on the domestic market and use the profits to modernize their equipment. The quotas were pushed by KDU-CSL chairman and Minister of Agriculture Josef Lux, and the more likely aim was to increase his party's popularity before the upcoming elections. Brussels retaliated swiftly with high tariffs on certain Czech meats and fruit juices. A defensive Czech government claimed it was protecting Czech interests, but withdrew the quota in May 1998 after threats of further trade restrictions from Brussels. The Commission signalled that negotiations would yield better results than violations: once the quotas were withdrawn, it promised Czech fruit growers PHARE money for modernization.

The 'screening' process, during which the Commission examined Czech legislation and practice in light of the thirty-one chapters of the *acquis communautaire*, officially launched negotiations in April 1998. Where the Czech Republic fell short during screening, Czech negotiators, led by Deputy Foreign Minister Pavel Telička, promised adoption of the acquis by a certain date. For all of their skill, Czech negotiators could not deliver on these promises: only the politicians could deliver, and whether they did provides a measure of how much the goal of joining the EU shaped the work of government and parliament. To avoid delays in the negotiations, the timetable of the next government for passing and implementing critical legislation had to be a very busy one.[45]

[44] Only 15% declared themselves against, while 24% were undecided. 'Občané podporují vstup ČR do EU', *Lidové Noviny* (20 Feb. 1998), 2.

[45] Michael Leigh, Chief Negotiator for the Czech Republic, European Commission, interview in Brussels (July 1998).

The Social Democrats take power

The elections of June 1998 produced a minority Social Democratic government led by Prime Minister Miloš Zeman.[46] The government was formed after the Social Democratic Party (CSSD) signed an 'opposition agreement' with its greatest ideological rival, Klaus's ODS. The ODS had done surprisingly well in the elections by forecasting doom if the left took power, yet it preferred to *give* power to the CSSD in order to undermine the two centrist parties. The KDU-CSL and the Freedom Union were, after all, peopled by politicians who had brought down Klaus in November 1997. For its part, the Freedom Union refused the CSSD's generous offer of a three-party coalition government with the KDU-CSL so as not to betray its right-wing voters, though once again personal antipathies played their part. What, then, was Zeman to do but sign the opposition agreement?

The opposition agreement allowed the two largest parties to divide up the spoils of power, never mind their declared ideological antagonisms. In exchange for important positions in the state administration, the ODS promised not to topple the CSSD government—but it did not promise to support its legislation. With the help of the CSSD, the ODS schemed to replace the electoral system of proportional representation with first-past-the-post in order to push the smaller parties out of parliament.[47]

The ODS distinguished itself in 1998 and 1999 as the only moderate party of the left or the right in post-communist Europe which opposed EU membership. This can be attributed to a mix of populism, ideology, and defensiveness. In the 1998 campaign and after, Klaus employed a confusing rhetoric of Euroscepticism which misrepresented the real costs and benefits of EU entry.[48] ODS leaders called Brussels a 'bureaucratic mastodon' on a par with CMEA, and proposed that the Czech Republic limit itself to

[46] The results for the five parties elected to the Czech parliament in June 1998 are as follows: the Social Democrats (CSSD) 32.3%, the Civic Democratic Party (ODS) 27.7%, the Communists (KSCM) 11%, the Christian Democrats (KDU-CSL) 9%, and the Freedom Union (US) 8.6%. The extreme right-wing Republicans (SPR-RSC) garnered 3.9% of the vote and the neo-communist pensioners (DZJ) 3.1%, thus failing to clear the 5% threshold.

[47] In 1999, Ramiro Cibrian, the Head of the Delegation of the European Commission in Prague, expressed the EU's misgivings about the possible change in electoral law and about the lack of political will for more salutary projects. 'Velvyslanec EU: Čeští politici delají pro vstup do unie málo', *Lidové Noviny* (4 June 1999), 2.

[48] For this argument, Milada Anna Vachudová, 'Matoucí retorika českého euroskpeticismu', *Lidové Noviny* (19 Oct. 1999), 11.

a custom-union with the EU on the model of Turkey. Ironically, the political ideology that the ODS claimed to espouse would be well-served by EU requirements. Far from forcing socialism on the Czech Republic, as Klaus claimed, they would compel the CSSD government to leave behind such ongoing socialist practices from the Klaus era as bailing out state banks and inefficient enterprises at the expense of the taxpayer.

Meanwhile, the economy had a rough two years, shrinking by 2.2 per cent in 1998 and roughly 0.3 per cent in 1999. Unemployment, a sign of restructuring, did well to triple to 9 per cent. The Zeman government inherited social and economic problems which were a challenge to tackle.[49] It was applauded for moving on soft-lending by selling off two banks and preparing two others for privatization. The government had to assume the banks' 'bad debts' before privatization, thus the state regained ownership of struggling, tunnelled-out Czech enterprises. (What next, a new round of privatization?) Reform of the country's wholly ineffectual bankruptcy laws also began, but only very gingerly. For months a four-way discussion between CSSD dinosaurs, CSSD progressives, the Commission, and the Czech National Bank raged on over the rules of a government scheme to revive 'key' enterprises with another injection from the state budget.[50] The recession did come to an end, with the World Bank predicting mild growth at 1.7 per cent in 2000 and 2.5 per cent in 2001.[51]

The Social Democrats hailed accession to the EU, and made meeting the requirements a cornerstone of their electoral programme. With negotiations already underway, the Czech Republic risked falling out of the first wave if reform was further delayed. Once in power, however, the CSSD faltered in preparing relevant legislation due to incompetence, disunity, and a lack of political will.[52] The

[49] For the CSSD's comprehensive and astute report on the state of the country, 'Zpráva vlády o stavu ceské spolecnosti', *Hospodářské noviny* (5 Mar. 1999).

[50] For the thoughtful views of the CSSD progressives, see the official government paper 'Economic Strategy of Joining the European Union: Growth-Competitiveness-Employment-Solidarity', written under the direction of Pavel Mertlík and Jan Mládek. The paper prioritizes restarting growth, restructuring enterprises, privatizing banks, and reforming the public administration.

[51] 'Czech Republic: Toward EU Accession', *World Bank Country Study* (Sept. 1999); and 'Belly up? A Survey of the Czech Republic', *Business Central Europe* (Dec. 1999/Jan. 2000), 45–56.

[52] The CSSD's proposal to pass accession-related legislation by decree was rejected by parliament in May 1999. On EU preparations, Václav Bartuška, 'S návratem do Evropy jsou potíže', *Mladá Fronta Dnes* (26 July 1999), 1; and Katarina Šafaríková, 'EU zatim s Čechy počita, otázkou je, jak dlouho', *Lidové Noviny* (3 Sept. 1999), 2.

upshot was the negative 'Regular Report' of October 1999 which noted that little progress had been made and ranked the Czech Republic well behind Hungary, Estonia, and Poland. The Report criticized the slow pace of legislative alignment and economic reform across the board. Bank privatization and an overhaul of the judiciary were among the bright spots. Meanwhile, on many issues, Zeman and Klaus were sounding more and more alike. There was a risk that the CSSD would assume the anti-EU rhetoric of the ODS: Mimicking its partner's disapprobation of the EU could provide an easy way to avoid the work and the compromise necessary to prepare for accession.

The opposition agreement led to rising political dissatisfaction. Preferences for the Freedom Union rose sharply, but so did those of the Czech Republic's entirely unrepentant Communist Party of Bohemia and Moravia (KSCM).[53] Intellectuals and centrist politicians expressed concern at the political stagnation and the slow preparations for EU membership. These became the central themes of the civic initiative 'Impuls 99', founded in August 1999. On the tenth anniversary of the Velvet Revolution, former student leaders called on existing party chairmen to end their choke hold on Czech politics; their petition 'Thank you, now go' resonated strongly with the electorate.

The divisive politics of 1997, 1998, and 1999 made productive cooperation difficult to imagine.[54] By the beginning of 2000, however, the CSSD was working hard to prepare necessary legislation (as part of a celebrated 'legislative tornado') while a subdued ODS was helping to get the legislation through parliament. Two messages seemed to be getting through: the Czech Republic would be better off if it joined the EU in the first wave and, barring an acceleration of reform, it would likely be excluded from it.[55] As far as the EU was concerned, how the Czech Republic measured up in the Regular Reports of 2000 and 2001 would decide the matter.

[53] For a comparison with its reformed neighbours, Mitchell Orenstein, 'A Genealogy of Communist Successor Parties in East-Central Europe', *East European Politics and Society*, 12: 3 (Fall 1998), 472–99.

[54] On Czech political culture and parties, Jiří Pehe, 'Českým politickym stranám chybí vize', *Lidové Noviny* (31 Mar. 1998), 8; 'Krize a záludnosti virtuální politiky', *Lidové Noviny* (10 Apr. 1998), 10; and 'Nesnesitelná lehkost české politiky', *Mladá Fronta Dnes* (18 Oct. 1999), 6.

[55] On EU costs and benefits, Susan Senior Nello and Karen Smith, *The European Union and Central and Eastern Europe: The Implications of Enlargement in Stages* (Aldershot: Ashgate, 1998); and Petr Kolář, 'Dopady evropské integrace na Českou republiku', Study prepared for a meeting of the Lípa group, Brno (Apr. 1999).

The Road to NATO Membership

Czech foreign policy guided by Foreign Minister Josef Zieleniec from 1992 to 1997 treated NATO membership as indispensable to the security of the Czech Republic and worked consistently to obtain it. NATO succeeded in shaping the reform of the Czech military and the Czech Republic's entire (shallow) conception of its own security. Czech political parties, however, failed to treat membership in NATO as a matter of state interest: legislation required for accession became embroiled in various domestic political fights, and was not accorded the political weight that it deserved. This was a symptom of a broader disregard for reformulating the security concept of the state, stemming in part from the absence of perceived threats. By nature, NATO required much less 'pre-emptive' integration than the EU and for this reason posed less of a problem for the Czech political class and the Czech state. Even so, Czech politicians showed that they would succumb to the requirements of NATO membership only at the eleventh hour.

The drive for NATO membership enjoyed the support of only a slim majority of Czechs.[56] In the Klaus-dominated period of Czech politics, few politicians exerted themselves to explain to the public the benefits and responsibilities of NATO membership, or to underscore that NATO could prevent the security failures which had twice in this century spelled the end of Czechoslovak democracy. Klaus viewed NATO membership as a matter of prestige, and gave little thought to the Czech Republic's security environment or to its future role in NATO.[57] In private, he reportedly opposed NATO membership and favoured deep cuts in the defence budget. In public, he questioned NATO policies, for example in Bosnia, and exhibited his trademark overconfidence in the Czech Republic's qualifications for membership. Taking a broader view, Havel explained that the Czech Republic belonged to West European civilization and should take part in its defence.

The absence of a pro-NATO campaign created political space for the Communists and the extreme-right Republicans to paint NATO as the tool of (respectively) American and German imperialists.

---

[56] Opinion polls in 1996 and 1997 showed that as few as one-third of Czechs supported NATO membership, while one-third were against and one-third did not know. By early 1998, those in favour had increased to 54%, while 24% were against and 22% did not know. *Lidové Noviny* (12 Feb. 1998), 2.

[57] Jiří Šedivý, Director of the Institute of International Relations, interview in Prague, June 1998.

Only strong pressure from the Czech Republic's future allies in late 1997 finally compelled the government to concentrate on bolstering popular support for NATO membership.[58] In this sense, an outside actor forced the government into a dialogue with its own people on an issue of unusual importance. Western pressure included direct reprimands from American secretary of state Madeleine Albright, who no doubt wondered why she was battling American critics of enlargement so fiercely on behalf of the torpid Czechs.

Albright laid down three requirements for prospective members: the adoption of a new strategic concept, the improvement of military interoperability, and the acceptance of a 'new responsibility' for European security. The Czech 'National Strategy Concept', in the making for five years, was only finished in 1998.[59] As for interoperability, it became clear in 1997 that the greatest hurdle for the Czech military would be knowledge of English and that NATO grants for language training had been squandered. The Czechs struggled to find English-speaking military officers and civilians to serve in various functions at NATO. Prospective members were also to be judged by their participation in joint projects and the level of their defence spending (to reach 2 per cent of GDP). The Czechs were widely praised for the conduct of their troops serving in IFOR/SFOR, and for participating actively in Partnership for Peace (PfP). However, unlike most PfP members, the Czechs did not create a joint unit with another PfP state, despite an abiding interest on the part of the Poles.[60] Defence spending did increase, rising to 1.7 per cent of GDP in 1997.

Along with Poland and Hungary, the Czech Republic was invited to begin negotiations on joining NATO in July 1997. By the time the Tosovsky government took office in December 1997, it was evident that Czech membership depended on the US Senate, which would be influenced only indirectly by the progress of reforms in the Czech military. The Tosovsky government nevertheless made the requirements of NATO membership a priority, and managed to push the treaty of accession through the Czech parliament. This,

[58] Officials emphasized that the Czech Republic will receive more from the NATO budget than it will contribute (an estimated $18.3 million/year), and that no nuclear weapons or foreign troops will be stationed on Czech soil.

[59] Martin Kontra and Jaroslav Špurný, 'Třetí pokus se jmenuje NATO: Ospalost hlavní prekázkou na ceste k diplomatickému úspechu století', *Respekt*, 9: 9 (9 Mar. 1998), 9–11.

[60] Zdeněk Brousil, 'Príprava na vstup do Aliance', *Vojenské Rozhledy*, 6: 4 (1997), 12–19.

however, proved quite a challenge. Without Poland and Hungary in the mix, Czech indifference to NATO might well have cooled NATO's interest in expansion.

The Social Democratic Party (CSSD) never took a strong stand in favour of NATO; instead of convincing its 'conservative' left-wing electorate of NATO's advantages, it preferred a vague, shifting approach to membership. This amounted to supporting NATO membership as a matter of foreign policy, but sporadically catering to anti-NATO voters on the domestic political scene. Although only one-half of the Social Democrat electorate supported Czech membership, Zeman had made no attempt over the previous five years to persuade the other half. Playing to Czech parochial sentiments in view of the upcoming elections, the Social Democrats insisted on a referendum and voted in early 1998 to defer the parliament's ratification of NATO accession.[61] The Social Democrats also voted to delay a law on the protection of sensitive information. They feared that pro-NATO votes in parliament before the June 1998 elections would cause their anti-NATO electorate to vote for Republicans or Communists.[62] In the end, however, they backed down from their referendum demands, and the US Senate and the Czech parliament ratified the NATO accession treaty before the elections.

The Kosovo crisis

When NATO launched airstrikes against the Federal Republic of Yugoslavia in the spring of 1999, the government, political parties, and public of the Czech Republic emanated substantially less support for the alliance than those of Poland or Hungary. The lack of political consensus on NATO was vividly displayed, and the CSSD again seemed intent on following public opinion rather than shaping it. Czech politicians were unable to formulate the interests of the Czech state with respect to the Yugoslav conflict, or the responsibilities of the Czech government with regard to its new allies.[63] A hostile political reaction was not warranted by any immediate threats

---

[61] A Czech referendum on NATO virtually precluded ratification before the induction ceremonies planned for March 1999, as the Czech Constitution would have had to first be amended to include provisions for a referendum.

[62] Until it was passed, Czech representatives at NATO (unlike their Polish and Hungarian counterparts) waited in the hallway during negotiations pertaining to classified information.

[63] Ivan Gabal, 'Český politici se k utoku NATO nehlásí', *Lidové Noviny* (26 Mar. 1999), 1.

to the security of the Czech Republic, such as stray missiles or waves of refugees, nor by the expectation of high economic costs. The Zeman government did support the alliance in deeds, if not in words. It met all of its formal obligations including the provision of air-space, airfields, roads, and rail facilities for the transit of NATO military forces. Foreign Minister Jan Kavan consistently presented a pro-NATO foreign policy on behalf of the government (although the Ministry of Foreign Affairs co-authored a peace initiative with its Greek counterpart which was met with displeasure in other NATO capitals).

But the Kosovo crisis revealed deep divisions within the Social Democratic Party itself, and belied previous claims that the party unambiguously supports Czech membership in NATO. To start things off, Prime Minister Zeman lied to the Czech public, denying that the government had assented to the airstrikes which he charac-terized as the work of primitive troglodytes. Some weeks later, Vice-Prime Minister Egon Lánsky declared that Milosevic's ethnic cleansing of Kosovo was morally justified because of the NATO bombing.[64] A few CSSD deputies, claiming traditionally strong ties between Serbs and Czechs, set sail to Belgrade to express their sup-port for Milošević. While the CSSD stood divided and irresolute, the ODS stood united—in its condemnation of NATO. For the whole of the 1990s, Klaus had taken an unusually amicable stand toward the Yugoslav regime of Slobodan Milošević.[65] In March 1999 he defended Milošević, for example by proclaiming that the air-strikes had caused the ethnic cleansing campaign in Kosovo.[66]

The Czech public could only be confused and unconvinced by incon-sistent and telescopic political pronouncements on the Yugoslav crisis. Support for the strikes stood at 34 per cent (with 48 per cent against) in April, while support for the Czech Republic's accession to NATO had declined to 49 per cent by early March. Havel warned that 'Czech politicians who publicly condemn NATO's military intervention are responsible for the creation and the support of isolationist and, from the long-term perspective, very dangerous moods in society.'[67] The Czech media, the Freedom Union and

---

[64] Martin Schmarcz, 'Lánský: vina NATO', *Lidové Noviny* (6 Apr. 1999), 10.

[65] Vilaim Buchert, 'Klaus selhává v zahraniční politice dlouho', *Mladá Fronta Dnes* (30 Mar. 1999), 12.

[66] Ondřej Drábek, 'Za odsun Albáncu muze NATO', *Lidové Noviny* (8 Apr. 1999), 1; and Václav Klaus, 'Kosovo: nevytvařejme nové falešné myty', *Lidové Noviny* (30 Mar. 1999), 11.

[67] 'Názory na úder dále štepí politickou scénu', *Mladá Fronta Dnes* (27 Mar. 1999), 2.

the Christian Democrats also strongly criticized the CSSD and the ODS, observing that the Czech Republic was proving to be an unreliable new ally. Other NATO members remarked upon the disunity in Prague and the scant solidarity proffered by their new ally. But since the Czech Republic was far removed from the conflict, its disposition was largely irrelevant for the prosecution of the war.

Racism and the Roma

Much of the criticism of the Czech Republic by international institutions and Western governments has been directed at the treatment of the Roma minority. The tragedies of history and the split of Czechoslovakia left the Czech Republic with fewer national problems than most of its post-communist neighbours. No substantial populations of ethnic Czechs live beyond the borders, and the Czechs share their state with only one significant minority, the Roma. But the Roma—who number up to 300,000—have suffered widespread discrimination and occasional violence.

Anti-Roma and anti-German sentiments have been the province of the extreme right-wing Republican Party of Miroslav Sládek. The party's platform called for the assimilation of ethnic minorities and resistance to an alleged German economic takeover.[68] The Germans, who numbered some 3 million before they were expelled after the Second World War, still evoke hatred and fear at the prospect of their return. Support for the Republican Party rose from 6 per cent in the 1992 elections to 8 per cent in the 1996 elections. While Czech political life was sullied by Sládek's public ranting and parliament was constantly disrupted by his party's obstructionist behaviour, the Republicans played a negligible direct role in national politics. The Republicans received only 3.9 per cent of the vote in the June 1998 elections and failed to enter parliament.

The Czech state has generally chosen not to prosecute the Republicans, for example, for publishing the magazine *Republika* which promotes anti-Semitism, racial intolerance, and xenophobia. At a demonstration against the Czech-German declaration in January 1997, Sládek observed that 'we can only regret that during the war

---

[68] Sladek's was the only party whose platform called for the return of Transcarpathian Ruthenia, annexed by the Soviet Union in 1945, though in December 1991, KDU-CSL leader Josef Lux briefly called for its return as well. Petr Janyska, 'Začátek nové éry', *Respekt*, 2: 51 (23 Dec. 1991), 2.

we killed so few Germans'. Sládek was then charged with inciting racial hatred, but acquitted in January 1998. The courts failed to convict Republicans of inciting racial hatred on many other occasions as well.[69] For example, on 25 July 1996, Sládek stated in parliament that 'the Gypsies should be penally responsible from birth because that is practically their biggest crime'. In June 1998 the Republicans called for the end of 'the rampage of black racists' as part of a vitriolic anti-Roma election campaign. Although the Republicans are no longer represented in parliament, echoes of their sentiments are shared by enough Czechs to make the treatment of Roma the greatest challenge for the consolidation of Czech democracy.

The social, economic, and educational position of the Roma in Czech society has declined steadily since 1990. In some areas, the unemployment rate for Roma is over 80 per cent. While in 1970 only 20 per cent of the children in 'special schools' were Roma, the figure in 1997 was 60 per cent. As their daily lives have worsened, Roma have found themselves confronting ever more racism. While Sládek's party and skinheads have been its most visible and brutal face, racism has become widespread among ordinary citizens and also among 'moderate' politicians of the left and right, especially at the local level. Up to 90 per cent of Czech respondents have said that they would not want to have a Roma as a neighbour. For their part, the government, the police, and the courts have failed to make a stand against the rise of racially motivated crime.

To the extent that discrimination and violent attacks have led significant numbers of Czech Roma to flee their country, it is clear that this community has been far from feeling itself to be a part of the democratic state. That the isolation of Roma was partly self-imposed is beyond question: but the issue at hand is whether the Czech Republic's largest national minority has formed a part of the political community, and whether international actors have extended any influence on its behalf. It is worth recalling that Roma, unlike other national minorities, have no home state to defend their interests. When Czech authorities do not protect them, they can attempt a move west, or an appeal to international institutions.

---

[69] Tomáš Nemeček, 'Proč zavřeli Sládka', *Respekt*, 9: 4 (19–25 Jan. 1998), 2; and Jan Kubita and Vladimír Dubsky, 'Státní orgány přistupují ke stíhání SPR-RSC velmi kiknavě', *Lidové Noviny* (5 June 1998), 3.

Citizenship

In 1993 and 1994, the Klaus government was indifferent to the plight of the Roma, and resisted Western pressure for improvement.[70] It initiated few programmes to promote interethnic understanding, and was unwilling to collaborate with non-governmental organizations that seek to help the Roma community. Calling it a redundancy, Klaus fiercely resisted international pressure to create an ombudsman (such as the Parliamentary Commissioner for National and Ethnic Minority Rights in Hungary). The need for such a figure in the Czech government was evident as ministries were unable to cooperate, and episodic outcries against racism died down leaving no one in charge of a comprehensive policy. These problems were manifest as the Czech Citizenship Law came into effect.

By design, the Citizenship Law of January 1993 denied citizenship to as many as 100,000 'Czechoslovak' Roma.[71] The law required 'Slovak' applicants to prove that they had a clean criminal record over the previous five years and were resident in the Czech Republic for two years. Many Roma resident in the Czech Republic at the time of the split were consequently left without citizenship. Some Roma were deported, while others were given train tickets to Slovakia by local authorities and pressured to leave. Most stayed in the Czech Republic but found the bureaucratic obstacles to obtaining citizenship insurmountable.[72] Consequently, several international institutions began helping Roma to obtain Czech citizenship.

The citizenship law was criticized by international organizations and Western governments, including the United Nations High Commission on Refugees, the OSCE, the US State Department, the US Congress, the International Helsinki Foundation, Amnesty International, Human Rights Watch, and the Council of Europe. Only an April 1996 amendment brought some improvement, allowing the Ministry of Interior to waive the five-year clean criminal

---

[70] Despite being a signatory of international conventions on safeguarding the memory of victims of fascism, the Klaus government ignored international pressure to remove a pig farm from the site of a concentration camp where hundreds of Roma were murdered. The Tošovský government made its removal a priority.

[71] Jiřina Šiklová and Marta Miklusáková, 'Denying Citizenship to the Czech Roma', *East European Constitutional Review*, 7: 2 (Spring 1998), 58–63; and 'Human Rights and Democratization in the Czech Republic', Commission on Security and Cooperation in Europe (Sept. 1994), 18–27.

[72] 'Czech Republic Human Rights Practices, 1995', US Department of State (Mar. 1996).

record requirement on a case-by-case basis. This amendment was a direct result of international pressure and followed on the recommendation of the Council of Europe. The Czech government held out for three years because it risked no meaningful sanctions. During the 1992–6 period, the EU did not yet have any tools with which to pressure the Czechs.[73] NATO and the 1995 Stability Pact were chiefly concerned with relations among East European states which the Roma, having no protector state, did not aggravate.

Violence

On the related but distinct problem of the general treatment of the Roma minority, we observe the same pattern: a disturbing problem, government stonewalling between 1992 and 1997, and effective Western pressure. Compared to other European states, the officially reported incidence of violent, racially motivated attacks on Roma and dark-skinned foreigners has not been high. From 1990 to 1997, 1,210 racially motivated attacks were recorded in the Czech lands by the Documentation Center for Human Rights. (In a country where the police have generally been thought indifferent or sympathetic to such attacks, it is likely that many more have gone unreported.) Of 1,210 attacks, only one-third were officially qualified as racially motivated; and of the nineteen incidents in which people were killed, only two were qualified as racially motivated.[74] Only about 10 per cent of attackers ended up in court, and more then 95 per cent of those convicted received suspended sentences.[75]

Police in the Czech Republic have been accused by human rights organizations and Roma leaders of doing little to investigate even violent crimes against the Roma, and judges have usually refused to rule a crime to have been racially motivated even when it was plainly so.[76] Light sentences, sometimes appallingly so, send the message that racially motivated violence is not considered a serious

---

[73] Technically it could have suspended the Europe Agreement, which contained a clause on the protection of minority rights. Had the law not been amended by 1997, it could have invoked the Copenhagen requirements to keep the Czech Republic out of the first wave.

[74] Miroslav Korecky and Renata Kalenská, 'Boj s rasismem skončil u slibů', *Lidové Noviny*, 28 (Jan. 1998), 5.

[75] Vladimír Dusánek, 'Rasové násilí,' *Mladá Fronta Dnes* (10 Feb. 1998), 4.

[76] Only five people were convicted in the Czech lands for racially motivated crimes in 1991; this number had risen to 146 in 1997. *Mladá Fronta Dnes* (10 Feb. 1998), 4.

crime.[77] For example, the court in Písek refused to rule the brutal murder of the Rom Tibor Danihel by skinheads as racially motivated: the skinheads clearly understood that the court was sympathetic to their racist views, and laughed openly at Roma witnesses during the trial.[78] Meanwhile, the Czech Commercial Inspectorate, to which complaints about discrimination against the Roma in public services, shops, and restaurants are to be submitted, has usually decided in favour of the perpetrators. Indeed, in 1997 only one restaurant owner had *ever* been prosecuted by the Inspectorate for refusing to serve Roma customers.

The problem of racist violence was largely ignored by the Czech government until 1995. At that time, a set of policies designed to counter racism was designed and central government politicians became more engaged in problems affecting the Romany community. In October 1996, parliament unanimously passed a resolution denouncing racism and xenophobia in the Czech Republic. One hundred and twenty new positions were created in the police force for specialists in the fight against racism and extremism. As events of 1997 were to show, however, these policies and pronouncements did not reverse the growing tide of racism against the Roma.

Exodus

After an August 1997 television documentary portrayed Canada as a wealthy country free of racism, several hundred Roma families left for Canada. Some local authorities reacted by encouraging Roma to leave the country, and one ODS deputy mayor famously offered them money to buy plane tickets on the condition that they abandon their tenancy rights. Between January and August 1997, Canada had granted refugee status to 22 Roma from the Czech Republic. Over 1,200 applied before Canada reinstated visa requirements for Czech citizens in September 1997.[79] Another wave of Roma left for the United Kingdom in October 1997. In January 1998, about 800 Roma were seeking political asylum in the United Kingdom or

---

[77] 'Roma and Sinti, Czech Republic: Report to the OSCE Implementation Meeting on Human Dimension Issues' (Warsaw, 1997), International Helsinki Federation for Human Rights; and 'Czech Republic Human Rights Practices, 1998', US Department of State (Feb. 1999).

[78] Václav Trojan, 'Rasismus má u nás hluboké kořeny', *Lidové Noviny* (19 Feb. 1998), 10.

[79] 'Czech Republic Human Rights Practices, 1997', US Department of State (Jan. 1998).

France.[80] About ten Roma families had been granted asylum since 1990 in the United Kingdom. However, between October 1997 and January 1998, the British authorities had returned 563 Czech and Slovak Roma to their countries. Still, after the brutal murder of a young Romany woman in the Czech Republic in February 1998, a Roma family which left in the October 1997 exodus was granted asylum by the British courts.[81] The murder reportedly moved Canadian courts to grant asylum to several Roma from the Czech Republic as well. Meanwhile, reports of state-tolerated racist violence in the Czech Republic caused concern in the US Senate in the run-up to the vote on NATO expansion.

In the face of this international embarrassment, many Czech politicians maintained that the Roma were economic migrants, not refugees fleeing from racism. The Klaus government did in its waning days emphasize its willingness to work to improve the situation of the Roma, and held talks with Roma leaders. In September 1997, it agreed to create a new commission for Romany affairs to advise the government but also rejected as too critical the assessments of a report written on the treatment of the Roma by one of its own ministers. The parliament ratified the Council of Europe's Framework Convention for the Protection of National Minorities in December 1997, but the Czech Republic has much work to do before the spirit of this convention will enter the government or society. To begin, the government will have to report to the Council of Europe what anti-discrimination measures have been taken by state organs: in 1997, state organs took no such measures.[82] Meanwhile, the Roma exodus and racist violence have occasioned only the beginning of a long overdue public discussion on racism in Czech society.

The Czech Republic's reputation was not helped by prominent reports in the Western press beginning in May 1998 that new ghettoes would be built in the Czech Republic: the ODS mayors of two Czech towns planned walls around 'noisy' apartment complexes inhabited by Roma. Despite vast amounts of international media attention and worldwide condemnation, the city council of Ustí nad Labem constructed its wall by the cover of night in October 1999. The Czech parliament, president, and political class helplessly

[80] 'V Evropě prý žádá azyl osm set Romů', *Lidové Noviny* (28 Jan. 1998), 5.

[81] 'Britský soud uznal, ze tři Romové byli v Čechách diskriminováni' and 'Po Kanade získali Romové z České republiky azyl rovněž ve Velké Británii', *Lidové Noviny* (28 Feb. 1998), 1–2.

[82] Martin Palouš, 'Základní cíle ceské zahraniční politiky a lidská práva', *Mezinárodní Politika*, 12: 1 (Jan. 1998), 9.

condemned it. Romano Prodi, European Commission President, declared 'Europe will never accept new walls separating European citizens from one another.'[83] For Czech Roma, the wall symbolized the discrimination which compelled them to emigrate to the West. In late November 1999, the Zeman government finally persuaded the stubborn local authorities to remove the wall, in exchange for state subsidies.

EU pressure

Before the exodus of Roma to the West, the Commission had already criticized the treatment of the Roma minority in its July 1997 'Opinion'. The Commission placed significant emphasis on the integration of Roma into Czech society as a condition for membership. It has been at something of a disadvantage in this policy area: since the EU member states have not harmonized their minority policies, the treatment of ethnic minorities is not among the thirty-one chapters of the *acquis*. Nevertheless, the Copenhagen criteria include the protection of ethnic minorities, and the EU can insist that the treatment of the Roma meet its expectations as a requirement for accession.

The Accession Partnership states that further work must be done to integrate the Roma into Czech society before accession, and PHARE money has been allocated for this purpose.[84] Among the priorities are the fight against racism in the police force and the judiciary, and the creation of a new education policy for Roma children. In response, the Tosovsky and Zeman governments have devoted considerable attention to these problems. For assessments of the Roma situation, the Commission has relied on the OSCE High Commissioner on National Minorities, the Council of Europe, and other expert institutions, whose importance have thereby been amplified.[85] The Roma have already proven that they can migrate

[83] Robert Anderson, 'Romany wall demolished', *Financial Times* (25 Nov. 1999), 3.

[84] 'Czech Republic: Accession Partnership', European Commission (Mar. 1998), 3. For EU leverage to take on its full potential force, Czech officials must be able to imagine that negotiations on all 31 chapters of the *acquis* are complete, but Czech accession to the EU is blocked by inadequate efforts to integrate the Roma into Czech society.

[85] European human rights groups advised the EU to require candidates to improve their treatment of the Roma minority. European Parliament Member Graham Watson asked the Commission in February 1998 to put particular pressure on the Czech government. 'Zahraniční odborníci kritizují vztah českých úřadu k Romům', *Lidové Noviny* (24 Feb. 1998), 3.

in large numbers, which will make their treatment a particularly sensitive issue for EU members. As the Czech Republic nears EU membership, humanitarian and self-interested advocacy of the Roma cause in Western Europe will increase.

Conclusions

The character of the influence of international factors on the consolidation of Czech democracy changed with time, as the Czech polity passed through the four stages set out in the introduction. International influence was most profound during the first stage (1989–92), but also most diffuse: the democratic and prosperous 'West'—a vague but hegemonic idea—provided the model and the goal of reform after the revolutions of 1989. In the Czech lands, as in Poland and Hungary, the Western model was so deeply internalized as to become a truly domestic factor. The liberal democratic choice of these polities after 1989 thus had little to do with the immediate influence of outside actors.[86]

The 'West', caught unawares by the fall of communism, offered spiritual support and modest economic assistance. However, the governments of Czechoslovakia, along with those of Poland and Hungary, sought to establish the West as the clear destination of their liberal democratic projects by making membership in the EU (and later NATO) an overarching goal of state policy, and the anticipated domestic requirements of membership the guidelines of reform. They were disappointed but resolute when the EU and NATO refused for years to commit to eastern enlargement. Once these institutions decided to enlarge, the conditionality of accession gave the West increasing influence over the details of reform.

In the second stage (1992–7), the Klaus governments' ability to pursue a westward orientation while rejecting policies recommended by the West necessarily limited the direct influence of Western actors. While the Civic Forum governments of 1990–2 engaged in a dialogue with the West about the course of domestic reform, the ODS-led governments wanted the transformation project to be 'homemade'. Klaus had his own strategy—a mix of Czech provincialism, free market ideology, and political pragmatism—for bringing the Czech Republic into the prosperous, democratic fold,

---

[86] Milada Anna Vachudová and Timothy Snyder, 'Are Transitions Transitory? Two Models of Political Change in East Central Europe Since 1989', *East European Politics and Societies*, 11: 1 (Winter 1997), 1–35.

and he secured a striking degree of domestic political freedom to carry it out.

During this second stage, Western influence on the independent Czech Republic was delimited by two factors. First, the Czech governments' liberal democratic project impressed Western observers, particularly in comparison to the neo-communist and nationalist projects undertaken by governing elites elsewhere in post-communist Europe. For years the Czech transformation was considered a great success, without most Westerners (or Czechs) looking too closely at the details. Klaus managed to convince the West (and the Czech public) that the Czech political and economic transition was all but complete.

Second, the institutions which stood to exercise the greatest leverage on the policy choices of Czech governments—NATO and especially the EU—only gradually developed the tools necessary to compel reform in those areas where the Czech project was eventually revealed to have fundamental flaws. Until 1997, international pressure only forced change in one clear case: the 1993 Citizenship Law. This of course speaks to the weakness of international influence and to the attitude of the Czech government, but also to the fact that, for all of its faults, the Czech Republic was not much of a miscreant in comparison to other post-communist states.

All of that, however, began to change in 1997. As the Commission studied Czech reform more closely in preparing its Opinion on the Czech application for EU membership, it found serious problems, some of which were reflected in the economic downturn and the corruption scandals of 1997. Meanwhile, the exodus of Czech Roma alerted the West (and some Czechs) that racism posed a grave problem. The illusion of Czech superiority was dispelled, and the Klaus government was toppled in November 1997. The end of the Klaus era coincided with the EU's direct engagement in the details of Czech reform. By identifying its shortcomings and offering the incentive of EU membership, the EU steered subsequent Czech governments toward resolving the deficiencies of the Czech reform process. The third stage of international influence on the Czech polity was brief: the six months of the interim Tosovsky government which held power until the early elections of June 1998. The Tosovsky government took the conditionality inherent in the EU accession process more seriously, and addressed mounting international criticism of economic reform, the state administration, and the treatment of the Roma minority.

The fourth stage of international influence on the consolidation of Czech democracy began when the Social Democratic Party formed a minority government in July 1998. The Zeman government was tasked with difficult economic reforms which drove up unemployment and prices. By repeating for years that radical reform was complete, Klaus ensured that this suffering seemed senseless to Czech society and undermined the effectiveness of EU membership as an argument for difficult reform. In 1998 and 1999, the disunity and ineptitude of Zeman's CSSD combined with the obstructionism and anti-EU populism of Klaus's ODS put in question the ability of the Czech Republic to tend to the requirements of EU membership.

The Czech case shows that the conditionality of the EU depends on a certain tension between confidence in securing membership and fear of suffering rejection due to inadequate reform. The small, highly industrialized, relatively rich Czech Republic began the 1990s with rather less work to do to prepare for EU membership than many of its post-communist neighbours. It could therefore suffer a variety of mistakes and delays in its reform process without compromising its place among the first group of post-communist states to join the EU. Indeed, its political and economic misadventures can be attributed in part to its comfortable position. Eventually, however, the scarcity of reform made the threat of exclusion from the EU's first wave a credible one. In the eleventh hour, this threat seemed to be galvanizing the government and opposition into action.

13

Slovakia: Misreading the Western Message

Ivo Samson

This chapter shows the failure of Western pressure aimed at improving the democratic record of successive Slovak governments led by the former prime minister, Vladimír Mečiar, until 1998. A new, proud, and insecure state tried to assert and manifest its independence from foreign actors. Unlike in Poland, Hungary, and the Czech Republic Western pressure was often considered as being alien to Slovak culture and in conflict with Slovak national interest. But the Mečiar government also misread the Western determination to bring about democratic reforms in Slovakia. It wrongly believed that regardless of its many democratic flaws Slovakia would soon become a member of the European Union and NATO, simply because of its unique geostrategic importance and decent economic performance. It apparently believed that allowing free and relatively fair elections in Slovakia would be enough to satisfy Western actors. But the United States and Western European countries also expected Slovakia to fully respect the right of ethnic minorities, liberalize the media, restrict the powers of secret services, and strictly observe constitutional provisions. In other words, the mere establishment of an electoral type of democracy could not be sufficient, and the West wanted Slovakia to embrace a Western-type of liberal constitutionalism before considering its possible membership in the EU and NATO. In its 1997 Opinion on the Slovak application to the EU the European Commission concluded that 'although the institutional framework defined by the Slovak constitution responds to the needs of a parliamentary democracy where elections are free and fair, nevertheless the situation is unsatisfactory, both in terms of the institutions and the extent to which they are rooted in political life'.[1]

---

[1] EC Commission, 'Commission Opinion on Slovakia's Application for Membership of the European Union', *Bulletin of the European Union*, suppl. 9 (1997).

Among the shortcomings of Slovak democracy the Commission mentioned, in particular, its treatment of the Hungarian and Roma minorities, the arbitrary use of the police and secret services, and insufficient independence of the judiciary. According to the Commission 'the operation of Slovakia's institutions is characterized by the fact that the government does not sufficiently respect the powers devolved by the constitution to other bodies, and that it too often disregards the rights of the opposition'.[2]

The Czechoslovak Legacy and Joining the Western Project

The manner by which Slovakia, a successor state of the Czechoslovak Federation, achieved independence created unfavourable conditions for its democratic consolidation. The partition of Czechoslovakia was not the result of a consensus between the political elites and the population. The partition was enforced by political parties after parliamentary elections, and not in accordance with their pre-election programmes. Neither of the two parties that decided on the partition (the Czech ODS and the Slovak HZDS) had an explicit popular mandate to split Czechoslovakia. The majority of Slovaks (the same is true of the Czechs) did not agree with the division of Czechoslovakia. To all intents and purposes, this division was accomplished against their will. Czechoslovakia had been a relatively stable state with good chances of admission to both the EU and NATO. The unusual circumstances surrounding its partition may explain the passivity of Slovak citizens regarding subsequent political developments. Moreover, unlike in the Czech Republic, the division of Czechoslovakia was officially presented in Slovakia as a rejection of rapid and radical transformation.

Slovakia's post-communist transformation linked the partition of the common state with a non-Western model of economic reform. The political (mostly intellectual) elites, which had held political power in Slovakia until mid-1992 and supported radical transformation, had opposed the creation of an independent Slovak state. With the passage of time, the existence of the independent Slovak Republic (SR) has been accepted by the majority of population.[3] As

[2] EC Commission, 'Commission Opinion on Slovakia's Application for Membership of the European Union', *Bulletin of the European Union*, suppl. 9 (1997).

[3] According to statistical findings in the Czech Republic and Slovakia, the existence of these independent states has become accepted as a matter of fact in the years following the partition.

a result, these political forces became alienated from the average voter.

There are good reasons to believe that the preservation of a common state would have led sooner or later to serious disturbances. On this basis, one may argue that the decision to partition may have been correct.[4] As a result of the partition, Slovakia became a new actor on the international scene. The international weight of the new state has been exaggerated in Slovakia. If Czechoslovakia was a middle-sized country, Slovakia must be regarded as a small country in the European context. It has assumed a weak regional position in the Central European region, where it became the weakest and smallest member of the Visegrad Group.[5] Czechoslovakia was traditionally perceived as a link between Western and Eastern Europe. Now that the Czech Republic is in the North Atlantic Treaty Organization (NATO), this traditional role may be assumed by Slovakia. Moreover, Slovakia stands to become a strategic link between two new NATO countries: Hungary and Poland. Its isolation from the first waves of NATO and European Union (EU) enlargement has complicated Slovakia's process of democratization.

Successful democratization was weakened by the refusal of the EU to open negotiation talks with Slovakia in 1997 as well as by Slovakia's violation of the rules set down in its Association Agreement (or European Agreement—henceforth, EA).[6] Slovak politics were characterized by a gap dividing official statements and declarations from political output and genuine decisions. These circumstances laid the foundations for continual conflict on the domestic political scene from 1995 to 1998. When it came to proclamations, Slovakia presented few differences to other associated countries. Officially, the Slovak government did everything necessary to demonstrate its readiness for admission to the EU and NATO. However, an analysis of the actual results of Slovakia's integration policy produces very different conclusions

Slovakia's basic foreign policy statement, the Programme Statement of the Slovak Government, placed great emphasis on its

[4] As K. Wolf has stated: 'In the meantime, even the hard-core Czechoslovaks must admit that even if the citizens had decided to preserve the common state in a referendum, it would have finally broken up in a big crash and certainly not calmly, maybe not even peacefully.' See K. Wolf, *Podruhé a naposled, aneb, Mirové dělení Československa* G plus G, 1998).

[5] By 1998, the Visegrad Group referred to the formally existing grouping that had lost its regional importance with the NATO enlargement decision adopted at the Madrid Summit.

[6] The original 'federal' EA (in the form of the Interim Agreement) was signed in October 1993, and has been in force since February 1995.

expected admission to the EU. The Slovak application to the EU was accompanied by a Memorandum, which stated the conviction that Slovakia had made sufficient progress in its 'economic, political, and social transformation' to apply for full membership.[7] Full membership, expected, in this view, to occur around the year 2000, was enshrined as Slovakia's strategic objective. As such, the Slovak government pledged to fulfil the political conditions required from associated countries, adopted at the Copenhagen summit in June 1993 and further specified at the summit in Essen in December 1994. Over the course of the negotiations on the EA, Slovakia's Western partners demonstrated a steadily decreasing willingness to take into consideration its particular requirements.[8] In the EA, Slovakia declared its commitment not only to economic criteria envisaged by the EU, but also democratic ones. While economic indicators made Slovakia a strong pretender to EU membership, it was the alleged democratic deficit manifested by the government of Prime Minister Mečiar which jeopardized its early entrance to the EU.

Slovakia was rejected for first wave membership at the NATO Madrid summit and was not recommended for opening negotiations with the EU. At the time, in the Slovak government's view, these rejections were the result of the failure of Western policy. In fact, it is the Slovak government which failed to take Western concerns seriously. Slovakia, evidently, did not believe that the West would follow through on its warnings. This chapter examines the factors that have influenced Slovak perceptions and policies. If the West did fail in its relations with Slovakia, this failure lay in the implementation of its policy. Indeed, initial warnings concerning democratic deficit should have been accompanied by more pressure and even direct threats to cancel the EA. The principal questions, therefore, raised by Slovakia's 'isolation' are: why did Slovakia fail to meet the democratic admission criteria for NATO and EU membership and why did the West fail to achieve its democratic and other objectives in Slovakia before the autumn of 1998?

One must remember that for the first two years after the division of Czechoslovakia the SR was a firm member of the group heading the Central Eastern European (CEE) applicant countries. However, by late 1997, Slovakia found itself behind such countries as Romania and Slovenia in the queue for NATO membership.

---

[7] See the commentary by Hervé de Charette on the Slovak application for membership in the EU in *Pravda* (28 June 1995).

[8] See *Documents: Foreign Policy of the Slovak Republic, I–II* (Bratislava: Slovak Foreign Ministry, 1993).

Slovakia has not only been eliminated from the first round of enlargement, but there were serious doubts before the change of government in autumn 1998 whether it would be invited to join in a possible second round. From being one of the forerunners in the enlargement of the EU, Slovakia became the least promising of the associated states. The failure of Slovakia's integration policy will be examined at several levels. It is not difficult to pinpoint factors that contributed to Slovakia's growing isolation. It is, however, more difficult to assess the reasons for the Slovak failure.

Slovak policy towards its ethnic minorities has been the greatest stumbling block to meeting the EU admission criteria.[9] The Constitution of the Slovak Republic and the Declaration of Independence offer a contradictory understanding of the meaning of citizenship for non-Slovak ethnic groups. Slovakia is presented as a nation-state, and Slovaks are declared the state-forming nationality. Following the partition, the Slovak parliament declared the Slovak language as the state language, and Slovak nation/identity was placed under state and even police protection.[10] As ethnic minorities form between 14 and 20 per cent of the population, a large proportion of the population seems to have been excluded from enjoying full civic rights.[11] Until 1998–9, the language and the culture of these minorities were not protected by the state. The use of minority languages and cultural symbols could even lead to prosecution. 'Non-Slovak citizens' have become members of 'non state-forming' minorities, whose limited civic rights contradict international norms.[12] As early as 1993, the Slovak government pledged to take into account Western concerns on this issue. The Slovak government, thereby, silenced international opposition to Slovakia's admission to the Council of Europe. However, by 1998, the Slovak government had still not met all of the Council of Europe's obligations on these problems.[13]

---

[9] It should be noted that in Slavic languages 'national' is a synonym for 'ethnic'. In this way, being a 'Slovak' reflects ethnicity first, and only then citizenship.

[10] *Act of the National Council of the Slovak Republic on the Official Language* (15 Nov. 1995).

[11] M. Kusy, 'The Hungarian Minority in Slovakia under the Conditions of the Slovak Nation State', *Perspectives*, 6–7 (1996), 63.

[12] Among others, the *UN Declaration of the Rights of Individuals Belonging to National or Ethnic, Religious and Linguistic Minorities* and the *Skeleton Agreement of the Council of Europe* to which Slovakia acceded in February 1995.

[13] A. Duleba, 'Democratic Consolidation and the Conflict over Slovak International Alignment', in Sona Szomolanyi and John A. Gould (eds.), *Slovakia: Problems of Democratic Consolidation* (Bratislava: Slovak Political Science Association, Friedrich Ebert Foundation, 1997), 212.

These policies are comparable to those adopted by inter-war Czechoslovakia. Slovakia seems to be following a similar national principle, that proved so detrimental at that time to the viability of Czechoslovakia. In the inter-war period, Czechs and Slovaks were declared state-forming nationalities and the minorities (mainly Germans and Hungarians) were simply called upon to observe civic principles. In the final account, their loyalty to the republic proved to be minimal. In a similar manner, Slovakia's transformation has assumed clear, and potentially damaging, ethnic connotations.

Prior to the partition, Slovakia believed itself to be indispensable to Czechoslovakia. The adoption of a Slovak constitution and the Slovak Declaration of Independence were designed to provide Slovakia with a stronger negotiation position within Czechoslovakia. As a result of Prague calling Bratislava's 'game' and pushing for real partition, Slovakia became 'independent' against its will, under Czech pressure.

Similar miscalculations were repeated by the Slovak government before the NATO summit in Madrid. Slovakia ignored warnings from the USA concerning its (un)democratic practices, perceiving itself as indispensable for NATO because of its sensitive geopolitical position. The US government then proceeded to eliminate Slovakia from the list of first round candidates. In talks with the EU, Slovakia's government again disregarded EU warnings, and continued contested policies. Clearly the ruling elite of Slovakia was too self-absorbed with domestic political struggle and ignored or misread the Western determination to improve Slovakia's democratic record. The policies of the nationalist left-wing government, in fact, streng-thened the position of extreme nationalist forces on the Slovak political scene.

Slovak Political Development and External Policy

The key figure in Slovak politics after independence was Vladimír Mečiar, who joined the top leadership of the Public Against Violence (PAV) in April 1991. Initially PAV sought to bring together anti-communists, reform communists, and even communists occupying top positions in the state apparatus until the November transfer of power. Mečiar created the Movement for a Democratic Slovakia, which gained a majority in the 1992 and 1994 parliamentary elections, and until 1998 remained the key factor in Slovak politics. The ruling Movement was composed of former communists who had transformed themselves into populists and nationalists.

The hybrid nature of this political force was surprising, as was its ability to retain widespread support from different strata of society. The Movement succeeded in reconciling two divergent Slovak traditions: the nationalist, and even fascist, on the one side, with the communist, on the other. The absence of a significant anti-communist opposition in Slovakia prior to 1989 clearly facilitated this rapprochement of polar opposites. In this respect, political developments in Slovakia were more like those in the Balkans and parts of the former USSR. Indeed, these developments were less similar to the situation in Hungary and Poland, where the success of the organized opposition under communist rule was impressive. They differed also from the situation in the Czech lands, where a loosely organized opposition was visible, if not as successful as its Polish and Hungarian counterparts. Slovak politics also witnessed more confusion over the lines of parliamentary alliance and opposition in general. In these circumstances, President Michal Kovac often performed the functions of an 'opposition', towards the cabinet headed by Vladimír Mečiar.

Patterns of political change, and the shifting fortunes of opposition forces, can be traced through three phases. The first phase was characterized by the sudden rise to power of the 'anti-communist' opposition, with specific Slovak features—a number of leading figures in the PAV were not only former (pre-1968) communists, but many had been prominent communists until 1989. The second phase, which started in early 1991, saw the increasing 'national-ization' of the PAV, accompanied by its retreat from anti-communism, and followed, finally, by its reconciliation with the former communist *nomenklatura*. These shifts occurred ostensibly in the name of the 'higher principle' of national interests (defined in ethnic terms). In the third phase, from 1993 to 1998, the most important institutions of the state were again put under control of collaborators with the former regime—and again, in accordance with the new state ideology of national interests. This control ranged from the secret services, to the headquarters of the government parties, industrial management as well as the boards of large enterprises. To a large degree, the representatives of the pre-1989 regime secured control over institutions decisive for state activities.

These developments were not entirely unpredictable. By 1992, Mečiar's Movement for a Democratic Slovakia had already exploited nationalist sentiments in Slovak politics. Moreover, the negative effects of post-1989 transformation (unemployment, first of all) were felt more in Slovakia than in Czech lands. In surveys conducted in 1991 and 1994, Slovakia demonstrated the greatest degree of dissatisfaction with democracy in comparison to the Czech lands, Hungary, and Poland. In 1991, 55 per cent of Slovaks were dissatisfied with democracy; while in the Czech lands, those dissatisfied represented 25 per cent, in Hungary 19 per cent, and Poland 21 per cent. In 1994, this dissatisfaction had reached 62 per cent in Slovakia (Czech lands 9 per cent; Hungary 43 per cent; Poland 40 per cent).[14] The Czechs, as the main proponents of democracy, were made responsible for Slovak dissatisfaction. However, despite widespread public dissatisfaction with democracy following independence, Mečiar was able to put together coalitions and gain far more votes than the opposition parties. Support for Mečiar was perhaps based on the fact that he would not allow 'too much' democracy.

Slovak governing elites at the time consisted of more or less unreconstructed former communists who made use of the post-1989 dissatisfaction with democracy, and the rise of ethnic nationalism, to fashion a new political identity. As an aggressive combination of nationalism and isolationism formed an integral part of their domestic legitimacy, these elites engaged in behaviour that created rifts with some of its neighbours and with its potential EU partners. This behaviour weakened the prospects of achieving Slovakia's declared strategic objective of integration with the West. The Mečiar government seemed to prefer to hold onto power internally, at the cost of Slovakia's place in the first group of post-communist candidates for EU and NATO membership.

The 'Slovak way'

The constitutional transformation process in Slovakia proceeded smoothly. The problems that existed, such as the absence of a Minorities Language Act, could theoretically be rectified very quickly. In practice, however, this 'constitutional normality' obscured many problematic peculiarities of the 'Slovak Way'. First, a section of the Slovak political elite suffered from growing xenophobia. This elite sought popular support through the pursuit of a specifically Slovak path of transformation. In 1997, as Slovakia's integration policy collapsed, many politicians reacted in hysterical fashion to Western criticism.

Another important feature concerns the manner in which governmental power was exercised. This factor bore closely on Slovakia meeting the requirements for NATO and EU membership.

---

[14] Charles Gati, 'The Mirage of Democracy', *Transition*, 2: 6 (1996), 8–11.

The aftermath of the parliamentary elections in 1994 produced an imbalance in Slovak political forces. As a result, the government coalition sought to obtain an overall majority in parliament by illegal means, as it realized its inability to achieve constitutional changes without such a majority.[15] The government resorted to methods which were unethical and incompatible with democratic principles. During his presidential term (up to October 1997), the Slovak president referred thirty-three bills back to parliament. In fifteen cases, the Constitutional Court judged the bills to be unconstitutional. In one case, the governmental majority in the parliament repeatedly refused to observe the constitution and the findings of the Constitutional Court.[16]

After the 1994 elections, these governmental practices contributed to the polarization of Slovak society. Relations between the Hungarian minority and the government worsened considerably. Western concerns about these developments were expressed on numerous occasions. The frequent visits by the Organization for Security and Cooperation in Europe (OSCE) High Commissioner for National Minorities, Max van der Stoel, as well as representatives from the Council of Europe and the EU, were important in this respect. Western criticism was also expressed in two series of demarches in 1994 and 1995, and in a critical resolution of the European Parliament in 1996. 1997 saw criticism from H. Bosch, chair of the Joint Interparliamentary Committee, and warnings from European politicians as well as from the US ambassador to Slovakia.[17]

---

[15] According to the view of the governmental majority, in 1994, one of the opposition parties, the Democratic Union (DU), was elected to parliament in spite of its illegal registration. A special Parliamentary Investigation Commission was set up with the aim to oust it from parliament. The government even made use of the police to check this party's petition sheets. Instead of finding the election procedures of the DU unlawful, the Constitutional Court declared the establishment of the Commission illegal, and it had to be dissolved. See the *Findings of the Constitutional Court from 29. 11. 1995* (No. 2/1996).

[16] P. Suger, 'Coho symptomom su kauzy Ustavneho sudu', *Nove slovo*, 46 (1997).

[17] See the demarche of the EU of November 1994 expressing 'misgivings about some phenomena' in Slovakia after the parliamentary elections. See also the EU demarche issued on 25 Oct. 1995 and the US demarche of 27 Oct. 1995, which expressed misgivings about the 'contemporary political and institutional tension in the country' and reminded Slovakia of its obligations to observe the criteria of the EA, and of the basic criteria of democratic behaviour anchored by the Copenhagen summit. See also the resolution of the European Parliament issued in December 1996: 'European Parliament: Joint Motion for a Resolution', *Sme* (14 Dec. 1996).

These declarations sought to draw the attention of the Slovak government to measures that it would need to take in order to confirm that Slovakia was heading towards democracy and the protection of human rights and civic liberties.[18] The Slovak government reacted in a manner reminiscent of communist times. Western concerns were presented as a slander campaign against independent Slovakia, directed by a coalition of internal opposition forces and enemies in the pay of the USA. Many leading figures in the government coalition referred openly to the existence of a conspiracy against Slovakia.

Government policy continued to be dominated by this isolationist line imposed by radical nationalists. Opponents of the 'integration policy' in the government exploited Western statements about the level of democracy in Slovakia in order to place in question the validity of Slovak integration. This position was presented by the pro-government media as a defence of the national interest. In the political sphere, defensive perceptions and isolationist tendencies continued to thrive, highlighting a drift towards increasing Slovak isolation.

Geopolitics as an obstacle to integration

In 1990, each of the new states of CEE faced the challenge of determining its position in the international order. Responding to this challenge became a critical issue in Slovakia, as there was general conviction that Czechoslovak foreign policy had in fact represented Czech interests. In defining a Slovak policy, Slovak political, military, and academic circles focused on what has been considered the unique geographical position of Slovakia with regard to CEE and Europe as a whole. Since the early 1990s, the study of geopolitics became the most popular discipline in Slovak political science. Slovak foreign policy has become characterized by an unhealthy dose of geographical determinism. Slovak policy towards future integration in the EU and NATO—still within the framework of Czechoslovakia—was even then driven by a firm belief in the importance of Slovakia's geopolitical position. Admission to European organizations was expected because of international recognition of this uniqueness, and not necessarily on the basis of economic or democratic record.

[18] Western criticism of Slovakia between 1993 and 1997 has been summed up in two reports: *Human Rights and Democratization in Slovakia*, issued by the Helsinki Commission of the US Congress in October 1993 and *Human Rights and Democratization in Slovakia*, prepared by the Staff of the Commission on Security and Cooperation in Europe in September 1997.

In the early 1990s, two agencies under the government took the lead in such geopolitical analysis.[19] These agencies based their research on classical theories, seeking to apply the geopolitics of the beginning of the century to the complex relations resulting from the collapse of the bipolar system. The factors of 'space' and territory were key concepts in calculations of Slovakia's central position in Europe.[20] Many problems that Slovakia experienced with the EU between 1995 and 1997 were due to the application of such geopolitically founded policy views on the future of Europe and the wider world. In particular, Slovak governments (with a brief interruption in 1994) adhered to three principles: Euro-centrism; a focus on Central Europe; and, finally, a deep Slovak-centrism. The focus on these principles helps to explain the anti-American orientation of the government after 1994–5.[21]

On the basis of these analyses, pre-1998 Slovak assessments of future developments in Europe and the transatlantic region were quite stark. According to government experts, Europe would not succeed in forming a political union. This failure would lead naturally to the emergence of a Russian-German axis, which Slovakia could join. As a result of these interesting, but hardly rigorous, analyses, Slovak foreign policy practically collapsed in 1997. Another important reason behind this collapse was the schizophrenic character of this policy. The Slovak government declared its desire for integration; at the same time, politicians, at the highest level, openly spoke out against integration. Slovakia formally applied for membership in the EU; at the same time, it saw the EU (in the form of political union) as doomed to disintegration. This unsound geopolitical foundation helps to explain Slovakia's contradictory, and sometimes even incomprehensible, foreign policy behaviour.

The new states in the Western part of CEE have held that, because of their Western culture and geographical position, their integration

---

[19] These were the Institute of Political Science, attached to the Slovak Academy of Sciences and the Center for Strategic Studies, attached to the Ministry of Defence.

[20] See the extensive study, *Geopolitický a geoekonomický vyvoj vo svete a post-avenie Slovenskej republiky*, presented to the government in February 1994; in M. Ziak, *Slovensko od komunizmu kam?* (Bratislava: Archa, 1996), 178.

[21] 'Today one can see clear signals that the world as a whole rejects the principle of a hegemonic leader being a guarantee of further development . . . the USA will not succeed in preserving the role of a hegemonic leader for a long time. The world is not willing any more to accept this role, even if the USA, as several authors believe, can preserve its position as the number one economic great power until 2005.' See *Slovensko od Komunizmu Kam?*, Ziak, 179. The material has not yet been published.

plans deserved special treatment. The emergence of the political concept of 'Central Europe' was also conspicuous in Slovak policy and perceptions.[22] Slovak analysts stressed the unique position of Slovakia in Central Europe. In this view, which informed the government's policy, Slovakia's historical, cultural, and political orientation is neither Eastern nor Western, but 'Central European'.[23] From the early 1990s until late 1997, a number of proposals and models of the geopolitical taxonomy of Slovakia appeared in political analyses and in government documents. In most of them, Central Europe appeared as the most important part of Europe, with Slovakia at its centre. Slovak analyses contesting this perspective were marginalized.[24]

Neutrality as a Security Concept

Slovakia's commitment to withstanding external pressures was also manifested by its adherence to the concept of international neutrality. Slovak security policy was especially influenced by this concept.

Bratislava first toyed with the idea of endorsing neutrality in the first months of 1993. However, as a successor state to Czechoslovakia, it had no choice then but to declare an enduring commitment to Czechoslovakia's pro-integration policy and the policy of the Visegrad Group, which included the Cracow Declaration of October 1991.[25] As such, the concept of neutrality was not mentioned in the Programme Declaration of the Slovak Government, although leading politicians in the government endorsed it officially shortly afterwards.

Public opinion on the question of neutrality was quite confused. A 1996 survey found that supporters and opponents were balanced at approximately 30 per cent; the remainder were undecided.[26] By

---

[22] Ivo Samson, 'The Concept of Central Europe', in *History and Politics*, Proceedings from a symposium (Bratislava, 1994), 59–65.

[23] A. Hrnko, 'Stredna Europa v polovici 90. rokov', *Sme* (2 Feb. 1995).

[24] R. Chmel, 'Sme v strednej Europe ci nie sme?' (Is Slovakia in Central Europe or not?), *Vychod—Zapad*, 1 (1995); J. Kohutiar, 'Žijeme v srdci Europy?', *Sme* (7 Oct. 1995).

[25] H. Polackova, 'Regional Cooperation in Central Europe: Poland, Hungary, Czech Republic and Slovakia', *Perspectives*, 3 (1994), 120.

[26] M. Butora (ed.), *Slovensko 1996: Suhrná správa o stave spoločnosti a trendoch na rok 1997* (Bratislava: Institut pre verejne otazky, 1997).

late 1997, support had increased to 36 per cent.[27] (In 1995, 22 per cent of neutrality supporters also favoured Slovakia joining NATO. In 1997, 10 per cent of neutrality supporters still believed that neutrality was compatible with NATO membership.) Polls suggest that neutrality has become attractive for people who hold anti-reform views, reject the principles of the market economy, and demonstrate limited ethnic tolerance. The concept of neutrality has become a standard slogan in nationalist rhetoric. Following the Madrid summit, it was combined increasingly with anti-Americanism. Intensely held anti-American sentiments are widespread among mainly elderly people who still view the inter-war and communist periods positively. In 1990–3, terms such as US 'masonism', 'cosmopolitism', and 'world hegemony' appeared only in marginal periodicals. By 1996–7, these expressions had penetrated the vocabulary of the government parties, including the leading officials of the ruling movement. It is notable that Russia has fully supported the idea of Slovak neutrality, which it has declared a willingness to guarantee.[28]

Why did the West fail to persuade Slovakia of the benefits of integration into Western security structures? Three factors, beyond the control of the international community, explain this failure. The first had to do with Slovak power calculations regarding its domestic policy. In the government's view, Slovakia's full integration into Western structures would bring Slovakia's domestic behaviour under constant scrutiny by democratic states.[29] EU criticism of developments in Slovak affairs was interpreted as unjustifiable intervention. The second factor involves Slovak perceptions of negative influences emanating from the West. Many of the problems afflicting Slovak society, such as crime, substance abuse, and unemployment, were seen as 'spillover' from abroad. In this view, Slovakia's voluntary isolation would represent an obvious panacea to these problems.

Thirdly, Slovakia's cultural tradition contains Russified elements, a vein of anti-Semitism and a distrust of the West. The urban-rural

[27] These opinion polls were conducted by the IVO (Institute for Public Affairs) in the first half of October 1997: 36 per cent were in favour of neutrality, 42 per cent were for NATO membership, 24 per cent were undecided, or not interested in the problem. See *Sme* (24 Nov. 1997).

[28] The Presidential Spokesman, Sergei Yastrzembsky, the Russian Ambassador to Slovakia S. Zotov, and Aleksandr Lebed gave 'assurances' about Russia's willingness to guarantee Slovak neutrality. See *TASR* (31 Mar. 1997).

[29] Ivo Samson, 'Proclamations, Declarations and "Realpolitik" in the Current Slovak Integration Policy', *Perspectives*, 6–7 (1996), 51–62.

divide in Slovakia is important in this respect.[30] The rural electorate represents the majority of the anti-integration group. Slovakia's political culture also includes a respect for authoritarianism, which found expression in fascism during the war and communism subsequently. In the mid-1990s, nationalist and former communist groups formed a natural alliance rallying against the integration of Slovakia into the EU and NATO. These groups seized on the concept of neutrality as an opportunity to prevent a reccurrence of their perceived 'historical defeats' of 1944–5 and 1989–90.

In this political climate, it is paradoxical that the Slovak armed forces have met most of the conditions set forth for membership in NATO. Indeed, Slovakia has achieved progress on ensuring the interoperability of forces and civilian control over the armed forces. Apparently, these conditions did not play an important role in the decision concerning Slovakia's candidature in NATO's enlargement plans. After 1997, criticism appeared in Slovakia about the state of civil–military relations. These reproaches focused on the parliament's lack of control over the defence budget and strategic defence planning. Criticism also focused on the parliament's lack of control over the intelligence services, and the passivity of the parliamentary Council for Defence and Security.[31]

Regional and International Contexts of Slovakia's Democracy

Slovakia's anomalous development in the Central European region underlines its lack of historical experience with independent statehood. In contrast to its neighbours, Slovakia cannot draw upon either a genuine history of independence or even a formal one as an independent state in Soviet-controlled Eastern Europe. Moreover, three of its four Central European neighbours held hegemonic control over Slovakia in the past. As a result, Slovak policy has been characterized by two contradictory tendencies, combining a desire for integration into Europe with an enduring distrust of external influences.

[30] S. Szomolanyi, 'Identifying Slovakia's Emerging Regime', in Szomolanyi and A. Gould, *Slovakia*, 22.

[31] See M. Wlachovsk, 'Armáda SR a národná bezpečnosť', in M. Bútora and M. Ivantsyn (eds.), *Slovensko 1997. Suhrna sprava o stave spoločnosti a trendoch na rok 1998* (Bratislava: Institut pre verejne otazky, 1998); M. Bútora and P. Huneik, *Global Report on the Society and Trends from 1998* (Bratislava: Institut pre verejne otazky, 1998), 324–5.

The profound difference between Slovak and other Central European definitions of national identity must be taken into consideration. In Slovakia, national identity was based on language before it became associated with territory. This process led to tensions with the Czechs and Hungarians, fuelled by a desire to avoid assimilation. This historical experience has been reflected in Slovakia's policy towards European integration, in which negative attitudes towards foreign influences are manifest. It is possible that anti-assimilationist tendencies in Slovak policies may have reached a natural climax in 1998. However, the appearance of a Slovak state long after the birth of the Slovak nation created distinct problems in Slovakia's relations with the outside world.[32]

Slovakia linked its economic and security policy to the Russian Federation in 1993, when two important agreements were signed between Slovakia and Russia.[33] The so-called Basic Treaty contained significant Slovak concessions to Russian perspectives on future European security.[34] Slovakia is the only Central European state that endorsed the Russian objective of establishing the OSCE as the coordinator of all European security organizations, including NATO and the WEU. The 1993 Treaty on Military Cooperation extended political and economic cooperation between the two countries into the military sphere.[35] This agreement included the use of Slovak territory for joint Slovak-Russian military exercises, the repayment of former Soviet debts (in military technology and Soviet weaponry), and closer cooperation in the military-industrial sector.

These treaties, however, did not stop Slovakia from expressing an interest in full integration into NATO. Slovakia thus adopted an ambiguous position between two European security strategies:

[32] One historical argument is often accepted as historical fact: the Slovaks are represented as the 'oldest Slavic nation' that 'christianized Russia', and that had its own state already in the ninth century AD. This presentation of history is not confined to academic discussions. Top politicians in the executive use these arguments openly.

[33] See Ivo Samson, 'Slovakia between an Orientation towards Russia and Western Integration' in BIOST, Cologne, 1997 (*Berichte des BIOST*, No. 2/1997).

[34] The Treaty on Friendship and Cooperation (1993) included the following article: 'The contracting parties confirm that security is indivisible and the security of both countries is linked with the security of all countries—the members of the OSCE.' See A. Duleba, *The Blind Pragmatism of Slovak Foreign Policy*, (Bratislava: SFPA, 1996), 55. This article was declared as 'probably the most important one' by Boris Yeltsin, *Pravda* (27 Aug. 1993).

[35] This was signed in August 1993. Unlike the Basic Treaty, this treaty did not require ratification by parliament. The treaty has not been fully revealed. Its items, however, have become partly known, due to interviews with competent military personnel.

on the one hand a Western strategy that aimed to provide for credible defence against any potential Russian relapse into great power imperialism; on the other hand a Russian strategy that has sought to ensure that Russia retains the authority of a great power in decisions about European security.

The development of Russian–Slovak relations became a sore point in government–opposition relations in Slovakia in the months leading up to the 1998 elections. The opposition raised the question of whether Slovakia's economic dependency on Russia, in terms of energy supplies, would not create a degree of political dependency. This question became all the more important after the collapse of Slovakia's European integration policy in 1997. Slovakia needed a strong partner in Europe, and Russia was seen by many to be the appropriate alternative in the face of the West's refusal to embrace Slovakia.[36]

The two most prominent issues in Slovak–Hungarian relations have been the problems raised by the Gabcíkovo-Nagyamaros dam and the tensions surrounding the ethnic Hungarian minority in Slovakia. The first was resolved by a decision of the International Court in the Hague in September 1997. There have been subsequent problems in the implementation of this decision, but the issue largely left the political plane in 1999. However, the issue of minorities remains critically important among the regional/international factors affecting Slovakia's democratization. The main problem is not merely the existence of national minorities within Slovakia.[37] It resides more in the interconnection between these minorities and developments on the international stage. The so-called *Hungarian factor* played an important role in Slovak domestic policy between 1993 and 1998 (the Hungarian minority represents about 10.5 per cent of the population). Although the Slovak constitution contains provisions guaranteeing the rights of national minorities that are compatible with European standards, the relations between Slovaks and the Hungarian minority in Slovakia produced serious international implications for Slovakia.[38]

[36] See A. Duleba, 'Slovensko a Rusko' (Slovakia and Russia) in Bútora and Ivanyutyn, *Slovensko 1997*, 294–5.

[37] Uncertainty about the exact number of minorities is due to the unknown situation of the Roma community. Officially, the Roma form only about 1.5% of the population. In reality, the numbers of this minority are several times higher, and will increase in the future because of high birth rates. See O. Dostál, 'Národnostné menuiny', in Bútora and Ivanyutyn, *Slovensko 1997*, 155.

[38] See the discussion by D. Brzica, Z. Poláčková, and Ivo Samson, 'The Slovak Republic: Bridge between East and West?', in Peter Katzenstein (ed.), *Mitteleuropa: Between Europe and Germany* (Oxford: Berghahn Books, 1997), 224.

The controversy centred on the minorities' right to use their own language in official discourse. After the State Language Act of November 1995, such a right was not codified in a special Minorities' Language Act. The delay surrounding this Act attracted a steady stream of criticism from the EU. The signing of the Basic Treaty between Slovakia and Hungary in 1995, and its ratification by the Slovak parliament in March 1996, resolved some of the outstanding problems. However, during the ratification process, Slovak deputies approved additional resolutions limiting the application of measures that had been anchored in the treaty.[39]

The Hungarian factor has made Slovakia's political transformation very different from that of the Czech Republic, Hungary, and Poland. Whereas the traditional Czech and Polish 'ethnic adversaries' could not be exploited in domestic politics owing to their disappearance after 1945, in Slovakia, nationalist former communists (as in Serbia, Croatia, and Romania) dominated domestic politics from 1994. Decisive power after 1989 in Slovakia was not transferred to pre-1989 opposition leaders on a comparable level. In spite of relatively strong religious dissent, Slovakia lacked the civic-democratic dissent present in these other countries. Soon after 1989, those politically active moderate democrats were pushed aside by the former communists, who used ethnic nationalism to redefine themselves politically.[40] In conditions of political and economic instability, ethnic tensions increased, as the majority of the Slovak population became unwilling to accept ethnic diversity as a natural element of its modern statehood.[41]

In seeking the roots of Slovakia's 'deviation' from the course adopted by the other Central European states, one must avoid the facile conclusion of making Slovak government policy solely responsible for its integration failure. Such a conclusion would confuse cause and effect, and disregard the interrelation between these two. In spite of many authoritarian features, Slovakia became a parliamentary democracy, with the government representing half of the population. The reasons why the other half supported

---

[39] See E. Sándor, 'The Slovak-Hungarian Basic Treaty', in M. Bútora and P. Huněík, *Global Report on Slovakia* (Bratislava: Institut pre verejne otazky, 1996), 61.

[40] Timothy Snyder and Milada Vachudová, 'Two Types of Political Change in Eastern Europe since 1989', *East European Politics and Society*, 1 (1997), 3.

[41] Ivo Samson, 'Die Sicherheitspolitik der Slowakei in den ersten Jahren der Selbtstandigkeit' (Security Policy of the Slovak Republic in the First Years of Independence), Dissertation (Giessen, 1997), 276, reference to *Domino efekt*, 27 (1995). See also Snyder and Vachudová, 'Two Types of Political Change', 3.

limited democracy have to be sought in the cultural sphere. At the same time, cultural/civilizational determination must also be avoided.[42] The example of Slovakia is eloquent: a country that had been a part of the Hapsburg Empire with a 1,000-year-old Catholic tradition seemed in early 1998 to have less chance than Romania and Bulgaria of integration with Europe.

Yet Slovakia's dialogue with the West failed predominantly because of the paradoxes of its domestic political development. These paradoxes emerge from a comparison with other states in the region. The political scene in the Czech Republic differs from that of Hungary and Poland, but remains broadly compatible. By contrast, political developments in Slovakia seemed atypical. Moreover, while clear similarities exist with the political development of Serbia, Croatia (until January 2000), and Romania (until late 1996), Slovak political development still appears to be distinctive. The formal successors to the Communist Party of Slovakia were not the alternative to right-wing political parties. In Slovakia, the ruling movement—composed mostly of former communists— was officially not post-communist. This ruling movement did not formally represent the continuation and rebirth of the former Communist Party. Needless to say, the leading figures of the ruling movement were all former communists. Unlike Serbia, Croatia, or Romania, the transition to a ruling nationalist movement did not originate in a renamed communist party, and the leading figures in the ruling movement began their career in 1989–90 partly in a strong anti-communist drive.

Conclusions

Slovakia's misperception of its geopolitical uniqueness led to serious misunderstandings about Western reactions to the development of Slovak domestic and foreign policy. Slovakia sought to become a bridge between East and West that would draw political and economic profit from both sides. After the resounding collapse of this policy, government officials, and large parts of the public, reacted with anti-Western invective, implying that Western criticism was a first step towards direct military intervention. Parallels have

[42] As Timothy Garton Ash stated, 'it is quite sufficient to look at the victims of the Croatian ethnical cleansings in Bosnia, and the image of a Croat as a defender of Western values against the Serbian Orthodoxy will appear ridiculous', in 'Paradoxy strednej Europy' (Paradoxes of Central Europe), *Sme v strednej Europe* (6 Nov. 1997).

been drawn with the demarches and the military interventions of Germany in 1938–9 and the USSR in 1968. It is these features of Slovak political behaviour that led Zbigniew Brzezinski to state that Slovakia was not yet mentally ripe for integration with the West.[43]

Until the parliamentary elections in 1994, all political parties represented in the Slovak National Council supported dual integration (in the EU and NATO). However, the parliament formed after these elections, and especially the government coalition between 1994 and 1998, included two parties whose leading officials questioned the correctness of Slovakia's orientation towards the EU, and, particularly, NATO. By late 1996, two of the three parties in the government coalition had formally declared an anti-integration position. It seems that the status quo that existed in Central Europe before the possibility of enlargement gained pace in 1996–7, in fact, had best suited the government's foreign policy objectives.

Since the change of government in September 1998, Slovakia has started to reverse some of the misperceptions and democratic failures covered in this chapter. In mid-1999, a new language law was adopted to guarantee the use of alternative languages in public life in areas where minority groups represent at least 20 per cent of the population. The status of ethnic Hungarians was further enhanced by the inclusion of a Hungarian party in the ruling coalition and relations with Hungary began to be mended. Political and economic reforms, combined with an intense lobbying effort and the wider implications of a shift in EU thinking, led to the start of official EU accession negotiations with Brussels in March 2000. However, undoing the legacy of the early years of independence could take longer and, in this respect, two scenarios seem worth noting.

First, the new government will have to spend several years proving to Europe that it really has set a 'new course' in domestic and foreign policy. In an optimistic scenario, Slovakia might become a member of the EU in or shortly after the first enlargement round and would have no problems with being integrated in a second round of NATO enlargement, were such a round considered.

In a pessimistic scenario, the new government will undertake steps in the direction of a successful transformation. However, the EU will prolong the accession process and adopt a longer wait-and-see policy in response, to ensure that Slovakia's transformation is irreversible. In this case, Slovakia would lose time, but would still retain principal Western support (such as in supporting

---

[43] See interview with Zbigniew Brzezinski in *Nove slovo*, 45 (1997).

programmes like PHARE) and could continue a transformation process together with other EU associated countries. Any possibility of EU membership, however, would be postponed for a decade or more.

In both cases, the new government needs time to remove the obstacles to its integration and domestic transformation process. First, it will have to further promote reconciliation in a politically, socially, and ethnically polarized society. Some of the issues involved —such as the prosecution of alleged criminal activities by the secret services, amendments to the constitution, radical economic reform—are potential sources of social and political instability, and could even hamper attempts at transformation. Without these steps, however, the completion of Slovakia's transformation might remain in question, taking the form of a dubious attempt to separate economic development from full democracy in the manner of the 'Asian tigers'.[44]

[44] See a friendly, but critical, study by Dieter Bricke, the former General Consul in Slovakia; *Die Slowakei auf dem Weg in die Europäische Union* (Ebenhausen: Stiftung Wissenschaft und Politik, 1995), 47–9.

Building Democracy in Romania: Internal Shortcomings and External Neglect

Tom Gallagher

Communist rule ended violently and abruptly in Romania in 1989, but in the 1990s a protracted and incomplete transition from that social system has occurred. Romania thus stands apart from Central European states with whom it prefers to be grouped and even with several in South-East Europe (SEE) or the Balkans, the geographical category into which international observers and many ordinary Romanian citizens feel Romania best fits.[1]

Until the 1996 election victory of centre-right reformers, Romania experienced a transition from communist rule controlled by second-ranking members of the old regime; until the mid-1990s, when at last it appeared possible that they could be peacefully substituted in office, they were widely seen as reluctant democrats wedded to illiberal practices, with a near-monopolistic approach to political power.

The situation appeared recognizable to scholars familiar with Romania's long-term political evolution. In the past imported ideologies have been modified and drained of their reformist content to suit local elite requirements.[2] This has led to huge discrepancies between constitutional forms and actual practices. Since Romanian independence in 1881, rhetoric about reform has often been a screen enabling a narrow oligarchy, whether aristocratic, mercantile, communist, or post-communist to pursue self-serving policies

---

[1] For an examination of the debates concerning Romania's geopolitical position, see Tom Gallagher, 'To Be or Not to Be Balkan?: Romania's Quest for Self-Definition', *Daedalus*, 126: 3 (Summer 1997).

[2] Although written in the late 1940s, the following work remains valid by pointing to such long-term trends in elite behaviour: Henry J. Roberts, *Rumania: Political Problems of an Agrarian State* (New Haven: Yale University Press, 1951), esp. 337–42.

that produce a dangerous gulf between state and society. A legacy of foreign occupation stretching over centuries, and sharp internal cleavages—economic, cultural, and above all ethnic—retarded the progress of democratization.

From 1881 to 1938 Romania enjoyed over fifty years of stable constitutional rule which distinguished it from all other states in SEE, but institutions and civic culture were not democratic (nor are they today according to one of Romania's foremost political scientists).[3] The inability of a poorly institutionalized state to integrate new territories with large minority populations acquired after 1918 led to the collapse of democracy twenty years later. For the next sixty years indigenous forms of development were pursued in turn by right-wing populists and national communists, following an interlude of communist rule shaped by internationalist (i.e. pro-Soviet) norms.

The self-image of Romania as 'a Latin country which has always believed itself to be an extension of the west towards the East', helps to explain why it has often differentiated itself from its neighbours.[4] It may share the Orthodox religion with its Slav neighbours, but it stays aloof from most of them, especially Russia, which is seen as a long-term foe of Romanian independence. Along with Hungary, Romania is the only non-Slavic nation-state in the Danubian basin, but cooperation has been thwarted by the debilitating quarrel over Transylvania, part of Romania since 1918, but mainly Hungarian-ruled for hundreds of years before that. Even with its long-standing Romanian majority, this province has undeniable Central European characteristics. Thus Romania finds itself crossed by important cultural fault-lines. The pre-1918 state shaped by Byzantine culture and proximity to Ottoman power coexists with relatively new territories where the Romanian majority has been exposed to German influence and where minorities enjoyed influence greater than their numbers. The great powers exploited such internal cleavages and Romania suffered devastating invasions in both world wars (never recovering Bessarabia and North Bukovina seized by the Soviet Union in 1940). It is hardly surprising that recently acquired independence and dire threats to territorial integrity have allowed nationalism to occupy a salient role in political culture. Nor is it any more surprising that, often

---

[3] See Alina Mungiu-Pippidi, *Reforma Sistemului Politic Romanesc, de la Democratia electorala la democratia liberala: a doua transitie* (Bucharest: Centrul Pentru Reforma Institutionala Rapoarte Asupra Politicilor Publice, 1998), 3.

[4] Dorina Nastase, *The World Today* (May 1997), 123.

against a background of misrule, rulers have consistently sought legitimacy from citizens by invoking nationalism and portraying themselves as executors of 'the national mission'.

In this chapter I argue that the process of building democracy in Romania is dependent on a favourable external environment and active backing from abroad. The communist regime's determination to retain absolute control over politics and society and oppose any liberal initiatives in economics blocked off the possibility of a democratic transition largely resourced and driven from within. However, at least until 1999 Western interest in Romania and concern for the success of its democratic experiment has been weak, with most involvement coming from NGOs and international economic bodies whose influence over Western policy towards Romania is relatively limited. The difficulties in the way of Romania consolidating a fragile democracy by pursuing a strategy dependent on successful integration with Western economic and security organizations are spelt out. Instead, the case is made for a new approach to democracy-building from domestic reformers and international organizations that recognizes Romania's special problems, one that is not based around unrealistic targets which the country is unable to meet for the foreseeable future.

Fluctuating International Influence

Romania today is the second largest of the former Soviet satellites in Eastern Europe (EE) and there has been intermittent interaction with the West (even though the importation of Western political values is of debatable significance). Independence was acquired through the skill of Romanian politicians in dealing with the Western powers, ensuring that Ottoman overlordship was not substituted by Russian control. After 1960, the West enjoyed a wider range of diplomatic and commercial contacts with Romania than with any other Warsaw Pact state, despite the unyielding character of a Marxist-Leninist regime soon to be infused with 1930s-style ultranationalism. The bid by Nicolae Ceaușescu, general secretary of the Romanian Communist Party (PCR) from 1965 to 1989, to acquire autonomy from the Soviet Union made him seem a weak link in Soviet power and thus a leader apparently worth cultivating.[5] Prestigious state visits from General De Gaulle and US President

---

[5] For the British attitude to Ceaușescu, see Mark Percival, 'Britain's Political "Romance" with Romania in the 1970s', *Contemporary European History*, 4: 1 (1994).

Nixon occurred in 1968 and 1969. In 1972 Romania was invited to join both the World Bank and the International Monetary Fund (IMF). It obtained preferential trading status from the European Union (EU) in 1973 and was awarded Most Favoured Nation trading status in 1974, the only EE state enjoying such a distinction.[6] Moreover, in 1967 Romania was the first communist state to recognize the Federal Republic of Germany.[7]

The West indirectly contributed to the chain of events that led to the violent collapse of the Ceauşescu regime in 1989. While it preferred to overlook systematic human rights abuses until the last years of the dictatorship, it made available massive loans to Ceauşescu that were used to finance ill-conceived industrialization schemes that resulted in massive policy failures. At considerable cost to his people, Ceauşescu set out to repay these loans by 1990, but in December 1989 popular protests and a rebellion by second-ranking communists brought about his downfall.

Numerous conspiracy theories seek to explain the sequence of events leading to the overthrow and execution by his underlings of a previously unchallenged communist dictator. One that has enjoyed unusual staying-power despite the absence of corroborating evidence is that Presidents Bush and Gorbachev at their Malta summit in November 1989 worked out the details of Ceauşescu's removal and his substitution by communist reformers who would not disturb the balance of power in the area.[8] In 1990 one of the most common chants of protestors angry at Western inaction as the political vacuum was filled by men with roots in the communist regime was 'Malta Yalta', indicating their belief that the democracies were ready to abandon Romania to Russian captivity for a second time.[9]

But, however unpalatable, Western passivity as coup leaders led by Ion Iliescu moved quickly to confirm their authority by holding

---

[6] Ronald Linden, 'After the Revolution: A Foreign Policy of Bounded Change', in Daniel Nelson (ed.), *Romania after Tyranny* (Boulder, Colo.: Westview Press, 1992), 204.

[7] *Adevarul* (Bucharest daily paper) (6 Nov. 1997).

[8] A former US ambassador in Bucharest, now a Republican Congressman in Washington, has published a memoir of his years in Bucharest in which he fiercely criticized Bush for his alleged propensity to brush aside human rights concerns and deal with the Romanian communist leadership on their terms. See David B. Funderburk, *Intre Department de Stat Si Dictatura Comunista Din Romania 1981–1985* (Constanta: Editura Dacon, 1994), 183–8.

[9] The most persuasive defence of this viewpoint in print was provided by Reuben H. Markham, *Rumania under the Soviet Yoke* (Boston: Meador, 1949), a book which was reissued in Romania in 1997.

elections in May 1990 before their competitors had the chance to organize themselves, probably has a more mundane explanation. No Western country saw Romania as being in its zone of influence. Neither Germany nor France had obvious economic or strategic interests there. Unlike Poland or Hungary, Romania lacked a large and vocal émigré community in the USA able to persuade politicians to adopt a vigilant approach to events in their former homeland.

Initially, there was relief in western capitals that Iliescu was able to co-opt the party and state bureaucracy which recognized that this paternalistic ex-communist was in a good position to safeguard their interests in troubled times. Anxiety built up, however, following Romanian-Hungarian clashes in the city of Tirgu Mures in March 1990 in which official complicity, at least at lower levels, seemed apparent.[10] Analysts were already advising Western policy makers that the politics of ethnicity had the potential to sabotage the transition to open politics being attempted in EE.[11] Anxiety gave way to displeasure when the state used violence against its political opponents. In May 1990 the US ambassador was recalled to Washington for consultations regarding violence and intimidation in the election campaign.[12] In June when the government used vigilante workers to beat up opposition protestors in the capital, there was widespread outrage. The EU froze agreements with Romania and the US government condemned 'in the strongest possible terms, the Romanian government's brutal suppression . . . of legitimate forms of dissent and public protest'.[13]

But the West was disinclined to take punitive action against ex-communists seemingly turning Romania into a façade democracy. As events in Yugoslavia would demonstrate only too clearly, policy makers are reluctant to act as organizers, leaders, or peacemakers in a region where there are serious doubts about the potentialities of local elites and their populations to aspire to good government and modern forms of political conduct. Besides, the undeniable winner in May 1990 was Iliescu and his National Salvation Front (FSN).

[10] For the Tirgu Mures events, see Tom Gallagher, *Romania after Ceausescu: The Politics of Intolerance* (Edinburgh: Edinburgh University Press, 1996), ch. 3.

[11] See Zbigniew Brzezinski, 'Post-Communist Nationalism', *Foreign Affairs* (Winter 1989–90), 1–25; John Mearsheimer, 'Back to the Future: Instability in Europe after the Cold War', *International Security*, 15: 1 (Summer 1990), 5–56.

[12] Tom Gallagher, 'A Feeble Embrace: Romania's Engagement with Democracy, 1989–94', *Journal of Communist Studies and Transition Politics*, 12: 2 (June 1994), 145.

[13] Holly Carter, *Since the Revolution: Human Rights in Romania* (New York: Human Rights Watch, 1991), 59–60; see also Nestor Ratesh, *The Entangled Revolution* (London: Praeger, 1991), 149–50.

The Front's denial of state assets to a fragmented opposition made its victory a runaway one. But Iliescu was genuinely popular on account of relaxing the savage austerity of the Ceaușescu era and collectivized villagers, elderly citizens, and heavy industrial workers, all with reason to feel insecure about the future, found noisy electoral competition unsettling and were more comfortable with socialist paternalism.[14]

Little noticed as Western governments averted their gaze from Romania was the voluntary help provided by thousands of ordinary citizens and trained professional people from across Western Europe who were moved by the television footage from Romania at the end of 1989 to seek to help rebuild that shattered society. Such efforts reveal the existence of an international civil society capable of surmounting political and geographical barriers often more effectively than powerful and well-financed governmental and multilateral organizations.[15] Private assistance meant to offer relief from the multiple hardships millions of Romanians were facing was soon followed by attempts to promote democracy and free institutions from private foundations, not least the Open Society Foundation, which was the brainchild of millionaire George Soros. These non-governmental initiatives are often ignored when drawing up a balance-sheet of external intervention in post-communist states, but there is no shortage of evidence to suggest that in Romania they may have been crucial in sustaining democratic values in the first half of the 1990s.[16]

NGOs played an active role in promoting free media, in monitoring local elections and then presidential and parliamentary elections in 1992, and in encouraging the government to show greater respect for human rights. The Iliescu regime was susceptible to international pressure in these areas. It felt it could give ground without undermining the basis of its rule. Indeed external monitoring of elections did not prevent widespread allegations of vote-rigging from domestic sources in the national polls of 1992.[17] As will be seen, it was far less happy about accepting advice from Western

[14] See Gallagher, *Romania after Ceausescu*, 101, 103.

[15] See Mary Kaldor, 'Cosmopolitanism v Nationalism: The New Divide?', in Richard Caplan and John Feffer (eds.), *Europe's New Nationalism: States and Minorities in Conflict* (Oxford: Oxford University Press, 1996).

[16] For the impact of democracy assistance both state-sponsored and private, see Thomas Carothers, *Assessing Democracy Assistance: The Case of Romania* (Washington: Carnegie Endowment for International Place, 1996).

[17] For a review of the evidence, see Henry F. Carey, 'Irregularities or Rigging: The 1992 Romanian Parliamentary Elections', *East European Quarterly*, 29: 1 (Mar. 1995), 43–66.

creditors concerning how to introduce market mechanisms into a state-led economy. Nor did the electoral arithmetic after 1992 when it was dependent on ultranationalist parties for its parliamentary majority allow it to respond positively to requests from the Council of Europe, the European Parliament, and the OSCE that it provide better safeguards for its ethnic minorities. Nor until Romania formally applied to join the EU in 1995 and NATO in 1996 was there external scrutiny of key state institutions and laws and the degree to which they were compatible with the standards required by these organizations. In the early 1990s the ruling FSN had been able to draw up a new Constitution and restructure on its own terms, or leave relatively unaltered, institutions such as the judiciary, the intelligence services, and the armed forces.[18]

Following the outbreak of warfare in ex-Yugoslavia, Romania began to be seen, rather unexpectedly, as an island of stability in the Balkan maelstrom. The restoration of Most Favoured Nation trading status by the US Congress in October 1992 was followed by the signing on 17 November of an association agreement with the EU, the first major diplomatic successes obtained by Romania since 1990. Statements by US officials in 1993–4 that the presence of extreme nationalists in the government was a Romanian affair seemed to confirm that Iliescu could pursue an idiosyncratic approach to democracy building without incurring severe penalties.[19] Of particular satisfaction was Romania's admission to the Council of Europe in October 1993. Membership was then seen as a gateway to wider European integration and Romania could claim that its human rights record was beyond serious reproach now that it could gain entry to such a prestigious body. But, soon afterwards, by admitting Croatia and Russia despite appalling human rights records, membership of the Council of Europe began to lose its lustre and ratings Romania received from human rights monitors such as Freedom House and the US government's Bureau of Democracy, Human Rights, and Labor would place it near the bottom of the European league until well into the 1990s.

---

[18] Unlike Bulgaria, the 1991 Constitution permitted parties based on ethnic criteria, such as the UDMR, the voice of the Hungarian minority. For years thereafter, Romanian ultranationalists, including members of Iliescu's party, sought to alter the constitution to ban the UDMR and it is unclear whether Iliescu was restrained by the adverse reaction likely to have occurred in the West if such a step was taken.

[19] *22* (Bucharest political weekly), (26 Oct. 1994). Such fears were reinforced by the interview US special envoy to South-East Europe Richard Schifter gave to the same journal in its 9 Nov. 1994 issue.

When, in 1995, the minimalist Western approach to the Bosnian conflict was replaced by NATO-led military intervention, the repercussions were not long being felt in Romania. Following the Dayton peace accord of November 1995, there was growing interest in the stability of the former communist states bordering ex-Yugoslavia, especially among US officials. The need to isolate nationalist hard-liners in Bosnia and promote moderate forces capable of arranging compromises across the various ethnic divides, was at the centre of the strategy identified with Richard Holbrooke, a former US assistant secretary of state. The architect of the Dayton accord realized that the success or failure of the initiative depended, in part, on efforts to delegitimize conflictual nationalism in SEE.[20] It is probably no coincidence that the criticism made by US Ambassador Alfred Moses on 22 February 1996 about the presence of ultranationalists in the Romanian government came not long after a visit to Bucharest by Holbrooke to discuss with Romanian officials the aims behind his Bosnia peace plan.[21]

With NATO prepared to include the former communist states of SEE inside a common European security umbrella provided they met a daunting range of civil and military conditions, far more attention began to be paid to the Romanian situation. US pressure contributed to a breakthrough in Romanian–Hungarian state relations in 1996 and the signing of a bilateral treaty between the two states on 14 September.[22] Iliescu was unable to exploit the treaty for electoral advantage. The tone of the messages of congratulation from Western leaders was noticeably cooler than the ones sent to Bucharest in 1997 as Romanian–Hungarian relations dramatically improved under a very different administration and it was not without significance that in October 1995 France had awarded the Legion d'Honneur to Corneliu Copusu, a veteran survivor of communist prisons who had stitched together an opposition electoral alliance which would shortly challenge Iliescu's hold on power.

In the November 1996 presidential and parliamentary elections, voters opted for a new president and for parties that were felt to have more credibility in Western capitals. The industrial workers

[20] *Unfinished Peace: Report of the International Commission on the Balkans* (New York: Aspen Institute/Carnegie, 1996) shows how the US-led Bosnian peace initiative increased the importance of states adjacent to ex-Yugoslavia in the eyes of Washington policy makers.

[21] *Adevarul* (26 Feb. 1996).

[22] For an analysis of the background to the bilateral agreement, see Tom Gallagher, 'Danube Detente: Romania's Reconciliation with Hungary after 1996', *Balkanologie*, 1: 2 (Dec. 1997), 88–94.

who had kept Iliescu in power since 1990 rejected him because his poorly institutionalized regime with a daunting record of incompetence was seen as jeopardizing their interests.[23] With 95 per cent of Romanians endorsing NATO entry, foreign policy issues played a not insignificant role in securing what amounted to a peaceful change of regime.[24] The choices Iliescu had been forced to make about the degree to which he was serious about integrating with the West undermined the cohesion of his regime and may have signalled to Romanians who took an interest in foreign affairs that the new times required new and untarnished people at the helm.

Thus despite Romanian events being a low priority for the West, external forces at different moments have played an influential role in strengthening weak democratic institutions and preventing a slide into post-communist autocracy. The strongly authoritarian instincts of the 1990–6 Iliescu regime were checked by the willingness of multilateral bodies like the EU and NATO to link financial and diplomatic backing with active respect for human and minority rights. Arguably, the victory of opposition reformers in the 1996 elections was enhanced by signs that the West was at last prepared to offer security guarantees to South-East Europe and envisage integrating countries making progress with democratization and economic reforms into pan-European institutions (though at a slower pace than Central European states).

Romanian Responses to the Outside World 1990–1996

Romania's perception of international events also influenced the progress of democratization after 1989. For a while, in 1990 the ruling FSN's attention was directed inwards as it sought to consolidate its authority in a society badly traumatized by an iron-fisted dictatorship and the violent nature of its demise. Little thought seems to have been given to how the West was likely to view the human rights abuses that occurred as the new regime took shape. The appointment as ambassadors to major Western capitals of Moscow-trained holdover from the communist era or else low-grade backers of the FSN, suggests that foreign relations were accorded

---

[23] Liliana Popescu, 'A Change of Power in Romania: The Results and Significance of the November 1996 elections', *Government and Opposition*, 32: 2 (Spring 1997), 172–86; see also *Evenimentul Zilei* (Bucharest daily paper) (5 Nov. 1996) for an analysis of voting shifts.

[24] See *22* (20–6 Mar. 1996); also Dan Ionescu, 'Hammering on NATO's Door', *Transition*, 2: 16 (9 Aug. 1996), 37.

a low priority.[25] Emil Constantinescu, the liberal academic who became head of state in 1996, vividly described the form of post-communism emerging in Romania and how inimical it was to core Western values:

We are not talking about classic communism . . . but rather of a form that is both old since it awakens latent nationalism and new because of its goal, which is to preserve all that can be preserved, both in men and structures, of the old regime: as many as possible of the large enterprises, as many monopolies as possible, especially in the areas of energy and agriculture, as many of the political and economic leaders as possible, and as much as possible of an isolationist and anti-Western mythology, ready to halt all openings towards Europe and the rest of the world.[26]

Perhaps Iliescu hoped that, as in the communist era, cosmetic changes would be sufficient to allow Western financial and diplomatic support to buttress his rule. In April 1991, when France's President Mitterand became the first Western leader to pay Iliescu an official visit, it suggested that such a devious strategy might indeed be worth pursuing. Evidence that Iliescu was still far from certain about whether to align with the West even in an opportunistic way was provided in the same month when Romania became the only former Moscow satellite to sign a comprehensive treaty with the Soviet Union. The April 1991 treaty of friendship gave Moscow an effective right of veto over any Romanian alliance with a Western country. If it had not been abrogated by the collapse of the Soviet Union six months later, it might have placed Romania more firmly in the Soviet sphere of influence than it had been before 1989; and thereafter, senior officials remained anxious to appease Russian sensibilities. In July 1993, General Dumitru Cioflina, the chief of the army, stated that Romania was not going to enjoy closer relations with NATO than the ones it already had with Russia.[27] While on a visit to Moscow in July 1995, Prime Minister Nicolae Vacaroiu declared that he was ready to realign the Romanian economy with Russia's because Western economic support had been so disappointing.[28]

Iliescu may have had reasons to keep relations with Moscow in good repair (such as access to cheap energy supplies) but isolation,

---

[25] The Bucharest daily *Adevarul* wrote on 22 Apr. 1998: 'in all the world's civilized countries, the best people are selected for diplomacy. Unfortunately, for us the Ministry of Foreign Affairs has become a sort of elephant's graveyard to which various political failures are sent, compromised individuals who need to be lost somewhere.'

[26] *Le Monde* (22 Feb. 1997).   [27] Ibid.

[28] *Lupta*, 249 (St-Cloud, France) (7 July 1996).

or alignment with an internally exhausted Russia, were not realistic objectives for post-communist Romania.[29] Besides, it is clear Iliescu hoped that Romania could benefit from Western economic and diplomatic support while being able to shape its own internal approach to democracy. Admission to European institutions, generous aid, official visits, and cordial interstate relations gradually became key goals. If accomplished, they could increase political stability and undermine opposition charges that Romania remained a pariah state under Ceauşescu's successors.

The first indication that Iliescu was not going to challenge Western interests as Slobodan Milosevic, the post-communist leader of Serbia was doing in 1991–3, came in the second half of 1990 during the Gulf Crisis. Romania held the presidency of the UN Security Council when Saddam Hussein invaded Kuwait and the necessity of her backing for the US-led action against Iraq was more important than it would normally have been.[30] It was extended willingly by Iliescu even though Romania lost up to $3 billion because of the embargo imposed on what had been one her most important trading partners.[31]

The UN embargo imposed on rump Yugoslavia (Serbia and Montenegro) in 1992 was even more damaging to the Romanian economy, leading to estimated losses of $7 billion as a result of the disruption of trade.[32] An admission in 1998 by Virgil Magureanu, the former head of the Romanian intelligence service that Romania had not wholly abided by the sanctions confirmed what a number of Western analysts had long suspected.[33] The decision to allow large supplies of oil to be shipped to Serbia came from President Iliescu himself, according to his top aide.[34] It was also to Serbia that Iliescu made his first official visit abroad in 1990 and Milošević was

---

[29] One of the milder charges made by his political and media critics was that the five years Iliescu spent as a student in Moscow in the 1950s left him with deeply ingrained communist habits which rendered him incapable of bringing Romania into the family of democratic nations. See Sorin Mircea Botez, 'An Alternative Romanian Foreign Policy', in Nelson, *Romania after Tyranny*, 267–8.

[30] Walter M. Bacon Jr., 'Security as Seen from Bucharest', ibid. 195.

[31] The Ministry of Foreign Affairs of Romania, *White Book on Romania and NATO, 1997* (Bucharest: Ministry of Foreign Affairs, 1997), ch. 7, 6.

[32] *Monitorul* (the news agency based in the Romanian city of Iasi) (18 Feb. 1998), http://www.nordest.ro/. Ministry of Foreign Affairs of Romania, *White Book on Romania and NATO, 1997*, ch. 3, 6.

[33] See Petru Mihai Bacanu, in *Romania libera* (then the leading Bucharest opposition daily) (10 Aug. 1995).

[34] *Monitorul* (11 Mar. 1998).

received in Bucharest in 1994 with all due ceremony when he was still widely seen as an international pariah.[35]

Attitudes to Moscow and Belgrade at specific moments showed how real was the temptation for some neo-communist backsliding. The Vacaroiu government's willingness to take Western credits but spend them for political purposes that were inimical to reform (resulting in the suspension of the IMF's agreement with Romania in late 1995) was probably the most daring example of bogus change. But Iliescu and his entourage lacked the vision and the energy to follow the maverick path and look for yet another indigenous solution to Romania's daunting handicaps in the economic sphere. They were essentially mediocre politicians looking for some sort of *modus vivendi* with the West in the hope they could still enjoy the autonomy to pursue a semi-authoritarian course in Romania.[36] This option became unrealistic as soon as Romania began to look seriously at integration into Euro-Atlantic security structures.

In January 1994, when NATO announced a cooperation programme with prospective new members called the Partnership for Peace, Romania was actually the first former Soviet bloc state to join. A process of reforming the Romanian military and bringing it closer to the model of armies in long-established democracies was established. Greater civilian control was asserted, several hundred hard-line nationalist officers were retired in 1995, and professional competence was given a higher priority than in other branches of the state. By early 1996 invitations had been extended to former Warsaw Pact states to join NATO and Romania applied in April of that year. The leading states in NATO seem to have concluded that SEE could not be left in a security vacuum after the war in the former Yugoslavia.

NATO made it clear that a candidate nation's chances of joining the Western military alliance depended on its performance in democratizing its society, reforming its economy, settling differences with adjacent states, and restructuring its military, in accordance with Western democratic standards. Romania's credentials for NATO membership were weaker than those of most other applicants. The country's political system, though pluralist, was displaying growing oligarchic tendencies. The transition from communism was proving painful and slow in the economic realm. Above all,

---

[35] Tom Gallagher, *Romania after Ceausescu*, 133–5.

[36] For their mediocrity, see Aurelian Craiutu, 'Light at the End of the Tunnel: Romania 1989–1998', in G. Pridham and T. Gallagher (eds.), *Experimenting with Democracy: Regime Change in the Balkans* (London: Routledge, 2000), 183.

the failure of bilateral treaty negotiations with Hungary and the Ukraine, and the delay in normalizing relations with Moldova, suggested to many NATO planners that Romania might be a consumer of security rather than a provider of it. Reviewing Iliescu's record, one local analyst concluded that 'the outcome of the disjunction between declaration and behaviour was the marginalization of Romania [and] the grave weakening of its international political position'.[37]

But Romania's gradual entry into a liberal international system limited his room to manœuvre. The external monitoring of human rights and governmental practices which he allowed meant the façade democracy that perhaps he would have been most comfortable with slowly gave way to a competitive system with enough genuine elements to secure his peaceful removal from office.

Dimensions of the Post-1996 Reform Push

In the euphoria of the moment, the unexpected transfer of power to the opposition alliance known as the Romanian Democratic Convention (CDR) following elections in November 1996 was hailed as a relaunch of the revolution stalled since 1990. But it was a repudiation of the incompetent Iliescu regime rather than a positive endorsement for the opposition. No blueprint for economic reform had been worked out in advance by the Christian Democrat and National Peasant Party (PNTCD), the dominant force in the victorious alliance and the only major party of pre-war vintage in the region to be restored to government in the 1990s. To form a viable government, the PNTCD swallowed its reservations and formed a coalition with the Democratic Party (PD) which had broken away from the Iliescu camp in 1992. It was a marriage of convenience between an ill-matched couple, inveterate anti-communists and reform-minded junior ex-communists. For such a coalition to honour its promise to relaunch a moribund economy and halt tumbling living standards, a culture of compromise would need to replace the partisanship which had disfigured Romanian politics since 1989.

In 1995 a rare degree of consensus had been exhibited by all the major parties when unanimous backing was given in parliament for Romania's application for EU entry. So popular was the desire to 'return to Europe' among the Romanian public that similar

---

[37] Gabriel Andreescu, 'Evaluare politicii externe romanesti', *Sfera Politicii*, 52 (1997).

endorsement was given to Romania's NATO bid even from extreme nationalist parties. Under President Constantinescu, a post-nationalist agenda of fence-mending with neighbours and reconciliation with minorities was emphasized. The new head of state argued that the chief threats to Romanian security were internal in origin rather than external, which was a fresh departure in Romanian politics.[38] He emphasized the moral danger and subversion of democratic values posed by corruption, the danger of the penetration of criminal organizations into the very heart of government; and the need to switch from a parasitic and exploitative capitalism to a growth-generating one which did not forget its responsibility for contributing to the public good.[39] In 1997 corrupt officials were removed from different branches of the state. But lack of enthusiasm for the anti-corruption drive from the courts and the prosecution service soon blunted its effectiveness. A cigarette smuggling scandal involving senior members of the president's military entourage in 1998 showed how hard it was for the president to rely on trusted personnel who shared his aim of creating a law-based state where there was equality for all before the courts.[40]

The president has important mediating powers rather than executive ones, so the brunt of the reform challenge was faced by the government headed by Victor Ciorbea. This upright and economically literate premier soon discovered how great was the shortage of loyal and competent officials willing to launch a shock therapy programme under which Romania implemented reforms that Central European states had dragged out over 7–8 years. An unholy alliance of anti-reform bureaucrats and managers of loss-making state firms was hard to dislodge even in the absence of its former political patrons. But popular enthusiasm about the ability of the state to protect the common good gave the Ciorbea government the breathing-space to challenge the sacred cow that the state must rule in the name of the ethnic majority alone. Ministers from the UDMR, the Hungarian minority party, were appointed to the new government, even though they were not essential for its survival. Proposed changes to the law gave Hungarians the right to be schooled in their own mother tongue at all levels of education, as well as the right to use their language in courts of law and the local administration. A cautious entente

[38] See *Le Monde* (22 Feb. 1997).
[39] For an analysis of how corruption is threatening democratization prospects in the Balkans as a whole, see James Pettifer, 'The Rise of the Kleftocracy', *The World Today* (Jan. 1997), 13–15.
[40] See *22* (5–11 May 1998).

with Hungary blossomed and what leaders from both states described as a strategic regional partnership began to emerge. Measures to strengthen bilateral economic and military cooperation were agreed in top-level visits.[41] Ciorbea openly stated in 1997 that he wished Romania to benefit from Hungarian investment and its greater experience of market economics so as to help relaunch the Romanian economy.[42] The previous government had portrayed such investment as tantamount to the recolonization of the country.

The new post-nationalist agenda of interethnic and interstate cooperation rightly earned Romania numerous plaudits from world leaders as its relations with Hungary moved from being a subject of occasional international concern to a positive example for resolving a thorny ethnic problem. Notice was also taken of the breakthrough in relations with the Ukraine that includes territory lost by Romania to the Soviet Union in 1940. A bilateral treaty on 2 June 1997 recognized that the borders between the two states were 'inviolable' and paved the way for practical measures of regional cooperation that will determine whether treaties with formerly suspicious neighbours are empty formulae or else augur a new era of partnership.[43] Progress in regularizing ties with Russia was much slower. No longer did Russia share a land frontier with Romania, but Russia was helping to shore up the self-styled breakaway Republic of Transnistria on the right bank of the river Dniester which, with the support of the Russian 14th Army, had refused to become part of the new state of Moldova that had declared independence from Moscow in 1991. With Moldova negotiations were long in train for a bilateral treaty. Bucharest wished for a document that 'contains nuances demonstrating the special nature of relations between the two states', their historic affinities based on common language and the fact that historically the territory comprising the state of Moldova is viewed by most Romanians as part of their traditional homeland, while the Chisinau authorities preferred the classic form of treaty between two sovereign states.[44] The signing of a bilateral treaty with Russia, scheduled for 27 April 1996, was postponed at the last minute by the Iliescu government owing to a storm of protest raised by the then

---

[41] For a description of the progress made, see Gallagher, 'Danube Detente', 98–100.

[42] See *Monitorul* (12 Mar. 1997), http://www.nordest.ro/.

[43] Reuters report 'Romanian-Ukrainian Leaders Hail Political Pact', carried by *Central Europe On-Line*, Prague (3 June 1997), http://www.centraleurope.com/.

[44] The quoted remarks are from a press briefing given by Foreign Minister Andrei Plesu on 17 Mar. 1998, see *Adevarul* (18 Mar. 1998).

opposition at the fact that condemnation of the 1939 Molotov-Ribbentrop pact (paving the way for the Soviet annexation of the Romanian province of Bessarabia in 1940) was not in the main treaty, but placed in a separate annexe.[45]

Romania's image as a stabilizing force in a disorderly Balkan neighbourhood won it high-level support in NATO, especially from Latin members with France in the vanguard. But it was not enough to overcome scepticism about Romania's abilities to cure its economic ills and not be a financial drain on the organization. Lingering doubts also remained that Romania would be a consumer rather than a provider of security. The rebuff delivered after the NATO summit in Madrid on 12 July 1997 had no adverse effects on public opinion and did not generate the nationalist backlash feared in some quarters. An opinion poll in late May showed that 29 per cent of voters blamed Iliescu's PDSR for any failure of Romania's NATO bid compared with 16 per cent holding the Ciorbea government responsible.[46] There was little noticeable public anger that Hungary had been selected and Romania spurned. Nor had there been a public outcry over the government's liberal minority policy, because it was widely seen as helping to end Romania's international isolation. The Romanian electorate showed patience and even maturity though it was hard not to disguise the fact that the government was using a foreign policy goal symbolizing 'the return to Europe' to extract more moral sacrifices from a hard-pressed population.[47]

But the government parties were unable to promote a culture of cooperation that would enable the coalition to survive in difficult times. Disputes over patronage between the PNTCD and the PD meant that reform plans hastily worked out in the winter of 1996–7 were never really implemented. Government came to a standstill in the first quarter of 1998 as the PD refused to support the budget

[45] Telegrama Daily News service, Chico California (1 May 1996), http://www.infocom@fsc.eunet.ro.

[46] The poll was carried out by the Romanian Institute for Public Opinion Surveys (IRSOP) and details were carried in *Evenimentul Zilei*, English On-Line Edition (14 June 1997).

[47] A poll carried out by the Centre for Urban and Rural Sociology between 16 and 24 Aug. 1977 posed the question 'how long can your family put up with the current reform programme?': 23% responded one year, 24% said between three and five years, 21% said around five years. These figures suggested that the fatalistic and short-term attitudes to be found in underdeveloped states of simply living from day to day and not having broad horizons are absent from a large segment of the Romanian population. Full results of the poll were carried in *Monitorul* (3 Sept. 1997) on http://www.nordest.ro/.

or other important bills until the PNTCD replaced Ciorbea with a more acceptable premier. Infighting among the ruling centre parties at a time of mass social hardship benefited the ugly nationalist fringe of Romanian politics whose poll ratings rose in 1997–8.

The widespread verdict of the sixteen-month Ciorbea government was that it had been in office but not in power. The power of the managers of state firms remained as strong as ever as did the capacity of these loss-making operations to swallow up huge amounts of public funds. While price controls had been lifted in 1997 and the currency freed, there had been minimal progress in restructuring the unproductive state-led economy. The failure of the Ciorbea government to match rhetoric with action had a demoralizing effect at home and eroded foreign confidence in the ability of Romania to throw aside a totalitarian legacy and catch up with its neighbours.

International Perspectives on Romanian Reform 1996–2000

South-East Europe was already a growing security concern for the West thanks to the Bosnia crisis when the dramatic results of the 1996 Romanian election occurred. The outcome suggested that there were parts of the Balkans where democracy could sink native roots in unpromising conditions. In a few months Romania went from being 'a no hope' outsider for NATO entry to being a serious contender. However irresolute he might sometimes have been in domestic politics, President Constantinescu soon acquired the reputation of being one of the most eloquent champions of reform to have emerged in EE since 1989. By contrast with his predecessor who had received few invitations to prestigious Western states, Constantinescu was soon enjoying a high profile in the West. There was no shortage of commentators ready to pronounce that Romanian political life was beginning to outgrow the Balkan stereotypes dominated by images of partisanship, collectivist values, and nationalism. On several occasions in 1997, US president Clinton expressed his admiration for the Romanian–Hungarian entente, claiming that it was a model for resolving intractable interethnic disputes.[48]

---

[48] Speaking at The Hague on 28 May 1997 on the fiftieth anniversary of the Marshall Plan's launch, Clinton singled out Romania as a country 'where democracy has prevailed over intolerance'. See *Lupta*, 288 (7 June 1997), 2.

Public statements emanating from NATO in 1996–7 indicated that it was efforts to bring the Romanian military into line with the armed forces capability of member states that most impressed NATO planners. In promoting its case for first-wave entry, Bucharest described the Romanian military as a stabilizing force both internally and in the regional context. There was no praetorian tradition in Romania, the armed forces had not been integrated into the Warsaw Pact (although Romania was a member), and 80 per cent of military equipment was produced at home.[49] The Foreign Ministry's White Book on Romania and NATO emphasized that:

Defence policy is made by civilian authorities. The military do not decide what are the national security risks, nor do they make the decisions on the ways and means to counteract them. Under the current legislation, the Armed Forces cannot impose their point of view with regard to any particular problem of interest to the society as a whole.[50]

In 1998 the military's image was tarnished owing to the involvement of senior elements in corruption and to the determination of top commanders to secure an amnesty for officers who had given the orders to fire on unarmed civilians in December 1989.[51] These events suggested that there was still a long way to go before the malign influence of the Ceauşescu era could be eradicated from the armed forces. But of greater concern to the West was the existence of no less than nine intelligence services that at different times have enjoyed considerable freedom of action from their nominal political masters.[52] Iliescu had created parallel structures in this sphere as in the domain of law enforcement in order to prevent his authority being challenged.[53] The existence of state bodies with near identical functions that often sought to neutralize each other's effectiveness impeded the efforts of reformers to dismantle the communist legacy in many areas of state activity.[54] At least the Romanian Information Service (SRI), the chief domestic intelligence service

[49] *EIU Co report, 2nd Quarter 1997* (London: Economist Intelligence Unit), 2.

[50] *White Book*, ch. 5, 9.

[51] The most reliable coverage of a multimillion cigarette smuggling racket involving officers guarding the president was provided in the Bucharest weekly *22* from 21 Apr. to 19 May 1998; for the amnesty bid, see H. R. Patapievici writing in *22* (28 Apr.–3 May 1998).

[52] For a description of these services, see *Monitorul* (5 June 1998), http://www.nordest.ro/.

[53] One source commented in 1997 that '[t]he current tendency in Romania, probably a legacy from the past, is to impose counter-checking powers for everything and at all levels'. See *Democracy in Romania* (Stockholm: Institute for Democracy and Electoral Assistance, 1997), 116.

[54] See Mungiu-Pippidi, *Reforma Sistemului Politic Romanesc*, 10–11.

and successor to the Securitate (in some eyes the chief power in the land before Ceauşescu's overthrow) had undergone a process of reform.[55] But the SRI's capacity to distort or even derail the democratization process was still regarded as considerable. In January 1999, following the narrow failure of an uprising by miners from the Jiu Valley protesting against IMF-backed plans to trim their industry, a rueful president admitted that he had learnt far more about what was happening from the media than from the intelligence services.[56]

Virgil Magureanu, who remained in charge of the SRI until April 1997, was one of the chief architects of the 1990–6 Iliescu regime and had been heavily implicated in the coup that toppled Ceauşescu.[57] His resignation as head of SRI in that month was widely seen as an attempt to assuage fears in the Western intelligence community about including as a NATO member a state where the security services had, until recently, played an omnipotent role in national affairs.[58]

Overlapping authority, poor management, and inability to define priorities were aspects of the Romanian administrative culture that left negative impressions on external officials vetting Romanian credentials for Euro-Atlantic integration.[59] The gap between the government announcing a decision and its actual implementation is greater in Romania than in many other countries. Western creditors, represented by the International Monetary Fund and the World Bank, grew increasingly exasperated during the death agonies of the Ciorbea government about the incapacity of the ruling parties to renounce politicking in order to pass a budget, never mind tackle structural reform. In May 1998 the World Bank suspended an accord designed to achieve the latter aim. Shortly beforehand, its Bucharest representative, Francois Ettori had warned that the marathon crisis had 'opened up a widening gap

---

[55] See the interview with the new director Costin Georgescu in *22* (21–7 Apr. 1998).

[56] *Evenimentul Zilei*, English Online edition (30–1 Jan. 1999).

[57] For the above information about Magureanu, see Dennis Deletant, *Ceausescu and the Securitate* (London: Hurst 1995), 398.

[58] Jonathan Eyal, director of studies at the Royal United Services Institute in London and political counsellor to King Michael I, argued that the intelligence services in Romania were probably much less infiltrated by the Soviet secret service or its successor than was the case in Hungary, the Czech Republic, or even Poland. See Jonathan Eyal, 'Eu nu cred in un guvern de tehnocrati', *22*, Bucharest (13–19 Jan. 1998).

[59] See the criticisms outlined by the NGO which published *Democracy in Romania, Institute for Democracy and Electoral Assistance* (Stockholm: 1997), esp. at xxviii–xxix. See also Eyal, 'Eu nu cred in un guvern de tehnocrati'.

between Romania and other countries of Eastern Europe . . . Also threatened were Romania's chances of entering the European Union along with other countries.'[60]

In July 1997 the European Commission had recommended that Romania, along with five other states, be left out of the accession process getting underway at the end of the year because they appeared to be far from meeting the criteria from EU entry, something Premier Ciorbea admitted himself.[61] The economic gap not only between Romania and EU states but between Romania and successful EU aspirants from Eastern Europe such as Poland and Hungary was immense. The volume of foreign investment per head of population in Romania between 1989 and 1996 and the volume of exports per head from Romania in 1996 were both lower than for all other former communist states in Eastern Europe.[62] But in December 1997 the gloom was lifted somewhat at the Luxembourg summit of EU heads of government, when it was decided to extend simultaneous invitations to all eleven aspirant members, but to proceed at a slow pace with countries like Romania which clearly fell far short of entry requirements. Further encouragement for Romania was offered in March 1998 when the EU decided that the pre-accession states least prepared for entry would receive a disproportionately large share of funds from the EU so as to catch up with the fast-track candidates.[63] In the year 2000 Romania was due to receive 650 million Euro to help it meet EU standards on a wide range of indicators.

In October 1999 Gunter Verheugen, the EU Commissioner for Enlargement, obtained the agreement of the Romanian government (headed by Radu Vasile since April 1998) that the EU would play an active role in supervising the formulation and implementation of the country's medium-term economic strategy between 2000 and 2004. Inevitably, Romanian sovereignty is infringed under such an arrangement. But the government had come to recognize that its failure to reach key policy targets vital in order to keep alive its EU integration hopes (not least the restructuring of loss-making state industries) stemmed from the post-communist state's limited administrative capacity.

In December 1999 EU pressure resulted in the passage of a law meant to depoliticize the top bands of the civil service, improve

[60] *22* (14–20 Apr. 1998), 1.

[61] *Evenimentul Zilei*, English Online edition (17 July 1997).

[62] Dennis Deletant et al., 'An Analysis of Negotiations for Romanian Membership of the EU', unpublished manuscript (London: 1997), 6.

[63] *Adevarul* (13 Mar. 1998).

coordination between ministries, and regularize appointment procedures. Instilling a public service ethos in a bureaucracy with Romania's legacy of misrule will not happen overnight, but such a law may encourage competent and motivated officials to stay in the public service rather than move to the better-paid private sector.

At the Helsinki summit in the same month, the EU formally invited Romania to take part in talks for full membership. Romano Prodi, the EU Commission president was hopeful that Romania's application was bound to succeed when he was in Bucharest in January 2000 for talks with the new Romanian premier Mugur Isarescu, the former state bank governor at the head of the same four-party coalition in office since 1996.

Romania's bid to join NATO has failed to generate the momentum of its EU application despite President Clinton declaring on a visit to Bucharest on 11 July 1997, after the Madrid summit, that 'the door to NATO is open, will stay open, and we will help you pass through it'.[64] If nothing else, this visit showed that Washington felt it important to provide top-level support to Romania's reformers, perhaps out of a belief that their success could have a stabilizing influence in South-Eastern Europe as a whole.[65] But Romanians took most comfort from the official NATO statement issued at the end of the Madrid summit, negotiated between Secretary of State Madeleine Albright and her French counterpart Hubert Vedrine which in diplomatic language mentioned that Romania was at the forefront of countries due to join NATO in a second wave of expansion.[66] However, the attention span of the West towards the problems of South-East Europe has always been limited unless unrest threatens the security of the wider European theatre.

Kosovo: A Catalyst?

The 1998–9 Kosovo crisis, culminating in NATO's military campaign against Serbia that began on 24 March 1999 transformed Romania from a Balkan backwater to a 'front-line state'. NATO required

[64] *Monitorul*, English Online edition (12 July 1997).

[65] In mid-June 1997, Clinton had written to his Romanian counterpart inviting him to the White House and promising to support Romania in progress towards 'integration in the near future in the community of the western nations and institutions'. Constantinescu turned down the invitation, realizing that it might not go down well and that a mildly nationalist attitude was more in tune with public opinion. See *Monitorul*, English Online edition (19 June 1997).

[66] See Bogdan Chireac, 'Contractul cu America', *Adevarul* (19 Mar. 1998).

military facilities from Romania as well as Bulgaria in its drive to force Slobodan Milosevic to give meaningful autonomy to the Albanian majority in Kosovo and to halt ethnic cleansing. The strategic importance of Romania increased as an aerial war got underway and plans for a ground invasion of Kosovo were hastily drawn up. The importance of the South-East European flank to NATO's security, something that most NATO planners had underestimated, seemed vindicated by the Kosovo war.

On 22 April the Romanian parliament approved NATO's demand for an unlimited use of Romanian airspace. On 18 April Romania had denied Russia use of its airspace to fly humanitarian aid to Belgrade. When it came to choosing between religious and historical ties with Serbia and persisting, in dangerous circumstances, with a pro-Western foreign policy that hitherto had enjoyed massive popular backing, the Romanian government quickly concluded that it had no alternative but to align with NATO.

The pro-NATO stance of a previously fractured government was impressive, especially in light of the fact that public opinion, under the influence of a nationalist media, was turning against NATO. The government was encouraged by a string of declarations, such as that of President Clinton on 12 April that the West 'should try to do for Southeastern Europe what we helped to do for western Europe after World War II and for Central Europe after the Cold War'.[67]

On 10 June 1999 the German foreign minister Joschka Fischer formally launched a stabilization plan for the Balkans that involved the EU being the main source of funds for a project designed to prevent future conflict and integrate the region with the rest of Europe. But Romania was disappointed when Fischer, on a visit to Bucharest on 8 July, said that the Stability Pact should not be understood as a means of granting material and financial rewards for economic losses, its aim being to promote 'economic development opportunities in the region on a long-term basis'.[68] German caution contrasted with the declaration of US Secretary of State Madeleine Albright on 10 June that 'Europe has to pay for the reconstruction of the Balkans', the US having assumed much of the military burden.[69]

---

[67] Tom Gallagher, 'Romania: Is the West Watching?', *International Herald Tribune* (23 July 1999).

[68] *Nine O'Clock* (9–11 July 1999).

[69] Tom Gallagher, 'The West and the Challenge to Ethnic Politics in Romania', *Security Dialogue*, 30: 3 (Sept. 1999), 302.

When the fiftieth anniversary NATO summit passed in April 1999 with no progress in Romania's application, President Constantinescu complained that 'an admission date [to NATO] some time before 2002 is an unjust and faraway prospect for our countries which have assumed the same risks as other NATO countries'.[70] The liberal president's patience seemed to snap when he declared on 13 July that 'Every day personalities from NATO and the EU come to Bucharest and tell us that during the conflict we behaved like member states of NATO. But nobody offers us security guarantees or speaks about recovering our losses in respect of the embargo [on trade with Yugoslavia] . . . While we are patted on the back and congratulated, our losses mount day by day.'[71]

Romania was left with two concrete assurances from NATO delivered presumably because of its highly supportive stance in the Kosovo crisis. During the conflict, high-level support for its EU membership bid emanated from Britain and Germany, hitherto unenthusiastic about the prospect of Romanian entry.[72] Romania (along with other multiethnic states in the region) was also promised that no change of boundaries was planned in Yugoslavia as part of an eventual peace settlement, a reassurance designed to dampen the claims of nationalists who were arguing that Kosovo offered a precedent which might lead to the detachment of Transylvania from Romania.[73]

During the Kosovo crisis while Romania found itself courted by Western powers, it also watched as NATO went to elaborate lengths to mollify the Russian authorities in order to obtain at least their reluctant acquiescence for its actions in Kosovo. Despite statements from Blair, Prodi, and Albright identifying Romania with the Western family of nations, fears remained that Western countries might do a deal with Russia which would place a country like Romania in the Russian sphere of influence in return for NATO expansion elsewhere. In 1994, Ion Mircea Pascu, shortly to become deputy defence minister, actually expressed the view that Germany and Russia had reached a secret understanding to that effect in the early 1990s.[74] In 1997 Russia was increasingly

---

[70] *South-East Europe Newsline*, Radio Free Europe (27 Apr. 1999).

[71] *Adevarul* (14 July 1999).

[72] Tony Blair promised active British backing for Romania's EU bid when he addressed the Romanian parliament on 4 May 1999. See *Ziua*, Bucharest daily paper (5 May 1999), http://ziua.ro.

[73] Tom Gallagher, 'Romania, NATO, and Kosovo: Right Instincts, Wrong Tactics?', *Politica Externa*, 3: 7–8 (Autumn–Winter 1999–2000), 92.

[74] Emil Hurezeanu, 'Rusia in Balcani', *22* (9–15 Aug. 1995).

adamant, through the pronouncements of its then foreign minister, Evgheni Primakov, that 'the extension of NATO has already reached its maximum point and that the interests of European stability require a stop to be imposed in the process'.[75] At the same time, Moscow reportedly offered Romania security guarantees and economic incentives in return for abandoning its bid to join NATO.[76]

More than in most former communist states, the success of the democratic transition in Romania depends on the supportive external environment. Poorly institutionalized parties lacking clear-cut ideologies or governing programmes, authoritarian power-structures, the weakness of civil society, and declining living and health standards, do not offer a propitious domestic environment. Without clearly focused and long-term Western help, the prospects of success for what is an audacious experiment in fostering pluralism in a society ravaged by totalitarianism (after fifty years of relatively democratic rule) are slim. Indeed as the range and scale of Romania's problems became evident after 1996 along with the incapacity of domestic reformers to deal adequately with them, constructive outside engagement began to appear a *sine qua non* in order to sustain a feeble reform process, particularly in the economic sphere.

It is unclear what will be the long-term fate of a developmental strategy for Romania partly crafted and supervised by the EU, especially if the PDSR (well ahead in the polls since 1999) returns to power in elections due at the end of 2000. Previously, the issue of decriminalizing homosexuality was the one that produced the most frequent interventions from elected officials in the European Parliament and the Council of Europe.[77] But the government was unable to persuade its own parliament that liberal European values were superior to conservative ones, as championed by the Orthodox Church, the main opponent of law reform in this area.

Indignation has long been expressed in the Bucharest press that the West has imposed strict conditions on the treatment of a range of minorities while itself continuing to discriminate against Romania as a whole.[78] Romania's inclusion in a EU blockade of

[75] Primakov made this comment while on a visit to Finland in June 1998. See *Adevarul* (4 June 1998).

[76] *Adevarul* (26 Mar. 1998).

[77] 'Romania Hopes to Scrap Anti-Gay Laws', *Central Europe Online* (21 May 1998), http://www.centraleurope.com/.

[78] The nearest thing to a daily paper of record in Romania, *Adevarul*, has made this a favourite topic in editorials too numerous to mention, mostly written by Cristian Tudor Popescu and Bogdan Chirieac.

countries for which strict visa requirements need to be met has become a *cause célèbre*. It makes obtaining a visa to travel to EU states extremely difficult for most Romanians and it was only in early 2000 that the EU signalled its willingness to take Romania off the list of European countries from whom visas are required. Many Romanians contrast the fact that tariff barriers have been lowered (in line with Romania's EU agreement), allowing West European goods to flood the country, thus jeopardizing local agriculture and industry) while Romanian citizens are effectively blockaded from travelling westwards.[79]

In the EU, fear of unwelcome immigrants from countries like Romania and Bulgaria (with the mobile Roma minority at the top of the list) outweighs concern that nations involuntarily severed from the rest of Europe during the Cold War, still lack easy access to the West. When President Constantinescu raised the issue of visas on a visit to Germany in March 1998, he got an unavailing response from his hosts. Indeed, it appears that to justify their approach, the Bonn authorities leaked to the press the results of an investigation that accused staff in the Romanian embassy of accepting bribes from suspected Romanian criminals in return for granting forged visas.[80]

There was general goodwill for Romania after it ditched rulers widely seen as neo-communist in 1996. But the degree of attention has been uneven and optimism in the West about its potential for switching to the fast-track of economic and institutional reform was soon dashed by the political turbulence of 1998. Only countries with cultural links to Romania have shown a real interest in its fate. France, and to a lesser degree the other South European states are the main examples.[81] Despite being the EU state with the biggest interest in stabilizing the former communist states to its east, Germany, under Chancellor Helmut Kohl, made it clear to Romania that progress with its NATO and EU bids largely depended on its own efforts to speed up reform at home.[82] Accordingly, hopes that Germany's ruling Christian Democrats might warm to the

---

[79] *Evenimentul Zilei*, English Online edition (6 June 1998), http://www.expres.ro/.

[80] *Romania, Country Report, 2nd Quarter 1998* (London: Economist Intelligence Unit, 1998), 15.

[81] At the summit of G-8 nations in June 1997, Italy's premier Romano Prodi declared that Romania and Slovenia needed to be included to strengthen stability in South-East Europe. When it was clear that his words were falling on deaf ears in Washington, he declared 'this is a big mistake Mr President [Clinton]'. *Monitorul* (24 June 1997).

[82] *Adevarul* (6 November 1997).

Romanian cause because Christian Democrats were the majority force in Romania's ruling coalition proved illusory.

The United States lacks the organic links with Romania that large émigré communities provide. Romania may have become a greater priority for Britain as a result of the Kosovo crisis, but it is unclear how long this will last. Russia still regards Romania as its backyard despite no longer sharing a land-frontier with the Danubian state, a cause of real, and perhaps not unjustified, apprehension in Bucharest.

Policy Drift Encourages Nationalism

Lack of progress with foreign policy goals seen as crucial for strengthening democracy has seen the return of a quasi-nationalist discourse even from the pro-Western government. In May 1998, the new prime minister, Radu Vasile proclaimed that the new budget was '100% Romanian', having observed that his predecessor might well have been called 'IMF', given the leverage the latter had enjoyed over economic policy in 1997.[83] In June 1998, Vasile seemed to reject the president's thesis that the major threat to Romania came from its internal debility not from external threats when he predicted that foreign intelligence agencies interested in destabilizing Romania were likely to intensify their activities in the period before NATO's April 1999 summit.[84] It came as no surprise for some that when ejected from the premiership and expelled from the PNTCD at the end of 1999 Vasile and his supporters looked for a new political home in a small ultranationalist party.

In an increasingly introspective atmosphere, much of the enthusiasm for Romanian–Hungarian détente also evaporated. Elements in both the PNTCD and the PD started to adopt intransigent attitudes towards the Hungarian minority as the need to appeal to a home audience took precedence over adhering to European norms on minority rights. Christian Tudor Popescu, the influential chief editor of *Adevarul*, was arguing in mid-June 1998 for the need to redefine Romanian politics by abandoning the obsession with Euro-Atlantic integration and concentrating on avoiding economic collapse, so as 'to avoid at any price the disintegration of the unitary Romanian state'.[85] An increasingly populist media (private television being to the fore) has influenced both

[83] *22* (19–25 May 1998).   [84] *Monitorul* (10 June 1998).
[85] *Adevarul* (11 June 1998).

public opinion and a political elite where clear-cut ideological differences are not always easy to discern. If a realignment of politics occurs in the wake of the defeat of the PNTCD-led attempt to mount fundamental reforms, the new nationalist discourse could prove appealing, especially if a new governing majority emerges from the left-centre of Romanian politics.

By 1998, disquiet was expressed at senior EU levels that laws designed to offer minority protection and which Romania had been told would be necessary if her applications to join the EU and NATO were to go forward, were unable to command a majority even among the parties which had signed up to a pro-Western prospectus on the defeat of Iliescu in 1996.[86] Thus it was no small achievement that the Hungarian UDMR remained inside the coalition as its term approached its end in 2,000, moderates being able to argue that enough progress had been made in securing minority rights to justify staying in.

The emphasis on trans-border cooperation with states from which Romania had previously held aloof receded in importance after a brief flurry of interest in Euro-regionalist concepts during 1997. Romania obstinately preferred to see itself as being 'in the immediate proximity of the Balkan peninsula', rather than a Balkan state *per se.*[87] At the first meeting ever convened of the heads of all South-East European states, held in Crete on 3–4 November 1997, Romania's unwillingness to be involved in a problematic geopolitical region was obvious. Greece's initiative for 'the institutionalisation of a permanent structure of Balkan co-operation' (one backed by Richard Holbrooke, the architect of the United State's proactive policy in the region since 1995) was rejected by Romania.[88]

A fragmented political elite in Romania sees European integration as necessary for national recovery (and perhaps even survival), but there are deep reservations about renouncing the nationalist complexes that the founders of the European integration project challenged in the 1940s and 1950s. Since 1995 whenever prospects for integration with European institutions has faltered, so has Romanian enthusiasm for a post-nationalist agenda. It is no

---

[86] See Cristiana Terenche, 'Nedumerire si neliniste la Bruxelles', *Romania libera* (21 Mar. 1998).

[87] This was first proposed by Teodor Melescanu, foreign minister from 1992 to 1996. See Sorin Matei, 'Romania nu va fi primiti in primul val in NATO', http://www.geocities.com/CapitolHill/3763, artn.3.html.

[88] *Adevarul* (5 Nov. 1997), in the lapidary words of Premier Ciorbea: 'new forms of co-operation merit close analysis, and a clash must be avoided with other forms of co-operation'.

coincidence that Romania seemed to discard its anti-Hungarian complex in the first half of 1997 when it looked like having a real chance
of being invited to join NATO at the July Madrid summit. There
were cordial top-level bilateral meetings, declaration of a strategic
partnership between Romania and Hungary, and laws were drawn
up in Bucharest to give the Hungarians some of the cultural and
linguistic rights they had long been demanding. But when Romanian expectations were dashed, laws strengthening minority rights
failed in parliament despite the government's technical majority and
the Hungarian party found itself isolated inside the coalition.[89]

There is no sign of the culture shift which will allow new forms
of governance based on subsidiarity to replace the centralized
nation-state on the jacobin model which has not served Romania
very effectively in over a century of independence. Decentralization is a key part of the European integration process but legislation allowing sub-state poles of government to enjoy autonomy from
the centre has been slow to emerge. Nationalist mentalities based
on rigid defence of sovereignty and suspicion of neighbouring states
have considerable staying-power in Romania. Even though there
is abundant evidence that decentralization has been a key to the
political stability and economic success of former dictatorships like
Germany and Spain, these role models are unlikely to prove persuasive for much of the politico-administrative elite in Romania.

Conclusion

Romania has benefited far less from external efforts to promote
democracy than most other ex-Warsaw Pact states. Measures such
as US President George Bush's decision to annul Poland's large debt
to the USA have not been taken in Romania's case. Instead the
country's economy was further weakened by Western insistence
that Bucharest comply with tough sanctions against former close
trading partners Iraq and Yugoslavia in the early 1990s.

A more favourable attitude started to be shown towards
Romania by the West following the 1996 presidential victory of Emil
Constantinescu. He is unambiguously committed to Euro-Atlantic
integration and broad adherence to the same goal has been shown
by the unwieldy four-party coalition that provided three governments in the 1996–2000 period.

[89] Information in this section is derived from Tom Gallagher, 'Danube Detente',
102–5.

But it was only in the aftermath of the 1999 Kosovo conflict that the EU Commission and key state players in the EU and NATO showed a willingness to provide concentrated assistance to Romania which is required if it is to begin to bridge the gap between it and more favoured EE aspirants for EU entry. The EU commission's offer of a partnership with the government to jointly shape and implement an economic and administrative reform strategy, Commissioner Prodi's keenness to advance Romania's EU application, the large amount of PHARE aid donated to Romania in 2000, and the EU's stated intention to devote more time and energy to second-stream candidates like Romania than front-runners offers a striking contrast with previous Western attitudes.

But it remains to be seen how concentrated Western attention will prove to be, especially if the PDSR returns to office in forthcoming elections. EU Enlargement commissioner Verheugen warned in February 2000 that Romania would face the isolation being visited upon Austria's new right-wing coalition, if populists and nationalists entered government at the end of the year.

It is clear that Brussels now recognizes that the obstacles in the way of Romania shedding its politically authoritarian and economically collectivist past are of such a magnitude that a special approach is required towards it from the gatekeepers of Euro-Atlantic integration. An approach involving active external engagement on the ground in rebuilding public institutions and a competitive economy is being pursued in a country where a large part of the power structure is still attached to authoritarian and collectivist values in politics and economics.

Anti-reformers who might, for convenience, be described as 'nomenklatura nationalists' are stronger in Romania than in most other post-communist states. They demonstrated their ascendancy by blocking economic reform between 1989 and 1996. But their advance has been contained by the fact that the main proponent of authoritarian politics in the region remains Russia. Russia appears keen to involve Romania in a series of economic agreements that would make the Romanian economy depend on its cheap energy supplies in return for political compliance. This would suit the powerful lobby of managers in the state-led Romanian energy sector who are hostile to genuine reform. But for most Romanians Russia remains 'a pole of repulsion' owing to long-term Russian bids to stifle Romanian independence. So it is difficult for Romanian interests hostile to the Western democratic project to take measures which are seen as analogous to ones being promoted by 'red-brown' forces in Russia itself. (Similarly, the surprising weakness of

Russian-influenced organized crime in Romania can probably be ascribed to the fact that even for local criminal forces Russia remains an anti-model).

Pro-Western Romanians were relieved when the Russian elections at the end of 1999 resulted in a comprehensive defeat for the communists. But it remains to be seen if Vladimir Putin's nationalist bloc will prove to be less hostile to Romania's path of Euro-Atlantic integration than an unambiguously left-wing administration in Moscow.

Divided and demoralised reformers accepted the active assistance of multilateral organizations in order to draw up a strategy for economic recovery meant to prepare Romania for EU entry after 2007. But drawing closer to the West was unable to save them from electoral rejection at home. By 2000, most of the population, around 40% of which was facing absolute poverty, was no longer prepared to accept further economic misery in return for progress on foreign policy goals which previously had enjoyed overwhelming support. Stemming unemployment and poverty and dealing harshly with the corruption that was widely perceived to have got out of control took precedence over staying on good terms with NATO, the IMF or the EU. A nervous President Constantinescu abandoned a second-term bid rather than face the wrath of voters on the campaign trail. The PDSR obtained a near majority of seats in the 26 November election but it was the beneficiary of a negative vote rather than the repository of hopes that it would do better than the outgoing coalition. Far more unsettling was the remarkable success of the anti-western Greater Romania Party which reconciled the extremes of left and right. It mopped up many of the votes of the collapsed centre as well as the young, acquiring 25% of seats in parliament compared to a handful in 1996. Its fiercely anti-minority leader C.V. Tudor, formerly Ceauşescu's court poet, became the prime beneficiary of the rift between the main parties and society at large where the chief political players are often viewed as a separate caste ready to promote their group interests at the expense of most ordinary Romanians. The PRM is a haven for former and serving members of the security forces and has influential supporters in a string of government ministries. Unless the other parties behave in a more public-spirited way than they have done since 1989, nationalist mentalities will acquire an even stronger grip on the electorate than before, opening up the possibility of political isolation and renewed authoritarianism in Romania.

15

Bulgaria and Macedonia: Voluntary Dependence on External Actors

Kyril Drezov

During the Cold War, Bulgaria and Macedonia belonged to two strikingly different communist entities: Bulgaria was a loyal part of the Soviet bloc, while Macedonia was a constituent republic of the Yugoslav federation. For about forty years, the preservation of Yugoslav unity and independence in the face of Soviet pressure was a major Western concern. Yugoslavia, with Macedonia, was considered part of 'the Free World', while Bulgaria was viewed as belonging to 'the Other'. Yet, despite diverging Cold War histories, Sovietized Bulgaria and Yugoslav Macedonia shared deep-rooted common traditions that went back to the Ottoman and pre-Ottoman periods of their history. These similarities became more pronounced once Soviet and Yugoslav controls were lifted. Under the Ottomans, the contemporary territories of both countries were part of a single linguistic and ethnographic area, and, between 1870 and 1912, the religious and educational affairs of these territories were directed by a Bulgarian Exarchate based in Istanbul. As a result of these experiences, both countries remain intimately connected (and often divided) by common history, traditions, and language.[1] 'The Macedonian Question' was a charged emotional issue in pre-1944 Bulgarian politics, although it is very much a minority preoccupation at present (none of the major Bulgarian dailies has a permanent correspondent in Skopje, and news from Macedonia appears only episodically in the Bulgarian media). On the other hand, the Bulgarian factor (the so-called 'Macedonian B-complex'

---

[1] The official languages of Bulgaria and Macedonia use two very different alphabets and terminologies. On the other hand, the everyday speech and grammar used by Bulgarians and Macedonians is no more different than English is from American.

as coined by Gane Todorovski, a leading Macedonian poet and diplomat) plays a very powerful role in present-day Macedonian politics.[2] Every politician or prominent intellectual visiting Bulgaria is closely followed. The leaders of the main anti-communist party have been routinely described in the media as 'Bulgarophiles' and 'agents of Sofia'.[3]

Whatever their attitudes to one another, after the lifting of Soviet and Yugoslav controls, both Bulgaria and Macedonia showed themselves more susceptible to Western concerns than their post-communist neighbours. In early 1990, Bulgarian politics were characterized by round table talks and negotiated transition, while, at the same time, Romania, under Iliescu, resurrected one-party controls and harassed the opposition. In 1991–2, Macedonia managed to disengage itself peacefully from Yugoslavia, and the local Albanian leaders were brought into the government—at a time when Milosevic was repressing Kosovo Albanians and waging proxy wars in Croatia and Bosnia. Both Bulgaria and Macedonia had shown similar 'sensitivity' to external factors before 1989—when Bulgaria was far more enthusiastic in its aping of the Soviet Union than most of the other satellites, and Macedonia had the reputation of being unreservedly pro-Yugoslav, unlike Slovenia, Croatia, and even Serbia.

In this chapter, my main hypothesis is that historically both Bulgaria and Macedonia have tended to adapt to an externally determined environment by opting for self-limiting behaviour. The concept of 'self-limiting behaviour' (or 'voluntary dependence') describes a situation when a subordinate ruling elite chooses not to exercise all the opportunities for sovereign decision-making that exist in a given hegemonic system, and, in return, expects—and sometimes receives—special favours from the hegemonic power.[4] This

---

[2] Quoted from *Srbinovski M. Makedonskite avgievi shtali* (Skopje: 1995), 24.

[3] The use of language and translation has become caught up in this. In the last week of November 1997, a visit of Skopje poets to Sofia was called off, because translation was not provided for some of their poems in public recitals; in mid-October, President Gligorov was criticized for not using an interpreter when he met his Bulgarian counterpart: *Dnevnik* (14 Oct. 1997); on 20 Aug. 1997 *Nova Makedonija* published a letter signed by 'a group of citizens' who accused the 'fascist' leaders of IMRO-DPMNU of following 'directives from Sofia' and demanded that they be arrested, and their party banned.

[4] According to Dimitar Tsanov, 'Zhivkov's policy line was a balanced mix of Soviet pretensions and (Bulgarian) national interests, combined with a striving for economic prosperity'; see Smyanata: Kak i zashto se stigna do 10 noemvri, (Sofia: Universitetsko izdatelstvo, 1995), 16. In 1963, Zhivkov justified his policy of drawing closer to the Soviet Union in the following way: 'Romanian and Chinese

chapter endeavours to show that similar 'survival techniques' define the post-communist positioning of Bulgaria and Macedonia. An examination of the specific patterns of democratization in Bulgaria and Macedonia is followed by an analysis of the international factors that have been most influential in shaping events in both countries. The focus will be on two factors: the impact of the general international environment on Bulgaria and Macedonia, and the actions of external powers to influence events in these countries. The way in which these factors have impinged on specific domestic developments is explored through several case studies.

Democratization and International Influences

Bulgaria and Macedonia share some broad similarities that set them apart from other post-communist countries. Both transitions were peaceful and negotiated, but both were ultimately dominated by the former *nomenklatura*. Parties representing the biggest ethnic minorities were early and successfully co-opted into parliament and government. Both countries have often been described in the West as 'islands of stability' in a turbulent region. For most of the 1990s, both Bulgaria and Macedonia were happy to subordinate their national interests to Western strategic concerns. Yet, paradoxically, at the very same time, the elites and the populations of both countries have harboured feelings that they are being neglected and discriminated against by the West, particularly in comparison with Visegrad countries.

Democratization and consolidation

Bulgaria reached an important degree of democratic consolidation by late 1994—after indisputably free and fair parliamentary elections in 1991 and 1994 (and presidential elections in 1992), several peaceful transfers of power between governments of very different political orientation, and the rooting of the institutions envisaged in the June 1991 non-communist constitution (of these, particularly important were the independent judiciary and the Constitutional

comrades insist that sovereignty should be respected. For the common people, sovereignty means that they have enough to eat and to live. This is what sovereignty is all about—happiness and prosperity for the people. We work for the people, not for some abstract concept'; see *Materiali na plenuma na Tsentralniya Komitet na BKP ot 31 yuli 1963*, Sofia (quoted in *Narodna Kultura* (29 Dec. 1989), at 5).

Court).[5] The role of international factors, such as Gorbachev's perestroika, the demonstration effect of other Central European transitions, and Western monitoring of elections, was decisive at the beginning of Bulgaria's democratization. This externally driven process of Bulgaria's democratization shaped the identity of the major agent for change in Bulgaria—the Union of Democratic Forces founded on 7 December 1989. 'Democracy' became the buzzword of the Bulgarian transition. Concerns about 'the nation' and 'the market' remained strictly subordinate to it. The role of international factors in Bulgaria's democratization rapidly declined after the adoption of a new constitution in July 1991, and the victory of the anti-communist Union of Democratic Forces in the October 1991 parliamentary elections. After these events, the consolidation of Bulgarian democracy has been largely internally driven.

In contrast to Bulgaria, external factors played a more limited role in the early phases of Macedonia's transition. Soviet perestroika was barely known, and in any case, considered largely irrelevant to the seemingly more liberal Yugoslav setting. However, in the 1980s, the Macedonian public was barely touched by the liberalization experienced in some other parts of Yugoslavia. The creeping disintegration of Yugoslavia in 1990–1 brought forth concerns about Macedonian statehood and nationhood. These concerns shaped the identity of the major agent for change in Macedonia, the Internal Macedonian Revolutionary Organization-Democratic Party for Macedonian National Unity founded on 17 June 1990 (by including the acronym IMRO, this party consciously sought to establish continuity with a succession of 'national-revolutionary' organizations

---

[5] In desribing the consolidation process in Bulgaria, I follow Parrot's understanding that 'consolidation denotes the condition of a political system in which all major political actors and social groups expect that government leaders will be chosen through competitive elections and regard representative institutions and procedures as their main channel for pressing claims on the state,' in 'Perspectives on Post-communist Democratization', in Karen Dawisha and Bruce Parrott (eds.), *Democratic Changes and Authoritarian Reactions in Russia, Ukraine, Belarus and Moldova* (Cambridge: Cambridge University Press, 1997), 6. One of the unfortunate consequences of relying on terms developed to explain very different transitions—from the Latin and Mediterranean countries—is the neglect of possible intrinsic linkages between the political and economic transformations in former communist countries. Unlike authoritarian or fascist/Nazi systems, communism was based on a fundamental reshaping of the polity and economy as part of a single, ideologically driven process. Consequently, to declare 'democracy' in a post-communist country, consolidated on the basis of only political criteria—as is the current consensus among political scientists—can be thoroughly misleading. If a 'self-sustained capitalist economy' is added to the usual political criteria, then not a single post-communist country has even remotely approached democratic consolidation.

under the same name that had existed before the communist takeover). State building and nation building became the main concerns of the Macedonian transition, with 'democracy' being strictly secondary to these. In contrast to Bulgaria, between 1992 and 1996 Macedonia experienced a cumulative reversal in its democratization process. Between November 1992 and October 1994, the largest party in parliament (the anti-communist IMRO-DPMNU) was excluded from government, and marginalized in parliament. Moreover, after the partly rigged, and partly boycotted, elections of 1994, all opposition forces were effectively excluded from Parliament and marginalized in a Macedonian society tightly controlled by a 'party of power' with roots in the former *nomenklatura*. International factors, in the shape of the preventive deployment of United Nations troops and the active involvement of the USA since 1993, played a key role in buttressing the Macedonian state and nation. But international actors generally allowed concerns for Macedonia's stability to triumph over concerns for the quality of Macedonia's democracy, as exemplified in Western monitoring of the 1994 parliamentary and presidential elections. After February 1996 Macedonia started to move again in a more pluralist direction, but it has remained far from accomplishing a democratic transition, let alone consolidation. Free and fair parliamentary elections in the autumn of 1998—which marked a major change by bringing to power a mostly anti-communist government—were followed by more dubious presidential elections one year later. Similar to the practice in 1994, the 1999 presidential elections were rubber-stamped by Western monitors more concerned about stability than democracy—only this time the beneficiary was the anti-communist IMRO-DPMNU.

State and nation building

Bulgaria and Macedonia are at very different stages in state- and nation-building terms. For all its dependence within the Soviet bloc, Bulgaria was a universally recognized state with uncontested borders, separate army (albeit part of a unified Warsaw pact structure), national bank and currency, foreign embassies, and membership in the UN and many other international institutions. Macedonia struggled to establish all of these from scratch after 1991, and this significantly complicated its transition. Even ten years later the Macedonian name and language are still contested, its border with Yugoslavia is undemarcated, and Macedonia's sizeable Albanian population (close to a quarter of the population according to the 1994 census, and a majority in territories adjacent to Albania and Kosovo) has had minimal commitment to the existing institutions.

This last factor threatens the very survival of the Macedonian state. Both the Party for Democratic Prosperity (PDP), led by Abdurahman Aliti (in government 1992–8), and the Democratic Party of the Albanians (DPA), led by Arben Xhaferi and Menduh Thaci (in government since 1998), are officially committed to the transformation of Macedonia into a two-part federation of Slav Macedonians and Albanians, which would lead to a complete over-haul of the existing constitution and legal order. While alternat-ing in government both PDP and DPA have shown an inclination to pursue this aim through the existing political institutions, and correspondingly have been rewarded with key government and diplo-matic posts, but both parties have been vehemently anti-systemic while in opposition. In contrast, the politicians of the major Turkish and Muslim party in Bulgaria—the Movement for Rights and Freedoms, led by Ahmed Dogan—have never contested the legitim-acy of the Bulgarian state, its borders, legal order, and symbols. Before 1990, Bulgaria's Turks appealed to specifically Bulgarian traditions in their fight against forced assimilation, such as the multiethnic vision of the revered nineteenth-century Bulgarian revolutionary Vasil Levski, and Bulgaria's pride in having saved its Jewish community from deportation during the Second World War. Since 1990, the politicians of the mainly Turkish and Muslim Movement for Rights and Freedoms worked to enhance the posi-tion of the minority strictly within the limits of the existing insti-tutions, and within the limits of the Bulgarian constitution and laws.

Marketization and Westernization

The fact that Macedonia lagged behind Bulgaria in terms of democratization should not obscure Macedonia's advantages over Bulgaria in the marketization of its economy. Macedonia never experi-enced sustained collectivization. Its predominantly private agri-culture has made the country largely self-sufficient in foodstuffs. Bulgaria's agriculture has been in tatters following an ill-conceived decollectivization, and the country imports agricultural products on a large scale.[6] Although Macedonia's service sector was archaic, and more reminiscent of a Middle Eastern country than a European one, the Macedonians did not have to recreate small businesses from

---

[6] 80% of the fruits and vegetables used in the Bulgarian food-processing industry are imported, mostly from Greece and Turkey; see interview with Krasen Stanchev, director of the Institute for Market Economy, *Kapital* (Sofia: 23–9 Mar. 1998).

scratch after 1989—as was required in Bulgaria. Macedonian advantages in the industrial sector were less clear, but for all its faults, Macedonia's privatization advanced further than Bulgaria's. The economic differences between the two countries in the 1990s were largely attributable to differences in their previous communist models. Bulgaria was a fully developed communist state along standard Soviet lines, with full nationalization of production and services, collectivization of agriculture, and five-year plans. Yugoslavia never established the full communist model, and, instead, had largely private agriculture and services, and decentralized industry (since 1965). In short, Bulgaria's transition from communism in the economic sphere faced greater challenges than Macedonia's.[7]

In terms of their openness to the world, the position of the Macedonian state and nation in the Yugoslav federation (the latter developed features of a confederation after the adoption of the 1974 constitution) compared favourably to the tightly controlled Soviet republics, and even to sovereign states of the Soviet bloc like Bulgaria. Macedonians were exposed to less anti-American and anti-Western propaganda, and had access to a freer press than Bulgarians. They were better travelled and had greater experience of Western realities. Macedonian agriculture was not collectivized, its enterprises had greater freedom to produce, trade, and export. As a result, Macedonian communists were quicker to mimic 'social democracy', and rely on American support, in comparison with their ideologically more conservative Bulgarian counterparts. Macedonian politicians with long Yugoslav experience, like President Gligorov, proved more adept at dealing with Westerners than the multitude of inexperienced politicians that passed through the swinging doors of the Bulgarian transition. Finally, Macedonia made a smoother and more convincing transition to a market economy in comparison to the near disaster of marketization in Bulgaria.

Exogenous Factors in the Democratization of Bulgaria and Macedonia

If one identifies the old historical 'core' of the West with the lands once ruled by Charlemagne (France, the Low Countries, West

---

[7] Paradoxically, the experience of deeper communization in Bulgaria might have facilitated the emergence of a far more robust anti-communist opposition in comparison with Macedonia—which in turn was a major factor in Bulgaria's early democratic consolidation.

Germany, and North Italy), then, of all former Soviet satellites in Europe, Bulgaria was the least connected with 'the West'. In the Middle Ages, Bulgaria was central to the Slav-Orthodox 'project'. This helps to explain the later affinity of Bulgaria with Russia, and Bulgaria's centuries-old attraction to the Russian 'pole'. Bulgaria was only episodically involved in anything to do with the West. Under Ottoman rule, the Bulgarians were the Balkan nation furthest from Western influence, with nothing comparable to the centuries-old contacts that existed between the Albanians and Italians, between the Serbs and Austrians, and between the Greeks and the Mediterranean world. After gaining independence in the late nineteenth century, Bulgaria had entered into formal alliances with forces inimical to the new 'core' countries of the West—France, Britain, and the United States. Bulgaria allied itself, first, with the Second and the Third Reichs, and, subsequently, with the Soviet Union. These alliances produced lasting damage to its image in the West. As for Macedonia, until 1944 it represented only a geographic term for Westerners. In a brief rise to fame at the turn of the century, it gave rise in the West to two lasting images—'la salade macedoine', and the Macedonian *comitadji* (later the IMRO terrorist)—half-brigand, half-revolutionary, both romantic and threatening.

The post-1989 transitions in Bulgaria and Macedonia underlined the peripheral place of both countries to Western influences and concerns. These transitions were doubly derivative—inspired in the first place by non-Western factors (democratization in the USSR and in Central Europe), which were themselves inspired by Western models. Correspondingly, until 1991 (when both Yugoslavia—SFRY—and USSR collapsed), both imitated other transitions and effected only indirect Westernization. The main role, at that time, was played by non-Western factors. After 1991, Bulgaria and Macedonia entered a period of direct adaptation to Western models and institutions. The old orientations towards Moscow (for the Bulgarians) and Belgrade (for the Macedonians) were gradually supplanted by new attitudes.

The evolution of the Soviet and Russian Factor in Bulgaria

The cataclysms of 1989–91 eroded the closest relationship that had ever existed between the USSR and a satellite country. At least since the 1960s, Bulgaria was perceived as the East European country closest to the Soviet Union. The main features of this 'special relationship' consisted, first, in that the Bulgarian ruling elite —the *nomenklatura*—was Russianized to a substantial degree through education and intermarriage. Secondly, the Bulgarian army was considered more reliable than the other East European armies by the Soviet Union. As a result, military cooperation with it was secured without the permanent stationing of Soviet troops. Thirdly, Bulgarian intelligence personnel were treated as 'insiders' by their Soviet counterparts, and the two services enjoyed a very close working relationship. Finally, compared with other European CMEA members, the Bulgarian economy grew most dependent on the Soviet one (the USSR accounted for about 60 per cent of over-all Bulgarian trade throughout the 1970s and 1980s).

Between August and December 1990, the extremely pro-Soviet post-Zhivkov leadership of the Bulgarian Socialist Party (formerly the Bulgarian Communist Party)—by that time the main decision-making body in Bulgaria—was replaced by an elaborate power-sharing mechanism, centred on the UDF-controlled presidency and including a coalition government. As a result, the most important vehicle of traditional Soviet domination over Bulgaria was destroyed.

However, important elements of the huge network, built over forty-five years, remained in place until early 1997. The BSP attempted, with some success, to transform itself from a fossilized *apparat* into a Russophile mass party (resembling, in this respect, some traditional Bulgarian parties from the turn of the century). Moreover, members of the former *nomenklatura* continued to control most government agencies and—most importantly—the management of most public enterprises as well (which, in the past, had direct links to Soviet ministries and enterprises). This gave them excellent opportunities for asset-stripping in the post-1989 period of 'initial accumulation', and for lucrative private deals with their former Russian colleagues. Furthermore, the army was left to reform itself—ensuring that its traditionally pro-Soviet command structure remained intact. The extent to which links between the Bulgarian intelligence agencies and their Soviet counterparts were preserved remains unclear for lack of reliable information. However, unlike in some of the other former Soviet satellites, in Bulgaria, such links were never publicly discontinued. In addition, all heads of security services appointed until early 1997 maintained a close connection with the BSP.

It is clear that, in comparison with other East European countries, all of these groups were far less delinked from the Soviet Union until early 1997. These enduring connections, coupled with their initially stronger Soviet ties, underline an unusually strong Soviet, and later Russian, profile in Bulgaria.

The 'Belgrade factor' in Macedonia

Throughout 1990 and the first half of 1991, the Slovenian and the Croatian elites were increasingly vocal in their demands for independence. At the same time, Macedonian attitudes towards 'dissociation' (the official term for separation of a federal republic) were much more ambivalent than the ones in the northern Yugoslav republics.

Unlike the Slovene and Croatian identities, which existed independently for a long period before the emergence of SFRY, the Macedonian identity and language were themselves a product of federal Yugoslavia, and took shape only after 1944. Again unlike Slovenia and Croatia, the very existence of a separate Macedonian identity was questioned—albeit to a different degree—by both the governments and the public of all the neighbouring nations (Greece being the most intransigent). Moreover, Macedonia had a fast growing and well-organized Albanian community, which comprised between one-fourth and one-fifth of the population—the highest percentage of minority population in a Yugoslav republic (not counting Bosnia-Hercegovina, where Serbs, Croats, and Muslims were considered constituent nations of this republic). Finally, Macedonia was one of the least developed parts of Yugoslavia (ahead only of Kosovo and Montenegro), and, thus, heavily dependent on federal subsidies. In comparison with Slovenia and Croatia, Macedonia was likely to have much greater difficulties in ensuring economic survival.

Bearing all this in mind, in 1990–1 the Macedonian leadership (the communist President Kiro Gligorov, the coalition government, and the pro-Markovic speaker of parliament) sided with Bosnian President Izetbegovic in advocating support for a loose federal structure for Yugoslavia—in contrast to the centralized option advocated by Serbia and Montenegro, and the community of independent states sought by Slovenia and Croatia. This variant (known as the Gligorov-Izetbegovic compromise) was strongly supported by the international community, but met only a lukewarm response from Serbia, and firm rejections from Slovenia and Croatia.

The Macedonian elite then faced a stark choice—either to follow Slovenia and Croatia in their quest for independence, or to remain in some sort of new Yugoslav federation, as advocated by Serbia. With similar neo-communist ruling elites in both Serbia and Macedonia, and the heavy dependence of the Macedonian economy on Serbia, everything seemed to push Macedonia to remain in a Serb-dominated rump Yugoslavia. In the Macedonian case, pro-Yugoslav attitudes often masked a dependence on Serbia.

Macedonian society was penetrated by an external factor (Serbian and Yugoslav interests) to a far greater degree than Bulgarian society was ever penetrated by Moscow. Even after 1944—when self-government was granted to Vardar Macedonia—the 'umbilical cord' with Serbia was not severed in at least several major respects. The same small nucleus of wartime 'pro-Yugoslav' communists remained in power after 1944.[8] Moreover, the Macedonian alphabet and literary language that were codified in 1944–5 incorporated some unmistakably Serbian characteristics.[9] For a period of forty-five years the Macedonian population was drawn away from the previously dominant Bulgarian culture, and had come closer to the Serbs in world-view, lifestyle, and popular culture. Industrial development was, indeed, heavily oriented towards Serbia—in 1992, about 70 per cent of the Macedonian economy was linked to Serbia. In short, by 1990 the Macedonian nation bore an indelible Serbian imprint—to a far greater degree than the Bulgarian nation was ever influenced by Russia.

That in such circumstances Macedonia followed Slovenia and Croatia to become the third republic to 'disassociate' itself from Yugoslavia was a tribute, first and foremost, to the constant pressure for independence exerted by IMRO. However, despite its declared independence, Macedonia still felt in some respects a part of Yugoslavia. The Belgrade-printed media dominated the local market. All governments formed by Prime Minister Branko Crvenkovski between September 1992 and November 1998 were dominated by members of the renamed communist party and other traditionally pro-Yugoslav forces. Even the coming to power of IMRO-DPMNU in 1998 has failed to achieve a decisive break with Yugoslav and Serbian influences in all spheres of national life.

---

[8] Palmer and King state: 'The Macedonians, who have attained high federal or party positions of authority, have been staunchly pro-Yugoslav and many have past Serbian connections.' These very people and their physical descendants are still prominent in the political, economic, and cultural circles of ex-Yugoslav Macedonia. See S. Palmer and R. King, *Yugoslav Communism and the Macedonian Question* (Hamden, Conn.: Archon Books, 1971), 135 and 140.

[9] Concerns about enduring Serbianization of the Macedonian tongue are expressed in the mass media even seven years after Macedonia's independence. According to the writer, Eftim Gashev: 'Nowadays the Macedonian literary tongue is a curious mish-mash of foreign, mostly Serbian expressions, that had been somewhat Macedonized. For decades, Macedonia had a dependent status within the hierarchy of federal Yugoslavia, where the Serbian tongue as language of the majority had a dominant role in the cultural sphere as well. Our inferior status and vassalage ensured a free and uncontrolled expansion of this foreign culture in Macedonia', *Dnevnik* (22 July 1998).

The emergence of Western actors

Unlike the profound effect of Soviet perestroika on democratization in Bulgaria, direct Western inputs in the democratization processes in Bulgaria and Macedonia were not particularly important. In the case of Macedonia, such inputs helped reverse democratization.

The involvement of the USA and the European Union (EU) in Bulgaria and Macedonia in the 1980s and 1990s was dominated by strategic concerns, rather than by an interest in their democratization. In Bulgaria these geopolitical concerns tended to promote democratization, while in Macedonia, they were largely inimical to democratization. In Bulgaria the former communists were deemed suspect because of their long-standing links with Moscow and perceived unfriendliness to Turkey and the Turks, while in Macedonia the former communists were 'the good guys' at least until the end of 1998, and the anti-communists were suspect because of their perceived unfriendliness to the minorities.

Before the fall of Zhivkov Western efforts in Sofia were concentrated on two fronts: first, support for Turkey in its attempts to undo the forced assimilation campaign against Bulgarian Turks dating back to 1984–5, and second, monitoring and support of the nascent anti-government organizations (the first of them was established in early 1988). The first was done mostly through diplomatic channels, while the second was directed by Radio Free Europe. Its transmissions ensured publicity to the dissidents in Bulgaria, and, in the climate of the late 1980s, this guaranteed some immunity from state persecution.

After the removal of Zhivkov and the abandonment of the anti-Turkish assimilation campaign in the end of 1989, Western governments tried to nudge the new regime in Sofia along the same road of reform as the countries in Central Europe. The usual diplomatic contacts with government circles, and the activities of Radio Free Europe, were combined with direct and regular contacts with the emerging opposition forces in Bulgaria. This marked the beginning of direct Western impact on the Bulgarian political scene. From that time onwards, the Soviet Union lost its monopoly position in Bulgarian politics, and all outside forces started competing on more or less equal terms for the favours of the local political elite.

In Macedonia the key turning point was its declaration of independence in the autumn of 1991, and especially the withdrawal of JNA forces in April 1992. Subsequently Serbia lost its monopoly position in Macedonian politics, and had to compete with other outside forces—first and foremost, the Western governments, who had much more to offer to the Macedonian elite than bankrupt Serbia.

Externally Shaped Developments in Bulgaria and Macedonia

This section examines several key events in the democratic transitions in Bulgaria and Macedonia that can be causally linked to international factors.

Bulgaria: the emergence of open opposition to the Zhivkov regime

Bulgaria was unique among all former Soviet satellites in the fact that a political campaign in the hegemonic state—Gorbachev's glasnost and perestroika in the USSR—created the basis for the first open opposition to the communist regime since the 1940s. The very thoroughness of Bulgaria's Sovietization had created channels for a massive influx of 'subversive' ideas from the USSR—through a universal knowledge of Russian, an extensive set of Russian bookshops, and the wide availability of Soviet press (with books and printed media much cheaper than Bulgarian ones), and one Soviet television channel broadcast with the two Bulgarian channels. Previously, the Soviet media had been considered utterly boring, but, in 1987–90, ordinary Bulgarians and Communist Party members alike massively subscribed to Soviet newspapers and magazines, and avidly watched Soviet television.[10] After one year of fermentation, the first openly dissident groups emerged in early 1988, seeking registration. The names of two of the most popular groupings founded in 1988–9 clearly show the inspiration behind them: Discussion Club in Support of Glasnost and Perestroika and Ecoglasnost. Also, it is notable that Communist Party members, and people with strong communist and secret police connections predominated among the organizers and activists of these glasnostinspired independent associations.[11]

---

[10] Although there was an upsurge of interest in Soviet publications in all East European countries, what happened in Bulgaria was quite unique: for example, in the period under discussion, Bulgaria, a country with 8.5 million population, got nine-tenths of all international subscriptions to one of the standard-bearers of glasnost, *Literaturnaya Gazeta*.

[11] 44 of the 81 founding members of the Discussion Club in Support of Glasnost and Perestroika (founded in November 1988) were communist party members, see Dimitar Ivanov, *Politicheskoto protivopostavyane v Balgaria 1956–1989* (Sofia:

The downfall of Todor Zhivkov

Although Zhivkov was pushed out of office by a cabal of colleagues from his own Politburo, their action was clearly coordinated with Moscow. This formed part of a Soviet push to get rid of anti-Gorbachev leaders in the Soviet bloc. The Soviet ambassador in Sofia, Viktor Sharapov (a KGB general), was directly involved in persuading Zhivkov to resign.[12] Zhivkov fell from power in the autumn of 1989 not because a majority of Bulgarians so desired—on the contrary, for many of them, Zhivkov seemed to be winning in the war of nerves with the Turkish government. Indeed, in August, Turkey decided to close its border to Bulgarian Turks, reneging on an earlier promise to accept all Bulgarian Turks who wanted to resettle in Turkey. Moreover, between August and October, about 40 per cent of the Turkish expellees streamed back to Bulgaria, dissatisfied with the treatment that they received in Turkey, thus handing another important propaganda victory to Zhivkov. His removal from office was dictated by the imperatives of Gorbachev's domestic and foreign policy.

The reversal of anti-Turkish renaming policies

The campaign to rename all Turks in Bulgaria was decided by a small group surrounding Zhivkov in 1984, and took both ethnic Turks and ethnic Bulgarians by surprise. Still, protests against it by ethnic Bulgarians were few. And whatever sympathy existed for the wronged Turks was largely destroyed by several indiscriminate terrorist acts perpetrated by ethnic Turks in 1985–7. The exodus of 369,000 Turks in the summer of 1989 (of whom 155,000 returned

Ares Pres, 1994), 141 (Ivanov is a former head of a section in the Secret Police department in charge of dissent in the Communist Party). However, the very first independent organization—the Association for Human Rights founded in January 1988—was organized by people who had spent years in prison for anti-communist activity; later, its original leaders were purged or expelled from the country and by spring 1989, this organization had been taken over by Rumen Vodenicharov, one of the major agents provocateurs in the Bulgarian non-communist opposition. In 1989–90, Vodenicharov was one of the most visible UDF leaders, was elected member of parliament, and used his talents to sabotage UDF's parliamentary activity. In 1992, he stood against Zhelev as a vice-presidential candidate, on behalf of the renamed communist party, and later distinguished himself by organizing hysterical rallies against the planned removal of the major Soviet monument in Sofia, and by fanning crude anti-Turkish propaganda.

[12] The best account of the Soviet involvement in the removal of Zhivkov is provided by Tsanov, *Smyanata.*

to Bulgaria by the end of the year) directly pitted Turks and Bulgarians against each other in the mixed population districts. The damage to interethnic relations then seemed irreparable.[13] In the spring and summer of 1989, only the budding opposition groups in Bulgaria—the largest of which had 215 members—supported the demands of ethnic Turks. These groups were vilified as traitors by the government.[14] The military threat from Turkey (Prime Minister Ozal, at one point, suggested that Bulgaria should be treated like Cyprus in 1974), and the mass return of dissatisfied expellees to Bulgaria seemed to vindicate Zhivkov's renaming policy in the opinion of many Bulgarians.

These feelings persisted after the removal of Zhivkov. At the first mass opposition rally in Sofia, Rumen Vodenicharov, then chair of the Independent Society for Defence of Human Rights, was whistled at by the crowd (the only such case at this rally) when he called for a reversal of the renaming policies. After this incident, most opposition leaders avoided the issue whenever possible. Again it was a small group in the Communist Party leadership that decided on a reversal of the renaming policies in late December 1989. They acted out of a combination of motives. The first was a genuine dislike of Zhivkov's policies for humanitarian reasons (this was the main motivation of Alexander Lilov, who later became the chair and the main ideologue of the renamed Communist Party), combined with an appreciation of Western humanitarian concerns (this was the motivation of some of Bulgaria's top diplomats, and of Communist Party leader Petar Mladenov, formerly Zhivkov's foreign minister for eighteen years), and the knowledge that the Soviet leadership expected such a reversal.[15] Soviet desires were perhaps decisive. These had the support of pro-Soviet security personnel in Bulgaria. The wavering Communist Party was pushed

[13] The figures are taken from Mikhail Ivanov and Ilona Tomova, 'Etnicheski grupi i mezhduetnicheski otnosheniya v Balgariya', paper presented to a German-Bulgarian Media Seminar, Bankya (26–30 Aug. 1993); Mikhail Ivanov was, at that time, President Zhelev's adviser on ethnic problems.

[14] The names and short biographies of all members of the Discussion Club in Support of Glasnost and Perestroika are listed in Dimitar Ivanov, *Politicheskoto protivopostavyane v Balgaria*, 281–92.

[15] Although the Soviets were careful not to pronounce publicly on such a sensitive issue, their negative attitude to the renaming campaign in Bulgaria was an open secret. In his memoirs, Kostadin Chakarov, one of Zhivkov's main advisers and ghost writers, unequivocally states that the Soviet Union and Gorbachev consistently refused to support Zhivkov's policy towards Turkey and the Bulgarian Turks in the 'hot Summer' of 1989, see Kostadin Chakarov, *Vtoriyat etazh, K sie M* (Sofia: K sie M, 1990), 94.

into action by Rumen Vodenicharov, who in late December organized groups of Pomaks (Bulgarian Muslims) to protest daily at the parliament building in Sofia. The mass protest rallies that engulfed a third of Bulgaria in January 1990—after the reversal of Zhivkov's renaming policies—show how unpopular this decision was amongst most ordinary Bulgarians and local party officials in the mixed population districts.

The advent of democratic politics

The inspiration for the emergence of mass opposition, the round table talks, and reform in the Communist Party came from abroad. The creation of the Union of Democratic Forces on 4 December 1989 was modelled on existing umbrella groupings in Central Europe. The idea of round table talks was copied from the more advanced states in transition, as were the major demands of the opposition, in December and January, for an end to the leading role of the Communist Party and the abolition of primary party cells at the workplace and in the military.[16] 'Democracy' replaced perestroika as the opposition buzzword less than a month after the removal of Zhivkov, and the Communist Party itself had to give up Soviet-style perestroika ambitions before long. In January 1990, Alexander Lilov decided on a new strategy, after a careful study of the transformation of communist parties in Central Europe. The Hungarian model of disbanding the Communist Party and reconstituting it as a new Socialist Party was rejected (although 'socialist' was preferred over other names). The model of the East German SED was adopted, which provided for internal democratization and a new name, without any disbanding of the party. Thus, by early 1990, both the Communist Party and the opposition in Bulgaria were firmly committed to a 'Central European' path of democratic transition—a negotiated change leading to free elections and multi-party politics.

Western concerns about Soviet–Bulgarian security cooperation

In the first half of 1991, the most important issue in Soviet–Bulgarian relations was the negotiations for a new treaty to replace the 1967 treaty of mutual assistance. The most significant part of the earliest (Bulgarian-prepared) draft was the explicit

---

[16] For an account of the early period of transition in Bulgaria, see Richard Crampton, *A Concise History of Bulgaria* (Cambridge: Cambridge University Press, 1997), 216–20.

mutual assistance mechanism enshrined in the text. It made this draft unique, even in comparison with the much criticized Soviet–Romanian treaty (signed in April 1991 but never ratified by the Romanians). The Bulgarian draft was elaborated over several months by Foreign Ministry experts following guidelines by the National Security Council with the presidency. It is notable that this body then was under the control of Vice-President Atanas Semerdjiev, who, for twenty years, under Zhivkov had directed Bulgarian military intelligence and the General Staff, and was also minister of the interior in the two post-Zhivkov governments before his election as vice-president in August 1990. Prior to its presentation to the Soviet side, the draft was discussed neither by the government nor by the respective parliamentary commissions. It had obviously won only the consent of President Zhelev, former leader of the opposition. According to one of its clauses, each side would be obliged to provide military assistance to the other in the case that it was attacked. This formula masked a unilateral Soviet guarantee for Bulgarian security.

At that time (March–May 1991), even the Soviets were not prepared to go that far. The Soviet draft suggested an emasculated version of the Bulgarian mutual assistance mechanism, in addition to what really interested them at the time—a clause precluding the signatories from joining alliances that might be deemed hostile to the other side (that is, any form of Western security cooperation). The initial Soviet draft was a variant of the Soviet–Romanian Treaty of Cooperation, Good Neighbourliness, and Friendship signed on 5 April 1991 for a term of fifteen years, and was meant to be the first of a network of bilateral treaties to replace the Warsaw Pact. The Soviets insisted that all these treaties contain a clause that would preclude the signatories from joining any alliance that could be directed against either side, as well as other clauses requiring regular consultations on security issues and some coordination of foreign policies and diplomatic activities. The vagueness of these clauses could leave them open to unilateral Soviet interpretation at some future moment, thereby giving the USSR a veto over the foreign and security policies of the countries involved. The fundamental aim of the treaties was to prevent any of the former Soviet satellites from cooperating with NATO and the Western European Union.

However in May 1991, the already exchanged Bulgarian and Soviet drafts were leaked to the Radio Free Europe Bulgarian service, causing a public uproar. On the eve of Popov's visit to Moscow, in late May 1991, 159 leading Bulgarian intellectuals signed an open letter accusing the BSP of masterminding 'a dangerous

treaty' with the USSR. Under intense internal and external pressure, the Bulgarian leadership was forced to give up its plans for
a new mutual assistance treaty with the USSR. Other factors that
were key to this change of heart were the direct warnings by US
diplomats in Sofia that Bulgaria should not sign a treaty which
might hinder Bulgaria's defence options.[17]

The constitutional ban on ethnic parties

Article 11.4 of the 1991 Bulgarian Constitution, which forbids the
creation of ethnic and religious parties, was severely criticized
by the Council of Europe. Bulgaria was admitted as member in
May 1992 only because, in the opinion of the Council, Bulgarian
authorities would be flexible in the application of this article.
Major examples of this 'flexibility' to which the Council of Europe
implicitly referred occurred in September 1991. On the basis of
Article 11.4 of the Constitution, the Central Electoral Commission
banned the Movement for Rights and Freedoms (a mostly Turkish
and Muslim party) from participation in the parliamentary elec-
tions scheduled for October. After that 'the European Union and
CSCE pressured the Bulgarian government in order to compel the
Supreme Court to revise the decision of the electoral commission'.[18]
MRF's constitutionality was challenged in the Constitutional
Court, but a ruling against it failed by one vote.[19]

The issue of EU and NATO membership

Bulgaria signed an association ('Europe') agreement with EU in 1993,
and declared its desire to join NATO in February 1997. On both
counts, Bulgaria has lagged behind the Visegrad countries.

---

[17] For the controversies surrounding this treaty, see Haramiev Drezov,
'Bulgarian-Russian Relations on a New Footing', *RFE/RL Research Report* (9 Apr.
1993), 36.

[18] Raymond Detrez, *Historical Dictionary of Bulgaria* (Lanham, Md: Scarecrow
Press, 1997), 225.

[19] MRF, as it exists now, is the product of many interventions: (1) it emerged
unchallenged in January 1990, because competing Turkish organizations and
leaders had been purposefully eliminated by that time by the Bulgarian security
apparatus: unlike other Turkish leaders, MRF's founder and leader Ahmed Dogan
had a record of collaboration with Zhivkov's police and was considered more
'malleable'; (2) it was registered for the first elections in June 1990, under BSP
pressure, in order to deny the ethnic Turkish vote to UDF; (3) it was registered
for the second parliamentary elections in October 1991, under Western pressure,
and played a key role in all governments for the next three years.

The promises that Bulgaria could eventually join both organizations create a specific constraint on Bulgaria's transition. Bulgarian governments have to consider the effect of their actions on relations with EU countries, and on the chances for Bulgaria to prepare for membership. Because of the promise of eventual membership, Bulgaria could not create a free trade area with Russia, while a similar area was agreed with Turkey, as the latter maintains a customs union with the EU. These promises had effects on internal politics also. During the mass demonstrations in January 1997, the BSP government refrained from using massive force against demonstrators, partly because it feared condemnation from Western governments.

To sum up, Western interventions in Bulgarian politics sought to limit Soviet and Russian influences, and to preserve a political voice for the Turkish minority. Overall, these interventions were beneficial to the non-communist parties, and contributed to Bulgaria's overall democratization. The promises of eventual membership in EU and NATO act as a constraint on possible 'misbehaviour' from Bulgarian governments.

Macedonia: the advent of multi-party politics and elections

Even the most Westernized Yugoslav republics (Slovenia and Croatia) discovered multi-party politics well after the collapse of communist regimes in Central Europe. Only in December 1989 did the communist parties of Croatia and Slovenia publicly call for the establishment of a multi-party system.[20] In January 1990, the Yugoslav League of Communists effectively disintegrated into republican parties. Although non-communist parties had emerged in Macedonia since November 1989, Macedonian communists committed themselves to multi-party politics only in summer of 1990. The first serious step towards 'indigenization' was taken in June 1990 with the creation of the Internal Macedonian Revolutionary Organization-Democratic Party for Macedonian National Unity (IMRO-DPMNU), which soon became the strongest anti-communist party in Macedonia. Throughout 1990–1, both the communists and IMRO followed patterns already developed in other Yugoslav republics: the Macedonian League of Communists transformed

---

[20] For a summary of the first steps towards democracy in Yugoslavia, see Lenard J. Cohen, *Broken Bonds: Yugoslavia's Disintegration and Balkan Politics in Transition* (Boulder, Colo.: Westview Press, 1995), 83.

itself into the League of Communists of Macedonia-Party for Democratic Changes (later Social Democratic Alliance of Macedonia), while IMRO emulated the Slovene and Croat pro-independence stances. Macedonia became the only Yugoslav republic where the local branch of the Alliance of Reform Forces of Yugoslavia (founded in the autumn of 1990 by the then prime minister of Yugoslavia, Ante Markovic) did well in the first republican elections, and later became an important party in its own right in Macedonia —first, as the Alliance of Reform Forces—Liberal Party, and later as Liberal Party (it brought together the most reform-minded cadres of the Macedonian League of Communists).

The first multi-party elections in Macedonia were held in November–December 1990, with IMRO gaining 38 of 120 seats, and forming the largest single group in parliament. However, the parties with *nomenklatura* roots jointly controlled more seats—55 belonged to Slav parties (Social Democrats, Liberals, and Socialists) and 23 belonged to the ethnically determined Albanian Party for Democratic Prosperity. After September 1992, all of the above parties were integrated into a Macedonian 'party of power' (the Liberals left government in February 1996, and in 1997 merged with the opposition Democrats). The second parliamentary elections were held in October 1994 amid protests and irregularities. Their second round was boycotted by opposition parties—IMRO and the Democratic Party—and these same parties declared as fraudulent the election of ex-communist Kiro Gligorov in the first round of the first direct presidential elections that were held concurrently with the parliamentary elections. The third parliamentary elections were held in the autumn of 1998 and were accepted as free and fair by all sides. These elections gave a majority of 62 seats to a coalition dominated by IMRO, which subsequently formed a government with the Democratic Party of the Albanians, thus gaining 11 more seats. The government parties won the second presidential elections in the autumn of 1999 amid irregularities and protests from the ex-communist Social Democrats, who refused to recognize the winner Boris Trajkovski as legitimate president of Macedonia.

Macedonia's separation from Yugoslavia

IMRO was committed to independence from the start, while the parties with communist roots wanted to keep Macedonia in some sort of federal or confederal Yugoslavia. The main push for independence was external—after the independence declarations of Slovenia and Croatia in June 1991, Macedonian President Gligorov stated that 'Macedonia might be forced to become independent' (*sic!*). Macedonian communists kept the Yugoslav option open even in the independence referendum of 8 September 1991: voters were asked whether they supported an independent Macedonia which would have the right to join an association of sovereign Yugoslav republics. The Constitution adopted in November 1991 included Article 120, which described the conditions under which Macedonia could form a union or association with another state. Sovereignty remains a hotly debated issue in Macedonia—the IMRO have accused the former communist parties of pro-Yugoslav leanings, while the latter have accused the IMRO of pro-Bulgarian attitudes.

Western support for the former communists

In this respect, the situation in Macedonia was different from Bulgaria. In Macedonia, the former Communist Party in power had no previous links with Russia, was not constrained by pro-Russian sympathies, and could offer full cooperation to Western powers. Moreover, since September 1992 the former communists had a working coalition with the main Albanian party, and could be counted on to keep ethnic peace (in contrast to them, the main non-communist party, IMRO-DPMNU, looked dangerously anti-Albanian). Thus, Western interventions sought to keep the former communists and their coalition in power, rather than promote 'democracy' in Macedonia.

The choice of 'stability' over 'democracy' in Macedonia was most blatant during the second parliamentary elections in October 1994. According to the US State Department's 'Macedonia Country Report on Human Rights Practices' for 1996, in these elections: 'Opposition groups charged the Government with massive fraud and announced a boycott of the second round. International monitors, under the auspices of the Council of Europe and the then Conference on Security and Cooperation in Europe (CSCE), found the elections to be generally free and fair despite widespread irregularities attributed largely to careless organization.'[21] Such government carelessness, however, is difficult to reconcile with electoral fairness: only three months before the October 1994 elections the

---

[21] 'Macedonia Country Report on Human Rights Practices for 1996,' released by the Bureau of Democracy, Human Rights, and Labour on 30 Jan. 1997.

same administration had meticulously prepared and conducted a much more difficult population census. Nor could anyone explain why there were fewer irregularities during the very first multi-party elections in the autumn of 1990, when such irregularities could have been more easily written off to inexperience.

The problem was different. The heads of foreign missions in Skopje, and the CSCE and EU delegations monitoring the elections with 540 observers, were presented with an awkward dilemma. Advice to the government to accept opposition demands would have resulted in a larger share of pro-opposition (mostly IMRO) votes in any new parliamentary and presidential elections; this surely would have complicated the position of Gligorov and his former communist Alliance for Macedonia (perceived in the West at that time as the only guarantee for 'stability' in Macedonia). Conversely, support for the government position would undermine the cause of 'democracy' in Macedonia, by leading to the complete exclusion of the Slav Macedonian opposition from parliament, and by pushing both government and opposition to dangerous extra-parliamentary methods. Forced to choose between 'stability' and 'democracy', the EU and CSCE observers chose 'stability'. In its press conference on 17 October, the CSCE observer delegation effectively endorsed the government position by advising all parties to participate in the second round, while admitting that irregularities had occurred in the first round. The Head of the US Permanent CSCE Mission in Skopje, Norman Anderson, made things even clearer by issuing blunt warnings against an opposition-led boycott of the second round. The opposition did not heed the advice, and the former communist coalition secured a four-year mandate without the opposition in parliament—with full blessings from 'the international community'. One year later, in November 1995, Macedonia was admitted to the Council of Europe.

It took IMRO four years to overcome the debilitating effect of the 1994 elections and to convince Western governments that it will not impair 'stability'. It became legitimate in Western eyes only after the formation of a coalition government with the ethnic Albanian DPA following the 1998 parliamentary elections. Consequently, in the presidential elections 1999 it was the IMRO and DPA candidate, Boris Trajkovski, who was perceived as the new factor of 'stability'. His election was welcomed by Western monitors and politicians despite glaring irregularities, and this time it was the ex-communists who bitterly complained about Western indifference to the quality of Macedonian democracy.

Conclusions

Both Bulgaria and Macedonia were latecomers in the democratic transitions. Until the very last moment, they clung to the old hegemon, even though the economic attractions of subordination had largely dissipated. Moreover, both countries turned to democratic politics, and an emphasis on sovereignty, later than the Central European nations. A slow transition from communism led to the subordination of democratic politics to *nomenklatura* interests—in Bulgaria until early 1997 and in Macedonia until late 1998. Finally, in the 1990s Western involvement in Bulgaria and Macedonia was dominated primarily by strategic concerns, rather than by an interest in their democratization.

If recent history is any guide, the foreign policies of Bulgaria and Macedonia are likely to give little trouble to the West. The two countries have long traditions of self-limiting foreign policies and internal malleability to suit the requirements of a foreign hegemon. So far, neither of them has put the pursuit of its own national interests over and above Western interests. Bulgaria and Macedonia have emerged as two dependable partners (perhaps even satellites) of the West in a very dangerous region.

However, such self-restraint should not be mistaken for lack of national ambitions, nor should it be taken for granted. Self-restraint in Bulgarian (and Macedonian) politics traditionally came from a feeling of impotence against overwhelming power, and from the expectation that there will be rewards for 'responsible behaviour'. In other words, it is a classic survival technique. No one expected Bulgaria to challenge the Soviet Union under Brezhnev, because there was a very real mix of fear and benefits for the Bulgarian elite. Similarly, one could not have expected Macedonian communists to challenge Tito at the height of his power. Both Brezhnev and Tito knew how to combine carrots and sticks in a strategy that would maximize the compliance of smaller dependencies.

The main danger to the 'Western project' in Bulgaria and Macedonia is that the encounter of these states with the West in the 1990s has led to many serious disappointments. These include perceived double standards in recognizing the independence of former Yugoslav republics like Macedonia (in early 1992, the EU recognized Slovenia and Croatia instead of Slovenia and Macedonia as proposed by the EU-appointed Badinter Commission), the lack of consultation with the regional countries on the introduction and hardening of sanctions against rump Yugoslavia, and the absence of realistic suggestions for compensating embargo losses. Also, both states face no realistic chance of joining the EU or NATO in the near term—in fact, there is a perception that they have been consistently relegated to second-class status, in comparison with every other former communist country from Croatia to Estonia (similar to Romanians, Bulgarians and Macedonians are subjected to a tough and irritating visa regime). It has to be said, however, that *vis-à-vis* the EU, Bulgaria is in a more advantageous position than Macedonia: the former is at least formally in a group of ten countries that have already started membership negotiations, while the latter is firmly relegated by the EU to 'the Western Balkans', a collection of most former Yugoslav republics and Albania, with no chance of 'Europe' agreement or membership negotiations in the near future.

Still, despite these disappointments, the elites of both Bulgaria and Macedonia continue to believe that the future of their countries is irrevocably tied to Europe. This clearly distinguishes them from Russian and some other CIS elites, who have discussed Eurasian alternatives to integration with the European and Western structures. It is likely that this 'hope against all hope' will stubbornly survive further disappointments, as governments in both countries see no alternative to their present pro-European and pro-Western policies. However, the hard-pressed populations of Bulgaria and Macedonia might one day grow tired of leaders that constantly promise something perhaps as elusive as communism —in this case, membership in the Western club.

16

Former Yugoslavia: International Efforts to Link Peace, Stability, and Democracy

Radovan Vukadinovic

The involvement of the international community in the area of former Yugoslavia has sought to advance the clear Western objectives of the consolidation of democracy, transformation to a market economy, and the protection of human and minority rights. It has also to sought to promote regional peace and security. The lack of preparation of the international community for the violent disintegration of Yugoslavia initially led to confusion in its policies. Passing through a period of gradual and rather unsuccessful involvement, the international community has become fully engaged in the former Yugoslavia. Given the conflicts in Croatia and Bosnia-Hercegovina, as well as the Kosovo crisis in 1999, external actors have attributed priority to peace building over the promotion of democratic goals. In this perspective, the process of democratic transition will be embarked upon in the region following the establishment of peace.

This chapter defines the 'international community' as comprising all external actors engaged in seeking to resolve the Yugoslav crisis, including the joint activities of the European Union (EU), USA, and Russia. These parts of the international community, despite differing positions and interests, have succeeded most in advancing these aims. If under the term of 'democratic changes', one includes everything that has led the nations of the former Yugoslavia towards the creation of independent states, the pursuit of peace, and closer ties to wider Europe, then external involvement must be viewed at different levels. At these different levels, the involvement of the international community has had different consequences according to the features of each new state.

The first part of this chapter analyses the role of international factors in the disintegration of Yugoslavia. The second part examines the Dayton Accord, as an example of direct external engagement to promote peace to the region. The third part analyses the main Western plans, the regional approach of the EU and US approaches, which seek the promotion of security through cooperation in the region. This part also assesses the policies adopted by external actors, and their efficiency in seeking the objective of regional peace and security.

The Disintegration of Yugoslavia and International Actors

Yugoslavia's disintegration took place in parallel to the fall of the Berlin Wall and the collapse of socialist regimes in Eastern Europe.[1] The Yugoslav state had been viewed by many as artificial since its creation at the end of the First World War. This state had played a peculiar role in East–West relations during the Cold War. In the complex conditions of the late 1980s, the Yugoslav state found itself facing a severe internal crisis, towards which the international community displayed an alarming lack of interest. 'Operation Desert Storm' in Kuwait, developments in Eastern Europe and the possibility of a Soviet collapse attracted most international attention. As a result, developments in Yugoslavia were driven exclusively by local forces. These local political forces successfully held democratic elections, upon which base, the newly elected national leaderships initiated a process for the peaceful dissolution of the Yugoslav federation. These new elites failed to achieve this objective.[2]

External actors became directly involved only after military force had been used in Slovenia and war had broken out in Croatia and Bosnia-Hercegovina. The efforts invested by the EU, the Organization of Security and Cooperation in Europe (OSCE), the United Nations (UN), and the Western European Union (WEU) seemed to turn this part of Europe into a sort of 'crisis management laboratory'. Early on, the first major differences in external approaches to the crisis became visible. The British and French governments then advocated the preservation of the federal state, while the German government gradually accepted the creation of

---

[1] Renéo Lukic and Allen Lynch, *Europe from the Balkans to the Urals: The Disintegration of Yugoslavia and the Soviet Union* (Oxford: Oxford University Press, 1996), 144–9.

[2] Radovan Vukadinovic, *The Break up of Yugoslavia: Threats and Challenges* (The Hague: Clingendael, 1992).

new states. The US position at first consisted of only mild objection to the disintegration of Yugoslav federation. Only after the West European states had done so did the USA declare that it was satisfied that Slovenia, Croatia, and Bosnia-Hercegovina met required political standards, and that these new states represented the 'peaceful and democratic expression of the will of citizens of these states for sovereignty'.[3]

Slovenia

Slovenia benefited from the most favourable initial conditions for undertaking the consolidation of its independence. Slovenia's historical experience, ethnic homogeneity, its lack of contested problems with its neighbours, and the peaceful withdrawal of Yugoslav armed forces from its territory, created a solid foundation for the newly independent state. These circumstances also set the basis for Slovenia's rapid incorporation into wider European cooperative mechanisms.[4] After its accession to the Central European Free Trade Agreement (CEFTA), an agreement on associate membership was reached with the EU, followed by participation in the Partnership for Peace (PfP), and the development of closer ties to the North Atlantic Treaty Organization (NATO). Slovenia was listed as one of the six candidates for full membership in the EU. The development of Slovene democratic institutions—enshrining democratic politics, a respect for human rights, freedom of the press, and a market economy—has enabled the new state to develop along a path very distinct from other countries created from the former Yugoslavia. In a wider sense, Slovenia has become a frontier between Europe and the Balkans. As it has been defined in some EU documents, Slovenia represents 'a dividing line between Europe and the South-Eastern Europe'. Therefore, Slovenia's relatively peaceful secession from the former Yugoslavia created conditions for the development of democratic institutions, and the implementation of Western priorities. This enabled Slovenia to go further than any other of these states in developing relations with the EU and NATO.

Croatia

Croatia faced many more obstacles in its pursuit of independence. At first, as Yugoslavia collapsed, a confrontation with Serb rebels

---

[3] US Department of State Dispatch, 4/3 (1992).

[4] B. Bucar and S. Kuhnle (eds.), *Small States Compared: Politics of Norway and Slovenia* (Bergen: Alma Mater, 1994), 13–16.

caused an outbreak of armed conflict. As a result of this conflict, the international community became engaged in the role of mediator. Initially, the international community sought to promote the autonomy of the Krajina region. However, in 1995, the Croatian government 'liberated' the Krajina region, and reincorporated the area of Eastern Slavonia. Over the course of this conflict, a number of external actors became involved in Croatia, ranging from UNPROFOR to UNTAES. The enduring presence of OSCE monitors in Eastern Slavonia demonstrated both the might and impotence of international organizations. These organizations were unable to stop the war from taking place at the outset, or to prevent the shelling of Dubrovnik and the destruction of Vukovar. The international community in fact entrenched the existence of the so-called Republic of Srpska Krajina, until the point when the Croatian government decided to recapture the region through direct action. This action brought fierce criticism of Croatia from the international community. Croatian negotiations with the EU were suspended, and substantial international pressure was applied. A limited international presence in Croatia was maintained in order to assist Croatia in resolving ongoing problems, and to supervise the policies adopted by the government.

Croatia, pressured by aggressive Serbian behaviour, had little time and energy to create the foundations for democracy. Although, during this period, there were few opportunities available for policies directed at strengthening democracy in Croatia, the international community still persisted in addressing this question in a limited manner.[5] The West was quite rigorous in its demands. Croatia was not admitted to the PHARE programme. International pressures persisted during Croatia's admission process to the Council of Europe (COE), which insisted that Croatia strengthen the democratic foundations of society, and enshrine respect for human and minority rights. During 1998 Croatia found itself on the brink of international sanctions because of delays in the implementation of agreed provisions for the return of Serbian refugees. This international threat was exploited by certain Croatian political forces, which argued that it would be better to suffer sanctions than to lose national dignity. The memory of the war remains very present in Croatian thinking, and Croatia's national identity remains fragile, yet strongly, expressed. These enduring realities of Croatian political life weakened the potential effectiveness of international pressure, and delayed the process of democratization until after the

---

[5] Lj. Cucic, *U.S. Foreign Policy and Croatia* (Zagreb, 1995), 86–93.

death of President Franjo Tudjman in late 1999 and the elections of January/February 2000.

Bosnia-Hercegovina

Bosnia-Hercegovina has undergone two wars between its three nations over the last four years. These wars have claimed over 200,000 lives, and left over 2 million people homeless. The international community has been deeply involved in Bosnia and Hercegovina, in a range of activities from the provision of humanitarian aid to extensive military deployments in IFOR and SFOR. This involvement has resulted in a resolution of the Croat-Muslim conflict, and tentative peace between Croat-Muslim and Serb forces, embodied in the Dayton Accord.

The West has accepted the belief that only democratic politics and society will be able to underpin the creation of the unique multi-ethnic state of Bosnia-Hercegovina. Western states and organizations, therefore, have sought to promote democracy in both of the entities and in all three nations. The special position and authority vested in EU representatives has opened the possibility for the development of relations between the entities making up the new state. These relations touch upon issues of daily life, media, the educational system, the creation of political parties, and other modes of cooperation. In the long term, this process of 'importing democracy' may unify Bosnia-Hercegovina as an unique democratic state. In order to achieve this objective, the international community has developed some of the necessary tools of leverage. First and foremost, these include a direct civilian and military presence on the ground. The provision of international economic aid has been linked to developments in the democratization process (such as the return of refugees, and the promotion of multi-ethnicity).

Macedonia

Macedonia was the only republic of the former Yugoslavia that managed to leave the federation without a single shot being fired. The Macedonian government has had carefully to balance relations with its neighbours. Relations with Greece have improved, but remain ambiguous, because of Greek objections over the issue of Macedonia's official name. More sensitive problems have emerged over internal issues that have significant external dimensions, particularly regarding Macedonia's Albanian minority. The western parts of Macedonia are exposed to the spillover of developments in Kosovo and Albania. Any new escalation of tensions there could soon be transferred to Macedonia. External actors have been engaged in seeking to promote peaceful interethnic relations within Macedonia, with regard to this issue. As a result of their early and positive engagement, foreign states have underpinned the consolidation of Macedonia's independence. The deployment of UN troops in Macedonia has represented the most effective form of preventive diplomacy witnessed to date. Moreover, at a period of economic difficulty, the international community has provided critically needed foreign aid. A satisfactory level of democratic development has led to Macedonia's accession to the Council of Europe. This, in turn, has enabled further development of democratic processes, despite significant controversies surrounding the late 1999 presidential election and the persistent risk of ethnic polarization spilling over from neighbouring Kosovo. A more detailed analysis of the Macedonian case is presented in the chapter by Kyril Drezov.

Yugoslavia

Rump Yugoslavia, created as a result of Milošević's nationalist and conflictual policies, has had to face years of Western sanctions, which have impacted on all aspects of Yugoslav life. As a result of the suppression of democratic processes in this state, regional movements for increased autonomy (in Vojvodina), and more extensive rights (in Montenegro), have gained pace. After many years of discrimination, Albanian groups in Kosovo embarked in 1998 upon an armed struggle for their independence. At first, the international community maintained an uneasy balance between placing firm pressure on Serbia, which was partly counter-productive as it was exploited by Milošević, and alleviating this pressure, due to the belief that Milošević remained a significant political actor, necessary for implementation of the Dayton Accord and for the maintenance of a degree of stability in Yugoslavia. In March 1999, however, the West's inclination to deal with Milošević, out of a lack of alternatives and for fear of further instability, was outweighed by the perceived failure of the Rambouillet process and persistent violence in the province—resulting in NATO's air campaign. The primary objective of the international community has remained to ease tensions in the short term, by containing ethnic confrontation and keeping Belgrade at bay through KFOR, while stopping short of sponsoring Kosovan independence. However, the promotion of democracy, a market economy, and respect for human and minority rights, while remaining a longer-term objective, has received stronger pledges, and the Kosovo crisis prompted the formulation of a broader international Stability Pact for the Balkans.

Under Milošević's leadership, Serbia did not benefit from any movement towards democratization. Entangled in the fall-out from the Kosovo conflict, Milošević counted on further exploiting Serbian national sentiments, and the Serb desire to retain control over this region. Once again, Milošević's policies obstructed any prospect for internal democratization. However, the Milošević regime was also forced to confront a growing reformist movement in Montenegro. This movement, in combination with the opposition in Belgrade and reformist forces in the Republika Srpska, may presage the shape of post-Milošević politics.

Western priorities

This analysis raises the following questions: what should be the international community's main goal in this region? Should it be the construction of democratic societies or the promotion of security? In addressing this dilemma, many have argued that security is unsustainable without democracy. Others have maintained that democracy may not develop without at least some level of security. The picture that emerges from this region is complex. If one considers Slovenia, it is obvious that its level of democracy has helped to resolve its security concerns. In Bosnia-Hercegovina, the prospects for democracy remain dependent on extensive economic and political support from the West, and particularly, a large international military presence. However, the policies of the international community may not suffice to create conditions for peace and security in these three nations. The case of Serbia presents a distinct answer to this dilemma. Following its involvement in Croatia and Bosnia-Hercegovina, and despite growing calls for change in the aftermath of the 'loss' of Kosovo, Serbia became entrenched in an authoritarian regime. Democratization in Kosovo, whose status remains unclear, will be an uphill struggle, as a result of and feeding into persistent ethnic tensions linked to the war and to ethnic Albanian attempts to secure independence despite the international community's reservations. Moreover, whether Macedonia will manage to escape from such a vicious circle, and whether the UN presence will provide a sufficient level of security to protect its democracy, remains to be seen.

The relationship between democracy and stability is complex and varied throughout this region. A simple prioritization of the maintenance of stability and the promotion of security may ignore the interrelated processes of democratization. A staged approach to these two objectives may be most appropriate. Viewing the objectives of the international community in realist terms, the process of state building has obtained so far, and should continue to receive, first priority from the international community. This state-building process, despite enduring shortcomings, has been mostly completed. In a second phase, the international community has to devote its efforts to maintaining peace and stability in the region, in order to avert renewed conflicts. Only after this, during a third phase, should the international community then address the question of building democratic states and societies. Armed conflicts, thus far, have exacerbated regional animosities and tensions. At the present, these circumstances may be inappropriate for the strengthening of democracy in all of these states, particularly when one takes into account the complex history of war that characterizes this region.

Dayton and after

The implementation of the Dayton Accord has resulted in the extensive involvement of the international community in this region. In this, external actors have sought to create the new state of Bosnia-Hercegovina (composed of two entities—Republic Srpska and the Croat-Muslim Federation), and to secure a balance of power between Croatia and Yugoslavia. The maintenance of regional peace and security will depend to a large degree on the political, economic, and social reintegration of Bosnia-Hercegovina. The military component of this policy, namely the peacekeeping operation, has so far been most effective. The creation of new state institutions, and the processes of democratic development, remain nascent. Ethnic divisions have not been eased, nor has a unique state of three equal ethnic communities emerged.

At first, the architects of the Dayton Accord failed to address directly the daunting task of democratizing the three authoritarian regimes. The international community hoped that the leaderships of the three ethnic communities would resolve their disputes peacefully, and naturally create effective and democratic state structures. In practice, the implementation of the Dayton Accord has entrenched nationalist forces in these entities, through the formation of zones controlled exclusively by one or another ethnic group at local, cantonal, and entity levels. Even the National Assembly has been designed on the principle of ethnic proportionality, rather than that of civil democracy.[6]

The implementation of the Dayton Accord quickly became almost impossible as a result of the exclusive nationalist policies adopted in these entities.[7] These circumstances stimulated the international community to adopt a more resolute position.[8] The international community demanded that Croatia remove the nationalist leaders in Mostar. It also placed pressure on Zagreb to assist with the extradition of those accused of war crimes. Bosnia has been heavily criticized, because of corruption affairs and the embezzlement of financial transfers. The most decisive pressure was applied on the Republika Srpska, the strongest bastion of opposition to the Accord. The international allies started to arrest those accused of war crimes. They also seized the television transmitter from the Pale leadership. The organization of new elections at first weakened considerably Karadžić's supporters. The first government, then led by President Biljana Plavšić, advocated an acceptance of the Dayton Accord—including the arrest of alleged war criminals, the return of all refugees and full cooperation with the international community.

On this basis, subsequent governments of the Republika Srpska might have received the full support of the international community, on the back of a reform programme providing for the return of all refugees, freedom for the mass media, a large scale privatization programme, a separation of the state and Church, and the formation of stable relations with neighbouring countries. The implementation of such a programme would go far towards achieving the international community's objective of creating a democratic Bosnia and Hercegovina. It would also have an impact on this new state's relations with the Yugoslav Federation. As a result of such changes, the international community might seek to make use of a more amenable Republika Srpska in order to improve relations with the Yugoslav Federation.[9] At the same time, this Republic could also be used as a means to apply pressure on the Federation to accept the new political reality in Bosnia-Hercegovina. The election of the extremist Nikola Poplasen as president of the Republic

[6] M. Sopta (ed.), *Bosnia Hercegovina: Future Political Scenarios in Bosnia Hercegovina beyond Dayton* (Zagreb, 1997), 202–3.

[7] Ibid. 206.

[8] This pressure was applied on all three sides, and clearly articulated in the speeches of Mrs Albright.

[9] The main aim is to create a civil and multiethnic democracy that will lead to the emergence of a unified Bosnia-Hercegovina.

in September 1998 set back such possibilities. Poplasen later attempted to prevent the moderate majority from returning to power under Prime Minister Milorad Dodik. Although he was seemingly sidelined, the subsequent attempt by his deputy Mirko Sarović to seize the presidency in January 2000 caused further instability. Dodik remained prime minister, but his support base was shaken by the persistent uncertainty. However, in the view of the international community, the only democratic alternative in the region remains the creation of a unique state. This objective requires the community to undertake direct management, financial support, and constant supervision. Thus, in November 1999, Bosnia-Hercegovina's three-man presidency was coaxed by the international community into signing the New York declaration, which projected the long-delayed establishment of some of the atttributes of a unitary state, such as a joint police force and border guard.

The international community recognized the need to create a new system of relations within this region that will assist its integration into the wider structure of relations in Europe. The realization of this objective has hardly been simple. However, some progress has been achieved already. A process of strengthening regional trust and mutual confidence has started.

Limited progress has been notable at several levels. First, until the Kosovo crisis, relations between Croatia and Yugoslavia had been normalized. Secondly, while this normalization is unlikely to recover due to the fact that the post-Tudjman government and president of Croatia are siding more firmly with the West, some further progress is to be expected in forging cooperative relations between Croatia and Bosnia-Hercegovina. Zagreb retains an interest in protecting Croats in the neighbouring state but has started to unravel the special relationship that existed between Tudjman's Croatian Democratic Union (HDZ) and its Bosnian branch (the HDZBiH). Meanwhile, Bosnia-Hercegovina continues to seek the resolution of important trade and transportation issues. Nevertheless, full normalization will take some time. Refugee returns between the two states have been very limited and raise complicated issues, while the Tudjman-era HDZBiH commands support among Bosnian Croats.

External actors have sought to prod the new states in the direction of democratization. Thus, the international community was very critical of Tudjman's Croatia for its control of the mass media and its treatment of minorities. External actors have become more insistent on local cooperation with the International Tribunal in The Hague. In Bosnia-Hercegovina, the international community organized elections, monitored the media, and sought to develop a programme of democratic education. Relative to the rest of Europe, these developments do not seem spectacular. However, this progress seems remarkable when one considers the background of war that exists in the region, let alone the atrocities that were committed, and the numbers of dead and homeless.

Moreover, domestic political forces in the new states became increasingly supportive of the objective to integrate them into the Europe, a process that was boosted by the pledges of the Stability Pact. These developments will open channels of communication between north–south and east–west, as well as the possibility of the more rapid integration of this south-eastern region into wider European processes. Despite ongoing problems, the involvement of external actors clearly highlights a commitment to achieve these long-term objectives.

International Plans for Cooperation

The EU's regional approach

At a meeting of the Council of Ministers on 28 October 1996, the EU adopted a document entitled Future Contractual Relations with Some Countries of South-Eastern Europe.[10] On the basis of the positive situation emerging after the Dayton Accord, this document stated that EU objectives in the region were the promotion of political stability and economic prosperity, the start of political and economic reforms, and the recognition of human rights, minority rights, and democratic principles. The document linked each state's relations with the EU to the strengthening of cooperation with its neighbours. Two key features were highlighted in the document. First, the reconstruction of the former Yugoslavia was ruled out. Secondly, one state's unwillingness to undertake these responsibilities would not affect another country's desire to cooperate. This '5 + 1 – 1' group (Albania as +1, and Slovenia as –1) was divided into two groups. The first group consisted of those countries with obligations related to the Dayton Accord (FR Yugoslavia, Croatia, and Bosnia-Hercegovina). Macedonia and Albania, which had made some progress in developing relations with the EU, formed the second group.

The EU decided to negotiate agreements on cooperation with these states on a case-by-case basis, with an emphasis on supporting

[10] *Vjesnik* (14 Dec. 1996).

regional cooperation. As a result, these countries were (apart from Serbia, but including Montenegro), expected to cooperate in the fields of energy, telecommunications, transport, agriculture, and environmental protection. The EU expressed an interest in developing three corridors (the Ljubljana gate, the Panonian corridor, and the Morava-Vardar corridor). The normalization of north–south and south–west trade and transportation highlights the potential benefits resulting from this regional approach. Each cooperation agreement was also required to include a 'strict commitment to the elements necessary for peace and stability of the region, such as human and minorities rights, the right for refugees to return to their homes, democratic structures and political and economic reforms'.[11]

Taking this approach further, the Stability Pact for South-Eastern Europe grew out of the desire of NATO members to avoid another war in the region following the Kosovo crisis. This desire yielded an agreement between the countries of the Balkans (apart from Yugoslavia), the EU, the G8, Hungary, and Turkey (as well as several observers). In order to establish linkages between receiving aid and improving civil, political, and human rights in the region, the pact established three 'working tables': on democratization and human rights; economic reconstruction, development, and cooperation; and security issues (including justice and home affairs). In due course, the EU's aim as part of the Stability Pact is to negotiate Stabilization and Association Agreements (SAAs) with Albania, Bosnia, Croatia, Macedonia, and Yugoslavia. These agreements, one step further than cooperation agreements, will include the objective of a ten-year transition to free trade areas with the EU, during which the EU will offer asymmetric trade preferences, opening up some of its markets prior to reciprocation by the recipient country. Macedonia was the first country singled out for developing an SAA. However, the poor administrative capacity of states in the region weakens the potential effects of such initiatives across the Balkans, highlighting the importance of state building.

While the Stability Pact has raised hopes in the countries concerned, the EU's approach may be vulnerable to the same criticisms as earlier strategies. It has in the past been argued that insisting on regional cooperation as a precondition for relations to the EU is contrary to the EU Agreement where it is stated that each European country may apply for membership.[12] These criticisms

[11] *Vjesnik* (14 Dec. 1996).
[12] I. Simonovic and A. Plenkovic, 'The Croatian European Story', *Croatian International Relations Review*, 3 (1996), 6–7.

have engendered widespread feelings that the project seeks to restore former Yugoslavia, and, in particular, to push Croatia back into the Balkans.[13]

The EU sought to reinforce regional cooperation as a bulwark against future instability. This policy falls in line with EU efforts to develop cooperation in other regions (Baltic, Central Europe, Black Sea). In presenting regional cooperation as an alternative to instability, the European Union has clearly underlined its main objectives: that is, the strengthening of cooperation between neighbouring states and the creation of conditions for preventing renewed conflict. On this basis, the EU has sought to develop the region's ties to wider Europe, and to foster the implementation of European standards and democratic principles.[14] As such, this regional approach has not been isolated or ad hoc. It was firmly grounded in general EU principles. The validity of the approach has also been reinforced by recent developments in the region. Brussels remains convinced that only this approach will promote the strategic aims of realizing peace, developing mutual cooperation, and linking these countries with the European Union.

US pragmatism: SECI

President Clinton launched the 'South-Eastern Europe Coopera-tion Initiative' (SECI) in a letter written in July 1996 to the foreign ministers of the Balkan states. At the time, it seemed to represent but one of many such proposals lacking firm grounding. It rapidly became apparent that this initiative was well planned, and sought to advance several important and long-term American goals. After years of non-involvement, the US government had finally signalled its commitment to this part of Europe, and realized the need for a long-term US presence.

The SECI initiative has become the channel through which the USA has sought to create conditions for peace and stability in the region, ranging from problems in Bosnia-Hercegovina to

[13] In this context, it is interesting to note the position of the Croatian ambas-sador to Brussels in 1997: 'Not a single conversation conducted so far, from the middle to the highest EU level, nor a single strategy paper document, has disguised any allusion to some institutionalization, or disguised creation, of a confederal or federal pseudo-Yugoslavia' (*sic*); J. Vranitzany-Dobrinovic, 'The EU, the SECI and Croatia', *Croatian International Relations Review*, 3: 6/7 (1997), 14.

[14] On the list of criteria to define Eastern European relations with the EU, includ-ing democratic development, legal compatibility, and political stability, see Werner Weidenfeld (ed.), *Central and Eastern Europe on the Way into the European Union* (Gutersloch: Bertelsmann Foundation, 1996).

Greek–Turkish relations. This initiative has also been designed to demonstrate to European countries that conflict resolution in the region is impossible without American engagement. As such, it highlights the critical role that NATO has assumed in post-Cold War European security, as a touchstone for strong Atlanticism— a role underscored by its much-debated bombing campaign against Serbia over Kosovo. Another US objective has been to prevent any spread of radical Islamic ideas from a fundamentalist nucleus in Bosnia-Hercegovina to other parts of the Balkans. The initiative also serves to constrain the emergence of Russia as a major power in the Balkans and to block Russia's access to Southern Europe.

The first draft of the 'Statement of Goals of the South-Eastern Europe Initiative' was signed by Albania, Bosnia and Hercegovina, Bulgaria, Macedonia, Greece, Hungary, Moldova, Romania, and Turkey (6 December 1996). Slovenia, Croatia and Yugoslavia also are to participate as SECI members. On the basis of this wide membership, the US government sought to link together South-Eastern Europe, the Balkans, and part of the former Soviet Union (Moldova). SECI has not been presented as an alternative to other regional approaches, particularly those developed by the EU. On the contrary, SECI was designed to supplement these other initiatives, by promoting close cooperation between the governments of the region, and by placing emphasis on the need for regional planning. In particular, SECI was designed to focus on determining regional programmes that are lacking, ensuring a greater involvement of the private sector in regional economic and environmental activities, and broadly assisting in creating a regional climate supportive to the private sector.[15] In order to fulfil these objectives, each member state was assigned a high-level officer to assist member states and to coordinate cooperation with the UN Economic Commission, international financial institutions, the EU, USA, and other interested countries.

Of the initial signatories, only Hungary showed unease with the initiative, fearing that it may push Hungary into the Balkans, and exclude it from European integration. Following Hungary's NATO accession in March 1999 and progress in its EU membership negotiations, its objections have been set aside. As a result, Hungary has become the northern outpost of SECI. In contrast, Yugoslavia was not invited to the meeting in Geneva, because of its democratic deficit.

[15] *Vjesnik* (12 Jan. 1997).

Slovenia opposed the initiative from the outset. The Slovene government has argued consistently that the Balkan region starts beyond its south-eastern borders. It considers itself an integral part of the Central European process. These perceptions are deeply felt in Slovene politics and society. As in Hungary, the Slovene government has been fearful that participation in SECI might close the doors for its accession to the EU. In the Slovene case, there has also been widespread animosity to any idea of being included with the south, as this would raise the spectre of a revival of the Yugoslav state.

By far the greatest criticism to the idea emerged in Croatia, both from the then leading party (HDZ) and the opposition, now in power. The initiative has been attacked as an attempt to draw Croatia back into Yugoslavia. In this view, SECI would categorize Croatia as a Balkan state, and not a Central European and Mediterranean country. Many political statements have presented the SECI and the European regional approach as the gravest dangers to Croatia. The government decided to participate in some SECI activities that it finds useful, but will not commit itself to full membership. In 1997, the Croatian government went so far as to initiate a discussion on amending the Constitution with a statement that would prohibit any integration connecting Croatia with the Balkans, and particularly, with Yugoslavia.[16]

In this perspective, accession to SECI would push Croatia towards a group of countries with which it has no longer anything in common, and from which it wishes to escape, because of its Yugoslav past. The Croat government has been reluctant, also, to link itself with such 'underdeveloped' states as Albania and Moldova. The Croatian government has sought recognition of its wider European, and not Balkan, civilizational identity.

However, US policy affirmed that the entire Balkan and South European region is critical to its strategic objectives. Such criticism of SECI seems to be unfounded. Moreover, US policy demonstrated a willingess to be flexible in adjusting the project to particular circumstances. In any case, it is highly unlikely that the initiative will be abandoned, as it has already gained some momentum. Most of the states in the region have accepted to join SECI, recognizing in it an opportunity to advance their own interests.[17] Moreover,

[16] *Vjesnik* (23 Feb. 1997).

[17] Erhard Busek, stated that the USA sought to avoid in SECI 'any form of initiative that would be similar to the form of ties that existed in the former Yugoslavia'; see *Vjesnik* (8 Feb. 1997).

SECI foresees joint projects with the Stability Pact, Montenegro, and Kosovo in the fields of transport, environment, and energy. In late 1999, SECI Head Erhard Busek also became coordinator for the economic council of the Stability Pact.

International Leverage

As discussed above, the international community has had a range of instruments of leverage at its disposal. Military instruments were first used by the international community during the war in Croatia, followed by the deployment of UNPROFOR, IFOR, and SFOR in Bosnia-Hercegovina, and NATO's Kosovo and the stationing of KFOR in that province. These operations differed widely in the degree of their use of force, as well as their effectiveness in achieving stated objectives. Apart from peacekeeping and air attacks, military instruments have been used also to reward states such as Slovenia and Macedonia, mainly through cooperation in the Partnership for Peace. On condition that it finally fulfils all the clauses related to internal democratization, as well as those touching upon its relations with Bosnia-Hercegovina, Croatia may now be admitted to the Partnership for Peace programme. Similar options have been raised for Bosnia-Hercegovina. The 'soft' use of military tools, through bilateral and multilateral cooperation, has played a role in fostering dialogue, and may eventually lead to shifts in civil–military relations, throughout these states, in the direction of further democratic control.

Economic means have assumed a central position in the policies of external actors. To some extent, Bosnia-Hercegovina remains entirely dependent on international support. This dependence has been linked to the demands set forth by the international community. Tudjman's Croatia experienced problems in obtaining international credit, which was made conditional on its cooperation with the International Tribunal. Extensive sanctions still prevent Yugoslavia from normal interaction with the international community. In addition to sanctions, the international community has employed other economic measures to stimulate changes in the behaviour of a given state. Talks with Croatia on its participation in the PHARE programme were suspended after operation 'Storm' in 1995. The continuation of these negotiations has been linked to progress in Croatia's internal democratization. Therefore, the international community has used a 'carrots and stick' approach towards the region in economic terms, as well as military. The relative success of the 'stick' of sanctions over the 'carrot' of assistance and trade in advancing international objectives of democracy as well as stability merits close attention.

Political and diplomatic means have not provided the international community with significant leverage, unless accompanied with military and economic measures. Membership in the Council of Europe has been an important matter of prestige for these states. Membership has been a means by which to distinguish themselves from such states as Bosnia-Hercegovina (though Sarajevo's application is to be considered in April 2000) and Yugoslavia. However, this membership is seen as only the first step on a long path towards stronger European and Transatlantic ties.

Placed in a wider context, the transformation of the countries of the former Yugoslavia may be compared with that of the countries of Southern Europe. Those states had experienced fascist, semi-fascist, and authoritarian regimes. However, democratic political forces in those countries succeeded in establishing the rule of law. Without the rule of law, the social-cultural preconditions for the development of democracy cannot take root: that is, a civil society, an independent media, and a culture of political participation. It is possible to affirm on the basis of the experience of Southern Europe that there is no reason for the process of democratization and Europeanization to bypass the countries of former Yugoslavia.

Indeed, the emergence of authoritarian regimes and delays in democratization have been a function largely of the war experience. Peace would open up throughout the region opportunities for democratic transformation along the lines of Western models of development. The political elites in these countries have not unanimously accepted authoritarian models of development. Many members of these elites are favourably inclined towards liberal development, in which a market economy, the rule of law, and a respect for human and minorities' rights mark the first steps towards increasing democratization. This process will need to be assisted by consistent and firm international engagement in the region. In the long term, this process will allow for the inclusion of these countries into the European family of democratic societies.

The correlation between the domestic and international aspects of democratization has become clearly visible. It can be argued that the collapse of the Yugoslav socialist model spurred the start of the democratic transformation in all of these countries, with the exception of Yugoslavia. This democratization process has been supported through various international measures. The experience of involvement in the Yugoslav wars had a sobering effect on the international community. However, this experience also highlighted those instruments and measures that are most effective in advancing international objectives. On the assumption that the international community has the political, will to do so, it can make use of a wide array of military, economic, political and diplomatic measures to underpin the democratic transition and consolidation of these new states.

However, a proper relation between internal and international activities should be carefully maintained, especially in countries that are sensitive about their new independence acquired in such difficult circumstances (Croatia and Bosnia-Hercegovina). International measures that ignore this national sensitivity will be counter-productive, and may even obstruct the process of democratization. The West must be careful so as not to create circumstances in which all its efforts will become seen and mistrusted locally as negative stimuli. International institutions, external actors, and foreign resources cannot guarantee the crafting of democracies in the region. However, these can establish democratization as a process that must be accepted and emulated by all strong forces in these new states.

Belarus and Ukraine: Democracy Building in a Grey Security Zone

Taras Kuzio

Democratization can be contagious in specific geographic regions. Samuel Huntington described the wave of democratization during 1974–90 as the 'Third Wave'. Meanwhile, Juan Linz and Alfred Stepan discussed the *Zeitgeist* and diffusion among tightly grouped countries as ensuring the likelihood of the domino effect of democratization.[1] Twenty-three of the twenty-nine countries democratizing during Huntington's 'Third Wave' had previous democratic experience. Therefore, it can be better described as 'redemocratization'. Of the twenty-seven post-communist states, possibly only ten had an earlier pre-communist experience with democracy.[2] Within the former USSR, the majority of the successor states are building democratic polities from scratch.

Belarus, surrounded by Poland, Ukraine, Latvia, Lithuania, and Russia, which are all participating to different degrees in a democratizing 'Fourth Wave', has not been influenced by this latest democratizing process. Between 1990 and 1994, democratization and marketization in Belarus progressed slowly. Since the election of Alyaksandr Lukashenka in July 1994, Belarus has returned to the authoritarianism of the Mikhail Gorbachev era. In contrast, Ukraine has made strides towards democratization and marketization under both Presidents Leonid Kravchuk (December

[1] Juan J. Linz and Alfred Stepan, *Problems of Democratic Transition and Consolidation: Southern Europe, South America, and Post-communist Europe* (Baltimore: Johns Hopkins University Press, 1996), 72–6.

[2] Karen Dawisha lists ten countries—Albania, Estonia, Latvia, Lithuania, Bulgaria, the Czech Republic, Hungary, Poland, Russia, and Yugoslavia. See her *Post-communism's Troubled Steps toward Democracy: An Aggregate Analysis of Progress in the 27 New States* (College Park, Md.: Center for the Study of Post-communist Societies, University of Maryland, 1997).

1991–July 1994) and Leonid Kuchma (July 1994–). Using Andreas Schedler's concepts of democratic consolidation, we see that Ukraine has evolved beyond 'Electoral Democracy' towards 'Liberal Democracy'. It still has some way to go before it becomes an 'Advanced Democracy'. In contrast, democratic erosion has taken place in Belarus since 1994. The country has returned to the status of an 'authoritarian regime' from that of an 'electoral democracy'.[3]

Belarus and Ukraine have followed different paths since the disintegration of the USSR. This chapter argues three points. First, during the early phase of the transition and drive to modernization, civic elements have been weak because of seven decades of totalitarianism. Initially, the transition to states, democratic polities, and market economies may rely on ethnic mobilization. However, ethnic mobilization has also been weak, because of the post-colonial conditions prevalent in countries such as Ukraine and Belarus. The strength of ethnicity and national identity at the start of the transition process can have a direct impact upon the choice of strategy, speed, and domestic policies adopted by the ruling elites. The post-Soviet states with the greatest degree of national unity and ethnic mobilization (Georgia, Armenia, Lithuania, Latvia, and Estonia) have been also those where reform progressed fastest.

Secondly, if the elites choose a reform path, as in Ukraine, they have little choice but to choose also a foreign policy orientation of 'returning to Europe', from where they will obtain security assurances, inspiration, and technical and financial assistance. Alternatively, if they shift away from democratization towards an authoritarian regime, as in Belarus, they are more likely to seek integration into Eurasian and not European and transatlantic structures.

Thirdly, the international community can play a highly positive role by providing incentives and assistance that persuade those countries which have embarked on democratization to continue the process in the hope of reaching the final destination of democratic consolidation. This positive influence is made more difficult if authoritarian domestic conditions prevent such influence from being exerted. While the international community has supported the transition process in post-communist countries, the external influence of Russia is more negative. As witnessed in Belarus, geopolitical considerations may prevail over democratization. Russia has therefore supported the imposition of an authoritarian regime in Belarus for its own selfish geopolitical purposes.

[3] Andreas Schedler, 'What is Democratic Consolidation?', *Journal of Democracy*, 9: 2 (Apr. 1998), 91–107.

This chapter is divided into four parts. The first part places the transition in Ukraine, Belarus, and the rest of the former USSR within a theoretical and comparative framework by focusing upon domestic factors. The second part discusses the international influences faced by a country that is participating in the reform process (Ukraine), and Russian influences upon a country which is not (Belarus). The last two parts examine Ukraine's 'return to Europe' and Belarus' 'return to Eurasia'.

Domestic Factors in the Post-Soviet Transition

East Central Europe, southern Europe, and Latin America share similar problems in the transition to democracy and market reform. The former USSR has been different for two reasons, both of which make its comparison with the other three regions problematic, and its transition more uncertain: First, these states possessed a totalitarian, in contrast to an authoritarian, legacy; and, second, at the start of the transition, these new states did not possess modern nations, with developed institutions.[4] Post-Soviet transition is therefore post-colonial and post-totalitarian.

Totalitarianism

Ernest Gellner argued that the outcome of the transition from totalitarianism in the direction of liberal democracy is unpredictable.[5] Totalitarianism was a closed political system with no separation of state and society, and no area where political power did not penetrate. The near total destruction of civil society, and the atomization of the population, led to transformation from above in the post-Soviet states. The small middle class of private entrepreneurs from the service and foodstuffs sectors found in former authoritarian-communist regimes is absent in totalitarian regimes. Moreover, the disintegration of totalitarian systems brought forth the great problems of an ideological and spiritual vacuum, moral degradation, nihilism, and corruption.

The post-communist transformation in the former USSR also took place under generally unfavourable conditions. The USSR disintegrated during a time of acute socio-economic crisis and after

---

[4] See the pessimistic survey of the non-Russian successor states of the former USSR by Alexander J. Motyl in *Freedom Review*, 28: 1 (Jan.–Feb. 1997), 50–60.

[5] Ernest Gellner, 'An Identity Crisis in the East', *Independent* (29 Apr. 1996).

decades of 'stagnation'. The consolidation of democracies, market economies, nations, and states is more likely during periods of economic growth.[6] According to former Ukrainian presidential economic adviser Anatoly Halchyns'kyi, the Poles, Czechs, and Slovenes launched their reform programmes at a point when their economies were not in as acute a crisis, had suffered lower declines in output, and benefited from political (read national) accord.[7] The depth of the socio-economic crisis has created unfavourable conditions for the inculcation of new loyalties in the emerging post-Soviet nations and states, particularly in regions such as eastern Ukraine and Belarus. Gertrude Schroeder has argued that an economic reform programme can be sustained only if the population remains strongly supportive of state independence and willing to tolerate the short-term hardships of the transition.[8] In eastern Ukraine and Belarus, support for independence has declined since 1992, which has translated into votes for the anti-reform and anti-independence Communist Party. With the collapse of the *ancien régime*, the disappearance of the 'imperialist centre' and the lack of a strong national identity, disillusionment quickly sets in, creating a legitimacy crisis for the new state and its support for reform.[9]

Quasi-nations and states

The former Soviet states, unlike their counterparts in Latin America and southern and Central Europe, did not inherit modern nations or states. Their political-economic transition has been accompanied by nation and state building which complicates and distorts this process.[10] This 'four pronged transition' has meant that the chances for the early emergence of civil society may be slim.[11] Nation and state building has forced the elites to make difficult choices when choosing strategies for political and economic reform.[12] George

---

[6] Linz and Stepan, *Problems of Democratic Transition and Consolidation*, 76–81.

[7] *Uriadovyi Kurier* (14 Oct. 1997).

[8] Gertrude E. Schroeder, 'On the Economic Viability of New Nation-States', *Journal of International Affairs*, 45: 2 (Winter 1992), 551.

[9] Seymour Martin Lipset, *The First New Nation: The United States in Historical and Comparative Perspective* (New York: W. W. Norton & Co., 1963), 16.

[10] See Taras Kuzio, *Ukraine: State and Nation Building*, Routledge Studies of Societies in Transition 9 (London: Routledge, 1998).

[11] John A. Hall, 'In Search of Civil Society', in John A. Hall (ed.), *Civil Society: Theory, History, Comparison* (Cambridge: Polity Press, 1996), 22.

[12] Gabriel A. Almond and Sidney Verba, *The Civic Culture: Political Attitudes and Democracy in Five Nations* (Princeton: Princeton University Press, 1963), 504.

W. Breslauer noted correctly the lack of a theory that would indicate the conditions under which a chosen economic reform model is compatible with state and nation building.[13]

Democratization is made more difficult if there is no agreement at the time of independence on whether the population wishes to be governed by the new centre and agrees with the boundaries of the new state.[14] Of the twenty-seven post-communist states, Dawisha lists eight that only changed their regime and did not have to build a new state. These eight (the three Baltic states, Albania, Bulgaria, Hungary, Poland, and Romania) possessed a distinct advantage over the other nineteen. Those that had to establish new states, many for the first time, inherited little sense of collective belonging and solidarity. Within these new states, passion, energy, and time has been devoted to creating a cohesive identity, debating an international orientation, inculcating a new civic culture, contesting borders, arguing about the content of the national idea, and dealing with restless national minorities demanding group rights. These debates have often served to divide the population even further, and have distracted them from focusing upon state building and democratization.[15]

Dankwart Rustow argued in his celebrated article nearly three decades ago that a central background condition for marketization and democratization is national unity, which must precede political-economic change. Robert Dahl has also stated that the greater number of citizens in a state who do not wish to be a part of it, the more difficulties there will be in consolidating democracy.[16] Rustow understood national unity as follows:

It simply means that the vast majority of citizens in a democracy-to-be must have no doubt or mental reservations as to which political community they belong to . . . Democracy is a system of rule by temporary majorities. In order that rulers and policies may freely change, the boundaries must adjure, the composition of the citizenry be continuous.[17]

National unity, in the sense Rustow describes, did not exist in any of the Soviet republics when the USSR disintegrated in late 1991.

[13] George W. Breslauer, 'The Impact of the International Environment: Theoretical and Methodological Considerations', in Karen Dawisha (ed.), *The International Dimension of Post-communist Transitions in Russia and the New States of Eurasia* (Armonk, NY: M. E. Sharpe, 1997), 7.

[14] Dawisha, *Post-communism's Troubled Steps*, 9–10.   [15] Ibid. 14–15.

[16] Robert A. Dahl, *Democracy and its Critics* (New Haven: Yale University Press, 1989).

[17] Dankwart Rustow, 'Transitions to Democracy: Towards a Dynamic Model', *Comparative Politics*, 2: 3 (Apr. 1970), 350, 351.

In both Belarus and Ukraine, national unity was lacking at the start of their post-communist transition process. Whenever colonial powers retreat they leave 'administrative voids'. This particularly applies to the non-Russian states of the former USSR. Ukraine inherited only 13,000 administrators compared to half a million found in the United Kingdom, a country with a comparable population size.[18] These weak institutions have meant that the states themselves are also 'weak', possessing little positive sovereignty (that is, control over their domestic affairs).[19] The Ukrainian historian Stanislav Kul'chyts'kyi argued that only three of the former communist states inherited the infrastructure and institutions of the former imperial metropolis—Russia, the Czech Republic and Serbia, from the USSR, Czechoslovakia, and Yugoslavia respectively.[20] Many of the remainder, particularly within the former USSR, 'had to undertake state building practically from scratch'.[21] Therefore, the non-Russian states of the former USSR are also undergoing an 'imperial transition', similar to that experienced by the former colonial dependencies of the Western empires.[22] Former prime minister of Ukraine, Kuchma, complained that his task was made all the more difficult by the fact that he lacked a mandate, finances, and capable officials.[23]

The absence of united national identities, elites and bureaucrats, recognized borders, legal systems, private economic sectors, citizens with access to hard currency who had knowledge of, and access to, the outside world, together with elements of civil society (the Church, the media, political movements, and civic groups) made transition in the former USSR very different from that experienced elsewhere. Linz and Stepan acknowledged that the elites of many of the former Soviet republics, with the exception of Russia, supported national liberation struggles against the state (which was

[18] See Judy Hague, Aidan Rose, and Marko Bojcun, 'Rebuilding Ukraine's Hollow State: Developing a Democratic Public Service in Ukraine', *Public Administration and Development*, 15: 4 (Oct. 1995), 417–33.

[19] Mette Skak, *From Empire to Anarchy: Postcommunist Foreign Policy and International Relations* (London: Hurst & Co., 1996), 26, 36.

[20] Mary McAuley points out that Russia and the USSR were closely merged: 'Hence any disentangling of Russia from the USSR was going to be something very different from a seemingly similar process involving the other republics.' See her *Russia's Politics of Uncertainty* (Cambridge: Cambridge University Press, 1997), 16.

[21] S. V. Kul'chyts'kyi, 'Derzhavotvorchyi protses v Ukraiini', *Ukraiins'kyi Istorychnyi Zhurnal*, 6 (1996), 69.

[22] Skak, *From Empire to Anarchy*, 18, 21, 69.

[23] *The Times* (21 May 1993).

not the case elsewhere). This situation 'almost pushed matters of democratic crafting off the normative and institutional agenda of politics'.[24]

Strong states are required for the consolidation of democracy, to defend civil society, implement policy and the rule of law, collect taxes, and provide for the welfare and other rights of citizens. State building is usually quicker and less problematical than nation building. In the former Soviet republics, new civic nations are being forged, which may create nation-states and democratic polities in the medium term. Sovereign states are a prerequisite for democracies because no states, no democracies: 'the absence of an organization with the attributes of a modern state . . . precludes democratic governance over the whole territory of the state'.[25]

Belarus and Ukraine

Both Belarus and Ukraine embarked upon democratization and marketization in the absence of national unity or political communities. Ukraine inherited a more favourable legacy than that bequeathed to Belarus. These inherited legacies played a prominent role in the transition processes in Belarus and Ukraine in two ways. First, these legacies influenced the starting period, speed, and type of transformation chosen by its elites. Secondly, they influenced their foreign orientations and attitudes towards integration with European and transatlantic structures, or Eurasia.[26]

A survey of mobilization in the former USSR on the eve of the disintegration of the Soviet Union illustrated the following points. Kathleen Montgomery and Thomas F. Remington found that the former Soviet states were divided into three groups, in terms of their counter-elite mobilization: 'high penetration', 'partial success', and 'low penetration'. Ukraine and Belarus (together with Russia and Moldova) formed part of the 'partial success' group, where the counter-elites had won between 15–40 per cent of the vote in the March 1990 parliamentary elections.[27]

[24] Linz and Stepan, *Problems of Democratic Transition and Consolidation*, 387.
[25] Ibid. 18.
[26] See Taras Kuzio and Marc Nordberg, 'Nation and State Building, Historical Legacies and National Identities in Belarus and Ukraine: A Comparative Analysis', *Canadian Review of Studies in Nationalism*, 26: 1–2 (1999), 69–90.
[27] Kathleen Montgomery and Thomas F. Remington, 'Regime Transition and the 1990 Soviet Republican Elections', *Journal of Communist Studies and Transition Politics*, 10: 1 (Mar. 1994), 57–79. Only Georgia, Armenia, and the three Baltic states entered the 'high penetration' group where the opposition won parliamentary majorities in March 1990.

The strength or weakness of the national idea in Ukraine and Belarus, and regionally within both countries, has had direct influence on the strength of their domestic constituencies in support of reform, independent statehood and a pro-Western orientation. Within Ukraine, the strength of the national idea in certain regions, its revived historical political culture, and the greater degree of language proficiency of the titular ethnic group have played a role in sustaining the post-transformation and nation-state building project.

Ukraine, in contrast to Belarus, was able to fall back upon a national communist tradition which helped provide additional support for a national movement that never encompassed the entire country.[28] These national communists helped to provide Ukraine with a large endorsement for independence in its December 1991 referendum. But, of course, they also contributed to delays and distortions in the transition until after October 1994.[29] A large and active national democratic lobby, therefore, was indispensable to sustaining the transformation process. The strength of national democratic support cannot be measured in terms of electoral strength. In Belgium, Scotland, and Ukraine, ethno-regional movements have not come to power. Nevertheless, such movements have effectively shaped the domestic and foreign policy agenda in all three countries.[30]

In contrast, Belarus resembled a large country without a nationally conscious capital city, and afraid to gamble on holding a referendum on independence. The absence of this referendum was used by Lukashenka to his advantage, as he has based his legitimacy upon the March 1991 referendum for a 'revived (Soviet) union'. Russified, denationalized masses, who have ambivalent or regional identities, as in the majority of Belarus and certain regions of Ukraine, are 'amorphous', difficult to mobilize, and more susceptible to populist support for Soviet nostalgia. This nostalgia translates into electoral support for the left.

---

[28] The leader of the Belarusian Popular Front, Zenon Pazniak, admitted: 'I must say that among the leaders of Belarus there are no politicians and personalities of Kravchuk's stature' (*Moscow News*, no. 48, 1992).

[29] See Taras Kuzio, *Ukraine: Perestroika to Independence*, 2nd edn. (London: Macmillan, 2000).

[30] See Saul Newman, 'Losing the Electoral Battles and Winning the Policy Wars: Ethnoregional Conflict in Belgium', *Nationalism and Ethnic Politics*, 1: 4 (Winter 1995), 44–72.

External Factors and Influences

The international community

To what degree can international agencies assist in the democratization process? The theoretical literature traditionally has argued that the main impetus for democratization came from within countries, as a consequence of political culture and/or modernization leading to domestic pressure. The international factor, therefore, was regarded as less important.[31]

However, international assistance has played and will continue to play a prominent role in the post-communist transition in Central and Eastern Europe, because it assists in the reform project and rewards those that are doing well. This has provided for a close relationship between international assistance and the progress of the transition process.[32] Countries, such as Ukraine, which support democratization, have sought to 'return to Europe', which has provided powerful leverage for the West and international institutions over their domestic policies. Ukraine, unlike Belarus, has seen its strategic foreign policy goals as integrating into European and Transatlantic structures. Domestic reformers, nation and state builders, such as the Ukrainian President Kuchma, have sought to enlist international support, 'even if only insubstantial and symbolic forms of endorsement are available from outside'.[33] States in the throes of nation and state building, whose domestic institutions are still under construction, will seek to obtain external support for their negative sovereignty, state independence, and territorial integrity.[34] This is particularly the case if the country has felt

[31] Laurence Whitehead, 'International Aspects of Democratization', in Guillermo O'Donnell, Philippe C. Schmitter, and Laurence Whitehead (eds.), *Transitions from Authoritarian Rule: Prospects for Democracy* (Baltimore: Johns Hopkins University Press, 1986), 4, 20; and Geoffrey Pridham, 'The International Dimension of Democratisation: Theory, Practice, and Inter-regional Comparisons', in Geoffrey Pridham, Eric Herring, and George Sanford (eds.), *Building Democracy? The International Dimension of Democratisation in Eastern Europe* (London: Leicester University Press, 1994), 10.

[32] Dawisha, *Post-communism's Troubled Steps*, 38.

[33] Whitehead, 'International Aspects of Democratization', 9.

[34] Robert H. Jackson defines quasi-states as those former colonies where 'few (of these) states are "nations" either by long history or common ethnicity or successful constitutional integration'. See his *Quasi-States: Sovereignty, International Relations and the Third World* (Cambridge: Cambridge University Press, 1990), 41. Jackson describes these former colonies as only possessing 'negative sovereignty'.

threatened by a powerful neighbour (for example, Ukraine with regard to Russia).

Two major themes dominated Ukrainian security policy after it became an independent state in 1992.[35] First, Ukraine sought international security guarantees for its sovereignty, independence, and territorial integrity. Ukraine successfully obtained security assurances (not guarantees) from the world's declared nuclear powers in December 1994, in return for ratifying the Nuclear Non-Proliferation Treaty, and in July 1997 from the North Atlantic Treaty Organization (NATO), largely out of gratitude for supporting NATO enlargement. Since 1994, the shift in Western policy away from Russo-centrism, which focused exclusively upon nuclear weapons, and the subsequent recognition of Ukraine as the 'linchpin of European security' provided Ukraine with greater freedom of manœuvre to focus upon its domestic problems.[36] Secondly, Ukraine, as the country which gained the most from post-war territorial changes, sought to obtain legal recognition of its borders by its neighbours. This was achieved in spring 1997 when Russia and Romania signed treaties with Ukraine. Both houses of the Russian parliament only ratified the treaty in December 1998 and February 1999.

In return for providing support for Ukraine's positive and negative sovereignty, Western governments and institutions sought to influence its post-communist transformation project. Through membership of international institutions, Ukraine has indicated its willingness to participate in organizations which will promote transparency and permeability, and will provide a positive link

That is, 'they possess juridical statehood while as yet disclosing little evidence of empirical statehood' (at 25). If state and nation building is successful in creating a modern nation and state, a country such as Ukraine would then possess 'positive sovereignty'. This Jackson defines as the 'sociological, economic, technological, psychological and similar wherewithal to decide, implement and enforce public policy both domestically and internationally' (at 29).

[35] See Taras Kuzio, *Ukrainian Security Policy* (Washington: Praeger and the CSIS, 1995). For discussions of changes in Ukrainian foreign policy under President Kuchma see O. F. Belov et al. (eds.), *Natsional'na Bezpeka Ukraiiny, 1994–1996 rr. Naukova Dopovid' NISD* (Kyiv: National Security and Defense Council and the National Institute for Strategic Studies, 1997), as well as ch. 6, 'New Foreign and Defense Policies', in Taras Kuzio, *Ukraine under Kuchma: Political Reform, Economic Transformation and Security Policy in Independent Ukraine* (London: Macmillan, 1997), 179–226.

[36] Evidence of this can be found in Sherman W. Garnett, *Keystone in the Arch: Ukraine in the Emerging Security Environment of Central and Eastern Europe* (Washington: Carnegie Endowment, 1997); and Tor Bukkvoll, *Ukraine and European Security* (London: Pinter and the RIIA, 1997).

between assistance and the transformation process. This influence and assistance, which is diffused through its domestic reform programme (by the IMF, the EU, the EBRD, and the World Bank), has enhanced Ukrainian self-confidence (by NATO), ensured that it adopts only peaceful methods in resolving ethnic conflict (by the OSCE), and pursued democratization (by the OSCE, the EU, the National Endowment for Democracy, the Soros Foundation, and the International Foundation for Electoral Systems). The desire of Ukraine to 'return to Europe'[37] has provided Western governments and institutions with strategic leverage which should aim, Adrian Hyde-Price has argued, 'to enmesh these countries in an ever-deepening network of political, economic and social interdependence'.[38]

The West and international organizations could not provide assistance to Ukraine prior to 1994, because only in that year was the nuclear weapons question resolved and did Ukraine launch its first reform programme. Ukraine's pro-Western foreign policy has been based on the fear that closer Commonwealth of Independent States (CIS) integration would weaken its sovereignty. This pro-Western foreign policy has been recognized and rewarded by key Western countries and NATO, which have seen Ukraine after 1994 as a strategic component of European security. Ukraine's pro-Western foreign policy has been supported, however, only on condition that its domestic reform programme continues. Ukraine has had to accept advice and recommendations from organizations such as the IMF, the World Bank, USAID, the EBRD, the Council of Europe, and the OSCE.

Relations with the EU may cause difficulties for Ukraine's perception of the utility of the international community. Ukraine is not a member even of the 'slow track' group of prospective EU members. Although a 'strategic partnership' between Ukraine and the EU was established in December 1999, it reduced the influence of Brussels over Kyiv's domestic reform programme.[39]

---

[37] See Taras Kuzio, 'Europe or Eurasia? National Identity, Transformation and Ukrainian Foreign Policy', in Rick Fawn (ed.), *Ideology and National Identity in Post-communist Foreign Policies* (forthcoming).

[38] Adrian G. V. Hyde-Price, 'Democratization in Eastern Europe: The External Dimension', in Geoffrey Pridham and Tatu Vanhanen (eds.), *Democratization in Eastern Europe: Domestic and International Perspectives* (London: Routledge, 1994), 245.

[39] See Taras Kuzio, 'The EU and Ukraine: A Troubled Partnership', in John Redmond and Jackie Gower (eds.), *EU Enlargement* (Aldershot: Ashgate, 2000), 154–62.

Ukraine has been the leading CIS state within NATO's Partnership for Peace programme. It signed a Charter with NATO in July 1997 and has not ruled out future membership.[40] Unlike Russia and Belarus, Ukraine supported the enlargement of NATO as the enlargement of a zone of security towards itself. A study of Ukrainian elite opinion found that 'NATO creates little or no fear in the minds of virtually all specialists in Ukraine as a direct military threat to their security.'[41] Ukraine has sought to define itself as a 'European', or, more specifically, a 'Central European' state through membership of the Central European Initiative and by seeking membership of the Central European Free Trade Association. Kyiv has also outlined its ambitious strategic agenda of seeking EU and WEU membership. This pro-Western orientation of Ukrainian security policy also includes exploring new markets for Ukrainian exports in mainly Third World countries (for example, Latin America), in order to reduce its foreign trade dependency upon Russia and the CIS.

Poland was a key strategic partner for Ukraine in this goal of 'returning to Europe' through Central Europe. In return for supporting Ukraine's evolutionary integration westwards, Poland secured three goals. First, it secured a stable and pro-Western eastern flank. Second, this support discouraged Ukraine from joining any pan-Slavic bloc with Russia which would be inevitably anti-Western. Third, Warsaw has been able to encourage Kyiv not to regard NATO enlargement as a threat to its security. By not opposing NATO enlargement, Ukraine prevented the creation of a potential anti-NATO expansion alliance of the three eastern Slavic states, which may have derailed the NATO enlargement and subsequently the democratization process. The Ukraine-NATO Charter may have represented the West's recognition of Ukraine's positive role in facilitating this enlargement.

International institutions have been unable to exert much leverage over the Lukashenka regime in Belarus. Belarus has little need for assistance from the IMF or the World Bank, whose criteria for providing assistance would be too strict for Lukashenka to swallow. Instead, he has successfully sought subsidies from Russia,

[40] See Taras Kuzio, 'Ukraine and NATO: The Evolving Strategic Partnership', *Journal of Strategic Studies*, 21: 2 (June 1998), 1–30.

[41] P. Terrence Hopman, Stephen D. Shenfield, and Dominique Arel, *Integration and Disintegration in the Former Soviet Union: Implications for Regional and Global Security*, Occasional Paper 30 (Providence, RI: Thomas J. Watson Jr. Institute for International Studies, Brown University, 1997), 58. See also Taras Kuzio, 'The Baltics, Ukraine and the path to NATO', *Jane's Intelligence Review*, 9: 7 (July 1997), 300–3.

which are provided in exchange for strategic considerations, not as a means to influence a non-existent domestic reform programme. Lukashenka has largely ignored calls by the OSCE, Council of Europe, or the EU to begin dialogue with his dissolved parliament and the democratic opposition. If countries, such as Belarus under the maverick Lukashenka, do not seek to participate in the democratizing 'Fourth Wave' they turn their backs on 'Europe' (and, by implication, upon Western governments and international institutions). The foreign orientation of such countries is directed instead towards returning to Eurasia, from where they feel they were unwillingly ejected in December 1991.

Russia's choice: geopolitics over democracy

But what of Belarus' patron state Russia? This relationship resembles that which existed between the USA and Central and South America throughout most of the twentieth century, and that between France and Francophone Africa from the 1950s. In these cases, geopolitics superseded the patron's (the USA, France, and Russia) concerns for democratization.[42]

Russian democrats, including former President Boris Yeltsin, who support reform and anti-communism at home, have largely backed the authoritarian, anti-reform Lukashenka in Belarus, who was openly nostalgic about the former USSR. The extent to which Russian democrats backed union with Belarus could be seen in the unanimous ratification of the Russian-Belarusian treaty by the Russian State Duma and the Federation Council, the lower and the upper houses of parliament, by 363 : 2 and 144 : 0 votes respectively.[43] At a time of acute payments crisis and wage arrears in autumn 1997, Russia subsidized Belarus to the tune of $1.5–2 billion per annum.[44] Even politicians with impeccable reform credentials, like Boris Nemtsov, have argued that 'The Russian-Belarusian union is tremendously important, irrespective of Lukashenka's personality. Whatever that personality may be, the union represents an enormous gain for Russia geopolitically, psychologically, and spiritually.'[45]

It may seem strange that Russian democrats, such as Nemtsov, have supported anti-reformists in neighbouring Belarus, when one would assume that democratic and market reform in that country

---

[42] Pridham, in 'International Dimension of Democratisation', 11.

[43] *Interfax* (6 June 1997); and *Reuters* (10 June 1997).

[44] Andrei Illarionov, the director of the Russian Institute of Economic Analysis, quoted by *Interfax* (9 Oct. 1997).

[45] *Jamestown Monitor* (8 Oct. 1997).

would be in the interests of Russia. Even somewhat less radical Russian democrats, such as former Deputy Prime Minister Valery Serov and Moscow Mayor Yury Luzhkov, have also backed Lukashenka.[46] A few in the democratic camp, such as leading Yabloko member, Vladimir Lukin, found his eccentricities more embarrassing, yet preferred to ignore the authoritarian nature of his regime in the interests of geopolitics and the cause of CIS integration.

Russia's support for geopolitics over reform in its 'near abroad' has been made all the more complicated by the peculiar legacies of tsarist and Soviet nationalities policies and historiography, which promoted both Russification and Little Russianization in Belarus and Ukraine. Between half and three-quarters of Russians do not regard Ukrainians as a separate ethnic group. This has influenced their perception of Ukrainian independence as somehow 'artificial' and 'temporary', with the Ukrainian *narod* eager to 'reunite' with Russia, but prevented from doing so by the USA, which does not want to see Russia as a great power, and by former communist and now nationalist elites.[47] As President Yeltsin complained: 'We cannot get it out of our systems that the Ukrainians are the same as we are. That is our destiny. Our common destiny.'[48]

Russia's geopolitical designs on its 'near abroad' may be similar to US and French former policies in Latin America and Francophone Africa. But when Russia looks towards Belarus and Ukraine, these geopolitical impulses have been strengthened by inherited deformed national identities. Democratizing Russia is still coming to terms with its loss of empire and great power status, with little tradition of a nation-state to fall back on. It has been torn between two policies: supporting nation and state building within its borders; or empire building among the eastern Slavs and/or the CIS, where geopolitics would take precedence over reform.

The importance to Russia of geopolitics over democratization in Belarus was reflected in the creation of a 'common defence space'

[46] See the remarks by Russian Deputy Prime Minister Valery Serov in *Moskovskiy Komsomolets* (2 Apr. 1997), and Moscow Mayor Y. Luzhkov in *Obshchaya Gazeta* (8–14 May 1997).

[47] See T. Kuzio, 'National Identity and Foreign Policy: The East Slavic Conundrum' in Taras Kuzio (ed.), *Contemporary Ukraine: Dynamics of Post-Soviet Transformation* (Armonk, NY: M. E. Sharpe, 1998), 221–44 and Taras Kuzio, 'The East Slavic Conundrum: History and National Identity', paper presented to the conference on 'National Identities; History, Geography, Images' at the Institute for Contemporary Historical Research, University of London (20–2 Apr. 1998).

[48] *Radio Rossii* (21 Nov. 1997).

after December 1997 when both countries signed nine military agreements. This 'common defence space', which encompasses Belarus and western Russia, was portrayed in anti-US terms as a response to the eastward enlargement of NATO. The importance for Russia of obtaining Belarus as a geopolitical ally will be at the expense of any democratization or marketization in Belarus, by converting it into a Russian dominion.[49] As Adam Watson points out, the greatest test of any country's sovereignty is its ability to conduct its own foreign policy, which in the case of Belarus has been limited.[50] Russian policies in Belarus, therefore, have entrenched the Lukashenka regime. A Russian geopolitical ally such as Lukashenka could only be one who is both anti-NATO and anti-Western, turning his back on 'Europe' and domestic reform.

A 'Return to Europe' under Kuchma

Ukraine has followed a very different path to Belarus since becoming an independent state. The foreign policies of its two presidents (Kravchuk, 1991–4 and Kuchma, 1994–) have followed a consistent strategic course of 'returning to Europe', coupled with domestic reform. This reflects the close correlation between domestic reform, national identity, and foreign geopolitical orientation.[51] Such a choice was given to the Ukrainian electorate in the second round of the presidential elections on 14 November 1999 when Kuchma (representing reform and 'return to Europe') faced Petro Symonenko, the communist leader (representing a return to the past domestically and a pro-Eurasian foreign orientation).[52]

Under Kravchuk, an alliance of national communists and national democrats dominated the parliamentary, presidential, and

[49] In the USSR, only Belarus has sought union with Russia.

[50] A. Watson, *The Evolution of International Society* (London: Routledge, 1992), 316. A dominion is defined as where an external hegemon only allows the country's leaders to deal with *internal* issues. They, 'nevertheless retain their identity as separate states and some control over their own affairs'. A hegemon is defined by Watson as a power which lays down the law in a system of states that determines 'the external relations between member states while leaving them domestically independent'.

[51] See Taras Kuzio, 'Defining the Political Communuity in Ukraine: State, Nation and the Transition to Modernity', in Taras Kuzio, Robert S. Krawchuk, and Paul D'Anieri (eds.), *State and Institution Building in Ukraine* (New York: St Martin's Press, 1999), 213–44.

[52] On the elite foreign policy consensus in Ukraine since 1992 see Paul D'Anieri, *Economic Interdependence in Ukrainian–Russian Relations* (Albany, NY: State University of New York Press, 1999).

governmental leaderships. Ukraine's reform programme, therefore, corresponded to Huntington's 'transplacement' (Linz's 'extrication') model, where the elites and opposition compromise, because neither is strong enough to replace or repress the other. Huntington's concept of transplacement fits with developments in Ukraine:

Uncertainty, ambiguousness, and division of opinion over democratization thus tended to characterize the ruling circles in transplacement situations. These regimes were not overwhelmingly committed either to holding on to power ruthlessly or to moving decisively towards democratization.[53]

The moderates in the *ancien régime* (the national communists) allied themselves to the moderates within a section of the opposition Rukh, in a centrist process of transplacement. This transplacement was opposed by two groups: first, by the radicals in the *ancien régime* (the so-called 'imperial communists' or Huntington's 'standpatters'); and second, by the radicals in the counter-elites (the section of Rukh led by V'iacheslav Chornovil, together with the New Ukraine bloc). Both sides benefited from transplacement, by democratization proceeding ahead, making a return to repression unlikely. Meanwhile, the old elites were not put on trial or forced to flee into exile in the new state.

The following crucial elements required for the success of transplacement are found in Ukraine (but not in Belarus): the existence of national communists (or 'regime moderates'); a strong counter-elite with its heartland in western Ukraine which provided the initial push to independence (or 'moderate opposition'); a greater degree of national identity, historical memory, and level of language proficiency; and the presence of greater domestic resources which are available for the enrichment of the old and the new elites.

Ukraine's democratic-national communist alliance made possible a consensus on maintaining Russia at a distance, while seeking to promote a pro-Western security policy. At the same time, they looked upon the CIS as either, at best, a forum for 'civilized divorce', or, at worst, an entity through which some of the pain of economic transformation could be mitigated. The national communists wished to maintain Russia at a distance because they felt threatened by, and disliked, the radical reform programme launched by Yeltsin in January 1992. The national democrats meanwhile, hailing mainly from western Ukraine and Kyiv, regarded Russia as the Eurasian/Asian 'Other', with Ukraine the last eastern outpost of 'European civilization'.

---

[53] Samuel P. Huntington, *The Third Wave: Democratization in the Late Twentieth Century* (Norman, Okla.: University of Oklahoma Press, 1991), 156–7.

The Kravchuk leadership limited Ukraine's engagement in the CIS to associate member status in the Economic Union, and rejected membership of the Inter-Parliamentary Assembly and the Tashkent Collective Security Treaty. Ukraine also refused to ratify the CIS Charter, thereby making it *de jure* not even a member of the CIS, but only a 'participant'.[54] Under Kuchma, Ukraine continued to follow the Kravchuk line of rejecting CIS political or military integration, or the creation of any multilateral institutions, while preferring to utilize the CIS as a forum to develop bilateral, mainly economic, relations.

Under Leonid Kuchma, Ukraine sought, however, to utilize discontent within the CIS at Russia's actions, as well as common geopolitical interests, to forge the GUUAM bloc (Georgia-Ukraine-Uzbekistan-Azerbaijan-Moldova). GUUAM has sought to oppose Russian-backed separatism, support territorial integrity, and develop, together with Turkey, the immense oil resources of Azerbaijan to the benefit of all five countries, thereby lessening their dependence upon Russian energy supplies.[55]

Assistance from international financial institutions and Western governments have become important external elements of support for the Ukrainian domestic reform programme. These were provided for three reasons. First, this support represented gratitude for Ukraine's agreement to denuclearize. Secondly, these institutions supported the launch of the IMF-backed economic reform programme in October 1994. Finally, this support symbolized the West's growing recognition of Ukraine's strategic importance.

Kuchma has sought to obtain external support for his 'four-pronged' transition of political reform, marketization, state and nation building by continuing Kravchuk's aim to 'return to Europe'.[56] Kuchma's more pragmatic approach to the CIS and relations with Russia has not dampened his desire to orient the country towards the West. Ukraine's historical memory and political culture have made integration with Russia, the CIS, or within Eurasia, unattractive because its elites have believed that 'close relations with Russia always entail subjugation, economic exploitation, and cultural assimilation'.[57]

[54] As described to this author by Andriy Vesselovs'kyi, acting head of the Policy Planning Department of the Ministry of Foreign Affairs, Kyiv, 15 Oct. 1997.

[55] See Taras Kuzio, 'Geopolitical Pluralism in the CIS: The Rise of GUUAM', *Problems of Post-Communism*, 47: 3 (May–June 2000), 25–35.

[56] This 'four pronged transition' was outlined by Volodymyr Cherniak to the VI congress of Rukh (*Chas*, 29 Dec. 1995) and by Ukrainian Foreign Minister Udovenko to the Royal Institute of International Affairs, London, on 13 Dec. 1995.

[57] Hopman, Shenfield, and Arel, *Integration and Disintegration*, 38.

For Ukraine to pursue its four-pronged transition (or trans-placement), its elites have felt the need to maintain a discreet distance between themselves and Russia. 'Cooperative integration', they fear, could lead to 'integration under Russian domination'. Consequently, the Ukrainian elites view any active engagement in the CIS as leading to a loss of its sovereignty.[58] This fear of Russia did not abate among Ukrainian elites after the signing of the Russian-Ukrainian treaty in May 1997. On the contrary, the majority of Ukrainian elites still believed that Russia has not outgrown its 'big brother syndrome', or reconciled itself fully to Ukrainian independence. The perceived threat from the Yeltsin administration is not military, but that of economic, cultural, and political domination.[59] Ukrainian elites felt that Russians saw them as another 'Belarus', whose cultural and linguistic closeness presupposed a common state under Moscow's control.

The most popular policy favoured by the Ukrainian elites *vis-à-vis* Russia has been 'cooperative independence'—not 'cooperative integration' or 'union'. 'Cooperative independence', as pursued by Kuchma since 1994, allowed Ukraine to normalize relations with Russia and to maintain Eurasia at a distance, without breaking with it completely—while focusing most upon 'returning to Europe'. 'Cooperative independence' would ensure Western support for Ukraine's reform programme, while neutralizing any threats to Ukrainian state and nation building from Russia.

Consequently, as reflected in Tables 17.1 and 17.2, there has been a high correlation between domestic supporters of reform and those who hold a westward foreign orientation. Supporters of reform were committed to a multi-party system, as competing parties are considered important and strongly back independence.

Centrist political parties represented liberal and social democratic constituencies. These favoured a strong emphasis upon economic issues and a heavy dose of pragmatism in foreign policy. They were committed to a medium- to long-term agenda of 'returning to Europe' while maintaining good relations with Russia and restricting Ukraine's participation in the CIS to bilateral economic cooperation (not integration). Centrist political parties and parliamentary factions supported Ukraine's current neutral and non-bloc status as a future stepping stone to integration into European and transatlantic structures.

Centre-right national democrats, on the other hand, adopted a more 'romantic' approach to foreign policy issues. Like their centrist

---

[58] Hopman, Shenfield, and Arel, *Integration and Disintegration*, 30.
[59] Ibid. 17, 27–8.

TABLE 17.1. *Public attitudes in Ukraine to different models of development*

Political model	Reformist views	Centrist views	Communist views
USA	23	18	8
Germany	13	8	4
Russia/USSR	1	3	13
Economic Model			
USA	11	12	8
Germany	19	16	7
Russia/USSR	1	2	16
Economic Preferences			
Limited gov.	59	64	15
Command Econ.	32	29	77
Radical reform	73	60	27
No reforms	4	6	39
Private land	84	90	63
Land as commodity	83	73	41
Political Parties			
Multi-party system	64	65	29
Competing parties	75	73	38
For party-affiliated candidates	40	24	57

Source: Elehie Natalie Skoczylas, *Ukraine 1996: Public Opinion on Key Issues* (Washington: International Foundation for Electoral Systems, 1997), 48. These figures are derived from an IFES May 1996 survey.

colleagues, they backed reform. Nevertheless, they supported Ukraine's non-participation in the CIS, renunciation of its neutral and non-bloc status, and its immediate application to join European and transatlantic structures. They therefore have had little interest in pragmatically cooperating in the CIS or maintaining good relations with Russia.

In contrast, only Communist supporters preferred both a single-party system and sought to reorient Ukraine backwards to a revived Soviet Union or to a new union (for example, by joining the Belarusian-Russian union). Only the radical left supported all-round integration within the CIS, with Ukraine formally joining the CIS by ratification of the CIS Charter. This integration would include Ukraine's membership of the CIS Inter-Parliamentary Assembly and the Tashkent Collective Security Treaty.

Ukraine's domestic transformation has proved to be more successful at the political rather than economic level. This transformation

TABLE 17.2. *Foreign orientations of Ukrainian political parties*

Radical Left	Social Democratic/Liberal (Centrist Pragmatics)	Centre-Right and Radical Right (National Democratic Romantics)
Revived USSR; CIS Military/Political and Economic Bloc;	Neutrality / Non-Bloc Status; CIS Economic Integration;	Withdrawal from CIS; NATO Membership;
—Communist Party —Party of Slavic Unity —Civic Congress —Socialist Party —Peasant Party —Progressive Socialists	—Hromada —Agrarian Party[a] —People's Democratic Party[a] —Social Democratic Party —Interregional; Bloc Reforms —Liberal Party —Green Party —Constitutional Democratic Party —SDP (United)[a] —Labour Party —Regional Revival[a] —Labour Ukraine[a]	—Republican Party —Rukh —Democratic Party —Peasant Democratic Party —Christian Democratic Party —Congress of Ukrainian Nationalists —Party of Reform and Order —Forward Ukraine! —Liberal Democratic Party

[a] These represent President Kuchma's 'parties of power'.

process accelerated after 1994, after which the West and international organizations began to play an important role in providing assistance, advice, and pressure. Nevertheless, there were notable areas of success in the overall reform process after Kuchma came to power. In 1996, 85 per cent of members of parliament voluntarily took the oath of allegiance to the Ukrainian state, reflecting growing support for independence (the oath became compulsory for deputies elected after the 1996 constitution). This vote underlined growing confidence in the consolidation of Ukrainian statehood and nation building.[60]

At the political level, parliamentary and presidential elections in 1994 and 1998–9 transferred power smoothly, and highlighted

[60] Hopman, Shenfield, and Arel, *Integration and Disintegration*, 46.

the consolidation of a multi-party system. The legitimacy of the new state was also enshrined in the adoption of a post-Soviet constitution in June 1996. Partly on this basis, Ukrainian politics have established better balance between the powers of parliament and those of the president, which has prevented the creation of an authoritarian regime and the emasculation of parliament (as in Belarus and Russia). This process also consolidated the rule of law with the reform of the judiciary. Ukraine also witnessed the expansion of independent printed and electronic media. At the international level, the controversial issue of Crimean separatism has been resolved peacefully, generally without recourse to violent protest, and a new constitution was adopted in December 1998 that recognized the peninsula as part of Ukrainian territory.[61] Finally, the last two sections of Ukraine's borders were legally recognized at the executive level by Russia and Romania in agreements in spring 1997.

Nevertheless, many problems remained. The Ukrainian state was still 'weak' in terms of two traditional methods for gauging state strength—tax collection, and success in combating corruption and crime. Ukraine inherited few of the necessary institutions to run such a large state. Therefore, President Kuchma was being rather optimistic when he claimed that state building had been 'completed' by 1996. This was particularly the case with regard to local institutions and centre-periphery institutional relations.[62]

Ukraine (and Belarus) was still not a consolidated democracy, because this can only exist in states which have overcome problems of nation building.[63] Ukraine was also still far from democratic consolidation as defined by Lipset.[64] In this, consolidated democracies are states where democracy is the only game in town, and where, in the event of a crisis, change can only come about through the democratic process. In such a state, no significant political groups should seek to overthrow the regime by violence.[65] Elements of the *ancien régime*, which impede democratic consolidation may have to be removed.[66] Civil society remained weak. The large number of

[61] See the report of the poll conducted by Democratic Initiatives and Sotsis-Gallup in *Den'* (1 Oct. 1997).

[62] Robert Dahl, *Polyarchy* (New Haven: Yale University Press, 1971).

[63] Linz and Stepan, *Problems of Democratic Transition and Consolidation*, 7.

[64] Seymour Martin Lipset, *Political Man: The Social Bases of Politics* (Baltimore: Johns Hopkins University Press, 1960).

[65] Juan J. Linz and Alfred Stepan, 'Toward Consolidated Democracies', *Journal of Democracy*, 7: 2 (Apr. 1996), 14–33.

[66] G. Munck, 'Democratic Transitions in Comparative Perspective', *Comparative Politics*, 26: 3 (Apr. 1994), 355–75.

political parties in Ukraine has been symbolic of Sartori's 'unstable democracies', characterized by 'extreme pluralism'.[67] Also, corruption and the size of the shadow economy remained intolerably high. Privatization, together with economic reform in general, has lagged behind democratization. Rent seeking, which has maintained Ukraine in the no man's land between a command and a market economy, was a preference for many centrist members of parliament over the creation of a genuine market economy.[68]

A 'Return to Eurasia' under Lukashenka

Russified or Russian-speaking populations throughout the former USSR have often exhibited the greatest degree of nostalgia for the Soviet Union.[69] The majority of Belarusian elites always favoured various forms of union with Russia. These elites, perhaps not surprisingly, were also the most hostile to reform: 'Elites wanting to integrate with Russia displayed negative, perhaps even xenophobic, views of the outside world.'[70] These views typify the Lukashenka regime.

The March 1991 referendum for a 'revived (Soviet) union' was endorsed by 83 per cent of Belarusians, the highest figure outside Central Asia and higher than the all-Union average.[71] No referendum on independence was held in December 1991, as had been held in Ukraine. Belarus, therefore, became an independent state in 1992 as one of the least national of the Soviet successor states (already as early as 1960, there were few remaining Belarusian-language schools).[72] Lukashenka openly derided the former state language,

[67] Giovanni Sartori, 'European Political Parties: The Case of Polarised Pluralism', in Joseph La Palombara and Myron Weiner (eds.), *Political Parties and Political Development* (Princeton: Princeton University Press, 1966), 137–76; and Giovanni Sartori, *Parties and Systems: A Framework for Analysis* (Cambridge: Cambridge University Press, 1976).

[68] See the excellent discussion of this phenomenon in Oleh Havrylyshyn, 'How Patriarchs and Rent Seekers are Hijacking the Transition to a Market Economy', *Perspectives on Ukraine*, 2: 3 (May–June 1995).

[69] Hopman, Shenfield, and Arel, *Integration and Disintegration*, 28.

[70] Matt Warsaw, 'Reintegration with Russia, Soviet Style', *Transition*, 1: 20 (3 Nov. 1995), 60.

[71] Kathleen Mihalisko, 'The All-Union Referendum in Belarus: Appeals to the Community of Slavs', *Report on the USSR* (29 Mar. 1991), 7.

[72] D. Marples, *Belarus: From Soviet Rule to Nuclear Catastrophe* (London: Macmillan, 1996), 37. See also Steven L. Guthier, 'The Belarusians: National Identification and Assimilation, 1897–1970', *Soviet Studies*, 29: 1, 2 (Jan., Apr. 1972), 37–61, 270–83.

Belarusian, as 'inferior' to the 'two great languages in the world—Russian and English'.[73] The last main Belarusian-language newspaper in Minsk (*Svaboda*) was banned in November 1997, reflecting a continuation of the policy of Russification conducted by the tsarist and Soviet regimes.

Between 1992 and 1993, there were two competing trends in Belarusian domestic and foreign policy.[74] The minority trend, backed by parliamentary speaker Stanislav Shushkevych and the Popular Front, supported the same position as their counterparts in Ukraine (independence, reform, and 'return to Europe'). These policies had only a minority following in the parliament and government, as was underlined by Belarus' joining the Tashkent Collective Security Treaty in 1993, and the country's full membership in the Economic Union, and CIS Customs and Payments Unions. Shushkevych, unlike Kravchuk and his allies, 'failed to put forth any kind of blueprint for democratic statehood'.[75]

Belarus drifted gradually back to Eurasia between 1992 and 1993. After 1994, it retreated completely to the status of a Russian dominion. This drift was facilitated by the West's Russo-centric policies between 1991 and 1994, which focused exclusively upon the Russian Federation and were only interested in nuclear weapons in the non-Russian republics of the former USSR. The West then found it difficult to see Ukraine and Belarus as anything other than a part of 'Russia'. Ironically, Western interest in Belarus surfaced only after Lukashenka created an authoritarian regime, by which time it was too late. Even then, the West followed double standards. The West, eager not to offend Yeltsin, muted its criticism of *both* his violent dissolution of parliament in autumn 1993 and his support for the Lukashenka regime after 1995. Moscow's geopolitical interest in Minsk increased in response to the enlargement of NATO, and to the detriment of political and economic reform in Belarus. As relations between Russia and the West deteriorated the domestic reform agenda in Belarus suffered because Russian resolve strengthened to maintain a friendly regime in power, even if it was authoritarian.

[73] *Reuters* (2 Apr. 1996).

[74] See Michael Urban and Jan Zaprudnik, 'Belarus: A Long Road to Nationhood', in Ian Bremmer and Raymond Taras (eds.), *Nations and Politics in the Soviet Successor States* (Cambridge: Cambridge University Press, 1993), 99–120.

[75] K. J. Mihalisko, 'Belarus: Retreat to Authoritarianism', in Karen Dawisha and Bruce Parrott (eds.), *Democratic Changes and Authoritarian Reactions in Russia, Ukraine, Belarus and Moldova* (Cambridge: Cambridge University Press, 1997), 247.

Majority opinion in the Belarusian elite supported limited reform, and was largely anti-Western, backing union with Russia. This was the position taken by both Vyacheslav Kebich, prime minister under Shushkevych, and Lukashenka, then head of the parliamentary committee on corruption. During the 1994 presidential elections, the first to be held in Belarus, the two leading contenders, Kebich and Lukashenka, were both pro-union and pro-Eurasian. Ironically, Russia backed Kebich, but was left with Lukashenka, a known admirer of the former USSR.

The regime established in Belarus, after the election of Lukashenka in 1994, closely resembles that commonly referred to as 'Sultanistic'.[76] Sultanistic regimes include those of the former Central African Empire (Emperor Bokassa), Romania (Nicolai Ceauşescu), and North Korea (Kim Il Sung).[77] The absence of a strong national consciousness in Belarus makes Sultanism under Lukashenka possible. Russians, both democrats and their radical opponents on the left and right, supported Lukashenka when he argued that there are few ethnic, religious, or linguistic differences between Belarusians and Russians (a view held by most Russians about Ukrainians as well). Hence, the 'natural state' for both countries was in union.[78] The majority of Russians and Belarusians have accepted the views, propounded by tsarist and Soviet historiography and nationalities policies, that all three eastern Slavs are regional branches of a *Rus'kiy narod*.

All of the characteristics of a sultanistic regime inhibit the democratization process.[79] These include extreme patrimonialism, in which the polity is perceived as the personal domain of the sultan, as well as the fusion of the private and public domains. Such regimes are characterized by the absence of a guiding ideology; loyalty to the ruler is built upon 'a mixture of fear and rewards to his collaborators', who are chosen from family, cronies, and business associates. The absence of the rule of law, where the bureaucracy is subverted to the arbitrary decisions of the Sultan and the

[76] David R. Marples, 'Belarus: An Analysis of the Lukashenka Regime', *Harriman Review*, 10: 1 (Spring 1997), 28. For a more detailed analysis see Stephen Eke and Taras Kuzio, 'The Socio-Political Roots of Authoritarian Populism in Belarus', *Europe-Asia Studies*, 52: 3 (May 2000), 523–47.

[77] Huntington, *The Third Wave*, 112.

[78] These views were stated by Russian State Duma speaker Gennady Seleznev in *Rabochaya Tribuna* (14 Mar. 1997).

[79] Linz and Stepan, *Problems of Democratic Transition and Consolidation*, 51–4 and 70–1; and Juan J. Linz, 'Totalitarian and Authoritarian Regimes', in Fred I. Greenstein and Nelson W. Polsby (eds.), *Handbook of Political Science*, iii (Reading, Mass.: Addison-Wesley, 1975), 259–63.

security forces prefer not to utilize the courts, is another feature. Such regimes suffer from a low level of institutionalization, and the absence of political pluralism. Opponents of the regime tend to come from disappointed former members of his staff. In such regimes, modern communications and developed society coexist with isolated and poor rural masses. This type of regime can only be removed through violence, usually by overthrowing the Sultan whose actions have destroyed the middle ground of domestic politics.

The majority of these attributes were present in Belarus under Lukashenka. Lukashenka represented a 'special type of politician', who differed from others in the former Soviet Union, and was highly unpopular throughout the CIS.[80] The Lukashenka regime professed no ruling ideology. Lukashenka admitted after winning the presidential elections in 1994: 'I am neither with the left, nor with the right. I am with the people and against those who are deceiving and robbing them.'[81] Lukashenka was a populist who appeals to the nostalgia held by a large proportion of the population for the stability and security of the Soviet era, as the 'saviour of Slavic civilization'.[82] Lukashenkism was, therefore, backward looking, based upon Little Russianism, promoted through Soviet nationalities policies and historiography, which is pan-Slavic and anti-Western. But this has not represented a clear ideology able to sustain the regime and provide a vision for the future. It vacillated between supporting full union with Russia (a product of Little Russianism), or a theoretical union which would respect sovereignty (based upon a Soviet Belarusian national identity created largely within the confines of Soviet Belorussia).[83] This absence of a clear ruling ideology has been Lukashenka's ultimate weakness.[84]

The Lukashenka regime was characterized by many authoritarian tendencies which came under intense criticism by Western

---

[80] *Kuranty* (17–23 Sept. 1997).   [81] *UPI* (11 July 1994).

[82] *Narodnaia gazeta* (12 Apr. 1995).

[83] On these issues, see the interesting, but, at times, controversial, article by Dmitri Furman and Oleg Bukhovets, 'Belarusian Self-Awareness and Belarusian Politics', translated from *Svobodnaia mysl*, 1 (1996) into *Russian Politics and Law*, 34: 6 (Nov.–Dec. 1996), 5–29. Furman and Bukhovets believe that the Soviet state prevented, on the one hand, the total fusion of Belarusians into the Russian nation. On the other, it also prevented the evolution of the Belarusian ethnos into a nation. This created a Soviet Belarusian identity, which understands it is different to the Russian, but without the self-confidence of a 'we' imparted by being a modern nation. Furman and Bukhovets, therefore, see Belarusians in a manner similar to say the Provençals or Bretons in France, who 'naturally' assimilated into the French nation.

[84] K. Mihalisko, 'Belarus: Retreat to Authoritarianism', in Dawisha and Parrott, *Democratic Change and Authoritarian Reaction*, 277.

governments and the international community. The authoritarian regime has violated Belarus' status as a party to numerous international agreements on human rights. The disbanding of the legally elected parliament, after a highly dubious referendum in November 1996, created a puppet bicameral parliament under the president's control, based upon a constitution modelled on the December 1993 Russian one. Not surprisingly, only Russia recognized the outcome of this referendum and the alleged 'legality' of the parliament.

The authoritarian regime in Belarus has also continued to suppress and place tight controls upon the mass media. It has used bureaucratic means to close down and hamper their independent operation, controlling printing and publishing and banning criticism of the government and president. The right to free assembly has been heavily circumscribed, with demonstrators obtaining short prison sentences. Journalists were regularly harassed and physically attacked. During elections and referendums, the media were not allowed to play the role traditional to democracies as channels of alternative information and criticism. This placed in doubt the 'fairness' of the May 1995 and November 1996 referendums and election.[85]

Sultanistic regimes leave little room for manœuvre for the opposition. The regime has become dominated by a personality cult with the state regarded as the sultan's personal fiefdom. An honourable way out, through round table negotiations between the ruling regime and counter-elites, proves impossible. The moderate former parliamentary speaker Shushkevych stated that 'civilized dialogue with Lukashenka is impossible'.[86] Lukashenka has successfully destroyed the centre ground, and created a wide opposition ranging from national communists, liberal democrats, to nationalists.[87] The youth wing of the Popular Front is believed to be behind the Belarusian Liberation Army, which has claimed responsibility for a number of terrorist explosions and assassinations.

What role have international organizations and Western countries played in the Belarusian post-Soviet transformation process?

[85] See the Belarus League for Human Rights and Article 19, *Suppression of Freedom and Expression and Media Freedom in Belarus* (London: Article 19, Sept. 1997).

[86] Interviewed in *Kievskiye vedomosti* (22–3 Oct. 1997).

[87] The deputy chair of the Popular Front, Stanislau Husak, said of the Belarusian national communists that: 'They understand the price for statehood and independence. They understand what the nation is. They move under our white-red-white banners. Nevertheless, there are very few of them.' *Vysokyi Zamok* (13 May 1997).

As noted earlier, between 1991 and 1994, Western policies reflected a mixture of indifference and lack of interest, and were highly Russophile. To some degree, these Russophile policies have been continued by the EU, which has not thought fit to include any of the CIS countries within its 'slow track' group of prospective members. After 1994, at which point some Western countries and organizations began to adopt less Russo-centric policies towards the CIS, Lukashenka's election destroyed any hopes that the slow pace of democratization, begun in the early 1990s, would continue. The West and international organizations found it difficult to influence domestic events in Belarus because of three factors. First, it did not want to offend Russia which supported Lukashenka at home and abroad. Second, Lukashenka, despite his eccentricities, had been elected by a very large majority over his rival, Vyacheslau Kebich. He continued to maintain a large base of domestic popularity. Western governments and institutions stopped recognizing Lukashenka as the legitimately elected president of Belarus only after his term officially expired in summer 1999. Third, the democratic opposition remained weak, divided, and unable to pose a serious threat to the Lukashenka regime.

Lukashenka's foreign policy has been a direct product of his domestic authoritarian policies. As portrayed by the Belarusian analyst, Vyacheslau Paznyak, it represents a mixture of socialism, pan-Slavism, and nostalgia for the former USSR.[88] The political parties which supported Lukashenka and these policies were the same as those in Ukraine (the radical left, pan-Slavists, and Internationalist Fronts). On domestic questions, pragmatic centrists on foreign policy (the equivalent of President Kuchma's supporters in Ukraine) have been allied to the national democrats against Lukashenka.[89] Consequently, Belarus presented a similar foreign policy breakdown to that which exists in Ukraine, where pragmatists and romantics have held different foreign policy strategies of how to reach the goal of 'Europe', while both support domestic reform. In both Ukraine and Belarus, therefore, supporters of democratization will not support anything other than bilateral economic cooperation within the CIS.

In his world-view, Lukashenka maintained a Cold War era hostility to the West, NATO, and international financial institutions.[90]

[88] Vyacheslau Paznyak, 'Belarus: In Search of a Security Identity', in Roy Allison and Christoph Bluth (eds.), *Security Dilemmas in Russia and Eurasia* (London: Royal Institute International Affairs, 1997), 160.

[89] Hopman, Shenfield, and Arel, *Integration and Disintegration*, 39.

[90] Ibid. 18–19, 29.

This has given external actors little prestige in Belarus and few possibilities to exert any influence. Belarus has become one of the few countries whose elites are uninterested in economic integration into the world economy, preferring, instead, reintegration within the CIS. These elites have also remained committed to Soviet-style planning and production targets, placing low value upon international assistance.[91]

These factors led to a disappointing inability of the West and international organizations to influence domestic policies in Belarus. The Parliamentary Assembly of the Council of Europe suspended the special guest status of Belarus in January 1997 (even though Lukashenka was merely copying Yeltsin's actions of three years earlier, *albeit* in a less violent manner). The IMF and World Bank have been unable to exert any influence or provide any assistance to Belarus in the absence of a reform programme. Lukashenka opposed any wide-ranging Belarusian cooperation within NATO's Partnership for Peace programme, and did not support a Russian or Ukrainian Charter with NATO. Unlike Ukraine, the Belarusian leadership has expressed no interest in future EU membership.[92] Ambassador Louis Moreno, head of the EU Commission in Belarus, Ukraine, and Moldova, warned in 1998 that 'if democratic changes do not begin in [Belarus], it would be naive to expect a change in Europe's attitude to [Belarus].'[93] He believed that if Lukashenka continued to refuse to hold round table negotiations with the deposed parliament and democratic opposition, it would be impossible for Europe to take any steps in the direction of Belarus.

Conclusions

Ukraine and Belarus followed different paths after becoming independent states in 1992, because of the different national legacies they inherited from tsarist and Soviet rule. These different legacies of external and totalitarian rule influenced the ability of pro-reform elites to mobilize the population in favour of an agenda of 'returning to Europe'; an agenda which includes the pursuit of democratization, marketization, and state and nation building. Those elites, as in Ukraine, who have pursued these domestic policies have sought to integrate into European and transatlantic structures. Those elites, as in Belarus, who have returned to authoritarianism,

---

[91] Hopman, Shenfield, and Arel, *Integration and Disintegration*, 24–5, 62.
[92] *RFE/Rl Newsline* (23 Oct. 1997).   [93] *Belapan* (4 Feb. 1998).

have no interest in a pro-Western foreign policy, because they have sought to return to the Eurasian past. The international community and organizations, therefore, have greater possibilities to influence Ukraine than Belarus.

At the domestic level, the inherited level of national consciousness and identity has played a direct role in influencing the domestic and foreign strategies of the ruling elites in Belarus and Ukraine. The ability to mobilize the population in favour of reform and a pro-Western foreign policy was directly related to the strength of inherited national identity, historical memory, and political culture. Reform and a pro-Western foreign policy of 'returning to Europe' is most evident in those former Soviet states where national identity was stronger, and the titular population not divided by Russification (for example, western-central Ukraine, the three Baltic states, Armenia, and Georgia).

Ukraine was closer than Belarus to these five states in the 'high penetration group', in the ability of its elites to pursue reform and a pro-Western foreign policy. Belarus lacked domestic counter-elites. Its high degree of Russification and weak national identity translated into opposition to reform, lack of interest in any 'return to Europe', and support for a revived union with Russia. The Russified populations of post-Soviet states, such as in Ukraine and Belarus (including the Transdniester separatist Republic of Moldova), were likely to be the most sovietized, lacking any clear national identity and, hence, supportive of pro-Eurasian unions. As Huntington reminded us, 'political leaders cannot through will and skill create democracy where preconditions are absent.'[94] Western policies, therefore, should not only focus upon democratization and marketization, but also recognize that state and nation building are important pillars upon, and within, which democratic polities are crafted. The success or failure of democratization and marketization is therefore directly related to the national question.

In Ukraine, the alliance of national communists and national democrats was sufficient to provide the momentum necessary for Huntington's transplacement to operate. Kravchuk's rule represented an interregnum between two systems, where moderates in *both* the *ancien régime* and opposition sought to compromise by excluding radicals in *both* camps. The inability of the counter-elites to secure support throughout Ukraine meant that transformation could not take place. Instead, a compromise in the form of transplacement led to slower progress in reform. Ukraine's transplacement provided

---

[94] Huntington, *The Third Wave*, 108.

legitimacy to the new state (through the referendum on independence) and led to the gradual evolution of the *ancien régime*'s moderate elites towards the national, economic, and political views of the opposition. To enable Kuchma, a product of the Kravchuk transplacement era, to promote reform, state and nation building required him to promote also a pro-European foreign policy. This, in turn, gave international organizations and Western governments the ability to exert influence over Ukraine's domestic policies.

In Belarus, the weakness of the national idea, the absence of national communists, and the lack of a sizeable democratic opposition (Belarus only produced one dissident in the post-Stalin era) meant that the reform process and state- and nation-building agenda were always in doubt. With few moderates in the *ancien régime* camp, the conservative stand-patters were able to thwart the rise of the opposition (the Popular Front was not registered until summer 1991, eighteen months after Rukh in Ukraine). The rise of Lukashenka after 1994 destroyed the politics of the centre ground and turned the country away from 'Europe' to a backward-looking Eurasian orientation searching for salvation from reform through reintegration with Russia. In the absence of a domestic programme of reform and state or nation building, Western governments and international institutions have found—and will continue to find—it difficult to influence the Lukashenka regime.

Russia and the West: To Belong or not to Belong?

Marie Mendras

With the turn of the century, Russia fares badly on the democratization scale. Deterioration, and not consolidation, of the essential constituents of democratic society has unmistakably been under way since the summer of 1999. The second war waged by Russian troops in Chechnya and Vladimir Putin's predetermined election to the presidential post in March 2000 are two major symptoms of a growing disregard for democratic rule, civil rights, and the rule of law.

In the turmoil of the military campaign and Yeltsin's succession, a few pillars of the institutional reform of the early 1990s are still standing but not unscarred. Legislative and executive powers continue to require the sanction of the electorate. The conditions of voting, however, raise many questions, most notably the absence of fair campaigning and the pressures on powerful rivals not to compete. These contributed to the easy victory of Vladimir Putin. Private property and free enterprise remain, in principle, untouched. In practice, the scale of corruption and public money diversion and the many scandals of financial-political deals greatly affect the honesty and competitiveness of Russia's 'new capitalism'.

How should we assess Western responsibility for Russia's at first promising and later distressing domestic history in the 1990s? The issue at stake is influence, and influence is one of the most difficult and elusive factors in interpreting change. This is particularly so in Russia, a vast country, long a major power and an inward-looking society where internal dynamics and historic legacies heavily determine the behaviour of elites and individuals. This chapter focuses on what we view as a major theme in Russia's relations with the democratic world: its attraction to Western, mainly European, ways of life and values, together with a propensity to resist influence and subordination.

Adjusting to Foreign Influence?

The enduring economic crisis in Russia, amplified by the financial crisis of 1998, has demonstrated the vulnerability of a large industrialized country when it combines domestic weaknesses with growing dependence on the outside world. Western governments, as well as ruling elites in Russia, underestimated the weight of the Soviet legacy and the complexity of the Russian situation in comparison with such East European states as Poland and Hungary. The new Russian Federation has not experienced a soft and progressive 'transition' to democracy and capitalism. In many respects, foreign actors remained oblivious to this until 1998, having acted as if Russia's fate were an unswerving, if slow and difficult, path towards a Western-style democratic and economic system.

The attitudes of the Russian ruling elites in the early Yeltsin period were characterized by a widespread openness to foreign influence and aid, a willingness to abide by international rules, and an attraction to Western stability and prosperity. This chapter will show that doubts about Russia's increasing interaction with the outside world and about the validity of a 'Western model' for Russia were raised in Russia as early as in 1993, in connection with disturbing domestic developments. In the decade between 1989 and 1999, Russian attitudes towards the West underwent a clear evolution. First, the period between 1989 and 1992 featured a spectacular opening with widespread attraction to the West. Second, a backlash occurred between 1993 and 1995, with the increasing disenchantment of the Russian population, suffering continuing economic dislocation, and the critical attitude of Russian elites to foreign interference. Third, a more balanced view of the West emerged in 1996–8, with the rise of less emotional positions regarding relations with the outside world. Finally, a new period of tensions with the West has emerged in the aftermath of the 1998 financial crisis, NATO strikes against Serbia, and the second war in Chechnya.

The dramatic developments of 1998–9 then occurred in a context of already deteriorating relations with and attitudes towards the West, resulting partly from growing disenchantment with reforms and Yeltsin's mismanagement. This crisis did not radically alter Russian attitudes to the West, but reinforced existing trends. Opinion polls following the August 1998 financial crisis showed that the Russian population held the leadership in Moscow and

Russian business circles responsible for the crisis.[1] The West has not become an easy scapegoat for the failed transformation.

In this chapter, I focus on developments in the Russian polity and society in the 1990s. The discussion centres on the following questions: first, how has Russia evolved in a drastically transformed environment? Second, how has the Russian state managed its relations with other states and different cultures? How open or closed has Russian society become to foreign influence and interaction with non-Russian actors? More generally, has the concept and exercise of Western influence over Russia promoted or obstructed the emergence of a sense of 'commonness' between Russia and Europe? To what extent have Russians believed that they have chosen their destiny or that it has been imposed upon them by Western influence?

For the first time in its recent history, Russia has found itself in an international environment over which it has little influence. These circumstances represent a change of great significance. Before 1991, the Soviet state was a superpower. However, as a political system and as a society, the Soviet Union was isolated from global developments and the evolution of other industrialized states. The wall that the Soviet Union had built around the communist fortress blocked interaction with European, American, and Asian societies. Paradoxically, the USSR existed in a well-protected and isolated space and was still able to play a decisive role in world politics and international relations.

In the 1990s, Russia brought down the fortress walls and it can no longer protect itself effectively against outside influence. Moreover, the new Russian state has abandoned the pretence that it can decide its own destiny independently of external developments. At the same time, Russia's reduced status in international affairs has deprived it of its previously powerful influence, in particular over the European continent.

More open, less protected, and no longer very powerful, Russia has found itself in a difficult period of redefinition of its status and identity. The process of redefining Russia's identity has been troubling for the society at large and, in particular, for the ruling elites. Indeed, much has been at stake in this redefinition process in terms of the self-esteem of the political leadership and reconstruction of the national spirit. Moreover, Russian society and elites have been

---

[1] Unpublished data, VTsIOM (All-Russian Centre for the Study of Public Opinion) (Oct. 1998).

attracted to the Western way of life but, at the same time, have sought to avoid coming 'under the influence' of the West.

The issue of foreign influence has become a complex question involving many actors, both inside and outside Russia.[2] Did Russia in the late 1990s move toward more or less interaction with foreign countries compared with the early 1990s? Did Western governments seek to influence developments in Russia or did they assume a lower profile than in the late Gorbachev and early Yeltsin periods? Did the Russian government and leading elites accept and welcome more exchange, and even more interference from the outside world, and make use of foreign impulses and ideas? Moreover, at what point did Russian elites perceive Western 'advice', or expressed 'preferences', as Western pressure, constraint, and even threat?

After the Westernizing trend in the Russian government between 1989 and 1993, the pendulum swung back to a more moderate position, based on the general consensus that Western aid and proximity were welcome so long as Russia did not become more vulnerable or externally dependent. As a result of the 1998 crisis, foreign aid came to be perceived simultaneously as an inescapable necessity and an infringement of Russia's freedom of choice. Aid and advice have led to deep feelings of subordination to external forces. Partly as a result, both Russian and Western decision makers have become caught in a spiral where there is little time for long-term strategy formulation.

When measuring influence or pressure, the first question to be addressed is whether influence from a foreign government, society, or organization has been purposefully intended. Diffused external influence is felt by all states with open borders. In Russia, the media have conveyed a vast range of values and helped to promote diversity in a society that had been sustained on the meagre diet of Soviet communism. The diversity in consumer goods that has become available has given Russians a taste of how other nations live, eat, and entertain themselves. New hobbies, tastes, and habits are starting little by little to change the Russian way of life and must have had an impact on the way that people think. Russia has become a country where Chinese cuisine, French perfumes, German cars, and English detective stories have become part of daily life in many cities (if not in the countryside nor in small towns). Has this increasing acculturation to foreign modes of living and values

[2] See George Breslauer, 'The Impact of the International Environment, Theoretical and Methodological Considerations', in Karen Dawisha (ed.), *The International Dimension of Post-communist Transitions in Russia and the New States of Eurasia* (Armonk, NY: M. E. Sharpe, 1997), 3–12.

promoted democratization within Russia? At this early stage, the real impact of these indirect influences remains difficult to measure.

In order to address this question, the following premises need first to be clarified. The first is that foreign influence over Russia was and continues predominantly to be influence from the West. Second, it is essential to distinguish between indirect/unintended influence—that is, the attraction of a the Western way of life—and direct/intended influence from governments and other foreign actors. Third, intended influence represents a form of transaction and has a cost. Any external actor might be willing to bear such costs in order to reap potential benefits. However, expected rewards cannot always be well defined in advance. Even if some of the targeted goals are political and cultural (for example, to contribute to the consolidation of the rule of law), there remains always an economic or strategic interest for the external actor in the transaction (for example, to develop a market, influence consumer tastes, and compete with other foreign actors). Experience has demonstrated that political influence for the sake of political influence has rarely been successful. Intended influence is most effective when both the recipient and the initiator have relatively accurate and similar views on the economic and social costs and benefits of a transaction.

Attraction to the West

Paradoxically, the Western world resided at the very centre of the Soviet system as its rival 'self'. The myth of a hostile and unjust Western civilization legitimized the nature of Soviet society and rule. Economic and political arbitrariness were justified in terms of the confrontation with the USA in particular. The Soviet population had to accept the sacrifices imposed by what was a virtual and permanent state of war. The West was not only a convenient scarecrow but also a standard, even a model. Competition with the West, therefore, was the very essence of the Soviet system. In negating Western civilization, the Soviet leadership was forced to constantly refer to it.[3] From the early 1960s onwards, Soviet ideology shifted to adopt a more defensive and conservative anti-Western position. As Western culture was so powerful and attractive, the Soviet leadership and ideology sought to protect Soviet society from its influence by all means.

[3] Marie Mendras, 'The Soviet Union and Its Rival Self', *Journal of Communist Studies*, 6: 1 (Mar. 1990), 1–23.

Soviet slogans of socialist achievement represented insistent self-justifications which neither the Soviet *nomenklatura* nor the people took seriously. Soviet ideology created a system of values that absolved everyone of responsibility by stating that the USSR was not responsible for any failures as it was the victim of relentless Western opposition. This doctrine did not produce genuine belief in the West's aggressive designs, nor did it sustain faith in Soviet socialism. Most Soviet people were distrustful of the leadership in the 1970s and 1980s. Nevertheless, Soviet popular and elite mentalities were distorted by this constant denial of responsibility for one's own fate. The easy temptation to blame others for national difficulties has endured within current Russian ruling circles, if less so in the general Russian population.

Mikhail Gorbachev launched perestroika because the USSR lagged behind the Western world. The constraint of competition with the rival system meant that there could be no real autarky of the Soviet polity and economic system. 'We live in one and the same world,' argued Gorbachev.[4] The Soviet Union's proximity to Europe was hailed as a key to the 'unlocking' of the socialist camp. Gorbachev admitted that the USSR could not continue to be a closed society in an open world. Domestic choices were inevitably influenced by external developments. Relations with the West needed to be accommodated to this reality of interdependence. At that point, the influence from Western countries was indirect, captured in the West's powerful pressure on the USSR to develop the Soviet economy and society and to reduce the pace of the arms race.[5] This political pressure was combined with a diffused attraction to the Western way of life perceived amongst segments of the Soviet elite and population.

Western political culture had not been totally eradicated from the consciousness of the Soviet elite. The primacy of the West over other cultures was generally accepted. In the last years of the Gorbachev era, Western democracies were clearly adopted as a model for Soviet reform. In 1991–2, across the Russian spectrum there was talk of a Russian transition towards the Western system. The prosperity of average Europeans and Americans, compared to the

---

[4] Mikhail Gorbachev's 'new thinking' was developed in many texts and speeches, and in his book *Perestroika: New Thinking for our Country and the World* (New York: Harper & Row, 1987).

[5] See Tsuyoshi Hasegawa and Alex Pravda (eds.), *Perestroika: Soviet Domestic and Foreign Policies* (London: Sage Publications, 1990); Marie Mendras, 'La Fin du protectionnisme politique', *Le Débat* (Paris), 56 (Sept.–Oct. 1989), 85–96.

average Russian, was most attractive. For a majority of Russians in the early 1990s, the improvement in material conditions prevailed over all other objectives. Institutional reforms, the protection of human rights, and freedom of the media were not as valued as an increase in living standards.[6] One possible reason for this may have resided in the fact that basic rights and freedoms had already been granted by Gorbachev in the late 1980s. These basic rights and freedoms had been won peacefully, without struggle or social rebellion (with the exception of the Baltic states and the Caucasus). Russians did not have to fight for these newfound liberties and freedoms, which may explain why they have been increasingly taken for granted.

Within the Soviet *nomenklatura* those who favoured change in the 1980s sought to become richer, with the aim of 's'embourgeoiser'. The Soviet system had limited the possibilities for bureaucrats (with the exception of a few top leaders in Moscow and in the republics) to accumulate private wealth because of the shortage of consumer goods and the absence of convertible currency. The *nomenklatura* was constrained in a closed system of clientelism and the reproduction of limited privileges. Officials, plant managers, as well as the intelligentsia sought more opportunities for better living standards.[7] Perestroika must be seen as reform from above, including not only the secretary general and the Central Committee members but also significant parts of the ruling elite in Moscow and in the republics and regions.[8]

Since the creation of the new Russian Federation, Russian elites have continued to steer the process of change from above.[9] However, these elites have become incomparably more diverse than under the communist system. Private businessmen, foreign partners, and many new professions (such as lawyers and bankers) have become critical players alongside the 'old elite' of cadres

[6] See the excellent sociological analysis of Iouri Levada, *L'Homme soviétique ordinaire* (Paris: Presses de Sciences-Po, 1995).

[7] On the stakes in détente and reform of important segments of the 'aristocratizing élite', see Alexander Yanov, *Détente after Brezhnev: The Domestic Roots of Soviet Foreign Policy* (Berkeley and Los Angeles: Institute of International Studies, University of California, 1977).

[8] This interpretation is shared by David M. Kotz, with Fred Weir, in *Revolution from above: The Demise of the Soviet System* (London: Routledge, 1996).

[9] On clientelism and corruption, and the adaptation of Russian bureaucracies to the market economy, see the special issue, Marie Mendras (ed.), 'Qui gouverne la Russie?', *La Revue Tocqueville/The Tocqueville Review*, 19: 1 (1998), 1–135 (articles in French and in English).

which have remained in positions in the local, regional, and federal authorities.[10] By and large, post-Soviet elites have shown a surprising ability to adjust to the formidable changes of the last ten years. This may be explained not only by their past frustration with the communist system but also by the fact that some aspects of Western life were attractive to them.

The powerful attraction of the Western model guided, to a large extent, the institutional choices made in the USSR/Russian Federation in 1989–93.[11] This has been less the case since the adoption of a new constitution in 1993. In the earlier period, Western advice was closely listened to by the Soviet and Russian leadership. In 1989–93, Moscow was the West's 'good pupil', willingly accepting advice, criticism, and interference. Russian elites sought to live in what has been referred to as a 'civilized country'. 'Civilization' then meant an institutional framework and political behaviour that was thought to be approved by Russia's Western counterparts.

These circumstances raise the fundamental question of Russian perceptions and misperceptions of Western rules and habits. It is important to note that the perceptions and expectations of those Western states that attract Russia may very well differ from Russian perceptions and expectations. In the process, the 'importer' may rebel against the 'exporter' of cultural, political, and economic values. This is precisely what happened in Russian-European and Russian-American relations in 1993–4. At that point, Russian politicians began to emphasize the non-altruistic and calculating behaviour of Western governments who sought to use their influence to 'weaken' and 'subordinate' Russia. As will be discussed later, concerns about subordination have grown steadily ever since.

---

[10] On Russian elites today, see David Lane, 'Russian Political Elites, 1991–1995, Recruitment and Renewal', *International Politics*, 32 (1997), 169–92; Olga Kryshtanovskaya and Stephen White, 'From Soviet Nomenklatura to Russian Elite', *Europe-Asia Studies*, 48: 5 (1996), 711–33; James Hughes, 'Sub-national Elites and Post-communist Transformation in Russia: A Reply to Kryshtanovskaya and White', *Europe-Asia Studies*, 49: 6 (Sep. 1997), 1017–36.

[11] On political and institutional developments in Russia after 1989, many works have been published. To quote a few: Richard Sakwa, *Russian Politics and Society*, 2nd edn. (London: Routledge, 1996); Stephen White, Alex Pravda, and Zvi Gitelman (eds.), *Developments in Russian Politics 4* (London: Macmillan, 1997); Karen Dawisha and Bruce Parrott (eds.), *Democratic Changes and Authoritarian Reactions in Russia, Ukraine, Belarus and Moldova* (Cambridge: Cambridge University Press, 1997); and articles in the journal *East European Constitutional Review*.

The Assertiveness of the West

Between 1989 and 1993 the Soviet and Russian leadership did not simply 'import' Western institutions or seek to copy a Western blueprint. The Soviet exit from communism was a complex process in which the West was the main reference point. The West was seen as the only alternative, and Europe was geographically and culturally close. Russia's relationship with Europe has been and is likely to remain both important and ambivalent. Europe will be the key to Russia's integration into the international system in the decades ahead as a modern (possibly democratic) state and open society. The Russian leadership has remained attracted to its former rivals. At the same time, the leadership has been very concerned that Russia should avoid any striving to become like these Western states.

At the economic level, Western 'capitalism', 'private property', and 'free market' were the catchwords of the critical years during 1990–2, which featured the demise of Gorbachev and the launch of the Yeltsin–Gaidar reforms. At that point, the Russian government officially welcomed Western advice and desperately sought Western aid and cooperation. The mood changed after 1993, with growing popular resentment towards the hardships of market reform. Despite this resentment, a form of market economy has developed in Russia.

At the political level, those early years of turmoil represented the high point in the import of Western terminology and political know-how. The late Soviet leadership and early Yeltsin government formally endorsed the objectives of representative democracy, the rule of law, and the defence of individual freedoms and rights. Cooperation with the West in the field of constitutionalism, law, and justice was intense after 1989.

In terms of culture, or to use the Russian term 'civilization', the victory of the West seemed at first total and unequivocal. In Russian discussions, the West was held up as the only standard to emulate. The prevalent view that communist societies had proved inefficient, whereas the Western way of life had shown its superiority, both in global efficiency and in terms of individual well-being. Soviet/Russian and Western views immediately before and after the collapse of the Soviet regime were based on the perception that the Western system had proved its superiority and Russia had to become fully 'Western-centric'. Western governments therefore felt assertive with regard to the Russian transition. International

(Western-controlled) institutions like the International Monetary Fund and the World Bank were asked to support Russia in its reform and process of Westernization. The mood in the West was victorious and optimistic. When the Berlin Wall fell, it generated a rapid chain of political collapse eastward with hardly a tremor westward.

It was assumed that Russia needed the West and that post-Soviet rulers needed the support of their counterparts in Europe and America to face the challenge of potential destabilization by communist or nationalist groups in their own country. It was taken for granted that Russians felt 'liberated' from the communist yoke and wished to converge with the more prosperous and liberal Europe. In the prevalent view, a 'new Russia' was emerging which could only be better than the previous 'evil empire'. To believe that Russian society and ruling elites had so easily closed the so-called 'parenthesis' of seventy years of communism to resume their place in the free world, of course oversimplified a very complex post-Soviet reality. In the early 1990s there was a general mood of optimism as to where Russia was going. Russia wanted to make a peaceful transition toward Western principles and culture, with Western support and influence. As Western influence seemed to be welcomed by the Russian government, Western states at times failed to note worrying political and social developments.

Western governments initially concentrated on two major issues: first, nuclear disarmament and non-proliferation throughout the region; and second, the need for economic and political stabilization, particularly in Russia, Ukraine, Belarus, and the three Baltic states. Interest in the stability of the Caucasus and Central Asia was seen by many Western states to be secondary to the peaceful transition of Russia and the western former Soviet republics. The US government concentrated its efforts on nuclear disarmament and security issues, and on promoting rapid economic reform. For example, the USA was instrumental in securing the denuclearization of Ukraine and Kazakhstan. European governments showed more concern for political issues. In this view, the stability of Russia, Ukraine, the Baltic states, and the Caucasus were critical for the peaceful Europeanization of the Central European states and further progress in European integration.

Quite naturally, the US administration was keen to maintain with Boris Yeltsin the cooperative momentum that it had achieved with Mikhail Gorbachev. Disarmament negotiations remained at the heart of US-Russian political relations. The new Russian government proved cooperative in the US pursuit of non-proliferation. In January 1994, the presidents of Russia, Ukraine, and the United

States signed an agreement about the denuclearization of Ukraine. This relatively smooth transfer of responsibilities to the new regimes in these new states may be partly explained by the limited changes that occurred in the apparatuses in charge of diplomacy. Former Soviet diplomats, technicians, and politicians, trained in the traditional field of arms control, maintained a continuity in this dimension of US–Russian relations between 1991 and 1994. For Yeltsin and his government, at this early stage, military-strategic issues were secondary to internal economic change and the consolidation of their political authority.

West European governments were satisfied with the smooth rapprochement of Eastern European states with the West. Until 1995, when NATO enlargement became a contentious issue, Moscow watched benignly as its former satellites moved quickly toward integration into West European institutions. This peaceful transition owed little to Western pressure or influence on Russia. It occurred mainly because of the East European determination to leave the Russian sphere of influence and because of Moscow's incapacity to obstruct the process. The first Yeltsin government lacked a formal policy toward Eastern Europe. Similarly, the consolidation of the independence of the former Soviet republics was not the result of Western pressure on Russia. Until as late as 1994, scepticism toward the 'viability' of Ukraine, Armenia, or Kazakhstan as independent states ran high amongst Western politicians and diplomats. With the exception of the Baltic states, the new states found little understanding and support in the West which was concerned not to hurt Russian pride further by close partnership with the former Soviet republics. Moreover, Russia remained the predominant interlocutor for strategic and disarmament negotiations. It is clear, therefore, that the West played little role in preventing Russian 'neo-imperialist temptations'. Russian attempts to interfere in Georgia, Ukraine, or Tajikistan were not seriously opposed by the international community.[12]

Direct influence from Western governments and international institutions was much more powerful in the economic realm, based on the consensus that international support had to be provided to assist Russia in undertaking the necessary economic reforms. The objective of an irreversible economic transformation was seen in

---

[12] On Russia's policy toward the former republics, see Christoph Royen, 'Conflicts in the CIS and their Implications for Europe', and Victor Kremeniuk, 'Post-Soviet Conflicts: New Security Concerns', in Vladimir Baranovsky (ed.), *Russia and Europe: The Emerging Security Agenda* (Oxford: Oxford University Press and SIPRI, 1997), 223–45 and 246–66.

the West as the key to fostering the irreversibility of Russia's transition from the communist system. Developments in domestic Russian politics did not raise much concern in the West until the violent events of October 1993, when President Yeltsin sent tanks against the parliament to quell the deputies' rebellion.

There has been considerable controversy over the economic priorities that were urged on the Russian government by Western experts and international institutions.[13] The efficiency of the IMF, the World Bank, and the European Bank for Reconstruction and Development has also been repeatedly questioned in recent years.[14] Beyond the diversity of opinion, a consensus has emerged on the very significant overall impact of foreign actors on Russian economic change since 1992. The 1998 rouble collapse exemplified the structural dependence of the Russian economy on foreign aid because of grave internal flaws in economic management. The many financial scandals made it impossible to conceal or play down the deeply corrupted nature of Russian public finance as well as semi-private semi-state business. Prominent figures, first and foremost President Yeltsin, his family and entourage, were involved in the Bank of New York-Mabetex scandal of 1999.

Western policies toward Russia were dominated initially by strategic and economic concerns. The fact that basic rights and freedoms seemed to have been secured earlier apparently reassured foreign governments as to the democratic nature of the Russian regime. However, the issue of drafting a new constitution, which emerged prominently in Russian domestic debates in 1991–3, demonstrated that the Russian political elite was divided over many aspects of the state-building and reform project. More striking at the time was the lack of attention given to social problems in Russia by external Western actors. Few Western officials and economic advisers even addressed the questions of the human cost of reform or of Russian society's ability to sustain systemic transformation.[15] Behind Western policy at this time stood the assumption that the post-Soviet population could but welcome such reforms as it would

[13] Jacques Sapir, *Le Krach russe* (Paris: La Découverte, 1998); Michael Ellman and Robert Scharrenborg, 'The Financial Panic and the IMF', *Problems of Post-Communism* (Sept.–Oct. 1998), 17–25.

[14] See, for example, Paolo Miurin and Andrea Sommariva, 'Financial and Technical Assistance to Central and Eastern Europe: A Critical Appraisal of the Role of International Institutions', *Washington Quarterly*, 17: 3 (Summer 1994), 91–105.

[15] Marie Mendras, 'La préférence pour le flou: pourquoi la construction d'un régime démocratique n'est pas la priorité des Russes', *Le Débat* (Paris), 107 (Nov.–Dec. 1999), 35–50.

offer eventually a better life than under the planned economy. In reality, in the short term, the 'shock therapy' of 1992 hit a majority of Russians who suffered a serious decline in living standards.

In the United States, more pragmatic politicians bitterly criticized the 'romantic period' in US policy of 1991–4. According to US Senator Bill Bradley (Dem.):

> the romantics (in the Administration) tried to support 'reformers' against 'opponents of reform', assuming that we could, clearly and easily, identify both and that the interests of the United States and of Russian reformers coincided . . . this simple formula created among many Russians the illusion of painless reform and the expectation of massive U.S. aid . . . But the formula is wrong. Russian politics is not a struggle between reform and anti-reform, because people and politicians favor combinations of both.[16]

Western governments also failed to take into account the effect on Russian elites of the accumulation of a great deal of foreign interference in a restricted period of time. For people who traditionally had tried to manage their country without paying much attention to outside factors, this overwhelming Western presence proved too much to accept over time. By 1993–4, the mood had changed in Russia. Russian elites had become more concerned with their own future and wanted to leave a lasting imprint on the new Russia. This objective became more important for many Russian politicians than pleasing Russia's Western partners.

Disenchantment: The Limits of Influence

In 1993–4, the West became seen in Russia as a constraint to be resisted. Russians started to feel that the goal of Westernization was not realistic in Russian conditions. Expectations had been high; hence, disenchantment was equally high. As the Russian sociologist Elena Danilova noted, Russian society's doubts and disillusions translated into a serious 'crisis of trust'.[17] Danilova argued that 1993 represented the turning point when Russians turned their back on politics and gave all their attention to social and material problems.

As far as the geopolitical and strategic posture of Russia was concerned, many Russian intellectuals and experts regretted the

---

[16] Bill Bradley, 'Eurasia Letter: A Misguided Russia Policy', *Foreign Policy*, 101 (Winter 1995–6), 83.

[17] Elena Danilova, 'Problema sotsialnoi identifikatsii naseleniia postsovetskoi Rossii', *Monitoring obshchestvennogo mneniia* (VTsIOM, Moscow), 3: 29 (May–June 1997), 15.

'excessively generous concessions' made repeatedly by Russian leaders to their Western counterparts.[18] They shared the bitter sentiment that the Kremlin had been too pliable in negotiations with the West. In this view, at stake was not only the diminished posture of Russia in international affairs. The economic influence and interference, political paternalism and strategic predominance of the West nurtured a growing frustration and hostility within the Russian elite. Russian politicians and experts increasingly understood that economic and strategic issues were intrinsically linked and that it was difficult to isolate Russian security policy from foreign influence if the Russian economy was already under international, mainly Western, supervision.

Even more important than strategic and economic disillusionment were domestic developments between 1993 and 1996 which disrupted the relationship with Western partners and encouraged more inward-looking trends in the Russian political class. As the politically engaged analyst and Duma deputy Alexei Arbatov noted:

The violent October 1993 crisis in Moscow and the parliamentary elections in December of the same year together formed a clear threshold in Russian developments. Domestically those two events signified the failure of the Russian leadership to implement market economic reforms by way of 'shock therapy' and to establish a functioning democracy to deal with the country's internal and external problems. The foreign policy implications were no less important: the 'romantic,' cosmopolitan and Western-centred policy started to give way to a much more Russian-centred and geopolitically defined course of action.[19]

At the same time, Arbatov added that Russian foreign policy would not be:

characterized as expansionist or aggressive. It is severely constrained by economic and political problems at home; by the reaction of public opinion, the mass media and parliament; by difficulties and vulnerabilities in relations with neighbouring republics; and by dependence on Western economic aid, credits and investment. It will be restricted by the current multifaceted arms control regime and contained by Western strategic preponderance, as well as by the weakness of the Russian armed forces and the degradation of the defence industries.[20]

---

[18] Georgi Arbatov, 'Eurasia Letter: A New Cold War?', *Foreign Policy*, 95 (Summer 1994), 102.

[19] Alexei Arbatov, 'Russian Foreign Policy Thinking in Transition', in Baranovsky, *Russia and Europe*, 135.

[20] Ibid. 158.

Not everybody would agree with Arbatov's assessments of the constraints, both domestic and international, that limited Russia's external policy. Most Russian experts, however, acknowledged the difficulty of devising a foreign policy in circumstances of domestic political and economic turmoil.

Strangely, the dramatic events of October 1993 disturbed the elites in Moscow more than Western governments. The West did not wish to question the positive role of Yeltsin in Russia's democratic breakthrough. Yet, the facts were incontrovertible: the Russian parliament building was bombed; many people were killed because force was preferred to negotiation; the president ruled by decree; and Yeltsin imposed his own version of the Constitution adopted in December 1993. During the troubled months October to December 1993, foreign states adopted a low profile and avoided interfering in these developments. The ultimate test was the legislative elections and the referendum on the Constitution on 12 December 1993. To the relief of Western governments, respect for universal suffrage, even in such controversial conditions, seemed to confirm Yeltsin's attachment to democratic principles.[21]

These principles were put to the test in 1995–6, when a very ill Boris Yeltsin was tempted to postpone the presidential elections. This test raises interesting questions: did the Russian leader hold elections mainly because of Western pressure or because of a concern not to jeopardize foreign economic aid? These considerations certainly played a part, but probably not the main part. In a study of voting patterns in Russia, I have argued that politicians and their entourage do not like to have to bow to the electorate, because of the risk of being kicked out of office. Nevertheless, Russian politicians have accepted the necessity of a form of arbitration between them.[22] It has been recognized that unless a leading group resorts to violence or *coup d'état*, and/or returns to a strict hierarchical system inside a closed group (scenarios which do not look probable in Russia today), the competition for power needs be arbitrated. Voting, even with extensive interference of financial groups and networks and a measure of fraud, is still seen as the best means available. Central and regional elites in Russia are not all deeply committed to the principle of representative democracy. The regional elections of 1996, the legislative election of December 1999, and the presidential vote of March 2000 demonstrated the numerous

[21] Marie Mendras, 'Lettre de Moscou: la Russie vote et se divise', *Pouvoirs*, 69 (1994), 173–81.

[22] Marie Mendras, 'L'élection présidentielle de 1996 en Russie', *Revue française de science politique*, 47: 2 (Apr. 1997), 173–203.

shortcomings of the Russian political system. Politicians have adjusted to the strictures of voting, but they have also often sought to influence the process to raise their chances. By and large, the political elite in Russia has proved less committed than society to the necessity of democratic elections. To comfort oneself with the concept of 'electoral democracy' is short-sighted and may lead to erroneous evaluations of Russian elites' commitment to key principles and mechanisms of a rule-of-law state.

Western monitoring of democratic standards in Russian politics has been a form of diffused external influence. External states and international organizations have tended to evaluate the situation in Russia according to institutional progress in legislation: that is, in terms of the adoption of a new civil code, court reforms, and the abolition of the death penalty. It is much more difficult to assess political and civic behaviour and the good use of democratic mechanisms. The many flaws related to the rule of law in Russia have resulted not so much from the lack or defective nature of legislation but from the distorted application of rules and principles. Mentalities and behaviour have been much more difficult to reform than codified documents.[23] In order to secure further respect for democratic culture and the rule of law, small well-targeted co-operation projects have been most successful. At a micro-level, with non-governmental actors, foreign advice has been most productive.[24]

At the same time, on important matters of state behaviour, only governments and international institutions, with their authority and potential for influence, can confront the Russian leadership over misguided policies that violate basic principles and endanger security. The international community failed to adopt such a position in the case of Chechnya.

The two wars in Chechnya are Yeltsin's and his successor's greatest shame and the international community's greatest failure in its treatment of post-Soviet Russia. From December 1994 until August 1996, the Russian army destroyed most of this North Caucasian republic and killed tens of thousands of civilians. More Russians than Chechens died in the war: Russian inhabitants in

[23] Hendley, K., 'Legal Development in Post-Soviet Russia', *Post-Soviet Affairs*, 13, No. 3 (1997), 231–56, and 'Rewriting the Rules of the Game in Russia: The Neglected Issue of the Demand for Law', *East European Constitutional Review* (Fall 1999), 89–95.

[24] This point is made by most observers of Russia. It is aptly argued by George Breslauer, 'Aid to Russia: What Difference Can Western Policies Make?', in Gail Lapidus (ed.), *The New Russia: Troubled Transformation* (Boulder, Colo.: Westview Press, 1995).

the capital Grozny had nowhere to escape to and Russian conscripts were sent to fight without the necessary preparation and equipment. The first war in Chechnya has been extensively analysed.[25] Even in Moscow's higher military and political circles, there has been clear recognition that the war was a mistake. It was badly planned, astonishingly poorly managed, and conducted without any clearly defined strategy. The Russian defeat was total, in military and political terms: Chechnya became *de facto* independent, even if devastated and riddled with clan strife; most Russians who lived in the republic fled or were killed; the Russian military experienced their worst trauma since the war in Afghanistan.

In Moscow the first armed conflict was officially presented not as a war but as a 'crisis' and an 'internal affair' of the Russian Federation. Two legitimating reasons for the use of force were offered by the Russian government: First, force was used to enforce the respect of human rights in Chechnya against the allegedly dictatorial and brutal rule of the republican leader Dudaev. Second, force was used to defend the integrity of the Russian Federation. At the outset of the armed conflict, most Western governments did not condemn Russian actions and openly or tacitly endorsed Moscow's claims. This embarrassed silence persisted for several months in 1995 until the level of destruction and killings reached such a level that any reasonable government could no longer remain quiet. However, by then, it was too late and Western policy lacked determination. Even the Council of Europe, which delayed Russia's admission because of the war, finally invited Russia to join before any withdrawal of Russian troops from the region. It is notable that the Council of Europe proved far more determined to secure the abolition of the death penalty.

The second war was launched in September 1999. Officially, the Russian government was 'waging a war against terrorism' in a response to an armed incursion in Daghestan in August and two explosions in Moscow killing about 300 residents. The responsibility of Chechnya's elected President Maskhadov could not be established in either case. The freshly nominated Premier Vladimir Putin nevertheless labelled Chechnya a country of terrorists and bandits, denied Maskhadov's legitimacy and implicitly denounced the agreement signed between the Maskhadov and Yeltsin in May 1997. The Russian military command headed into an all-out war of destruction taking a heavy toll of human life. During the first six months of

---

[25] See Anatol Lieven's excellent book, *Chechnya: Tombstone of Russian Power* (New Haven: Yale University Press, 1998).

the war, thousands of civilians died and over 200,000 fled their republic, mostly to neighbouring Ingushetia.

Why did Western governments and institutions fail to make use of their influence in order to exert pressure on Yeltsin? Even Russian officials and experts were surprised at the onset of the first conflict in December 1994 that the international community did not voice disapproval.[26] A number of reasons explain Western restraint. First, the West's experience with the war in the former Yugoslavia discouraged it from involvement in the conflict. Second, the need to keep Russia engaged in disarmament negotiations was seen as a more important objective. Third, the West feared the effects of further dislocation in the former Soviet empire. Moreover, there was a notable lack of sympathy for Chechnya throughout the West. Another consideration was that Western governments felt ill at ease with the conflicting principles of the need to protect territorial integrity and the right to self-determination. The international community also failed to take issue on whether the war was 'just'. Moreover, the Russian decision to invade Chechnya highlighted all too clearly the weakness of the Russian state, government, and leadership. The Western concern was 'not to further weaken Yeltsin'. After Yeltsin's re-election in July 1996, Western governments were relieved that a 'communist reaction' had been narrowly avoided, which reflected the West's superficial understanding of Russia's internal predicament. In late 1999 to early 2000, international reactions to the war remained mainly vocal, and ambivalent. No Western government unequivocally condemned the Russian aggression in the first place. Concerns were merely voiced about the 'disproportionate' toll of civilian lives. Strengthened by the popular support for his military solution in Chechnya, Vladimir Putin was not ostracized by his foreign counterparts. He also played on the comparison with NATO strikes against Serbia in the Kosovo war to 'justify' Russia's use of force against Chechnya.

Foreign governments may also have unwillingly accepted that it would be very difficult to influence the Russian ruling elite during the uneasy period of succession. Foreign states and international institutions were confronted with a very confusing and unpredictable Russian polity. The persistent financial crisis, the role of big financiers and businessmen in politics, flourishing corruption, the increasing disparities between Russian regions, and the uncertainties over Yeltsin's succession have created unstable and unpredictable conditions for cooperation. When Boris Yeltsin resigned on

---

[26] Discussions with the author in Moscow (11–19 Dec. 1994).

31 December 1999, inviting his compatriots to elect Prime Minister Vladimir Putin to the presidential post, foreign governments were relieved that a solution had been found. The fact Putin went on to win the 26 March 2000 election in the midst of a brutal war in Chechnya, thanks to servile media and unfair campaigning, did not raise much international concern.

The difficulties faced in implementing programmes in areas as crucial as environmental protection or health have exemplified the inhospitable conditions for cooperation. In order to conduct relations with Russia, or to engage in economic activities, an external actor must develop an ability to keep varied contacts with different groups and networks.[27] The conditions for effective and direct external influence that existed in the late 1980s and early 1990s have largely disappeared.

Since the fall of the Soviet Union, political dialogue between the West and Russia has progressively lost its intensity and significance. Summit meetings and intergovernmental committees have become strikingly disconnected from the other domains of interaction. The growing role of non-governmental and non-public actors at all levels helps to explain this situation. Another reason has been the relative lack of interest on the part of European governments and the US administration in a rich and sustained political exchange with the Kremlin. Security matters have lost their previous primacy and urgency. The Russian armed forces are gradually becoming more internally focused on the management of the national territory and its borders. The new concept on security, published in January 2000, does not clarify matters much. As is common in Russia, it is a long text that displays the numerous ills of society and flaws of the ruling system, and complains about the negative attitude of foreign governments in very general terms.

Threats to the national security of the Russian Federation in the international sphere can be seen in the attempts of other states to hinder the strengthening of Russia as a centre of influence in the mutipolar world, prevent the implementation of its national interests and weaken its positions in Europe, the Middle East, the Transcaucasus, Central Asia and Asia Pacific.[28]

---

[27] On the drift of the Russian state, see Stephen Holmes, 'Plaidoyer pour un État libéral et fort en Russie', *Esprit*, 7 (July 1998), 97–111; and Marie Mendras 'La Faiblesse des institutions politiques en Russie', *Esprit*, 7 (July 1998), 91–6.

[28] 'National security concept of the Russian Federation', approved by presidential decree No. 1300 of 17 Dec. 1999, translated from *Rossiiskaya gazeta* (18 Jan. 2000).

Many of the developments that Western governments have consistently promoted (such as European integration and NATO enlargement) have concerned Russia. However, most of these changes have taken place without Moscow's acquiescence. In the tense debate over NATO's enlargement, the Yeltsin administration found itself in the position of a 'non-voting' actor. Moscow was asked to express its position and negotiate accommodations but it was not given the possibility to stop the process. It seems that discussions between NATO and Russia have had, and continue to have, as much of an economic as a security content.

There are not many subjects discussed productively with Russian authorities at the higher political level, besides the START 2 agreement, military proliferation issues, and questions of monetary policy. Many issues are dealt with at the technical and administrative level, without political arbitration. Heads of state have sometimes intervened politically when bilateral dialogue has gone askew and important financial interests are at stake. However, high-low visits are no longer as decisive as they were in earlier periods when substantial commercial contracts could only be signed at the highest level.

Russia remains under pressure to abide by a growing number of international rules, foreign economic conditions, and gentleman's agreements. These militate against reversing direction and adopting a semi-protectionist stance. Despite this, many Russian politicians have become tempted to do so. The effects of 'globalization' and the fear of competition have led to increasing talk in Russia about the 'Russian way' and the 'uniqueness of Russia'. Such talk worked as a formidable boost to Vladimir Putin's rapid ascension to power against the backdrop of the war in Chechnya, making ample use of the primitive but productive credo of restoring 'order' and 'patriotic pride'.[29]

The 'Uniqueness' of Russia

Russia's elites and society have not rejected interaction and openness with the outside world. However, there has been a widespread perception that Russia might be incapable of following the pace of global change. Fear has arisen over Russia being plunged in a world of intense economic, financial, and cultural competition. Only a small

---

[29] See Vladimir Putin's electoral appeal published in several newspapers, including *Izvestiya* and *Komsomolskaya pravda* (25 Feb. 2000).

minority at the extreme end of the Russian political spectrum has argued that the West has isolated Russia in order to keep it weak and not competitive. For the large majority of Russians, Russia's backwardness has been the result of history and poor management. Specific conditions, such as climate, territorial size, and the diversity of its population made of the Russian empire and the USSR a unique case. Backwardness is not seen as fatal, yet the Russian people have found it difficult to imagine that Russia could have the same accelerated development as Japan after 1945 or the Asian dragons in the 1970s.

Russians see their country as large, heavy, robust, and slow. They often mention the rich potential of their country in primary resources and in human capital. However, it is rare to hear the opinion voiced that, had Russia not been sovietized after 1917, it would today be a country like the United States. This prevalent view has stood in contrast with the attitudes of the populations in Eastern Europe and the Baltic states who have no doubt that, had they not been satellized, they would have followed the West European pace of development. The belief in the uniqueness of Russia, for better and worse, has become well entrenched in the Russian mentality. There is a widespread desire to live better and to become as 'civilized' as Europe and respected as an equal by the West.[30] However, in the Russian population and elite, there also is a strong attachment to a unique Russian culture.

Public opinion polls have highlighted the ambivalence in Russian views of the West, combining attraction towards and rejection of the dominant Western model. According to a 1997 survey, 60 per cent of respondents indicated that they would prefer to have a Western standard of living, while 30 per cent noted that they would prefer to return to the situation of the USSR under Brezhnev;[31] 44 per cent believed that 'Russians must learn to work and live under the conditions of private property and market economy,' but only 10 per cent agreed that 'Russians must make use of economic aid from the US and other Western countries';[32] 47 per cent indicated a desire to have their children study in the West, against 34 per cent who would not (18 per cent failed to answer).[33] The survey

[30] In Iver Neumann's words, 'the forging of Russian identity by a process of internal integration has as its twin the external differentiation of Russia from Europe,' in 'Russian Identity in the European Mirror', *European Security*, 3: 2 (Summer 1994), 281.

[31] T. I. Kutkovets and I. M. Kliamkin, 'Russkie idei', Informatsionno-analiticheskii biulleten, *Institut sotsiologicheskogo analiza*, Moscow 1–2 (Jan.–Feb. 1997), 42.

[32] Ibid. 37.   [33] Ibid. 44.

also showed that a majority of Russians wished to have friendly relations with Russia's European neighbours, but did not envision Russia as part of the West.[34]

The authors of this survey concluded that many Russians saw no serious alternative to the Western model and that 'ideas of restoration, communist or imperial, appeal to no more than 15 to 20 per cent of the population'.[35] They added that it is 'the huge historical responsibility of the reform-minded political elite' to show that 'Westernism (*zapadnichestvo*) today does not contradict but agrees with the national interest of Russia'.[36]

In actual fact, opinion polls since then have tended to demonstrate that Russians do not want to be caught in an 'either/or' dilemma: either to become like the West or stay as they are. These polls have highlighted that many Russians long for a 'Russian way' that accommodates Western-style 'modernity' with Russian 'specificities'.[37] The 1998 financial and political crisis has reinforced this attitude. Hostility against the West has not increased but there has been less trust in a 'Western solution' for Russia. This is due in part to the lack of trust amongst Russians in their own ruling elites. A January 1999 poll showed an almost unanimous distrust of the federal government. Over 90 per cent believe that the government had done a bad, or very bad, job in 'guaranteeing the payment of wages and pensions, in providing social protection, in fighting organized crime'.[38] Vladimir Putin's declared commitment to restoring law and order may change public sentiments but as of early 2001 it is too early to tell.

Europe has been seen as a monument of accomplishment for many in Russia, as it has been at various historical periods. However, the prevalent desire amongst Russians is not to fuse in one mould with Europe but to remain distinct. Distinctness and proximity to Europe and self-accomplishment and recognition from Europe have become the ideal of a very large spectrum of Russian opinion. The war in Kosovo has deepened the divide between Europe and America in Russian perceptions. In the spring of 1999, many in Russia shared the sentiment that the United States were primarily responsible for the NATO strikes and for waging an

---

[34] T. I. Kutkovets and I. M. Kliamkin, 'Russkie idei', Informatsionno-analiticheskii biulleten, *Institut sotsiologicheskogo analiza*, Moscow 1–2 (Jan.–Feb. 1997), 37.

[35] Ibid. 33.   [36] Ibid. 31.

[37] See in particular the analysis of the sociologists of VTsIOM in their publication, *Monitoring obshchestvennogo mneniia* (Moscow), 6 issues a year.

[38] USIA Office of Research and Media Reaction, *The People Have Spoken: Global Views of Democracy*, 11 (Sept. 1999), 24.

illegitimate conflict in a 'sovereign' country, Serbia and its 'Yugoslav Federation'.[39] European countries were not considered as bellicose and intrusive as the United States.

Willingly or unwillingly (with a few important exceptions of course), the Russian population has adapted to the new domestic environment and to the loss of the Soviet Union.[40] Dissatisfaction has run high as have expectations. The forced adjustment to less authoritarianism, less security, and more initiative, was welcomed by those who had the means to face a more competitive and less controlled socio-economic environment. For others, it was a forced and painful adaptation. However, those segments of the population who have felt victimized by Russia's reform project have also lacked the means, and probably the will, to resist change actively. This resilient part of Russian society has felt cheated by history, seeing itself as a silent victim of 'change from above, made for those above'. As opinion polls have demonstrated, a significant minority (around 30 per cent) have expressed nostalgia for the lost security provided by the former communist state, even though day-to-day living was not easy and pleasant in most parts of Soviet Russia.[41] Working and living conditions were mediocre, if not poor, but ambitions were equally limited. It was a 'low-risk/low-opportunity' system. The great majority of the inhabitants of the USSR were prisoners of this system. As a result, they naturally developed a very conservative mentality, in the literal sense of hostility to any unpredictable change. This was most prevalent among the older, less educated, and poorer groups of the Russian population.[42]

Only a select few in the USSR in the 1980s (many more in the Baltic states) could contrast Soviet low living standards to Western prosperity. It is impossible to measure the satisfaction or dissatisfaction of the Soviet population under Brezhnev because there was no serious alternative available. Satisfaction may only be evaluated when those concerned have a choice. Hence, the confused nostalgia expressed in the late 1990s in polls has not meant that Russians were satisfied with the Soviet regime, but that they had learned to live with it and did not expect much progress

[39] Author's interviews in Russia, Mar. 1999, and VTsIOM survey data.

[40] Mark Urnov, 'Nekotorye faktory adaptatsiya rossiiskogo obshchestva k situatsii posle avgustovskogo krizisa 1998 g', *Monitoring obshchestvennogo mneniia*, 2: 40 (Mar.–Apr. 1999), 7–11.

[41] See Kutkovets and Kliamkin, 'Russkie idei', 42–3 and the diagrams on the attitude to reforms in *Monitoring obshchestvennogo mneniia*, every issue, at 3–5.

[42] Aleksandr Golov, 'Reputatsiia rynochnoi ekonomiki u rossian', *Monitoring obshchestvennogo mneniia*, 3: 29 (May–June 1997), 33.

from it.[43] In 1987–9, expectations rose rapidly, with the double promise that things would get easier economically and that life would altogether be more agreeable. In 1990–2, living conditions significantly worsened as the Soviet state broke up and price liberalization increased inflation and destroyed individual savings. Russian society entered a state of shock, losing its certainties and secure points, from which it has not yet recovered. Its apparent support of the second war in Chechnya late 1999–2000[44] may be the result of this mix of insecurity and humiliation, in a context where the domestic media are under stricter control and feeding pro-war propaganda.

Yeltsin played the historical role of the father of the nation keeping a sinking ship afloat. As such, Yeltsin reassured Russian society that it still represented a whole, even after the loss of the other Soviet republics. This role had more significance for Russians than the 'victory of democracy over communism'. There has been a widespread misunderstanding in the West that the Soviet population applauded democracy and decommunization. It is true that few mourned the demise of Gorbachev and the Communist Party. However, the Russian population did not have a clear idea of what it sought for the new Russian Federation. Western democracy and market economy have remained linked to abstract notions of 'progress' and 'modernization'.

Only several years after the Soviet collapse did Russia start to address the question of the desirability of moving toward a Western system. This question reflected a fear that in so doing Russia would permanently lag behind, being incapable of competing with international pressures and foreign societies. The presence of Europe and Asia can be found in all aspects of Russian daily life. However, the Russian way of life has remained distinct.

Long hostile to its 'Asian roots', Russia has slowly shifted to develop relations with Asia, mostly in the form of economic exchanges.[45] Economics and trade have eroded the predominance of the West. Asian, as well as some Middle Eastern, enterprises have become

[43] For an interesting analysis of Russia's assessment of the past, see B. V. Dubin, 'Proshloe v sevodniashnykh otsenkakh rossiian', *Monitoring obshchestvennogo mneniia*, 5: 25 (Sept.–Oct. 1996), 28–34.

[44] Most opinion polls in Nov.–Dec. 1999 and in Jan.–Feb. 2000 indicated a majority of respondents agreeing with 'military operations in Chechnya in order to get rid of all the bandits' (as the question is often formulated in VTsIOM surveys. See the VTsIOM internet site and VTsIOM *Monitoring obshchestvennogo mneniia*.

[45] See Milan Hauner's work on *Asia in the Soviet-Russian Consciousness: What is Asia to Us?* (London: Unwin Hyman, 1990).

increasingly prominent in Russia. Russian politicians and diplomats have lagged behind the fast pace of economic change. In the future, economic as well as political and cultural ties with Asian societies will undoubtedly grow stronger. Russian interaction with such states as China, Japan, Korea, and India will develop, particularly in Russia's adjacent regions. Similarly, relations with Turkey, Iran, and the Middle Eastern countries have become stronger in the south-western provinces of Russia. Openness and economic globalization has thus emerged as a challenge to the Russian state as a federal entity. The fragility of the federal government in Moscow has fostered regionalization and an increasing differentiation in terms of local development and foreign contacts among Russian regions and republics.[46]

Conclusions

Despite daunting internal problems, the opening of Russia and its irreversible immersion into world affairs has fundamentally changed the country from what was in the 1980s a closed, communist system. In a number of cases, Russia has shown the will to play by international norms. And those norms are predominantly Western, created by American or European politicians, lawyers, and other decision makers. In other situations, rulers have proved immune to foreign advice and criticism. The use of brutal force in Chechnya, the overextended political and financial control over the media, and the lack of systematic strategy to fight corruption in state administrations are a few glaring examples.

Russian ruling elites have remained ambivalent about the relationship with major foreign states, as they have sought to avoid significant external involvement in Russian domestic affairs. At the same time, these elites have become weary of isolation and the danger of being left aside from important international developments. Vladimir Putin's words and deeds since autumn 1999 are in keeping with this general pattern.

Ultimately, Western states will exercise more pressure on Russia through indirect and diffused means rather than through direct influence and conditional cooperation. The diffuse but permanent influence of the West, especially Europe, has remained very strong

---

[46] Marie Mendras (ed.), *Russie: le gouvernement des provinces* (Geneva: CRES, 1997); see also the special issue of *Communist Economies and Economic Transformation*, under the direction of Philip Hanson (Sept. 1998).

in Russia. The European cultural and social heritage has a special position in Russia. This heritage, and the attraction it creates, will not be nurtured by the new millionaires or the self-assured bureaucrats. It may only be fostered by other strata of society that have a greater desire to belong to the Western world and share, not simply an economic standard of living, but also similar ways of life, in the broad sense of the term, encompassing values, aesthetics, culture.

19

Conclusions: Foreign Made Democracy

Jan Zielonka

The countries reviewed in this book reveal the enormous scope and variety of external pressures impinging upon democracy building in Eastern Europe. These pressures came from all corners of the globe and involved both governmental and non-governmental actors. They took various forms: from direct purposeful intervention to indirect, diffuse influence. Some of these initiatives succeeded in strengthening democracy, while others undermined the pro-democracy campaign. Economics, security, culture, and politics all played a part in shaping democracy, sometimes as distinct and sometimes as mutually reinforcing, interlinked factors. The picture is complex indeed, but it appears that democracy in East Europe is to a significant extent foreign made. Although one can hardly ignore the importance of domestic factors on democracy building, this book concentrates on external policies and pressures, revealing a complex set of relationships between internal and external influence on democracy in the region.[1] This concluding chapter will identify a set of variables responsible for the enormous impact of external factors on democratic consolidation in Eastern Europe: (*a*) the historical legacy, (*b*) the liberal-democratic ideological paradigm, and (*c*) the forces of globalization. Next, it will conceptualize the interplay of external and internal factors impinging upon democracy. Positive and negative types of external impact on democracy will be scrutinized later. The chapter will conclude with an evaluation

I would like to thank Svetlozar Andreev, Leslie Holmes, Margot Light, and Alex Pravda for their helpful critiques in the process of preparing this chapter.

[1] The two other volumes prepared within the European University Institute's project on Democratic Consolidation in Eastern Europe focus chiefly on domestic factors. The first volume in the series deals with constitution-making and institutional engineering and the third focuses on democratic orientation and civil society in Eastern Europe.

of the conscious Western effort to craft or engineer democracy in Eastern Europe. Despite inconsistent signals and the lack of a broader strategic design for Europe, the West has succeeded in creating an environment conducive to democratic reform in the post-communist arena. Linking membership of Western institutions to democracy and other reforms has been a characteristic feature of the crafting effort. As Alex Pravda argues in the introduction to this book, the more wide-reaching and integrated the conditionality package, and the more tightly linked to membership in an attractive club, the greater the impact of the Western pro-democracy leverage has been.

Historical Legacy

All countries undergoing democratic transition claim to have a particular, if not unique history. However, in Eastern Europe this history has had one characteristic feature: vulnerability to foreign influence. For at least the last two centuries all the countries of Eastern Europe have been victims of international power politics which at times brought about oppression, and at other times liberation.

Several countries in the region began constructing democratic regimes in the aftermath of the First World War, only to fall victim to either fascist and/or Soviet external aggression. Of course, in Poland, Czechoslovakia, and Lithuania, weak political parties, heightened ethnic animosities, and economic underdevelopment greatly contributed to the failure of the democratic experiment at that time. Nevertheless, external military intervention was clearly decisive in bringing the nascent democracies down. Since the Second World War most of the countries analysed in this volume have been subject to various levels of Soviet influence. The strength of the external Soviet grip initially prevented democratic revival. But eventually it faltered, making democratic revival possible—if not requisite.

Gorbachev's reforms fundamentally restructured the domestic political scene in every country in Eastern Europe, and had clear implications for democratic development there. Poland's Solidarity movement in the 1980s had an equally important impact throughout the region. And even disparate incidents in a single country— such as the opening of Hungary's borders to East German refugees —produced waves of domino effects in neighbouring states which later proved crucial for the rebirth of democracy.

Western policies—or perhaps simply the mere existence of the successful Western world—also contributed to the fall of the Soviet empire. Cold War policies were not specifically geared towards bringing democracy to Eastern Europe; at best the West was trying to improve the human rights record in the East.[2] Nevertheless, as Marie Mendras asserts in her chapter, the West represented the main reference point for all political forces in Eastern Europe—communists and anti-communists alike. Opposition leaders demanded Western-style liberty and 'returning to Europe', which meant returning to the family of democratic nations. In contrast, communist leaders promised to catch up with the West economically while providing citizens with a greater degree of social justice than in the West. When it became apparent that the communists had failed to deliver on these promises, the opposition grew in strength and the oppressive machinery collapsed. Ultimately, most of the countries of Eastern Europe endorsed the successful *other*: Western-style democracy.

This historical susceptibility to various types of foreign pressures has greatly influenced democratic developments since 1989. In Poland and the Baltic countries the legacy of foreign invasion has indelibly coloured current thought on democracy building. One cannot understand the restrictive citizenship laws in Latvia and Estonia without referring to the security concerns rooted in Russian-Baltic history. Nor can one understand why Poland perceived NATO membership to be a major—if not the decisive—step towards its democratic consolidation without viewing Poland in its historical context. It is equally difficult to comprehend the apparently enthusiastic endorsement of the Western democratic blueprint by such seemingly non-Western polities as Macedonia or Bulgaria without taking into account what Kyril Drezov named the historical legacy of 'voluntary dependence'. Bulgarian and Macedonian leaders have always displayed self-limiting behaviour that helped them cope with various types of external hegemony throughout history. László Valki's chapter, in contrast, shows how Hungarian democracy building has been shaped by the historic implications of the 1920 Trianon Treaty, which deprived Hungary of one-third of its population and two-thirds of its territory. And in her chapter, Marie Mendras confirms that it is impossible to explain democratic developments in Russia without referring to the complex historical legacy of the Soviet Union and pre-communist Russia.

---

[2] I develop this argument in the conclusions to Vojtech Mastny and Jan Zielonka (eds.), *Human Rights and Security: Europe on the Eve of a New Era* (Boulder, Colo.: Westview Press, 1991), 240–1.

When one adopts this long-term historical perspective it is difficult to argue that domestic pressures have been much more important for democracy in Eastern Europe than external pressures. Likewise it is difficult to claim that external pressures can only be crucial in the transition stage, but not in the subsequent stage of democratic consolidation.[3]

Ideological Paradigm

Before 1989 democrats had to compete with other seemingly attractive alternatives. Not only did fascism and communism appeal to millions of Europeans, but also ideologically less pretentious forms of authoritarianism were seen as plausible solutions for countries facing economic malaise and political instability. As Mark Robinson and Gordon White argue, from the late 1960s to the mid-1980s the dominant consensus in the West held that economic development could best be assured by strong, authoritarian regimes.[4] Moreover, during this period some dictatorial regimes were seen as legitimate simply because they were anti-communist. This reasoning no longer held sway in the 1990s: democracy has been endorsed by words— if not by deeds—by all major political forces in Europe and the United States. This consensus created an unprecedented historical situation: Eastern European countries found themselves operating in an international environment which considers democracy to be 'the only game in town', to paraphrase Linz and Stepan's expression.[5] The Asian 'model' combining rapid economic growth with an authoritarian political system was culturally too alien to represent a workable alternative. And the collapse of Asian markets in the late 1990s scared off those few in Eastern Europe who had been tempted to try the 'Asian' alternative.

Faith in democracy was linked to the triumphant notion that economic liberalism is the height of rationality and brings comfort and satisfaction to the greatest number of citizens. Democracy was

[3] See Philippe C. Schmitter, 'The Influence of the International Context upon the Choice of National Institutions and Policies in Neo-Democracies', in Laurence Whitehead (ed.), *The International Dimensions of Democratization* (Oxford: Oxford University Press, 1996), 48.

[4] Mark Robinson and Gordon White (eds.), *The Democratic Developmental State: Politics and Institutional Design* (Oxford: Oxford University Press, 1996), 1.

[5] Linz and Stepan use the expression 'the only game in town' in the domestic rather than international context. See Juan J. Linz and Alfred Stepan, *Problems of Democratic Transition and Consolidation* (Baltimore: Johns Hopkins University Press, 1996), 5.

also seen as a recipe for peace: democracies do not fight each other, it was argued. The triangle—democracy, free markets, and peace —became a sort of a neo-medieval religion that countries should not only adhere to themselves, but also actively promote abroad through a modern form of a moral crusade. Promotion of democracy in Eastern Europe also has been seen as a means of enhancing Western interests. Does not democracy represent the surest way to make Europe and the world more secure and prosperous? In her chapter, Karen E. Smith provides a revealing quote from an article written by the US deputy secretary of state, Strobe Talbott:

The larger and more close-knit the community of nations that choose democratic forms of government, the safer and more prosperous Americans will be, since democracies are demonstrably more likely to maintain their international commitments, less likely to engage in terrorism or wreak environmental damage, and less likely to make war on each other.[6]

Not only states, but also international organizations engaged in the democracy-promotion campaign—from the European Union and the Council of Europe to NATO, the World Bank, and the IMF. Several important NGOs have also participated in this crusade, and in fact were able to generate more financial and human resources for democracy aims than certain governments and IGOs. For instance, according to 1998 statistics, the Soros Foundation has invested more in democracy-related projects in Russia than the European Union or its largest member states, such as Germany or Great Britain.[7]

The result of this international environment was that even the most unlikely proponents of democracy—such as Albania or Belarus—initially embarked on a democratic path. There was no workable alternative among culturally similar countries and these new states succumbed to the vigorous pro-democracy campaigns conducted by external forces. Indeed there was little space for domestic considerations when faced with such a democracy-conducive international environment. Although this statement ought to be qualified, the situation was certainly special compared to other democratic transitions.

These qualifications concern the sincerity of the West's pro-democracy project and the ability of some Eastern European countries

---

[6] Strobe Talbott, 'Democracy and the National Interest', *Foreign Affairs*, 75: 6 (Nov./Dec. 1996), 48–9.

[7] See *The Economist* (12 Dec. 1998). See also Kevin F. F. Quigley, *For Democracy's Sake: Foundations and Democracy Assistance in Central Europe* (Washington: Woodrow Wilson Center Press, 1997), 122–3.

to meet the democratic expectations of the outside world. This book gives several examples of Western policies putting security above democratic considerations, with the policy towards Russia being the most notable example. Moreover, Western policies towards Eastern Europe have often created the impression that they are more about responding to the interests of Western bankers, farmers, or steel producers than about enhancing democratic prospects in the post-communist world. And to a great extent, Western policies have neglected the democratic needs of individual countries and have been indifferent to their specific problems.

Ultimately, some governments (most notably Belarus) decided to ignore Western calls for democracy. This was partly due to domestic developments, but partly due to the West's benign neglect policy towards them. Other governments, in countries such as Slovakia, misread the West's determination to promote democracy. As Ivo Samson's chapter illustrates, the government led by Vladimír Mečiar wrongly assumed that the geostrategic position of Slovakia would prompt the West to include Slovakia in the EU and NATO despite its serious democratic deficiencies. Other governments tried hard to respond positively to Western calls for democracy, but failed when confronted with the economic and cultural realities of their countries. Here Albania represents the most obvious example. Some governments initiated a minimal level of democracy (based simply on free elections), but postponed the construction of Western-style liberal constitutionalism. In this book the cases of Russia and Ukraine seem to have followed this course.

Despite these qualifications, no alternative to the democracy-promotion project has been conceived thus far. A decade after the fall of the Berlin Wall, democracy is still the clearly stated objective of both Eastern European and Western governments (with the exception of Belarus and part of the former Yugoslavia). Yet, despite these good intentions, there is probably less confidence today in what can actually be accomplished in the complex post-communist environment. Confidence has also dissipated in the West's determination to support its democratic rhetoric with concrete action, especially when it involves sacrifices of blood or wealth. But democracy still has no real competition as a political ideology as it had in the past. The horror of the wars in the Balkans and in the Caucasus have only reinforced its appeal. Therefore, Eastern European countries are confronted with a democracy-friendly international environment which significantly limits their freedom to manœuvre domestically.

Transnational Pressures

This book also refers to the mounting transnational pressures working on the countries of Eastern Europe, which have serious implications for democracy. Despite the rhetoric of economic self-sufficiency, communist countries never operated in total isolation from the non-communist world. In fact, the failure to withstand global economic competition, the difficulty to insulate itself from the impact of the transnational media system, and increased migratory pressures have all contributed to the collapse of the Soviet system. However, with the end of communism and the Cold War division of Europe, the impact of globalization on Eastern Europe has become much more profound and complex. The long-standing restrictions on cross-border movement of people, goods, ideas, and property have now been largely removed and these countries have found themselves at the mercy of various powerful—even vicious—transnational pressures. The change was truly dramatic in scope and pace and caught the region off guard. The countries of Eastern Europe were too inexperienced and too fragile to be able to cope effectively with the unexpected and powerful impact of globalization. Transnational pressures have not always been detrimental to democracy. As mentioned earlier, the free flow of ideas across Eastern borders exposed these countries to the liberal democratic values which have dominated global discourse over the last decade. The opening of markets may well have contributed to the rise of international economic crime and even to massive financial crashes in some countries. But in other cases market liberalization stimulated economic rationalization, and even produced astounding economic growth. Whatever the balance of positive and negative effects, globalization was largely responsible for four important developments relevant to our discussion.

First, and most obviously, globalization has eroded the sovereignty of the new democracies in the region.[8] More often than not, Eastern European states have found themselves incapable of controlling capital flows, defending their currencies, maintaining a certain level of welfare protection, restricting migration, combating transnational crime, or shaping the media system. This has made it difficult for these governments to be democratically accountable. After all, democratic accountability requires a certain amount of

[8] See Csaba Gombar, Elemer Hankiss, et al., *The Appeal of Sovereignty: Hungary, Austria, and Russia* (Boulder, Colo.: Social Science Monographs, 1998).

state sovereignty. If the state is made powerless against global forces, democratic accountability is weakened. Thus, just as Eastern European states succeeded in regaining their sovereignty from the Soviet system, it was snatched away again by the unidentified if not mysterious transnational force of globalization. And again as in the Soviet period, the state is often perceived not as the ultimate representative of national interests, but of 'foreign' interests, however dimly understood and comprehended.

Secondly, globalization has forced the new democracies of Eastern Europe to attempt constructing a new type of 'competition state', to use Philip G. Cerny's expression.[9] In order to survive under transnational pressures, these countries have abandoned policies aimed at protecting citizens from the disruptive effects of the market—promoting wage stability, imposing controls on 'speculative' international capital flows, maintaining full employment, and the like—and have pursued policies of increased marketization. Therefore, economic activities have been abruptly deregulated and government spending has been drastically reduced. Such policies usually have been unpopular with the electorate, but time and again governments have been willing to break campaign promises in order to make their states competitive enough to cope with globalization. States that failed to become competitive experienced full-blown institutional collapse, as experienced in Russia, Ukraine, and Albania. Those that succeeded in becoming competitive—Poland, Hungary, Estonia, Slovenia, and the Czech Republic—enforced the decisions made by world markets, transnational private interests, and international quango-like regimes.[10]

Thirdly, globalization has induced the new democracies of Eastern Europe to cooperate with the international institutions responsible for organizing global order and coping with transnational pressures. Institutions such as the International Monetary Fund, the World Bank, the World Trade Organization, the European Union, and the European Bank for Reconstruction and Development have been helping these states take advantage of globalization rather than fall prey to its ill-effects. However, this assistance has been linked to a set of very strict conditions that are often

[9] Philip G. Cerny, 'Paradoxes of the Competition State: The Dynamics of Political Globalization', *Government and Opposition*, 32: 2 (1997), 251–74.

[10] According to Cerny, a 'quango', or quasi-autonomous non-governmental organization, is an authoritative body licensed by the state to carry out public regulatory functions but made up of appointed representatives of private sector interests; a variant of state corporatism. See Cerny, 'Paradoxes of the Competition State', 258.

at odds with the demands of the local electorate. True, international institutions are frequently used by local politicians as scapegoats for carrying out unpopular and painful (but nevertheless necessary) policies. It is also true that cooperation with these international institutions frequently is seen as a sign of the desire to return to Europe and the Western world after years of living under the Soviet yoke. That said, conditions imposed by the EU or the IMF leave little space for domestic considerations and create the impression that crucial decisions are not being made in national parliaments but rather in Washington DC or Brussels. And the scope of this external 'intervention' should not be underestimated. Countries aspiring to join the European Union, for instance, have been asked to fully implement the *acquis communautaire* which contains some 20,000 laws and regulations covering a wide range of issues in both the public and private spheres.

Fourthly, globalization has stimulated the reorganization of the political space in Eastern Europe. Increasingly, the main dividing line in the region is between those who want to take advantage of globalization and those who are afraid of it. The former seek to overcome geographic, legal, and cultural boundaries, while the latter seek to restore them. The former welcome foreign capital and goods, while the latter want to protect 'national' economic actors. The former opt for a multicultural society which is open to foreign influence, while the latter cherish 'pure' national traditions and culture. The former argue for speedy membership in international institutions, while the latter jealously guard the principle of national sovereignty and territorial integrity. The division between these parties of 'globalization' and 'territoriality', to use Charles Maier's words, cuts across traditional party lines and ideologies.[11] Globalization produces both economic winners and losers. It erodes traditional norms and values. It challenges parochial types of cultural identity. The conflict between the two parties is therefore unavoidable and has serious implications for democratic politics. Both parties formally claim their adherence to democracy. But the party of territoriality is associated with xenophobia and nationalism, while the party of globalization is held responsible for rapidly rising poverty rates and administrative unaccountability.

Although all Eastern European states have been affected by globalization, this does not mean that the state has become marginal. The cases of Russia and Ukraine clearly show that meaner, more

---

[11] See Charles S. Maier, 'Territorialisten und Globalisten: die beiden neuen "Parteinen" in der heutigen Demokratie', *Transit*, 14 (Winter 1997), 5–14.

repressive modes of state organization are being adopted to prevent the collapse of public institutions which are unable to live up to the challenge of globalization.[12] And even states that succeeded in coping well with globalization have offered their citizens insufficient levels of participation, consultation, representation, transparency, and accountability in response to these transnational pressures.[13]

External versus Internal Pressures

International and transnational factors have clearly shaped democratic politics in Eastern Europe, but the question remains: how much impact have they had? Which factors were truly decisive: external or internal? This book suggests that there can be no straight and simple answer to these questions. This is not only due to the increased fusion between domestic and international politics—a trend which Wolfram F. Hanrieder perceived more than twenty years ago.[14] It is also because the impact of domestic and external factors varies over time in different countries without any clear logic or pattern. In other words, individual states have pursued a strategy of adjustment to both internal and external pressures giving preference to one over the other during different phases of democratization. They have been involved in a difficult balancing act to meet various challenges arising both within and outside their borders. The only observable pattern is the convergence and divergence of internal and external factors.[15] Namely, when external factors

[12] This has been a pattern predicted by Peter Evans in Peter Evans, 'The Eclipse of the State? Reflections on Stateness in an Era of Globalization', *World Politics*, 50: 1 (Oct. 1997), 64.

[13] Jan Aart Scholte's study on Romania illustrated this point very well. See Jan Aart Scholte, 'Globalization, Governance and Democracy in Post-Communist Romania', *Democratization*, 5: 4 (Winter 1998), 52–77.

[14] See Wolfram F. Hanrieder, 'Dissolving International Politics: Reflections on the Nation-State', *American Political Science Review*, 72: 4 (1978), 1276–87. For a more recent analysis of this fusion see James N. Rosenau, *Along the Domestic–Foreign Frontier: Exploring Governance in a Turbulent World* (Cambridge: Cambridge University Press, 1997) or Robert O. Keohane and Helen V. Milner (eds.), *Internationalization and Domestic Politics* (Cambridge: Cambridge University Press, 1996). However, as Alex Pravda argues in the introduction to this book the distinction between domestic and foreign factors is still useful for analytical purposes.

[15] In his introduction, Alex Pravda points to three specific variables impinging upon the impact of external factors on democratic consolidation: issue area, the domestic political context, and the international position of the state. Hans Peter Schmitz and Katrin Sell have identified three dominant modes of external impact

reinforced the domestic development already taking place—in other words, they converged—then the result has been largely predictable, as the cases of Hungary, the Czech Republic, and Poland demonstrate. As Antoni Kamiński argues in his chapter, Poland's remarkable progress in democracy building reflects its 'European compatibility potential'. Poland was culturally close to the West and the policies of both Polish and Western actors largely converged. This was not the case in some other post-communist countries where Western political culture was poorly rooted and where local elites pursued policies distinct from those of the West. The divergence of internal and external pressures has been most striking in the cases of Belarus under the rule of President Aleksander Lukashenka, Romania under President Ion Iliescu, and Albania under President Sali Berisha. Divergence was also present in the case of Slovakia under the rule of Prime Minister Vladimír Mečiar, even though Slovakia was culturally closer to the West than many other countries in the region. Cultural similarity could explain how domestic pressure produced a regime change there in 1998. The new government led by Prime Minister Mikulas Dzurinda adopted policies that converged with external forces, firmly geared towards the consolidation of democracy in Slovakia.

This last case indicates the need to distinguish between policies and processes both at the domestic and foreign levels.[16] Whether a country drifts towards democracy or autocracy is not only a function of actors' policies, but also of broader historical, ideological, and economic processes at work. These processes are not simply a product of rational calculations or meticulously conceived designs. In fact, they are seldom controlled by any single government or international organization. This book makes frequent reference to them: the collapse of the Soviet empire, ethnic conflicts, waves of migration, capital flows, and the rise and fall of various ideological doctrines. Some of these processes reflect pressures within

on democratization: socialization, adaptation, and outright pressure. See Hans Peter Schmitz and Katrin Sell, 'International Factors in Processes of Political Democratization: Towards a Theoretical Integration', in Jean Gruel (ed.), *Democracy without Borders: Transnationalization and Conditionality in New Democracies* (London: Routledge, 1999), 39. For other typologies of external impacts on democratization, see Dankart A. Rustow, 'Democracy: A Global Revolution?', *Foreign Affairs*, 69: 4 (Fall 1990), 75–91. Also, Paul W. Drake, 'International Factors in Democratization', *Estudios/Working Paper*, 61 (Nov. 1994), 10–26.

[16] Laurence Whitehead suggests distinguishing between state-to-state interactions, non-governmental political transactions, and more diffuse social processes. See Laurence Whitehead, 'Three International Dimensions of Democratization', in Whitehead (ed.), *The International Dimensions of Democratization*, 4.

individual countries, but many reflect external influence. Clearly, the overall capacity of state institutions to cope with these pressures ultimately determined the balance between the impact of policies and processes. In Albania the state was extremely weak and thus fell prey to both external and internal processes beyond its control. In Belarus, on the other hand, there was a combination of external isolation, the iron grip of President Lukashenka over state institutions, and weak domestic response due mainly to the premodern, unstructured economy and underdeveloped civil society. Above all, Belarus had no tradition of independent statehood, nor even a national awakening comparable to that experienced in neighbouring countries, such as Ukraine. Hungary, with its large ethnic population abroad, high level of foreign direct investment and foreign debt, and extremely open domestic electoral market was particularly vulnerable to the working of various broader processes, but this has been offset by the relatively high capacity of state institutions to cope with these pressures.

Figure 19.1 presents a simple scheme illustrating possible adjustment strategies to different types of pressures. States need to cope with four basic factors: (1) policies of domestic actors, (2) policies of foreign actors, (3) domestic structural processes, and (4) international structural processes.

When all four factors pull in the direction of democracy, states cannot but adjust to the democracy-prone environment. In reality, however, the situation is much more complex. The exact direction

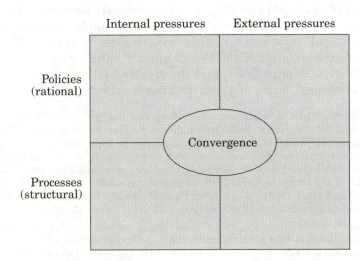

Fɪɢ. 19.1 *States' strategies of democratic adjustment*

and intensity of pressures exerted by individual factors varies, giving states an option to follow different adjustment strategies. In some cases they give in to the pressure of domestic policies and in others to external pressures. States may also try to minimize the impact of certain structural processes—if not ignore them all together—at least for a short while. And of course, much depends on whether these various types of pressures have a positive or negative impact on democracy.

Negative and Positive Impact

Bearing in mind the relative success of democracy in Eastern Europe, one is tempted to assume that the external environment has had only a positive impact on democracy building in the region. If there have been problems, they have been largely attributed to domestic factors such as economic backwardness, an underdeveloped party system, weak administrative structures, nationalism, authoritarian leadership, or conflict-ridden politics. However, this book clearly shows that external factors also have had a negative impact on democracy in the region. The problem is not so much that certain policies and processes are by definition detrimental to democracy—civil war, collapse of financial markets, uncontrolled mass migration, misguided economic requirements by financial institutions, and Russian or Serbian security pressure are the most often cited examples. The problem is that certain policies and processes may have a positive impact in some countries, but a negative impact in others. Varying circumstances may also change the nature of certain external factors at work. And as always, the positive or negative impact of certain pressures depends on the broader historical context and subjective evaluations. As Stephen Whitefield and Geoffrey Evans show in their chapter, Eastern Europeans do not always appreciate the beneficial effects of Western pressures: polls indicate that Eastern Europeans value democracy and the market much more than they value the West.

This leads us to another important observation. Namely, politics is largely about power and it would be wrong to evaluate the impact of external pressures in pure abstract terms while ignoring the emergence of actual winners and losers in the political or economic domain.

Several cases analysed in this book show how individual external factors can have either a positive or negative impact depending on specific circumstances. For instance, Ewa Morawska in her chapter shows that a century ago, masses of Eastern European migrants played an active role in the development of democratic ideas and practices in their home countries. This, however, is not the case today because contemporary migrants' positions as informal-sector workers—or 'gray' or 'black' market traders—has isolated them from contact with host-country democratic institutions. Their predecessors a century ago operated within the mainstream political and economic structures of host countries, which had given them experience with democratic practices that could be used back home.

In his chapter, S. Neil Macfarlane shows that ethnic disputes are not only about machinations of unprincipled ethno-chauvinist political entrepreneurs which can have only a detrimental impact on democracy. Ethnic disputes are also about creating constitutional structures that foster trust, checks on power, and security. In other words, ethnic disputes are also about creating the most appropriate democratic unit in a multiethnic community. For instance, it would be wrong to analyse the Slovenian secession from Yugoslavia or the Estonian secession from the Soviet Union in terms of an ethno-chauvinist power struggle detrimental to democracy. For Slovenes and Estonians, ethnic disputes and secessionist politics represented a means of escaping from their respective authoritarian federal states and of constructing a democratic nation-state of their own.

Susan Senior Nello's chapter shows that a similar package of economic liberalization, privatization, and financial austerity produced economic growth and democratic stability in countries such as Poland, Slovenia, and Hungary, while producing economic and democratic crises in Bulgaria, Albania, and Russia.

This book also indicates that certain external factors may have both a positive and negative impact on democracy depending on the time and place. For instance, the ongoing violent conflict in the Balkans has imposed many economic hardships on countries such as Bulgaria, Romania, and Hungary with negative implications for the democracy promotion campaign. But the Balkan conflict also induced greater cooperation between local Bulgarian, Romanian, and Hungarian elites, who could not but realize that abandoning the democratic route and choosing the route of unchecked confrontation may lead to self-destruction. Similarly, Western aid to Eastern European NGOs has strengthened the basic pillar of each democracy—namely civil society. However, aid has also stalled the spontaneous emergence of indigenous NGOs in these countries. NGOs have thus become a symbol of foreign dependence rather than of grassroots initiative.

This leads to another important finding of this book. The strong pro-democracy pressure from the West (whether in the form of calculated policies or structural processes) has often had negative side effects despite good intentions. First, the dominance of market-based, Western-style democracy has effectively ended the debate on alternative models of democratic governance which might better suit the complex post-Soviet and largely premodern environment of Eastern Europe. Some even argue that the neo-liberal economic prescription behind the so-called 'Washington consensus' was indifferent to, if not in conflict with, democratic ideals.[17] Second, Western pro-democracy pressure has largely constrained any effective self-rule by Eastern European 'democratic' governments. These governments had little choice but to accept a catalogue of written and unwritten conditions presented by various Western actors, fearing that their fledgling states might slide into chaos, isolation, and misery if those requirements were not met. Third, Western pro-democracy pressure limited incentives for the emergence of spontaneous participatory democracy and contributed to a political culture of foreign dependence.

Of course, the assumption was that Western pressure would result in stable democracy, which, after all, is about the 'power of the people' and as such is in the interest of the people throughout the region. But one can question whether the benefit of Eastern European people was always the prime goal behind Western pressure. The pro-democracy campaign was also—if not primarily—about securing peace and economic profit for the West. The West believed that democracy would create new markets for Western goods and stabilize its eastern borders. It is also evident that specific national, class, and sectarian interests were behind the policies and processes affecting the states of Eastern Europe. The policies of major Western states involved in Eastern Europe—Germany and the USA most notably—were primarily guided by their own national interests. Eastern Europe was also a playground for competition among major international institutions such as NATO and the EU. And Western bankers, farmers, and traders have not necessarily been concerned with democracy in their approach to Eastern Europe. This is not to suggest that we have returned to the familiar pattern of struggling for power, primacy, or even hegemony, which had prevented genuine democracy from reaching

---

[17] See e.g. Joseph E. Stiglitz, 'Whither Reform? Ten Years of the Transition'. Paper prepared for the Annual Bank Conference on Development Economics, Washington (28–30 Apr. 1999). Available at http://www.worldbank.org/research/abcde/stiglitz.pdf

Europe in various places for so many years.[18] Nor is this to suggest that Eastern Europe became a victim of a new type of class or colonial exploitation. Relations between Eastern Europe and the West cannot be seen in terms of a zero-sum game. This book leaves little doubt that policies of Western states and processes generated by the Western world have had an overall positive impact on democracy building in the region. But the external pressure on Eastern Europe should be seen in the broader political and historical context in which various partisan interests are at play, with democracy being only a part of this picture.

Crafting Democracy

Democratic theory has often used the terms 'crafting' or 'engineering' democracy in the domestic context.[19] However, this book reflects the fact that crafting democracy has been a matter of international politics as well. Since the late 1980s Western governments have consciously aimed their policies at enhancing the democratic cause in Eastern Europe and have applied a variety of diplomatic, economic, and security means to meet their democratic objectives. But it is important to emphasize that Western crafters were never in full control over democratic developments in Eastern Europe. Moreover, the West has been crafting not only democracy but also the market economy, security, and other matters. These various crafting projects were not necessarily in harmony. Nor was there a natural harmony between the various means applied by the West *vis-à-vis* Eastern Europe. Although Western politicians often claimed to possess an overall strategic design for creating a peaceful and democratic Europe, their rhetoric was vague and ambiguous and their policies lacked a clear sense of direction. As Alex Pravda states in his introduction, the whole exercise of democracy promotion often amounted to less than the sum of its parts.

First of all, the distinction between conscious external policies and structural processes should be recalled in this context. Crafting is

[18] For a historical analogy argument see John J. Mearsheimer, 'Back to the Future: Instability in Europe after the Cold War', *International Security*, 15: 1 (Summer 1990), 5–55. For my critique of this argument see Jan Zielonka, *Explaining Europaralysis* (London: Macmillan, 1998), 25–54.

[19] See Guiseppe Di Palma, *To Craft Democracies* (Berkeley and Los Angeles: University of California Press, 1990) and Giovanni Sartori, *Comparative Constitutional Engineering: An Inquiry into Structures, Incentives and Outcomes* (London: Macmillan, 1994).

about policies, but these policies are more effective when enforcing processes already taking place. This is what Karl Deutsch once labelled 'autonomous probability of events' and what is also implied by Figure 19.1 in this chapter. The distinction between policies and processes is meant to indicate that not everything is in the hands of Western governments, but that uncontrollable economic, social, and political processes operate on various sub-national, national, and transnational levels. To put it differently, not all democratic successes and failures can be attributed to right or wrong Western polices. Sometimes policy makers claim too much credit, while at other times they receive too much blame.[20]

Another point already mentioned but worth repeating in the context of crafting is the issue of intended and unintended policy consequences. Western policy makers did not intend to curb self-rule when they insisted on democratic reform as a precondition for various types of favours. However, sometimes they left their weak Eastern European partners with no alternative but to follow a ready-made blueprint, and this was seen as arbitrary imposition by many observers. Likewise Western aid to local NGOs in the region was not intended to make them lame ducks, totally dependent on Western donors. In short, international actors are never in full control of their policy outcomes. Even carefully prepared and well-executed policies may have some unintended side effects.

The compatibility of different Western objectives has also been questioned in this book. Democracy was only one among many other policy aims Western actors were pursuing in Eastern Europe. And each time Western actors appeared to give priority to economic or security objectives they were accused of betraying their commitment to democracy. This was especially evident in the case of Russia, where broader strategic considerations prevailed over democratic goals for most of the period discussed in this book. But democratic commitments have also been compromised by dissonant Western policies in Latvia, Estonia, Ukraine, and Croatia.[21]

Western policy makers insist that their objectives in various fields are complementary rather than contradictory—creating a

---

[20] In other words, the neo-liberal, capitalist West cannot be held responsible for all democracy failures in Eastern Europe as Marxists and nationalists would have it. But to believe that everything that came from the West was beneficial for democracy in the region is equally erroneous.

[21] For instance, Croatia was admitted to the Council of Europe despite its serious democratic deficiencies at the time. Estonia has been allowed to open accession negotiations with the EU despite its clear discrimination against the Russian minority.

more secure and economically more prosperous Eastern Europe
is helping democracy and also the other way around. This claim is
basically correct, though some qualifications are necessary. For
instance, the economic project is largely about financial profits, while
democracy is largely about distributive justice. The security project
is largely about stability, but concern over stability in autocratic
states prevents any democratic breakthroughs. And there were
also numerous examples of Western support for certain Eastern
European leaders despite their dubious democratic credentials.
This book also reveals how the tension between various crafting
projects manifests itself in practice. In the case of Romania, for
instance, Tom Gallagher shows that the level of defence expenditures undertaken by Romania under Western pressure has put
this nascent democracy under enormous strain. And Susan Senior
Nello shows that economic austerity measures undertaken by
Romania in response to Western pressure undermined popular support for the elected government and generated political instability.

The problem is not only with harmonizing different policy objectives, but also in matching these objectives with adequate instruments. Crafting usually envisages the use of instruments from one
field to enhance objectives in another field. For instance, actors use
economic incentives and sanctions to enhance democratization.
However, the question of which instrument is linked with which
policy goal is up for debate. During the Cold War, Americans
argued that everything could be linked to everything, while Europeans (and especially Germans) insisted that economic means
should not be used for political objectives.[22] In the post-Cold War
period the American argument has clearly prevailed and has been
framed in characteristic institutional terms. Eastern Europeans have
been promised membership in various Western institutions such
as NATO, EU, and the Council of Europe on the condition that they
meet a number of strict criteria—democracy being an important
one. Democracy was demanded in every case even though each of
the three above-mentioned institutions has a distinct purpose:
NATO is largely about security, the EU is largely about economics,
and the Council of Europe is largely about culture. Even specialized
financial institutions, such as the International Monetary Fund
and the World Bank, expected democratic reforms from their new
Eastern European members. And so we can observe a kind of fusion

---

[22] For a genesis of this argument see Pierre Hassner, 'A Time for Linkage? Western
Leverage for Human Rights and Security in Eastern Europe', in Mastny and
Zielonka, *Human Rights and Security*, 59–64.

between different means and ends. The question is no longer about the 'exchange rate of different types of power', to use Pierre Hassner's words, but about managing both internal and external dimensions of each individual institution—the famous widening versus deepening dilemma.[23]

The fusion of different means and ends was geared towards reinforcing the West's message and making it more coherent. However, it often contributed to confusion because it made it more difficult for Eastern European states to see a clear set of priorities. The countries of Eastern Europe have been confronted with a large number of conditions without a clear indication of which ones are truly important. Was the Slovak Prime Minister Mečiar's neglect for democracy a defiant, calculated move or a mistake resulting from misreading the West's priorities? The fusion between different means and ends also made it difficult to assess the level of Western commitment to democracy. For instance, which part of the EU's budget devoted to the eastern enlargement was meant for promotion of democracy?[24] Is there any evidence that the Union's ambition to establish workable democracies in Eastern Europe is matched by an adequate economic commitment to the project?

Crafting democracy through various international institutions (rather than through national governments) was a clear boost for collective rather than unilateral efforts. But this book also shows that while institutionalization of relations with Eastern Europe reduced national brinkmanship, it never eliminated it altogether. Some large Western countries such as France, Great Britain, the United States, and Germany never ceased to engage in bilateral diplomacy with individual Eastern European states. Moreover, the first post-Cold War decade witnessed a drastic increase in institutional competition. NATO, EU, WEU, OSCE, and the Council of Europe hardly ever work in tandem, but try to grab as much authority and resources for dealing with Eastern Europe as possible.[25]

Another important finding of this book concerns the lack of any long-term vision for Europe as part of the democracy-crafting

---

[23] Ibid.

[24] As Karen Smith notes in her chapter, only 1% of the PHARE budget was devoted to democracy promotion. Other studies point to the fact that, contrary to official pledges, democratic and democratizing states have not received a greater share of Western developmental aid. See Steven W. Hook, 'Building Democracy through Foreign Aid: The Limitations of United States Political Conditionalities, 1992–96', *Democratization*, 5: 3 (Autumn 1998), 156–80.

[25] I dealt with the problem in more depth in Zielonka, *Explaining Euro-paralysis*, 191–7.

project. Although Western actors insist on the triangle policy—democracy, free market, and peace—they hardly ever define the vision of Europe they are trying to create. How can the promise of joining Western institutions mobilize broad support in the East if no one knows what is involved in practice? The European Union inflated its 'power of attraction' by failing to identify—let alone admit—any East European country as a future member even after ten years had passed since the fall of the Berlin Wall. The Union never specified what sort of borders it hopes to create in the East, nor has it explained how its institutions are going to work after its enlargement to the East. NATO initially denied any intentions to enlarge and instead created the North Atlantic Cooperation Council. But later it rapidly changed its mind and opted for a limited and speedy enlargement into three Eastern European countries. In 1999, however, it changed its mind again and opened the prospect of further enlargement to the East. Of course, the pace and scope of events in Eastern Europe made any long-term strategic planning difficult. Besides, democracy as such is an evolving process rather than a fixed formula.

That said, Eastern Europeans could have been given some kind of guarantee that their struggle for democracy would open doors to Western institutions where they would be treated as sovereign and equal partners. Democrats in the Balkans and the area formerly belonging to the Soviet Union have found the lack of such guarantees most disappointing. Moreover, the West's ambiguous rhetoric and muddled sense of direction made its policies towards Eastern Europe vulnerable to chaotic sequences of events and sectarian pressures. The efficiency of Western policies has also suffered since it was difficult to know which instruments were needed for the set of vague—if not contradictory—objectives. In the absence of a clear vision and long-term policy goals, it is difficult to judge whether or not Western policies have been truly successful.

In the final analysis, this book leaves little doubt that the external environment was largely conducive to democracy building in Eastern Europe, despite the complications and qualifications. There was a large degree of convergence between the Western desire to bring democracy to the region and the global processes at work in Eastern Europe in the 1990s. Democratic policies made in the West and in the East also largely converged, although this was more the case in countries such as Poland, the Czech Republic, and Hungary than in Russia, Belarus, and Albania. The West has tried to engineer democracy in Eastern Europe through the conditional inclusion of democratic champions in its own institutions.

However, this policy has had many flaws and in the end has produced the desired effects indirectly rather than directly. In other words, the West created an environment conducive for democracy building and this has helped those local elites in Eastern Europe who were interested in accomplishing democratic consolidation. The instrumental approach, using direct leverage and linkage, has proved less effective. Local autocrats such as Mečiar, Lukashenka, or Berisha proved to be surprisingly immune to Western pressures for democratization.

Three more general conclusions can be drawn from this book. The first concerns the interplay between internal and external factors affecting democracy building. In view of the evidence provided it is no longer possible to claim that internal factors are more important than external ones, especially if the latter category includes not only the policies of external actors, but also external processes such as globalization or ideological trends.[26] If one was asked which factors are truly important, external or internal, the answer ought to be that both are important, although the very nature of interplay between these two factors varies at different times and places. Figure 19.1 in this chapter provides an illustration of this interplay.

The book also makes it difficult to maintain that external pressures are more effective in shaping democratic procedures (constitutions, electoral rules, etc.) than democratic processes (such as a shared understanding of the rules of the democratic game, common norms and values, and habits of reciprocity and compromise).[27] For instance, migration can effectively influence the way migrants internalize certain democratic practices experienced in their new countries and 're-export' them to their homelands, as Ewa Morawska shows in her chapter. Foreign-made ideological

---

[26] This view has also been expressed in the Southern European context by Geoffrey Pridham. See Geoffrey Pridham, 'The International Context of Democratic Consolidation: Southern Europe in Comparative Perspective', in Richard Gunther, P. Nikiforos Diamandouros, and Hans-Jürgen Puhle, *The Politics of Democratic Consolidation: Southern Europe in Comparative Perspective* (Baltimore: Johns Hopkins University Press, 1995), 202. For an opposing view in the Southern and Eastern European context see Leonardo Morlino, *Democracy between Consolidation and Crisis: Parties, Groups, and Citizens in Southern Europe* (Oxford: Oxford University Press, 1998), 4; and Margot Light, 'The USSR/CIS and Democratization in Eastern Europe', in Geoffrey Pridham, Eric Herring, and George Sanford (eds.), *Building Democracy? The International Dimension of Democratization in Eastern Europe* (London: Leicester University Press, 1994), 144.

[27] Margot Light, 'Exporting Democracy', in Karen E. Smith and Margot Light (eds.), *Ethics and Foreign Policy* (forthcoming).

paradigms can also shape internal democratic processes, as can global mass communication and trade exchanges. At the same time, democratic procedures can be immune to external pressures. As Julio Faundez argues, a constitution cannot be regarded as an 'intellectual commodity that can be used to sell, impose, or transplant political models'. What works for some countries does not work for others, even under the influence of similar external pressures.[28]

The final conclusion concerns the uses and misuses of comparative research on democracy. Whatever the interplay of internal and external factors in individual settings, this book reveals that a careful empirical examination of each case proves indispensable for any attempt aimed at comparative generalizations. In other words, *transitologists* and *consolidologists*, to use Karl and Schmitter's words, did not make the work of area specialists less important, let alone obsolete.[29] To understand democratic developments in Eastern Europe we certainly need to rely on both empirical work conducted by country or region specialists, as well as theoretical work conducted by transitologists and democratic theorists. As Valerie Bunce rightly asserted several years ago: 'The wall separating eastern European studies from comparative politics came down long before the collapse of the wall separating eastern from western Europe.'[30] There is no need to recreate either of these walls.

[28] Julio Faundez, 'Constitutionalism: A Timely Revival', in Douglas Greenberg et al. (eds.), *Constitutionalism and Democracy: Transitions in the Contemporary World* (Oxford: Oxford University Press, 1993), 358. A similar conclusion was reached in the first volume on democratic consolidation in this series.

[29] See Philippe C. Schmitter and Terry Lynn Karl, 'The Conceptual Travels of Transitologists and Consolidationists: How Far to the East Should They Attempt to Go?', *Slavic Review*, 53: 1 (1994), 173–85.

[30] Valerie Bunce, 'Should Transitologists be Grounded? *Slavic Review*, 54: 4 (1995), 111–27.

Select Bibliography

Ágh, A., *The Politics of Central Europe* (London: Sage, 1998).

Allan, P., and Skaloud, J. (eds.), *The Making of Democracy* (Prague: Czech Political Science Association, 1997).

Allison, R., and Bluth, C. (eds.), *Security Dilemmas in Russia and Eurasia* (London: Royal Institute International Affairs, 1997).

Almond, G. A., and Verba, S., *The Civic Culture: Political Attitudes and Democracy in Five Nations* (Princeton: Princeton University Press, 1963).

Ardittis, Solon (ed.), *The Politics of East–West Migration* (London: St Martin's Press, 1994).

Åslund, A., *Gorbachev's Struggle for Economic Reform* (London: Pinter Publishers, 1989).

Bäckman, J., *The Inflation of Crime in Russia* (Helsinki: National Research Institute of Legal Policy, 1998).

Bade, K., *Deutsche im Ausland—Fremde in Deutschland: Migration in Geschichte und Gegenwart* (Munich: Verlag C. H. Beck, 1992).

Baldersheim, H., and Ståhlberg, K. (eds.), *Nordic Region-Building in a European Perspective* (Aldershot: Ashgate, 1999).

Baranovsky, V. (ed.), *Russia and Europe: The Emerging Security Agenda* (Oxford: Oxford University Press and SIPRI, 1997).

Berend, I., *Central and Eastern Europe, 1944–1993: Detour from the Periphery to the Periphery* (Cambridge: Cambridge University Press, 1996).

Blank, S., *Prague, NATO, and European Security* (Carlisle Barracks, Pa.: Strategic Studies Institute, 1996).

Bock, S., and Schünemann, M. (eds.), *Die Ukraine in der europäischen Sicherheitsarchitektur* (Baden-Baden: Nomos Verlagsanstalt, 1997).

Bremmer, I., and Taras, R. (eds.), *Nations and Politics in the Soviet Successor States* (Cambridge: Cambridge University Press, 1993).

Bricke, D., *Die Slowakei auf dem Weg in die Europäische Union* (Ebenhausen: Stiftung Wissenschaft und Politik, 1995).

Brubaker, R., *Nationalism Reframed: Nationhood and the National Question in the New Europe* (Cambridge: Cambridge University Press, 1996).

Bucar, B., and Kuhnle, S. (eds.), *Small States Compared: Politics of Norway and Slovenia* (Bergen: Alma Mater, 1994).

Bukkvoll, T., *Ukraine and European Security* (London: Pinter and the RIIA, 1997).

Bútora, M., and Skladony, T. W. (eds.), *Slovakia 1996–1997* (Bratislava: Friedrich-Ebert-Stiftung, 1998).

Caplan, R., and Feffer, J. (eds.), *Europe's New Nationalism: States and Minorities in Conflict* (Oxford: Oxford University Press, 1996).

Carnovale, M. (ed.), *European Security and International Institutions after the Cold War* (New York: St Martin's, 1995).

Carothers, T., *Assessing Democracy Assistance: The Case of Romania* (Washington: Carnegie Endowment for International Peace, 1996).

Chayes, A., and Chayes, A. Handler (eds.), *Preventing Conflict in the Post-communist World: Mobilizing International and Regional Organizations* (Washington: Brookings Institution, 1996).

Cohen, L. J., *Broken Bonds: Yugoslavia's Disintegration and Balkan Politics in Transition* (Boulder, Colo.: Westview Press, 1995).

Connor, W., *Ethnonationalism: The Quest for Understanding* (Princeton: Princeton University Press, 1994).

Cornelius, W., Martin, P., and Hollifield, J. (eds.), *Controlling Immigration: A Global Perspective* (Stanford, Calif.: Stanford University Press, 1994).

Crampton, R., *A Concise History of Bulgaria* (Cambridge: Cambridge University Press, 1997).

Crawford, G., *Promoting Democracy, Human Rights and Good Governance through Development Aid: A Comparative Study of the Policies of Four Northern Donors* (Leeds: Leeds University Press, 1996).

Crocker, C., Hampson, F., and Aall, P. (eds.), *Managing Global Chaos: Sources of and Responses to International Conflict* (Washington: USIP Press, 1996).

D'Anieri, P., *Economic Interdependence in Ukrainian–Russian Relations* (Albany: State University of New York Press, 1999).

Dahl, R. A., *Democracy and its Critics* (New Haven: Yale University Press, 1989).

—— *Polyarchy: Participation and Opposition* (New Haven: Yale University Press, 1971).

Dankwart, A. Rustow, and Erickson, Kenneth Paul (eds.), *Comparative Political Dynamics* (London: HarperCollins, 1991).

Dawisha, K. (ed.), *The International Dimension of Post-Communist Transitions in Russia and the New States of Eurasia* (Armonk, NY: M. E. Sharpe, 1997).

—— *Post-Communism's Troubled Steps toward Democracy: An Aggregate Analysis of Progress in the 27 New States* (College Park, Md.: Center for the Study of Post-Communist Societies, University of Maryland, 1997).

—— and Parrott, B. (eds.), *The Consolidation of Democracy in East-Central Europe* (Cambridge: Cambridge University Press, 1997).

—— —— (eds.), *Democratic Changes and Authoritarian Reactions in Russia, Ukraine, Belarus and Moldova* (Cambridge: Cambridge University Press, 1997).

Deletant, D., *Ceausescu and the Securitate* (London: Hurst, 1995).

Della Porta, D., and Mény, Y. (eds.), *Democracy and Corruption in Europe* (London: Pinter, 1997).

Delwit, P., and Wael, J.-M. de (eds.), *La Démocratisation en Europe centrale* (Paris: Éditions Complexes, 1998).

Detrez, R., *Historical Dictionary of Bulgaria* (Lanham, Md.: Scarecrow Press, 1997).

Diamond, L., and Plattner, M. (eds.), *Nationalism, Ethnic Conflict, and Democracy* (Baltimore: Johns Hopkins University Press, 1994).

Di Palma, G., *To Craft Democracies* (Berkeley and Los Angeles: University of California Press, 1990).

Dreifelds, J., *Latvia in Transition* (Cambridge: Cambridge University Press, 1996).

Duleba, A., *The Blind Pragmatism of Slovak Foreign Policy* (Bratislava: SFPA, 1996).

Dwan, R. (ed.), *Building Security in Europe's New Borderlands: Subregional Cooperation in the Wider Europe* (Armonk, NY: M. E. Sharpe, 1999).

Ekiert, G., *The State against Society: Political Crises and Their Aftermath in East Central Europe* (Princeton, NJ: Princeton University Press, 1996).

Ellman, M., Gaidar, E., and Kolodko, G., *Economic Transition in Eastern Europe* (Oxford: Blackwell, 1993).

Elster, J., et al., *Institutional Design in Post-communist Societies: Rebuilding the Ship at Sea* (Cambridge: Cambridge University Press, 1998).

Fassmann, H., and Munz, R. (eds.), *European Migration in the Late Twentieth Century* (Aldershot: Edward Elgar, 1994).

Featherstone, M., et al. (eds.), *Global Modernities* (London: Sage, 1994).

Flemming, J., and Rollo, J. M. C., *Trade, Payments and Adjustment in Central and Eastern Europe* (London: Royal Institute of International Affairs, 1992).

Frejka, T. (ed.), *International Migration in Central and Eastern Europe and the Commonwealth of Independent States* (New York: UN Economic Commission for Europe, 1996).

Fullerton, M., Sik, E., and Toth, J. (eds.), *From Improvisation toward Awareness? Contemporary Migration Politics in Hungary* (Budapest: Institute for Political Science of the Hungarian Academy of Sciences, 1997).

—— —— —— (eds.), *Refugees and Migrants: Hungary at a Crossroads* (Budapest: Institute for Political Science of the Hungarian Academy of Sciences, 1995).

Gallagher, T., *Romania after Ceausescu: The Politics of Intolerance* (Edinburgh: Edinburgh University Press, 1996).

Garnett, S. W., *Keystone in the Arch: Ukraine in the Emerging Security Environment of Central and Eastern Europe* (Washington: Carnegie Endowment, 1997).

Gastil, R. (ed.), *Freedom in the World: Political Rights and Civil Liberties, 1993–1994* (New York: Freedom House, 1994).

Gellner, E., *Nations and Nationalism* (Oxford: Basil Blackwell, 1983).

Ghebali, V.-Y., *L'OSCE dans l'Europe post-communiste, 1990–1996: vers une identité paneuropéenne de sécurité* (Brussels: Bruylant, 1996).

Giddens, A., *The Constitution of Society* (Berkeley and Los Angeles: University of California Press, 1984).

Gombar, C., Hankiss, E., et al., *The Appeal of Sovereignty: Hungary, Austria, and Russia* (Boulder, Colo.: Social Science Monographs, 1998).

Goodwin, C. D., and Nacht, M., *Beyond Government: Extending the Public Debate in Emerging Democracies* (Boulder, Colo.: Westview Press, 1995).

Gorbachev, M., *Perestroika: New Thinking for our Country and the World* (New York: Harper & Row, 1987).

Gow, J., *Triumph of the Lack of Will: International Diplomacy and the Yugoslav War* (London: Hurst, 1997).

Grabbe, H., and Hughes, K., *Enlarging the EU Eastwards* (London: Royal Institute of International Affairs, 1998).

Greenberg, D., et al. (eds.), *Constitutionalism and Democracy: Transitions in the Contemporary World* (Oxford: Oxford University Press, 1993).

Greenfeld, L., *Nationalism: Five Roads to Modernity* (Cambridge, Mass.: Harvard University Press, 1992).

Gruel, J. (ed.), *Democracy without Borders: Transnationalization and Conditionality in New Democracies* (London: Routledge, 1999).

Gunther, R., Diamandouros, P. N., and Puhle, H.-J., *The Politics of Democratic Consolidation: Southern Europe in Comparative Perspective* (Baltimore: Johns Hopkins University Press, 1995).

Hall, J. A. (ed.), *Civil Society: Theory, History, Comparison* (Cambridge: Polity Press, 1996).

Handelman, S., *Comrade Criminal* (London: Michael Joseph, 1994; New Haven: Yale University Press, 1995).

Hansen, E. (ed.), *Cooperation in the Baltic Sea Region, the Barents Region and the Black Sea Region: A Documentation Report* (Oslo: Fafo, 1997).

Hasegawa, T., and Pravda, A. (eds.), *Perestroika: Soviet Domestic and Foreign Policies* (London: Sage Publications, 1990).

Hauner, M., *Asia in the Soviet-Russian Consciousness: What is Asia to Us?* (London: Unwin Hyman, 1990).

Held, D., *Democracy and the Global Order: From the Modern State to Cosmopolitan Governance* (Cambridge: Polity Press, 1995).

—— (ed.), *Prospects for Democracy: North, South, East,* West (Cambridge: Polity Press, 1993).

Hoerder, D., and Moch, L. (eds.), *European Migrants: Global and Local Perspectives* (Boston: Northwestern University Press, 1996).

Holmes, L., *The End of Communist Power* (Cambridge: Polity, 1993).

—— and Roszkowski, W. (eds.), *Changing Rules* (Warsaw: Institute of Political Studies, Polish Academy of Sciences, 1997).

Horowitz, D., *Ethnic Groups in Conflict* (Berkeley and Los Angeles: University of California Press, 1985).

Huntington, S. P., *The Third Wave: Democratization in the Late Twentieth Century* (Norman: University of Oklahoma Press, 1991).

Ingelhart, R., *Modernization and Postmodernization: Cultural, Economic and Political Change in 43 Societies* (Princeton: Princeton University Press, 1996).

Iwaskiw, W. (ed.), *Estonia, Latvia, Lithuania: Country Studies* (Washington: Federal Research Division, Library of Congress, 1996).

Jackson, R. H., *Quasi-States: Sovereignty, International Relations and the Third World* (Cambridge: Cambridge University Press, 1990).

James, H., *International Monetary Cooperation since the Bretton Woods Agreements* (New York: Oxford University Press, 1996).

Joenniemi, P. (ed.), *Neo-nationalism or Regionality? The Re-structuring of Political Space around the Baltic Rim* (Stockholm: NordRefo, 1997).

Jowitt, K., *New World Disorder: The Leninist Extinction* (Berkeley and Los Angeles: University of California Press, 1992).

Kamiński, A. Z., *An Institutional Theory of Communist Regimes: Design, Function and Breakdown* (San Francisco: ICS Press, 1992).

Karklins, R., *Ethnopolitics and Transition to Democracy: The Collapse of the USSR and Latvia* (Baltimore: Johns Hopkins University Press, 1994).

Keohane, R. O., and Milner, H. V. (eds.), *Internationalization and Domestic Politics* (Cambridge: Cambridge University Press, 1996).

Kirchner, E., and Wright, K. (eds.), *Security and Democracy in Transition Societies*, Conference Proceedings (Essex, 1998).

Klingemann, H., and Fuchs, D. (eds.), *Citizens and the State* (Oxford: Oxford University Press, 1995).

Koechler, H. (ed.), *The Crisis of Representational Democracy* (Frankfurt: Lang, 1987).

Kotz, D. M., with Weir, F., *Revolution from above: The Demise of the Soviet System* (London: Routledge, 1996).

Krejčí, J., and Machonín, P., *Czechoslovakia, 1918–1992* (Oxford: Macmillan, 1994).

Kuzio, T. (ed.), *Contemporary Ukraine: Dynamics of Post-Soviet Transformation* (Armonk, NY: M. E. Sharpe, 1998).

—— *Ukraine under Kuchma: Political Reform, Economic Transformation and Security Policy in Independent Ukraine* (London: Macmillan, 1997).

—— *Ukraine: State and Nation Building* (London: Routledge, 1998).

—— Krawchuk, R. S., and D'Anieri, P. (eds.), *State and Institution Building in Ukraine* (New York: St Martin's Press, 1999).

Lane, D. S., *The Rise and Fall of State Socialism* (Oxford: Blackwells, 1996).

Lapidoth, R., *Autonomy: Flexible Solutions to Ethnic Conflicts* (Washington: USIP Press, 1996).

Lauristin, M., et al., *Return to the Western World: Cultural and Political Perspectives on the Estonian Post-Communist Transition* (Tartu: Tartu University Press, 1997).

Leftwich, A. (ed.), *Democracy and Development* (Cambridge: Polity Press, 1996).

Levada, I., *L'Homme soviétique ordinaire* (Paris: Presses de Sciences-Po, 1995).

Liebich, A., and Warner, D. (eds.), *Citizenship East and West* (London: Kegan Paul International, 1995).

Lieven, A., *Chechnya: Tombstone of Russian Power* (New Haven: Yale University Press, 1998).

Lieven, A., *The Baltic Revolution: Estonia, Latvia, Lithuania and the Path to Independence* (New Haven: Yale University Press, 1993).

Linklater, A., *The Transformation of Political Community: Towards a Post-Westphalian Order* (Cambridge: Polity Press, 1998).

Linz, J., and Stepan, A., *Problems of Democratic Transition and Consolidation* (Baltimore: Johns Hopkins University Press, 1996).

Lippert, B., and Schneider, H. (eds.), *Monitoring Association and Beyond: The European Union and the Visegrád States* (Bonn: Europa Union Verlag, 1995).

Lotter, C., *Die parlamentarische Versammlung der westeuropäischen Union* (Baden-Baden: Nomos Verlagsgesellschaft, 1997).

Lotter, C., and Peters, S. (eds.), *The Changing European Security Environment* (Weimar: Boehlan Verlag, 1996).

Lukic, R., and Lynch, A., *Europe from the Balkans to the Urals: The Disintegration of Yugoslav and the Soviet Union* (London: Oxford University Press, 1996).

Lynn-Jones, S., and Miller, S. (eds.), *Global Dangers: Changing Dimensions of International Security* (Cambridge, Mass.: MIT Press, 1995).

McAuley, M., *Russia's Politics of Uncertainty* (Cambridge: Cambridge University Press, 1997).

MacFarlane, S. N., and Thränert, O. (eds.), *Balancing Hegemony: The OSCE in the CIS* (Kingston, Ont.: Queen's University Centre for International Relations, 1997).

Mainwaring, S., O'Donnell, G., and Valenzuela Samuel, J. (eds.), *Issues in Democratic Consolidation: The New South American Democracies in Comparative Perspective* (Notre Dame, Ind.: University of Notre Dame Press, 1992).

Maravall, J. M., *Regimes, Politics and Markets: Democratization and Economic Change in Southern and Eastern Europe* (Oxford: Oxford University Press, 1997).

Markham, R. H., *Rumania under the Soviet Yoke* (Boston: Meador, 1949).

Marples, D., *Belarus: From Soviet Rule to Nuclear Catastrophe* (London: Macmillan, 1996).

Mastny, V., and Zielonka, J. (eds.), *Human Rights and Security: Europe on the Eve of a New Era* (Boulder, Colo.: Westview Press, 1991).

Mayhew, A., *Recreating Europe: The European Union's Policy towards Central and Eastern Europe* (Cambridge: Cambridge University Press, 1998).

Mendelson, S. (ed.), *Evaluating NGO Strategies for Democratization and Conflict Prevention in the Formerly Communist States* (New York: Carnegie Endowment for International Peace, 2000).

Mendras, M. (ed.), *Russie: le gouvernement des provinces* (Geneva: CRES, 1997).

Merritt, G., *Eastern Europe and the USSR: The Challenge of Freedom* (London: Kogan Page, 1991).

Meyer, G. (ed.), *Die politischen Kulturen Ostmitteleuropas im Umbruch* (Tübingen: Francke Verlag, 1993).

Midlarsky, M. I. (ed.), *The Internationalization of Communal Strife* (London: Routledge, 1992).

Morlino, L., *Democracy between Consolidation and Crisis: Parties, Groups, and Citizens in Southern Europe* (Oxford: Oxford University Press, 1998).

Morokvasic, M., and Rudolph, H. (eds.), *Migrants: les nouvelles mobilités en Europe* (Paris: Éditions L'Harmattan, 1996).

Nelson, D. (ed.), *Romania after Tyranny* (Boulder, Colo.: Westview Press, 1992).

Nelson, J. M., with Eglinton, S. J., *Encouraging Democracy: What Role for Conditioned Aid?* (Washington: Overseas Development Council, 1992).

Norgaard, O., Hindsgaul, D., Johannsen, L., and Willumsen, H., *The Baltic States after Independence* (Cheltenham: Edward Elgar, 1996).

O'Donnell, G., Schmitter, P. C., and Whitehead, L. (eds.), *Transitions from Authoritarian Rule: Comparative Perspectives* (Baltimore: Johns Hopkins University Press, 1986).

O'Neil, P. (ed.), *Post-Communism and the Media in Eastern Europe* (London: Cass, 1997).

Palmer, S., and King, R., *Yugoslav Communism and the Macedonian Question* (Hamden, Conn.: Archon Books, 1971).

Plakans, A., *The Latvians: A Short History* (Stanford, Calif.: Hoover Institution Press, 1995).

Pridham, G., and Gallagher, T. (eds.), *Experimenting with Democracy: Regime Change in the Balkans* (London: Routledge, 2000).

—— and Vanhanen, T., *Democratization in Eastern Europe: Domestic and International Perspectives* (London: Routledge, 1994).

—— Herring, E., and Sanford, G. (eds.), *Building Democracy? The International Dimension of Democratisation in Eastern Europe* (London: Leicester University Press, 1994; rev edn., 1997).

Przeworski, A., *Democracy and the Market: Political and Economic Reforms in Eastern Europe and Latin America* (Cambridge: Cambridge University Press, 1991).

Quigley, K. F. F., *For Democracy's Sake: Foundations and Democracy Assistance in Central Europe* (Washington: Woodrow Wilson Center Press, 1997).

Ramet, S., *Balkan Babel: The Disintegration of Yugoslavia from the Death of Tito to Ethnic War* (Boulder, Colo.: Westview, 1996).

Ratesh, N., *The Entangled Revolution* (London: Praegar, 1991).

Remacle, E., and Seidelmann, R. (eds.), *Pan-European Security Redefined* (Baden-Baden: Nomos Verlagsgesellschaft, 1998).

Roberts, H. J., *Rumania: Political Problems of an Agrarian State* (New Haven: Yale University Press, 1951).

Robinson, M. and White, G. (eds.), *The Democratic Developmental State: Politics and Institutional Design* (Oxford: Oxford University Press, 1996).

Rose, R., Mishler, W., and Haerpfer, C., *Democracy and its Alternatives* (Cambridge: Polity, 1998).

Rosenau, J. N., *Along the Domestic–Foreign Frontier: Exploring Governance in a Turbulent World* (Cambridge: Cambridge University Press, 1997).

Rueschemeyer, Dietrich, Stephens, Evelyne Huber, and Stephens, John D., *Capitalist Development and Democracy* (Cambridge: Polity, 1992).

Sakwa, R., *Russian Politics and Society*, 2nd edn. (London: Routledge, 1996).

Sapir, J., *Le Krach russe* (Paris: La Découverte, 1998).

Sartori, G., *Comparative Constitutional Engineering: An Inquiry into Structures, Incentives and Outcomes* (London: Macmillan, 1994).

Sassen, S., *The Global City* (Princeton: Princeton University Press, 1991).

Schöpflin, G., *Politics in Eastern Europe, 1945–1992* (Oxford: Blackwell, 1995).

—— and Hosking, G. (eds.), *Myths and Nationhood* (London: Hurst, 1997).

Schumpeter, J., *Capitalism, Socialism and Democracy* (London: George Allen & Unwin, 1943).

Seidelmann, R., *Crises Policies in Eastern Europe* (Baden-Baden: Nomos Verlagsanstalt, 1996).

Senior Nello, S., and Smith, K., *The European Union and Central and Eastern Europe: The Implications of Enlargement in Stages* (Aldershot: Ashgate, 1998).

Senn, A. E., *Lithuania Awakening* (Berkeley and Los Angeles: University of California Press, 1990).

Skak, M., *From Empire to Anarchy: Postcommunist Foreign Policy and International Relations* (London: Hurst & Co., 1996).

Skalnik Leff, C., *The Czech and Slovak Republics: Nation versus State* (Boulder, Colo.: Westview, 1997).

Smith, A. D., The Ethnic Origins of Nations (Oxford: Blackwells, 1986).

—— *Theories of Nationalism* (New York: Holmes & Meier, 1983).

Smith, G. (ed.), *The Baltic States: The National Self-Determination of Estonia, Latvia, and Lithuania* (London: Macmillan Press, 1994).

Sorensen, G., *Political Conditionality* (London: Frank Cass, 1993).

Splichal, S., *Media beyond Socialism* (Boulder, Colo.: Westview, 1994).

Stanley Vardys, V., and Sedaitis, J., *Lithuania: The Rebel Nation* (Boulder Colo.: Westview Press, 1997).

Stark D., and Bruszt, L., *Postsocialist Pathways: Transforming Politics and Property in East Central Europe* (Cambridge: Cambridge University Press, 1998).

Sterling, C., *Crime without Frontiers* (London: Warner, 1995).

Strekal, O., *Nationale Sicherheit der unabhängigen Ukraine (1991–1995): zur Analyse der Sicherheitslage und der Grundlagen der Sicherheitspolitik eines neu entstandenen Staates* (Baden-Baden, in print for Nomos-Verlag, 1998).

Taagepera, R., *Estonia: Return to Independence* (Boulder, Colo.: Westview Press, 1993).

Telo, M. (ed.), *De la nation à l'Europe: paradoxes et dilemmes de la social-démocratie* (Brussels: Bruylant, 1993).

—— (ed.), *Démocratie et construction européenne* (Brussels: Éditions de l'Université de Bruxelles, 1995).

—— and Remacle, E. (eds.), *L'Union européenne après Amsterdam: adaptations institutionelles, enjeux de la différenciation et de l'élargissement* (Brussels: Rapport remis à la Fondation Paul-Henri Spaak, 1998).

Tismanyanu, V., *Reinventing Politics: Eastern Europe from Stalin to Havel* (New York: Free Press, 1992).

Todorova, M. N., *Imagining the Balkans* (New York: Oxford University Press, 1997).

Tökés, R., *Hungary's Negotiated Revolution* (Cambridge: Cambridge University Press, 1996).

Volten, P. (ed.), *Bound to Change: Consolidating Democracy in East Central Europe* (New York: Institute for East West Studies, 1992).

Walzer, M. (ed.), *Toward a Global Civil Society* (Oxford: Berghahn Books, 1995).

Watson, A., *The Evolution of International Society: A Comparative Historical Analysis* (London: Routledge, 1992).

Webster, W. (ed.), *Russian Organized Crime* (Washington: Center for Strategic and International Studies, 1997).

Weiner, M., *The Global Migration Crisis: Challenge to States and to Human Rights* (Cambridge, Mass.: MIT Press, 1995).

Weiss, T., *Beyond UN Subcontracting* (London: Macmillan, 1998).

White, S., Pravda, A., and Gitelman, Z. (eds.), *Developments in Russian Politics 4* (London: Macmillan, 1997).

Whitehead, L. (ed.), *The International Dimensions of Democratization: Europe and the Americas* (Oxford: Oxford University Press, 1996).

Williams, K., *The Prague Spring and Its Aftermath: Czechoslovak Politics, 1968–1970* (Cambridge: Cambridge University Press, 1997).

Williams, M., *International Economic Organisations and the Third World* (New York: Harvester Wheatsheaf, 1994).

Williams, P., *Russian Organized Crime* (London: Cass, 1997).

—— and Savona, E. (eds.), *The United Nations and Transnational Organized Crime* (London: Cass, 1996).

Zecchini, S. (ed.), *Lessons from the Economic Transition: Central and Eastern Europe in the 1990s* (Dordrecht: Kluwer Publishers, 1997).

Zellner, W., and Dunay, P., *Zwischen Integration, Nachbarschafts- und Minderheitenpolitik: Ungarns Aussenpolitik 1990–1997* (Baden-Baden: Nomos Verlagsanstalt, 1998).

Zielonka, J., *Explaining Euro-paralysis* (London: Macmillan, 1998).

—— (ed.), *Paradoxes of European Foreign Policy* (Dordrecht: Kluwer Law International, 1998).

Index